INTERRACIALISM

INTERRACIALISM

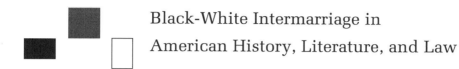

Black-White Intermarriage in
American History, Literature, and Law

Edited by
Werner Sollors

OXFORD
UNIVERSITY PRESS

2000

OXFORD

UNIVERSITY PRESS

Oxford   New York
Athens   Auckland   Bangkok   Bogotá   Buenos Aires   Calcutta
Cape Town   Chennai   Dar es Salaam   Delhi   Florence   Hong Kong   Istanbul
Karachi   Kuala Lumpur   Madrid   Melbourne   Mexico City   Mumbai
Nairobi   Paris   São Paulo   Shanghai   Singapore   Taipei   Tokyo   Toronto   Warsaw

and associated companies in
Berlin   Ibadan

Copyright © 2000 by Oxford University Press, Inc.

Published by Oxford University Press, Inc.
198 Madison Avenue, New York, New York 10016

Oxford is a registered trademark of Oxford University Press.

Library of Congress Cataloging-in-Publication Data
Interracialism : Black-white intermarriage in American history,
   literature, and law / edited by Werner Sollors.
      p.   cm.
   Includes bibliographical references and index.
   ISBN 0-19-512856-7; ISBN 0-19-512857-5 (pbk.)
   1. Interracial marriage—United States—History.
2. Miscegenation—United States—History.   3. Racially mixed people—
United States—History.   4. Miscegenation—Law and legislation—
United States—History.   5. Miscegenation in literature.
6. Racially mixed people in literature.   I. Sollors, Werner.
HQ1031.I8   2000
306.84'6'0973—dc21   99-32521

9 8 7 6 5 4 3 2 1

Printed in the United States of America
on acid-free paper

In memoriam

A. Leon Higginbotham, Jr.
(February 25, 1928–December 14, 1998)

Acknowledgments

I am indebted to T. Susan Chang and to the anonymous readers at Oxford University Press for their encouragement in the planning stages for this volume, to Norma McLemore for superb copyediting, and to Will Moore for seeing the manuscript through the production process. I am grateful to Jessica Hook and Erica Michelstein for excellent research and editorial assistance and to Larry Benson, Lawrence Buell, and Derek Pearsall and the Hyder E. Rollins Publication Fund at Harvard University for defraying a substantial part of the permission fees. An NEH Fellowship allowed me to complete this edition.

The essays collected in this volume have been selected from a growing body of work on the subject, work to which reference is made in many footnotes and in the suggestions for further reading. It should particularly be emphasized that numerous helpful and some excellent monographs have been written on the topic, yet that this collection contains only essays, and no excerpts from published books. The editor wishes to thank Randall Kennedy and Jamie Wacks for the right to publish new work, to the University of Massachusetts Press for the right to include an essay by Du Bois that was not printed in his lifetime, and to the various copyright holders for permission to reprint previously published copyright materials:

and the Organization of American Historians, publisher of the *Journal of American History*.

Terms from the *Oxford English Dictionary* (2nd edition, 1989). By permission of Oxford University Press.

Sidney Kaplan, "The Miscegenation Issue in the Election of 1864." Copyright © 1949. By permission of the *Journal of Negro History* and the Association for the Study of African-American Life and History, Inc. Reprinted from Sidney Kaplan's *American Studies in Black and White: Selected Essays, 1949–1989* (Amherst: University of Massachusetts Press, 1991). Copyright © 1996 by the University of Massachusetts Press.

Sterling A. Brown, "Negro Character as Seen by White Authors," *Journal of Negro Education* 2 (1933): 179–203. Copyright © 1996 by Howard University. All rights reserved.

Penelope Bullock, "The Mulatto in American Fiction," Copyright © 1945. By permission of *Phylon*, Clark Atlanta University.

Jules Zanger, "The 'Tragic Octoroon' in Pre–Civil War Fiction," *American Quarterly* 18 (1966): 63–70. Copyright © The American Studies Association. Reprinted with permission of the Johns Hopkins University Press.

William Bedford Clark, "The Serpent of Lust in the Southern Garden." Copyright © 1974. By permission of the author.

William L. Andrews, "Miscegenation in the Late Nineteenth-Century American Novel." Copyright © 1979. By permission of the author.

Arthur P. Davis, "The Tragic Mulatto Theme in Six Works of Langston Hughes." Copyright © 1955. By permission of *Phylon*, Clark Atlanta University.

Langston Hughes, "Introduction" to Mark Twain's *Pudd'nhead Wilson*. Reprinted by permission of Harold Ober Associates, Inc. Copyright © 1959 by Bantam Books. Copyright renewed 1987 by George Houston Bass.

Simone Vauthier, "Of African Queens and Afro-American Princes and Princesses: Miscegenation in *Old Hepsy*." Copyright © Presse de la Sorbonne Nouvelle, Paris, 1980. By permission of the author and the publisher.

"*Othello* in America: The Drama of Racial Intermarriage," by Tilden G. Edelstein, from *Region, Race, and Reconstruction: Essays in Honor of C. Vann Woodward*, by James M. McPherson and J. Morgan Kousser. Copyright © 1982 by Oxford University Press. Used by permission of Oxford University Press.

"Jean Toomer and American Racial Discourse," by George Hutchinson, from *Texas Studies in Literature and Language* 35.2, pp. 226–250. Copyright © 1993 by the University of Texas Press. All rights reserved. Published with the permission of the author.

Glenn Cannon Arbery, "Victims of Likeness: Quadroons and Octoroons in Southern Fiction." Copyright © 1989. By permission of the author.

Karen Sánchez-Eppler, "Bodily Bonds: The Intersecting Rhetorics of Feminism and Abolition." Copyright © 1988 by The Regents of the University of California. Reprinted from *Representations* 24 (fall 1988), pp. 28–59, by permission of publisher and author.

Eduardo González, "American Theriomorphia: The Presence of *Mulatez* in Cirilo Villaverde and Beyond," in *Do the Americas Have a Common Literature?*, ed. Gustavo Pérez Firmat (Durham, N.C.: Duke University Press), pp. 177–193. Copyright © 1990, Eduardo Gonzalez. All rights reserved. Reprinted with permission.

W. E. B. Du Bois, "Miscegenation," reprinted from *Against Racism: Unpublished Essays, Papers, Addresses, 1887–1961, by W. E. B. Du Bois*, ed. Herbert Aptheker (Amherst: University of Massachusetts Press, 1985). Copyright © 1985 by the University of Massachusetts Press.

Robert K. Merton, "Intermarriage and the Social Structure: Fact and Theory," *Psychiatry.* Copyright © 1941. By permission of the author.

Hannah Arendt, "Reflections on Little Rock." Copyright © 1955. By permission of Lotte Kohler, Trustee, Hannah Arendt Literary Trust.

William H. Turner, "Black Man/White Woman: A Philosophical View," reprinted from Doris Y. Wilkinson, *Black Male/White Female: Perspectives on Interracial Marriage and Courtship* (Cambridge, Mass.: Schenkman, 1975), 170–175. By permission of the author and Doris Y. Wilkinson.

Joel Perlmann, *Reflecting the Changing Face of America: Multiracials, Racial Classification, and American Intermarriage* (Publications of the Jerome Levy Institute, no. 35, 1997). Reprinted by permission of the author and of the Jerome Levy Economics Institute.

Every effort has been made to trace all copyright holders, but if any have been inadvertently overlooked the publisher will be pleased to make the necessary arrangement at the first opportunity.

Contents

■ ▓ ☐

Part II Literature

INTERRACIALISM

Introduction

■ ▨ ☐

A marriage between a person of free condition and a slave,
or between a white person and a negro, or between a white
person and a mulatto, shall be null.
           1786 Virginia bill, drafted by Thomas Jefferson
                                (Jefferson 557, bill 86)

I

What is American about American culture? Many readers inside and outside of the United States are now suspicious of this line of questioning, for does it not exaggerate what distinguishes this country from other countries, and is this not an "exceptionalist" approach that stylizes the United States as unique? We have become skeptical of sweeping views of American history and literature that isolate the frontier or mobility, notions of virgin land and abundance, or peculiar forms of pastoralism as the distinguishing features of the United States. Instead, we have turned toward internationalist approaches and toward the study of regions and ethnic and gender groups to avoid generalizations about the United States.

One theme that has been pervasive in U.S. history and literature and that has been accompanied by a 300-year-long tradition of legislation, jurisdiction, protest, and defiance is the deep concern about, and the attempt to prohibit, contain, or deny, the presence of black-white interracial sexual relations, interracial marriage, interracial descent, and other family relations across the powerful black-white divide. Many fears have been attached to the formation of the otherwise ideal American social institution: the heterosexual family. Thus a complicated area defined only by the racial difference of bride and groom was designated where family founding was considered "null and void," and children of interracially married couples were deemed illegitimate. This focus on marriage, children, legitimacy, property, and family created a paradox in American society, idealizing the concept of family while destroying certain families.

The powerful black-white divide was mirrored in other interracial relationships. Prohibitions of other forms of interracialism in the United States, critics Eva Saks, Peggy Pascoe, and Randall Kennedy observe in this volume, have existed for long periods of time. Anti-miscegenation laws came to include, in various states, American Indians, Chinese, Japanese, Hawaiians, Filipinos, and other groups—but *all* such laws restricted marriage choices of blacks and whites, making the black-white divide the deepest and historically most pervasive of all American color

3

lines, even though the percentage of blacks among America's people of color is now declining (a fact Joel Perlmann's essay illuminates). And, though growing, the rate of intermarriage between blacks and whites has remained significantly lower than that of other racial minorities—less than one in ten for black men and one in twenty-five for black women. Such facts suggest, as the Census demographer Roderick Harrison writes, "that the black-white color line is still with us, and that the integration of blacks is going to be a different story than the assimilation of Asians and Hispanics" (Fletcher 1998:2).

Some readers might expect to see the definition of "forbidden couples" expanded here to gay and lesbian partners. While miscegenation laws may no longer exist, many legal decisions surrounding interracial marriages have reemerged as possible precedents in debates surrounding same-sex marriages (see Koppelman 1988). The resounding congressional support for the 1996 "Defense of Marriage Act" (which passed the House 342 to 67 and the Senate 85 to 14) suggests that legislative bodies are still far from ready to extend marital legal benefits to homosexual partners. Yet the thrust of the historical prohibitions of interracial marriage justifies a concentrated discussion of the forbidden heterosexual couple on the following pages: the homosexual couple was generally prohibited, regardless of race (though racial difference may have intensified community reaction against homosexuals, as A. Leon Higginbotham, Jr., and Barbara K. Kopytoff suggest in an early Virginia case). The heterosexual couple, however, was designated as legitimate or criminal *only* according to the racial sameness or difference of the contractants.[1] And whereas many countries have prohibited homosexuality, and most still deny a right to homosexual marriage, the case of a three-century-long curtailment of what many motherlands and colonies permitted, and what all democracies have tended to view as an elementary human right, marks a strong idiosyncrasy of the English colonies and the American republic. These contexts justify this collection's focus on black-white heterosexual marital, sexual, and family relations in the United States.

While many countries have practiced brutal forms of ethnic discrimination, accompanied by hate literature and inhumane laws (including marriage prohibitions for certain spans of time), few people around the world have shared the peculiar ways in which *black-white marital* relations were prohibited in several English colonies on the American continent (starting with Maryland in 1661). They would be startled to learn that, in a great number of American states—often the majority—such prohibitions survived the Revolution, the Civil War, two world wars, the League of Nations, and the first few presidencies of the United Nations, before being declared unconstitutional by the Supreme Court only on June 12, 1967, in the *Loving v. Commonwealth of Virginia* decision (in-

---

1. Andrew Koppelman stresses that sexual sameness and difference is constructed in a parallel way when he cites and comments on Justice Traynor's statement in *Perez v. Sharp* (which held miscegenation statutes to be unconstitutional): "A member of any of these races [one might substitute "either of these sexes"] may find himself barred by law from marrying the person of his choice and that person to him may be irreplaceable" (p. 162).

cluded in this volume). Even the representation of interracial relations was restrained at times, from Southern states' disputes about interracial themes in books (see William D. Zabel, in this volume) to the infamous American "Motion Picture Production Code" of 1934 that urged filmmakers to uphold the "sanctity of the institution of marriage and the home," but simultaneously stated: "Miscegenation (sex relationship between the white and black races) is forbidden" (Kydd 1996: 55–56). And even the word used to describe interracial sexual and marital relations, *miscegenation,* is an Americanism. Sidney Kaplan's essay in this volume reveals how the word was coined by two New York journalists in an 1863 pamphlet, a political hoax designed to hurt abolitionists and Republicans who were invited to endorse it. Derived from Latin *miscere* and *genus,* the made-up word that faintly echoes the term for the European class mismatch, *misalliance,* and replaced *amalgamation.* It became a catchall term, used in phrases like "miscegenation law" that are hard to translate into some other languages. Could the question of what is American about American culture be answered with "prohibiting black-white heterosexual couples from forming families and withholding legitimacy from their descendants"?

II

Constructing miscegenation law was a difficult task for lawmakers and judges. Although they may have invoked a divine or natural order, the ramifications of drawing a line between legal and illegal families were mindboggling and led to some absurd situations, many of which are illuminated in the essays in this book. One line of argument was to stress equality as well as difference (as in "separate but equal"), but at least to the twenty-first century ear this emphasis reveals the inherent paradox. In *Green v. State* (1877), for example, the Alabama Supreme Court ruled in defense of interracial marriage bans:

> Manifestly, it is for the peace and happiness of the black race, as well as of the white, that such laws should exist. And surely there can not be any tyranny or injustice in requiring both alike, to form this union with those of their own race only, whom God hath joined together by indelible peculiarities, which declare that He has made the two races distinct. (Lombardo 1988:426)

At the same time, the state's right to meddle in private matters (patterned on the state's right to prohibit incest) had to be intensified in order to make such "peace and happiness" possible. And when challenged in *Pace v. State of Alabama,* the U.S. Supreme Court ruled in a remarkable decision of 1883 (included in this collection), thirteen years before *Plessy v. Ferguson,* that punishing interracial couples more harshly than intraracial couples for "fornication or adultery" did not constitute racial discrimination. The "punishment of each offending person" in the interracial relationship, "whether white or black, [was] the same." Since both "Tony Pace, a negro man, and Mary J. Cox, a white woman," had received the same sentence of two to seven years' penitentiary or hard labor, and since the offense "cannot be committed without involving the persons of both races," the

Supreme Court felt that the State of Alabama had not used racial discrimination. This was "equality" with a vengeance.

Since the racial difference between the partners alone constituted a crime with such severe punishments, a whole science of drawing the color line and of "reading race" emerged (leading to the rise of experts and to strange legal proceedings even in civil cases such as the one Jamie Wacks analyzes in her essay in this collection); it was developed heterogeneously in different states. Contrary to many assertions, the so-called one-drop rule (according to which *any* African ancestry, no matter how far removed, made an American "black") was never widely applied, and many contradictory racial definitions coexisted. George S. Schuyler points out in "Who Is 'Negro'? Who Is 'White'?" (1940) that a

> person with less than one-eighth "Negro blood" may marry a "white" person, say, in Nebraska, North Dakota, Maryland, Louisiana, Missouri, Mississippi, or South Carolina, where he is not legally a "Negro," and receive the sanction of law and society; but that marriage will be null and void in Arizona, Montana, Virginia, Georgia, Alabama, Oklahoma, Arkansas, and Texas. (p. 54)[2]

These definitions changed over time. As Higginbotham and Kopytoff and Kennedy show in this book, problems would necessarily emerge with the enforcement of such acts. Defining someone as "one-fourth" or "one-eighth" meant that one could argue that proof of "full-blooded" Africanness had to be given for the decisive ancestor from whom counting proceeded (see *Ferrall v. Ferrall* in the essays by Saks and Kennedy in this book). Virginia's 1924 "Act to Preserve Racial Integrity" (reprinted in this collection) extended racial definition to an almost mystical level by suggesting that "the term 'white person' shall apply only to the person who has no trace whatsoever of any blood other than Caucasian" (see Sherman 1988). This version of the one-drop rule, modeled on membership in an aristocracy, came late from one of the first states to prohibit interracial marriages, and it specifically excluded American Indian ancestry. The Louisiana Supreme Court had to arrive at the following statement in 1908: "that a negro is necessarily a person of color; but not that a person of color is necessarily a negro" (Daggett 1953:20; see Domínguez 1986:30). The definition of a "white person" (examined by Charles Chesnutt in this book) had its correspondent problems, exemplified in the tautological procedure of the *Texas Criminal Statutes* of 1906: "All persons not included in the definition of 'negro' shall be deemed a white person within the meaning of this article" (art. 347; see Jenks 1916:678). Such definitions were of great significance not only in the area of criminal law but also

---

2. See also W. A. S. 1927, 862–863n: "Some of the statutes prohibit marriages between white persons and persons of African descent (Georgia, Oklahoma, Texas), or between white persons and persons of negro blood to the third generation (Alabama, Maryland, North Carolina, Tennessee), or between white persons and persons of more than one-fourth (Oregon, West Virginia), or one-eighth (Florida, Indiana, Mississippi, Nebraska, North Dakota), or one-sixteenth (Virginia) negro blood; other statutes in more general terms prohibit marriages between white persons and Negroes or mulattoes (Arkansas, Colorado, Delaware, Idaho, Kentucky, Louisiana, Missouri, Montana, Nevada, South Carolina, South Dakota, Utah, Wyoming)."

for civil lawsuits surrounding property disputes, in which the factor of one family member's race could decide whether a divorce settlement or an annulment was in order (as in the Rhinelander case, here analyzed by Jamie Wacks), or whether an inheritance had to be shared.

As more races entered the range of prohibitions, the formulations became more and more complex, and Arizona became famous for passing a law in 1913 (on which Kennedy, Zabel, and Pascoe reflect, and which is reprinted in this volume) that had very curious side effects. As Roger D. Hardaway writes in "Unlawful Love: A History of Arizona's Miscegenation Law":

> By extending the prohibition against interracial marriage to descendants of "persons of Caucasian blood" and to descendants of "negroes, Mongolians or Indians," the [Arizona] law [of 1913] placed a person of mixed Indian-white blood, for instance, in an untenable position. As the descendant of a white person, he could not legally marry a Negro, a Mongolian, and Indian or anyone descended from a member of these races. Conversely, as a descendant of an Indian, he could not marry a white person or anyone descended from a white person. He could not even marry someone who, like himself, was of mixed Indian-white ancestry. In short, he could not legally marry anybody! (Hardaway 1986:379)

This was, however, an inadvertent exception, for very few laws were enacted prohibiting the intermarriage among members of different non-white races in the United States. "Racial integrity" usually referred only to the "purity" of (or the intended purification of) the white race.

Virginia Judge Leon M. Bazile (who originally sentenced Mildred and Richard Loving in the case that led to the landmark U.S. Supreme Court decision of 1967) argued, "Almighty God created the races white, black, yellow, malay and red, and he placed them on separate continents. And but for the interference with his arrangement there would be no cause for such marriages. The fact that he separated the races shows that he did not intend for the races to mix" (the verdict is cited and overturned in *Loving v. Commonwealth of Virginia*, in this volume). It took such an amazing amount of legislative and judicative energies to translate this supposed divine plan into legal reality that the theory of human-made differences has seemed more plausible to scholars.

III

The exceptional legal pressures on black-white interracialism in the United States become more apparent when one considers international contexts. As W. E. B. Du Bois shows in his essay "Miscegenation" (included in this book), interracial relations apparently did not constitute a historically deep-seated or pervasive taboo throughout the world. And Frank Snowden reports in his excellent book *Blacks in Antiquity*, "No laws in the Greco-Roman world prohibited unions of blacks and whites" (Snowden 1970:195). Bernard Lewis comments on the Muslim world, "The voice of Islamic piety on miscegenation is clear and unequivocal—there are no superior and inferior races and therefore no bar to racial intermarriage" (Lewis 1990:85). Is the American prohibition then part of the modern world of the African slave trade? Here Carl Degler makes an important point. Degler noted that while "Portuguese law forbade marriage between whites and Negroes or Indians" in colonial Brazil, "the church and the society accepted such unions informally" (Degler 1973:213, 216). Patricia Seed offers an assessment of a related situation in Mexican history: There, at first, "interracial sexual contact took place primarily outside marriage," but in the eighteenth century "a dramatic increase occurred in interracial marriage" (Seed 1988:146). Prohibition was also highly uncommon in the non-English slaveholding colonies that would become part of the United States. "One of Antonio de Ulloa's acts in his first year in office as first Spanish governor of Louisiana was to grant permission to a Frenchman to marry a Negro woman," Virginia Domínguez (1986:25) writes about a 1768 case. The French *Code noir* for most of the time it was in effect did not prohibit interracial marriage, but penalized couples for having sex outside marriage (a fact Carter G. Woodson emphasized in his pioneering essay, "The Beginnings of Miscegenation of the Whites and Blacks," which is included in this book).

Given these policies of other colonies, one wonders whether the English colonies might have inherited an *English* idiosyncrasy. But apparently this was not the case either. George Schuhmann writes explicitly that there "was no prohibition of interracial marriage at common law or by statute in England at the time of the establishment of the American Colonies" (Schuhmann 1968:70; see also Applebaum 1964:50, Getman 1984:125, and Saks, p. 61, in this volume). One must accept J. A. Rogers's conclusion that although "any prohibition of marriage between white and black at all began in the New World," the "United States is the only country in the New World which has carried its law against the marriage of white and black from its colonial period into its national one" (Rogers 1941–1944:3.15). Of course, there have been occasional restrictions on black-white relations in other countries, perhaps most notably in the apartheid era of South Africa. Even that case was modeled on U.S. segregation (see Higginbotham and Kopytoff, p. 138n245, in this volume) and lasted a much shorter time than American bans of interracial marriage: the legal prohibition of racially mixed marriages was in effect in the South African Union for less than forty years, from 1949 (when the "Immorality Act" was passed) to 1985 (when apartheid was officially ended).[3]

Legalized hostility to miscegenation may well have stamped and defined American culture, yet this hostility appears not to have been determined *by* the culture, and a cultural-relativist approach to the issue would be difficult to sustain. First, numerous cultural practices violated the legal norms, some of which led to legal consequences, including Supreme Court decisions, that are analyzed in part I of this book; laws, after all, rarely prohibit what humans do not practice. Second, numerous Americans raised their voices against these laws, and their

---

3. Another example of proscribing interracial marriages, inspired in part by the racial laws of the United States (see Krieger 1936) were the so-called Nuremberg laws enacted by German fascists. In his 1935 essay on "Miscegenation" (included in this volume) W. E. B. Du Bois argued that the "moral and physical problems of race mixture are tense and of present interest chiefly in Germany, South Africa and the United States."

pronouncements anticipated the verdict of future ages. A Massachusetts act of June 22, 1786, stipulated: "That no person by this Act authorized to marry, shall join in marriage any white person with any Negro, Indian or Mulatto, on penalty of the sum of *fifty pounds* . . . ; and that all such marriages shall be absolutely null and void" (*Massachusetts* 1893:10). Yet Lydia Maria Child and William Lloyd Garrison—as well as William Ellery Channing and forty-two other Bostonians (see Johnston 1970:335ff.) campaigned against the Massachusetts intermarriage ban so successfully that it was repealed in 1843. Child expressed her fear in 1839 that "posterity will look back with as much wonder at the excited discussions on this subject as we now do to the proceedings of learned lawyers and judges, who hung witches for raising a storm" (Child 1982:110–111). Garrison was equally prophetic in questioning the state's right to interfere with the private realm of marriage when he argued in 1843, "It is not the province, and does not belong to the power of any legislative assembly, in a republican government to decide on the complexional affinity of those who choose to be united together in wedlock; and it may as rationally decree that corpulent and lean, tall and short, strong and weak persons shall not be married to each other as that there must be an agreement in the complexion of the parties" (Washington 1970: 84).[4] Charles Chesnutt, whose 1889 survey "What Is a White Man?" this collection includes, also argued prophetically about these laws: "Some day they will, perhaps, become mere curiosities of jurisprudence; the 'black laws' will be bracketed with the 'blue laws,' and will be at best but landmarks by which to measure the progress of the nation."

These opinions, voiced by cultural "insiders" at a time when interracial marriage was banned in the majority of states, were just as strong as were those phrased by foreign observers. Lord James Bryce called the American intermarriage

---

4. Garrison's example foreshadows an antiapartheid allegory written more than a century later, E. V. Stone's "The Kingdom of Ethnaria" (Cape Town, 1959):

> Once upon a time there was a kingdom of Ethnaria, but all was not well, for it was discovered that the great virtues of the people, such as pride, selfishness, arrogance, hatred and greed, were in danger of being watered down or even lost altogether, through indiscriminate marriage and association. As a first step, it was decreed that all long-nosed people should be kept separate from their less endowed fellows, as the nation was in danger of losing the ability to look down its nose. Again, the long-sighted members of the community were to be kept free from association with the short-sighted, the tall from the short, the blue-eyed from the brown-eyed, the hairy from the glabrous, the freckled from the clear, the bow-legged from the knock-kneed, the left-handed from the right-handed, and the stout from the thin. Step by step the policy was enforced. Each group had its separate area, and although there were some attempts made to evade the law, marriage between the groups was kept to a minimum, while the King had emblazoned on its coat of arms the legend, *Divided we stand; united we fall.*
>
> The only thing that remained to be done in order to perfect the system, was to separate the male from the female. In spite of pessimistic warning that this would result in the death of the nation, it was agreed by the King, in consultation with the Monarch, that those who criticised the plan were just agitators, and that if the ship should go down, it would do so with its colours flying.
>
> Once upon a time there was a kingdom of Ethnaria.

ban "one of the least defensible of all laws" in 1888 (Rogers 1988:80); and Tocqueville's traveling companion Gustave de Beaumont wrote in 1835: "Intermarriages
are certainly the best, if not the unique, means of fusing the white and the black
races. They are also the most obvious index of equality" (Beaumont 1958 [1835]:
245). Many other observers voiced criticism or expressed incomprehension of
these laws. As Randall Kennedy's essay illuminates, even Southern courts were
at times keenly aware of the exceptional nature of the antimiscegenation statutes.
Thus a South Carolina court ruled in 1873 that, while it considered interracial
marriages as "immoral" and "revolting," it realized that this was not "the common sentiment of the civilized and Christian world" since many European countries and U.S. states did not prohibit interracial marriage.

Naturally, the institution of literature—the topic of part II of this book—could
not help but become part of the debate. Whether an interracial marriage was
portrayed as successful or considered impossible had important political consequences, and Beaumont himself used the form of a novel to make his argument
against the American custom of banning intermarriage. In this remarkable work,
Marie, ou l'esclavage aux états-unis, the hero, Ludovic, understands American race
prejudice in terms of a perverted sense of antiaristocratic sentiment, telling Nelson, the white father of Marie, his beloved mixed-blood bride-to-be: "If your
custom is not to admit the transmission of honors by blood, then why does it
sanction inherited infamy? One is not born noble, one is born ignominious! Now,
you must admit that these are horrid prejudices!" Yet Ludovic assumes that the
institution of marriage could not possibly be affected by those prejudices when
he tells Nelson: "However, a white man, if such was his wish, could marry a free
woman of color," and the following dialogue ensues:

Nelson: No, my friend, you are mistaken.
Ludovic: What power could hinder him?
Nelson: The law. It contains an express prohibition, and declares such a marriage
   null.
Ludovic: A hateful law! But I shall defy that law. (Beaumont 1958 [1835]:63)

Many American novels, plays, and poems participated in the debate, from Dion
Boucicault's *The Octoroon*—in the American version of which the titular heroine
Zoe poisons herself, but in the English versions of which the white hero George
Peyton gets to marry her (see Degen 1975)—to William Dean Howells's novel
An Imperative Duty and Mark Twain's *Pudd'nhead Wilson,* and from William
Faulkner's *Absalom, Absalom!* to Allen Tate's *The Fathers.* Many essays in the
present collection, especially those in part II, examine this literature, ranging from
Lydia Maria Child, Harriet Beecher Stowe, and Mary Denison to Mark Twain,
Charles Chesnutt, and Jean Toomer. I would like here merely to add a few more
examples. In Epes Sargent's novel *Peculiar* (1864), a Northern divine is invoked
with the argument: "What a strange reason for oppressing a race of fellow-beings,
that if we restore them to their rights we shall marry them! (p. 149). Madame
Delphine tells Père Jerome in George Washington Cable's *In Old Creole Days*

(1879), " 'tis not Miché Vignevielle w'at's crezzie. . . . Tis dad *law!* Dad *law* is crezzie! Dad law is a fool" (p. 6). And in William S. Henry's novel *Out of Wedlock* (1931), Reverend Nathaniel Pius asks Pastor Edward Jones: "Do you believe it impossible for God to join in the bond of holy wedlock a white man to a Negro woman?" Jones answers: "No, I don't believe it impossible, but it is improbable that he does it in Texas" (pp. 31–32).

The laws banning interracial marriages are often thematized, and at times (for example in Frank Webb's *The Garies and Their Friends* and Pauline Hopkins's *Contending Forces*) become plot-constitutive in American literature. Today, creative work in literature and film continues to revisit a debate it still considers alive at the cultural level: one only has to think of John Gregory Brown's *Decorations in a Ruined Cemetery*, Danzy Senna's *Causasia*, Spike Lee's *Jungle Fever*, and James Ivory's *Jefferson in Paris*.

A final example comes from a pioneer of interracial studies, J. A. Rogers, in whose 1917 novel, *From "Superman" to Man,* the Negro Pullman porter Dixon combines the kinds of arguments advanced by Beaumont and Garrison and memorably pronounces that the "right to select one's mate is one of the most ancient, most sacred of individual rights, and when the state interferes in this, except in the case of the mentally unfit, it but adds humor to the witticism—'This is a free country' " (Rogers 1988:80). This character in Rogers's little-known 1917 novel anticipates Hannah Arendt's 1959 argument as well as Justice Warren's 1967 Supreme Court decision in *Loving v. Commonwealth of Virginia,* both of which are included in this book.

It is telling that the German-Jewish refugee Arendt prefaced her "Reflections on Little Rock" with the comment, "Like most people of European origin I have difficulty in understanding, let alone sharing, the common prejudices of Americans in this area." In her essay she firmly insisted:

> The right to marry whoever one wishes is an elementary human right compared to which "the right to attend an integrated school, the right to sit where one pleases on a bus, the right to go into any hotel or recreation area or place of amusement, regardless of one's skin or color or race" are minor indeed. (p. 496, this volume.)

That essay was so controversial in 1959 that *Commentary,* which had commissioned it, refused to publish it, and when it finally did appear in *Dissent,* it was accompanied by an editorial disclaimer and two sharp rebuttals, one of which called Arendt an "ardent champion" of intermarriage; in the subsequent issue of *Dissent,* Sidney Hook wrote that Arendt gave "priority to agitation for equality in the bedroom rather than to equality in education." Yet eight years later Chief Justice Warren virtually adopted Arendt's (or shall we say, Rogers's porter Dixon's?) arguments when, in ending the era of "miscegenation" laws, he stated: "Marriage is one of the basic civil rights of man, fundamental to our very existence and survival. . . . Under our Constitution, the freedom to marry or not to marry, a person of another race resides with the individual and cannot be infringed upon by the State." Just as laws shaped and gave themes to literature, literature may also have affected the realm of the law.

IV

The present collection calls attention to the significance of black-white interracialism and its repression by bringing together for the first time pioneering, provocative, informative, and outstanding work on this topic in American history, literature, and law.[5] More than thirty years after the end of this form of American exceptionalism, at a time when American black-white intermarriage rates are dramatically on the rise—though still comparatively low (see Farley, forthcoming)—the time is right to examine the strange ramifications of this fear of mixing, particularly odd in a melting-pot culture. At the same time, while the collection specifically focuses on the United States, its findings should interest a much broader audience concerned about the past and future of race relations and civil rights in many lands in this new century.

The collection is divided into three major sections, focusing on history and the law, literature, and social theory. These divisions are necessarily loose, as there is an interdisciplinary spirit at work here. Many of the legal essays also draw on literature, and some of the others on law; and several essays in part I and part II are significant theoretically and could have been included in part III. The collection concludes with a short list of further readings, all book-length works.

The volume provides essential information to students and general readers and should stimulate more research. This book is about interracialism in American history, law, and literature; it would be desirable to find more work done on interracialism in areas including the visual arts (Dalton 1992, 1993; and Wilson 1991) or film (Cripps 1993a, b; and Kydd 1996),[6] and to find the interdisciplinary thrust of the work presented here expanded and extended in future studies.

Many shared themes emerge in this book. It concerns an area of inquiry in which even the most descriptive essays indicate a moral agenda. The political nature of interracialism becomes apparent in many contributions; one indication of it is the frequency of references to American presidents in connection with interracial concubinage and marriage plots, and with interracial descendants. The essays in this volume allude to Thomas Jefferson's position toward egalitarianism that was paradoxically undercut by his role as a slaveholder and his possible relationship with Sally Hemings (at the center of media attention in 1998 in connection with public belief in the certainty of DNA evidence, but the subject of American fiction since the days of William Wells Brown's *Clotel, or the President's Daughter*). It is possible that the author of the Declaration of Independence had a son who could not vote or serve on juries; they mention the rumor that

5. Except where indicated, the essays are reprinted in their entirety here; and the reader interested in pursuing further some of the issues raised on these pages will appreciate that the full notes of the original essays are included here. The different disciplinary backgrounds make for different systems of annotation, but lawyers, literary critics, and historians will be happy to find that the essays in their own disciplines have not been reformatted and homogenized to another citation system.
6. Interracial films in the United States alone include *The Birth of a Nation* (1915), *Scar of Shame* (1927), *Imitation of Life* (1934 and 1959), *Anna Lucasta* (1949 and 1958), *Lost Boundaries* (1949), *Pinky* (1949), *Raintree County* (1957), *Shadows* (1960), *One Potato, Two Potato* (1964), *Guess Who's Coming to Dinner* (1967), *Hairspray* (1988), *Jungle Fever* (1991), and *Jefferson in Paris* (1995).

Andrew Jackson had to protest that he had a half-brother who was sold as a slave. The essays report that John Tyler's daughter tried to reach foreign soil with her secret lover, before being captured and sold into slavery by her own father, the president; they quote from Lincoln's horrified recoiling at the possibility of interracial marriage in a debate with Douglas; they refer to Andrew Johnson's concubine, and even to the integration supporter Harry Truman who recited the clichéd question, "Would you want your daughter to marry a Negro?", assuming that the answer of a white journalist would have to be "no." In a country in which a person of color (or a woman of any race) has yet to become president, these stories of presidents—and of their mothers, brothers, sons, and daughters—are steps in the unfinished process of imagining the country as a multiracial family, of fully living up to the ideal of *fraternité*.[7] The reader repeatedly wonders whether legislators were trying to establish "racial purity" when they invoked a supposedly longstanding racial order they were merely preserving. "Racial integrity" often appears as goals for the future, and not as the legacy of a past.

Essayists must report their findings in contexts the reader can understand. These contexts range from historical excavation to psychoanalysis, from internationally comparative and contrastive approaches to new historicist models of investigation, and from century-old pathbreaking explorations of what would now be called "whiteness studies" to recent work informed by a focus on the human body. Written from a variety of perspectives, and published over the course of over a century, these essays by literary critics, professors of law, historians, sociologists, philosophers, poets, and journalists combine the seriousness of rigorous archival work with some of the urgent and painful questions that have led to the rise of cultural studies.

Interracialism: Black-White Intermarriage in American History, Literature, and Law presents important work on the three centuries of legalized opposition to interracial family structures in the United States. This book constitutes a progress narrative, as the *Loving v. Commonwealth of Virginia* Supreme Court decision of 1967 removed the legal underpinning of an American peculiarity that would currently find few intellectual defenders. Yet if the problem of the twentieth century was, as W. E. B. Du Bois predicted in 1903, "the problem of the color-line" (p. vii), what is the problem of the twenty-first century? Has the United States permanently abolished a legal framework that for centuries isolated it from other countries, a framework that critics have compared to fascist laws? Or is the country merely entering, as Peggy Pascoe warns, a period of a new ideology—that of "the deliberate nonrecognition of race"—with its own, perhaps even more sinister consequences? Is the problem of the twenty-first century the problem of color blindness? Or do Americans still have to struggle out of the shell of the old racial ideology of which so many aspects remain? Joel Perlmann compellingly identifies the "bizarre" assumption of all current U.S. Census projections (including those about "the browning" of America) "that a child born to an interracial couple

7. See the collection *Sally Hemings and Thomas Jefferson: History, Memory, and Civic Culture*, ed. Peter S. Onuf and Jan Ellen Lewis (Charlottesville: University Press of Virginia, 1999).

today will take the race of the mother and that, starting tomorrow, neither that child nor any other American will marry across race lines." Is the lasting legacy of "miscegenation law" that too many people and institutions focus inappropriately on race? Or is it that not enough people and institutions recognize race in the United States? *Interracialism* asks readers to address this question; and much depends on how they will answer it.

References

Applebaum, Harvey M. 1964. "Miscegenation Statutes: A Constitutional and Social Problem." *Georgetown Law Journal* 53:49–91.

Beaumont, Gustave de. 1958. *Marie* [1835]. Engl. trans. Barbara Chapman. Stanford: Stanford University Press.

Cable, George Washington. 1893. "Madame Delphine" [1879]. *In Old Creole Days*. New York: Scribners.

Child, Lydia Maria. 1982. *Selected Letters, 1817–1889*. Ed. Milton Meltzer and Patricia G. Holland. Amherst: University of Massachusetts Press.

Cripps, Thomas. 1993a. *Slow Fade to Black: The Negro in American Films 1902–1942*. 2nd ed. Oxford: Oxford University Press.

————. 1993b. *Making Movies Black: The Hollywood Message Movie from World War II to the Civil Rights Era*. Oxford: Oxford University Press.

Daggett, Harriet Spiller. 1953. *Legal Essays on Family Law*. Baton Rouge: Louisiana State University Press.

Dalton, Karen C. 1992. "Currier & Ives's Darktown Comics: Ridicule and Race." Presented at the Museum of the City of New York, 2 May.

————. 1993. "Caricature in the Service of Racist Stereotypes: Evolution of Nineteenth-century Caricatures of African Americans." Delivered at American Antiquarian Society Seminar in American Art History, 23 February.

Degen, John A. 1975. "How to End *The Octoroon*." *Educational Theatre Journal* 27: 170–178.

Degler, Carl N. 1973. *Neither Black Nor White: Slavery and Race Relations in Brazil and the United States* [1971]. Repr. New York: Macmillan.

Domínguez, Virginia R. 1986. *White by Definition: Social Classification in Creole Louisiana*. New Brunswick, N.J.: Rutgers University Press.

Du Bois, W. E. Burghardt. 1903. *The Souls of Black Folk: Essays and Sketches*. Chicago: A. C. McClurg.

Farley, Reynolds. 1999. "Racial Issues: Recent Trends in Residential Patterns and Intermarriage." In *Diversity and Its Discontents: Cultural Conflict and Common Ground in Contemporary American Society*, ed. Neil J. Smelser and Jeffrey C. Alexander. Princeton: Princeton University Press, 1999.

Fletcher, Michael A. 1998. "Mixed Marriages Give U.S. Melting Pot New Life." *International Herald Tribune* (December 30): 2.

Gaines, Francis Pendleton. 1925. *The Southern Plantation: A Study in the Development and the Accuracy of a Tradition*. New York: Columbia University Press.

Getman, Karen A. 1984. "Sexual Control in the Slaveholding South." *Harvard Women's Law Journal* 7.1 (spring): 115–152.

Henry, William S. 1931. *Out of Wedlock*. Boston: Richard G. Badger.

Hodes, Martha, ed. 1999. *Sex, Love, Race: Crossing Boundaries in North American History*. New York: New York University Press.

Jefferson, Thomas. 1950. *The Papers of Thomas Jefferson*. Vol. 2, ed. Jackson Boyd. Princeton, N.J.: Princeton University Press.

Jenks, Albert E. 1916. "The Legal Status of Negro-White Amalgamation in the United States." *American Journal of Sociology* 21 (March): 666–678.

Johnston, James Hugo. 1970. *Race Relations in Virginia and Miscegenation in the South, 1776–1860*. Amherst: University of Massachusetts Press.

Koppelman, Andrew. 1988. "The Miscegenation Analogy: Sodomy Law As Sex Discrimination." *Yale Law Journal* 98.1 (November): 145–164.

Hardaway, Roger D. "Unlawful Love: A History of Arizona's Miscegenation Law." *Journal of American History* 27 (winter 1986): 377–390.

Krieger, Heinrich. 1936. *Das Rassenrecht in den Vereinigten Staaten*. Neue Deutsche Forschungen, Abt. Staats-, Verwaltungs-, Kirchen-, Völkerrecht und Staatstheorie, vol. 6. Berlin: Junker und Dünnhaupt Verlag.

Kydd, Elspeth. 1996. " 'Touched by the Tar Brush': Miscegenation and Mulattos in Classical Hollywood Cinema." Ph.D. diss., Northwestern University.

Lewis, Bernard. 1990. *Race and Slavery in the Middle East: An Historical Enquiry*. New York: Oxford University Press.

Lombardo, Paul A. 1988. "Miscegenation, Eugenics, and Racism: Historical Footnotes to *Loving v. Virginia*." *University of California Davis Law Review* 21.2 (winter): 421–452.

Massachusetts, Acts and Laws of the Commonwealth of. 1893. Repr. Boston: Wright and Potter.

Nelson, John Herbert. 1968. *The Negro Character in American Literature* [1926]. Repr. College Park, Md.: McGrath.

J. A. Rogers. 1941–1944. *Sex and Race*. 3 vols. New York: Helga M. Rogers, n.d. (vols. copyright 1941, 1942, and 1944 respectively).

———. 1988. *From Superman to Man* [1917]. Repr. St. Petersburg, Fla.: Helga M. Rogers.

Sargent, Epes. 1864. *Peculiar: A Tale of the Great Transition*. New York: Carleton.

Schuhmann, George. 1968. "Miscegenation: An Example of Judicial Recidivism." *Journal of Family Law* 8: 69–78.

Schuyler, George S. 1940. "Who Is 'Negro'? Who Is 'White'?" *Common Ground* 1 (autumn): 53–56.

Seed, Patricia. 1988. *To Love, Honor, and Obey in Colonial Mexico: Conflicts over Marriage Choice, 1574–1821*. Stanford, Calif.: Stanford University Press.

Sherman, Richard B. 1988. " 'The Last Stand': The Fight for Racial Integrity in Virginia in the 1920s." *The Journal of Southern History* 54.1 (February): 69–92.

Snowden, Frank M. 1970. *Blacks in Antiquity*. Cambridge, Mass.: Belknap Press of Harvard University Press.

Stone, E. V. "The Kingdom of Ethnaria." *Africa South* 3.1 (Cape Town, 1959): 47–48.

W.A.S. 1927. "Intermarriage with Negroes—A Survey of State Statutes." *Yale Law Journal* 36 (April): 858–866.

Washington, Joseph R., Jr. 1970. *Marriage in Black and White*. Boston: Beacon Press.

Wilson, Judith. 1991. "Optical Illusions: Images of Miscegenation in Nineteenth- and Twentieth-Century American Art." *American Art* 5.1 (summer): 89–107.

PART I

The History of "Miscegenation" and the Legal Construction of Race

This collection begins with the texts of selected laws (Arizona and Virginia) and the momentous Supreme Court decisions of *Pace v. State of Alabama* (1883) and *Loving v. Commonwealth of Virginia* (1967) that mark the modern trajectory of legal thinking about black-white interracialism. The essays that follow span more than a century. The legally trained writer Charles W. Chesnutt (whose oeuvre of interracial literature is briefly discussed in this collection by Penelope Bullock and William L. Andrews and is mentioned by several others) provides a provocative survey of the heterogeneous definitions of "What Is a White Man?" in different states in the 1880s. His dwelling on the particularly liberal definition of whiteness in South Carolina, where "reputation and reception into society" and "admixture of blood" mattered (perhaps to increase the number of whites), has particular resonance for Chesnutt, whose novel *The House Behind the Cedars*, published a decade later, had a plot that was clearly affected by this issue. Carter G. Woodson, the founder of African-American history, offers the first scholarly, comparative, and informative account of "The Beginnings of Miscegenation of the Whites and Blacks," first published in 1918, in an essay that juxtaposes legislative prohibition with stories of lived lives, culled from a variety of sources. It is an essay that established a field, and from which much later work drew its inspiration. William D. Zabel's essay on "Interracial Marriage and the Law" (originally published in *Atlantic Monthly* in 1965) is valuable for a different reason: two years before *Loving v. Commonwealth of Virginia*, Zabel reviews the legal situation surrounding interracial marriage historically, with a focus on legal absurdities (including the Arizona law) in order to make a strong case for the Supreme Court to strike down these laws. Even though the issue might prove to be "incendiary to some whites and insignificant to most Negroes," he finds that no laws are "more symbolic of the Negro's relegation to second-class citizenship."

Part I continues with essays from the 1980s and 1990s, decades after the Supreme Court decision had declared the miscegenation statutes unconstitutional. Clearly animated by cultural studies approaches, Eva Saks's "Representing Miscegenation Law" (1988) is both a provocative survey and a Foucault-inspired institutional analysis of the laws and decisions prohibiting interracial sex and marriage. Tellingly, her far-ranging essay is framed by a literary focus on Dion Boucicault's *Octoroon* (followed by references to *Othello*, *Absalom, Absalom!*, and *Pudd'nhead Wilson*). It calls attention to the origin of the word *miscegenation*, emphasizes the paradoxes in decisions including *Pace v. State of Alabama*, *Loving v. Commonwealth of Virginia*, and the politics of the "miscegenous body" in the legal establishment of "race." Saks also highlights the modern connections with eugenicism and fascism. In "Racial Purity and Interracial Sex in the Law of Colonial and Antebellum Virginia," the renowned legal scholars A. Leon Higginbotham, Jr., and Barbara K. Kopytoff offer a magisterial, in-depth survey and the most thoroughly researched analysis of the legal situation in Virginia up to the Civil War, with a forward glance beyond that period and up to the "Racial Integrity Law" of 1924. The authors review legislation and judication in their historical contexts and offer provocative new readings of frequently cited cases—such as the 1630 whipping of Hugh Davis "for abusing himself to the dishonr of God and shame of Christianity by defiling his body in lying with a negro." Since the gender of the Negro is not identified the "extremely strong language may have reflected the Council's revulsion at a homosexual relationship" (p. 102n98). Higginbotham and Kopytoff include consensual sex and rape cases and view the concepts of racial purity, interracial sex, and interracial marriage as being "at the root of American racism that has entangled almost every aspect of American society." Law professor Randall Kennedy surveys, in "The Enforcement of Anti-Miscegenation Laws" (part of a forthcoming book), an entire series of theoretically significant practical issues that were raised when laws were tested in actual cases, ranging from problems in classification and the knowledge of racial identity to problems of proof and questions of comity, and focusing especially on divorce and annulment cases. Kennedy treats the messiness of racial classification, the heterogeneity of policies in different states, and the surprising refusal of most courts to grant husbands annulments on racial grounds—a fact that flies in the face of what one would expect from the logic of white supremacy. "Reading Race, Rhetoric, and the Female Body in the *Rhinelander* Case," Jamie Wacks's examination of a New York high-society case, is an in-depth study of one of the most remarkable modern interracial annulment attempts. Working with the trial transcript (previously considered lost), Wacks shows narrative patterns and the prurient and voyeuristic extremes to which legal experts could go in order to determine "race," or a husband's knowledge of his wife's race, in courtroom proceedings. In "Miscegenation Law, Court Cases, and Ideologies of 'Race' in Twentieth-Century America," the historian Peggy Pascoe takes her point of departure from *Kirby v. Kirby* and from other cases that challenged miscegenation laws, with a focus on Arizona. She reviews the decline of an old racist ideology and attempts to trace the rise of what she heretically terms "modernist racial ideology" according to which granting public recognition to racial categories was considered the same as racism itself. Many of the essays mention briefly, or analyze in depth, some of the same cases, so that part I offers different perspectives on not only the most famous rulings, but also on such cases as *Ferrall v. Ferrall, In re Monks Estate, Kirby v. Kirby*, or the quoting of Hitler's *Mein Kampf* in *Perez v. Sharp*.

LAWS AND DECISIONS

The Virginia "Act to Preserve Racial Integrity" of 1924*

1. Be it enacted by the General Assembly of Virginia, That the State Registrar of Vital Statistics may as soon as practicable after the taking effect of this act, prepare a form whereon the racial composition of any individual, as Caucasian, negro, Mongolian, American Indian, Asiatic Indian, Malay, or any mixture thereof, or any other non-Caucasic strains, and if there be any mixture, then the racial composition of the parents and other ancestors, in so far as ascertainable, so as to show in what generation such mixture occurred, may be certified by such individual, which form shall be known as a registration certificate. The State Registrar may supply to each local registrar a sufficient number of such forms for the purposes of this act; each local registrar may personally or by deputy, as soon as possible after receiving such forms, have made thereon in duplicate a certificate of the racial composition as aforesaid, of each person resident in his district, who so desires, born before June fourteenth, nineteen hundred and twelve, which certificate shall be made over the signature of said person, or in the case of children under fourteen years of age, over the signature of a parent, guardian, or other person standing in loco parentis. One of said certificates for each person thus registering in every district shall be forwarded to the State Registrar for his files; the other shall be kept on file by the local registrar.

Every local registrar may, as soon as practicable, have such registration certificate made by or for each person in his district who so desires, born before June fourteen, nineteen hundred and twelve, for whom he has not filed a registration certificate or a birth certificate.

2. It shall be a felony for any person wilfully or knowingly to make a registration certificate false as to color or race. The wilful making of a false registration or birth certificate shall be punished by confinement in the penitentiary for one year.

3. For each registration certificate properly made and returned to the State Registrar, the local registrar returning the same shall be entitled to a fee of twenty-five cents, to be paid by the registrant. Application for registration and for transcript may be made direct to the State Registrar, who may retain the fee for expenses of his office.

4. No marriage license shall be granted until the clerk or deputy clerk has reasonable assurance that the statements as to color of both man and woman are correct.

---

* From Ivan McDougle, *Mongrel Virginians: The Win Tribe* (Baltimore: Williams & Wilkins, 1926), 203–205.

If there is reasonable cause to disbelieve that applicants are of pure white race, when that fact is stated, the clerk or deputy clerk shall withhold the granting of the license until satisfactory proof is produced that both applicants are "white persons" as provided for by this act.

The clerk or deputy clerk shall use the same care to assure himself that both applicants are colored when that fact is claimed.

5. It shall hereafter be unlawful for any white person in this state to marry any save a white person, or a person with no other admixture of blood than white and American Indian. For the purpose of this act, the term "white person" shall apply only to the person who has no trace whatsoever of any blood other than Caucasian; but persons who have one-sixteenth or less of the blood of the American Indian and have no other non-caucasic blood shall be deemed to be white persons. All laws heretofore passed and now in effect regarding the intermarriage of white and colored persons shall apply to marriages prohibited by this act.

6. For carrying out the purposes of this act and to provide the necessary clerical assistance, postage and other expenses of the State Registrar of Vital Statistics, twenty per cent of the fees received by the local registrars under this act shall be paid to the State Bureau of Vital Statistics, which may be expended by the said bureau for the purposes of this act.

7. All acts or parts of acts inconsistent with this act are, to the extent of such inconsistency, hereby repealed.

"Marriage and Divorce" in 1913 Arizona*

All marriages of persons of Caucasian blood, or their descendants, with negroes, Mongolians or Indians, and their descendants, shall be null and void.

Pace v. State of Alabama, 1883†

Constitutional Law—Equal Protection of the Law—
Crimes between Different Races.

> *When one of two sections of a Code prescribes generally a punishment for an offense committed between persons of different sexes, and the other prescribes a punishment for offenses committed by persons of different races as well as different sexes, the two sections are consistent with each other,*

---

* From *Revised Statutes of Arizona*, ed. and annotated by Samuel L. Pattee (Phoenix: McNeil, 1913), 1310.

† From 106 U.S. 583; 1 S. Ct. 637; 1882 U.S.

and the latter section is not obnoxious to the fourteenth
amendment to the federal constitution as denying "to one
person the equal protection" of the laws.

In Error to the Supreme Court of Alabama.

Section 4184 of the Code of Alabama provides that "if any man and woman live together in adultery or fornication, each of them must, on the first conviction of the offense, be fined not less than $100, and may also be imprisoned in the county jail or sentenced to hard labor for the county for not more than six months. On the second conviction for the offense, with the same person, the offender must be fined not less than $300, and may be imprisoned in the county jail, or sentenced to hard labor for the county, for not more than 12 months; and for a third or any subsequent conviction with the same person, must be imprisoned in the penitentiary or sentenced to hard labor for the county for two years."

Section 4189 of the same Code declares that "if any white person and any negro, or the descendant of any negro to the third generation, inclusive, though one ancestor of each generation was a white person, intermarry or live in adultery or fornication with each other, each of them must, on conviction, be imprisoned in the penitentiary or sentenced to hard labor for the county for not less than two nor more than seven years."

In November, 1881, the plaintiff in error, Tony Pace, a negro man, and Mary J. Cox, a white woman, were indicted under section 4189, in a circuit court of Alabama, for living together in a state of adultery or fornication, and were tried, convicted, and sentenced, each to two years' imprisonment in the state penitentiary. On appeal to the supreme court of the state the judgment was affirmed, and he brought the case here on writ of error, insisting that the act under which he was indicted and convicted is in conflict with the concluding clause of the first section of the fourteenth amendment of the constitution, which declares that no state shall "deny to any person the equal protection of the laws."

J. R. Tompkins, for the plaintiff in error.

H. C. Tompkins, for the defendant in error.

FIELD, J. The counsel of the plaintiff in error compares sects. 4184 and 4189 of the Code of Alabama, and assuming that the latter relates to the same offence as the former, and prescribes a greater punishment for it, because one of the parties is a negro, or of negro descent, claims that a discrimination is made against the colored person in the punishment designated, which conflicts with the clause of the Fourteenth Amendment prohibiting a State from denying to any person within its jurisdiction the equal protection of the laws.

The counsel is undoubtedly correct in his view of the purpose of the clause of the amendment in question, that it was to prevent hostile and discriminating State legislation against any person or class of persons. Equality of protection under the laws implies not only accessibility by each one, whatever his race, on the same terms with others to the courts of the country for the security of his person and property, but that in the administration of criminal justice he shall not be subjected, for the same offence, to any greater or different punishment. Such was the view of congress in the re-enactment of the civil-rights act, after the adoption of the amendment. That act, after providing that all persons within the jurisdiction of the United States shall have the same right, in every state and territory, to make and enforce contracts, to sue, be parties, give evidence, and to the full and equal benefit of all laws and proceedings for the security of person and property as is enjoyed by white citizens, declares that they shall be subject "to like punishment, pains, penalties, taxes, licenses, and exactions of every kind, and none other, any law, statute, ordinance, regulation, or custom to the contrary notwithstanding." 16 St., c. 114, § 16.

The defect in the argument of counsel consists in his assumption that any discrimination is made by the laws of Alabama in the punishment provided for the offense for which the plaintiff in error was indicted when committed by a person of the African race and when committed by a white person. The two sections of the Code cited are entirely consistent. The one prescribes, generally, a punishment for an offense committed between persons of different sexes; the other prescribes a punishment for an offense which can only be committed where the two sexes are of different races. There is in neither section any discrimination against either race. Section 4184 equally includes the offense when the persons of the two sexes are both white and when they are both black. Section 4189 applies the same punishment to both offenders, the white and the black. Indeed, the offense against which this latter section is aimed cannot be committed without involving the persons of both races in the same punishment. Whatever discrimination is made in the punishment prescribed in the two sections is directed against the offense designated and not against the person of any particular color or race. The punishment of each offending person, whether white or black, is the same.

Judgment affirmed.

Loving v. Commonwealth of Virginia, 1967*

Proceeding on motion to vacate sentences for violating state ban on interracial marriages. The Circuit Court of Caroline County, Virginia, denied motion, and writ of error was granted. The Virginia Supreme Court of Appeals, 206 Va. 924, 147 S.E.2d 78, affirmed the convictions, and probable jurisdiction was noted. The United States Supreme Court, Mr. Chief Justice Warren, held that miscegenation statutes adopted by Virginia to prevent marriages between persons solely on basis of racial classification violate equal protection and due process clauses of Fourteenth Amendment.

Convictions reversed.

1. Marriage
   Marriage is social relation subject to state's police power.

* From 388 U.S. 1; 87 S. Ct. 1817; 1967 U.S.

2. Marriage

Under Fourteenth Amendment, power of state to regulate marriage is not unlimited. U.S.C.A.Const. Amend. 14.

3. Constitutional Law

Mere equal application of statute containing racial classifications is not sufficient to remove classifications from Fourteenth Amendment's proscription of all invidious racial discriminations. U.S.C.A.Const. Amend. 14.

4. Constitutional Law

Fact of equal application of statutes containing racial classifications does not immunize statutes from heavy burden of justification which Fourteenth Amendment requires of state statutes drawn according to race. U.S.C.A.Const. Amend. 14.

5. Constitutional Law

Equal protection clause of Fourteenth Amendment requires consideration of whether classifications drawn by any statute constitute arbitrary and invidious discrimination. U.S.C.A.Const. Amend. 14.

6. Constitutional Law

Clear and central purpose of Fourteenth Amendment was to eliminate all official state sources of invidious racial discrimination in states. U.S.C.A.Const. Amend. 14.

7. Constitutional Law

At very least, equal protection clause of Fourteenth Amendment demands that racial classifications, especially suspect in criminal statutes, be subjected to most rigid scrutiny, and, if they are to be upheld, they must be shown to be necessary to accomplishment of some permissible state objective, independent of racial discrimination which it was object of Fourteenth Amendment to eliminate. U.S.C.A.Const. Amend. 14; Code Va.1950, §§ 1–14, 20–50, 20–53, 20–54, 20–57 to 20–59.

8. Constitutional Law

Restricting freedom to marry solely because of racial classifications violates central meaning of equal protection clause. U.S.C.A.Const. Amend. 14.

9. Constitutional Law
Miscegenation

Miscegenation statutes adopted by Virginia to prevent marriages between persons solely on basis of racial classification violate equal protection and due process clauses of Fourteenth Amendment. Code Va.1950, §§ 1–14, 20–50, 20–53, 20–54, 20–57 to 20–59; U.S.C.A.Const. Amend. 14.

10. Marriage

Marriage is one of basic civil rights of man.

11. Constitutional Law

Fourteenth Amendment requires that freedom of choice to marry not be restricted by invidious racial discrimination. U.S.C.A.Const. Amend. 14.

12. Marriage

Freedom to marry, or not marry, person of another race resides with individual and cannot be infringed by state. U.S.C.A.Const. Amend. 14.

Philip J. Hirschkop, pro hac vice, by special leave of Court, Bernard S. Cohen, Alexandria, Va., for appellants.

R. D. McIlwaine, III, Richmond, Va., for appellee.

William M. Marutani, Philadelphia, Pa., for Japanese American Citizens League, as amicus curiae, by special leave of Court.

Mr. Chief Justice WARREN delivered the opinion of the Court.

This case presents a constitutional question never addressed by this Court: whether a statutory scheme adopted by the State of Virginia to prevent marriages between persons solely on the basis of racial classifications violates the Equal Protection and Due Process Clauses of the Fourteenth Amendment.[1] For reasons which seem to us to reflect the central meaning of those constitutional commands, we conclude that these statutes cannot stand consistently with the Fourteenth Amendment.

In June 1958, two residents of Virginia, Mildred Jeter, a Negro woman, and Richard Loving, a white man, were married in the District of Columbia pursuant to its laws. Shortly after their marriage, the Lovings returned to Virginia and established their marital abode in Caroline County. At the October Term, 1958, of the Circuit Court of Caroline County, a grand jury issued an indictment charging the Lovings with violating Virginia's ban on interracial marriages. On January 6, 1959, the Lovings pleaded guilty to the charge and were sentenced to one year in jail; however, the trial judge suspended the sentence for a period of 25 years on the condition that the Lovings leave the State and not return to Virginia together for 25 years. He stated in an opinion that:

> Almighty God created the races white, black, yellow, malay and red, and he placed them on separate continents. And but for the interference with his arrangement there would be no cause for such marriages. The fact that he separated the races shows that he did not intend for the races to mix.

After their convictions, the Lovings took up residence in the District of Columbia. On November 6, 1963, they filed a motion in the state trial court to vacate the judgment and set aside the sentence on the ground that the statutes which they had violated were repugnant to the Fourteenth Amendment. The motion not having been decided by October 28, 1964, the Lovings instituted a class action in the United States District Court for the Eastern District of Virginia requesting that a three-judge court be convened to declare the Virginia antimiscegenation statutes unconstitutional and to enjoin state officials from enforcing their convictions. On January 22, 1965, the state trial judge denied the motion to vacate the sentences, and the Lovings perfected an appeal to the Supreme Court of Appeals of Virginia. On February 11, 1965, the three-judge District Court continued the

---

1. Section 1 of the Fourteenth Amendment provides:

> All persons born or naturalized in the United States and subject to the jurisdiction thereof, are citizens of the United States and of the State wherein they reside. No State shall make or enforce any law which shall abridge the privileges or immunities of citizens of the United States; nor shall any State deprive any person of life, liberty, or property, without due process of law; nor deny to any person within its jurisdiction the equal protection of the laws.

case to allow the Lovings to present their constitutional claims to the highest state court.

The Supreme Court of Appeals upheld the constitutionality of the antimiscegenation statutes and, after modifying the sentence, affirmed the convictions.[2] The Lovings appealed this decision, and we noted probable jurisdiction on December 12, 1966, 385 U.S. 986, 87 S.Ct. 595, 17 L.Ed.2d 448.

The two statutes under which appellants were convicted and sentenced are part of a comprehensive statutory scheme aimed at prohibiting and punishing interracial marriages. The Lovings were convicted of violating § 20–58 of the Virginia Code:

> *Leaving State to evade law.*—If any white person and colored person shall go out of this State, for the purpose of being married, and with the intention of returning, and be married out of it, and afterwards return to and reside in it, cohabiting as man and wife, they shall be punished as provided in § 20–59, and the marriage shall be governed by the same law as if it had been solemnized in this State. The fact of their cohabitation here as man and wife shall be evidence of their marriage.

Section 20–59, which defines the penalty for miscegenation, provides:

> *Punishment for marriage.*—If any white person intermarry with a colored person, or any colored person intermarry with a white person, he shall be guilty of a felony and shall be punished by confinement in the penitentiary for not less than one nor more than five years.

Other central provisions in the Virginia statutory scheme are § 20–57, which automatically voids all marriages between "a white person and a colored person" without any judicial proceeding,[3] and §§ 20–54 and 1–14 which, respectively, define "white persons" and "colored persons and Indians" for purposes of the statutory prohibitions.[4] The Lovings have never disputed in the course of this

---

2. 206 Va. 924, 147 S.E.2d 78 (1966).

3. Section 20–57 of the Virginia Code provides:

> *Marriages void without decree.*—All marriages between a white person and a colored person shall be absolutely void without any decree of divorce or other legal process. (Va.Code Ann. § 20–57 [1960 Repl. Vol.].)

4. Section 20–54 of the Virginia Code provides:

> *Intermarriage prohibited; meanings of term "White persons."*—it shall hereafter be unlawful for any white person in this State to marry any save a white person, or a person with no other admixture of blood than white and American Indian. For the purpose of this chapter, the term "white person" shall apply only to such person as has no trace whatever of any blood other than Caucasian; but persons who have one-sixteenth or less of the blood of the American Indian and have no other non-Caucasic blood shall be deemed to be white persons. All laws heretofore passed and now in effect regarding the intermarriage of white and colored persons shall apply to marriages prohibited by this chapter. (Va.Code Ann. § 20–54 [1960 Repl.Vol.].)

> The exception for persons with less than one-sixteenth "of the blood of the American Indian" is apparently accounted for, in the words of a tract issued by the Registrar of the State Bureau of

litigation that Mrs. Loving is a "colored person" or that Mr. Loving is a "white person" within the meanings given those terms by the Virginia statutes.

Virginia is now one of 16 States which prohibit and punish marriages on the basis of racial classifications.[5] Penalties for miscegenation arose as an incident to slavery and have been common in Virginia since the colonial period.[6] The present statutory scheme dates from the adoption of the Racial Integrity Act of 1924, passed during the period of extreme nativism which followed the end of the First World War. The central features of this Act, and current Virginia law, are the absolute prohibition of a "white person" marrying other than another "white person,"[7] a prohibition against issuing marriage licenses until the issuing official is satisfied that the applicants' statements as to their race are correct,[8] certificates of "racial composition" to be kept by both local and state registrars,[9] and the carrying forward of earlier prohibitions against racial intermarriage.[10]

Vital Statistics, by "the desire of all to recognize as an integral and honored part of the white race the descendants of John Rolfe and Pocahontas * * *." Plecker, The New Family and Race Improvement, 17 Va.Health Bull., Extra No. 12, at 25–26 (New Family Series No. 5, 1925), cited in Wadlington, The Loving Case; Virginia's Anti-Miscegenation Statute in Historical Perspective, 52 Va.L.Rev. 1189, 1202, n. 93 (1966).

Section 1–14 of the Virginia Code provides:

Colored persons and Indians defined.—Every person in whom there is ascertainable any Negro blood shall be deemed and taken to be a colored person, and every person not a colored person having one fourth or more of American Indian blood shall be deemed an American Indian; except that members of Indian tribes existing in this Commonwealth having one fourth or more of Indian blood and less than one sixteenth of Negro blood shall be deemed tribal Indians. (Va.Code Ann. § 1–14 [1960 Repl.Vol.].)

5. After the initiation of this litigation, Maryland repealed its prohibitions against interracial marriage, Md.Laws 1967, c. 6, leaving Virginia and 15 other States with statutes outlawing interracial marriage: Alabama, Ala.Const., Art. 4, § 102, Ala.Code, Tit. 14, § 360 (1958) ; Arkansas, Ark.Stat.Ann. § 55–104 (1947) ; Delaware, Del.Code Ann., Tit. 13, § 101 (1953); Florida, Fla.Const., Art. 16, § 24, F.S.A., Fla.Stat. § 741.11 (1965) F.S.A.; Georgia, Ga.Code Ann. § 53–106 (1961) ; Kentucky, Ky.Rev.Stat. Ann. § 402.020 (Supp.1966) ; Louisiana, La.Rev.Stat. § 14:79 (1950) ; Mississippi, Miss.Const., Art. 14, § 263, Miss.Code Ann. § 459 (1956) ; Missouri, Mo. Rev.Stat. § 451.020 (Supp.1966), V.A. M.S.; North Carolina, N.C.Const., Art. XIV, § 8, N.C.Gen.Stat. § 14–181 (1953); Oklahoma, Okla.Stat., Tit. 43, § 12 (Supp. 1965); South Carolina, S.C.Const., Art. 3, § 33, S.C.Code Ann. § 20–7 (1962) ; Tennessee, Tenn.Const., Art. 11, § 14, Tenn.Code Ann. § 36–402 (1955) ; Vernon's Ann.Texas, Tex.Pen.Code, Art. 492 (1952) ; West Virginia, W.Va.Code Ann. § 4697 (1961).

Over the past 15 years, 14 States have repealed laws outlawing interracial marriages: Arizona, California, Colorado, Idaho, Indiana, Maryland, Montana, Nebraska, Nevada, North Dakota, Oregon, South Dakota, Utah, and Wyoming.

The first state court to recognize that miscegenation statutes violate the Equal Protection Clause was the Supreme Court of California. Perez v. Sharp, 32 Cal.2d 711, 198 P.2d 17 (1948).

6. For a historical discussion of Virginia's miscegenation statutes, see Wadlington, supra, n. 4.

7. Va.Code Ann. § 20–54 (1960 Repl.Vol.).

8. Va.Code Ann. § 20–53 (1960 Repl.Vol.).

9. Va.Code Ann. § 20–50 (1960 Repl.Vol.).

10. Va.Code Ann. § 20–54 (1960 Repl.Vol.).

I

In upholding the constitutionality of these provisions in the decision below, the Supreme Court of Appeals of Virginia referred to its 1955 decision in Naim v. Naim, 197 Va. 80, 87 S.E.2d 749, as stating the reasons supporting the validity of these laws. In *Naim*, the state court concluded that the State's legitimate purposes were "to preserve the racial integrity of its citizens," and to prevent "the corruption of blood," "a mongrel breed of citizens," and "the obliteration of racial pride," obviously an endorsement of the doctrine of White Supremacy. Id., at 90, 87 S.E.2d, at 756. The court also reasoned that marriage has traditionally been subject to state regulation without federal intervention, and, consequently, the regulation of marriage should be left to exclusive state control by the Tenth Amendment.

[1, 2] While the state court is no doubt correct in asserting that marriage is a social relation subject to the State's police power, Maynard v. Hill, 125 U.S. 190, 8 S.Ct. 723, 31 L.Ed. 654 (1888), the State does not contend in its argument before this Court that its powers to regulate marriage are unlimited notwithstanding the commands of the Fourteenth Amendment. Nor could it do so in light of Meyer v. State of Nebraska, 262 U.S. 390, 43 S.Ct. 625, 67 L.Ed. 1042 (1923), and Skinner v. State of Oklahoma, 316 U.S. 535, 62 S.Ct. 1110, 86 L.Ed. 1655 (1942). Instead, the State argues that the meaning of the Equal Protection Clause, as illuminated by the statements of the Framers, is only that state penal laws containing an interracial element as part of the definition of the offense must apply equally to whites and Negroes in the sense that members of each race are punished to the same degree. Thus, the State contends that, because its miscegenation statutes punish equally both the white and the Negro participants in an interracial marriage, these statutes, despite their reliance on racial classifications do not constitute an invidious discrimination based upon race. The second argument advanced by the State assumes the validity of its equal application theory. The argument is that, if the Equal Protection Clause does not outlaw miscegenation statutes because of their reliance on racial classifications, the question of constitutionality would thus become whether there was any rational basis for a State to treat interracial marriages differently from other marriages. On this question, the State argues, the scientific evidence is substantially in doubt and, consequently, this Court should defer to the wisdom of the state legislature in adopting its policy of discouraging interracial marriages.

[3, 4] Because we reject the notion that the mere "equal application" of a statute containing racial classifications is enough to remove the classifications from the Fourteenth Amendment's proscription of all invidious racial discriminations, we do not accept the State's contention that these statutes should be upheld if there is any possible basis for concluding that they serve a rational purpose. The mere fact of equal application does not mean that our analysis of these statutes should follow the approach we have taken in cases involving no racial discrimination where the Equal Protection Clause has been arrayed against a statute discriminating between the kinds of advertising which may be displayed on trucks in New York City, Railway Express Agency, Inc. v. People of State of New York, 336

U.S. 106, 69 S.Ct. 463, 93 L.Ed. 533 (1949), or an exemption in Ohio's ad valorem tax for merchandise owned by a non-resident in a storage warehouse, Allied Stores of Ohio, Inc. v. Bowers, 358 U.S. 522, 79 S.Ct. 437, 3 L.Ed.2d 480 (1959). In these cases, involving distinctions not drawn according to race, the Court has merely asked whether there is any rational foundation for the discriminations, and has deferred to the wisdom of the state legislatures. In the case at bar, however, we deal with statutes containing racial classifications, and the fact of equal application does not immunize the statute from the very heavy burden of justification which the Fourteenth Amendment has traditionally required of state statutes drawn according to race.

The State argues that statements in the Thirty-ninth Congress about the time of the passage of the Fourteenth Amendment indicate that the Framers did not intend the Amendment to make unconstitutional state miscegenation laws. Many of the statements alluded to by the State concern the debates over the Freedmen's Bureau Bill, which President Johnson vetoed, and the Civil Rights Act of 1866, 14 Stat. 27, enacted over his veto. While these statements have some relevance to the intention of Congress in submitting the Fourteenth Amendment, it must be understood that they pertained to the passage of specific statutes and not to the broader, organic purpose of a constitutional amendment. As for the various statements directly concerning the Fourteenth Amendment, we have said in connection with a related problem, that although these historical sources "cast some light" they are not sufficient to resolve the problem; "[a]t best, they are inconclusive. The most avid proponents of the post-War Amendments undoubtedly intended them to remove all legal distinctions among 'all persons born or naturalized in the United States.' Their opponents, just as certainly, were antagonistic to both the letter and the spirit of the Amendments and wished them to have the most limited effect." Brown v. Board of Education of Topeka, 347 U.S. 483, 489, 74 S.Ct. 686, 689, 98 L.Ed. 873 (1954). See also Strauder v. State of West Virginia, 100 U.S. 303, 310, 25 L.Ed. 664 (1880). We have rejected the proposition that the debates in the Thirty-ninth Congress or in the state legislatures which ratified the Fourteenth Amendment supported the theory advanced by the State, that the requirement of equal protection of the laws is satisfied by penal laws defining offenses based on racial classifications so long as white and Negro participants in the offense were similarly punished. McLaughlin v. State of Florida, 379 U.S. 184, 85 S.Ct. 283, 13 L.Ed.2d 222 (1964).

[5, 6] The State finds support for its "equal application" theory in the decision of the Court in Pace v. State of Alabama, 106 U.S. 583, 1 S.Ct. 637, 27 L.Ed. 207 (1883). In that case, the Court upheld a conviction under an Alabama statute forbidding adultery or fornication between a white person and a Negro which imposed a greater penalty than that of a statute proscribing similar conduct by members of the same race. The Court reasoned that the statute could not be said to discriminate against Negroes because the punishment for each participant in the offense was the same. However, as recently as the 1964 Term, in rejecting the reasoning of that case, we stated "*Pace* represents a limited view of the Equal Protection Clause which has not withstood analysis in the subsequent decisions

of this Court." McLaughlin v. Florida, supra, 379 U.S. at 188, 85 S.Ct. at 286. As we there demonstrated, the Equal Protection Clause requires the consideration of whether the classifications drawn by any statute constitute an arbitrary and invidious discrimination. The clear and central purpose of the Fourteenth Amendment was to eliminate all official state sources of invidious racial discrimination in the States. Slaughter-House Cases, 16 Wall. 36, 71, 21 L.Ed. 394 (1873); Strauder v. State of West Virginia, 100 U.S. 303, 307–308, 25 L.Ed. 664 (1880); Ex parte Virginia, 100 U.S. 339, 344–345, 25 L.Ed. 676 (1880); Shelley v. Kraemer, 334 U.S. 1, 68 S.Ct. 836, 92 L.Ed. 1161 (1948); Burton v. Wilmington Parking Authority, 365 U.S. 715, 81 S.Ct. 856, 6 L.Ed.2d 45 (1961).

[7] There can be no question but that Virginia's miscegenation statutes rest solely upon distinctions drawn according to race. The statutes proscribe generally accepted conduct if engaged in by members of different races. Over the years, this Court has consistently repudiated "[d]istinctions between citizens solely because of their ancestry" as being "odious to a free people whose institutions are founded upon the doctrine of equality." Hirabayashi v. United States, 320 U.S. 81, 100, 63 S.Ct. 1375, 1385, 87 L.Ed. 1774 (1943). At the very least, the Equal Protection Clause demands that racial classifications, especially suspect in criminal statutes, be subjected to the "most rigid scrutiny," Korematsu v. United States, 323 U.S. 214, 216, 65 S.Ct. 193, 194, 89 L.Ed. 194 (1944), and, if they are ever to be upheld, they must be shown to be necessary to the accomplishment of some permissible state objective, independent of the racial discrimination which it was the object of the Fourteenth Amendment to eliminate. Indeed, two members of this Court have already stated that they "cannot conceive of a valid legislative purpose . . . which makes the color of a person's skin the test of whether his conduct is a criminal offense." McLaughlin v. Florida, supra, 379 U.S. at 198, 85 S.Ct. at 292, (Stewart J., joined by Douglas, J., concurring).

[8] There is patently no legitimate overriding purpose independent of invidious racial discrimination which justifies this classification. The fact that Virginia prohibits only interracial marriages involving white persons demonstrates that the racial classifications must stand on their own justification, as measures designed to maintain White Supremacy.[11] We have consistently denied the constitutionality of measures which restrict the rights of citizens on account of race. There can be no doubt that restricting the freedom to marry solely because of racial classifications violates the central meaning of the Equal Protection Clause.

---

11. Appellants point out that the State's concern in these statutes, as expressed in the words of the 1924 Act's title, "An Act to Preserve Racial Integrity," extends only to the integrity of the white race. While Virginia prohibits whites from marrying any nonwhite (subject to the exception for the descendants of Pocahontas), Negroes, Orientals, and any other racial class may intermarry without statutory interference. Appellants contend that this distinction renders Virginia's miscegenation statutes arbitrary and unreasonable even assuming the constitutional validity of an official purpose to preserve "racial integrity." We need not reach this contention because we find the racial classifications in these statutes repugnant to the Fourteenth Amendment, even assuming an even-handed state purpose to protect the "integrity" of all races.

II

[9] These statutes also deprive the Lovings of liberty without due process of law in violation of the Due Process Clause of the Fourteenth Amendment. The freedom to marry has long been recognized as one of the vital personal rights essential to the orderly pursuit of happiness by free men.

[10–12] Marriage is one of the "basic civil rights of man," fundamental to our very existence and survival. Skinner v. State of Oklahoma, 316 U.S. 535, 541, 62 S.Ct. 1110, 1113, 86 L.Ed. 1655 (1942). See also Maynard v. Hill, 125 U.S. 190, 8 S.Ct. 723, 31 L.Ed. 654 (1888). To deny this fundamental freedom on so unsupportable a basis as the racial classifications embodied in these statutes, classifications so directly subversive of the principle of equality at the heart of the Fourteenth Amendment, is surely to deprive all the State's citizens of liberty without due process of law. The Fourteenth Amendment requires that the freedom of choice to marry not be restricted by invidious racial discriminations. Under our Constitution, the freedom to marry or not marry, a person of another race resides with the individual and cannot be infringed by the State.

These convictions must be reversed. It is so ordered.

Reversed.

Mr. Justice STEWART, concurring.

I have previously expressed the belief that "it is simply not possible for a state law to be valid under our Constitution which makes the criminality of an act depend upon the race of the actor." McLaughlin v. State of Florida, 379 U.S. 184, 198, 85 S.Ct. 283, 292, 13 L.Ed.2d 222 (concurring opinion). Because I adhere to that belief, I concur in the judgment of the Court.

ESSAYS

What Is a White Man?*

CHARLES W. CHESNUTT

The fiat having gone forth from the wise men of the South that the "all-pervading, all-conquering Anglo-Saxon race" must continue forever to exercise exclusive control and direction of the government of this so-called Republic, it becomes important to every citizen who values his birthright to know who are included in this grandiloquent term. It is of course perfectly obvious that the writer or speaker who used this expression—perhaps Mr. Grady of Georgia—did not say what he meant. It is not probable that he meant to exclude from full citizenship the Celts and Teutons and Gauls and Slavs who make up so large a proportion of our population; he hardly meant to exclude the Jews, for even the most ardent fire-eater would hardly venture to advocate the disfranchisement of the thrifty race whose mortgages cover so large a portion of Southern soil. What the eloquent gentleman really meant by this high-sounding phrase was simply the white race; and the substance of the argument of that school of Southern writers to which he belongs, is simply that for the good of the country the Negro should have no voice in directing the government or public policy of the Southern States or of the nation.

But it is evident that where the intermingling of the races has made such progress as it has in this country, the line which separates the races must in many instances have been practically obliterated. And there has arisen in the United States a very large class of the population who are certainly not Negroes in an ethnological sense, and whose children will be no nearer Negroes than themselves. In view, therefore, of the very positive ground taken by the white leaders of the South, where most of these people reside, it becomes in the highest degree important to them to know what race they belong to. It ought to be also a matter of serious concern to the Southern white people; for if their zeal for good government is so great that they contemplate the practical overthrow of the Constitution and laws of the United States to secure it, they ought at least to be sure that no man entitled to it by their own argument, is robbed of a right so precious as that of free citizenship; the "all-pervading, all conquering Anglo-Saxon" ought to set as high a value on American citizenship as the all-conquering Roman placed upon the franchise of his State two thousand years ago. This discussion would of course be of little interest to the genuine Negro, who is entirely outside of the charmed circle, and must content himself with the acquisition of wealth, the pursuit of learning and such other privileges as his "best friends" may find it

* From Charles W. Chesnutt, "What Is a White Man?" *The Independent* 41. 2113 (May 30, 1889): 5–6 (693–694).

consistent with the welfare of the nation to allow him; but to every other good citizen the inquiry ought to be a momentous one, What is a white man?

In spite of the virulence and universality of race prejudice in the United States, the human intellect long ago revolted at the manifest absurdity of classifying men fifteen-sixteenths white as black men; and hence there grew up a number of laws in different states of the Union defining the limit which separated the white and colored races, which was, when these laws took their rise and is now to a large extent, the line which separated freedom and opportunity from slavery or hopeless degradation. Some of these laws are of legislative origin; others are judge-made laws, brought out by the exigencies of special cases which came before the courts for determination. Some day they will, perhaps, become mere curiosities of jurisprudence; the "black laws" will be bracketed with the "blue laws," and will be at best but landmarks by which to measure the progress of the nation. But to-day these laws are in active operation, and they are, therefore, worthy of attention; for every good citizen ought to know the law, and, if possible, to respect it; and if not worthy of respect, it should be changed by the authority which enacted it. Whether any of the laws referred to here have been in any manner changed by very recent legislation the writer cannot say, but they are certainly embodied in the latest editions of the revised statutes of the states referred to.

The colored people were divided, in most of the Southern States, into two classes, designated by law as Negroes and mulattoes respectively. The term Negro was used in its ethnological sense, and needed no definition; but the term "mulatto" was held by legislative enactment to embrace all persons of color not Negroes. The words "quadroon" and "mestizo" are employed in some of the law books, tho not defined; but the term "octoroon," as indicating a person having one-eighth of Negro blood, is not used at all, so far as the writer has been able to observe.

The states vary slightly in regard to what constitutes a mulatto or person of color, and as to what proportion of white blood should be sufficient to remove the disability of color. As a general rule, less than one-fourth of Negro blood left the individual white—in theory; race questions being, however, regulated very differently in practice. In Missouri, by the code of 1855, still in operation, so far as not inconsistent with the Federal Constitution and laws, "any person other than a Negro, any one of whose grandmothers or grandfathers is or shall have been a Negro, tho all of his or her progenitors except those descended from the Negro may have been white persons, shall be deemed a mulatto." Thus the color-line is drawn at one-fourth of Negro blood, and persons with only one-eighth are white.

By the Mississippi code of 1880, the color-line is drawn at one-fourth of Negro blood, all persons having less being theoretically white.

Under the *code noir* of Louisiana, the descendant of a white and a quadroon is white, thus drawing the line at one-eighth of Negro blood. The code of 1876 abolished all distinctions of color; as to whether they have been re-enacted since the Republican Party went out of power in that state the writer is not informed.

Jumping to the extreme North, persons are white within the meaning of the Constitution of Michigan who have less than one-fourth of Negro blood.

In Ohio the rule, as established by numerous decisions of the Supreme Court, was that a preponderance of white blood constituted a person a white man in the eye of the law, and entitled him to the exercise of all the civil rights of a white man. By a retrogressive step the color-line was extended in 1861 in the case of marriage, which by statute was forbidden between a person of pure white blood and one having a visible admixture of African blood. But by act of legislature, passed in the spring of 1887, all laws establishing or permitting distinctions of color were repealed. In many parts of the state these laws were always ignored, and they would doubtless have been repealed long ago but for the sentiment of the southern counties, separated only by the width of the Ohio River from a former slave-holding state. There was a bill introduced in the legislature during the last session to re-enact the "black laws," but it was hopelessly defeated; the member who introduced it evidently mistook his latitude; he ought to be a member of the Georgia legislature.

But the state which, for several reasons, one might expect to have the strictest laws in regard to the relations of the races, has really the loosest. Two extracts from decisions of the Supreme Court of South Carolina will make clear the law of that state in regard to the color-line.

> The definition of the term mulatto, as understood in this state, seems to be vague, signifying generally a person of mixed white or European and Negro parentage, in whatever proportions the blood of the two races may be mingled in the individual. But it is not invariably applicable to every admixture of African blood with the European, nor is one having all the features of a white to be ranked with the degraded class designated by the laws of this state as persons of color, because of some remote taint of the Negro race. The line of distinction, however, is not ascertained by any rule of law. . . . Juries would probably be justified in holding a person to be white in whom the admixture of African blood did not exceed the proportion of one-eighth. But it is in all cases a question for the jury, to be determined by them upon the evidence of features and complexion afforded by inspection, the evidence of reputation as to parentage, and the evidence of the rank and station in society occupied by the party. The only rule which can be laid down by the courts is that where there is a distinct and visible admixture of Negro blood, the individual is to be denominated a mulatto or person of color.

In a later case the court held:

> The question whether persons are colored or white, where color or feature are doubtful, is for the jury to decide by reputation, by reception into society, and by their exercise of the privileges of the white man, as well as by admixture of blood.

It is an interesting question why such should have been, and should still be, for that matter, the law of South Carolina, and why there should exist in that state a condition of public opinion which would accept such a law. Perhaps it may be attributed to the fact that the colored population of South Carolina always outnumbered the white population, and the eagerness of the latter to recruit their ranks was sufficient to overcome in some measure their prejudice against the Negro blood. It is certainly true that the color-line is, in practice as in law, more loosely drawn in South Carolina than in any other Southern State, and that no inconsiderable element of the population of that state consists of these legal white persons, who were either born in the state; or, attracted thither by this feature of the laws, have come in from surrounding states, and, forsaking home and kindred, have taken their social position as white people. A reasonable degree of reticence in regard to one's antecedents is, however, usual in such cases.

Before the War the color-line, as fixed by law, regulated in theory the civil and political status of persons of color. What that status was, was expressed in the Dred Scott decision. But since the War, or rather since the enfranchisement of the colored people, these laws have been mainly confined—in theory, be it always remembered—to the regulation of the intercourse of the races in schools and in the marriage relation. The extension of the color-line to places of public enter-tainment and resort, to inns and public highways, is in most states entirely a matter of custom. A colored man can sue in the courts of any Southern State for the violation of his common-law rights, and recover damages of say fifty cents without costs. A colored minister who sued a Baltimore steamboat company a few weeks ago for refusing him first-class accommodation, he having paid first-class fare, did not even meet with that measure of success: the learned judge, a Federal judge by the way, held that the plaintiff's rights had been invaded, and that he had suffered humiliation at the hands of the defendant company, but that "the humiliation was not sufficient to entitle him to damages." And the learned judge dismissed the action without costs to either party.

Having thus ascertained what constitutes a white man, the good citizen may be curious to know what steps have been taken to preserve the purity of the white race, Nature, by some unaccountable oversight having to some extent neglected a matter so important to the future prosperity and progress of mankind. The marriage laws referred to here are in active operation, and cases under them are by no means infrequent. Indeed, instead of being behind the age, the marriage laws in the Southern States are in advance of public opinion; for very rarely will a Southern community stop to figure on the pedigree of the contracting parties to a marriage where one is white and the other is known to have any strain of Negro blood.

In Virginia, under the title "Offenses against Morality," the law provides that "any white person who shall intermarry with a Negro shall be confined in jail not more than one year and fined not exceeding one hundred dollars." In a marginal note on the statute-book, attention is called to the fact that "a similar penalty is not imposed on the Negro"—a stretch of magnanimity to which the laws of other states are strangers. A person who performs the ceremony of marriage in such a case is fined two hundred dollars, one-half of which goes to the informer.

In Maryland, a minister who performs the ceremony of marriage between a Negro and a white person is liable to a fine of one hundred dollars.

In Mississippi, code of 1880, it is provided that "the marriage of a white person to a Negro or mulatto or person who shall have one-fourth or more of Negro blood, shall be unlawful"; and as this prohibition does not seem sufficiently em-phatic, it is further declared to be "incestuous and void," and is punished by the

same penalty prescribed for marriage within the forbidden degrees of consan-
guinity.

But it is Georgia, the *alma genetrix* of the chain-gang, which merits the questionable distinction of having the harshest set of color laws. By the law of Georgia
the term "person of color" is defined to mean "all such as have an admixture of
Negro blood, and the term 'Negro,' includes mulattoes." This definition is perhaps restricted somewhat by another provision, by which "all Negroes, mestizoes,
and their descendants, having one-eighth of Negro or mulatto blood in their veins,
shall be known in this State as persons of color." A colored minister is permitted
to perform the ceremony of marriage between colored persons only, the white
ministers are not forbidden to join persons of color in wedlock. It is further
provided that "the marriage relation between white persons and persons of African
descent is forever prohibited, and such marriages shall be null and void." This
is a very sweeping provision; it will be noticed that the term "persons of color,"
previously defined, is not employed, the expression "persons of African descent"
being used instead. A court which was so inclined would find no difficulty in
extending this provision of the law to the remotest strain of African blood. The
marriage relation is forever prohibited. Forever is a long time. There is a colored
woman in Georgia said to be worth $300,000—an immense fortune in the poverty
stricken South. With a few hundred such women in that state, possessing a fair
degree of good looks, the color-line would shrivel up like a scroll in the heat of
competition for their hands in marriage. The penalty for the violation of the law
against intermarriage is the same sought to be imposed by the defunct Glenn Bill
for violation of its provisions; *i.e.*, a fine not to exceed one thousand dollars, and
imprisonment not to exceed six months, or twelve months in the chain-gang.

Whatever the wisdom or justice of these laws, there is one objection to them
which is not given sufficient prominence in the consideration of the subject, even
where it is discussed at all; they make mixed blood a *prima-facie* proof of illegitimacy. It is a fact that at present, in the United States, a colored man or woman
whose complexion is white or nearly white is presumed in the absence of any
knowledge of his or her antecedents, to be the offspring of a union not sanctified
by law. And by a curious but not uncommon process, such persons are not held
in the same low estimation as white people in the same position. The sins of their
fathers are not visited upon the children, in that regard at least and their mothers'
lapses from virtue are regarded at least as misfortunes or as faults excusable under
the circumstances. But in spite of all this, illegitimacy is not a desirable distinction,
and is likely to become less so as these people of mixed blood advance in wealth
and social standing. This presumption of illegitimacy was once, perhaps, true of
the majority of such persons; but the times have changed. More than half of the
colored people of the United States are of mixed blood; they marry and are given
in marriage, and they beget children of complexions similar to their own. Whether
or not, therefore, laws which stamp these children as illegitimate, and which by
indirection establish a lower standard of morality for a large part of the population
than the remaining part is judged by, are wise laws; and whether or not the purity
of the white race could not be as well preserved by the exercise of virtue, and

the operation of those natural laws which are so often quoted by Southern writers as the justification of all sorts of Southern "policies"—are questions which the good citizen may at least turn over in his mind occasionally, pending the settlement of other complications which have grown out of the presence of the Negro on this continent.

The Beginnings of Miscegenation of the Whites and Blacks*

CARTER G. WOODSON

Although science has uprooted the theory, a number of writers are loath to give up the contention that the white race is superior to others, as it is still hoped that the Caucasian race may be preserved in its purity, especially so far as it means miscegenation with the blacks. But there are others who express doubt that the integrity of the dominant race has been maintained.[1] Scholars have for centuries differed as to the composition of the mixed breed stock constituting the Mediterranean race and especially about that in Egypt and the Barbary States. In that part of the dark continent many inhabitants have certain characteristics which are more Caucasian than negroid and have achieved more than investigators have been willing to consider the civilization of the Negro. It is clear, however, that although the people of northern Africa cannot be classed as Negroes, being bounded on the south by the masses of African blacks, they have so generally mixed their blood with that of the blacks that in many parts they are no nearer to any white stock than the Negroes of the United States.

This miscegenation, to be sure, increased toward the south into central Africa, but it has extended also to the north and east into Asia and Europe. Traces of Negro blood have been found in the Malay States, India and Polynesia. In the Arabian Peninsula it has been so extensive as to constitute a large group there called the Arabised Negroes. But most significant of all has been the invasion of Europe by persons of African blood. Professor Sergi leads one to conclude that the ancient Pelasgii were of African origin or probably the descendants of the race which settled northern Africa and southern Europe, and are therefore due credit for the achievements of the early Greek and Italian civilizations.[2]

---

* From Carter G. Woodson, "The Beginnings of Miscegenation of the Whites and Blacks." *The Journal of Negro History* 3.4 (October 1918): 335–353.

1. MacDonald, *Trade, Politics and Christianity in Africa and the East,* chapter on inter-racial marriage, p. 239; and *The Journal of Negro History*, pp. 329, 334–344.

2. *Report of First Race[s] Congress,* 1911, p. 330 [probably G. Spiller, ed., *Papers on Inter-Racial Problems Communicated to the First Universal Races Congress Held at the University of London, July 26–29, 1911* (London: P. S. King & Son, 1911) —Ed.]; MacDonald, *Trade, Politics, and Christianity*, p. 235; and *Contemporary Review*, August, 1911.

There is much evidence of a further extension of this infusion in the Mediterranean world.

"Recent discoveries made in the vicinity of the principality of Monaco and others in Italy and western France," says MacDonald, "would seem to reveal . . . the actual fact that many thousand years ago a negroid race had penetrated through Italy into France, leaving traces at the present day in the physiognomy of the peoples of southern Italy, Sicily, Sardinia and western France, and even in the western parts of the United Kingdom of Great Britain and Ireland. There are even at the present day some examples of the Keltiberian peoples of western Scotland, southern and western Wales, southern and western Ireland, of distinctly negroid aspect, and in whose ancestry there is no indication whatever of any connection with the West Indies or with Modern Africa. Still more marked is this feature in the peoples of southern and western France and of the other parts of the Mediterranean already mentioned."[3]

Because of the temperament of the Portugese this infusion of African blood was still more striking in their country. As the Portugese are a good-natured people void of race hate they did not dread the miscegenation of the races. One finds in southern Portugal a "strong Moorish, North African element" and also an "old intermixture with those Negroes who were imported thither from Northwest Africa to till the scantily populated southern provinces."[4] This miscegenation among the Portugese easily extended to the New World. Then followed the story of the Caramarii, the descendants of the Portugese, who after being shipwrecked near Bahia arose to prominence among the Tupinambo Indians and produced a clan of half-castes by taking to himself numerous native women.[5] This admixture served as a stepping stone to the assimilation of the Negroes when they came.

There immigrated later into Brazil other settlers who, mixing eagerly with the Amerindians, gave rise to a race called Mamelucos who began to mix maritally with the imported Negro women. The French and Dutch too in caring for their offspring by native women promoted the same. "They educated them, set them free, lifted them above servitude, and raised them socially to the level of the whites"[6] so that today generally speaking there are no distinctions in society or politics in Brazil. Commenting on this condition in Brazil, Agassiz said: "This hybrid class, although more marked here because the Indian is added, is very numerous in all cities; perhaps, the fact, so honorable to Brazil, that the free Negro has full access to all privileges of any free citizen, rather tends to increase than to diminish that number." After emancipation in Brazil in 1888, the already marked tendency toward this fusion of the slave and the master classes gradually increased.[7]

---

3. *Report of First Races Congress*, 1911, p. 330.
4. Johnston, *The Negro in the New World*, p. 98.
5. *Ibid.*, p. 78.
6. *Ibid.*, pp. 98–99.
7. Authorities consider the Amerindians the most fecund stock in the country, especially when mixed with an effusion of white or black blood. Agassiz, *A Journey in Brazil in 1868*.

The Spaniards mixed less freely with the Negroes than did the Portugese but mixed just the same. At first they seriously considered the inconveniences which might arise from miscegenation under frontier conditions and generally refrained from extensive intermingling. But men are but men and as Spanish women were far too few in the New World at that time, the other sex of their race soon yielded to the charms of women of African blood. The rise of the mixed breeds too further facilitated the movement. Spaniards who refused to intermingle with the blacks found it convenient to approach the hybrids who showed less color. In the course of time, therefore, the assimilation of the blacks was as pronounced in some of the Spanish colonies as in those which originally exhibited less race antipathy. There are millions of Hispanicized Negroes in Latin America. Many of the mixed breeds, however, have Indian rather than Negro blood.[8]

Miscegenation had its best chance among the French. Not being disinclined to mingle with Negroes, the French early faced the problem of the half caste, which was given consideration in the most human of all slave regulations, the *Code Noir*.[9] It provided that free men who had children from their concubinage with women-slaves (if they consented to such concubinage) should be punished by a fine of two thousand pounds of sugar. But if the offender was the master himself, in addition to the fine, the slave should be taken from him, sold for the benefit of the hospital and never be allowed to be freed; excepting, that, if the man was not married to another person at the time of his concubinage, he was to marry the woman slave, who, together with her children, should thereby become free. Masters were forbidden to constrain slaves to marry against their will. Many Frenchmen like those in Haiti married their Negro mistresses, producing attractive half caste women who because of their wealth were sought by gentlemen in preference to their own women without dot.

Among the English the situation was decidedly different. There was not so much need for the use of Negro women by Englishmen in the New World, but there was the same tendency to cohabit with them. In the end, however, the English, unlike the Latins, disowned their offspring by slave women, leaving these children to follow the condition of their mother. There was, therefore, not so much less miscegenation among the English but there remained the natural tendency so to denounce these unions as eventually to restrict the custom, as it is today, to the weaker types of both races, the offspring of whom in the case of slave mothers became a commodity in the commercial world.

There was extensive miscegenation in the English colonies, however, before the race as a majority could realize the apparent need for maintaining its integrity. With the development of the industries came the use of the white servants as well as the slaves. The status of the one differed from that of the other in that the former at the expiration of his term of service could become free whereas the latter was doomed to servitude for life. In the absence of social distinctions between these two classes of laborers there arose considerable intermingling growing

8. Johnston, *The Negro in the New World*, p. 135.
9. *Code Noir*.

out of a community of interests. In the colonies in which the laborers were largely of one class or the other not so much of this admixture was feared, but in the plantations having a considerable sprinkling of the two miscegenation usually ensued.

The following, therefore, was enacted in Maryland in 1661 as a response to the question of the council to the lower house as to what it intended should become of such free women of the English or other Christian nations as married Negroes or other slaves.[10] The preamble reads: "And forasmuch as divers freeborn *English* women, forgetful of their free condition, and to the disgrace of our nation, do intermarry with negro slaves,[11] by which also divers suits may arise, touching the issue of such women, and a great damage doth befall the master of such negroes, for preservation whereof for deterring such free-born women from such shameful matches, *be it enacted:* That whatsoever free-born woman shall intermarry with any slave, from and after the last day of the present assembly, shall serve the master of such slave during the life of her husband; and that all the issues of such free-born women, so married, shall be slaves as their fathers were." "And be it further enacted: That all the issues of *English,* or other free-born women, that have already married negroes, shall serve the master of their parents, till they be thirty years of age and no longer."[12]

According to A. J. Calhoun, however, all planters of Maryland did not manifest so much ire because of this custom among indentured servants. "Planters," said he, "sometimes married white women servants to Negroes in order to transform the Negroes and their offspring into slaves."[12a] This was in violation of the ancient unwritten law that the children of a free woman, the father being a slave, follow the status of their mother and are free. The custom gave rise to an interesting case. "Irish Nell," one of the servants brought to Maryland by Lord Baltimore, was sold by him to a planter when he returned to England. Following the custom of other masters who held white women as servants, he soon married her to a Negro named Butler to produce slaves. Upon hearing this, Baltimore used his influence to have the law repealed but the abrogation of it was construed by the Court of Appeals not to have any effect on the status of her offspring almost a century later when William and Mary Butler sued for their freedom on the ground that they descended from this white woman. The Provincial Court had granted them freedom but in this decision the Court of Appeals reversed the lower tribunal on the ground that "Irish Nell" was a slave before the measure repealing the act had been passed. This case came up again 1787 when Mary, the daughter of William and Mary Butler, petitioned the State for freedom. Both tribunals then decided to grant this petition.[13]

10. Brackett, *The Negro in Maryland*, pp. 32–33.
11. Benjamin Banneker's mother was a white woman who married one of her own slaves. See Tyson, *Benjamin Banneker*, p. 3.
12. *Archives of Maryland, Proceedings of the General Assembly*, 1637–1664, pp. 533–534.
12a. Calhoun, *A Social History of the American Family*, p. 94.
13. Harris and McHenry Reports, I, pp. 374, 376; II, pp. 26, 38, 214, 233.

The act of repeal of 1681, therefore, is self explanatory. The preamble reads: "Forasmuch as, divers free-born *English,* or white women, sometimes by the instigation, procurement or connivance of their masters, mistresses, or dames, and always to the satisfaction of their lascivious and lustful desires, and to the disgrace not only of the *English*, but also of many other Christian nations, do intermarry with Negroes and slaves, by which means, divers inconveniences, controversies, and suits may arise, touching the issue or children of such free-born women aforesaid; for the prevention whereof for the future, *Be it enacted:* That if the marriage of any woman-servant with any slave shall take place by the procurement of permission of the master, such woman and her issue shall be free." It enacted a penalty by fine on the master or mistress and on the person joining the parties in marriage.[14]

The effect of this law was merely to prevent masters from prostituting white women to an economic purpose. It did not prevent the miscegenation of the two races. McCormac says: "Mingling of the races in Maryland continued during the eighteenth century, in spite of all laws against it. Preventing marriages of white servants with slaves only led to a greater social evil, which caused a reaction of public sentiment against the servant. Masters and society in general were burdened with the care of illegitimate mulatto children, and it became necessary to frame laws compelling the guilty parties to reimburse the masters for the maintenance of these unfortunate waifs."[15] To remedy this laws were passed in 1715 and 1717 to reduce to the status of a servant for seven years any white man or white woman who cohabited with any Negro, free or slave. Their children were made servants for thirty-one years, a black thus concerned was reduced to slavery for life and the maintenance of the bastard children of women servants was made incumbent upon masters. If the father of an illegitimate child could be discovered, he would have to support his offspring. If not this duty fell upon the mother who had to discharge it by servitude or otherwise.[16]

As what had been done to prevent the admixture was not sufficient, the Maryland General Assembly took the following action in 1728:

Whereas by the act of assembly relating to servants and slaves, there is no provision made for the punishment of free mulatto women, having bastard children by negroes and other slaves, nor is there any provision made in the said act for the punishment of free negro women, having bastard children by white men; and forasmuch as such copulations are as unnatural and inordinate as between white women and negro men, or other slaves.

Be it enacted, That from and after the end of this present session of assembly, that all such free mulatto women, having bastard children, either within or after the time of their service, (*and their issue,*) shall be subject to the same penalties that white women and their issue are, for having mulatto bastards, by the act, entitled, An act relating to servants and slaves.

---

14. Hurd, *Law of Freedom and Bondage*, VI, pp. 249–250.
15. McCormac, *White Servitude in Maryland,* p. 70.
16. Act of Assembly, Oct., 1727.

And be it further enacted, by the authority aforesaid, by and with the advice and consent aforesaid, That from and after the end of this present session of assembly, that all free negro women, having bastard children by white men, (*and their issue,*) shall be subject to the same penalties that white women are, by the act aforesaid, for having bastards by negro men.[17]

Virginia which faced the same problem did not lag far behind Maryland. In 1630 the Governor and Council in Court ordered Hugh Davis to be soundly whipped before an assembly of Negroes and others for abusing himself to the dishonor of God and shame of a Christian by defiling his body in lying with a Negro, which he was to acknowledge next Sabbath day. In 1662 the colony imposed double fines for fornication with a Negro, but did not restrict intermarriage until 1691.[18] The words of the preamble give the reasons for this action. It says:

And for the prevention of that abominable mixture and spurious issue which hereafter may increase in this dominion, as well by negroes, mulattoes, and Indians intermarrying with English, or other white women, as by their unlawful accompanying with one another, *Be it enacted by the authoritie aforesaid, and it is hereby enacted,* That for the time to come, whatsoever English or other white man or woman being free shall intermarry with a negro, mulatto, or Indian man or woman bond or free shall within three months after such marriage be banished and removed from this dominion forever, and that the justices of each respective countie within this dominion make it their perticular care, that this act be put in effectuall execution.

If any free English woman should have a bastard child by any Negro or mulatto, she should pay the sum of fifteen pounds sterling, within one month after such bastard child should be born, to the church wardens of the parish where she should be delivered of such child, and in default of such payment she should be taken into the possession of the said church wardens and disposed of for five years, and such bastard child should be bound out as a servant by the church wardens until he or she should attain the age of thirty years, and in case such English woman that should have such bastard child be a servant, she should be sold by the church wardens (after her time is expired that she ought by law to serve her master) for five years, and the money she should be sold for divided as before appointed, and the child should serve as aforesaid.[19]

It was further provided in 1753 that if any woman servant should have a bastard child by a Negro or mulatto, over and above the year's service due to her master or owner, she should immediately upon the expiration of her time, to her then present master, or owner, pay down to the church wardens of the parish wherein such child should be born for the use of the said parish, fifteen pounds current money of Virginia, or be sold for five years to the use aforesaid; and if a free Christian white woman should have such bastard child by a Negro, or mulatto,

17. Dorsey, *The General Public Statutory Law and Public Local Law of State of Maryland,* from 1692–1839, p. 79.
18. Ballagh, *White Servitude in the Colony of Virginia,* pp. 72, 73.
19. Hening, *The Statutes at Large,* I, pp. 146, 552. II, 170; III, pp. 86–88, 252.

for every such offence, she should within one month after her delivery of such bastard child, pay to the church wardens for the time being, of the parish wherein such child should be born, for the use of the said parish, fifteen pounds current money of Virginia, or be by them sold for five years to the use aforesaid; and in both the said cases, the church wardens should bind the said child to be a servant until it should be of thirty-one years of age.

And for a further prevention of that "abominable mixture, and the spurious issue, which may hereafter increase in this his majesty's colony and dominion as well by English, and other white men and women, intermarrying with Negroes or mulattoes, as by their unlawful coition with them" it was enacted that whatsoever English, or other white man or woman, being free, should intermarry with a Negro, or mulatto man or woman bond or free, should by judgment of the county court, be committed to prison and there remain during the space of six months, without bail or main-prize, and should forfeit and pay ten pounds current money of Virginia, to the use of the parish as aforesaid. It was further enacted that no minister of the Church of England, or other minister or person whatsoever, within that colony and dominion, should thereafter presume to marry a white man with a Negro, or mulatto woman, or to marry a white woman with a Negro or mulatto man, upon pain of forfeiting and paying for every such marriage, the sum of ten thousand pounds of tobacco.[20]

It developed later that these laws did not meet all requirements, for there were in subsequent years so many illegitimate children born of such mothers that they became a public charge.[21] Those of Negro blood were bound out by law. According to Russell, "In 1727 it was ordered that David James a free negro boy, be bound to Mr. James Isdel 'who is to teach him to read ye bible distinctly also ye trade of a gunsmith that he carry him to ye Clark's office & take Indenture to that purpose.' By the Warwick County court it was 'ordered that Malacai, a mulatto boy, son of mulatto Betty be, by the Church Wardens of this Parish bound to Thomas Hobday to learn the art of a planter according to law.' By order of the Norfolk County court, about 1770, a free negro was bound out 'to learn the trade of a tanner.' "[22]

In making more stringent regulations for servants and slaves, North Carolina provided in 1715 that if a white servant woman had a child by a Negro, mulatto or Indian, she must serve her master two years extra and should pay to the Church wardens immediately on the expiration of that time six pounds for the use of the parish or be sold four years for the use aforesaid.[23] A clergyman found guilty of officiating at such a marriage should be fined fifty pounds. This law, according to Bassett, did not succeed in preventing such unions. Two ministers were indicted within two years for performing such a marriage ceremony. "In one case the suit was dropped, in the other case the clergyman went before the Chief

20. Hening, *Statutes at Large,* VI, pp. 360–362.
21. Meade, *Old Churches and Families of Virginia,* I, p. 366.
22. Russell, *Free Negro in Virginia,* pp. 138–139.
23. Bassett, *Slavery and Servitude in North Carolina,* p. 83.

Justice and confessed as it seems of his own accord. . . . In 1727 a white woman was indicted in the General Court because she had left her husband and was cohabiting with a negro slave. . . . So far as general looseness was concerned this law of 1715 had no force. Brickell, who was a physician, says that white men of the colony suffered a great deal from a malignant kind of venereal disease which they took from the slaves."[24]

By the law of 1741 therefore the colony endeavored to prevent what the General Assembly called "that abominable mixture and spurious issue, which hereafter may increase in this government, by white men and women intermarrying with Indians, Negroes, mustees, or mulattoes." It was enacted that if any man or woman, being free, should intermarry with an Indian, Negro, mustee or mulatto man or woman, or any person of mixed blood, to the third generation, bond or free, he should, by judgment of the county court forfeit and pay the sum of fifty pounds, proclamation money, to the use of the parish.[25] It was also provided that if any white servant woman should during the time of her servitude, be delivered of a child, begotten by any Negro, mulatto or Indian, such servant, over and above the time she was by this act to serve her master or owner for such offence, should be sold by the Church wardens of the parish, for two years, after the time by indenture or otherwise had expired.[26]

The miscegenation of the whites and blacks extended so widely that it became a matter of concern to the colonies farther north where the Negro population was not considerable. Seeking also to prevent this "spurious mixt issue" Massachusetts enacted in 1705 that a Negro or mulatto man committing fornication with an "English woman, or a woman of any other Christian nation," should be sold out of the province. "An English man, or man of any other Christian nation committing fornication with a Negro or mulatto woman," should be whipped, and the woman sold out of the province. None of her Majesty's English or Scottish subjects, nor of any other Christian nation within that province should contract matrimony with any Negro or mulatto, under a penalty imposed on the person joining them in marriage. No master should unreasonably deny marriage to his Negro with one of the same nation; any law, usage or custom to the contrary notwithstanding.[27]

There was much social contact between the white servants and the Negroes in Pennsylvania, where the number of the latter greatly increased during the first quarter of the nineteenth century. Turner says a white servant was indicted for this offence in Sussex County in 1677 and a tract of land there bore the name of "Mulatto Hall."[28] According to the same writer Chester County seemed to have a large number of these cases and laid down the principle that such admixture should be prohibited,

24. *Ibid.*, pp. 58–59. See also *Natural History of North Carolina*, p. 48; and Hawk's *History of North Carolina*, II, pp. 126–127.
25. Potter, *Revised Laws of North Carolina*, I., p. 130.
26. *Ibid.*, I, p. 157.
27. *Massachusetts Charters, etc.*, p. 747; Hurd, *Law of Freedom and Bondage*, VI, p. 262.
28. Turner, *The Negro in Pennsylvania*, pp. 29–30.

"For that hee," referring to a white man, "Contrary to his Masters Consent hath . . . got wth child a certaine molato wooman Called Swart anna." "David Lewis Constable of Haverford Returned a Negro man of his And a white woman for having a Bastard Childe . . . the Negroe said she Intised him and promised him to marry him: she being examined, Confest the same: the Court ordered that she shall receive Twenty one lashes on her bare Backe . . . and the Court ordered the negroe never more to meddle with any white woman more uppon paine of his life."[29]

Advertising for Richard Molson in Philadelphia in 1720, his master said, "He is in company with a white woman named Mary, who is supposed now goes for his wife"; "and a white man named Garrett Choise, and Jane his wife, which said white people are servants to some neighbors of the said Richard Tilghman."[30] In 1722 a woman was punished for abetting a clandestine marriage between a white woman and a Negro. In the *Pennsylvania Gazette*, June 1, 1749, appeared the notice of the departure of Isaac Cromwell, a mulatto, who ran away with an English servant woman named Anne Greene.[31]

The Assembly, therefore, upon a petition from inhabitants inveighing against this custom enacted a prohibitory law in 1725. This law provided that no minister, pastor or magistrate or other person whatsover who according to the laws of that province usually joined people in marriage should upon any pretence whatever join in marriage any Negro with any white person on the penalty of one hundred pounds. And it was further enacted that if any white man or woman should cohabit or dwell with any Negro under pretense of being married, such white man or woman should be put out of service as above directed until they come to the age of thirty-one years; and if any free Negro man or woman should inter-marry with a white man or woman, such Negro should become a slave during life to be sold by order of the justice of the quarter sessions of the respective county; and if any free Negro man or woman should commit fornication or adultery with any white man or woman, such Negro or Negroes should be sold as a servant for seven years and the white man or woman should be punished as the law directs in cases of adultery or fornication.[32]

This law seemed to have very little effect on the miscegenation of the races in certain parts. In Chester County, according to the records of 1780, mulattoes constituted one fifth of the Negro population.[33] Furthermore, that very year when the State of Pennsylvania had grown sufficiently liberal to provide for gradual emancipation the law against the mingling of the races was repealed. Mixed marriages thereafter became common as the white and the blacks in the light of the American Revolution realized liberty in its full meaning. Thomas Branagan said:

> There are many, very many blacks who . . . begin to feel themselves conse-quential, . . . will not be satisfied unless they get white women for wives, and are

29. *Ibid.*, p. 30.
30. *The American Weekly Mercury* (Philadelphia), August 20, 1720.
31. *The Pennsylvania Gazette,* June 1, 1749.
32. *Statutes at Large*, IV, p. 62.
33. Turner, *The Negro in Pennsylvania*, p. 31.

likewise exceedingly impertinent to white people in low circumstances. . . . I solemnly swear, I have seen more white women married to, and deluded through the arts of seduction by negroes in one year in Philadelphia, than for eight years I was visiting (West Indies and the Southern States). I know a black man who seduced a young white girl . . . who soon after married him, and died with a broken heart. On her death he said that he would not disgrace himself to have a negro wife and acted accordingly, for he soon after married a white woman. . . . There are perhaps hundreds of white women thus fascinated by black men in this city, and there are thousands of black children by them at present.[34]

A reaction thereafter set in against this custom during the first decade of the nineteenth century, when fugitives in the rough were rushing to that State, and culminated in an actual campaign against it by 1820. That year a petition from Greene County said that many Negroes had settled in Pennsylvania and had been able to seduce into marriage "the minor children of the white inhabitants."[35] This county, therefore, asked that these marriages be made an offence against the laws of the State. Such a marriage was the cause of a riot in Columbia in 1834 and in 1838 the members of the Constitutional Convention engaged in a heated discussion of the custom.[36] Petitions were frequently sent to the legislature asking that this admixture be penalized by law, but no such action was ever taken. Relying upon public opinion, however, the advocates of racial integrity practically succeeded. Marriages of whites and blacks eventually became so odious that they led to disturbances as in the case of the riot of 1849, one of the causes of which was that a white man was living with a Negro wife.[37] This was almost ineffective, however, in the prevention of race admixture. Clandestine intermingling went on and tended to increase in enormous proportions. The conclusive proof of this is that in 1860 mulattoes constituted one third of the Negro population of Pennsylvania.

Persons who professed seriously to consider the future of slavery, therefore, saw that miscegenation and especially the general connection of white men with their female slaves introduced a mulatto race whose numbers would become dangerous, if the affections of their white parents were permitted to render them free.[38] The Americans of the future would thereby become a race of mixed breeds rather than a white and a black population. As the lust of white persons for those of color was too strong to prevent this miscegenation, the liberty of emancipating their mulatto offspring was restricted in the slave States but that of selling them remained.[39]

These laws eventually, therefore, had their desired effect. They were never intended to prevent the miscegenation of the races but to debase to a still lower

34. Branagan, *Serious Remonstrances,* pp. 68, 69, 70, 71, 73, 74, 75, 102; *Somerset Whig,* March 12, 1818, and *Union Times,* August 15, 1834.
35. *Journal of Senate,* 1820–1821, p. 213; and *American Daily Advertiser,* January 23, 1821.
36. *Proceedings and Debates of the Convention of 1838,* X, p. 230.
37. *The Spirit of the Times,* October 10, 11, 12, 13, 17, 19, 1849.
38. Harriet Martineau, *Views of Slavery and Emancipation,* p. 10.
39. Hart, *Slavery and Abolition,* p. 182; *Censuses of the United States.*

status the offspring of the blacks who in spite of public opinion might intermarry with the poor white women and to leave women of color without protection against white men, who might use them for convenience, whereas white women and black men would gradually grow separate and distinct in their social relations. Although thereafter the offspring of blacks and whites did not diminish, instead of being gradually assimilated to the type of the Caucasian they tended to constitute a peculiar class commonly called people of color having a higher social status than that of the blacks but finally classified with all other persons of African blood as Negroes.

While it later became a capital offence in some of the slave States for a Negro man to cohabit with a white woman, Abdy who toured this country from 1833 to 1834 doubted that such laws were enforced. "A man," said he, "was hanged not long ago for this crime at New Orleans. The partner of his guilt—his master's daughter—endeavored to save his life, by avowing that she alone was to blame. She died shortly after his execution."[40] With the white man and the Negro woman the situation was different. A sister of President Madison once said to the Reverend George Bourne, then a Presbyterian minister in Virginia: "We Southern ladies are complimented with the name of wives; but we are only the mistresses of seraglios." The masters of the female slaves, however, were not always the only persons of loose morals. Many women of color were also prostituted to the purposes of young white men[41] and overseers.[42] Goodell reports a well-authenticated account of a respectable Christian lady at the South who kept a handsome mulatto female for the use of her genteel son, as a method of deterring him, as she said, "from indiscriminate and vulgar indulgences."[43] Harriet Martineau discovered a young white man who on visiting a southern lady became insanely enamored of her intelligent quadroon maid. He sought to purchase her but the owner refused to sell the slave because of her unusual worth. The young white man persisted in trying to effect this purchase and finally informed her owner that he could not live without this attractive slave. Thereupon the white lady sold the woman of color to satisfy the lust of her friend.[44]

The accomplishment of this task of reducing the free people of color to the status of the blacks, however, was not easy. In the first place, so many persons of color had risen to positions of usefulness among progressive people and had formed connections with them that an abrupt separation was both inexpedient and undesirable. Exceptions to the hard and fast rules of caste were often made to relieve the people of color. Moreover, the miscegenation of the races in the South and especially in large cities like Charleston and New Orleans had gone to the extent that from these centers eventually went, as they do now, a large

40. Abdy, *North America*, I, p. 160.
41. Child, *Anti-slavery Catechism*, p. 17; 2 *Howard Mississippi Reports*, p. 837.
42. Kemble, *Georgian Plantation*, pp. 140, 162, 199, 208–210; Olmstead, *Seaboard States*, pp. 599–600; Rhodes, *United States*, I, pp. 341–343.
43. Goodell, *Slave Code*, pp. 111–112.
44. Harriet Martineau, *Views of Slavery and Emancipation*, p. 13.

number of quadroons and octoroons,[45] who elsewhere crossed over to the other race.

White men ashamed of the planters who abused helpless black women are now trying to minimize the prevalence of this custom. Such an effort, however, means little in the face of the facts that one seventh of the Negroes in the United States had in their veins any amount of Caucasian blood in 1860 and according to the last census more than one fifth of them have this infusion. Furthermore the testimony of travelers in this country during the slavery period support the contention that race admixture was common.[46]

So extensive did it become that the most prominent white men in the country did not escape. Benjamin Franklin seems to have made no secret of his associations with Negro women.[47] Russell connects many of these cases with the master class in Virginia.[48] There are now in Washington Negroes who call themselves the descendants of two Virginians who attained the presidency of the United States.

The abolitionists made positive statements about the mulatto offspring of Thomas Jefferson. Goodell lamented the fact that Jefferson in his will had to entreat the legislature of Virginia to confirm his bequest of freedom to his own reputed enslaved offspring that they might remain in the State of their nativity, where their families and connections were.[49] Writing in 1845, the editor of the *Cleveland American* expressed regret that notwithstanding all the services and sacrifices of Jefferson in the establishment of the freedom of this country, his own son then living in Ohio was not allowed to vote or bear witness in a court of justice. The editor of the *Ohio Star* said: "We are not sure whether this is intended as a statement of actual fact, or of what might possibly and naturally enough be true." *The Cincinnati Herald* inquired: "Is this a fact? If so, it ought to be known. Perhaps 'the Democracy' might be induced to pass a special act in his favor." *The Cleveland American,* therefore, added: "We are credibly informed that a natural son of Jefferson by the celebrated 'Black Sal,' a person of no little renown in the politics of 1800 and thereafter, is now living in a central county of Ohio. We shall endeavor to get at the truth of the matter and make public the result of our inquiries."[50]

---

45. Featherstonaugh, *Excursion*, p. 141; Buckingham, *Slave States*, I, p. 358.

46. Writing of conditions in this country prior to the American Revolution, Anne Grant found only two cases of miscegenation in Albany before this period but saw it well established later by the British soldiers. Johann Schoepf witnessed this situation in Charleston in 1784. J. P. Brissot saw this tendency toward miscegenation as a striking feature of society among the French in the Ohio Valley in 1788. The Duke of Saxe-Weimar-Eisenach was very much impressed with the numerous quadroons and octoroons of New Orleans in 1825 and Charles Gayarré portrayed the same conditions there in 1830. Fredrika Bremer frequently met with this class while touring the South in 1850. See Grant, *Memoirs of an American Lady*, p. 28; Schoepf, *Travels in the Confederation*, II, p. 382; Brissot, *Travels*, II, p. 61; Saxe-Weimar, *Travels*, II, p. 69; Grace King, *New Orleans*, pp. 346–349; Fredrika Bremer, *Homes of the New World*, I, pp. 325, 326, 382, 385.

47. *Ibid.*, XXII, p. 98.

48. See Russell, *Free Negro in Virginia*, p. 127.

49. Goodell, *Slave Code*, p. 376.

50. *The Liberator*, December 19, 1845.

A later report of miscegenation of this kind was recorded by Jane Grey Swisshelm in her *Half a Century*, where she states that a daughter of President John Tyler "ran away with the man she loved in order that she might be married, but for this they must reach foreign soil. A young lady of the White House could not marry the man of her choice in the United States. The lovers were captured and she was brought to His Excellency, her father, who sold her to a slave-trader. From that Washington slave-pen she was taken to New Orleans by a man who expected to get twenty-five hundred dollars for her on account of her great beauty."[51]

Interracial Marriage and the Law*

WILLIAM D. ZABEL

In the past decade, the law and the Supreme Court have done a great deal to ensure the equality of all races and to guarantee equal civil rights. But in the area of interracial marriage, the statutes of nineteen states continue to deny the individual the freedom to marry the person of his choice. The vagaries of these statutes and the failure of the Supreme Court to act are here set forth by William D. Zabel, a practicing lawyer in New York.

When a reporter asked former President Harry S. Truman if interracial marriage—miscegenation—would become widespread in the United States, Mr. Truman said, "I hope not; I don't believe in it." Then Mr. Truman asked the reporter that hackneyed question often spouted at anyone advocating racial integration, "Would you want your daughter to marry a Negro?" The reporter responded that he wanted his daughter to marry the man she loved whoever he might be. "Well, she won't love someone who isn't her color," the former President continued, and, as if he had not said enough, added that racial intermarriage ran counter to the teachings of the Bible.

The question of miscegenation can make a man like Truman, whose past support of integration in other respects is not open to question, appear unthinking if not bigoted. The fact of interracial marriage can cause a young Radcliffe-educated "liberal" to refuse to attend the wedding of her only brother, or a civilized, intelligent judge to disown and never again speak to his daughter. How many persons are repelled or at least disconcerted at the mere sight of a Negro-white couple? Perhaps their number tells us how far we are from achieving an integrated society.

---

51. Swisshelm, *Half a Century*, p. 129.
* From William D. Zabel, "Interracial Marriage and the Law." *Atlantic Monthly* (October 1965): 75–79.

If usually tolerant and rational persons can react this way, it is not surprising that many experts consider the fear of miscegenation the strongest reason for the desire of whites to keep the Negro permanently segregated. Next in importance in the "white man's rank order of discrimination," according to Gunnar Myrdal in his classic study, *An American Dilemma,* are other social conventions, the use of public facilities, political franchise, legal equality, and employment. On the other hand, the social and legal barriers to miscegenation rank at the bottom of the Negro's list of grievances; quite naturally, he is more concerned with obtaining a job, decent living accommodations, and an education than with marrying "your daughter." A recent Ford Foundation study of more than seven hundred Negro families in Chicago concluded: "There is no evidence of a desire for miscegenation, or even interest in promoting it, except among a tiny minority."

Even though the Negro has finally attained equality under the law in most areas of American life, a Negro and a white still cannot marry in nineteen states having antimiscegenation statutes—mostly Southern and "border" states, but also including Indiana and Wyoming. No other civilized country has such laws except the Union of South Africa.

The United States Supreme Court has never ruled on the constitutionality of these statutes. In 1954, a few months after its historic decision prohibiting segregation in public schools, the Court refused to review the case of Linnie Jackson, a Negro woman who had been convicted under the Alabama miscegenation statute. Later, in 1956, the Court again avoided the issue, dismissing an appeal in a miscegenation case from Virginia. This dismissal was termed "wholly without basis in law" by a leading authority on constitutional law, Professor Herbert Wechsler of the Columbia Law School, because there was no appropriate legal reason for avoiding the decision.

In December, 1964, the Court upset the conviction of Connie Hoffman, a white woman, and Dewey McLaughlin, a Spanish-speaking merchant seaman from British Honduras. They had violated a Florida criminal law punishing extramarital cohabitation only if the offending couple were a Negro and a white person. The Court invalidated this statute as a denial of equal protection of the law guaranteed by the Fourteenth Amendment but refused to express "any views about [Florida's] prohibition of interracial marriage."

The Court may again be confronted with this question in a case instituted by a white construction worker and his part-Negro wife, Richard and Mildred Loving. They are seeking to have the Virginia miscegenation law declared unconstitutional so that they and their three children may reside in the state from which they have been banished. The Lovings have no connection with the civil rights movement and are not represented by attorneys of a Negro civil rights organization. Both had spent all their lives in Caroline County, Virginia, south of Fredericksburg. They were married in Washington, D.C., in 1958 and returned to Virginia. Five weeks later, they were charged with the crime of marrying each other, and because of this crime were convicted and sentenced to one year in prison. But Virginia County Circuit Judge Leon M. Bazlie suspended the sentences and provided instead that the Lovings leave Virginia "at once and do not return together or at the same time" for twenty-five years.

Should the Supreme Court avoid deciding this question because Negroes as a group are not concerned with it and because a decision of unconstitutionality might harm the civil rights movement? Before concluding that such a decision ought to be avoided if possible, or alternatively, how the question ought to be decided, we should consider the history and content of the miscegenation laws.

The use of laws to ban marriages between persons of different races developed primarily in this country as an outgrowth peculiar to our institution of slavery. Neither the common law of England nor its statutes provide precedents for America's miscegenation laws.

A Maryland statute of 1661 is generally considered the first miscegenation law in America, even though it did not prohibit interracial marriage and was motivated not by a theory of racial superiority, but by economic considerations. Socioeconomic conditions in the colonial period encouraged racial mingling. There was a severe shortage of Negro women in the colonies, and to a lesser extent, of white men of the same social class as the white female indentured servants. There indentured servants and Negro slaves, who often worked together in the fields and lived near each other in similar tenant huts, intermixed and intermarried. By the general custom of the time, a child of such a marriage would be a freeman because he acquired the status of his mother. "And forasmuch as divers freeborn English women . . . do intermarry with negro slaves" by which "a great damage doth befall the master of such negroes," the Maryland statute was passed to stop such marriages by making the female miscegenator a slave for the lifetime of her husband and all children of such marriages "slaves as their fathers were."

According to some historians, after this law was passed, plantation owners encouraged or forced white women, usually indentured servants, to marry Negroes in order to increase the number of slaves. Lord Baltimore, shocked by this practice, had the law changed in 1681 to penalize any master encouraging an interracial marriage and to make such women and their issue free. Masters stopped encouraging these marriages, but they still occurred. And the children of the interracial couples were the financial burden of the masters during their minority because they were the legal children of male slaves. Such children were, however, freed upon reaching maturity. New laws became necessary to compel the servant girls to reimburse the masters for the cost of supporting these children. These laws did not achieve their purpose, and so, finally, all Negro-white marriages were prohibited.

In 1691, Virginia passed a law prohibiting miscegenation to prevent "spurious issue." Any white person marrying a Negro was to be banished from Virginia forever. Considering the banishment of the Lovings in 1959, Virginia's policy has not changed much since 1691.

Eventually, miscegenation laws were passed in nearly all the colonies, including Massachusetts in 1705, which also was one of the first states to repeal its law, in 1843. During the nineteenth century as many as thirty-eight states prohibited interracial marriages. In the period surrounding the Civil War, nine states repealed their statutes. But through the years, Southern states made their laws harsher, Georgia and Virginia going so far as to require all citizens to register and identify their "race" although never establishing a practical means for enforcing the requirement. By 1951, there remained in effect twenty-nine miscegenation statutes. Ten states since 1951 have repealed their statutes. Of these, most were Western states, such as South Dakota (1957), Colorado (1957), Nevada (1959), Nebraska (1963), and Utah (1963), acting at least partially in response to the Negro social revolution.

All nineteen states with miscegenation laws prohibit Negro–white marriages. Other "races" which have been included in the various laws are Mongolians, Chinese, Japanese, Africans, Malayans, American Indians, Asiatic Indians, West Indians, mulattoes, Ethiopians, Hindus, Koreans, mestizos, and half-breeds. The laws border on burlesque. The Arizona law, repealed in 1962, at one time so defined a mulatto that he could not marry anyone, even another mulatto; then it was changed so that a mulatto could marry an Indian but could not marry a Negro, a Caucasian, or another mulatto.

Who is a Negro under such laws? There is no uniform definition, so it is difficult to know. The different definitions create racial chameleons. One can be Negro in Georgia because he had a one-half Negro great-grandmother, and by crossing the border into Florida, become a white because Florida makes him a Negro only if he had a full Negro great-grandmother. The most common definition uses an unscientific percentage-of-blood test usually classifying a Negro as "any person of one-eighth or more Negro blood." If a blood test is to be used and one-eighth Negro blood, whatever that means, makes you Negro, why does not one-eighth white blood make you white? Alabama, Arkansas, Georgia, and Virginia make anyone a Negro who has any ascertainable trace of Negro blood. The Delaware, Kentucky, Louisiana, West Virginia, and Wyoming laws provide no definition of a Negro, and Tennessee has two conflicting definitions. Oklahoma and Texas prohibit marriages between whites and Africans or descendants of Africans without defining an African.

It should not be surprising that in the usual case a jury may decide that a person is a Negro from his appearance—a test authorized by statute in Missouri. Neither the statutes nor science provides a method to determine whether a person is one eighth Negro or one of the other statutory formulas of fractionalized racial membership. Terms such as "octaroons," "quadroons," and "half-breeds" are misleading except in a fictional or social sense. Genes are not transmitted in predetermined or culturally labeled quantities as the draftsmen of these statutes thought. Detailed genealogies might be used to try to make the statutory racial calculus workable. But even where genealogies are available, they may be unreliable or insufficiently informative on the racial composition of the great-grandparent whose blood allegedly makes the accused a Negro. After all, from one third to three fourths of U.S. Negroes have some Caucasian ancestry.

In short, the statutory definitions of Negro are sometimes contradictory, often nonexistent, and usually a combination of legal fiction and genetic nonsense nearly impossible to apply as a practical matter. None of the statutory definitions seems sufficiently precise to meet the constitutional requirement of due process which nullifies a criminal statute that is so vague that men of common intelligence must guess at its meaning and differ about its application.

And the penalties under these statutes can be quite severe—ten years imprisonment in Florida or North Carolina. Georgia, South Carolina, and other states impose criminal penalties upon anyone issuing a license to a miscegenetic couple or performing their marriage ceremony. Virginia levies a fine on anyone performing such a marriage ceremony "of which the informer shall have one half." Because these laws make the proscribed marriages void, a spouse may be prevented from inheriting from his or her mate by other heirs who prove the forbidden interracial nature of the marriage; spouses have even lost the right to workmen's compensation benefits otherwise payable. In many states, children of such marriages are declared illegitimate and are thereby prevented from inheriting under intestacy laws.

Mississippi, not surpassed in its crusade to maintain segregation, has a unique law supplementing its ban on interracial marriage, making a crime the publication for "general information, arguments or suggestions in favor of social equality or of intermarriage between whites and Negroes," and punishing the violator by imprisonment or fine or both. This law could be invoked against me for writing this article, or the *Atlantic Monthly* for printing it.

The rule voiding miscegenetic marriages creates another disturbing problem. A mixed couple legally marries in a state where their marriage is valid, and later, quite innocently, enters a state with a miscegenation statute. This couple would be subject to criminal prosecution for miscegenation, fornication, or cohabitation in the state which will not recognize the validity of their marriage even though it was valid where celebrated. Delaware, Louisiana, Mississippi, Tennessee, and Texas actually declare such marriages invalid by statute.

Is it not alarming to know that in 1965 the new U.S. congresswoman from Hawaii, who is of Japanese descent, and her Caucasian husband could be criminally prosecuted under Virginia law if they were to reside there while Congress is in session?

These laws are completely contrary to the undeniable trend in this country to ensure Negroes equality under the law. They continue to exist even though the Fourteenth Amendment was intended to eliminate racial discrimination fostered by state legislation. Yet, surprisingly, fifteen state supreme courts and several lower federal tribunals have upheld these laws. Only the Alabama Supreme Court in 1872 (which reversed itself in 1877) and the California Supreme Court in 1948 have declared miscegenation statutes unconstitutional.

What are the legal issues? How does a state justify making a marriage between two competent, consenting adults a crime solely because one is Negro and the other white?

Some decisions without any reasoning sanction the statutes simply by referring to "laws" of nature or of God which interdict amalgamation of the races. In an early decision, the Missouri Supreme Court approved a miscegenation law because of the "well authenticated fact" that the issue of miscegenetic marriages "cannot possibly have any progeny and such a fact sufficiently justifies those laws which forbid the intermarriage of blacks and whites. . . ." This "fact" is pure fiction.

Other courts have reasoned that these laws do not discriminate by race because whites and Negroes are treated equally in that both races are prevented from intermarrying. This so-called "equal application" theory is supported by reference to a now discredited 1883 decision by the U.S. Supreme Court affirming a conviction of a Negro man and white woman for fornication even though the penalty was more severe than for the commission of the same act by two whites or by two Negroes. But the decisive question is not whether different races, each considered as a group, are treated equally. Races do not marry, individuals do; and the Fourteenth Amendment protects the personal right of an individual to marry. When a Negro is denied the right, solely because he is a Negro, to marry a white woman who wishes to marry him, the law discriminates against him and denies him a fundamental right solely because of his race, just as it denies the same right to the white woman.

Defenders of miscegenation laws maintain that the right to marry is subject to regulation by the state, and that the state has the power to ban miscegenetic marriages in order to prevent the violence and tension that will result from their legalization. Even if violence were certain to occur, this fact would not justify the statutes. No court should accept the reasoning that race tension can be eradicated by perpetuating by law the irrational prejudices that cause the tension. This reasoning not only is circular but also suggests that local law officials are unwilling or unable to maintain order—clearly not a rational basis to support a law depriving persons of constitutional rights. In fact, racial violence is almost nonexistent in areas where miscegenation is common, as in Brazil and Hawaii.

Virginia's highest court, in sustaining a miscegenation statute in 1955, emphasized the state's legislative purpose "to preserve the racial integrity of its citizens" and to prevent the creation of "a mongrel breed of citizens." Assuming racial purity to be a legitimate purpose, the only race kept "pure" is the Caucasian, because these laws do not prohibit, for example, Negroes from marrying Mongolians. If racial purity is a desirable goal, then why are only Caucasians protected, and why should a "pure Negro" be allowed to marry a person who is seven eighths Caucasian and only one eighth Negro? This occurs not from a lack of logic or from ignorance, but because these laws are designed to preserve the purity of the majority Caucasian race—which in itself is one aspect of their larger, unexpressed goal of preserving what many think of as our "white American culture."

Of course, the maintenance of racial purity is a meretricious basis for these laws. There is no evidence to support the existence of so-called "pure" races. Even the idea of a pure race has been termed a subterfuge to cloak ignorance of the phenomenon of racial variation. Race mixture has occurred extensively throughout history.

Often courts have accepted, either explicitly or implicitly, two erroneous assumptions in order to find a rational basis for the laws: (1) the white race will be harmed by intermixing because of its innate superiority over the Negro race and (2) the progeny of Negro-white marriages are inferior.

There is no scientific evidence to sustain the assumption that the white race is innately superior to the Negro race. One can still find "studies," such as those by Carleton Putnam in 1961 and W. C. George in 1962 (commissioned by the Alabama legislature), to support the theory of an inferior race. Most serious students of anthropology do not even consider this question a present problem for research, agreeing that the races of the world are essentially equal in native ability and capacity for civilization and that group differences are for the most part cultural and environmental, not hereditary.

As for the progeny of racial intermixing, there is not a single anthropologist teaching at a major university in the United States who subscribes to the theory that Negro-white matings cause biologically deleterious results. On the contrary, some conclude that because of a certain hybrid vigor, interracial marriage may be desirable and the offspring superior, citing the Hawaiian population, among others, to support this view.

In addition to their "scientific" arguments, defenders of the laws maintain that a state has an obligation to protect both the couples and their children from the psychological harm of social adjustments necessitated by miscegenation. Upholding the Louisiana miscegenation law in 1959, that state's supreme court stressed, without citing factual or other authority, that a state could prohibit miscegenetic marriages to protect the children of such marriages from "a feeling of inferiority as to their status in the community that may affect their hearts and minds in a way unlikely ever to be undone." (The quoted language used by the Louisiana court, with, I think, a touch of sarcasm, was taken from the 1954 U.S. Supreme Court decision prohibiting segregation in public schools.)

Even if one assumes there are findings of fact to support the legislature's judgment that miscegenation will cause social harm, must the U.S. Supreme Court bow to its judgment? The Court, consistent with its appropriate function in our political system, has developed a salutary presumption in favor of the constitutionality of state legislation. But if a law discriminates solely on the basis of race, then the Court considers the law constitutionally suspect and requires the state to justify the racial classification by some overriding legislative purpose.

There may yet be racial classifications which are constitutional, such as the use of different mortality tables for whites and Negroes or the keeping of racially segregated public records for statistical purposes. Nevertheless, the guarantee of equal protection of the laws must mean at the very least that there can be no valid legislative purpose for a state law which denies two competent, consenting adults the right to marry because of the color of their skins or the imagined racial composition of their blood. No legal scholar of note considers these laws constitutional nor thinks that a declaration of their unconstitutionality will require a new interpretation of the meaning of the Fourteenth Amendment.

Today interracial marriage is opposed because of social considerations by the majority of both Negroes and whites. Even those who approve in principle would find it difficult to advise their sons or daughters to enter into such a marriage knowing the unavoidable social problems which confront an interracial couple.

However, the number of interracial marriages does seem to be increasing. Andrew D. Weinberger, a New York lawyer who has studied miscegenation, estimates that there are one million such couples in the country, including a large

number of light-skinned Negroes who pass for white and whose marriages—
estimated at 810,000—are not generally known as mixed marriages. He estimates
known mixed marriages at 190,000. Neither their number nor the personal reasons
for these interracial marriages may be significant. It may be significant that many
leading Negroes in public life are partners in mixed marriages, including Edward
W. Brooke, Republican Attorney General of Massachusetts, the highest Negro
public officeholder in the United States, and James Farmer, national director of
CORE. More mixed marriages will occur as integrated education spreads, and
generally, these laws will be no obstacle. For example, after the disclosure of the
marriage of Charlayne Hunter, the first Negro girl to enter and graduate from
the University of Georgia, to a white Southerner and fellow student, they left
Georgia and now reside in New York City.

   Although an argument can be made that the Supreme Court would make a
serious error if it now struck down these laws, it misstates the question to ask
whether a decision should be deferred because the issue is incendiary to some
whites and insignificant to most Negroes. In their apparent lack of concern about
the existence of these laws, Negro spokesmen may underestimate both their symbolic meaning and their psychological force in the states which have such laws.
Consider the efforts in Alabama to remove Garth Williams' book for children,
The Rabbits' Wedding, from the shelves of the public libraries because the picture
of the two little rabbits who "were wed and lived together happily in the big
forest; eating dandelions" indicated that one was white and the other black. White
racists point to these laws to support their appeal to the ultimate superstition
fostering racial prejudice—the myth that Negroes are innately inferior to whites—
and to demonstrate that even the Supreme Court (by its silence) still deems the
Negro inferior in his right to enter into the most private and personal of relationships. There are no laws more symbolic of the Negro's relegation to second-
class citizenship. The fact that legislation cannot end prejudice does not mean
that laws which foster it should continue to exist.

   The elaborate legal structure of segregation has virtually collapsed with the
exception of the miscegenation laws. Whether or not the Supreme Court was wise
to avoid this question in 1954, it should now invalidate these laws. A free society
cannot tolerate legalized racial prejudice, unsupported by reason or morals and
capable of causing incalculable hurt to those designated inferior by law.

Representing Miscegenation Law*

EVA SAKS

Blood kin to both "the Quadroon" in *Uncle Tom's Cabin* (1850) and to *The Quadroon* (1856) by novelist and former slave overseer Mayne Reid, Dion Boucicault's
The Octoroon, or, Life in Louisiana (1859) descended on Broadway with some

---

* From Eva Saks, "Representing Miscegenation Law." *Raritan* 8.2 (fall 1988): 39–69.

success. In Boucicault's play on the Great White Way, the heroine Zoe, a Louisiana octoroon whose gentlemanly white father, Judge Peyton, had tried to adopt her and set her free, discovers upon his death that she is not a legal owner of her father's plantation but instead is part of it, and is to be sold along with it to satisfy the debts of the estate. Though Zoe looks white, she cannot marry her dashing cousin, young Master Peyton, because Louisiana miscegenation law makes a crime of the union of a white and an "octoroon." Instead of becoming mistress of Terrebonne plantation, the fair Zoe is auctioned off for twenty-five thousand dollars to the villainous Jacob M'Closky, who murders Judge Peyton's favorite male slave and is photographed while doing so by a "good Indian," who is falsely accused of the murder. Eventually, of course, money arrives from England to pay off the Peytons' creditors, the murderer is identified when his photographed image turns up in the Indian's satchel, and the plantation is saved—but not before Zoe takes poison, turns white, and dies.

American Jurisprudence (1941) defines the crime of miscegenation as "intermarrying, cohabiting, or interbreeding of persons of different races." In *The Octoroon*, it is miscegenation law that blocks Zoe's escape from the status of property to the contract of marriage. The octoroon's oscillating identity between property owner and owned property dramatizes the chief tensions of American miscegenation law: the gap between social and legal definitions of race and property; the power of legal language to construct, criminalize, and appropriate the human body itself, as Zoe was appropriated by law to her father's estate; and the ongoing crisis of representation entailed in litigating a crime in which legal definitions contradict physical signs and social codes, and the exacerbation of this problem in subsequent generations. Miscegenation law, as Boucicault recognized, occupied a central position in the American family romance, both because it governed the marriage contract, which had legal implications for inheritance and legitimacy, and because it upheld the purity of the body politic through its constitution of a symbolic prohibition against the dangerous mixing of "white blood" and "black blood," casting social practices as biological essences. Underwritten by the social sciences, miscegenation laws dramatically inscribed—and sometimes diverged from—the taboos of the body politic. Emphasizing these issues, I will analyze the American case law of miscegenation from the first reported case in 1819 through the last, which arose in 1970, after the United States Supreme Court held miscegenation statutes unconstitutional in *Loving v. Virginia* (1967).

Although miscegenation jurisprudence was dynamic, constantly interacting with historical events, miscegenation cases have a relative autonomy from other social definitions of miscegenation. This autonomy, along with their internal cohesiveness and cross-references, allow them to be analyzed as a genre: miscegenation discourse. This autonomous discourse also had normative effects.

There were three major causes for the autonomy of miscegenation discourse. First, it was autonomous because any given state's number of miscegenation cases was extremely limited. State courts were forced to refer frequently to cases from other states. All state miscegenation cases therefore drew on the same written sources.

Second, it was autonomous because it so frequently lacked external physical referents: the crime that it defined and punished was a crime of "blood," a metaphor that miscegenation law itself helped to invent and promote. The central criminal element of miscegenation was a difference in blood which existed only as a figure of speech: "white blood" and "black blood," which were mutually constitutive, and equally fictitious. In miscegenation law, judges not only presented descriptions reflecting physical facts (in mimetic language referring to objects both concrete and external to the case), but also composed new versions of social phenomena, *in* and *as* metaphor (in semiotic language). The legal, semiotic discourse of miscegenation was not mimetic; it did not describe visible material objects but instead provided signs of representation, like "blood."

Third, and related to the second, miscegenation law was autonomous because law's version of race and ownership could completely contradict the social meaning of these terms. *The Octoroon* dramatizes the conflict that ensues when the social owner is the legally owned, the social white is legally black, and the social family is legally no family at all. Because the deviance of social form from legal form makes social form an unreliable sign of legal form (and vice versa), this deviance causes a crisis of representation. Moreover, the subjects at stake in miscegenation, which were destabilized by this crisis, are among those most central to social life: language, family, property, and race.

Judges in miscegenation discourse used semiotic representation to create a new property in race: the metaphor of "blood," which functioned as title. However, this so-called new property held by the white family was ultimately subject to the same paradox complicating the old property: how does good title originate? What comes first—title or possession? How does title come to be the authoritative representation of property, trumping social expectations, as in *The Octoroon*?

Because legally defining property *is* a problem of representation, defining the new property of blood in miscegenation law's criminal bodies replays this problem on a new stage: how do courts represent the body, when possession of whiteness deviates from legal title to it? If blood is the signifier and signified of race, to what can judges refer to "prove" that something is the authoritative representation of blood? If race is a source of property rights, how are courts to adjudicate the rights of the products of miscegenation, offspring who are legal subjects of mixed blood and ambiguous race? An anxiety about representation, the body, ownership, and reproduction is the characteristic property of miscegenation discourse, and this conflict of representation is embodied in the cases' recurring symbol, what I call the miscegenous body. This symbol stands for the threatening clash and conjunction of difference: of black and white, of owner and owned, of property and the body, and of legal and social forms of representation itself. In this corporate form, every body is deviant and criminal.

In this image, the human body often stands for the national body. However, the national body also comes to stand for the human body in the imagery of Southern state court jurisprudence, a jurisprudence which simultaneously elaborated the state court's relation to the federal government and the white body's relation to the black's. The confusing question of which term represents which is a central problematic of the representations of miscegenation; this circularity is compounded by the problematic status of the body in the Southern state legal culture, in which the body of black Americans was only a Constitutional amendment removed from property. Whether the national body was conceived as a single human body, or whether the miscegenous human bodies were seen as a microcosm of the national body—"the little society composed of man and wife" of Tocqueville's *Democracy in America*—the jurisprudence of miscegenation was the site for working out political issues of Federalism and race, and the human body the fractured medium of this struggle.

The word *miscegenation* was coined in 1864 by crusading *New York Daily Graphic* editor David Croly, in his political pamphlet *Miscegenation: The Theory of the Blending of the Races, Applied to the White Man and the Negro.* However, the criminalization of interracial relations, especially marriage, had begun in the colonial period. Maryland passed this country's first miscegenation statute in 1661. This statute criminalized marriage between white women and black men. Unlike most British colonial law, the miscegenation statute had no English statutory or common law precedents (although Joseph Bishop's *Commentaries* (1852) would analogize an 1841 Kentucky miscegenation decision to an English opinion nullifying the marriage of a countess and her footman). The statute's genealogy instead includes moral and economic concerns: moral concerns of the parent country, England, which stemmed from the popular white mythology that blacks descended from the Ham of *Genesis,* and that their blackness was a punishment for sexual excess; economic concerns of Maryland and Chesapeake Bay, where marriage between a white woman and a black slave would produce legally free children, thereby depriving the slaveowner of potential slaves—a reduction in the stream of future earnings capitalized in the black body. Subsequent antebellum miscegenation statutes criminalized interracial sex and interracial marriage; such sex was, like all extramarital sex, prohibited as fornication but generally accepted (by the dominant culture) when occurring between white men and black women. Statutes prohibiting interracial marriage did not (arguably, nor were they meant to) deter white men from engaging in sex with black women, especially with their slaves; in fact, there were positive economic incentives for slaveowners to do so, since the progeny of interracial intercourse with white fathers would become the white fathers' property. Yet all Southern states passed statutes criminalizing interracial marriage, as did many Northern states. *The Octoroon* dramatizes this moral economy, in which the same characters who accept the prohibition against miscegenous *marriage* also enact the acceptability of the miscegenous *sex* which produced the Octoroon. As Tocqueville described this peculiar code: "To debauch a Negro girl hardly injures an American's reputation; to marry her dishonors him." Miscegenation law, which during slavery kept interracial children slaves, and after slavery bastardized them, originated as much in concerns about identifying the rights of (and in) future generations as in moral concerns. This is the law of the Octoroon's father, Judge Peyton; its focus is at least as much on "intermarrying" and "interbreeding" as on "cohabiting."

Miscegenation was a topic to which legislators paid increasing attention in the nineteenth century. This attention was heightened in mid-century, from 1840 through Reconstruction. (That legislators and judges paid increasing attention to the regulation and punishment of miscegenation at this time does not mean that interracial sex and marriage as social practices actually increased in frequency; the centrality of these practices to legal discourse was instead a sign that their relation to power was changing. The extent of uncoerced miscegenation before this period is a debated issue.) At the federal level, the framers of the Fourteenth Amendment endlessly discussed "miscegenation" and "amalgamation," as recorded in the *Congressional Globe* of the Fortieth Congress (1869). At the state level, there was an increase in the passage and enforcement of miscegenation laws. In substance, the federal government's Civil War amendments (1865–1870) and Civil Rights Acts (1866 and 1875) threatened the white South with the potential legal legitimation of interracial sex and intermarriage; in structure, these federal legal initiatives threatened the sovereignty of the individual Southern state courts that adjudicated miscegenation cases, since the empire of federal power was expanding through the United States Constitution, congress, and judiciary. This put the state court judges of miscegenous bodies—white men charged with upholding state criminal law against federal constitutional challenges—on the defensive on many levels: sexual, economic, professional, and political. Six Southern states actually incorporated prohibitions of miscegenation into their post–Civil War constitutions.

However, in the post-Reconstruction period, even the United States Supreme Court was prepared to contract the federal government's power over race relations. They held in *Pace v. Alabama* (1882) that the Alabama Code's punishment of interracial fornication more harshly than intraracial was constitutional under the Equal Protection clause of the Fourteenth Amendment because it punished the black and white parts of the miscegenous body equally; the following year, they struck down the Civil Rights Acts. *Pace* was both a rehearsal and an important symbolic antecedent for the "separate but equal" rhetoric of the United States Supreme Court's decision upholding the constitutionality of segregated passenger trains, *Plessy v. Ferguson* (1896). Thus did the crime of miscegenation play its symbolic part in maintaining the alienated status of American blacks.

The social sciences were both cause and effect of these legal changes. The nineteenth century marked the popularization of theories of heredity and eugenics descended from Darwinism. As Foucault notes in *The History of Sexuality*, blood achieved a new pseudoscientific status, while heredity would play an important role in the new disciplines of criminology and penology. The word "eugenics," which has Greek roots suggesting the "production of fine offspring," was introduced in 1883 by Galton, who drew on theories of Aryan superiority expounded in Gobineau's *Essai sur l'inégalité des races humaines* (1853); Gobineau transposed the idea of "race"—which had entered the English language in the sixteenth century to denote differences *between* species in anthropology and classificatory biology—from a linguistic to a physical group, and added the idea of a pure Aryan race. For the first time, "race" denoted a physical group *within* the human species. Furthermore, individual identity and subjectivity were constituted by fractions of blood: a person of one-eighth negro blood was an octoroon. (The very terms of the legal reification of blood as race—octoroons, quadroons, griffes—disappeared along with the culture and the laws that recognized them; describing someone as one-eighth black is now understood in both the scientific and the popular culture as having neither biological nor genetic meaning, but instead embodies a pragmatic recognition of how someone's ancestors were socially defined.) Theories of heredity begin to appear in miscegenation jurisprudence in Reconstruction, underwriting the modern institutionalization of blood and race. Social Darwinism, employing biology's survival mechanism to explain and justify social conditions, offered a philosophy of human hierarchy compatible with the general biologization that supported miscegenation laws.

From the turn of the twentieth century, xenophobia and racism combined to contribute to the currency of eugenics. Furthermore, an entire social science literature of hereditary deviance—a deviance of the blood—upheld the discipline and punishment of the dangerous miscegenous body in the interest of racial purity: Havelock Ellis's *The Criminal* (1891), Lombroso and Ferrero's *The Female Offender* (1895), Tredgold's *Mental Deficiency* (1914), Goddard's *The Criminal Imbecile* (1915). Despite intermittent challenges to their constitutionality, miscegenation statutes were upheld by both state and federal tribunals until the Supreme Court decided *Loving* (1967), and these courts invoked the authority of science and social science. Indeed, when the California Supreme Court decided *Perez v. Sharp* (1948), making theirs the sole state court ever to hold miscegenation statutes unconstitutional, they rejected the normative claims of eugenics yet continued to rely on science and social science as authority, to support their assertion of racial equality. Shortly after its school integration decision in *Brown v. Board of Education* (1954), which relied on current social science findings, the U.S. Supreme Court avoided these issues in *Naim v. Naim* (1955), in which they dismissed an appeal from the Virginia Supreme Court's decision which upheld miscegenation statutes against an Equal Protection challenge; by holding that *Naim* was "devoid of a properly presented federal question," the Supreme Court allowed Virginia to continue to exercise its "state's right" to "preserve racial integrity," as the Virginia judge had phrased it. In *McLaughlin v. State* (1963), the Supreme Court held that a Florida statute punishing interracial fornication more severely than intraracial fornication was unconstitutional but refused to address the more sensitive issue of interracial marriage, before *Loving*.

Miscegenation jurisprudence demanded an inversion of traditional moral categories: while punishing interracial fornication more severely than intraracial fornication, it punished interracial marriage most severely. As the legal creation of a property relation, and the institution where reproduction was legitimated, marriage was the subject policed most vigilantly by miscegenation law.

In slave states, the relative property rights of blacks and whites were clear. As summed up by Theodore Rosengarten in *Tombee: Portrait of a Cotton Planter:*

> Nothing but a white man's conflicting claim could limit a master's property rights in a Negro. . . . Chief of all property rights was the right to transfer ownership—to sell, deed, or bequeath title in a Negro to another white person.

In this social system, wealth was land and slaves. The Civil War and its legal offspring, the Civil War amendments and the Civil Rights Acts, upset this effectively feudal economy altogether.

White property was assaulted by five related developments of the immediate postwar period. First, Confederate money became worthless. Second, white southerners lost their property in slaves, as law turned blacks from living personal property into legal persons. Third, land values dropped, both in absolute price and as valued relative to the growing industrial wealth of the North. Fourth, Lincoln and his successors intimated that major land redistribution might be undertaken by the federal government; preliminary steps towards land redistribution were taken by General Banks in wartime Louisiana, and General Sherman's famous Field Order No. 15 specifically allocated forty-acre plots to freed slaves. Land distribution was the logical extension of emancipation: "If you had the right to take the Master's niggers, you had the right to take the Master's land too," reasoned one freedman quoted in Eric Foner's *Reconstruction: America's Unfinished Revolution, 1863–1867.*

Fifth, the value of white skin dropped when black skin ceased to signify slave status. However, this racial devaluation could be reversed if white blood could internalize the prewar status of white over black. Drawing on the social sciences as then understood, miscegenation jurisprudence was instrumental in stabilizing white property. In substance, it prevented the creation of legal homes and families and legitimate social exchange between blacks and whites by preventing marriage. This had critical legal consequences for the common law morality that held that "the bastard had no inheritable blood." (The fact that the bastard had none of his parents' blood for the purpose of *inheritance* did not mean he had none for the purpose of *heredity*.) Even statutes passed to relieve the plight of illegitimate offspring did not necessarily address the problems of descent created by miscegenation laws. Interpreting wrongful death acts designed to allow illegitimate "children" to inherit from their parents, Southern state courts frequently refused to designate illegitimate offspring *as* "children" within the meaning of the statutes; this was apparently because the offspring in question were "mulatto," suggests James Macauley Landis in *Statutes and the Sources of Law* (1934).

In imagery, state miscegenation cases emphasized the family, the home, the estate, and the state (as opposed to the federal) power. Above all, it created a symbol of race—blood—which was as independent from the visible as legal title was from possession. Moreover, it created an autonomous legal regime of "blood," which could conflict with the social regime of race.

Miscegenation law responded in varied ways to the assault on white property represented by the abolition movement and, later, the Civil War Amendments. On the political level, states passed stricter miscegenation statutes during Reconstruction. On a substantive level, genealogy was made the determinant of race, thereby marking former slaves permanently as black and, within the values of miscegenation, as a genetic underclass. This marking had important consequences in the civil laws governing property and property owners. And miscegenation law responded on a rhetorical level, using the metaphor of blood to signify race. By choosing the internal, biological *res* of blood, miscegenation jurisprudence transformed race into an intrinsic, natural, and changeless entity: blood essentialized race. (The reification of race as "blood," in the late nineteenth century, is part of a general judicial tendency of the period to hypostatize legal concepts, creating formalistic legal doctrines which were segregated from their factual and political context.)

According to its theoretical founding fathers, property is a right, not a thing. This translates, in the context of miscegenation, into its negative: for blacks, their property-in-race was not the negation of a thing but the negation of a right. Miscegenation jurisprudence turned a right back into a thing by injecting it into the body as blood, where it became the signifier of the body's legal rights; in Reconstruction, miscegenation law internalized the feudal economy the Civil War had supposedly ended. Miscegenation law used blood to control the legal legitimation of social unions and the legal disposition of property to the children of these unions; in doing so, it raised the classical issue of property in a new form: is blood a thing or a right? Is blood visible in possession, or invisible until written by the law as title?

The substantive element of cohabitation required courts to describe property while recounting the incriminating facts (for example, by describing where the defendants slept). These descriptions suggest the courts' prudishness regarding the parties' relationship. More importantly, they reveal that the legally significant facts were precisely those that would affect the disposition of property rather than people. In the judges' representations, property was not merely a backdrop for the moving bodies; instead, the human body was a medium for the transmission of property (through marriage and inheritance). The problem of representing the race of parties has turned into the problem of representing property. If property itself is the legal system of representation based on title, a threat to this system of representation was a threat to property rights. Miscegenation, which threatened the existing distribution of property and of blood (law's title to race), was therefore a crime by people against property. Miscegenation rhetoric attempted to stabilize property in race by investing white blood with value and arresting its circulation in the body politic. In so doing, miscegenation law constituted the human body as property.

The white race became a leading figure on the legal stage in this period, as did the corporation, which was held a legal "person" under the Fourteenth Amendment by the Supreme Court in *Santa Clara Co. v. Southern Pacific Railroad* (1886). But the corporation was property treated by law as a person, whereas the body in miscegenation was a person treated as property through the legal regime of blood, fractional holdings, and inheritance. To the law, a black person was not represented by a perceptible physical phenomenon like black skin, but instead consisted in black blood. Blood could not be proved empirically, any more than the "event" of miscegenation could be narrated in terms of the human actors: because the word *blood* was a displacement and appropriation of the human, it could not be portrayed *as* human. Legal race, as determined by legal blood, perpetuated the prewar economy of the human body, in which the body could be alienated because it was potentially another form of property.

Because sexual and marital choices are among the most intimate choices citizens make, and because choice as an ideal was sacrosanct in a legal culture based on contract and consent, courts had to stretch to provide rationalizations for their intervention in miscegenation cases. They therefore represented themselves as the paternalistic protectors of impoverished whites, on whom the courts bestowed the new property of race. As the court put it in *Green v. State* (Ala. 1877):

> [It] is . . . a fact not always sufficiently felt, that the more humble and helpless families are, the more they need this sort of protection. Their spirits are crushed, or become rebellious, when other ills besides those of poverty are heaped upon them.

Interracial sex and marriage had the potential to threaten the distribution of property, and their legal prohibition was an important step in consolidating social and economic boundaries.

Despite its concern with delineating boundaries between bodies and property, miscegenation jurisprudence failed to draw a critical boundary: that separating the human subject from property. In *State v. Treadaway* (La. 1910), the relatively lenient Louisiana court held that an "octoroon" was not "a person of the negro or black race" for the purposes of a criminal miscegenation prosecution because of the absence of statutory definition of "octoroon"; in doing so, the court presented a hypothetical situation which expressed this double anxiety over property-in-the-person:

> For instance, a notice that all negroes were to be driven out of New Orleans would no doubt set everyone wondering at what point the color line was to be drawn.

In this jurisprudence, the boundary of property-in-the-person ("the color line") is confused with the boundaries of real property, on which the first boundary is based ("out of New Orleans"). This is the same conflict of representation dramatized when the Octoroon, a person, becomes part of the property of her father. This conflict appears here, again, as a potential discrepancy between where law would set the "color line" and where society would set it, a discrepancy that turns the relationship of people to property into a problem of conflicting representations.

This discrepancy between the legal and the social definition of race appears in the cases that discuss the legal institutions of marriage and the family. The marriage contract is law's mechanism for the transmission of property. It also formalizes the parties' social relation; it represents to the world their relationship to property and to each other. Cases discussing marriage and family make explicit how social "race" and social ownership conflict with legal definitions.

Occasionally, a court adjudicated a conflict over property based on this gap between legal and social signifiers of race. In the 1910 North Carolina case of *Ferrall v. Ferrall* (N.C. 1910), a man tried to evade making a property settlement with his wife by voiding his marriage retroactively; his defense to her suit for alimony was that she was "negro within the prohibited degree." Apparently their marriage had initially been permitted because his wife was socially or visibly white. Mr. Ferrall sought to use the autonomous discourse of miscegenation law to defeat the social code which had accepted his wife as white. The court refused to deprive the wife of her social position as white, rejecting her husband's attempt to invoke the legal rule of "blood" to trump the legal rule of marriage:

Years ago the plaintiff married a wife who, if she had any strain of negro blood whatever, was so white he did not suspect it until recently. She has borne his children. . . . The plaintiff by earnest solicitation persuaded the defendant to become his wife in the days of her youth and beauty. She has borne his children. Now that youth has fled and household drudgery and child-bearing have taken the sparkle from her eyes and deprived her form of its symmetry, he seeks to get rid of her, not only without fault alleged against her, but in a method that will not only deprive her of any support while he lives by alimony, or by dower after his death, but which would consign her to the association of the colored race which he so affects to despise. . . . The law may not permit him thus to bastardize his own children.

Focusing on the woman's literal and figurative labor ("household drudgery," "child-bearing"), the court treats "blood" as a form of property that accrues over time, based on an individual's labor—almost a pension. Consistent with its holding, the court portrays the wife as an active subject, and vindicates her personhood by recognizing her rights. Moreover, the court refuses to employ law's autonomous, scientistic test of race, blood, and instead allows social judgments to prevail. Here, the law is mimetic: it reflects and enforces a prior, external social arrangement, rather than imposing its own semiotic system of adjudicating property rights through the metaphor of blood. The boundaries of the culture are not the boundaries of the law. In defining boundaries, the law might refer to social codes, as in *Treadaway*—"Few in all likelihood would understand that many people who have the appearance, education, and culture of white [would be included in a decree banishing negroes]"—or the law might rely on a higher authority: "[God] intends that they shall not overcome the natural boundaries He has assigned to them," as in *Gibson v. State* (Ind. 1871).

The family law in *Ferrall* suggests a larger theme of miscegenation: white blood allowed courts to conceive all whites as members of a family. Because the entire white family shared "race-as-property," blood was therefore a form of collective property. However, this only exacerbated the task faced by miscegenation law: defining the boundaries of this extended family, and making this property stable by making it inalienable.

Tracing the defendant's genealogy became the equivalent of a title search, the search for an authoritative legal representation of race. However, it also led to the same problem besetting any title search: how did title *originate*? In the context of race, this metaphorical title to blood, if traced back far enough, revealed the actual, historical fact of legal title: the "title in a Negro" which could be sold, deeded, or bequeathed to another white person, in the transfer of ownership that was "chief of all property rights." Blood therefore revealed itself as part of a social rather than biological pattern. While this historical origin explained the social status of blacks, it absolutely challenged the legal and "scientific" myth that the boundary between the races was natural, ahistorical, and biological. It was, like other property boundaries, like the legal family itself, the positive creation of the law. Blood was merely law's representation, one that tried to render natural and scientific that which was instead legal and metaphorical.

The flux in blood and the problem of its representation resulted in an anxiety about family. Where were family boundaries? Where did they begin and end, and what combinations of blood were appropriate? Was the appearance of a family sufficient to guarantee its legal status? *Bell v. State* (Tenn. 1872) revealed the pressure that was on the legal system's semiotic system of representation:

> Extending the rule [of recognizing out-of-state marriages to a miscegenation context] . . . we might have in Tennessee the father living with his daughter, the son with his mother, the brother with the sister, in lawful wedlock, because they had formed such relations in a State or country where they were not prohibited. The Turk or Mohammedan, with his numerous wives, may establish his harem at the doors of the capitol.

This problematization of family was reflected in this suggestive and typical association of miscegenation and incest. This conjunction appears as frequently in state criminal codes, which usually listed miscegenation next to incest as two crimes of "blood," as it does in Faulkner's *Absalom, Absalom!* The strange affinity of the taboo of "too different" with "too similar" was affirmed by an antebellum Mississippi statesman quoted in Eugene Genovese's *Roll, Jordan, Roll:* "The same law which forbids consanguineous amalgamation forbids ethnical amalgamation. Both are incestuous. Amalgamation is incest." The taboo of too different (amalgamation/miscegenation) is interchangeable with the taboo of too similar (incest), since both crimes rely on a pair of bodies which are mutually constitutive of each other's deviance, a pair of bodies in which each body is the signifier of the deviance of the other. Neither body can represent the norm, because each is figured as deviance from an other. (This complex of anxiety and taboo also evokes the jurisprudence of sodomy, another area of the law in which a pair of bodies constitutes deviance upon conjunction. Because they are too similar to each other, and too different from the "norm," the bodies of sodomy are legally Other. "Miscegenation was once treated as a crime similar to sodomy," notes one dissent in *Bowers v. Hardwick* [U.S. 1986].)

Bell's hysterical defense of the home was highly selective: it called for a fortification of the white house, not the American home. According to Herbert G. Gutman's *The Black Family in Slavery and Freedom 1750–1925*, black Reconstruction legislators attempted to promote the values of legitimate and respectable interracial domesticity by lobbying for the legalization of interracial marriage and inheritance and the criminalization of interracial "concubinage" (the customary form of white male/black female extramarital relationships). But white legislators refused, preferring to pass laws criminalizing interracial marriage and inheritance but *de*criminalizing concubinage! Only the white home, the "Terrebonne" of the white family, was consolidated by miscegenation law.

The divergence between legal and social forms is clear in *Green v. State* (Ala. 1877), where the court used the glorified, symbolic "marriage relation" to end an existing social union, sending a black man and a white woman to jail because they were married, yet describing their goal as the preservation of marriage and the home:

> [The institution of marriage] is indeed, "the most interesting and important in its nature of any in society." It is through the marriage relation that the *homes* of a people are created—those homes in which, ordinarily, all the members of all the families of the land are, during a part of every day, assembled together. . . . These homes, in which the virtues are most cultivated and happiness most abounds, are the true *officinae gentium*—the nurseries of the States.

Again, a social union, an apparent marriage, could deviate from legally cognizable marriage, just as social ownership deviated from legal ownership. In this legal version of family, the role of marriage is to keep property "in the [white] family." This may explain why *Green*'s focus on the home sometimes degenerated to a focus on the *house*, on real property *simpliciter*. This "real estate rhetoric" suggests some of the distributional tensions underwriting the substantive law of miscegenation.

For example, in *Hovis v. State* (Ark. 1924) the court acquitted the unmarried defendants despite their frequent sexual adventures because they had not cohabited—in other words, because they had not placed their bodies in a prohibited relation to property. The crime, as "the law lexicographers define it: 'To dwell together in the same house.' " In terms of property law, such a conjunction implied the threat of common property—a tenancy in common. The law lexicographers, then, add the final, requisite element of property to the definition of the crime. Property is the missing link, the legal form necessary to constitute the crime of miscegenation. Again, the obvious social connection of the parties was not dispositive. The autonomous law lexicographers demanded something different: that the defendants place their bodies in a prohibited relation to real estate.

They also demanded investigation of the defendant's family to determine his blood. *Jones v. Commonwealth* (Va. 1885) attempted to draw boundaries between the white and the Negro family trees, in the process reducing the defendant to a *res:*

> [It] is necessary to establish first, that the accused is a person with one-fourth or more of negro blood, that is, that he is a negro. . . . We find, that the accused was not a full-blooded negro, but had white blood in his veins, but there was no evidence to show the quantity of negro blood in his veins, and no evidence of his parentage except that his mother was a yellow woman. If his mother was a yellow woman with more than half of her blood derived from the white race, and his father a white man, he is not a negro. If he is a man of mixed blood he is not a negro, unless he has one-fourth at least of negro blood in his veins.

In this passage, where the language of heredity coincides with the language of inheritance, miscegenation law reifies blood as inalienable estate. However, the problem of representation created by this form of property was implicit in this formulation: the legal test for proving "blood" was so purely semiotic, so autonomous and nonreferential, that the prosecution here could not meet the test with concrete evidence. The prosecution could prove the color of the mother's skin— "yellow"—but could not prove the color of her blood. Miscegenation law created

a system of representation in race-as-property that merely continued the problem
of representation inherent in the system of property itself.

> The state's witness testified that "Ophelia Smith *looked like* a white woman—*was*
> a white woman." The court committed no error in overruling the motion to
> exclude the expression "*looked like* a white woman." But, if it were error not to
> exclude this expression, it would be a harmless one, because the positive evidence
> of the witness was that "she *was* a white woman."

As suggested by this quotation from *Jones v. State* (Ala. 1908), the evidentiary
rules of representing race presented a conundrum. Did the state's witness in *Jones*
misrepresent Miss Smith's race?

The state's witness in *Jones* testifies to the discrepancy between "looked like"
and "was," between representation and identity in the logic of miscegenation.
What relationship between the two halves of his statement is represented by the
transcript's "—"? Did the fact that "Ophelia Smith *looked like* a white woman"
equal the fact that she "*was* a white woman," or did it merely provide evidence
for the fact that she "*was*" one? Perhaps the fact that she "*looked like*" a white
woman distanced her somewhat from *being* white, and, by suggesting that her
skin was not her identity but a representation of an identity, opened the door to
the disturbing possibility of misrepresentation—a forgery by Nature? If Nature
was forging, what was being forged?

This reversal of the natural order is reflected in the deeper mystery of the *Jones*
case: why did the defendant's lawyer object to the statement that she "looked
like," but not to the statement that she "was"? The court's curious justification
for overruling the objection to the admission of "looked like" is that the witness
had also offered evidence that she "was." But how did he know that she "was"
a white woman, if not by the fact that she "looked like" a white woman? What
does a white woman look like?

What Nature was forging, and what a white woman *looked like*, was miscegenation discourse's creation: the "white woman" with "white blood." That the
"white woman" and "white man," like the "negro," had to be frequently and
instrumentally redefined throughout the history of miscegenation discourse is as
much a function of the autonomous nature of miscegenation discourse as of the
changing social conditions that demanded this strategic redefinition. The notion
that race could be forged or hidden—the concept of "invisible blackness," embodied in Harriet Beecher Stowe's "white niggers"—produced the phenomenon
of "passing": blacks who passed as white.

This implied an ontological corollary: whites who passed as white. And indeed,
Moore v. State (Tx. 1880) held that the prosecution must not only prove that the
black defendant had black blood, but also that the white defendant had white
blood:

> [That the defendant was a white woman] was an essential fact, perhaps the most
> essential to be established by the prosecution. To permit a female, however lowly
> her conditions or vicious her associations may be, to suffer imprisonment in the
> penitentiary for two years, upon the opinion of a single witness "that she looks

like a white woman," would be an outrage upon law and justice, which courts cannot tolerate.

The clash between legal essentialism and mimetic hearsay is explicit here. However, now every witness's testimony will be insufficient, since presence itself has been destabilized as a form of representation.

Miscegenation law's identification system, based on the metaphor of blood, was committed to the separation of *looked like* (possession of whiteness without legal title to it) from *was* (good title to whiteness). In the discourse of blood, semiotic representation simultaneously becomes inevitable and problematic—inevitable, because appearance (looking like) is no longer sufficient proof; problematic, both because the appearance of social life for blacks and whites is now called into question, and because no other evidentiarily acceptable proof of blood exists. To substantiate blood, to substantiate what is neither a mimetic description nor a tangible entity but instead a semiotic figure, is impossible. Caught in an epistemological loop, courts were led right back to social codes based on appearance, which was where the problem had begun. (In this same period, the art and philosophy of photography were working through this same tension between "essence" and representation. In *The Stereoscope and the Stereograph* [1859], Oliver Wendell Holmes, Sr. proclaimed that "form is henceforth divorced from matter. . . . Men will hunt all curious, beautiful, grand objects . . . for their *skins*, and leave the carcasses as of little worth." In *The Octoroon*, a photograph is the dispositive evidence of a crime because it captures the identity of the murderer in a perfect policing representation; however, the drama depends on and derives from the *un*representativeness of the Octoroon's skin. The Gilded Age esthetic of photography, judiciously analyzed by Walter Benn Michaels in *The Gold Standard and The Logic of Naturalism,* reflects the problems of representability in miscegenation.)

An additional problem jurists faced in representing race was posed by the fact that, in the legal culture, race itself was already conceived as a representation of something else. In this conception of nature, race was nature's means of inscribing an organism in the social hierarchy. In *State v. Scott* (Ga. 1869), race was nature's sign of value:

> [Social] equality does not in fact exist, and never can. The God of nature made it otherwise, and no human law can produce it, and no human tribunal can enforce it. There are gradations and classes throughout the universe. From the tallest arch angel in Heaven, down to the meanest reptile on earth, moral and social inequalities exist, and must continue to exist through all eternity.

The problem of representing race, then, was two-fold. If race already represented a prior, original presence (two tiers), representing race meant *representing a representation* (three tiers). The second problem was that the most obvious physical manifestation of race, skin color, ceased to have the significance of a tangible property. The court in *Scott,* like other courts, was faced by a situation where the body was now an unreliable signifier; however, they continued to use it as proof, as did the court in *Jones v. State* (Ala. 1908):

Nor was there error in the action of the court, permitting the state to make profert of the person, Ophelia Smith, in order that they might determine whether or not she was a white woman.

This conception of the race-marked body as a readable text which represented race and, upon fulfillment of the relevant conditions, crime, is a recurrent motif in the case law of miscegenation. However, the problem with this new body-text was that it pointed not to blood, not to race, not to dispositive unmediated proof, but instead led the court only to other texts: to the body-texts of the defendant's family, in the title search for blood—parents, as in *Weaver v. State* (Ala. 1928), or children, as in *Agnew v. State* (Ala. 1921).

Although a defendant's color and relatives were not dispositive proof of his race, his race was dispositive proof of his moral identity. His culpability was contingent on how the court represented him, more precisely on his race. In *Jones v. Commonwealth* (Va. 1885), the subject is criminalized once it has been racialized:

> To be negro is not a crime; to marry a white woman is not a crime; but to be a negro, and being a negro, to marry a white woman is a felony; therefore it is essential to the crime that the accused shall be a negro—unless he is a negro he is guilty of no offense.

Paradoxically, the defendant without a race—that is, the defendant with no identity in miscegenation discourse—could avoid criminal guilt: the *Jones* court did not convict the defendant. Undoubtedly the court could have found a way to convict him, but the court's substantive decision is justified by language that suits their substantive result; they strategically characterize his identity and therefore criminality as contingent on legal rhetoric: "The statutory definition of negro has been repealed, and no definition of negro substituted."

This court reaches a result similar to the result in *Ferrall*, since both courts refuse to find that a litigant is "negro"; this court, however, accomplishes this substantive objective by an instrumental conception of legal discourse that is the exact opposite of the *Ferrall* court's. In *Ferrall*, the court repudiates the legal code of blood, and enforces the social code; in *Jones,* the court wields the legal code to subvert the social code and to acquit the defendant. In both cases, the courts come close to recognizing legal race as a problem of representation.

When courts characterized legal race as the construct of "statutory definitions" rather than as biological essence, the defendants could prevail. This characterization was itself a step away from the typical "scientific" racism of the nineteenth century, and so such courts may have been more generally sympathetic to the defendants' plight; such language was more probably the effect of racial tolerance than its cause. But in any case, the figuration of race made the court uneasy with the process of race-production. In *Ferrall*, the court was outraged by a man's attempt to avoid paying alimony by proving his wife was a "negro within the prohibited degree" and retroactively voiding his marriage. The court's description of the process of adjudicating someone's race is revealing; rather than using words that characterize race as a prelinguistic, external phenomenon that words merely name or mime—that is, as a mimetic relation between word and object—the court instead describes the adjudication as "branding," tacitly recognizing its own role in the inscription of race:

> [He] would *brand* them for all time, *by the judgment of the court*, as negroes—a fate which their white skin will make doubly humiliating for them. . . . Certainly of all men he should have welcomed *the verdict that decided his wife and children are white*. . . . The eloquent counsel for the [white husband attempting to void his marriage] depicted the infamy of social degradation from the slightest *infusion* of negro blood. He quoted from a great writer, not of law but of fiction, the instance of a degenerate son who sold his mulatto mother "down the river" as a slave. But his crime was punished, and surely was not greater than that of the husband and father, who for the sake of a divorce, would *make negroes* of his wife and children.

The court's reference is apparently to Mark Twain's *Pudd'nhead Wilson;* the husband, relying on a legal fiction, offers fiction as authority.

That legal race was law's inscription on the human body did not mean that lawmakers could necessarily control the semiotic code. In *Bartelle v. United States* (Okla. 1908), the court could not prevent the witness from substituting conclusory terms ("mulatto") for common descriptive ones ("brown"):

> Q. What is the color of her skin? A. I would call it mulatto. Q. Has she brown skin? Just describe her *appearance.* A. Well, if I was going to describe her, I should call her a light colored mulatto.

Courts looking for external, objective referents for blood (brown skin) were also implicitly attempting to forge a way of representing race that was referential, to invent mimetic terms that referred to something beyond figures of speech. However, the ironic result of this double search—for referents and for *referentiality*— was that courts often found only other legal texts, prior legal inscriptions.

The court in *Treadaway* (La. 1910) presented a catalog of referents for race. It began by positing a system of language that was mimetic, that was "coined for the very purpose" of miming a prelinguistic reality:

> There is a word in the English language which does express the meaning of a person of mixed blood and other blood, which has been coined for the very purpose of expressing that meaning, and because the word "negro" was not known to express it, and the need of a word to express it made itself imperatively felt.

However, despite the court's depiction of miscegenation discourse as a language of mimesis, the language (and locus) of race was evidently not so simple—as the court's own search manifests. Facing "the sole question [of] whether an octoroon is 'a person of the negro or black race' within the meaning of the statute" making "concubinage between a person of the Caucasian or white race and a person of the negro or black race . . . a felony," the court first looked for definitions of "negro" in "literature" (as the *Ferrall* court had). Next, the court found "colored" in the dictionary:

> One belonging to the Ulotrichi or wooly-haired type of mankind; a black man, especially of African blood, and particularly one belonging to the stock of Sene-

gambia, Upper Guinea, and the Sudan. In North Carolina, a person who has in his veins one-sixteenth or more of African blood.

Looking for an extralegal, objective point of reference for race, the court finds itself referred back to miscegenation discourse: "one-sixteenth or more of African blood." The Louisiana judge looking for a referent can get no further than the Code of North Carolina! Ironically, this same North Carolina Code was less than authoritative in North Carolina itself: in *Ferrall*, the North Carolina case decided the same year, the court ignored the wife's legal blood and held that her social role qualified her as white.

In *Pace v. Alabama* (1883), the U.S. Supreme Court decision relied on by Southern state courts for eighty years, the court suggested an image that recurs throughout miscegenation discourse. In *Pace*, the Court rejected a Constitutional challenge to the state's miscegenation statutes brought on the theory that the Equal Protection clause was violated by Alabama's statutory scheme, which punished interracial fornication more harshly than intraracial fornication. The court denied that these statutes were "inconsistent" with the Equal Protection clause by defining the meaning of equality in the context of miscegenation: "[blacks and whites are treated equally under miscegenation law because] the offence . . . cannot be committed without involving persons of both races in the same punishment."

This version of "Equal Protection" was a virtual parody of formal reasoning: the statute was not racially discriminatory, despite the fact that it punished interracial fornication more harshly than intraracial fornication, because it punished the black and the white party involved in interracial fornication *equally*: "Indeed, the offence against which this [law] is aimed cannot be committed without involving persons of both races in the same punishment. . . . The punishment of each offending person, whether white or black, is the same."

In articulating the rationale for miscegenation law, the justice represents the offense of miscegenation. This offense was a single entity created by two disparate bodies which, when joined, became a "miscegenous body." The conjunction of difference was the putative crime: "The discrimination is not directed against the person of any particular color or race, but against the offence, the nature of which is determined by the opposite color of the cohabiting parties."

This horror at the conflation of difference was replicated in the mythology of the "mulatto." Scientific, legal, and popular mythology deemed this offspring of interracial union inferior to both white and black. The product of difference was a monster ultimately deviant and inferior. He was deviant from and inferior to the black, who was already defined as deviant and inferior. The mulatto monster was therefore doubly deviant, the other of the other. Indeed, to a century in which pollution theory underwrote escalating public health regulation, he was virtually *an infection*. According to *State v. Scott* (Ga. 1869),

> The amalgamation of the races is not only unnatural, but is always productive of deplorable results. Our daily observation shows us, that the offspring of these unnatural connections are generally sickly and effeminate, and that they are inferior in physical development and strength to the full-blood of either race. It is

sometimes urged that such marriages should be encouraged, for the purpose of elevating the inferior race. The reply is, that such connections never elevate the inferior race to the position of the superior, but they bring down the superior to that of the inferior. They are productive of evil, and evil only, without any corresponding good.

Thus the threatening "miscegenous body" emerged in three dimensions: first, the individual body with two colors of blood in it. Second, the corpus delicti, *Pace*'s "offence," consisting of the two defendants; each was defined against the other, and the crime of each was his body's difference from his lover's. Collectively constituting *Othello*'s "beast with two backs," their crime *was* their collective identity, and their collective identity could only be a crime: miscegenation. Finally, the social body was conceived as doubly miscegenous: between 1850 and 1880, the South often portrayed itself as different from, yet conjoined with or imprisoned within, the United States—in L. W. Spratt's memorable 1858 phrase, "like twin lobsters in a single shell." Another recurrent theme is that the nation, in its socio-political identity, was becoming "miscegenous." Here the national body was explicitly conceived as a white body, while blacks were portrayed in a simile as the fraction of polluting blood within this body, an unassimilable *clot* in the national body and the white family—as in Samuel Sewall's earlier *The Selling of Joseph:* "There is such a disparity in their Conditions, Colour and Hair, that they can never embody with us and grow up into orderly Families, to the Peopling of the Land: but still remain in our Body Politick as a kind of extravasat Blood."

The conjunction of different bodies always signaled the breakdown of legal boundaries, which were the boundaries of property and representation. The cluster of differences represented by this symbol included the difference between legal and social codes of race, between the semiotic (blood) and the mimetic (skin, hair, associates). This symbol both constituted and undermined the semiotic system of blood, by challenging the boundaries of state, and estate, and identity.

> To all intents and purposes Roxy was as white as anybody, but the one sixteenth of her which was black outvoted the other fifteen parts and made her a negro.

Post–Civil War miscegenation discourse juxtaposed miscegenation's threat to white legal and political (especially electoral) power with its threat to white physical and domestic security. As Mark Twain in the above quotation from *Pudd'nhead Wilson* turned Roxy's body into a minority ballot, a congressman debating the effect of the new Fourteenth Amendment on American social life responded to a white colleague's fear that the miscegenous ballot would bleed into miscegenous bodies:

> And, should your ballot and that of a black man happen to be placed in juxtaposition, would you for that reason deem it incumbent on you to give your daughter in marriage to the "American citizen of African descent"? Why, on the same principle, are you not bound to become the father-in-law of one of those other voters who, though white, is somewhat more debased than the negro? . . . Why, by parity of reasoning, are you not bound to inaugurate practical amalga-

mation by sending your daughter into a wigwam as the wife of the half-tamed savage and the prospective mother of children of the forest?

This embodiment of political issues as miscegenous figures dramatized a central theme of miscegenation discourse: the dreaded "juxtaposition" produced problematic issues of both sexuality and of the federal government's *jurisdiction*. Roxy's body *is* the body politic, and the body in miscegenation discourse is the site of many political and jurisdictional battles. This miscegenous body was the medium for state courts' attempt to define and individuate the Southern state and its white capital, both of which were under siege. The body itself was conceived frequently in political terms, as in *State v. Gibson* (Ind. 1871):

> The question is one of difference, not of superiority or inferiority. Why the Creator made one black and the other white, we do not know, but the fact is apparent, and the races are distinct, each producing its own kind, and following the peculiar law of its constitution.

"Law" and "constitution" were the issues splitting the national body in 1871. The Indiana state court's references to law and constitution in this metaphorical way turned its prosecution of the white race's "peculiar law" into an affirmation of both white racial separatism *and* state sovereignty. The upholding of a race's right to follow the "peculiar" law of its constitution became a proxy for a state's right to its "peculiar" institution. Thus did Southern courts allegorize the body into the battlefield of Federalism.

Arkansas, among the first Confederate states to be readmitted to the United States in Reconstruction (in 1868), revealed its Civil War battle scars in the miscegenation rhetoric of *Dodson v. State* (1895): "[permitting miscegenation would] involve a surrender by the people of one of the attributes of sovereignty." In effect, the War was still being fought in such language. In *Kinney v. Commonwealth* (Va. 1878), the court invalidated the marriage of a Virginia couple who had gone to Washington, D.C., to get married. This formal pattern, which recurs throughout the history of miscegenation, was guaranteed to elicit the maximum panic from a state court judge in 1878. (It recalled the antebellum attempt to subvert property-in-the-person by crossing state lines of *Scott v. Sandford* (U.S. 1857), better known as *Dred Scott*.) The state court was concerned with asserting the sovereignty of the state as well as of the race, especially in 1878, the year after the United States Supreme Court had radically expanded its own jurisdiction over state courts in *Pennoyer v. Neff* (U.S. 1877), and three years after the Civil Rights Acts had enlarged the federal role in enforcing the new race relations:

> Laws would be a dead letter if . . . both races might, by stepping across an imaginary line, bid defiance to the law. . . . Connections and alliances so unnatural that God and nature seem to forbid them, should be prohibited by positive law.

The defendants' bodies become a pretext to discuss other politicized borders; they focus the court's anxieties about emerging black political power, and potential political "alliances" and "connections" between blacks, whites, and mulattoes in the postwar South. Certainly, governments, connections, and alliances sound more

like political discourse than like (nonmiscegenation) case law on prohibited fornication and cohabitation.

Needless to say, the Civil War Amendments engendered an entire corpus of
law governing race relations and race-related evidentiary issues, as well as a new
jurisprudence of federal jurisdiction. However, the mark of miscegenation discourse is its unique position in this struggle: the miscegenous body was caught
in flagrante delicto at the intersection of federalist and racial tensions. The same
Supreme Court justice, Justice Field, wrote the opinions that delineated the Fourteenth Amendment's consequences for both jurisdiction (*Pennoyer*) and for miscegenation (*Pace*). As later diagnosed in *Treadaway* (La. 1910), the human body
itself was a tense federation of conflicting states: "Scientifically or ethnologically,
a person with seven-eighths white blood in his veins and one-eighth negro blood
is seven-eighths white and one-eighth negro." As Mark Twain recognized, the
critical issue was how this blood would vote.

Although the image of the miscegenous body haunted miscegenation discourse,
it was conspicuously absent in the cases that struck down miscegenation statutes:
Perez v. Sharp (Ca. 1948), *Loving v. Virginia* (U.S. 1967), and *U.S. v. Brittain*
(Federal District Court, 1970). Traynor's *Perez* opinion embodied a new rhetoric
of individual human dignity:

> A member of any of these races might find himself barred by law from marrying
> the person of his choice, and that person to him may be irreplaceable. Human
> beings are bereft of dignity by a doctrine that would make them as interchangeable
> as trains.

This is a new theme in miscegenation cases: a judge who consciously tries to
construct a human body that is *dis*continuous with property, in dramatic contrast
to earlier reasoning, in which human boundaries represented, and were represented by, property boundaries. In both style and substance, Judge Carter's concurring opinion in *Perez* moved even further from *Pace*'s formal logic to a sensational theatricality:

> Suffice it to quote the following from petitioner's [pro-miscegenation law] brief:
> "The blood-mixing . . . with the lowering of the racial level caused by it, is the
> sole cause of the dying-off of old cultures; for the people do not perish by lost
> wars, but by the loss of that force of resistance which is contained only in the
> pure blood. All that is not race in this world is trash." This quotation is from
> Hitler's *Mein Kampf.*

Conjuring up *Mein Kampf* forced the issue of the new popular and scientific
consensus on what was human as well as of what endangered that humanity,
casting Traynor's repudiation of trains as an overruling of both the segregated
train of U.S. racism in *Plessy* (1896) and the more recent European trains to
genocide rationalized by eugenics and blood. In contrast, the more important
Supreme Court *Loving* opinion was downright dry, perhaps because the opinion
was potentially inflammatory or perhaps because the decision was so uncontro-
versial; in any case, the miscegenous body was bound to be regulated henceforth

by the social text rather than the legal. Only *Brittain*, the *American Digest*'s final "Miscegenation" entry, produced a reconstructed human figure to strike down Alabama's miscegenation law over the state's defense of mootness: "There is no reason for this Court to delay making such a declaration until another couple in just the right circumstances next feels the pinch of these laws." Redefining the body's position in miscegenation law, the court recognizes this law as a force inflicting itself on the human body in a painful way: it "pinches." Although the body still serves as a figure (since the law is personified as a person who "pinches"), the body also retains its sentience: it "feels." This case makes material the dignity of the human body. This new figure has a new relation to race, property, and representation. It is no longer enslaved by the semiotic system of blood. *Loving* and *Brittain* present a happy ending—but they may not represent the final curtain on miscegenation. When *The Octoroon* played London in 1861, Boucicault rewrote the ending to reflect popular prejudice (and keep Zoe alive). The play of miscegenation is always open to reproduction.

Racial Purity and Interracial Sex in the Law of Colonial and Antebellum Virginia*

A. LEON HIGGINBOTHAM, JR.
BARBARA K. KOPYTOFF

I. Introduction

There is probably no better place than Virginia to examine the origins of the American doctrine of racial purity and the related prohibitions on interracial sex and interracial marriage. Many people applaud Virginia as the "mother of Presidents" (four of the first five Presidents were Virginians)[1] and the "mother of revolutionaries," such as Thomas Jefferson, George Washington, and Patrick Henry. Yet few stress that colonial Virginia was also the "mother" of American slavery and a leader in the gradual debasement of blacks[2] through its institution of slavery.[3] Virginia was also one of the first colonies to formulate a legal definition

---

* From A. Leon Higginbotham, Jr., and Barbara Kopytoff, "Racial Purity and Interracial Sex in the Law of Colonial and Antebellum Virginia." *Georgetown Law Journal* 77.6 (August 1989): 1967–2029.

1. These were Presidents Washington, Jefferson, Madison, and Monroe.
2. When we use the term "black" in this Article in reference to pre–Civil War Virginia, we mean it to include all those who at that time were called Negroes or mulattoes. The two comprised a single legal category, but a single term was not generally used in legal writing of the time. After the Civil War, the term "colored" was used for both, and it has recently been replaced by "black." *See* 1888 CODE OF VIRGINIA tit. 4, ch. VI, § 49 (defining "colored" persons and Indians).
3. *See* A. L. HIGGINBOTHAM, IN THE MATTER OF COLOR: RACE AND THE AMERICAN LEGAL PROCESS ch. 2 (1978).

of race[4] and to enact prohibitions against interracial marriage and interracial sex.[5] For more than three centuries,[6] the Virginia courts and legislatures advocated and endorsed concepts of racial purity that we would call racist.

While Virginia was a pioneer in these areas of law both before and after the Civil War, the pre–Civil War law was significantly different from that of the early twentieth century. The law of racial purity in the eighteenth century defined "white" as a less exclusive term than did the law of the twentieth century: people some of whose ancestors were known to be African could be legally white. The laws banning interracial sex and marriage were less harsh on blacks before the Civil War than they were afterwards: they did not punish blacks at all for marriage or for voluntary sexual relations with whites.

This is not to say that Virginia was less racist and oppressive to blacks before the Civil War than it was in the late nineteenth and twentieth centuries, but merely that the legal mechanisms of oppression were somewhat different. Slavery had its own mechanisms for legal control. When it was abolished, white Virginians elaborated other mechanisms to preserve the racial hierarchy of the slave era, among them the laws regarding racial purity and interracial sex. This Article explores the origin of these laws and their development in colonial and antebellum Virginia.

The laws regarding racial purity and interracial sex in pre–Civil War Virginia sprang from two concerns. The first concern was with the maintenance of clear racial boundary lines in a society that came to be based on racial slavery. Starting in the late seventeenth century, white Virginians devised statutes to discourage racial intermingling and then statutes to classify racially the mixed-race children born when the earlier statutes were ineffective. The statutes punishing voluntary interracial sex and marriage were directed only at whites; they alone were charged with the responsibility for maintaining racial purity.

The second concern was with involuntary interracial sex—that is, rape. This was seen primarily as an aspect of power relations between the races. Virginia applied the early law of rape more harshly to blacks than to whites: it punished only black men for interracial rape and, in the nineteenth century, the state formulated anti-rape statutes directed specifically at blacks.

This Article documents the laws of racial purity and interracial sex in pre–Civil War Virginia. It explores the law and the myth of white racial purity, contrasts the different legal approaches to voluntary and involuntary interracial sex, and

---

4. *See* Ch. IV, 3 LAWS OF VA. 250, 252 (Hening 1823) (enacted 1705) (mulatto defined as child, grandchild, or great-grandchild of Negro [and presumably a white] or child of Indian [and presumably a white]).

5. *See* Act XII, 2 LAWS OF VA. 170, 170 (Hening 1823) (enacted 1662) (fine for interracial sex twice that for fornication): Act XVI, 3 LAWS OF VA. 86, 86–87 (Hening 1823) (enacted 1691) (interracial marriage punished by banishment from Virginia within three months).

6. The first prohibition against interracial sex came in a 1662 statute; Act XII, 2 LAWS OF VA. 170, 170 (Hening 1823) (enacted 1662). Virginia's prohibition on interracial marriage was declared unconstitutional in 1967. Loving v. Virginia, 388 U.S. 1, 12 (1967) (prohibition violated equal protection and due process clauses of fourteenth amendment).

discusses the contribution of this body of law to the development and maintenance of racial slavery in Virginia. Finally, it notes that these issues reflected a far broader process of the debasement of blacks by means of the law.

II. Definitions of Race and Racial Classifications

When Europeans, sub–Saharan Africans, and American Indians first encountered one another during the expansion of Europe, the three populations had effectively been separated for thousands of years and each had developed distinctive physical characteristics. The visible differences, especially between Africans and Europeans, were so striking that travelers usually commented on them: "indeed when describing Negroes they frequently began with complexion and then moved on to dress (or rather lack of it) and manners."[7] The causes of the physical variations were open to question, and theories to explain them abounded.[8] But the more important question in the Americas became the results of racial difference rather than its causes: that is, the legal and social significance of race.

In practical terms, the fact that the differences were so visible gave a particular ease to the operation of a racially based system of slavery. In theoretical terms, when people bothered to ponder the question, they often saw the differences among races as part of a natural ordering of creatures by Providence into a Great Chain of Being, from the highest to the lowest.[9] Clearly, such a conception of a hierarchical ordering of races need not imply slavery; the English thought that the Irish were an inferior "race" but did not advocate denying them all basic human rights.[10] Yet just as clearly, the idea of racial hierarchy *could* be, and came to be, used as a justification for slavery.

In a 1772 suit in Virginia by a group of Indians who claimed they had been unjustly enslaved, Colonel Bland, the lawyer for the slave owner, argued:

> That societies of men could not subsist unless there were a subordination of one to another, and that from the highest to the lowest degree. That this was conformable with the general scheme of the Creator, observable in other parts of his great work, where no chasm was to be discovered, but the several links run imperceptibly into one another. That in this subordination the department of slaves must be filled by some, or there would be a defect in the scale of order.[11]

In Colonel Bland's notion of the Great Chain of Being, Indians and Negroes were created inferior and were meant to be subservient. Although seldom ex-

---

7. W. JORDAN, WHITE OVER BLACK 4 (1968).

8. *See id.* at 11–20 (climate, disease, natural dyes, and Biblical curse among candidates).

9. The popularity of this idea increased in the 18th century. *See id.* at 216–24 (discussing development of idea of hierarchical ordering in Europe during 17th and 18th centuries); *id.* at 481–511 (discussing relevance of idea of hierarchical ordering of races to American thought).

10. *See* Curtis, *Anglo-Saxonism and the Irish*, in RACE AND SOCIAL DIFFERENCE 123–29 (P. Baxter & B. Sansom eds. 1972) (noting shift in meaning of word "race" in 19th century from more neutral and traditional meaning of a particular class or category to more biological and scientific meaning).

11. Robin v. Hardaway, 1 Va. (Jeff.) 58, 62–63 (1772).

pressed clearly and explicitly in eighteenth-century Virginia, the view was implicit throughout Virginia society, especially with regard to Negroes.

Since the racially based systems of slavery that developed in the New World were premised on the concept of the racial inferiority of the enslaved, it would have been far simpler had there been no intermingling of races, no anomalous offspring, no confusion of the "natural order" by beings who did not clearly belong to one rather than another of the three populations of Indians, Africans, and Europeans. But human sexual behavior did not respect the "natural order," and mixed-race children invariably sprang up wherever the races had contact. White Virginians were disturbed by the racial intermingling, especially white-Negro mixtures, and introduced laws to prevent what they saw as the "abominable mixture and spurious issue"[12] by penalizing whites who engaged in interracial sex. When that failed, they turned to drawing strict racial boundary lines, defining some mixtures as white and others as mulatto.[13] They also devised a separate rule to settle the status of mixed-race children as slave or free, depending on the status of the mother. This rule had general application to all children born in Virginia, whether of mixed race or not.[14]

Virginia did not create a perfect social system in which black equaled slave and white equaled free with no confusing middle ground. Virginia's racially based system of slavery was created in the context of continuous racial mixing,[15] legal anomalies, and recurrent attempts to patch holes in the fabric of the system. Looking at the system in terms of its anomalies and patches will help bring into focus some of the central conceptions of race and slavery of pre–Civil War Virginia.

A. The Law of Slave Status

Part of the reason that there was no complete correspondence of race with slave status in pre–Civil War Virginia was that the rule for the inheritance of slave status was, as written, technically independent of race. While white Virginians seemed increasingly to want Negroes to be slaves, the statutes avoided a direct and explicit statement equating race and status. In 1662, the House of Burgesses set down the law on the inheritance of slave status, and it remained virtually unchanged throughout the slave period in Virginia.[16] It was devised to settle the

---

12. Act XVI, 3 LAWS OF VA. 86, 86 (Hening 1823) (enacted 1691).
13. Ch. IV, 3 LAWS OF VA. 250, 252 (Hening 1823) (enacted 1705).
14. Act XII, 2 LAWS OF VA. 170, 170 (Hening 1823) (enacted 1662).
15. Jordan's impression is that racial mixing in North American colonies and the United States was more common in the 18th century than at any time since, but he stresses the impossibility of discovering the extent of race mixing. W. JORDAN, *supra* note 7, at 137. Jordan reports that at least one observer before him also held this perception. *Id.* at 137 n.1 (citing E. REUTER, THE MULATTO IN THE UNITED STATES 112 [1918]).
16. *See* Act XII, 2 LAWS OF VA. 170, 170 (Hening 1823) (enacted 1662) (child to inherit mother's status); Act I, 3 LAWS OF VA. 137, 140 (Hening 1823) (enacted 1696) (same): Ch. XLIX, 3 LAWS OF VA. 447, 460 (Hening 1823) (enacted 1705) (same); Ch. XIV, 5 LAWS OF VA. 547, 548 (Hening

status of the mulatto children of free white fathers and slave Negro mothers. The act read:

> Whereas some doubts have arrisen whether children got by any Englishman upon a negro woman should be slave or free. Be it therefore enacted and declared by this present grand assembly, that all children borne in this country shalbe held bond or free only according to the condition of the mother.[17]

There was a confounding of "negro" and "slave" in this early statute. It stated that the problem was the doubtful status of the mulatto children of "negro" women; yet "negro" must have meant "slave" or there would have been no question of the slave or free status of the children. In a world in which whites (here "Englishmen") were assumed to be free and Negroes were increasingly assumed to be slaves, a decision had to be made about the status of individuals who did not clearly belong to one race or the other: children whose parents represented two distinct races and two extreme statuses.

The statute did not say that all children of Negroes or of Negro women were to be slaves, probably because not all Negroes were then slaves.[18] It would have seemed extreme, no doubt, even to white Virginians of that time, to enslave the child of two free people just because one or both of them were black. Some blacks were landowners and held slaves themselves.[19] The statute said, rather, that all children would be "bond or free" according to the status of the mother.[20] The rule embodied in the statute was thus phrased only in terms of status, not in terms of race.

A rough correspondence of race and status was assumed; however, they did not correspond entirely then and they diverged over time, partly as a result of the

---

1819) (enacted 1748) (same); Ch. VII, 6 LAWS OF VA. 356, 357, (Hening 1819) (enacted 1753) (same).

17. Act XII, 2 LAWS OF VA. 170, 170 (Hening 1823) (enacted 1662) (emphasis omitted).

18. *See generally* J. RUSSELL, THE FREE NEGRO IN VIRGINIA, 1619–1685 (1913).

19. *See* Russell, *Colored Freemen as Slave Owners in Virginia.* 1 J. NEGRO HIST. 233, 234–37 (1916) (earliest evidence of black slave owner dated 1654).

20. It was contrary to English tradition for children to inherit the status of their mothers, but since the children who posed the problem were almost certainly illegitimate, it may also have been contrary to English tradition for them to inherit a position or status from their fathers. Indeed, the inheritance of slave status was itself anomalous in English law of that era. Villeinage had died out in England and all English men and women of the 17th century were free born, whether legitimate or not. When it existed, villeinage had been heritable in the male line. *See* Morris, *"Villeinage . . . as it existed in England, reflects but little light on our subject": The Problem of the "Sources" of Southern Slave Law,* 32 AM. J. LEG. HIST. 95, 105–07 (1988) (concluding common law of property rather than villeinage source of slave law). The decision to make slave status heritable in the female line marked a departure. The rule of having children take their mother's status is known in Civil Law as *partus sequitur ventrem.* Exactly how the doctrine came into use in Virginia is unclear. It is not known whether it came with slaves brought from Civil Law countries, or was borrowed by the legislators from Roman Law, or was independently invented by Virginians. We do know that the legislators did not in 1662 invent the idea that the progeny of female slaves were also to serve for life; we find evidence for that practice as early as the 1640s. *See* Jordan, *Modern Tensions and the Origins of American Slavery.* 28 J.S. HIST. 18, 23–24 (1962) (sales of Negroes for life and of Negro women with future progeny recorded in 1640s).

1662 statute. They failed to correspond because of free Negroes. Some Negroes imported into Virginia before 1662 had never been slaves, and others who had been born slaves were later emancipated. The children of free black women were free under the statute, as were mulatto children born to white women. Free mulattoes were classified with free Negroes in terms of race and position in society.[21] They also failed to correspond because, as white men mated with mulatto slave women, a class of very light-skinned slaves was produced. Some individuals, who were slaves because they were remotely descended in the maternal line from a Negro slave woman, had such a high proportion of European ancestry that they looked white.[22] Some would even have qualified as legally white under eighteenth- and nineteenth-century Virginia statutes that defined race in terms of a specific proportion of white and non-white ancestry. Yet legally, they were also slaves.[23]

21. *See infra* note 40 (discussing relative status of blacks and mulattoes).
   While we can sort out the legal categories of race, the numbers in each are uncertain. The population figures on which estimates are based are incomplete, especially for the early period, and they do not distinguish Negroes and mulattoes and sometimes do not distinguish slave and free blacks. Edmund Morgan has given population estimates for 17th-century Virginia in the appendix to AMERICAN SLAVERY, AMERICAN FREEDOM: THE ORDEAL OF COLONIAL VIRGINIA 404 (1975). He also has estimated the number of blacks, but he says those figures are largely conjectural. In 1674, by his estimates, Virginia had 1,000 to 3,000 blacks out of a total population of 13,392. By the end of the century, in 1699, he suggests, Virginia's population included 6,000 to 10,000 blacks out of 58,040. *Id.* at 423. We have even less idea how many of those blacks were free.
   The first U.S. census reports, from 1790, show that during the 18th century the free and slave black population increased at a far greater rate than the white. In 1790, the total black population was 305,493—of whom 12,866 were free—and the white population was 442,117. By 1860, the last U.S. census under slavery, the total black population was 548,907—of whom 58,042 were free—and the white population was 1,047,299. U.S. BUREAU OF THE CENSUS, NEGRO POPULATION IN THE UNITED STATES 1790–1915, at 57 (W. Katz ed. 1968) [hereinafter NEGRO POPULATION 1790–1915] (figures for black population); *id.* at 44–45 (figures for white population).
22. There are a number of references to slaves who looked white. *See* J. JOHNSTON, RACE RELATIONS IN VIRGINIA & MISCEGENATION IN THE SOUTH, 1776–1860, at 209–14 (1970) (contemporary accounts of fair-skinned slaves). The numbers of fair-skinned slaves increased over time, as the slave population "lightened."

> [T]he glaring fact is that throughout the South, mulatto slavery was on the rise in the decade before the Civil War. Slavery as an institution was becoming whiter and whiter, a direct contradiction to the fundamental white notion that slavery was meant for black people. In 1835, Chancellor Harper of South Carolina had declared that it was "hardly necessary to say that a slave cannot be a white man," but by the end of the ante-bellum period the facts said otherwise. Growing numbers of persons with predominantly white blood were being held as slaves.

J. MENCKE, MULATTOES AND RACE MIXTURE 20 (1979).
23. We have come across no case that held that a slave was free solely on the ground that he or she was legally white. The point was raised in Henry v. Bollar, 34 Va. (7 Leigh) 552 (1836), in which the plaintiffs alleged, among other things, "that they were in fact white persons, and therefore could never have been lawfully held in slavery." *Id.* at 556. The defendants in the case claimed that those suing for their freedom were mulattoes. *Id.* at 557. The court did not address the interesting question of whether persons who had so small a proportion of Negro ancestry that they were legally white could, in fact, be slaves. It found the plaintiffs free on other grounds,

Being legally white did not make one free if one's mother were a slave; being Negro or mulatto did not make one a slave if one's mother were free.[24] The law of the inheritance of slave status was technically independent of race. This led to anomalies in the society, to people whose status was not considered appropriate to their race in the white Virginians' ideal conception of their slave society.

To say that a person could legally be a slave if he or she were descended in the maternal line from a slave raises the question of whether the first woman in the line had been legally enslaved. It seems clear from the early documents that Virginians gradually made what Winthrop Jordan has called an "unthinking decision" to enslave Negroes, and they did so in the absence of any specific legal sanction for the practice.[25] It was only after the practice was well established that it was reinforced by positive law. Thus the first statute on the legality of enslavement came in 1670, eight years *after* the statute on the inheritance of slave status.[26]

The stated purpose of the statute was to settle the question of whether Indians who were bought as war captives from other Indians could be slaves. Negroes were not mentioned explicitly, but by curiously circumspect language the legislature indicated that imported Negroes were to be slaves. The act as published was captioned "what tyme Indians to serve."[27] It reads, in its entirety:

> Whereas some dispute have [*sic*] arisen whither Indians taken in warr by any other nation . . . that taketh them sold to the English, are servants for life or terme of yeares, It is resolved and enacted that all servants not being christians imported into this colony by shipping shalbe slaves for their lives; but what shall come by land shall serve, if boyes or girles, untill thirty yeares of age, if men or women twelve yeares and no longer.[28]

---

namely, that their owner, who had tried to free them both by will and by deed of emancipation, had been mentally competent to do so. *Id.*

24. For a brief period of fifteen years, starting in 1676, some Indians also could be legally enslaved, and a female ancestor from that period could produce a line of descendants who were legally slaves. Act I, 2 LAWS OF VA. 341, 346 (Hening 1823) (enacted 1676) (Indians taken during war held as slaves for life); Act I, 2 LAWS OF VA. 401, 404 (Hening 1823) (enacted 1676) (same); Act I, 2 LAWS OF VA. 433, 440 (Hening 1823) (enacted 1679) (same); Act IX, 3 LAWS OF VA. 69, 69 (Hening 1823) (enacted 1691) (abolition of all trade restrictions with Indians). The 1691 statute was later interpreted as having made enslavement of Indians illegal. *See* Gregory v. Baugh, 25 Va. (4 Rand.) 246, 252 (1827) (Green, J.) (discussion of these and other statutes regarding enslavement of Indians).

25. *See* W. JORDAN, *supra* note 7, at 44, 71–82 (strong pre-1640 historical uncertainty of Negro status and subsequent trend of increasing importance of slavery).

26. *Compare* Act XII, 2 LAWS OF VA. 283 (Hening 1823) (enacted 1670) (legality of slavery) *with* Act XII, 2 LAWS OF VA. 170 (Hening 1823) (enacted 1662) (inheritance of slave status).

27. Act XII, 2 LAWS OF VA. 283, 283 (Hening 1823) (enacted 1670). Hening notes, "The title of this act in Ch. City and P. Rand MSS. and edi 1733 and 1752, is 'An act declaring who shall be slaves'; in Purvis, 'An act concerning who shall be slaves.' " *Id.* at 283 n.* (italics omitted).

28. *Id.* at 283 (italics omitted). The treatment of Indians by the Virginia legislature and courts is an area which goes far beyond the coverage of this Article. However, even within the context of racial purity and interracial sex, the Virginia legal process demonstrated a hostility to Indians because they were non-white. At a later time, we hope to develop this theme more comprehensively.

Why was enslavement made to depend on manner of importation? If the legislators wanted to enslave Negroes but not Indians, why did they not say so? There seems to have been a curious avoidance of any mention of Negroes in the statute. In 1682, the statute was revised to eliminate the distinction based on the manner of importation, for the legislature had, in the interim, approved the enslavement of Indians.[29] This time the legislators offered explicit examples of the people whom they contemplated enslaving: "all [imported] servants except Turkes and Moores whilest in amity with his majesty, . . . whether Negroes, Moors, Mullattoes or Indians."[30] The list of likely slave peoples was dropped from the act in the 1705 revision; the revised act noted only which imported servants could not be enslaved, not which could be.[31]

Enslavement was also made to depend on religion, but this requirement was modified so as to circumscribe a population primarily of blacks and Indians. In the 1670 act, no Christians were to be sold as slaves. But in the 1682 statute, a Christian servant "who and whose parentage and native country are not christian at the time of their first purchase . . . by some christian" could be sold as a slave, notwithstanding his conversion to Christianity before importation.[32] This allowed slaves who had become Christians in the West Indies to be sold in Virginia as slaves. The provision echoed one in a 1667 statute declaring that slaves in Virginia would not be made free by virtue of their conversion to Christianity once there.[33] Now, conversion *before* importation would not release them either. Thus, religion did not truly circumscribe the population that Virginia legislators meant to exclude from slavery. In 1705, the legislature again revised the rule on enslavement. The language was simplified, but the substance was the same. The act exempted those who were Christians in their native country, "Turks and Moors in amity with her majesty, and others that can make due proof of their being free in England, or any other christian country, before they were shipped hither."[34] Now prior freedom in a Christian (civilized?) country would protect one from enslavement, but being Christian itself would do so only for those who were Christians in their "native country."[35]

Thus, the rule of enslavement, like the rule of the inheritance of slave status, was technically independent of race. Even a superficial familiarity with the history

29. *See supra* note 24 (enslavement of Indians legally valid until 1691).
30. Act I, 2 LAWS OF VA. 490, 491 (Hening 1823) (enacted 1682).
31. Ch. XLIX, 3 LAWS OF VA. 447, 447–48 (Hening 1823) (enacted 1705).
32. Act I, 2 LAWS OF VA. 490, 491 (Hening 1823) (enacted 1682).
33. "[T]he conferring of baptisms doth not alter the condition of the person as to his bondage or freedom." Act III, 2 LAWS OF VA. 260, 260 (Hening 1823) (enacted 1667).
34. Ch. XLIX, 3 LAWS OF VA. 447, 447–48 (Hening 1823) (enacted 1705). This provision would have exempted Jews and other non-Christians who came as servants from England. Slaves who had been manumitted in England before being brought to North America also were to be free.
35. Slaves could be imported until 1785, when slave status was limited to those who were slaves in Virginia on October 17, 1785, or were descendants of the female slaves: persons later brought in as slaves were to be free. Ch. LXXVII, 12 LAWS OF VA. 182, 182–83 (Hening 1823) (enacted 1785).

of the era would indicate that white Virginians did not truly intend that slave status and race be independent. As the 1682 statute shows, they saw slaves as "Negroes, Moors, Mullatoes or Indians."[36] Yet, for the most part, they avoided racial designations in their laws, making enslavement depend on other characteristics instead. Were white Virginians of the mid-seventeenth century reluctant to admit, even to themselves, what they were doing: establishing a slave society based on race?[37]

B. Statutory Definitions of Race in Virginia

We mentioned above the anomaly of people whose status was not appropriate to their race in Virginia slave society. There were also racial anomalies: people whose race was in itself ambiguous, who did not fit into one or another of the set categories of race that comprised the white Virginian's view of nature.

When the three races first met in Virginia, there was no question or problem as to which race an individual belonged. It was evident at first glance. As Judge Roane observed in *Hudgins v. Wright*:

> The distinguishing characteristics of the different species of the human race are so visibly marked, that those species may be readily discriminated from each other by mere inspection only. This, at least, is emphatically true in relation to the negroes, to the Indians of North America, and the European white people.[38]

Initially, there was no need for statutory definitions of race and there were no problems of racial identity to be solved by legislative fiat. However, as soon as the races began to mingle and reproduce, problems of racial identity arose. How should mixed-race offspring be classified?

Strictly in terms of genetic contribution, the child of one white parent and one black parent had the same claim to being classified as white as he did to being classified as black. He was neither, or either, or both. One could decide to call such half/half mixtures mulattoes, but that merely raised the question of classification again in the next generation. Was the child of a mulatto and a white to be deemed a mulatto or a white? Or should another name, like quadroon, be devised for such a person?

Of course, the important point was not the name but the set of rights and privileges that accompanied the classification. In Virginia, there were only three racial classifications of any legal significance, though there were far more combinations and permutations of racial mixture. Those three were "white," "Indian,"

---

36. Act I, 2 LAWS OF VA. 490, 491 (Hening 1823) (enacted 1682). The Moors that the Virginians meant to enslave were most likely Negroes while those "in amity with his majesty" who were not to be enslaved were most likely lighter-skinned people from North Africa.

37. Jordan notes that "[a]s late as 1753 the Virginia slave code anachronistically defined slavery in terms of religion when everyone knew that slavery had for generations been based on the racial and not the religious difference." W. JORDAN, *supra* note 7, at 95.

38. 11 Va. (1 Hen. & M.) 71, 74 (1806) (Roane, J., concurring) (emphasis omitted).

and "Negro and mulatto."[39] Mulattoes of mixed Negro and white ancestry had the same legal position as Negroes, although their social position may have been somewhat different.[40] These legal classifications, then, gave rise to the need for a legal definition of race. As Winthrop Jordan notes, "if mulattoes were to be considered Negroes, logic required some definition of mulattoes, some demarcation between them and white men."[41] Virginia was one of only two colonies to bow to the demands of logic by creating a precise statutory definition in the colonial period.[42]

As was noted above, slave status was legally independent of race. Slaves who looked white had no special legal privileges until the nineteenth century, and then their only advantage was that they were relieved of the burden of proof in freedom suits.[43] Race did, however, make a considerable difference for free people. Thus, the first legal definition of "mulatto" appeared in a statute dealing with the rights of free persons.[44]

In 1705, the Virginia legislature barred mulattoes, along with Negroes, Indians, and criminals, from holding "any office, ecclesiasticall, civill or military, or be[ing] in any place of public trust or power."[45] The mixed-race individuals defined as mulatto under the statute were "the child of an Indian, or the child, grandchild, or great grandchild of a Negro."[46] Whites had distinct legal advantages, but mulattoes had no greater rights than Negroes. Thus, the important dividing line was the white/mulatto boundary, not the mulatto/black boundary. The fact that some

---

39. Other aspects of an individual's heritage might, of course, determine important legal rights. For example, whether his mother was a slave or freewoman, or whether his mother was an unwed indentured white servant or a free white woman. See Act XII, 2 LAWS OF VA. 170, 170 (Hening 1823) (enacted 1662) (whether children bound or free depends solely on condition of mother); Act C, 2 LAWS OF VA. 114, 114–15 (Hening 1823) (enacted 1661) (birth of bastard child by servant extends term of indenture or subjects servant to fine).

40. *But see* Jordan, *American Chiaroscuro: The Status and Definition of Mulattoes in the British Colonies.* 19 WM. & MARY Q. 183, 186 (1962) [hereinafter Jordan, *American Chiaroscuro*] (finding no evidence of higher social position for mulattoes in the mainland colonies). An explicit statement that Negroes and mulattoes were the same in the eyes of the law did not occur until 1860. Then, in a statute defining "mulatto," the legislators said, "the word 'negro' in any other section of this, or in any future statute, shall be construed to mean mulatto as well as negro." VA. CODE ch. 103, § 9 (1860).

41. Jordan, *American Chiaroscuro, supra* note 40, at 185.

42. *Id.* North Carolina was the other. *Id.*

43. *Id.; see infra* notes 81–84 and accompanying text.

44. Ch. IV, 3 LAWS OF VA. 250, 251 (Hening 1823) (enacted 1705). Although the term "mulatto" was not defined by law until 1705, we find it used as early as March 12, 1655, when the record refers to a "Mulatto held to be a slave and appeal taken." MINUTES OF THE COUNCIL AND GENERAL COURT OF COLONIAL VIRGINIA 504 (H.R. McIlwaine 1st ed. 1924) [hereinafter MINUTES].

45. Ch. IV, 3 LAWS OF VA. 250, 251 (Hening 1823) (enacted 1705). This statute defines "mulatto" for purposes of holding office only. It could have been defined differently for other purposes, but there was no other statutory definition until 1785. As we shall see below, however, the courts did not apply the strict statutory definition.

46. *Id.* at 252. Presumably the other ancestors would all be white.

people were classified as mulatto rather than as Negro seems to have been simply a recognition of their visible differences.[47]

One notes in the statute's definition of "mulatto" the different treatment of those whose non-white ancestors were Indians as opposed to Negroes. A person with one Indian parent and one white parent was a mulatto. Someone with one Indian grandparent and three white grandparents was, by implication, legally white and not barred from public office under the statute. For Negro-white mixtures, it took two additional generations to "wash out the taint" of Negro blood to the point that it was legally insignificant. A person with a single Negro grandparent or even a single Negro great-grandparent was still considered a mulatto.

Why was there a difference in the legal treatment of white-Indian mixtures and white-Negro mixtures? Perhaps it was related to the degree to which a mixed-race individual looked white to eighteenth-century white Virginians. Perhaps it was also because Europeans tended to see Indians as higher on the scale of creation than Negroes, though still lower than themselves.[48]

Note that these definitions of race state the rule in theory; we do not suppose that they were rigidly followed in practice. We have found no case from this period in which a claim to being legally white was based on the exact proportion of white blood. At the time of the statute, in 1705, some eighty-five years after the first Negroes had arrived in Virginia, there would barely have been time for the four generations of offspring necessary to "dilute the taint" of Negro blood to the point that it did not count under law. Thus, few if any white/Negro mixtures would have qualified as white, though there were likely some white/Indian mixtures who did.

The Virginia legislature, meeting in 1785, changed the legal definition of mulatto to those with "one-fourth part or more of negro blood."[49] Thus, by impli-

---

47. After the Civil War, a single term, "colored," was often used for both Negroes and mulattoes in legal writing. See *supra* note 2 (discussing use of various terms designating race).

48. The favored treatment of Indians was still present in 1924 as indicated by an act of the Virginia legislature that made it unlawful for a white person to marry anyone but another white. A white was defined as someone with "no trace whatsoever of any blood other than Caucasian" or someone with no admixture of blood other than white and a small proportion of American Indian. 1924 Va. Acts ch. 371, § 5, at 535. This provision was the so-called "Pocohontas exception," designed to protect descendants of John Rolfe and Pocahontas, who were by then considered part of the white race. However, John Rolfe could not, in 1924, have married Pocahontas. Under the most likely interpretation of the statute, he would have been limited to whites or those who were no more than 1/16 American Indian. Wadlington. *The Loving Case: Virginia's Anti-Miscegenation Statute in Historical Perspective*, 52 VA. L. REV. 1189, 1202–03 (1966).

49. The statute was entitled "An Act declaring what persons shall be deemed mulattoes," and it stated:

> [E]very person whose grandfathers or grandmothers any one is, or shall have been a negro, although all his other progenitors, except that descending from the negro, shall have been white persons, shall be deemed a mulatto: and so every person who shall have one-fourth part or more of negro blood, shall, in like manner, be deemed a mulatto.

Ch. LXXVIII, 12 LAWS OF VA. 184, 184 (Hening 1823) (enacted 1785; effective 1787).

cation, those of one-eighth Negro ancestry (one Negro great-grandparent), who by the 1705 statute had been mulattoes, were now legally white.[50] There is no mention in the statute of Indian ancestry.[51] Interestingly, while the definition of mulatto in 1705 excluded from the category of white virtually all of those with any Negro ancestry at the time, the 1785 definition, some four generations later, did not attempt to do the same. Instead, under the 1785 act, a number of mixed-race people who previously would have been classified as mulatto could be considered white. This was the only time Virginia law was changed to allow persons with a greater proportion of Negro ancestry to be deemed white. All subsequent changes were in the opposite direction—making a smaller proportion of Negro blood bar one from being considered white.

Was this statute, as James Hugo Johnston suggests, an effort to bring the law into line with social practice? He says, "[i]t would appear that the lawmakers of the early national period feared that a declaration to the effect that the possession of any Negro ancestry, however remote, made a man a mulatto might bring embarrassment on certain supposedly white citizens."[52] He notes that before the Civil War, in no state did the law provide that a person having less than one-eighth Negro blood should be deemed a mulatto.[53]

Johnston also says that it was no doubt believed to be exceedingly difficult, if not impossible, to enforce a more drastic law of racial identity.[54] Yet in fact, Virginia did enact more drastic laws in the twentieth century. Under a 1910 statute, as small a proportion as one-sixteenth Negro ancestry made one "colored."[55] Then, in 1924 and 1930, *any* Negro blood at all meant that one was not legally white.[56]

Another possible explanation for the 1785 statute is that it reflected strategic considerations. If supposedly white men of power and position were declared to be mulatto and thus deprived of civil and political rights, they might have formed a dangerous alliance with other "less white" free mulattoes and Negroes whose rights were similarly denied. Their combined forces would have threatened the

50. In an 1877 case, McPherson v. Commonwealth, 69 Va. (28 Gratt.) 292, Judge Moncure declared that Rowena McPherson could marry a white man because "less than one-fourth of her blood is negro blood. If it be but one drop less, she is not a negro." *Id.* at 292. Negro in this context meant both Negro and mulatto, as they comprised one legal category.

51. Ch. LXXVIII, 12 LAWS OF VA. 184 (Hening 1823) (enacted 1785; effective 1787). In this statute, persons of mixed Indian and white ancestry are no longer classified mulattoes, but they appear as mulattoes again in the statutes drawing racial boundary lines starting in 1866. Ch. 17, § 1, 1865–1866 Va. Acts 84. A person who has one-fourth or more of Indian blood is an Indian, if he is not "colored."

52. J. JOHNSTON, *supra* note 22, at 193–94.

53. *Id.* at 193.

54. *Id.* at 194.

55. Ch. 357, § 49, 1910 Va. Acts 581.

56. Ch. 371, § 5, 1924 Va. Acts 534–35; Ch. 85, 1930 Va. Acts 96–97. After the Civil War there was a shift from the use of the term "mulatto" to "colored" in the statutes, the latter term comprising the former categories of Negro and mulatto. Ch. 17, § 1, 1865–1866 Va. Acts 84.

social control over the society of the remaining smaller number still classified as white. Georgia, to encourage the immigration of free mixed-race persons into the colony, provided in 1765 that free mulatto and "mustee"[57] immigrants might be declared "whites," with "all the Rights, Privileges, Powers and Immunities whatsoever which any person born of British parents" would have, except the right to vote and to sit in the Assembly.[58] Georgia legislators were apparently at that time more concerned about hostile Indians on their southern border than they were about the racial makeup of the colony's "white" population.[59]

These explanations are merely suggestions. We have no satisfactory answer as to why the 1785 Virginia statute allowed racially mixed persons who formerly were classified as mulatto to become legally white. The Act itself gives no clue as to the reason for the change. The percentage of allowable Negro ancestry in a legally white person was not changed again until the twentieth century, and Indian mulattoes were reintroduced in an 1866 statute making a person who was one-quarter Indian a mulatto, if he was not otherwise "colored."[60]

Objectively, the effect of statutes defining a mulatto as someone with a certain proportion of Negro or Indian ancestry, and implying that someone with a smaller proportion of non-white ancestry was legally white, was to make "white" into a mixed-race category. By the early twentieth century, when those classified as white had to have "no trace whatsoever"[61] of Negro "blood," there was indeed a great deal of untraced (and, in some cases, untraceable) Negro blood in the white population.

We see the notion that Negro ancestry can be gradually diluted into legal insignificance in the case of *Dean v. Commonwealth*.[62] There, a criminal defendant claimed that two witnesses were incompetent to testify against him because they were mulattoes, and mulattoes could not testify against whites.[63] The court found

---

57. "Mustee" was a term used in Georgia and the Carolinas to describe a person who was part Indian, "usually Indian-Negro but occasionally Indian-white." W. JORDAN, *supra* note 7, at 168–69.

58. THE COLONIAL RECORDS OF THE STATE OF GEORGIA, 659 (Chandler, comp. 1904–16), *quoted in* Jordan, *American Chiaroscuro supra* note 40, at 187.

59. *Id.* No one was actually naturalized under the statute. Note that Georgia was not willing to give Negroes the full rights and privileges of whites, nor were they willing to give naturalized mulattoes or mustees political power. It was "a begrudging kind of citizenship" that was extended by the legislature. *Id.*

60. Ch. 17, § 1, 1865–66 Va. Acts 84.

61. Ch. 371, § 5, 1924 Va. Acts 534–35. All of the acts setting out racial definitions, with the exception of the 1924 "Act to Preserve [white] Racial Integrity" defined "mulatto" or "colored" rather then "white." White is defined by implication. In the 1924 act, "white" is given an explicit definition for the first time in the statute which sets out whom whites could marry. It is the most restrictive of the racial definitions. It defines a white person as one "who has no trace whatsoever of any blood other than Caucasian; but persons who have [only] one-sixteenth or less of the blood of the American Indian . . . shall be deemed to be white persons." Ch. 371, 1924 Va. Acts 535. The 1930 statute defining as colored anyone "in whom there is ascertainable any Negro blood" is only slightly less restrictive. Ch. 85, 1930 Va. Acts 97.

62. 45 Va. (4 Gratt.) 210 (1847).

63. *Id.* at 210.

the witnesses competent, since they had less than one-fourth Negro blood, the legal dividing line under the statute then in force.[64] The description of legal "lightening" over the generations in the reporting of the case is telling:

> . . . [F]rom the testimony it appeared certainly, that they had less than one fourth of negro blood. Their grandfather, David Ross, who was spoken of as a respectable man, though probably a mulatto, was a soldier in the revolution and died in the service. The evidence as to the grandmother was contradictory; though she was probably white, the mother was so certainly.[65]

The grandfather would have been incompetent to testify because he was a mulatto, but the grandchildren were not.[66] The grandmother was probably white but the mother was certainly so. Thus, in mid-nineteenth century Virginia, mulatto parents and grandparents could have children and grandchildren who were legally white. That became legally impossible only in the twentieth century, when any trace of Negro blood would disqualify a person from being considered white under the law.[67]

Whites in pre–Civil War Virginia paid a strategic price to maintain their ideal of white racial purity. Had they declared, for example, that anyone with more than fifty percent white blood was legally white, they would have had less to fear from an alliance of free mulattoes and slaves. Then, however, their racial rationale for slavery would have been undermined because the number of legally white slaves would have increased greatly. It would have been hard to maintain that slavery was justified by the inferiority of the Negro if large numbers of slaves were classified as white under Virginia law. The white population was in fact racially mixed, but the proportion of non-white ancestry allowable in a white person was so small that it was not very visible. It was so small that, as we shall see, white Virginians could maintain the myth that it was not there at all.

C. Natural and Cultural Definitions of Race

Most anthropologists today reject the notion that the world's races are distinct types and prefer to speak instead of clusterings of physical traits that occur differentially in different populations.[68] If one moves south from northern Europe,

---

64. *Id.* at 210–11.
65. *Id.* at 210 (emphasis omitted).
66. In Chaney v. Saunders, 17 Va. (3 Munf.) 621 (1811), the plaintiff tried to introduce the deposition of a man who the defense claimed was one-fourth Negro. *Id.* at 622. A number of witnesses were called by both sides on the issue of the deponent's race. *Id.* The trial court ruled in favor of the defendant and would not allow the deposition to be read. *Id.* The district court reversed the ruling, but the Supreme Court of Appeals reversed again, on the ground that the trial court was better able to judge the credibility of the witnesses. *Id.* The Supreme Court called the evidence "extremely contradictory." *Id.*
67. *See supra* note 61 (20th-century Virginia statutes defining white and "colored" persons).
68. For anthropological views of race, see generally THE CONCEPT OF RACE (A. Montagu ed. 1964) (rejecting proposition that certain races should be assumed to exist and arguing that racial definitions are only meaningful at end of population inquiry); UNESCO, RACE AND SCIENCE 269,

through the Mediterranean and North Africa to sub-Saharan Africa, the changes in the populations are gradual; there is a continuum of physical characteristics. For seventeenth and eighteenth-century Virginia, however, the view that prevailed was one of ideal racial types, and the three populations that met and mixed in Virginia fit that model. Northern Europeans and sub-Saharan Africans represented extreme points on the Old World continuum of physical types, and they were plucked out of that continuum and replanted in the New World. American Indians were markedly different from the other two. There had been no intermingling of these three populations for many thousands of years and they exhibited great contrasts of physical traits. Thus, it was easy for colonial white Virginians, and it is easy for many of us even today, to think of Africans, American Indians, and Europeans in terms of ideal pure racial types and to see other populations representing other points on the Old World continuum—e.g., North Africans—as somehow "in-between" or "mixed."

It also is easy to see the three races as natural categories. But in the eighteenth century, when Virginia law drew racial boundary lines, it was not dealing with natural categories but with legal constructions. It drew a boundary line separating mulattoes from whites and changed the position of the line from time to time. What is interesting is that the idea of white racial purity was maintained even when the law recognized that a certain amount of racial mixture could be present. "Mulatto" was not every racially mixed child, but only mixtures up to a certain point. Beyond that point, the fact of mixture was not legally recognized until well into the twentieth century, when the definition of mulatto or "colored" was changed to include all people with any Negro ancestry.[69] By that time it was far too late to identify all those with any Negro ancestry in the legally white population. The racial boundary was drawn differently for white/Indian and white/Negro mixtures, it changed over time for both, and all of the "pure" racial categories defined by the law—white, Indian, and Negro—included in their defi-

---

273 (1961) (recognition that "views about race uniformity and purity and fixity of racial differences were wrong" and assertion that race is "a population, which differs from other populations in relative commonness of certain hereditary traits"): M. WEISS & A. MANN, HUMAN BIOLOGY AND BEHAVIOR: AN ANTHROPOLOGICAL PERSPECTIVE 526, 533 (1985) ("idea of the 'pure' race can be laid to rest" in favor of categorization based on "regular variation in a trait over space shown by the alteration in the frequency of one or more traits from population to neighboring population"). For a history of the concept of race in early 19th-century America, see W. STANTON, THE LEOPARD'S SPOTS: SCIENTIFIC ATTITUDES TOWARD RACE IN AMERICA 1815–1859 (1960).

69. In 1870, the U.S. Census Bureau defined the term "mulatto" to include "quadroons, octoroons, and all persons having any perceptible trace of African blood." NEGRO POPULATION 1790–1915, *supra* note 21, at 207. Instructions for the 1890 census defined "black" to include all persons "having three-fourths or more 'black blood.' " *Id.* Other persons with a lesser proportion of 'black blood' were classified as "mulatto" (3/8–5/8 black blood), "quadroon" (1/4 black blood), or "octoroon" (any trace of up to 1/8 black blood). *Id.* In 1910, "mulatto" was defined for census purposes as anyone having some "proportion or perceptible trace of Negro blood." *Id.* In 1850 and 1860, the terms "black" and "mulatto" were not defined. In 1850 enumerators were told to write "B" or "M" on the schedule for black and mulatto, but in 1860 they were given no such instructions. *Id.*

nitions mixed-race individuals. Yet the myth of natural categories of race was maintained, with all the moral force that the idea of a "natural order" could confer on such a categorization.

In *Kinney v. Commonwealth of Virginia*,[70] in holding that an interracial couple who married outside Virginia were in violation of Virginia anti-miscegenation law when they entered the state, the judge wrote:

> The purity of public morals, the moral and physical development of both races, and the highest advancement of our cherished southern civilization, under which two distinct races are to work out and accomplish the destiny to which the Almighty has assigned them on this continent—all require that they should be kept distinct and separate, and that connections and alliances so unnatural that God and nature seem to forbid them, should be prohibited by positive law and be subject to no evasion.[71]

The "two distinct races" to which the judge in *Kinney* referred—black and white—had been mixing for some 250 years, and yet the law still recognized only "two distinct races," each of which had many members of mixed ancestry. Thus, many of the "connections and alliances" between men and women who fell under the same racial classification in eighteenth and nineteenth-century Virginia law were, in fact, alliances of people one or both of whom was a product of racial mixing. In this respect, some of the alliances between legally white individuals were no different from some of the alliances between individuals the law labeled of different races (white and mulatto), yet it was only the latter alliances that the judge called "so unnatural that God and nature seem to forbid them."[72]

In nineteenth-century Virginia, the concept of a "pure white race" as a category of nature was a myth. It was a powerful myth, however, one used to support social and legal action, as in the *Kinney* decision, and to justify the oppression of non-whites. Pure white race as a legal concept was a vigorous and powerful cultural construct. It gained force in the late nineteenth and early twentieth centuries, and was called on to justify an ever harsher set of repressive legal measures against blacks.

---

70. 71 Va. (30 Gratt.) 284 (1877).
71. *Id.* at 287. The idea of a natural, divinely sanctioned separation of races was used to justify segregation in an 1867 Pennsylvania case, West Chester & Philadelphia Railroad Co. v. Miles, 55 Pa. (5 P.F. Smith) 209 (1867). The court stated:

> Why the Creator made one [race] black and the other white, we know not; but the fact is apparent, and the races distinct, each producing its own kind, and following the peculiar law of its constitution. Conceding equality, with natures as perfect and rights as sacred, yet God has made them dissimilar, with those natural instincts and feelings which He always imparts to His creatures when He intends that they shall not overstep the natural boundaries He has assigned to them. The natural law which forbids their intermarriage and that social amalgamation which leads to a corruption of races, is as clearly divine as that which imparted to them different natures. The tendency of intimate social intermixture is to amalgamation, contrary to the law of races.

> *Id.* at 213.

72. *Kinney,* 71 Va. at 287.

D. Applications of Racial Classifications by Courts and by the Legislature in Private Acts

In drawing a racial line, the real concern of white Virginians seems to have been to maintain the purity of the white race and to preserve it from visible "darkening." There was no similar concern with preserving the Negro race from "lightening." While the statutes defined "mulatto," and, by implication, "white," in terms of the proportion of white and non-white ancestry rather than in terms of physical appearance, in practice distinctions were based on appearance.[73] For most mixed-race children, there were no formal genealogies, no marriage records, no legal marriages. It would have been difficult to prove that one was one-sixteenth rather than one-eighth Negro, or one-eighth rather than one-fourth, and for the most part, no one seemed to try. People did not base their legal claims on the exact proportion of white and non-white ancestry; when people claimed to be white, the matter was generally settled by appeal to their appearance.

As discussed above, slave status as defined by statute was independent of race.[74] It was, however, important to know whether free persons were legally white or mulatto, for there were statutes imposing special burdens on free Negroes and mulattoes. Thus, Sylvia Jeffers and her children, emancipated in 1814 by the will of her deceased master, petitioned the Hustings Court of Petersburg, Virginia, in 1853 to be declared legally white.[75] The court granted their plea, and they were released from the civil and political disabilities from which they had suffered as free mulattoes. Sylvia Jeffers and her children were no more white, genetically or in appearance, after the court granted their petition than when they were slaves, but a declaration that they were legally white would have been of little use to them until they became free.[76]

In a similar petition, this time before the Virginia Assembly in 1833, five members of the Wharton family asked after they were freed to be released from the operation of a statute requiring all slaves emancipated since 1806 to leave the commonwealth within twelve months.[77] The Assembly granted their petition, saying in the preamble to the act, "it appears to the general assembly that [the petitioners] are not negroes or mulattoes, but white persons, although remotely descended from a colored woman."[78] In other petitions by "free persons of color"

---

73. One can compare racial definitions based entirely on ancestry, or genotype, with ones based primarily on appearance, or phenotype. For example, the latter type of definition is used in South African law. There a white person is one who "in appearance obviously is a white person and who is not generally accepted as a colored person; or is generally accepted as a white person and is not in appearance obviously not a white person," Population Registration Act of 1950 § 1 (1950), *quoted* in J. DUGARD, HUMAN RIGHTS AND THE SOUTH AFRICAN LEGAL ORDER 61 (1978).

74. *See supra* Part II.A.

75. J. JOHNSTON, *supra* note 22, at 206.

76. The fact that a slave looked white shifted the burden of proof in freedom suits. *See infra* text accompanying notes 81–93 (discussing *Hudgins v. Wright*).

77. Ch. 63, § 10, 1805 Va. Acts 35–36.

78. Ch. 243, 1832 Va. Acts 198, 198. An act passed earlier in the same session authorized the county courts,

made at around the same time, the petitioners listed specific circumstances justifying their pleas, and the assembly usually granted only an extension of time
beyond the twelve-month limit.[79] In the Whartons' case, racial appearance was
sufficient justification to exempt them entirely from the operation of the statute.
Note here that even the legislature that had devised the statutory definition of
mulatto and, by implication, of white, seemed to be using a definition based not
on proportion of ancestry as set out in the statute, but rather on appearance. They
were not declaring the Whartons white because of their exact proportion of white
ancestry, but because they had the appearance of white persons.[80] If the applicants
looked white, there was apparently little fear that they would darken and thus
corrupt the white race.

---

upon satisfactory evidence of white persons being adduced before any such court, to grant
to any free person of mixed blood, resident within such county, not being a white person
nor a free negro or mulatto, a certificate that he or she is not a free negro or mulatto, which
certificate shall be sufficient to protect and secure such person from and against the pains,
penalties, disabilities and disqualifications, imposed by law upon free negroes and mulattoes,
as free negroes and mulattoes.

Ch. 80, § 1, 1832 Va. Acts 51, 51.

Presumably this statute applied to Indians, Indian-white mixtures, or other mixtures lacking
the statutory proportion of Negro ancestry to make them mulatto. We may assume it did not
apply to Negro-white mixtures because no middle ground between mulatto and white was recognized. *See* Dean v. Commonwealth, 45 Va. (4 Gratt.) 210, 210–11 (1847) (child of white and
mulatto parents is either mulatto or white).

79. If the free colored person were allowed to remain in Virginia, the grant of privilege included a
clause revoking the extension if he or she were convicted of any offense. For specific instances of
these clauses, see, e.g., Act of Jan. 31, 1835, concerning Margaret, sometimes called Margaret
Moss, a free woman of color, Ch. 214, 1834 Va. Acts 239 (seven-year privilege, revocable upon
conviction of any crime); Act of Feb. 12, 1835, allowing Dick Skurry, a free man of color, to
remain in the commonwealth, Ch. 215, 1834 Va. Acts 239 (no time limit on privilege, but revocable
upon conviction); Act of Feb. 16, 1835, allowing Hope Butler, a free man of color, to remain in
the Commonwealth, ch. 216, 1834 Va. Acts 239 (same).

80. The text of the act in its entirety is as follows:

Whereas it appears to the general assembly, that William Wharton, Lemuel Wharton, Barney
Wharton, Nancy Wharton and Lewis Wharton, of the county of Stafford, who were
heretofore held in slavery by John Cooke, senior, deceased, and acquired their freedom since
May, eighteen hundred and six, are not negroes or mulattoes, but white persons, although
remotely descended from a coloured woman; and they having petitioned the general assembly
to be released from the operation of the statute requiring all slaves emancipated since May,
eighteen hundred and six, to remove beyond the limits of this commonwealth:

1. Be it enacted by the general assembly, That the said William Wharton, Lemuel Wharton, Barney Wharton, Nancy Wharton and Lewis Wharton, shall be, and they are hereby
released and discharged from all pains, forfeitures and penalties whatsoever, incurred by
them, or any of them, or to which they or any of them may be subject or liable, by reason
of their failure heretofore or hereafter to remove beyond the limits of this commonwealth.

2. This act shall be in force from the passing thereof, Act of Mar. 5, 1833, concerning
William Wharton and others, Ch. 243, 1832 Va. Acts 198 (1833) (italics omitted).

The legal importance of racial appearance was set out formally in the 1806 case of *Hudgins v. Wright*.[81] There, the court declared that racial appearance was to determine who bore the burden of proof in freedom suits. As Judge Roane said:

> In the case of a person visibly appearing to be a negro, the presumption is, in this country, that he is a slave, and it is incumbent on him to make out his right to freedom; but in the case of a person visibly appearing to be a white man, or an Indian, the presumption is that he is free, and it is necessary for his adversary to show that he is a slave.[82]

The presumption established in *Hudgins v. Wright* gave Nanny Pagee and her children their freedom in 1811.[83] The Supreme Court of Virginia held in her case that the jury's finding, from visual inspection, that "Nanny Pagee, is a *white* woman . . . was quite sufficient; it being incumbent on the defendant to have proved, if he could, that the plaintiff was descended in the maternal line from a slave. Having not proved it, she and her children must be considered as free."[84]

The statutes had imperfectly established the identity of black with slave and white with free. The judiciary stepped in with a modification in the form of a presumption setting the burden of proof differently in the case of those who appeared to be whites and Indians on the one hand and those who appeared to be Negroes on the other. The judiciary was not unanimous in wanting to impose the extra burden on blacks seeking freedom. In the lower court in *Hudgins v. Wright*, Chancellor George Wythe had declared that when one person claimed to hold another in slavery, the burden of proof always lay on the claimant, "on the ground that freedom is the birth-right of every human being, which sentiment is strongly inculcated by the first article of our 'political catechism,' the bill of rights."[85] The Virginia Supreme Court refused to endorse this view, finding that it infringed too far on the property rights of white Virginians. Judge St. George Tucker wrote:

> I do not concur with the Chancellor in his reasoning of the first clause of the Bill of Rights, which was notoriously framed with a cautious eye to this subject, and was meant to embrace the case of free citizens, or aliens only; and not by a side wind to overturn the rights of property, and give freedom to those very people whom we have been compelled from imperious circumstances to retain, generally, in the same state of bondage that they were in at the revolution, in which they had no concern, agency, or interest.[86]

---

81. 11 Va. (1 Hen. & M.) 71 (1806).
82. *Id.* at 74 (Roane, J., concurring). Judge Tucker made the same point in the leading opinion. *Id.* at 73–74 (majority opinion).
83. Hook v. Nanny Pagee, 16 Va. (2 Munf.) 500, 503 (1811).
84. *Id.* at 503 (emphasis in original).
85. 11 Va. at 71.
86. *Id.* at 74 (emphasis omitted).

If the individual claiming freedom was not, on inspection, unambiguously white, Indian, or Negro, the question of burdens, presumptions, and evidence became more complicated. One case contained an elaborate discussion of what evidence could be admitted to establish pedigree in the case of a mixed blood individual who claimed freedom based on descent in the maternal line from a free Indian. In *Gregory v. Baugh*[87] the plaintiff's maternal grandmother, Sybil, was "a copper-coloured woman, with long, straight, black hair, with the general appearance of an Indian, except that she was too dark to be of whole blood."[88] The plaintiff himself was a "man of color."[89] Among the questions that had to be decided was whether Sybil's dark color came from the maternal line, making her presumptively a slave, or from the paternal line, in which case she might be a free Indian. She might also have descended in the maternal line from an Indian who had been enslaved during a brief period when it was lawful to enslave some Indians. In that case, legally, she would be a slave.[90] The question of what evidence could be introduced to establish her ancestry occupied much of the case. No simple presumption in the plaintiff's favor was made here as in *Hudgins v. Wright*.[91]

In the case of light-skinned individuals of mixed ancestry, the question of whether the non-white blood came from the maternal or paternal line was of critical importance, as slave status was inherited only in the maternal line. Questions of evidence and proof became correspondingly more complicated. As Judge Roane noted in *Hudgins v. Wright*:

When, however, these races become intermingled, it is difficult, if not impossible, to say from inspection only which race predominates in the offspring, and certainly impossible to determine whether the descent from a given race has been through the paternal or maternal line. In the case of *Propositus* of unmixed blood, therefore, I do not see but that the fact may be as well ascertained by the Jury or the Judge, upon view, as by the testimony of witnesses, who themselves have no other means of information: but where an intermixture has taken place in relation to the person in question, this criterion is not infallible; and testimony must be resorted to for the purpose of shewing through what line a descent from a given stock has been deduced; and also to ascertain, perhaps, whether the colouring of the complexion has been derived from a negro or an Indian ancestor.[92]

87. 25 Va. (4 Rand.) 246 (1827).
88. *Id.* at 246.
89. *Id.*
90. *See Hudgins,* 11 Va. at 73 (Indians brought into Virginia could be legally enslaved between the passage of the act of 1679 and 1691) (Tucker, J.).
91. *Compare* Gregory v. Baugh, 25 Va. (4 Rand.) 246, 249 ("though evidence by hearsay and general reputation be inadmissible as to pedigree, it is not admissible to prove the freedom of the plaintiff's ancestor, and thence to deduce his own") *with Hudgins,* 11 Va. at 73 ("all American Indians are prima facia free: and that where the fact of their nativity and descent, in a maternal line, is satisfactorily established, the [burden] of proof thereafter lies upon the party claiming to hold them as slaves") (Tucker, J.).
92. 11 Va. at 73 (Roane, J., concurring).

In attempting to apply this dictum of *Hudgins v. Wright* regarding the introduction of evidence to show line of descent in a freedom suit, Judge Carr in *Gregory v. Baugh* cautioned against allowing the emotional bias in favor of liberty to cause one to bend the law of evidence. Quoting Chief Justice John Marshall's opinion in *Mima Queen and Child v. Hepburn*,[93] he stated:

> However the feelings of the *individual* may be interested on the part of the person claiming freedom, the *Court* cannot perceive any legal distinction between the assertion of this, and any other right, which would justify the application of a rule of evidence to cases of this description, which would be inapplicable to general cases, in which a right of property may be asserted.[94]

Carr felt compelled to add, "I have thought it proper to state these authorities in order to fortify the mind against that bias we so naturally feel, in favor of liberty."[95]

The legislature and the judiciary played complementary roles in establishing the racially based system of slavery that flourished in pre–Civil War Virginia. The legislature set out legal definitions of race and rules for the inheritance of slave status, but it refrained from an open declaration that Negroes were to be slaves and whites and Indians were to be free. Instead it relied on custom and circumlocutions, as in a 1670 statute making non-Christian servants imported by sea (Negroes) serve for life, and those imported by land (Indians) serve for a term of years.[96] It was the judiciary that took the bold and overt step of equating black with slave and white with free by assigning the burden of proof in freedom suits and by denying to Negroes the presumption of freedom contained in the Bill of Rights. It also cautioned itself, in hearing evidence, not to be emotionally swayed by the fact that an individual's freedom was at stake, but rather to treat the evidence as one would do in any ordinary property case.

The judiciary, which had developed the notion of slaves as property in elaborate detail, applied that perspective to blacks claiming their freedom; the property rights of white Virginians restrained the judiciary from extending the presumption of freedom to those who looked like slaves. By the nineteenth century, when *Hudgins v. Wright* was decided, the judiciary was well-versed in using the intricacies of the law of property and evidence as a shield behind which the humanity of the slave was hidden. The judges became involved with the legal patterns on the surface of the shield, not with the person behind it. But, as Judge Carr's admonition demonstrates, the preoccupation with legal intricacies at the expense of the person suing for his freedom was at times a strain, even at the appellate level where the judges were not directly faced with the individuals who claimed their freedom.

93. 11 U.S. (7 Cranch) 290 (1813).
94. *Id.* at 295, *quoted in Gregory*, 25 Va. at 247 (emphasis added).
95. 25 Va. at 247.
96. *Id.* at 251 (citing Act XII, 2 LAWS OF VA. 283, 283 [Hening 1823] [enacted 1670]).

III. Voluntary Interracial Sex and Attempts to Discourage It

A. Concern over Interracial Sex

As it became obvious to white Virginians that interracial sex posed a threat to white racial purity, they tried to suppress it. Apparently, they did not perceive the threat immediately. The first clear legal pronouncement on interracial sex came in the 1662 statute on the inheritance of slave status.[97] In Virginia before the 1660s, there was no unambiguous legal statement against interracial sex per se, as distinguished from illicit sex in general—that is, non-marital sex. There were several instances of public condemnation of couples who engaged in inter-racial sex, but the importance of the race factor was unclear. The early cases are inconsistent in their treatment of blacks. When, in 1630, the Council ordered "Hugh Davis to be soundly whipt before an assembly of negroes & others for abusing himself to the dishonr of God and shame of Christianity by defiling his body in lying with a negro," the Negro partner was not punished, and we cannot tell whether the sexual offense was made worse by the race of Davis's partner.[98] On the other hand, in 1640, when Robert Sweat had only to do public penance in church according to the law of England, for getting with child the Negro servant of another man, his Negro partner was to be "whipt at the whipping post."[99] In a case in 1649, penance in church was imposed on both the white man and his Negro partner:

> William Watts and Mary (Mr. Cornelius Lloyds [sic] negro woman) are ordered each of them to doe penance by standing in a white sheete with a white Rodd in theire hands in the Chappell of Elizabeth River in the face of the congregation on the next sabbath day that the minister shall make penince [sic] service and the said Watts to pay the court charges.[100]

This same punishment was sometimes used for white couples who were found guilty of fornication,[101] and the court records before the 1660s show fines or

---

97. Act XII, 2 LAWS OF VA. 170, 170 (Hening 1823) (enacted 1662) ("If any christian shall committ ffornication with a negro man or woman, hee or shee so offending shall pay double the fines imposed by the former act."). This "former act," Act C, 2 LAWS OF VA. 114, 114–115 (Hening 1823) (enacted 1661–62), established penalties for "the filthy sin of fornication" but contained no mention of interracial sexual relations.

98. MINUTES, *supra* note 44, at 479. Davis's race was not stated in the opinion. From this and the phrasing we may infer that he was white. The customary practice was to refer to whites, but not blacks, by full name, and to give no racial designation for whites. When blacks are referred to by first and last name, their race is noted. We also cannot tell the gender of the Negro. The extremely strong language may have reflected the Council's revulsion at a homosexual relationship.

99. *Id.* at 477.

100. Lower Norfolk County Order Book 139 (1646–50), *quoted in* W. BILLINGS, THE OLD DOMINION IN THE SEVENTEENTH CENTURY 161 (1975).

101. W. JORDAN, *supra* note 7, at 79 (citing 2 P. BRUCE, ECONOMIC HISTORY OF VIRGINIA IN THE SEVENTEENTH CENTURY 110 [1896]).

whippings commonly given as punishment for both partners in cases of fornication, regardless of race.[102]

From Virginia's Eastern Shore Counties, records of an unusual group of free black property owners have survived from the mid-seventeenth century.[103] These records shed interesting light on the attitude of early Virginians towards race and interracial sex. In those counties during that brief era, free whites and blacks who committed sexual offences were treated in a similar manner whether their partners were of their own race or not.[104] In 1654, a black couple, "Richard Johnson, Negro and Negroe woman of the Family of Anthony Johnson, Negro" and a white couple, Abraham Morgan and Ann Shawe (who by the time the case was decided had become husband and wife), were reported by the churchwarden for fornication and adultery. The churchwarden was obliged to report them, so that "according to Lawe Such offenders maye receive punishment."[105] No difference in the treatment of the two couples was noted.

White men who fornicated with black or white women were charged a standard fine of 500 pounds of tobacco.[106] John Oever was fined that amount in 1663 for fornicating with Margaret Van Noss, a white woman, and Charles Cumnell had been given the same fine in 1658 for "Committinge . . . Ellicit Fornication with a Negro woman of Mr. Michael."[107] There is no mention of punishment for either of these women, but black women who can be identified from the record as being free blacks were called to stand trial for their actions, whether their partners were white or black. In 1663, Jane Driggus, the daughter of a free black property owner, and her white lover, Denum Olandum, both had to pay court costs and to post bond to ensure their future good behavior when they had a mulatto bastard. In addition, Olandum had to promise to support the child.[108] In 1666, Sara King, a free Negro, was to stand trial along with her Negro lover, Thomas Driggus, servant to Lieutenant William Kendall, for fornication. When she failed to appear, the sheriff was ordered to take her into custody until she posted bond sufficient to guarantee her appearance.[109]

Free black men were required to support their free bastard children in the same manner as were white men. In 1663, John Johnson, a free black property owner, had a child by Hannah Leach, a white servant on a neighboring plantation.[110] Aside from posting bond to ensure the child's support, and his future good behavior,

102. E. MORGAN, *supra* note 21, at 333.
103. *See* T. BREEN & S. INNES, "MYNE OWNE GROUND": RACE AND FREEDOM ON VIRGINIA'S EASTERN SHORE 1660–76 at 68–109 (1980) [hereinafter T. BREEN] (describing in detail social and economic interrelationship of early white and free black communities).
104. *Id.* at 94–96, 107.
105. *Id.* at 94–95.
106. *Id.* at 95. The fine for interracial fornication was increased in 1662. *See infra* notes 123–24 and accompanying text (citing statutes).
107. T. BREEN, *supra* note 103, at 95.
108. *Id.*
109. *Id.* at 95–96.
110. *Id.* at 96.

Johnson had to "pay and sattisfie all . . . damages."[111] Presumably, that included payment to the woman's master for time she lost from work. Johnson also had to get a wet nurse for the child. Hannah Leach escaped whipping only because her master agreed to pay 1,000 pounds of tobacco.[112] Philip Mongum, another free black, had a child by Margery Tyer, a white woman. Like Johnson and Olandum, Morgan had to post bond to ensure his good behavior and the support of the child. He was also fined 500 pounds of tobacco for the sin of adultery, and was ordered to keep away from Tyer. She was given four lashes—perhaps there was no one to post bond to save her from corporal punishment—and was warned to keep away from Morgan or suffer further whipping.[113]

The punishments meted out to these free participants in illicit sexual unions seemed to depend more on their economic status and affluence than on their race. Regardless of the race of either party, men and women of property were fined, those who could not pay often were whipped, and men were required to pay damages and to support their free bastard children. Race did not make a noticeable difference when the offenders were known to be free.

There were other cases, however, in which the black partners went unnamed and unpunished. When Charles Cumnell was fined for fornicating with "a Negro woman of Mr. Michael,"[114] the fate of the woman was not mentioned. William Sriven was formally charged with "Committinge the sin of Fornication with a Negro woman," but his partner apparently was not charged.[115] The Irishman John Dorman was convicted of getting a "Negro woman" with child and had to pay damages and costs. Again, the woman apparently was not charged. Furthermore, John Dorman was not specifically required to post security to ensure that the parish would not have to bear the cost of raising the child.[116] The one unnamed Negro woman who appears to have been held accountable for her sexual behavior was attached to a black family. That was the "Negro woman of the Family of Anthony Johnson, Negro" with whom Richard Johnson, Negro, had committed fornication and adultery.[117]

Who were the three nameless Negro women of whom no notice was taken except to say that white men had sinned with them? We suggest that they were slaves, or servants for life, if the slave status had not yet been fully formalized. There was no need to order the man to post bond ensuring support for the bastard children because the parish did not need to be concerned that these bastard children would become economic burdens. Rather, the children would become economic resources to the mothers' masters. There would have been no point in fining the women or ordering them to post bond, because they had no money.

---

111. *Id.*
112. *Id.* One thousand pounds was the statutory fine for a "christian" (white person) who engaged in interracial sex after 1662. *See infra* notes 123–24 and accompanying text (citing statute). Hannah Leach would have had to serve extra time to work off the debt.
113. T. BREEN, *supra* note 103, at 107.
114. *Id.* at 95.
115. *Id.* at 95–96.
116. *Id.* at 96.
117. *Id.* at 95.

Their owners would not have posted bond to save them from whipping because they could not recover the money in the form of additional service. The women could, of course, have been whipped, but there is no record that they were.

Free blacks, on the other hand, were held to the same standard of sexual conduct as were whites. One might then be tempted to say that it was slave status rather than race that caused the difference in treatment in this early period, but that would be misleading. Race, after all, determined who could be enslaved.[118] Thus, a difference based on slave status was, in a sense, a difference based on race. A more accurate characterization might be to say that some free blacks could "rise above their race." These prosperous blacks of the Eastern Shore were not newly arrived Africans. They were highly acculturated men and women of African origin, property owners who were skilled at making a living in the new colony. Many of them were married and probably were Christians. The evidence from the Eastern Shore suggests that for a brief period they were treated as "black Virginians" rather than as members of an exotic and inferior race.[119]

In any case, the specific significance of race in the early cases is uncertain, at least insofar as "race" meant purely physical characteristics. When there was a difference in the treatment of Negroes in the early cases, it might have been due to their "pagan" or Muslim religion as well as to their physical type. Yet these aspects of the Negro's separateness—physical type, religion, even language— tended to be parts of a parcel to early white Virginians. When there were exceptions, like the free blacks of the Eastern Shore who had mastered the language and culture of the whites, they were treated much as the whites were. That, however, was only in the early days of the Virginia colony, before ideas of race and social status had hardened. Later, when the parcel fell apart, the whites focused on physical type rather than on religion, language, or other aspects of culture, probably because it was the only aspect of difference that was immutable. Thus, the role of race as physical type is unclear in the early cases. Negroes were sometimes, but not always, treated differently from whites. When they were, we attribute this difference in treatment to the fact that the whites saw them as fundamentally different sorts of human beings, not only because they had a different appearance, but because they had a different culture as well.[120] We cannot

118. *See supra* notes 15–36 and accompanying text (discussing race as basis for slavery). This was true in fact, though not in the technical language of the law.

119. *See* T. BREEN, *supra* note 103, at 110–11 (describing equalities of treatment between whites and free blacks on Eastern Shore of Virginia).

120. The legislature in 1667 downgraded its reliance on religious distinctions with the enactment of a statute providing that slaves were not to be freed by virtue of conversion to Christianity. Act III, 2 LAWS OF VA. 260, 260 (Hening 1823) (enacted 1667). But heathenism continued to be associated with Negroes. As Jordan explains it:

> What had occurred was not a change in the justification of slavery from religion to race. No such justifications were made. There seems to have been, within the unarticulated concept of the Negro as a different sort of person, a subtle but highly significant shift in emphasis. . . . The shift was an alteration of emphasis within a single concept of difference rather than a development of a novel conceptualization. . . .

sort out the exact dimensions of the perceived difference in the minds of early white Virginians, and most likely they did not sort it out themselves at that time.

The early cases show that adultery and fornication were, in themselves, grounds for punishment quite apart from the race of the participants. A number of early statutes explicitly condemned such actions.[121] They were periodically reenacted, as in a 1691 law against a series of moral offenses, of which fornication and adultery were but two; the others being "swearing, curseing, prophaneing God's holy name, Sabbath abuseing, [and] drunkenness."[122]

By 1662, however, the Virginia legislators had singled out interracial sex for special and harsher treatment. They declared, "that if any christian shall commit ffornication with a negro man or woman, hee or shee soe offending shall pay double the ffines imposed by the former act."[123] The former act to which this one referred set fines for fornication at 500 pounds of tobacco.[124] The "christian" to be fined double in the 1662 statute may be taken to mean any white person. Virginians tended to use the terms interchangeably at this early stage. Later, when called upon to distinguish them, they found race the more telling characteristic for legal discriminations.[125]

The prescribed treatment of white men and white women who engaged in interracial sex was even-handed in the 1662 statute: both were to be fined. But what of their Negro partners? Why were they not punished under this statute? They were not even mentioned. This statute is the first in a long series of statutes, starting in 1662 and continuing over 200 years until after the Civil War, that singled out whites for punishment in cases of voluntary interracial sex and marriage and ignored their non-white partners. While the records show that in a few early cases, as noted above, Negroes were punished along with their white partners under anti-fornication laws, the statutes specifically forbidding interracial sex and marriage were directed toward whites only.[126]

... [I]t seems likely that the colonists' initial sense of difference from the Negro was founded not on a single characteristic but on a congeries of qualities which, taken as a whole, seemed to set the Negro apart. Virtually every quality in the Negro invited pejorative feelings. What may have been his two most striking characteristics, his heathenism and his appearance, were probably prerequisite to his complete debasement.

W. JORDAN, *supra* note 7, at 96–97; *see also infra* note 202.

121. *See* Act II, 1 LAWS OF VA. 433, 433 (Hening 1823) (enacted 1657–58) (prohibiting adultery and fornication); Act C, 2 LAWS OF VA. 114, 114–15 (Hening 1823) (enacted 1661–62) (prohibiting fornication).

122. Act XI, 3 LAWS OF VA. 71, 71–72 (Hening 1823) (enacted 1691).

123. Act XII, 2 LAWS OF VA. 170, 170 (Hening 1823) (enacted 1662). The double fine was continued until 1696, when a new statute against fornication repealed the 1662 act and failed to reinstate that provision. 3 LAWS OF VA., 437, 438–39, Act I (Hening 1823) (enacted 1696).

124. Act C, 2 LAWS OF VA. 114, 115 (Hening 1823) (enacted 1661–62).

125. *See* J. BALLAGH, A HISTORY OF SLAVERY IN VIRGINIA 45–49 (1902) (discussing distinction between unlawful enslavement of Christians and lawful enslavement of converted heathens): W. JORDAN, *supra* note 7, at 91–98 (describing distinction between heathenism and race in early Virginia statutes). Again, race and religion were not at that time viewed as completely distinct.

126. This is not to say that Negroes were never punished for interracial sex after 1662. Slaves on the

B. Concern over the Production of Mulatto Children

Significantly, the new and harsher legal attitude toward interracial sex appeared in the 1662 statute designed to solve the "problem" of fitting the mulatto children of such unions into the social order.[127] This suggests that what prompted the harsher punishment was not simply the act of interracial sex itself, but its likely result: mulatto children.

While a number of statutes prescribed the same punishment for white men as for white women who engaged in interracial sex, it was the interracial sex of white women that seemed to concern the legislators most. That was evident from the wording of the early statutes. The 1662 statute noted in unemotional language that "some doubts have arrisen whether children got by any Englishman upon a Negro woman should be slave or free."[128] The statute set a fine for interracial sex double the normal one for fornication, but omitted the adjective "filthy" that modified "fornication" in the earlier act whose fine this one doubled.[129] The language suggests that the legislators were devising a practical solution to a practical problem. The act fined both white men and white women who engaged in interracial fornication, but it was the behavior of the men that prompted the law and set its tone.

In contrast, when the legislators were contemplating mulattoes produced by white women and non-white men, their revulsion is evident. A 1691 statute prohibiting interracial marriage stated:

> [F]or the prevention of that abominable mixture and spurious issue which hereafter may encrease in this dominion, as well by negroes, mulattoes, and Indians intermarrying with English, or other white women, as by their unlawfull accompanying with one another. Be it enacted by the authoritie aforesaid, and it is hereby enacted, that for the time to come, whatsoever English or other white man or woman being free shall intermarry with a negroe, mulatto, or Indian man or woman bond or free shall within three months after such marriage be banished and removed from this dominion forever.[130]

By their own declaration, what prompted the legislators to act was the realization that the punishment for interracial fornication was no deterrent to white women

---

plantation were generally subject to whatever discipline their masters chose to impose. Nor did it mean that whites were routinely punished for their lapses. White men were very rarely called to task for interracial sex. The fate of white women who engaged in interracial sex is discussed below. *See infra* Part II.c.

127. Act XII, 2 LAWS OF VA. 170, 170 (Hening 1823) (enacted 1662). This statute is one of several at that time that tried to resolve quandaries over the status of blacks. Another was the 1667 statute declaring that slaves would not be made free by virtue of their becoming Christian. Act III, 2 LAWS OF VA. 260, 260 (Hening 1823) (enacted 1667). The early uncertainty over the status of blacks was being resolved in ways that kept increasing numbers of them in lifetime servitude and sealed the same fate for most of their children.

128. Act XII, 2 LAWS OF VA. 170, 170 (Hening 1823) (enacted 1662).

129. *Id*; Act C, 2 LAWS OF VA. 114 (Hening 1823) (enacted 1661–62).

130. Act XVI, 3 LAWS OF VA. 86, 86–87 (Hening 1823) (enacted 1691) (emphasis omitted).

producing mulatto children if the women were married to the Negro or mulatto fathers of their children. The legislators therefore devised an extremely harsh punishment for such marriages: banishment of the white partner. The punishment was made to apply to white men as well as to white women, but it was the prospect of white women mating with non-white men that called forth the strong language not present in the earlier statute.[131]

A revision of this statute in 1705 adjusted the wording so that the interracial marriages of white men as well as white women were seen as leading to "that abominable mixture and spurious issue," and punishment for the white partner was changed to six months in prison, without bail, and a fine of ten pounds current money.[132] Indians were dropped from the statute.[133] The minister who knowingly performed such a marriage was fined 10,000 pounds of tobacco, half to go to the informer.[134] The provision was reenacted in 1753 and 1848.[135]

131. The statutory and judicial condemnations of white male/black female sexual relations seem to have been expressions of discomfort over the production of mulatto children rather than a distaste or personal revulsion for the sexual relations themselves. When they addressed black male/white female sexual relations, the relations themselves, as well as their likely result, disturbed the white male legislators.

132. Ch. XLIX, 3 LAWS OF VA. 447, 453 (Hening 1823) (enacted 1705). The motivation behind this change in punishment is unclear. Banishment removed the white offender from the colony and prevented him or her from producing any more "abominable mixtures" in Virginia. The short prison term merely interrupted the process. After the white partner had served his or her time, presumably the couple could go on living together within the sacrament of marriage and producing mulatto children. Morgan, on the other hand, sees the new penalty as "a less drastic but more effective deterrent to racial intermarriage among ordinary people," and notes that the colony would not thereby be deprived of a potential laborer. E. MORGAN, supra note 21, at 335.

In addition, indentured servants who married without the permission of their masters had to pay a fine or to serve them for an additional period of time. Act XX, 1 LAWS OF VA. 252, 252 (Hening 1823) (enacted 1642–43); Act XIV, 1 LAWS OF VA. 438–39 (Hening 1823) (enacted 1657–58): Act XCIX, 2 LAWS OF VA. 114, 114 (Hening 1823) (enacted 1662); Ch. XLVII, 3 LAWS OF VA. 441, 444 (Hening 1823) (enacted 1705); Act XXXII, 6 LAWS OF VA. 81, 84 (Hening 1819) (enacted 1748).

133. Some effort was made to encourage whites to marry Indians. In 1784, Patrick Henry introduced to the Virginia legislature a bill offering a reward to white men or women who married Indians— and additional bounties for any children produced—but the bill was not adopted. William Crawford promoted a similar bill before the U.S. Congress in 1824 but it also did not succeed. The motivation behind these bills was probably a desire to mitigate the danger of Indian attacks on the frontier. J. JOHNSTON, supra note 22, at 269–70.

134. Ch. XLIX, 3 LAWS OF VA. 447, 454 (Hening 1823) (enacted 1705). Johnston notes that in North Carolina, where a similar statute was in force, the Reverend John Blacknall was both the minister and the informer in a case of interracial marriage. Blacknall reportedly collected fifty pounds for performing the marriage, then turned himself in and collected half of the fifty pounds he was fined. He thus made twenty-five pounds on the deal. J. JOHNSTON, supra note 22, at 179–80.

135. Ch. VII, 6 LAWS OF VA. 356, 361–62 (Hening 1819) (enacted 1753); 1848 Acts of Va., Criminal Code, tit. II, ch. VIII, at 111–12. It was not until 1849 that marriages between whites and Negroes were declared void ab initio. VA. CODE ch. 109, § 1, at 471 (1849). Before that, the sacrament of marriage still prevailed, though the white partner was punished for entering into it contrary to secular law. See McPherson v. Commonwealth, 69 Va. (28 Gratt.) 292, 292 (1877) (marriage held valid and cohabitation judgment reversed when husband white and wife less than one-quarter black); Kinney v. Commonwealth, 71 Va. (30 Gratt.) 284, 286 (1878) (indictment of black man

It is significant that the prohibition on interracial marriage came in a statute that showed a growing concern over the presence of free Negroes and mulattoes in Virginia and enacted many measures designed to control their numbers. The act itself was entitled "An Act for Suppressing Outlying Slaves," and it noted the dangers in the possible alliances of free negroes and mulattoes with slaves.[136] One measure that the statute devised to reduce the danger was to require that an owner who set a slave free pay his transportation out of Virginia within six months.[137] Another was the one discussed above, discouraging interracial marriages by prescribing banishment for the white partner. Yet another was a severe penalty on white women who had mulatto bastards.[138] What the white Virginians seemed not to realize was that they had greatly increased the danger of alliance by classifying most mixed-race individuals with blacks rather than with whites in terms of their legal rights.

While the increase in free mulattoes was one of the motivating factors behind the harsh treatment of white women who had mulatto bastards, it was not the only one. Free and indentured Negro and mulatto women also produced free mulatto children, and there were no comparable special punishments for these women.[139] Nor were white men who sired free mulatto bastards subject to any punishment beyond the fine prescribed by statute for interracial fornication, and that was seldom applied.[140] The legislators seemed to feel a particular distaste that

---

for lewd cohabitation with white woman upheld when couple went to District of Columbia to be married but returned to Virginia domicile in ten days; court ruled Virginia law applied to "essentials" of marriage contract and, therefore, interracial marriage void).

136. See Act XVI, 3 LAWS OF VA. 86, 87 (Hening 1823) (enacted 1691) (claiming that freed slaves may endanger country by "entertaining negro slaves from their masters service, or receiving stolen goods, or . . . [growing old and becoming dependent] upon the country").

137. Id. at 87. The statute reads "out of the countrey" but this may be taken to mean the colony, as there was no single country in British North America.

138. A white woman, indentured or free, who had a mulatto bastard, had to pay 15 pounds sterling or be sold into service for five years. Act XVI, 3 LAWS OF VA. 86, 87 (Hening 1823) (enacted 1691).

By contrast, a law enacted in 1696 provided that if an indentured servant woman had a bastard (presumably not a mulatto), she had to give only one extra year of service to her master, in addition to a fine for fornication, which was "five hundred pounds of tobacco and casque" or 25 lashes. The master or mistress of the servant could claim an extra six months of service by paying the fine. Act I, 3 LAWS OF VA. 137, 139–40 (Hening 1823) (enacted 1696).

If a free white woman bore a white bastard, there was no punishment beyond that for fornication until 1769, when she had to pay 20 shillings. Even then, the law specified that she was not to be whipped for default of payment. Ch. XXVII, 8 LAWS OF VA. 374, 376 (Hening 1821) (enacted 1769).

139. There were only the penalties applicable to any woman servants who had bastard children. See supra note 138 (discussing statutes that imposed fines for bearing bastard children).

140. We have found only two appellate cases in which interracial fornication or cohabitation by white males was an issue. Commonwealth v. Isaacs, 26 Va. (5 Rand.) 523 (1826); Commonwealth v. Jones, 43 Va. (2 Gratt.) 477 (1845). White men could be called upon to support their bastard children, Act VIII, 2 LAWS OF VA. 168 (Hening 1823) (enacted 1642–43), and an early act required an indentured man servant who secretly married or fornicated with an indentured woman servant to serve extra time to the woman's master, Act XX, 1 LAWS OF VA. 252, 253

white women, who could be producing white children, were producing mulattoes. Black women who produced mulatto children were not seen as making the same direct assault on white racial purity; they were unable to produce white children and thus did not affect the white race. There was no comparable concern over their "lightening" of the Negro race. In addition, Morgan suggests that the legislators and their white male constituents may have wanted to save for themselves the white women, who were in short supply in the early years.[141]

There was a special group of cases concerning white women who produced mulatto children while being married to white men. Several such men applied to the House of Burgesses for a special act granting them a divorce. The question of whether a white woman was to be divorced, or punished under the criminal code, or both, for producing a mulatto bastard was sometimes complicated over uncertainty as to whether the child was a mulatto. It seems that this question may have been at issue in the case of Peggy and Richard Jones.[142] In that case a divorce was granted provisionally, pending the outcome of a jury trial deciding the husband's claim. The divorce would take effect, "provided that it shall be found by the verdict of a jury, upon . . . trial . . . that the child of said Peggy Jones is not the child of said Richard Jones, but is the offspring of some man of colour."[143] In other cases no reference was made to a trial.[144] The Jones child probably looked white enough so that there was some question as to whether Richard Jones might not be the father after all, and Peggy Jones may have contested the accusation of adultery.

It is interesting to note that when a couple classified as white produced a child whose racial identity was uncertain, the wife was suspected of having committed

---

(Hening 1823) (enacted 1642). But there were no special provisions or punishments for white men who fathered mulatto children.

141. E. MORGAN, *supra* note 21, at 336 (noting that county birth statistics [circa 1700] showed a substantial number of mulatto children born to white women, suggesting black competition for the affections of scarce white women).

142. Act of Nov. 25, 1814, divorcing Richard Jones from his wife Peggy, Ch. XCVIII, 1814 Acts of Va. 145.

143. *Id.* at 145.

144. Act of Jan 4, 1803, dissolving a marriage between Dabney Pettus and his wife Elizabeth, Ch. LXIV, 1802 Acts of Va. 46, 47 (divorce granted without trial when wife publicly acknowledged mulatto child as son of Negro slave); Act of Dec. 20, 1803, dissolving a marriage between Benjamin Butt, Jr. and Lydia his wife, Ch. VI, 1803 Acts of Va. 20, 20–21 (same); Ch. LIX, 1806 Acts of Va. 26, 26 (divorce granted without trial when "reasons to believe" that child born to white woman was fathered by Negro slave and not her white husband); Act of Jan. 10, 1817, divorcing Abraham Newton from his wife Nancy, Ch. 120, 1817 Va. Acts 176, 176 (divorce granted without trial when white woman gave birth to mulatto child five months after marriage to white man). In the case of Hezekiah Mosby and his wife Betsy, a trial was also ordered to determine the facts. Act of Jan. 25, 1816, authorizing the divorce of Hezekiah Mosby from his wife Betsy, Ch. CXXXV, 1816 Acts of Va. 246, 246–47. The fate of these women after the divorce is unknown, though they were subject to the act penalizing white women who had mulatto bastards with a heavy fine or five years of servitude. Act XVI, 3 LAWS OF VA. 86, 87 (Hening 1823) (enacted 1691); Ch. XLIV, 3 LAWS OF VA. 447, 453 (Hening 1823) (enacted 1705).

adultery with a Negro or mulatto man. Another possible explanation was that either the husband or the wife or both were in fact of mixed Negro-white ancestry, though legally white (if the proportion of Negro ancestry were small enough), or passing as white. Mixed-race parents would, on occasion, produce a child whose complexion was darker than either of theirs, a child who looked mulatto when they did not. That possibility was not explored. It may not have occurred to white Virginians, or it may have been suppressed. It may have been more disturbing to them than the attribution of adultery to the women, for it called into question the idea of clear racial classifications, an idea that was central to the maintenance of slave society in Virginia.

In addition to the question of a child's racial identity were questions of when evidence could be introduced to prove racial identity and what sort of evidence might be allowed. That issue was faced by the Virginia Court of Appeals in *Watkins and wife v. Carlton*[145] in 1840. The case was not an action for divorce, but rather a contest over part of the estate of John Carlton by three people who claimed to be his children. There was no challenge to the claims of the first two, Mary and Thomas, but the legitimacy of the third child, William, was at issue. Carlton had not modified his will after William's birth so as to include him, and the others claimed William's share, saying that he was a mulatto and was not their father's child.[146] William's lawyer had argued at trial that since there was a great variety in hair, complexion, and features of persons of "unmixed race,"[147] the presumption should always be in favor of legitimacy unless physical separation or impotence made it impossible that the husband could be the father.[148] The jury had agreed, and the judge in the lower court had refused to allow testimony by "professional and scientific men" on the question of the impossibility of a white couple producing a mulatto child.[149]

The lawyer for William Carlton made the important point, ignored by the appeals court, that the genetic difference between a person legally defined as a mulatto and a legally white person might be very small, and that the races could not always be reliably distinguished by inspection:

Now, he said, it would be very difficult, hardly possible, to distinguish with certainty a mulatto having only one fourth part of negro blood from a white person. The difficulty, the uncertainty, attending the proof of a person being white or mulatto, were strongly exemplified in the present case; it was always [a]

145. 37 Va. (10 Leigh) 560 (1840).
146. *Id*. at 560
147. *Id*. at 562. When the lawyer says "unmixed," we may take this to mean "accepted as white." That category included many mixed-race individuals, some of whom were also legally white because their proportion of Negro ancestry was below the legal limit.
148. *Id*.
149. Plaintiffs sought to introduce testimony by a physician that "there was no time at which such sexual intercourse could take place between a white man and a white woman, that the white man could, according to the laws of nature, be the father of a mulatto child born of the white woman." *Id*. at 565.

matter of opinion, founded on inspection, and it appeared from the depositions in this cause, that while some of the witnesses thought the defendant William a mulatto, others thought him a white person.[150]

In the attempt to determine whether William was illegitimate by looking at his color, the court did not consider the possibility that the Carltons' legitimate and legally white children could be as much as one-eighth Negro.[151]

Instead of considering such an awkward possibility, which may have been relevant given the conflicting testimony concerning William's race, the court used the terms "white" and "Negro" unreflectively, as absolute and ideal racial types. The president of the court added in a note: "Among the hundred millions of whites in *Europe*, there is no authenticated instance of the produce of the white race being other than white."[152] Undoubtedly the scientific experts, when called upon in the retrial of the case to testify as to whether a mulatto child could be the offspring of two white persons, also answered in terms of the ideal racial types of Europe and sub-Saharan Africa rather than in terms of the legal and physical realities of racial categories in nineteenth-century Virginia. The failure to recognize the realities of racial mixing in nineteenth-century Virginia served an important purpose in the society. Its recognition would have undermined the logic of Virginia's racially based system of slavery. By the 1840s, scientific racism, here in the form of expert witnesses, was being called upon to bolster that social system under attack.

C. Who Was Punished for Voluntary Interracial Sex and Why

We have noted that all of the statutes dealing specifically with voluntary interracial sex prescribe punishments for the white partners only. What were the reasons for such a glaring omission?

In the case of sexual relations between whites and their slaves, failure to punish the slave might have been a recognition that the slave had little choice in preventing the relationship, especially if the white were the owner. It might have been seen as bad policy or unreasonable to punish a slave for acquiescing to the

---

150. *Id.* at 569 (emphasis omitted).

151. Under the 1785 statute, a mulatto was someone with "one-fourth part or more of Negro blood." Thus someone with one-eighth Negro blood, that is, with one Negro great-grandparent, was, by implication, not mulatto but legally white. Ch. LXXVIII, 12 LAWS OF VA. 184, 184 (Hening 1823) (enacted 1785; effective 1787).

Mr. or Mrs. Carlton or both of them could have been one-eighth Negro. If both, then their children would have been one-eighth Negro and legally white. If Mrs. Carlton had committed adultery with a mulatto who was not more than one-fourth Negro, and if William were the product of that union, he would be legally white though illegitimate. If Mrs. Carlton were totally of European ancestry, the child would be one-eighth Negro and legally white. Even if Mrs. Carlton were one-eighth Negro (and thus legally white), a child borne of her by a mulatto who was one-fourth Negro would be legally white; it would have three-sixteenths Negro ancestry and would thus fall below the minimum one-fourth Negro blood required to designate one a mulatto.

152. *Watkins*, 37 Va., at 576 n.* (emphasis in original).

demands of his or her master, even to demands for illicit behavior. In addition, many of the usual punishments were meaningless when imposed on slaves or would result in punishing their masters. Years could not be added to life-long servitude; slaves could not be fined if they owned no property; and imprisonment would have deprived their masters of their work.[153]

It is more puzzling why the penalties imposed on whites were not also meted out to free blacks and mulattoes. A likely explanation seems to be that whites, or "Christians"—with whom they were equated—were simply held to a higher moral standard than non-whites in the eyes of the law, and that white racial purity, as well as sexual morality, was considered the special responsibility of the whites.[154] Furthermore, voluntary interracial sex was probably considered the prerogative of whites, albeit an immoral one. The wishes and interests of whites were seen as determining relations between the races. Perhaps whites were so secure in their position of power and superiority that they assumed such relations would not occur unless initiated by whites. After the early years of the colony, as the lines of the racial caste system hardened, the freedom of choice of blacks was ignored in this as in so many other areas of life.

Under the statutes, whites were to be punished for these unions and their non-white partners were not. Also, according to the statutes, white men and women were to be punished equally for such unions, at least when the unions did not produce children. In practice, however, we suspect that it worked differently. Black men may have been punished, either by their masters if they were slaves, or by the law, under the guise of punishment for other offenses. Though a review of county court cases would be needed to reveal the full dimensions of the gap between the law as written and as applied, we have a few cases that suggest how the law was applied. In one early case from lower Norfolk County, only the white woman was punished for fornication; her black partner was punished for something else. In two other cases, from the Virginia high court, the judges merely "winked" at the white men who kept black mistresses.

In 1681, Mary Williamson was found guilty of having fornicated with William, a Negro slave of William Basnett.[155] We assume she was white since no racial designation is given for her.[156] She was fined "five hundred pounds of tobacco and Caske" for the use of Linhaven parish "for which the said Basnett hath In open Court Ingaged himself, etc. security."[157]

---

153. Other punishments were available that would have affected the slaves and not their masters, but they were not used. Several statutes provided for the whipping of slaves in other contexts, but with regard to voluntary interracial sex there was no such punishment for the slave.

154. Another possible explanation is that blacks were thought to be less able to control their sexual desires. *See infra* note 203. But the notion that blacks were naturally lazy did not preclude punitive attempts by their owners to make them work harder; indeed, it justified such attempts.

155. *Id.*

156. *See supra* note 98 (discussing this assumption).

157. Lower Norfolk County Order Book 139 (1681–86) (unpublished manuscript) [hereinafter 1681–86 Order Book], *quoted in* W. BILLINGS, *supra* note 100, at 161.

Interestingly, Mary Williamson was not prosecuted under the 1662 statute providing double fines in cases of *interracial* fornication. Instead, either the general 1661–62 Virginia statute against fornication or local law was applied.[158] Under the general fornication statute, masters whose indentured servant committed fornication were to pay the servant's fine, and the servant was to serve an extra half year. If free, not indentured, and unable to pay, the offender would be imprisoned unless he or she found someone to pay.[159] If no one would pay, the offender was to be whipped. It is likely that Mary got to know William while working as Basnett's servant before the incident. But whether or not she had worked for him before, she owed Basnett an additional six months of service after he agreed to pay her fine.

An interesting feature of the case is that the slave William also was punished, but not, apparently, for the fornication:

> Whereas It hath appeared to the Court that William a negro belonging to William Basnett Squire hath very arrogantly behaved himself in Linhaven Church in the face of the Congregation, It is therefore ordered that the Sheriff take the said William Into his Custody and give him thirty lashes on his bare back.[160]

Since Mary was punished under a general law against fornication rather than under the special law which prescribed punishment for the white partner only, William could have been punished for the fornication too. It seems he was not. Both William and Mary were made to do penance in the church, during which William behaved arrogantly. The whipping was for his arrogance rather than for the fornication. In other earlier cases in Lower Norfolk County, when white couples were punished for fornication or adultery, they had to recite words of contrition as well as stand up in church. Perhaps it was in his public pronouncement that William failed to satisfy the congregation as to his sincere repentance.[161]

158. *See* Act C, 2 LAWS OF VA. 114, 114–15 (Hening 1823) (enacted 1661–62) (providing that a man or woman guilty of the "ffilthy sin of ffornication . . . shall pay five hundred pounds of tobacco fine, . . . to the use of the parish . . . and be imprisoned until they find security to be bound with them").

159. *Id.* at 115.

160. 1681–86 ORDER BOOK, *supra* note 157, at 139, *quoted in* W. Billings, *supra* note 100, at 161.

161. This practice followed English law. In 1641, in Norfolk County, Virginia, Christopher Burrough and Mary Somes were ordered,

> according to the statute of England, [to] do penance in their parish church the next sabbath day the minister preacheth at the said church, standing in the middle alley of the said church upon a stool in a white sheet, and a white wand in their hands, all the time of the divine service and shall say after the minister such words as he shall deliver unto them before the congregation there present.

Lower Norfolk Records (Apr. 12, 1641) (unpublished transcript), *quoted in* A.P. SCOTT, CRIMINAL LAW IN COLONIAL VIRGINIA 277 n.71 (1930). The type of speech required of the couple may be seen in a case of adultery that came up two years later. The couple had to acknowledge

> in these express words mentioned in a schedule hereunto annexed the schedule I B.H. or J.U. do here acknowledge and confess in the presence of this whole congregation that I have grievously sinned and offended against the divine majesty of almighty God and all

Cases in which white men were prosecuted for interracial sex rarely reached the highest courts of Virginia. We have found only two, despite the frequency with which mulatto children were born of black mothers. One reason lay in the rules of evidence: no black or mulatto could testify against a white at trial.[162] Therefore, another white would have had to bring the complaint. Another reason was that society tended to wink at the casual liaisons of white men and black women. The two cases that reached the General Court of Virginia did not concern casual or clandestine sex; both involved cohabitation, and open and stable relationships. In these cases, it seems that other whites did complain.

In *Commonwealth v. Jones*,[163] a case in the General Court of Virginia in 1845, a white man was prosecuted for "cohabiting with and keeping a female slave named Eveline."[164] The fact that the court was in this case called upon to decide whether a white man could be prosecuted under the criminal code for fornication with a slave suggests that the issue had not been presented before. The court had decided in a prior case, *Commonwealth v. David Isaacs and Nancy West*,[165] that cohabitation of a white man and a free mulatto woman was not a common law crime but that the man might be prosecuted under a statute prohibiting fornication.[166] In *Jones* the court held, similarly, that cohabitation of a white man with a slave was not a common law crime but was punishable under the criminal code.[167]

Given all the thousands of such relationships between white men and slave women that must have occurred in Virginia before 1845, why did the question arise at this late date? Why did not everyone wink at this breach of the law as they had done countless times before? The unusual circumstance in this case was that Jones was cohabiting not with his own slave, but with the slave of one Bennett M. Bagby, who presumably had not given his permission.[168] Jones was interfering with Bagby's dominion over his property, Eveline, and it may be that Bagby's complaint brought about the criminal prosecution. Had Eveline been Jones's own slave, it is doubtful that the prosecution would have been initiated, for then the prosecution, rather than the cohabitation, would have been interfering with the property rights of a white Virginian. On appeal, the Virginia high court rejected

---

Christian people in committing the foul and detestable crime of adultery and am heartily sorry and truly penitent for the same and do unfainedly beseech almighty God of his infinite goodness to be merciful unto me and forgive this offense, and I do heartily desire this congregation and all good people likewise to forgive me and pray for me.

Id.
162. Ch. XIX, 3 LAWS OF VA. 289, 298 (Hening 1823) (enacted 1705).
163. 43 Va. (2 Gratt.) 477 (1845).
164. *Id.* at 477.
165. 26 Va. (5 Rand.) 523 (1826).
166. *Id.* The court held that without evidence of fornication, the facts that the couple "occupied the same chamber, ate at the same board, and discharged toward each other the numerous common offices of husband and wife," were "not sufficient to sustain the prosecution of common law." *Id.*
167. *Jones*, 43 Va. at 477.
168. *Id.*

the defendant's argument that since the statute prohibiting fornication did not apply to his slave partner, he should be exempt from prosecution too. It rejected his reasoning, holding "that a person who is not a servant or slave, having illicit intercourse with a slave, is as much within the operation of the statute as if both offending parties were free."[169]

Though the question of statutory interpretation was resolved against the defendant, he received no punishment. The court set Jones free, declaring only that it did not have to declare its reasons for doing so:

> [A] majority of the Judges are of the opinion, that there are other errors disclosed by the record and proceeding of the cause, for which the judgment ought to be arrested; but there being a diversity of opinion among the Judges, as to the particular grounds upon which the judgment ought to be arrested, it becomes unnecessary to state them.
>
> It is therefore ordered, that it be certified to the Circuit Superior Court of Law and Chancery of the county of Powhatan, that the judgment on the verdict aforesaid ought to be arrested; and the defendant discharged and acquitted of the said prosecution.[170]

Jones had suffered the inconvenience and expense of a trial and an appeal, but the high court let him off without so much as a slap on the wrist. Why did they bother to uphold the principle of the law when they apparently did not mean to apply it to the white man in this case? The court may have been concerned about creating a precedent that could be used in the future. It may have wanted to preserve a tool for the use of the aggrieved owner of a slave whose time and attentions were being occupied by another white person without the owner's permission. If a lower court decided against someone like Jones in a subsequent case, the defendant could no longer appeal on the same grounds. The disposition of the case, however, suggests more than anything else the great extent to which restrictions on the sexual behavior of white men with slave women were dismissed lightly.

While we have no comparable cases concerning voluntary sexual relations between white women and slave men for that late period, there are reasons to think such relations were treated far less lightly. As discussed below, they may sometimes have been characterized as rape, thus bringing severe punishment to the black men.[171]

D. Offspring of Interracial Unions

Virginians from an early date lashed out at interracial sex in language "dripping with distaste and indignation."[172] The distaste turned to revulsion when they

---

169. *Id.* at 478.
170. *Id.* (emphasis omitted).
171. *See infra* Part IV.
172. W. JORDAN, *supra* note 7, at 139.

spoke of the resulting mulatto children, especially those with white mothers, as an "abominable mixture and spurious issue."[173]

Mixed-race offspring were disturbing to white Virginians for several reasons. First, they were anomalies. They simply did not fit into the whites' vision of the natural order of things: a great chain of Being comprised of fixed links, not of infinite gradations. Things which do not fit into the perceived natural order are seen as unnatural and often as dangerous and "abominable."[174] The term "spurious," used by the Virginia legislature for the children of marriages between whites and Negroes,[175] shows a fundamental uneasiness and aversion to the idea of racial mixture, an aversion that is not entirely explainable by practical considerations. The aversion was greatest toward the mulatto children of white women. Since mulattoes were classified with blacks, the prospect of a mulatto child of a black mother was not as disturbing as that of a mulatto child of a white mother. It seemed less anomalous. Second, the idea of a racially based system of slavery depended on a clear separation of the races. Mulattoes challenged that idea. Winthrop Jordan suggests that the psychological problem was handled in part by categorizing mixed-blood offspring as belonging to the lower caste, thus, in effect, denying their existence:

> The colonist . . . remained firm in his rejection of the mulatto, in his categorization of mixed-bloods as belonging to the lower caste. It was an unconscious decision dictated perhaps in large part by the weight of Negroes on his community, heavy enough to be a burden, yet not so heavy as to make him abandon all hope of maintaining his own identity, physically and culturally. Interracial propagation was a constant reproach that he was failing to be true to himself. Sexual intimacy strikingly symbolized a union he wished to avoid. If he could not restrain his sexual nature, he could at least reject its fruits and thus solace himself that he had done no harm. Perhaps he sensed as well that continued racial intermixture would eventually undermine the logic of the racial slavery upon which his society was based. For the separation of slaves from free men depended on a clear demarcation of the races, and the presence of mulattoes blurred this essential distinction. Accordingly, he made every effort to nullify the effects of racial intermixture. By classifying the mulatto as a Negro he was in effect denying that intermixture had occurred at all.[176]

Third, mulattoes created a practical problem for a racially based system of slavery. They had to be classified in terms of status as well as in terms of race, and as we have discussed earlier, race did not automatically determine one's status as slave or free.[177] The law of the inheritance of slave status was a response to

---

173. *See supra* text accompanying notes 99 & 130.
174. *See generally* M. DOUGLAS, PURITY AND DANGER: AN ANALYSIS OF CONCEPTS OF POLLUTION AND TABOO (1970) (discussing the attribution of danger to things that fall outside the culturally constructed order).
175. *See supra* text accompanying note 130.
176. W. JORDAN, *supra* note 7, at 177–78.
177. *See supra* Part II.

the question of how to classify the children of white men and slave women, and the 1662 statute gave them the status of their mothers.[178]

It has been suggested that, rather than having been dictated solely by racism, this policy might have reflected, among other things, the "prudential considerations of keeping a child with its mother and reimbursing the mother's master for its support."[179] But keeping a child with its slave mother hardly required such a drastic measure as making it a slave. Many free white children were raised from infancy by slave women. Had their mulatto children by white fathers been declared free, the slave mothers would probably have continued to raise them. Furthermore, masters could get reimbursement by making the child serve an indenture as well as by making it a slave. Whatever the precise combination of motives behind the rule of the inheritance of slave status, it had two notable practical effects: first, it separated the large majority of the children of interracial unions from whites by assigning them the status of slave; second, it provided slaveowners with easy and cheap ways to increase the number of slaves they held. In the psychological terms suggested by Jordan, it also allowed white men to deny their responsibility for racial intermixture far more effectively than they could have done had the child inherited its status from the father.

The rule that children were to take the status of their mothers meant that some mulattoes (the great majority) were slave and some were free. Free mulattoes fell into two categories that were treated very differently. Under a 1691 statute, a mulatto bastard child *of a white woman* was to be bound out as a servant by the church wardens until the age of thirty.[180] The statute prescribed no similar fate for the legitimate mulatto children of white mothers or the legitimate or illegitimate mulatto children of free black mothers. The same statute prescribed banishment within three months for white women who married Negro, mulatto, or Indian men, so that the mother, and any legitimate mulatto children who went with her, were removed from local society anyway. When, however, in 1705, the penalty was changed to six months in prison and a fine,[181] white women who served their time presumably were able to raise families of free legitimate mulatto children.[182] These children were not to be sold

---

178. *See supra* note 16.

179. E. Morgan, *supra* note 21, at 336 (1975).

180. Act XVI, 3 Laws of Va. 86, 87 (Hening 1823) (enacted 1671). In 1705, the age was changed to 31, Ch. XLIX, 3 Laws of Va. 447, 453 (Hening 1823) (enacted 1705), and, in 1765, it was reduced to age 21 for males and age 18 for females, the legislators having decided that thirty-one years of servitude "is an unreasonable severity toward such children." Ch. XXIV, 8 Laws of Va. 133, 134–35 (Hening 1821) (enacted 1765).

   It may be that the mulatto children of free black women who were not themselves indentured and the legitimate mulatto children of white women were so few in number that the legislators inadvertently omitted them or did not bother to include them in the harsh treatment.

181. Ch. XLIX, § XIX, 3 Laws of Va. 447, 453–54 (Hening 1823) (enacted 1705).

182. Johnston repeats that the 1830 census record for the county of Nansemand, Virginia, lists a number of free Negro heads of families with white wives, and in the 1844 Virginia census one census taken for the district of Southhampton noted "white mother" after the names of certain

into service for the benefit of the parish, for that provision applied only to bastard children, and while the products of the mixed marriages might have been spurious and abominable to the white Virginians, they were not illegitimate. The sacrament of marriage was effective even in the case of interracial marriage until 1849.[183]

Just as the legislators were much harder on white women who produced free mulatto bastards than they were on free black women who also produced free mulatto bastards, the legislators were also much harder on the free mulatto bastards descended from white women than they were on other free mulattoes.[184] What was the difference between the free mulattoes of white mothers and the others that the former should be treated more harshly? Perhaps it was an extension of the outrage the legislators felt toward the mothers of such children. Perhaps it was that they were evidence of the corruption of the white race in a way that the mulatto children of black mothers were not. Once Virginians had made the decision to classify mulattoes with blacks, the mulatto child of a white mother was an assault on racial purity. The mulatto child of a black mother merely exhibited a lighter shade within the range of skin color of the lower racial caste.[185]

---

mulatto children. He also cites other instances of mulatto children living with their white mothers and white women cohabiting with Negro men. J. JOHNSTON, *supra* note 22, at 265–67.

183. VA. CODE ch. 109, § 1, at 471 (1849) (any marriage between a white person and a Negro absolutely void without further legal process).

184. When female mulatto bastards of white women who were bound out as servants had children during their service, those children served the mother's master until they reached the age their mother was when she completed her service. Ch. IV, 4 LAWS OF VA. 126, 133 (Hening 1820) (enacted 1723). It was left to the courts to decide the fate of the third generation of children born to such mulatto women servants, and the courts did so. In Gwinn v. Bugg, 1 Va. (Jeff.) 48 (1769), the General Court interpreted the statute prescribing indenture for the mulatto bastards of white women to apply to the bastard children of females so indentured whether such children had been formally bonded out by the church wardens or had simply stayed on with the master of their mother. *Id.* at 48–49.

Despite the revulsion the legislators seemed to feel toward mulattoes, and especially toward free mulattoes with white mothers, the one "solution" they would not tolerate was for the mothers quietly to kill their children at birth. To discourage free women wishing to avoid penalties for producing bastards from killing their infants, the legislators prescribed the death penalty for any non-slave woman who killed her bastard child to conceal it. Ch. XII, 3 LAWS OF VA. 516, 516 (Hening 1823) (enacted 1710). Presumably, a mother who killed her child might always face the death penalty, but the legislators felt the practice in this case warranted a special statute.

185. The legitimate mulatto children of white women who were married to black men were, it seems, also exempted from particularly harsh treatment. We see this as an unwilling deference on the part of the legislators to the sacrament of marriage.

Similarly, white bastards were treated less harshly. The major concern was that they not be a financial burden to their respective parishes, and laws were enacted to make the fathers of these children accountable. The children themselves were, by a 1769 law, to be apprenticed until the boys reached age 21 and the girls reached age 18, but before this law, no special arrangements had been established for them. Ch. XXVII, 8 LAWS OF VA. 374, 376 (Hening 1821) (enacted 1769).

IV. Involuntary Interracial Sex: Rape

White Virginians were concerned with involuntary as well as voluntary interracial sex, with rape as well as with fornication and marriage. However, the concern over involuntary interracial sex sprang from a different source. The motivation behind the dissuasions for voluntary interracial sex seems to have been white racial purity and the maintenance of racial boundary lines. Only whites were called to task for polluting the white race—primarily the white women, whose mulatto children were a constant reminder of their mothers' defilement of the white race. In cases of interracial rape, in contrast, only black men were called to task. White men were not punished at all for the rape of black women, and black men were punished more severely than were white men who raped white women. Here, it was not racial purity that was the issue; indeed, we have not seen it mentioned in connection with the rape of white women by black men that mulatto children might result. Rather, it was the maintenance of power relations that concerned the white legislators. They came to see interracial rape as a direct assault on their domination and control over blacks and over white women.

A. The Early Prosecution of Black and White Men
for Rape in Virginia

The first settlers in Virginia were authorized by the King to punish a very limited number of crimes by death, among them rape.[186] Sexual crimes were taken very seriously in colonial Virginia. When the colony was established, sexual crimes made up half of the capital crimes.[187] By a 1796 statute, the death penalty was abolished for all crimes committed by free persons except first degree murder, and we may assume this limitation applied only to free *white* persons.[188]

Attempted rape initially was not a felony; it was, rather, aggravated assault and did not carry the death penalty for either black or white perpetrators. By the early nineteenth century, that had changed for blacks. In 1823, attempted rape of a white woman by a slave or free Negro or mulatto was made punishable by death.[189]

Note the direction of change in this area of law in the late eighteenth and early nineteenth centuries. The penalties for whites convicted of committing sexual crimes against white women decreased as part of a general restriction in the use of the death penalty against whites. In contrast, the penalties for Negroes and mulattoes convicted of committing sexual crimes against white women increased as part of a general hardening of the racial lines that began in the early nineteenth

---

186. A.P. Scott, *supra* note 161, at 4 (1930) ("They were authorized by the King to punish rebellion and mutiny, murder, incest, rape, and adultery by death.").
187. *Id.*
188. 1796 Va. Acts ch. II, § 1, at 4. Statutes not specifying race usually applied to whites only, and the 1823 statute, discussed below, which specified that *attempted* rape of a white woman by a free Negro was punishable by death made no sense if a completed rape of a white woman by a free Negro were not punishable by death. 1823 Va. Acts ch. 34, § 3, at 36, 37.
189. *Id.* § 3, at 37.

century and extended well into the twentieth. Before the statutory changes of 1796 and 1823, the differences in the way whites and blacks accused of rape were treated were apparent, but the gulf was not as great as it became later.

Before 1796, when the law gave no formal recognition to the differences in punishment of whites and blacks convicted of rape, the death penalty was ordered for men of both races convicted of raping white women. Arthur Scott canvassed a number of court records for the period before 1774 and found ten cases of rape and two of attempted rape.[190] In half of them, five cases of rape and one of attempted rape, the men were identified as Negro. In the other half, there were no racial designations and presumably the men were white. In all cases but one the race of the victim was not identified, and those victims were presumably white. One woman, raped by a Negro, was identified as a mulatto.[191] The Negro who was accused of raping a mulatto woman in 1773 must have been prosecuted under the common law, as the legislators had not deemed this possibility worthy of legislation.

Although the sample of early cases reported by Scott is extremely small, the details he gives suggest significant differences in the patterns of prosecution and treatment of Negroes and whites in cases of rape. Not surprisingly, the Negroes were treated more harshly, though there was a range of responses to both white and black defendants. Of the five whites accused of rape, two were convicted. One was condemned to death in 1627 for seducing four girls under the age of consent;[192] the other was convicted in 1774, though there is no record of his execution.[193] Of the three not convicted, one was a man whom, in 1670, the grand jury refused to indict, and the others were acquitted after trials in 1767 and 1773, respectively.[194] One servant, presumably white, who was convicted of attempted rape in the late seventeenth century, received thirty-nine lashes, had his hair cut off, was made to wear an iron collar, and had to serve several additional years.[195] The six Negroes fared less well. In three cases, the defendants were convicted of rape; in a fourth case, it is not known whether the accused rapist was ever apprehended. In the remaining two cases, the Negroes were convicted of lesser offenses. In no case was there an acquittal.[196]

The earliest Negro rape case noted was in 1678, when the Minutes of the Council and General Court report, "Strong measures to be taken for apprehending Robin, a negro who ravished a white woman,"[197] but we do not know whether he was ever apprehended and tried. In 1702, a Negro was executed for raping a woman, presumably white; in 1767, another was hanged for ravishing a woman identified as white; and, in 1773, a Negro was found guilty of raping a mulatto

190. A.P. SCOTT, *supra* note 161, at 207–08.
191. *Id.* at 208.
192. *Id.* at 207 (citing MINUTES, *supra* note 44, at 149 [H.R. McIlwaine 2d ed. 1979]).
193. *Id.* at 207.
194. *Id.*
195. *Id.* at 208.
196. *Id.* at 207–08.
197. *Id.*

woman.[198] Scott does not note the punishment in the last case, nor whether the Negro was slave or free, but the fact that there was any prosecution at all for the rape of a mulatto woman is significant. It meant that she was deemed worthy of the law's protection, at least against a Negro assailant.[199]

The Negroes who were not convicted of the rape charge were found guilty of the lesser offenses of attempted rape or assault and were given lesser punishments. The slave Jack, who was tried in 1742 for raping a white woman, was found not guilty of rape, but guilty of assault and was given thirty-nine lashes, the same punishment received by the white man convicted of attempted rape in the case noted above.[200] A free Negro, convicted in 1737 of attempting to rape a seven-year-old white girl, "was punished by one hour in the pillory where he was 'much pelted by the populace,' 29 lashes, and temporary servitude for payment of fees."[201]

The victims all were described as white or were not designated by race and may be assumed to have been white, except for the one mulatto woman raped by a Negro. Rapes of Negro and mulatto women by white men must certainly have occurred, especially of Negro and mulatto slaves, but, for a number of reasons, they were rarely, if ever, prosecuted. Scott found no such cases, nor did we. In the first place, whites could not easily be prosecuted for rapes of non-whites, since

---

198. *Id.*
199. In 1829, a slave was condemned to death for raping a free black woman. P. SCHWARTZ, TWICE CONDEMNED 207 (1988).
200. A.P. SCOTT, *supra* note 161, at 208.
201. W. JORDAN, *supra* note 7, at 157 n. 44 (quoting Williamsburg Gazette, Aug. 26, 1737). Scott's survey of rape in Virginia extends only through 1774. Ulrich B. Phillips compiled another survey for the period 1774 to 1864. Phillips, *Slave Crime in Virginia*, 20 AMER. HIST. REV. 336 (1915). Unfortunately, Phillips' figures cover crimes by slaves only, as they were based on vouchers for reimbursement of owners for their slaves executed for capital crimes. They do not include either free blacks or whites. Schwartz has compiled statistics on slave crimes, including rape, from Virginia court records from 1705–1865. P. SCHWARTZ, *supra* note 199, *passim*.

In 1691, the legislature, in "An act for suppressing outlying Slaves," Act XVI, 3 LAWS OF VA. 86 (Hening 1823) (enacted 1691), arranged to compensate owners of runaway slaves who "lie hid and lurk in obscure places killing hoggs and committing other injuries," when those slaves were killed in the process of resisting apprehension. *Id.* at 86. In 1705, the compensation was extended for all slaves put to death by law. Ch. XLIX, § XXXVIII, 3 LAWS OF VA. 447, 461 (Hening 1823) (enacted 1705).

Castration and other forms of dismemberment were drastic measures short of death that could be used to punish uncontrollable slaves and to serve as examples to others. In 1769, castration was forbidden as a punishment except in cases of attempted rape of a white woman by a slave. Ch. XIX, § 1, 8 LAWS OF VA. 358, 358 (Hening 1821) (enacted 1769). Presumably, it was not authorized at all after 1823, when the penalty for attempted rape of a white woman was changed to death. Ch. 34, § 3, 1823 Va. Acts 36, 37.

Phillips' survey showed that in the period from 1774 to 1864, vouchers were issued reimbursing owners for some 1418 slaves who were convicted of capital crimes. Of them, 73 were executed for rape and 32 for attempted rape. In two cases, the victims were children under the age of ten; in two other cases they were free mulatto women, though in one of those two latter cases the conviction was merely of "suspicion of rape." Phillips, *supra* at 33.

the latter could not testify against their attackers in court.[202] In addition, even if the testimony of blacks had been admissible against whites, convictions of white men for interracial rape would have been rare. The assumption of promiscuous Negro sexuality[203] and the assertion of white male dominance over blacks in the sexual sphere would have inclined white male prosecutors not to prosecute, and white male juries not to convict. Finally, there is the question of whether slaves were recognized as having any personal rights that could be violated by rape. While the Virginia Supreme Court did not face this question directly, the Mississippi Supreme Court decided they had none; rape of a slave woman was simply not a crime, even when committed by a slave.[204]

Another pattern that may be noted in these early cases is that while three of the five whites charged with rape were acquitted of all charges, none of the Negroes was. Those Negroes who were not convicted of rape were convicted of the lesser crimes of assault or attempted rape. While this might have been just part of the general arbitrary harshness in the treatment of Negroes, there may be another explanation as well: the role of consent as a defense in rape cases. Consent by the woman is a complete defense to rape or attempted rape except in the case of underage women. That defense might have been responsible for the acquittal of the three whites. In the trials of the Negroes, however, we may conclude that consent of the woman was either not pleaded or was not successful as a defense, because none of the accused was set free. Indeed, it would have been difficult to plead because the Negro himself could not testify against the white woman after 1705, nor could other Negroes support his testimony against a white person had

---

202. Ch. XIX, § XXXI, 3 LAWS OF VA. 287, 298 (Hening 1823) (enacted 1705). An act of 1705 regulating procedures in the General Court provided: "That popish recusants convict, negroes, mulattoes and Indian servants, and others, not being christians, shall be deemed and taken to be persons incapable in law, to be witnesses in any cases whatsoever." *Id.*

In 1732, another act again specified that Negroes were not allowed to testify against whites even though they were Christians because of their "base and corrupt natures." Ch. VII § V, 4 LAWS OF VA. 325, 327 (Hening 1820) (enacted 1732). In the eyes of the legislators, it was not, then, simply the fact that they were not Christian that made Negroes unfit to testify; it was something deeper in their nature, something not changed by mere conversion.

203. *See* W. JORDAN, *supra* note 7, at 32–40 (1968) (noting that common perception of slaves as "animals" and "beasts" led to conclusion that slaves were unusually libidinous and unrestrained in their sexual behavior).

204. *See* George v. State, 37 Miss. 316, 318–20 (1859) (holding that rape of a female slave under the age of ten by a slave was not a crime because English common law did not recognize slavery and thus recognized no rights of slaves and Mississippi extended no such rights through legislation: all rights in slave rested with master).

Virginia courts did explicitly deny slaves other rights, such as the right to own property and the right to make a contract on their own behalf. *See* Higginbotham & Kopytoff, *supra* note *, at 526.

No 18th-century Virginia court whose records have survived convicted a white man or a slave of raping a female slave. Two male slaves were so charged in 1873; one was not convicted and charges were dropped against the other for want of witnesses to testify. P. SCHWARTZ, *supra* note 199, at 156.

he been allowed to give it. The claim would have required support by testimony from other whites.

B. The Issue of Consent

While the issue of consent of white women to sexual relations with Negroes seems not to have been raised formally in the legal proceedings, it was very much present in the background. It appeared in a number of cases of alleged rape of white women by black men, as shown by James Hugo Johnston in his survey of rapes by Negroes and mulattoes reported to governors of Virginia between the years 1789–1833, but it was raised, apparently, only after conviction.[205] In nearly half of the cases surveyed by Johnston, twenty-seven out of sixty, the judges who imposed the mandatory death sentence recommended the condemned to the mercy of the governor. They did so either because they themselves doubted that the man was guilty, or because the jury or citizens of the community had sent petitions on the man's behalf. According to Johnston, the petitions presented evidence not admitted at the trial.[206]

In the six petitions quoted by Johnston, which he says are typical, the petitioners seemed to say either that the woman had consented in this case, or that she had consented so often to having sexual relations with Negroes in the past that she had lost the right to object before the law.

In the 1833 case of Tasco Thompson, a free Negro condemned to die for the attempted rape of Mary Jane Stevens, the jury that convicted him recommended mercy. In response to the Governor's query as to the reasons for their recommendation, the jury foreman, Sam H. Davis, under oath, had the following to say:

> 1st. The exceedingly disreputable character of the family of the said Stevens. It consisted of the mother and herself, with a younger sister, a small girl. It was notorious that the mother had long entertained negroes, and that all her associations, with one or two exceptions were blacks. All the evidence went to shew that she visited no white families save the one or two referred to, who were upon her own level. In a word she was below the level of the ordinary grade of free negroes.
>
> 2nd. [I]t was clearly proved that long settled malice had existed against the prisoner in the bosom of [Mrs. Stevens] who was looked upon as one of the getters up of the prosecution and who was proved to have declared before the offense that she would have the prisoner hung if it took her seven years.
>
> 3d. . . . There is no doubt that he repaired to the house of Mrs. Stevens in the belief that she would cheerfully submit to his embraces, as she doubtless had often done before, but finding her absent he probably supposed his embraces would be equally agreeable to her daughter [Mary Jane], and in making the attempt the jury considered the offense as differing only *in name* from a similar

205. J. JOHNSTON, *supra* note 22, at 257–63.
206. *Id.* at 258–59.

attempt made upon one of his color. They also considered that the law was made to preserve the distinction which should exist between our two kinds of population, and to protect the whites in the possession of their superiority; but here the whites had yielded their claims to the protection of the law by their voluntary associations with those whom the law distinguishes as their inferiors.

4th. As a prosecution would not have a claim in the case if the female concerned had been a colored girl, so the jury thought it hard to convict the prisoner for an offense not greater in enormity than had the prosecutrix been colored; but her maker had given her a white skin, and they had no discretion. They could only convict him capitally and urge the recommendation which they did.[207]

This document has been quoted at length because it presents an unusual window into the workings of the legal system and into the minds of white jurors who felt they were unjustly condemning a black man to death. First, note the harshness and rigidity of the law concerning sexual relations between black men and white women. At the time of this petition, there was a new statute, barely ten years old, making attempted rape of a white woman by a black man punishable by death. The new statute read: "And it be further enacted, That if any slave, free negro or mulatto, shall attempt to ravish a white woman, married, maid, or other, such offender, his aiders and abettors, shall be adjudged guilty of felony, and suffer death as in other cases of felony, by hanging by the neck; any law, custom, or usage, to the contrary notwithstanding."[208] Before the enactment of this statute, attempted rape had not carried the death penalty. Presumably that would still be the case in an attempted rape of a free mulatto woman by a Negro or mulatto, as jury foreman Davis's statement suggests. By the early nineteenth century, the legal position toward sexual relations between black men and white women had hardened and become rigid and more punitive toward black men. Furthermore, there was little room for maneuvering within the formal legal system. The jurors thought they had no choice in condemning Tasco Thompson to death, though they doubted the story of his accusers and thought the punishment was unjust.

A second point to note is that while the jury accepted the purpose of the new and harsher law as preserving and protecting the whites' position of superiority, they felt there was a limit to the extent of that protection. They considered that whites could, and in this case did, voluntarily relinquish their claims to superiority and therefore to the law's special protection by willfully allowing themselves to fall below the level of the Negroes. In Thompson's case, they held the white accusers more responsible, morally, than the accused black. If a white woman freely threw away her claims to superiority by having sexual relations with blacks, the jury felt it was unjust for a black man who complied to be condemned to

207. *Id.* at 262–63 (emphasis in original). A recommendation for mercy could result in transportation for sale elsewhere, or in the lesser punishment of whipping or imprisonment, or in pardon. Phillips notes that pardon would not appear in the vouchers he used for then there would have been no reimbursement to the owner, but that other punishments do. He did not, however, note any of the lesser punishments in rape cases. Phillips, *supra* note 201, at 338–39.

208. Act 34, § 3, 1823 Va. Acts 36, 37 (emphasis omitted).

death. Sexual relations between white women and black men were distasteful to them, but the jury did not want Thompson to die for participating in what it saw as the self-debasement of the Stevens family women.

Third, the jury recognized that an accusation of rape or attempted rape could be misused by a white woman simply for spite or vengeance, and they suspected that it had been in Thompson's case. Fourth, they clearly saw Mrs. Stevens as consenting to sexual intercourse with Negroes, even if her daughter had not on this occasion, and this mitigated the seriousness of Thompson's actions. Although all of these factors were in the jury foreman's response to the Governor's questions, there seemed to be no place for them in the formal legal proceedings.

Citizens were no less outspoken on behalf of slaves who they thought were unjustly sentenced to death for rape than they were for free Negroes like Thompson. For example, when a slave named Peter was sentenced to death for raping Patsy Hooker, sixty-two citizens of Hanover County petitioned the Governor in 1808 for mercy toward Peter.[209] They declared that "the said Patsy Hooker, from the best information they can get upon the subject, is a common strumpet, and she was the only witness introduced on the part of the Commonwealth in the prosecution of the said slave."[210] The petitioners seemed to disbelieve Patsy Hooker, but the legal system did not give the judge or jury the option of choosing to believe the word of a slave over the word of a white person. In another case, petitioners claimed that the accusing white woman already had mulatto children and had consented to having intercourse with the accused black on prior occasions; it was suggested that she also had consented on the occasion in question. Yet this apparently had not been an issue at trial. At trial, the accusation of rape by a white woman seemed virtually to ensure conviction of a Negro.[211] The issue of

---

209. J. JOHNSTON, *supra* note 22, at 261.
210. *Id.*
211. A white woman who had voluntary sexual relations with a black man and later found herself pregnant might claim rape in the hope of avoiding the harsh penalties meted out to white women who bore mulatto children.

    That may have been what led Katherine Watkins, wife of Henry Watkins of Henrico County, to pursue a claim of rape in September of 1681 against a mulatto belonging to Capt. Thomas Cocke some five weeks after the event allegedly took place. (W. BILLINGS, *supra* note 100, at 161–63 (quoting from Henrico County Deed Book, 1677–1692, at 192–95 [manuscript]). Of the four individuals who were deposed concerning her behavior, only one supported her story. The other three told of her drinking and her advances toward mulatto Jack, close to the date that the rape allegedly occurred, during which she kissed him, "put her hand on his codpiece," told him she loved him, and led him into a backroom. *Id.* at 162. When he left, she "fetched him into the roome againe and hugged and kist him." *Id.* at 163. She also "tooke Mingoe one of the Cocke's Negroes about the Necke and fling on the bedd and Kissed him and putt her hand into his Codpiece." *Id.* She made playful advances toward another Negro when she turned up the tail of his shirt and "said that he would have a good pricke." *Id.*

    The one deponent who supported Katherine Watkin's story that she was raped, Humphrey Smith, said that he had seen her mouth torn and swollen and was shown a bloody handkerchief with which she claimed Jack had stopped her mouth. Smith said that Jack had confessed to having gone to the Watkins' place three times to ask her forgiveness, and that the last time he

consent arose only after conviction. Then, if judges or jurors suspected that the white woman in a case of interracial rape had consented, they blamed her vigorously. The black man was not blamed at all. This is consistent with the statutes on voluntary interracial sex and marriage that punished the white partner, especially the white woman, and ignored the black partner.[212]

Voluntary sexual relations between black men and white women could be treated as rape. As the petitions to the Governor suggest, they sometimes were, but only if the woman claimed rape. If she said nothing, then, presumably, the relationship could continue and the law could continue to ignore it, as long as no mulatto children were produced. In 1825, a statute was passed that did acknowledge the role of consent in voluntary sexual relations between black men and white women but it did so in such a convoluted way that it underscores the difficulties the white legislators had in dealing with the subject. It reads:

Be it enacted by the General Assembly, That if any free negro or mulatto do ravish a white woman, married, maid or other, where she did not consent before nor after; or shall ravish a white woman, married, maid, or other, with force, although she consent after; the person so offending shall be adjudged a felon and shall suffer death, as in the case of felony, without benefit of clergy; any law, custom, or usage to the contrary withstanding.[213]

We should note first that this act was written to apply only to free Negroes and mulattoes, not to slaves, and second, that it dealt only with actual rape, not with attempted rape. The question seems to be one of distinguishing consensual

---

went, the husband Henry Watkins told Jack to keep off the Watkins' property or he would be shot. *Id.* at 163.

In explaining why she had not made her complaint earlier, Katherine Watkins blamed the delay on her sickness and that of her children. Her claim that her husband had not prosecuted because he was "inclinable to the quakers," *id.* at 161, does not sit well with his threat to shoot Jack if the mulatto appeared on his property again. Whether or not Jack did in fact rape Katherine on the occasion in question, her delay in initiating the charge does raise the question of whether she decided to do so only when she thought she was pregnant, and her husband's behavior in failing to prosecute suggests he may have been doubtful of the charge of rape. Unfortunately we do not know the disposition of the case.

212. When whites and blacks married, only the whites were punished. *See, e.g.,* Act XVI, 3 LAWS OF VA. 86, 87 (Hening 1823) (enacted 1691) (white partner banished from Virginia for life); Ch. XLIX, § XIX, 3 LAWS OF VA. 447, 453–54 (Hening 1823) (enacted 1705) (white partner imprisoned for six months); Ch. VII, § XIV, 6 LAWS OF VA., 356, 361–62 (Hening 1819) (enacted 1753) (white partner imprisoned for up to twelve months); Ch. VIII, § 4, 1848 Va. Acts 12, 13 (Hening 1823) (enacted 1849) (same).

When whites had mulatto bastards, only white women were punished. *See e.g.,* Act XVI, 3 LAWS OF VA. 86, 87 (Hening 1823) (enacted 1691) (imposing fine and five year servitude if woman unable to pay); Ch. VII, § XIII, 3 LAWS OF VA. 447, 453 (Hening 1823) (enacted 1705) (same); 6 LAWS OF VA. 356, 361 (Hening 1819) (enacted 1753) (same).

When whites engaged in interracial fornication, only the whites were punished. *See, e.g.,* Act XII, 2 LAWS OF VA. 170, 170 (Hening 1823) (enacted 1662).

213. Ch. 23, 1824 Va. Acts 22, 22 (1825) (emphasis omitted).

sexual relations from rape. For free Negroes and mulatto men, but not for slaves, this presented a problem deemed worthy of statutory consideration.

The statute appears to say that consent may never be assumed from a white woman's participation in an act of interracial sex, but that she must give it explicitly either before or after the act. Sexual intercourse between a free black man and a white woman was assumed to be rape unless the woman spoke up and said that she had consented. Further, if the court were to decide that force had been used, the woman could not save the man from death by declaring her consent afterwards, even if she wished to.

This statute, enacted in 1825, came two years after one making attempted rape of a white woman by a black man a capital offense.[214] Under the 1823 statute, a white woman could cause a black man to be put to death by doing little more than swearing in court that he had tried to rape her. This gave a great deal of power to white women to condemn to death black men against whom they bore some grudge. The legislators who conferred that considerable power on white women appeared to be less worried about the women who might abuse it than they were about white women who would not use it at all—about white women who willingly submitted to sexual relations with free blacks. They also may have been concerned with the perceived sexual dominance exercised by free black men over those white women who willingly had sexual relations with them. To address these concerns, the 1825 act allowed the conviction of a free black man for "raping" a white woman based solely on the testimony of others unless the woman would publicly say that she consented to sexual relations with the man. While a white woman who violated social taboos might have had no private regrets about what she did, it was quite another thing for her to make a public statement of it. Apart from the social opprobrium to which it would subject her, such a statement made her vulnerable to prosecution for interracial fornication. If the liaison were a casual one, the white woman might well be unwilling to subject herself to public condemnation, fines, and possible imprisonment, even if remaining silent meant condemning a man to death.

The 1825 statute made it easier to convict and condemn to death free black men who had had voluntary sexual relations with white women. The statute marks the first explicit recognition in an interracial rape statute of the possibility of consent by the white woman, but it does so in a context that appears to make it easier to prosecute black men for such relations by calling it rape.

Why was the 1825 statute, with its sleight-of-hand wording that could turn consensual sex into rape, applied only to free Negroes and mulattoes and not to slaves? In the case of a white woman who voluntarily had sex with her own slave, that could be seen as an aspect, though an unseemly one, of her dominion over him. When a white woman had sexual relations with the slave of another, he was still under the control of whites, and, more importantly, he was valued property. The owners did not want to be deprived of their valuable property, nor did the legislators wish the state to have to compensate owners for the loss of their slaves

---

214. Act 34, § 3, 1823 Va. Acts 36, 37.

just because some white women had been foolish enough to have sexual relations with them.[215] On the other hand, the legislators could well contemplate ridding themselves of free Negroes and mulattoes who, as we have seen, posed a threat to white Virginians, and had been arrogant enough to have sex with white women, even if they had done so at the latter's behest.

Both this statute and the 1823 statute making attempted rape of white women by blacks and mulattoes punishable by death[216] show an increasing uneasiness and rigidity toward interracial sexual relations on the part of the white men who drafted them. This suggests that such relations were beginning to take on increasing symbolic importance in the Virginia society of the nineteenth century.

Some juries, however, seemed reluctant to apply the new and harsh laws. An 1832 case shows a Virginia jury struggling with the question of attempted rape, as they did in the Thompson case a year later. In *Commonwealth v. Fields*,[217] the defendant also was tried under the 1823 statute prescribing the death penalty for attempted rape. In this case, the jury acquitted the defendant, but the reasoning sounds rather strained, or, to put it positively, imaginative. A free Negro named Fields was indicted "for violently and feloniously making an assault upon, and attempting to ravish a white woman." The jury acquitted him, and the General Court of Virginia upheld the jury's reasoning on the following special verdict:

> We find, from the evidence, that the prisoner did not intend to have carnal knowledge of the within named *S.L.* as alleged in the indictment, *by force*, but that he intended to have such carnal knowledge of her while she was asleep; that he made the attempt to have such carnal knowledge of her when she was asleep, but used no force except such as was incident to getting to bed with her, and stripping up her night garment in which she was sleeping, and which caused her to awake.[218]

The jury, after making these findings of fact, left it to the judge to apply the law to them, but recommended that if the law determined that the prisoner was guilty, and if the offense were not punishable by death, that he be imprisoned for six years. The General Court took the special verdict to allow acquittal, and thus Fields was set free.

Under Virginia law of the time, the result is surprising. It seemed clear that the jury believed Fields did try to have sexual intercourse with "S.L." without her consent. Under the 1823 statute, he could well have been found guilty of attempted rape and put to death.[219] Yet the trial judge (in setting the jury the

215. *See supra* note 201, ¶2.
216. *See supra* note 214.
217. 31 Va. (4 Leigh) 648 (1832).
218. *Id.* at 648–49 (emphasis in original).
219. Ch. 34, § 3, 1823 Va. Acts 36, 37. The 1825 statute made it clear that one could ravish without using force. In that act, a free Negro or mulatto who ravished a white woman by force was always guilty of rape; if he ravished her without force, he was guilty only if she failed to consent. Ch. 23, § 1, 1824 Va. Acts 22, 22 (1825). If a man under the 1825 statute could ravish a woman without using force, could he not then under the 1823 statute *attempt* to ravish her without using force? The question was not considered. Fields was not indicted under the 1825 act, presumably

task of finding a special verdict), the jury (in finding that no force was intended), and the appeals court (in finding attempted intercourse without force was not attempt to ravish within the meaning of the 1823 statute) were all generously interpreting law and fact in favor of the defendant. Was this a case like *Thompson* in which they thought the white woman was not worthy of the protection of the law, or did they think the punishment too harsh, or the sex consensual, or some combination of these factors?

Whatever the reason, it seems that those charged with applying the new harsh laws punishing sexual relations between black men and white women had more difficulty with them than had the legislators who devised them.[220]

C. The Purpose of the Anti-Rape Statutes

Thus far we have discussed the anti-rape statutes that protected white women, and we have noted that free Negro and mulatto women and slaves were not similarly protected. The anti-rape statutes and trials, however, went far beyond protecting the personal rights of white women, especially as the law developed in the nineteenth century. The 1823 statute making attempted rape of white women by blacks a felony punishable by death was not primarily an effort to secure greater protection for white women. Rather, its primary function and focus was the protection of a racial caste system. In the words of Sam Davis, the foreman of the jury in the *Tasco Thompson* case, "the law was made to preserve the distinction which should exist between our two kinds of population, and to protect the whites in the possession of their superiority."[221] The jurors and magistrates felt compelled to apply that law, even when they thought that the white women who claimed its protection were not victims of attacks by blacks, but willing sexual partners. They also thought that the law's application in a number of particular cases resulted in injustice to the accused and thus they petitioned the Governor for mercy for the condemned prisoner. Only in the occasional anomalous case, such as *Fields,* did they go so far as to acquit a black man. In other cases, a sympathetic jury at most recommended mercy, small comfort to a black man convicted of rape whose options were likely to be death by hanging if mercy were not granted or sale as a slave in the West Indies if it were. Even when white ju-

---

because that statute applied only to completed acts of intercourse, and Fields' attempt was not successful.

220. *See* J. JOHNSTON, *supra* note 22, at 263 (noting jury's discomfort with punishing black man for rape and not white woman though she consented). The only other change in the anti-rape laws in the early 19th century came in response to a potential loophole created by insufficiently broad statutory language. In Commonwealth v. Watts, 31 Va. (4 Leigh) 672 (1833), a free Negro named Watts claimed his attempt to ravish an 11-year-old white girl who had not yet reached puberty was not an attempt to ravish a white *woman* within the meaning of the 1823 statute. *Id.* at 672. The court disagreed and condemned Watts to death, *id.*, and the legislature in 1837 broadened the language of the statute to include "any white female person, infant or adult." Ch. 71, § 1, 1836–37 Va. Acts 49, 49 (1837).

221. *Quoted in* J. JOHNSTON, *supra* note 22, at 263.

rors believed that the law's result was unjust, as they did in the *Tasco Thompson* case, they upheld it.

As a by-product of laws designed to protect and preserve a racial caste system, white women did, in fact, receive far greater protection than non-white women, especially than slave women, who received no protection at all.[222] The whites valued both the bodily integrity of the white woman and the social integrity of the slave system far more highly than they valued the black or mulatto woman, who was seen primarily as something to be used: for work, for comfort, for pleasure, at will. Those black and mulatto women who were slaves were valued, by the law, in the same ways property in general was valued, as something in which the owner's rights were to be protected. The question of rights of slave women who were sexually assaulted simply did not enter the picture; it was not part of the legal landscape. Categorization as property precluded the recognition of their human rights. The rights of free black and mulatto women received scarcely more attention or recognition.

V. Conclusions

We have traced the roots of Virginia's law of racial purity and related prohibitions on interracial sex and marriage that arose during the era of slavery, and we have discussed the role played by such laws in maintaining the slave society. Unfortunately, those laws did not end with slavery. White Virginians were determined to uphold the racially based social, economic, and political hierarchy of their slave society, even after the institution of slavery had been outlawed.

Before emancipation, oppression had operated largely through the institution of slavery, but, as we have noted, slave status was technically independent of race. There were the anomalies of free blacks and of slaves who were visibly white. These people interfered with a perfect correlation of race and status. Oppression thus operated partly in terms of race and partly in terms of slave status.

After emancipation, there was no special status of slave and oppression became entirely racial. Thus, all those identified as Negro or mulatto had a special low status and were subject to special disabilities and oppression. As race became the sole means of identifying those who belonged to the lower caste, the legal definition of race became more exclusive and maintenance of white racial purity became more important.

In the early twentieth century, Virginians made the first change in their definition of mulatto in 125 years. From the Act of 1785 to 1910, a mulatto, or "colored" person[223] was someone who had one-fourth or more Negro blood.[224] In 1910, that category was expanded to include anyone with one-sixteenth or more

---

222. *See supra* note 204, last ¶.
223. Shortly after the Civil War, in 1866, the legislature shifted from the word "mulatto" to "colored" but continued with the same proportion of one-fourth or more. Ch. 17, § 1, 1865–66 Va. Acts 84, 84 (1866).
224. *See supra* notes 49–67 and accompanying text.

Negro blood, and many people previously classified as white became legally colored.[225] Then, in 1924, in a statute frankly entitled "Preservation of Racial Integrity," the legislators for the first time defined "white" rather than "mulatto" or "colored."[226] The statute, which forbade a white person to marry any non-white, defined "white" as someone who had "no trace whatsoever of any blood other than Caucasian" or no more than one-sixteenth American Indian blood.[227] In 1930, the Virginia legislature defined "colored" in a similar, though slightly less restrictive, way as any "person in whom there is ascertainable any negro blood."[228] As we have noted, these exclusive definitions represented an unattainable ideal, as the white population had in fact been a racially mixed population for hundreds of years.

Virginia also continued the ban on interracial marriage, making it a felony,[229] until the United States Supreme Court declared the law unconstitutional in *Loving v. Virginia*[230] in 1967. Far from having abated, the sentiment against interracial marriage expressed by the Virginia trial court in that case was at least as strong as that of the Virginia legislature in 1691 when it first outlawed interracial marriage, referring to the "abominable mixture and spurious issue" that it produced.[231] The myth of white racial purity also was invoked in *Loving*. Once used to support a slave society, this myth still survived a hundred years after slavery's demise to support the racial hierarchy that white Virginians tried to maintain.[232]

The following excerpts from the opinion of Virginia Circuit Court Judge Leon

---

225. Ch. 357, § 49, 1910 Va. Acts 581.
226. Ch. 371, § 5, 1924 Va. Acts 534.
227. *Id.*
228. Ch. 85, § 67, 1930 Va. Acts 97.
229. Ch. VII, § 8, 1877–78 Va. Acts 302 (1877).
230. 388 U.S. 1 (1967).
231. Act XVI, 3 LAWS OF VA. 86, 86 (Hening 1691).
232. The elusive search for a satisfactory definition of race still persists. The struggles of the U.S. Department of Labor to identify members of protected groups without establishing strict definitions can be seen in their current employment practices guidelines. The Department's solution is to use culturally accepted criteria without identifying what those criteria are. Instead, the guidelines merely say that the observers must be "adept" at judging race:

> A visual survey may be the most practical and secure way of identifying the race or sex of an individual . . . but the observer would need to be adept to the characterizations of each racial group. Help in this area might be obtained from friends or acquaintances of the individual who would possibly be able to determine to which group the individual is regarded by persons in the local community as belonging.
>
> Skin coloring is a prohibited basis for decision making, and it is also not a reliable means of racial identification. Some persons with dark skins are to be classified according to their culture or ethnic origin, as indicated below.
>
> Racial/ethnic minorities—Scientific definitions of race or anthropological origin are not generally of use in categorizing racial/ethnic minorities. As noted above, the enforcement agencies permit inclusion of individuals in the racial or ethnic group they appear to belong, to identify with, or are regarded in the community as belonging to. . . . The category "black" would apply to some persons from Central and South America, such as Brazil,

Bazile,[233] in *Loving* in 1965, exemplify the legal, religious, and philosophical rationale embraced by Virginia judges and legislators for some three centuries when they spoke of racial purity and interracial sex:

> Parties [to an interracial marriage are] guilty of a most serious crime.
>   . . . . Almighty God created the races, white, black, yellow, malay, and red, and he [sic] placed them on separate continents. And but for the interference with his arrangement there would be no cause for such marriages. The fact that he separated the races shows that he did not intend for the races to mix. The awfulness of the offense [of interracial marriage] is shown by the fact . . . [that] the code makes the contracting of a marriage between a white person and any colored person a felony. Conviction of a felony is a serious matter. You lose your political rights, and only the government has the power to restore them. And as long as you live you will be known as a felon. "The moving finger writes and moves on and having writ / Nor all your piety nor all your wit / Can change one line of it."[234]

Guyana, Surinam, or Trinidad, whose origins are the black racial groups of Africa, even though they may have adopted other cultures.

Employment Practices Guide (CCH) ¶ 403, at 606 (1987).

233. Transcript of Record at 8, *reproduced in* Loving v. Virginia, 388 U.S. 1, Appendix at 33 (1967) [hereinafter Transcript of Record].

234. *Loving*, 388 U.S. at 3, Appendix at 42.

Richard and Mildred Loving left Virginia to evade its miscegenation laws, married in Washington, D.C., and returned to the state to live together as husband and wife. Richard was described as white and Mildred as colored. They were convicted, on guilty pleas, and each was given a 25-year suspended sentence, if they left the state and if they would never return together to the state during that period. *Id.* at 2–3.

The statutes involved were sections 20–54 and 20–57 of the Virginia Code. Section 20–57 provided: "Marriages void without decree.—All marriages between a white person and a colored person shall be absolutely void without any decree of divorce or the legal process." VA. CODE ANN. § 20–57 (1960 Repl. Vol.). Section 20–54 of the Virginia Code provided:

> Intermarriage prohibited; meaning of term "white persons"—It shall hereafter be unlawful for any white person in this State to marry any save a white person, or a person with no other admixture of blood than white and American Indian. For the purpose of this chapter, the term "white person" shall apply only to such person as has no trace whatever of any blood other than Caucasian; but persons who have one-sixteenth or less of the blood of the American Indian and have no other non-Caucasic blood shall be deemed to be white persons. All laws heretofore passed and now in effect regarding the intermarriage of white and colored persons shall apply to marriages prohibited by this chapter.

Id. § 20–54.

The exception for persons with less than one-sixteenth "of the blood of the American Indian" is apparently accounted for, in the words of a tract issued by the Registrar of the State Bureau of Vital Statistics, by "the desire of all to recognize as an integral and honored part of the white race the descendants of John Rolfe and Pocahontas." Plecker, *The New Family and Race Improvement*, 17 VA. HEALTH BULL., Extra No. 12, at 25–26 (New Family Series No. 5, 1925), *cited in* Wadlington, *supra* note 48, at 1202 n. 93.

Section 1–14 of the Virginia Code provided:

> Colored persons and Indians defined—Every person in whom there is ascertainable any

The judge concluded that there was no constitutional basis, state or federal, to invalidate Virginia's prohibition of interracial marriages.[235]

> Negro blood shall be deemed and taken to be a colored person, and every person not a colored person having one fourth or more of American Indian blood shall be deemed an American Indian; except that members of Indian tribes existing in this Commonwealth having one fourth or more of Indian blood and less than one sixteenth of Negro blood shall be deemed tribal Indians.

VA. CODE ANN. § 1–14 (1960 Repl. Vol.).

Judge Bazile's opinion seems inconsistent with the more humanitarian values of post–World War II America—particularly since it was written after the seminal decision in Brown v. Board of Education, 347 U.S. 483 (1954)—and supports the finding that racism was still very vigorous in the Virginia judiciary.

235. Transcript of Record, *supra* note 233, at 12–15. Other court opinions that upheld the validity of antimiscegenation laws include: State v. Pass, 59 Ariz. 16, 121 P.2d 882 (1942); Jackson v. City & County of Denver, 109 Colo. 196, 124 P.2d 240 (1942); In re Shun T. Takahashi's Estate, 113 Mont. 490, 129 P.2d 217 (1942); In re Paquet's Estate, 101 Or. 393, 200 P. 911 (1921); *see also* Dodson v. State, 61 Ark. 57, 31 S.W. 977 (1895); Scott v. Georgia, 39 Ga. 321 (1869); State v. Jackson, 80 Mo. 175, 50 Am. Rep. 499 (1883); State v. Kennedy, 76 N.C. 251, 22 Am. Rep. 683 (1873); Lonas v. State, 50 Tenn. (3 Heiskell) 287 (1871); Frasher v. State, 3 Tex. Crim. App. 263, 30 Am. Rep. 131 (1877).

For other cases that did not involve interracial sex or interracial marriage but in which the court nevertheless cited or relied on antimiscegenation statutes, see Harris v. City of Louisville, 165 Ky. 559, 117 S.W. 472 (1915) (housing); Hopkins v. City of Richmond, 117 Va. 692 (1915) (housing); Plessy v. Ferguson, 163 U.S. 537 (1896) (separate but equal transportation); Civil Rights Cases, 109 U.S. 3 (1883) (public accommodation).

One of the most extensive racist explications of the fear of interracial mixture occurs in an education case, Berea College v. Commonwealth, 123 Ky. 209, 94 S.W. 623 (1906). A 1904 Kentucky criminal statute prohibited any person or institution from teaching whites and blacks within a distance of 25 miles of each other. *Id.* at 213, 94 S.W. at 623–24. In upholding the portion of the statute that prohibited integrated education, the Kentucky Supreme Court stated:

> The separation of the human family into races, distinguished no less by color than by temperament and other qualities, is as certain as anything in nature. Those of us who believe that all of this was divinely ordered have no doubt that there was wisdom in the provision; albeit we are unable to say with assurance why it is so. Those who see in it only nature's work must also concede that in this order, as in all others in nature, there is an unerring justification. There exists in each race a homogenesis by which it will perpetually reproduce itself, if unadulterated. Its instinct is gregarious. As a check there is another, an antipathy to other races, which some call race prejudice. This is nature's guard to prevent amalgamation of the races. A disregard of this antipathy to the point of mating between the races is unnatural, and begets a resentment in the normal mind. It is incompatible to the continued being of the races, and is repugnant to their instincts. So such mating is universally regarded with disfavor. In the lower animals this quality may be more effective in the preservation of distinct breeds. But among men conventional decrees in the form of governmental prescripts are resorted to in aid of right conduct to preserve the purity of blood. No higher welfare of society can be thought of than the preservation of the best qualities of manhood of all its races. If then it is a legitimate exercise of the police power of government to prevent the mixing of the races in cross-breeding; it would seem to be equally within the same power to regulate that character of association which tends to a breach of the main desideratum—the purity of racial blood. In less civilized society the stronger would probably annihilate the weaker race. Humane civilization is endeavoring to fulfill nature's

The post–Civil War Virginia courts had previously upheld the miscegenation laws because they assertedly were based on the "laws of God and the laws of property, morality and social order . . . [that] have been exercised by all civilized governments in all ages of the world."[236] In 1955, the Virginia Supreme Court adopted the theories of other courts that had declared miscegenation laws were valid because "the natural law which forbids their intermarriage and the social amalgamation which leads to a corruption of races is as clearly divine as that which imparted to them different natures."[237]

The Virginia Supreme Court then declared the state's miscegenation statutes were constitutionally valid:

[They] preserve the racial integrity of its citizens, . . . regulate the marriage relation so that it shall not have a mongrel breed of citizens . . . [and] prevent the obliteration of racial pride, [that would] permit the corruption of blood [and] weaken or destroy the quality of its citizenship. Both sacred and secular history teach that nations and races have better advanced in human progress when they cultivated their own distinctive characteristics and culture and developed their own peculiar genius.[238]

By 1965, when the *Loving* case was tried, many courts both in the North and the South had expressed fears about the "social amalgamation" of the races and the necessity of racial purity.[239] Some states had opposed interracial marriages and interracial sex "to prevent breaches of the basic concepts of sexual decency."[240]

---

edicts as to the preservation of race identity in a different way. Instead of one exterminating the other; it is attempted to so regulate their necessary intercourse as to preserve each in its integrity.

Id. at 221–22, 94 S.W. at 626.

236. Kinney v. Commonwealth, 71 Va. (30 Gratt.) 284, 285 (1878).

237. Naim v. Naim, 197 Va. 80, 84, 87 S.E.2d 749, 752 (1956). *Naim* involved a Chinese male and a white female who had a valid marriage ceremony in North Carolina and who returned to Virginia to reside as husband and wife.

238. *Id.* at 90, 87 S.E.2d at 756.

239. In 1995, "[m]ore than half of the States of the Union [had] miscegenation statutes." *Id.* at 84, 87 S.E.2d at 753. By 1966, 16 states (including Virginia) still outlawed interracial marriages. The Supreme Court in Loving v. Virginia, 388 U.S. 1 (1967), listed these state statutes and constitutions. They were, in addition to Virginia:

Alabama, ALA. CONST., Art. 4, § 102, Ala. Code, tit. 14, § 360 (1958); Arkansas, Ark. Stat. Ann. § 55–104 (1947); Delaware, Del. Code Ann., tit. 13 § 101 (1953); Florida, FLA. CONST., art. 16 § 24, Fla. Stat. § 741.11 (1965); Georgia, Ga. Code Ann. § 53–106 (1961); Kentucky, Ky. Rev. Stat. Ann. § 402.020 (Supp. 1966); Louisiana, La. Rev. Stat. § 1479 (1950); Mississippi, MISS. CONST., art. 14, § 263, Miss. Code Ann. § 459 (1956); Missouri, Mo. Rev. Stat. § 451.020 (Supp. 1966); North Carolina, N.C. CONST., art. XIV, § 8, N.C. Gen. Stat. § 14–181 (1953); Oklahoma, Okla. Stat., tit. 43, § 12 (Supp. 1965); South Carolina, S.C. CONST., art. 11, § 14, Tenn. Code Ann. § 36–402 (1955); Texas, Tex. Pen. Code, art. 492 (1952); West Virginia, W. Va. Code Ann. § 4697 (1961).

Id. at 6 n.5.

240. McLaughlin v. Florida, 379 U.S. 184, 193 (1964). The Supreme Court, however, did not agree

The concerns expressed by the many state legislatures that at various times prohibited interracial marriage have roots that go back three centuries in America. The prohibitions against interracial marriage were part of a long-standing aversion to interracial sex, marital and non-marital.

In 1944, twenty-three years before the United States Supreme Court declared miscegenation laws unconstitutional, the sociologist Gunnar Myrdal wrote:

> The ban on intermarriage has the highest place in the white man's rank order of social segregation and discrimination. Sexual segregation is the most pervasive form of segregation, and the concern about "race purity" is, in a sense, basic. No other way of crossing the color line is so attended by the emotion commonly associated with violating a social taboo as intermarriage and extra-marital relations between a Negro man and a white woman. No excuse for other forms of social segregation and discrimination is so potent as the one that sociable relations on an equal basis between members of the two races *may possibly* lead to intermarriage.[241]

Indeed, the issue of interracial sex and interracial marriage seems to have been more troublesome to the U.S. Supreme Court than even the issue of racial integration of public schools.[242]

---

with the state legislature that a statute prohibiting interracial cohabitation was necessary to preserve "sexual decency"; it concluded that the Florida statute violated the equal protection clause. *Id.* at 196.

More than a century before Judge Bazile's opinion, Chief Justice Roger Brook Taney, in Dred Scott v. Sanford, 60 U.S. (19 How.) 393 (1857), relied heavily on the existence of antimiscegenation laws as evidence that blacks were of an inferior class, that blacks could not be citizens of the United States, and that blacks had "no rights which the white man was bound to respect." *Id.* at 413. Taney's first legislative reference was to the Massachusetts laws of 1786 and 1705 which "forbids the marriage of any white person with any Negro, Indian or mulatto." *Id.*

241. G. Myrdal, An American Dilemma 606 (1944) (emphasis in original). *But cf.* O. Cox, Caste, Class and Race 386–387, 526–527 (1959), *cited in* D. Bell, Race, Racism and American Law 268–69 (2d ed. 1973) (segregation motivated by whites' desire to continue to exploit blacks economically).

242. *See generally* D. Bell, *supra* note 241, at 258–94 (selected articles discussing interracial sex and the law). Professor Bell has written:

> As late as 1955, in Naim v. Naim, the Supreme Court of Appeals of Virginia upheld its state's anti-miscegenation statute on the grounds that the legislature had complete power to control the vital institution of marriage. While its decision came after Brown v. Board of Education, the Virginia Court found that precedent a comfort rather than an obstacle to its conclusion. It noted that Brown found education a "foundation of good citizenship," but that so lofty a status was hardly deserved by interracial marriage. In short, the Virginia court literally challenged the Supreme Court to reverse its Naim v. Naim decision. Still hoping that the nation might accept and comply with Brown I and its "all deliberate speed" compliance mechanism set out in Brown II, the Supreme Court was in no mood for extending the racial revolution to the ever sensitive area of interracial sex. In a decision that Professor Herbert Wechsler condemned as "wholly without basis in law," the Supreme Court, after hearing oral argument in the Naim case, decided the record was incomplete with respect to the domicile of the parties (a white woman and Chinese man had been married in North Carolina and then returned to reside in Virginia), remanding the case to the Virginia court for a further remand to the trial court. On remand, the Virginia Court

The issues of racial purity and interracial sex form part of a background of a far broader process of debasement of blacks that uses the law to treat blacks more harshly than similarly situated whites.[243] The societal problem goes

---

of Appeals refused to comply with the mandate, concluding that there was no Virginia procedure available to reopen the case. Requested to recall the remand, the Supreme Court instead dismissed the appeal on the grounds that the second Virginia decision left the case devoid of a substantial federal question.

The Supreme Court's performance in Naim v. Naim may be explained as a "prudent avoidance" of an obvious test case. Prudence of that character caused substantial sacrifice earlier when the Supreme Court refused, only a few months after the decision in Brown v. Board of Education, to review the conviction under Alabama's miscegenation law of a black man who married a white woman.

Id. at 56–57 (footnotes omitted).

Philip Elman, who was on the staff of the U.S. Solicitor General from 1944 to 1961 and who handled all Supreme Court civil rights cases in which the United States was a party or an amicus curae, discusses Naim v. Naim as follows:

I first heard of that case after the Supreme Court had decided *Brown v. Board of Education* in 1954. . . .

Now, at that time the opposition to *Brown v. Board of Education* in southern states was very great. . . . And over and over again, the fear was expressed that *Brown* was going to lead to "mongrelization" of the races. The notion was that little black boys would be sitting next to little white girls in school, and the next thing would be intermarriage and worse. This was terrible stuff to be expressing, yet it was being said not only by the demagogues, the Bilbos and Talmadges, but also by more "respectable" southern politicians as a way of galvanizing opposition to the Supreme Court's decision.

Well, I knew that the last thing in the world the Justices wanted to deal with at that time was the question of interracial marriage. Of course, if they had to, they unquestionably would hold that interracial marriage could not be prohibited consistently with *Brown v. Board of Education*, but they weren't ready to confront that question. The timing was all wrong. . . .

[Solicitor General Simon Sobel and Justice Felix Frankfurter agreed with this conclusion.] In due course, the appeal was filed and the Supreme Court in a brief per curiam order dismissed it and sent the case back to the Virginia Court of Appeals on the ground that the record did not clearly present the constitutional issue. Now that was a specious ground. The record did present the constitutional issue clearly and squarely, but the Court wanted to duck it. And if the Supreme Court wants to duck, nothing can stop it from ducking.

And so the case went back to the Virginia Court of Appeals. . . . The Supreme Court again refused to take the case, on the ground that it failed properly to present a federal constitutional question. So that was the end of *Naim v. Naim*.

A decade later, when the climate was more agreeable and there were no longer factors justifying any further delay, the Supreme Court—in a case that very aptly was titled *Loving v. Virginia*—unanimously held that racial miscegenation laws are unconstitutional.

Elman, *The Solicitor General's Office, Justice Frankfurter, And Civil Rights Litigation, 1946–1960: An Oral History*, 100 HARV. L. REV. 845–47 (1987) (emphasis in original) (footnotes omitted).

243. In dissenting from the Supreme Court's conclusion that statistical evidence could not be used to consider whether the death penalty in Georgia was disproportionately imposed on black defendants who had been convicted of killing white victims, Justice Brennan wrote:

At some point in this case, Warren McCleskey doubtless asked his lawyer whether a jury was likely to sentence him to die. A candid reply to this question would have been dis-far beyond the scope of this Article[244] and beyond the boundaries of this country.[245]

In this Article, we discuss the evolution of the concepts of racial purity, interracial sex, and interracial marriage in colonial and antebellum Virginia, but we

---

turbing. First, counsel would have to tell McCleskey that few of the details of the crime or of McCleskey's past criminal conduct were more important than the fact that this victim was white. Furthermore, counsel would feel bound to tell McCleskey that defendants charged with killing white victims in Georgia are 4.3 times as likely to be sentenced to death as defendants charged with killing blacks. In addition, frankness would compel the disclosure that it was more likely than not that the race of McCleskey's victim would determine whether he received a death sentence: 6 of every 11 defendants convicted of killing a white person would not have received the death penalty if their victims had been black, while, among defendants with aggravating and mitigating factors comparable to McCleskey, 20 of every 34 would not have been sentenced to die if their victims had been black. Finally, the assessment would not be complete without the information that cases involving black defendants and white victims are more likely to result in a death sentence than cases featuring any other racial combination of defendant and victim. The story could be told in a variety of ways, but McCleskey would not fail to grasp its essential narrative line: there was a significant chance that race would play a prominent role in determining if he lived or died.

McCleskey v. Kemp, 481 U.S. 279, 320–21 (1987) (Brennan, J., dissenting) (citations omitted).

244. These issues are also part of a larger process of denigration of both black and white women in American society. On the issue of gender, though in a somewhat different context, the United States Supreme Court stated as recently as 1974 that women in America have been victimized by either "overt discrimination . . . or a socialization process of a *male dominated culture.*" Kahn v. Shevin, 416 U.S. 351, 353 (1974) (emphasis added). Even the famed egalitarian Thomas Jefferson purportedly believed "that women should be neither seen nor heard in society's decisionmaking councils," Frontiero v. Richardson, 411 U.S. 677, 684 n.13 (1973). Jefferson reportedly stated that, "were our state a pure democracy, there would still be excluded from our deliberations . . . women, who, to prevent depravation of morals and ambiguity of issues, should not mix promiscuously in gatherings of men." *Quoted in* M. GRUBERG, WOMEN IN AMERICAN POLITICS 4 (1968). *See generally* E. Brooks Higginbotham, *Beyond The Sound of Silence: Afro-American Women in History,* 1 GENDER & HIST. 50 (1989) (discussing effect of race on nature and intensity of discrimination against women in United States); *see also* Burnham, *An Impossible Marriage: Slave Law and Family Law,* 5 LAW & INEQUALITY 187, 199 (1987) (slave women deemed sexual property of owner, available for sexual abuse by owner, his sons, the overseer, or any other white male); Scales-Trent, *Black Woman and the Constitution: Finding Our Place, Asserting Our Rights,* 24 HARV. C.R.-C.L.L. REV. 9, 26–27 (1989) (arguing for distinct legal classification of black women, separate from black males and white women, due to unique oppression suffered by this group throughout history).

On the issue of race, the National Advisory Commission on Civil Disorder observed: "What white Americans have never fully understood—but what the Negro can never forget—is that white society is deeply implicated in the ghetto. White institutions created it, white institutions maintain it, and white society condones it." REPORT OF THE NATIONAL ADVISORY COMMISSION ON CIVIL DISORDER 2 (N.Y. Times ed. 1968).

245. In many ways, the pronouncements of Judge Bazile in *Loving* are indistinguishable from the racist views that have been and are now being advocated by many supporters of South African apartheid. In fact, South Africa did not enact miscegenation statutes until 1949, and government spokesmen justified their proposed statute on the ground that some 30 states in the United States of America had similar laws:

submit that these concepts were part of the root of American racism that has entangled almost every aspect of American society.[246]

> Look at the experience of other countries in this very same sphere of mixed marriage. Is it not something for the other side to think about that in thirty out of the forty-eight States of the United States they have legislation on similar lines to this? Is it not an argument to show that it is no reason for discarding such legislation, because it is not so effective as one would like it to be? I take it the difficulty is as great there as it is here, but thirty states have decided on legislation on these lines; thirty states have found it necessary to take legislative steps to keep down this social evil.

Union of South Africa, 68 DEBATES OF THE HOUSE OF ASSEMBLY, col. 6493 (25 May 1949) (statement of the Minister of the Interior, Union of South Africa) [hereinafter Minister's remarks]; *see also id.* at 6498, 6506 (other references to the United States miscegenation laws).

The Prohibition of Mixed Marriages Act of 1949, which forbids marriages between "a European and a non-European" and provides that any union entered into in contravention of this law "shall be void and of no effect," was one of the first laws to be passed by the National Party Government after it came to power. Act 55 (S. Af. 1949) (amended by Act 21 of 1968), *cited in* J. DUGARD, *supra* note 73, at 68–71. The law also made it a criminal offense for a marriage officer to perform an interracial marriage ceremony. Before 1949, mixed marriages were rare in South Africa and averaged fewer than one hundred per year between 1943 and 1946, but the South African government wished to legislate against such marriages in order to prevent coloreds from "infiltrating" the dominant white group by marriage. Minister's remarks, *supra,* at 6493 (reminding the South African legislature that "the numerical position [of whites] in the United States of America, in those thirty states [banning interracial marriage] is not half or a quarter so serious as the position in South Africa"). For a general discussion of South African miscegenation laws, see J. DUGARD, *supra* note 73, at 68–71. Dugard discusses the Act at pages 68–69. For a more detailed comparative analysis of United States and South African legal policies, see Higginbotham, Racism in American and South African Courts: Similarities and Differences (draft manuscript) (copy on file at *The Georgetown Law Journal*).

246. This entanglement, of course, starts with slavery, *see* A. HIGGINBOTHAM, *supra* note 3, at 40–47, 58–60 (discussing white male domination and interracial sexual relations in the context of the legalized debasement of blacks in Virginia during the colonial period), but it pervades contemporary American society as well:

Employment: Griggs v. Duke Power Co., 401 U.S. 424, 436 (1971) (invalidated use of intelligence test unrelated to terms of employment); Steele v. Louisville & N.R.R., 323 U.S. 192, 208 (1944) (labor organization may not discriminate on the basis of race when representing employees).

Housing: Tillman v. Wheaton-Haven Recreation Ass'n, 410 U.S. 431, 440 (1973) (swimming pool association forbidden to use geographic criteria for membership); Jones v. Alfred H. Mayer Co., 392 U.S. 409, 413 (1968) (unconstitutional to discriminate on the basis of race in selling lots in a private subdivision); Shelley v. Kraemer, 334 U.S. 1, 23 (1948) (racially restrictive covenants invalid).

Education: Swann v. Charlotte-Mecklenburg Bd. of Educ., 402 U.S. 1, 32 (1971) (interdistrict school busing ordered as remedy for school segregation); Brown v. Board of Educ., 347 U.S. 483, 496 (1954) (separate education for blacks and whites violated equal protection clause); McLaurin v. Oklahoma State Regents, 339 U.S. 637, 641 (1950) (graduate school segregational seating violated equal protection clause); Sweatt v. Painter, 339 U.S. 629, 636 (1950) (educational opportunities for black law students in Texas unequal, in violation of equal protection clause).

Voting: South Carolina v. Katzenbach, 383 U.S. 301, 326 (1966) (implementation of 1965 voting rights act in which Congress invalidated discrimination on the basis of race in voting); Reynolds v. Sims, 377 U.S. 533, 545 (1964) (apportionment of legislature found irrational); Gray v. Sanders, 372 U.S. 368, 379 (1963) (one man-one vote invalidates weighted voting that granted

The Enforcement of
Anti-Miscegenation Laws*

RANDALL KENNEDY

Hybridism is heinous. Impurity of races is against the law of nature. Mulattoes are monsters. The law of nature is the law of God. The same law which forbids consanguineous amalgamation forbids ethnical amalgamation. Both are incestuous. Amalgamation is incest.

Henry Hughes, Treatise on Sociology 31 *(1860)*

[Anti-miscegenation laws] make the father a nominal criminal, the mother a legal prostitute, and the children legal bastards in the arms of their recognized parents. They deprive the mothers and innocent children of the proper protection of the laws of their country, and nothing more . . . These State laws prohibiting the intermarriage of the two races do not prevent amalgamation, but encourage prostitution and abandonment of offspring. They are, therefore evil, and only evil.

Senator James Harlan, Cong. Globe, 42 2d Cong Sess., pt.1 at 878 *(1872)*

White race-purity is the corner-stone of our civilization. Its mongrelization with non-white blood, particularly with negro blood, would spell the downfall of our civilization. This is a matter of both national and racial life and death, and no efforts should be spared to guard against the greatest of all perils—the peril of miscegenation.

Letter from Lothrop Stoddard to John Powell, Feb. 1, 1924, quoted in Paul A. Lombardo, Miscegenation, Eugenics, and Racism: Historical

---

disproportionate power to rural areas); Baker v. Carr, 369 U.S. 186, 236–37 (1962) (existing legislative apportionment schemes held to violate 14th amendment).

Public accommodations: Katzenbach v. McClung, 379 U.S. 294, 304 (1964) (private restaurant that served out-of-state patrons sufficiently in interstate commerce to be within Civil Rights Act of 1964's prohibition of racial discrimination); Heart of Atlanta Motel, Inc. v. United States, 379 U.S. 241, 293 (1964) (public accommodations provisions of Civil Rights Act of 1954 are valid under the commerce clause); Burton v. Wilmington Parking Auth., 365 U.S. 715, 726 (1961) (refusal of private restaurant in a public building to serve on account of race violates equal protection clause).

Racial violence: Griffin v. Breckenridge, 403 U.S. 88, 107 (1971) (thirteenth amendment right to travel impinged); United States v. Johnson, 390 U.S. 563, 567 (1968) (criminal to intimidate a citizen in the free exercise or enjoyment of a constitutional right).

* This previously unpublished essay is part of a new book project by Randall Kennedy.

Footnotes to *Loving v. Virginia, 21 University of
California at Davis Law Review 421, 432 (1988)*.

Half an hour after midnight, on a chilly evening in 1929 in Sheffield, Alabama, two white police officers barged into a home where they found Elijah Fields, a fifty-year-old black man, in the company of Ollie Roden, a twenty-five-year-old white woman. The police maintained that they knocked on the door for about five minutes without receiving any response before entering Fields's house. When they did, they encountered Fields and Roden in an unlit bedroom. Both were fully dressed, except that she wore no shoes. Asked why he had failed to respond to the knocking, Fields said that he had been afraid to do so.

Fields and Roden were both indicted for miscegenation.[1] Under Alabama law it was a felony for a black person and a white person to intermarry or cohabit. At trial, Fields's witnesses, including Roden's parents, portrayed the episode as one big misunderstanding. Fields and Roden were not carrying on an affair. Rather, Fields had simply been acting as a good samaritan. Roden's father had asked Fields—a man whom he had known for many years—to transport his daughter from a hospital to a boarding house. Fields was in the process of doing so when intercepted by the police. The defense also emphasized Roden's physical infirmities. Some unidentified malady caused her feet and legs to be covered with open sores. That, apparently, is why she was wearing no shoes at the time of her arrest. Uncontradicted testimony also established that she was incontinent and suffering from an unceasing menstruation.

The prosecution emphasized the presumptive suspiciousness of finding a man and a woman together in an unlit bedroom in the man's house late at night. It also noted that police had previously seen Fields and Roden riding together alone in his car and that on at least one occasion Fields had allowed Roden to steer the car, with his hand on top of hers on the steering wheel—a gesture which, in the eyes of the state's attorney, was remarkably and illicitly friendly. In his summation, Assistant Attorney General James L. Screws declared at one point, "Gentlemen of the jury, suppose it had been your daughter who was treated like this white girl was treated by this negro"; at another point he declared, "You should convict . . . in order that similar occurrences may not happen to your daughter."[2]

Judge J. Fred Johnson, Jr., told the jury that state law provided that "a white woman and a black man . . . cannot intermarry or live together in adultery or fornication and [that] it is a felony if they do so." According to the judge, the state had to prove more than that the defendants had engaged in a single act of sexual intercourse or even an occasional act of illicit sex; rather, the state had to prove that Fields and Roden had an ongoing *relationship*—that they "did live

---

1. My description of this case is based upon an opinion rendered by the Court of Appeals of Alabama (*Fields v. State*, 132 So. 605 [1931]) and upon the record of the case (Record), which is on file at the Harvard Law School Library and which contains the indictment, the judge's jury instructions, objections made by defense counsel, and the testimony offered at trial.
2. Record, 5.

together in fornication" or did otherwise intend to continue having sex when the opportunity arose.[3]

The jury convicted Fields whereupon the judge sentenced him to a two-to-three-year prison term.

The Alabama court of appeals reversed, ruling that the jury lacked an adequate evidentiary basis for its finding of guilt. "Standing alone," the court concluded, the fact that Fields and Roden were found together in Fields's home at night, "under the circumstances testified to by the arresting officers," was an insufficient basis for conviction. The court also chastised the prosecutor for making blatant appeals to racial prejudice in his summation and the trial judge for doing too little to restrain the prosecutor. "The surrounding atmosphere," the court of appeals complained, "was not conducive to a fair and impartial trial for one of appellant's race accused of such an offense."[4]

Elijah Fields's travail illustrates the way in which, not so long ago, law enforcement officials were statutorily empowered to police associations perceived to be an affront to conventional codes of racial conduct, particularly those which demanded social distance between black men and white women. Initially, the officers who arrested Elijah and Ollie probably thought the couple was in violation of state law. After the arrest, however—when officials were apprised of Ollie's illness and hospitalization and her father's request to Elijah—it is difficult to believe that they continued to think that they had stumbled upon an illegal sexual crossing of the color line. A more likely scenario is that local officials wanted to emphasize (perhaps for reasons of electoral politics) that even the *appearance* of sexual intimacy between a black man and a white woman constituted a crime. One gets the impression that by the time of trial the prosecutor's real complaint was that Elijah and Ollie had acted recklessly by comporting themselves in such a way that onlookers might get the wrong impression of their relationship.

An especially poignant moment in Fields's trial occurred when the prosecutor asked him whether he "liked" Ollie. Clearly afraid that an affirmative response would prejudice the jury, Fields replied—"I am a negro"—meaning, essentially, that he knew his rightful "place" and that his rightful place precluded him from "liking" a white woman. "I don't especially like [Miss Roden]," he replied; "I am very fond of her father, and I wanted to help him."[5]

The state court of appeals ultimately saved Fields from prison (at least temporarily) by demanding at least some semblance of due process within the administration of segregationist law. But the reversal of his conviction probably did little to alleviate the *in terrorem* affect of the prosecution and conviction. After all, the expense and anxiety associated with even a winning defense in a criminal case

---

3. Record, 1–2.
4. *Fields v. State*, 606.
5. A similar moment awaited Ollie Roden. During her testimony, she stated at one point, "I am a white woman and though greatly afflicted . . . have never thought of having sexual intercourse with a negro" (Record, 19–20).

is enough understandably to frighten people. Moreover, when an appellate court reverses a conviction, the way remains open typically for a retrial. Whether Fields was retried is unknown. But in any event, any onlooker, particularly any black male onlooker, would surely have inferred from Fields's prosecution the advisability of staying far clear from any interracial familiarity that could possibly be subject to misinterpretation.

Perhaps the most significant thing about Fields's case has to do with the precise character of his supposed "crime." That crime did not occur when people of different races merely had sex together. Courts reversed scores of convictions for criminal miscegenation based merely on episodes of interracial sex.[6] Judges insisted that the state prove the existence of some sort of relationship. Tolerant of a loveless, perhaps commercial, interracial "quickie," Alabama law was intolerant of an authentic, stable interracial romance.

Nothing more vividly reflects American racial pathologies than the tendency to use power, especially state power, to discourage interracial love. Fear of interracial love, particularly its institutionalization in marriage, has given rise to "more statutes covering a wider geographical area than any other type of racially restrictive law."[7] Initially, sex was the locus of regulation. In 1662 in one of the first anti-miscegenation statutes in what is now the United States, Virginia doubled fines for persons who engaged in interracial as opposed to intraracial fornication.[8] As the racial regulation of intimacy matured, however, officials generally chose to police marriage more closely than mere sex. Indeed, the same officials who have insisted that interracial marriage poses a dire threat to white civilization, have often resisted efforts to prevent sex across the race line, especially when the trespassing involved white men. In 1895 when delegates to the South Carolina Constitutional convention contended that a prohibition against interracial marriage should be added to the state's constitution, Robert Smalls, a black politician, responded by saying that he would assent to such a provision *if*, in addition, it provided that men who had concubines of a different race would be forever barred from political office. Smalls's proposal caused an uproar. Observers understood that it was aimed at exposing the hypocrisy of white politicians who, on the one

---

6. See *Gilbert v. State*, 23 So. 2d 22 (Alabama Court of Appeals, 1945); *State v. Brown*, 108 So. 2d 233, 235 (Louisiana Supreme Court, 1959). See also Koppelman, "Same-Sex Marriage, Choice of Law and Public Policy," 921, 950.

7. Greenberg, *Race Relations and American Law*, 353.

8. Virginia's Act XII (Hening, *Laws of Virginia* 2 [New York, 1823]), enacted December 23, 1662, provided that "if any christian shall commit fornication with a negro man or woman, hee or she so offending shall pay double the fines [regularly imposed]." Even more consequential was another section of this act which provided that children fathered by white men and born of black slave women would inherit the legal status of their mothers, thereby becoming slaves for life: "Whereas some doubts have arisen whether children got by any Englishman upon a negro woman should be slave or free, Be it therefore enacted and declared . . . that all children borne in this country shall be held bond or free only according to the condition of the mother." For an excellent discussion of the colonial history of Virginia's anti-miscegenation provisions, see Higginbotham and Kopytoff, "Racial Purity and Interracial Sex in the Law of Colonial and Antebellum Virginia." [Higginbotham and Kopytoff's article is found in this volume, pp. 81–139. —Ed.]

hand, roundly condemned "amalgamation" and, on the other, frequented black prostitutes or enjoyed black concubines. Acting pursuant to that hypocrisy, the convention defeated Smalls's amendment but supported the proposed prohibition against interracial matrimony.[9]

By that time, such laws already had a long history in America. In 1691 Virginia became the first colony to outlaw interracial marriage. "For prevention of that abominable mixture and spurious issue"—meaning mixed-race babies—the Virginia Assembly decreed that whites who married blacks, mulattoes, or Indians would be banished from the dominion forever. Next to discourage or prohibit such marriages was Maryland (1692), followed by Massachusetts (1705), followed by Pennsylvania (1725). By 1800, ten of the sixteen states then constituting the United States proscribed interracial marriages. In 1913, when Wyoming became the last state to impose a statutory discouragement or prohibition on interracial marriage, forty-one states had enacted laws at one time or another that armed public authorities and private persons with weapons with which to create and police racial divisions in matters of sex and matrimony.[10] In 1967, when the U.S. Supreme Court belatedly invalidated anti-miscegenation statutes in *Loving v. Virginia*, seventeen states still prohibited interracial marriage.[11]

From the beginnings of the eighteenth century onwards, *all* anti-miscegenation laws in British North America prohibited blacks and whites from marrying one another. Similar prohibitions were imposed upon Native Americans and people of Chinese, Japanese, Filipino, Indian, and Hawaiian ancestry. There were no laws that prohibited Christians from marrying Jews or that prohibited interethnic marriages.

In the nineteenth century, many groups that we now think of simply as ethnic "whites" were then thought of as distinct races. Hence, Jews were thought of as a discrete race as were the Irish, Italians, Hungarians, and so on. However, despite sometimes intense social discriminations based on ethnic identities—"No Irish need apply"—state governments never prohibited interethnic marriages among whites. This is an example of the unique place of *color* in American life. Many groups of all sorts have discouraged their "members" from marrying outside the group. However, the only time State power has been mobilized to prevent such unions is when authorities feared marriage across the color line.

The targets and intensities of punishments varied widely. In some states, prior to the Civil War, officials subjected only whites to punishment for crimes of interracial intimacy. This probably stemmed from two beliefs. One was that blacks were too irresponsible and inferior to punish. A second was that whites were the

9. See Williamson, *After Slavery*.

10. Alaska, Connecticut, the District of Columbia, Hawaii, Minnesota, New Hampshire, New Jersey, Vermont, and Wisconsin are the jurisdictions that never enacted anti-miscegenation laws. See Fowler, *Northern Attitudes towards Interracial Marriage*, p. 336.

11. On the evolution of anti-miscegenation laws see Martyn, "Racism in the United States"; Applebaum, "Miscegenation Statutes," 49; Weinberger, "A Reappraisal of the Constitutionality of Miscegenation Statutes," 208; Wallenstein, "Race, Marriage, and the Law of Freedom," 371; Wadlington, "The *Loving* Case," 1189.

ones responsible for protecting the purity of their bloodlines. This second belief was closely related to yet another status distinction found in antebellum laws regulating intimacy: a gender distinction under which white women were deemed to be the primary gatekeepers to white racial purity and, concomitantly, the members of the white community who could, with justice, be most severely punished for racial transgressions, including—in order of increasing perfidiousness—having sex across racial lines, marrying across racial lines, and giving birth to a mixed-race baby. The peculiar burdens imposed upon white women by racial regulations of intimacy highlight a point worth special emphasis: The racial regulation of intimacy has not only pitted colored people against white people; it has also pitted men against women, both across racial lines and within racial groups.

After the Civil War, to comply with new federal requirements for formal racial neutrality, officials in some states felt compelled to punish blacks who married interracially to the same extent as their white spouses—an ironic effect of Reconstruction.[12] Similarly ironic is that in at least some jurisdictions anti-miscegenation laws were probably enforced more stringently *after* the Civil War than before it. Slavery provided such a massive boost to the collective self-esteem of whites that many of them were willing to overlook certain infractions of racial regulations, including those that prohibited interracial romance. With the traumatic abolition of slavery, however, and the even more unsettling assertion of civil and political rights by blacks during Reconstruction, southern whites suffered a tremendous blow to their collective, racial self-esteem. Many compensated by insisting relentlessly upon an exacting observance of formal and informal rules of racial caste. The result in many places appears to have been an enhanced criminal enforcement of anti-miscegenation laws, along with every other restriction that would reinforce the lesson of white supremacy and black subordination, white purity and black contamination.[13]

Punishments for violating anti-miscegenation laws included enslavement, exile, whipping, fines, and imprisonment. Some jurisdictions punished those who performed such marriages. Not to be outdone, Mississippi criminalized not only interracial marriage but advocacy of "social equality or of intermarriage between whites and negroes."[14]

Criminal punishments were not the only means of enforcing anti-miscegenation laws. Civil liabilities played an important role as well. Some jurisdictions made interracial marriages *voidable*—meaning that a party to the union could always freely repudiate it (thereby undercutting its stability). Others made interracial marriages *void*—meaning that, in the eyes of the state, parties to such an arrange-

---

12. See *Ex parte Francois*, 9 Federal Cases 5,047 (Circuit Court, Western District, Texas 1879); Mangum, *The Legal Status of the Negro*, 241.

13. See Hodes, *White Women, Black Men*; Mills, "Miscegenation and the Free Negro in Antebellum 'Anglo' Alabama," 16. Diane Miller Sommerville shows that the same held true for responses to rape, that black men charged with raping white women generally fared better in the antebellum South than the South of the Jim Crow era. See "The Rape Myth in the Old South Reconsidered," 481.

14. See Fowler, *Northern Attitudes towards Interracial Marriage*, 393.

ment had never been married. These efforts to deprive interracial unions of legal standing had far-reaching consequences. Children of void marriages became bastards with no legal claim to their parents' estates. Women partners in void marriages had no claim upon their husbands for alimony or child support, death benefits or inheritance. A sibling who initially stood to gain little or nothing upon the death of a married brother or sister could gain a lot by proving that the deceased relative was of a different race than the bereaved spouse and that, therefore, their marriage violated state law. In that event, money that would have gone to the spouse would now go to the siblings. Because anti-miscegenation laws opened up opportunities for enrichment along these lines, the civil enforcement of such statutes was often stubborn and aggressive.

It is impossible to determine precisely how much of a difference anti-miscegenation laws made to the way in which people actually lived their lives. There are, after all, many considerations beyond fears of criminal prosecution that shape behavior. For black men in certain times and places, for instance, fear of lynching probably played a more influential role in their conduct towards white women than fear of enforcement of anti-miscegenation laws. It is also impossible to determine to what extent such laws were enforced. We do not know the incidence of unlawful miscegenation or the level of resources allocated to enforcing anti-miscegenation statutes or even the number of criminal or civil suits brought to enforce these statutes. What we do know is that hundreds of cases were decided by appellate courts, which handed down opinions that reveal scores of fascinating and poignant (albeit largely forgotten) problems that judges dealt with in all manner of contradictory ways. As we shall see, these problems vary widely. They all reflect, however, the difficulties that officials encountered in seeking to preserve or create racial "integrity"—or at least the racial integrity of those defined as "white."

Along with *integrity, purity* was a salient watchword of those who mobilized state power to prevent racial "mixing," "mongrelization," and "amalgamation." But at every turn, this impulse to maintain a strict, clean, and consistent racial order was confounded by the force and consequences of human passion, compassion, and ingenuity. The anti-miscegenation laws were unable to preserve or recreate white racial chastity; desire, humanity, and hypocrisy kept getting in the way. This is by no means a unique story.

To paraphrase George M. Fredrickson: Across the world, the anarchic nature of the human libido has always created serious problems for the guardians of racial, ethnic, and religious boundaries and privilege.[15]

Problems of Classification

One difficulty that emerges whenever authorities attempt any sort of racial regulation is the task of placing racial labels onto individuals, especially when they dispute the ascription. It is widely believed that the race line—at least the one

15. See Fredrickson, *White Supremacy*, 94.

separating "whites" from "blacks"—has been governed by a simple formula, the "one-drop rule" under which one drop of black blood is sufficient to classify a person as black. Thus, in *Who Is Black?* F. James Davis asserts that the answer in the United States has long been that "a black is any person with *any* known African black ancestry."[16]

Over the years, many governments and individuals have embraced this proposition. Several states enacted laws, for example, that expressly defined a colored person as anyone with Negro forebears or anyone displaying any discernible trace of Negro ancestry.[17] Edna Ferber's novel *Show Boat* and its Broadway musical adaptation reflect this widespread understanding. In the novel, Steve, a white man, marries Julie, a Negro passing for white. Informed that the couple is married in violation of a state anti-miscegenation statute, a Mississippi sheriff arrives to arrest Steve and Julie. Desperate to avoid arrest, Steve pricks Julie's finger and sucks some of her blood. When the sheriff approaches, Steve says, "You wouldn't call a man a white man that's got negro blood in him, would you?" "No, I wouldn't; not in Mississippi," the sheriff replies; "One drop of nigger blood makes you a nigger in these parts"—a formulation that allows the couple to go free.[18]

The one-drop rule has served various social functions and expressed powerful racial beliefs. It has prevented the formal recognition of intermediate racial castes, assuaged anxieties about feared loss of racial purity, promoted racial solidarities, and articulated disgust aimed at the very idea of racial amalgamation. For all its significance, however, the one-drop rule has by no means exercised easy or uncontested dominance. Even where the one-drop rule has governed, there remained problems of proof: How can it be determined whether that one drop is present or absent? Furthermore, authorities in some jurisdictions have created canons of racial classification that depart from the one-drop rule.

For illustration of the complexities that arose in the context of making racial identifications in criminal prosecutions aimed at enforcing state anti-miscegenation law consider *McPherson v. Commonwealth (of Virginia)* (1877)[19] and *Keith v. Commonwealth [of Virginia]* (1935).[20]

McPherson stemmed from the prosecution of Rowena McPherson and George Stewart, who were charged with having illicit sexual intercourse with each other. Although the couple had been ceremonially married, the prosecutor alleged that their marriage was void because Stewart was white and McPherson black—or at

16. See Davis, *Who Is Black*, 5.
17. See Mangum, *The Legal Status of the Negro*, 6.
18. See Edna Ferber, *Show Boat* (Garden City, N.Y.: Doubleday, Page, 1926). The law of racial classification in Mississippi varied depending on the context. Anti-miscegenation laws defined a person as black if, in terms of ancestry, he was determined to be one-eighth or more Negro. By contrast, laws governing segregation in public schools insisted upon a one-drop rule: any Negro ancestry made one black. See *Moreau v. Grendich*, 114 Miss. 560 (Mississippi Supreme Court, 1917). See also *Tucker v. Blease* 81 S.E. 668 (South Carolina Supreme Court, 1914).
19. 69 Va. (28 Gratt.) 939 (1877).
20. 165 Va. 705, 1815 E.2d 283 (1935).

least sufficiently black to be covered by Virginia's anti-miscegenation statute. At that time, Virginia classified as "colored" anyone who was more than one-quarter black. Rowena McPherson appears to have conceded that she was, to some extent, black. She maintained, however, that she was insufficiently black to be labeled properly as colored.

At trial, McPherson and Stewart were found guilty by a jury and fined. On appeal, however, their convictions were overturned. The key to the case, in the eyes of the state appellate court, was the racial identity of Rowena McPherson's great-grandmother. Everyone appears to have conceded that Rowena McPherson's other forebears were white. Her great-grandmother, however, was a "brown skin woman."[21] Had the great-grandmother been "a full-blooded African or negro whose skin is black," the court would have judged Rowena to be one-quarter black and thus a Negro and ineligible to marry Stewart.[22] However, the McPherson family argued, and the court believed, that Rowena's great-grandmother "was a half Indian—a fact confirmed by the color of her skin." That fact was important to the court because, in its view, "[i]f any part of the said residue of the [great-grandmother's] blood, however small, was derived from any source other than the . . . negro race, then Rowena McPherson cannot be a negro."[23] In reaching its conclusion, the court of appeals of Virginia did not inquire into Rowena McPherson's self-perception of her race. Nor did it inquire into what, racially, her neighbors perceived her to be. Nor did it inquire into her personal characteristics and on that basis classify her as "white" or "colored." Rather the court conducted an investigation focused solely upon the apparent racial character of her lineage.

Fifty-eight years later, Virginia prosecuted another couple—Bascomb and Reda Keith—for violating the state's prohibition against interracial marriage. That law had been broadened considerably since the prosecution of McPherson and Stewart. At the time of the earlier prosecution, a person with some—but not too much!—Negro ancestry could legitimately marry a white person. By the time the Keiths were prosecuted, however, Virginia law had been amended to define as Negro anyone "in whom there is ascertainable any negro blood."[24] In other words, by the time of the later prosecution, Virginia operated pursuant to the one-drop rule.

The prosecution of the Keiths ultimately failed, however, even under the one-drop rule. A jury convicted the couple. But the Virginia supreme court of appeals overturned the convictions. The state alleged that the mother of defendant Bascom Keith was the daughter of Pat Keith and that Pat Keith "had negro blood in his veins."[25] The court ruled that regardless of Pat Keith's race, the conviction was improper because the state had failed to prove beyond a reasonable doubt that Pat Keith was related to Bascom Keith. This was a decisive error because Bascom

21. *McPherson v. Commonwealth*, 940.
22. Ibid.
23. Ibid.
24. *Keith v. Commonwealth*, 706. On changes in Virginia statutory scheme of racial classification, see Sherman, "The Last Stand," 56, and Lombardo, "Miscegenation, Eugenics, and Racism."
25. *Keith v. Commonwealth*, 707.

Keith denied that Pat Keith was his great-grandfather. In support of this denial, Bascom's mother testified that her mother had told her that her father was one Thomas Belcher, a white man.

One should not get the impression from these two cases that prosecutions were typically foiled when defendants challenged prosecutors' racial labels. In York, South Carolina, in 1881, a couple charged with criminal miscegenation defended themselves by asserting that the woman, contrary to appearances, was really "black." At trial, the judge instructed the jury to decide all doubt as to her white ancestry "in her favor"—whereupon they found her to be white and thus found her guilty.[26] Still, what the failed prosecutions in *McPherson* and *Keith* demonstrate is that imposing racial classifications on individuals has been (and remains) a more difficult, elaborate, and varied process than is commonly understood.[27]

That point is made even more vividly in certain civil contexts in which private parties sought to enforce anti-miscegenation laws. In *Bennett v. Bennett*, Virginia Bennett challenged the will of her deceased father, Franklin Capers Bennett.[28] Virginia Bennett was Franklin Bennett's daughter by his first wife. Virginia Bennett, however, received no mention (and hence no property) pursuant to the will. Franklin Bennett left his entire estate by will to his wife, Louetta Chassereau Bennett. Virginia Bennett attacked this bequest on two grounds. First, she asserted that the marriage between Franklin and Louetta was invalid because Louetta was Franklin's niece; Louetta's father was Franklin's half-brother. Second, Virginia Bennett asserted that the marriage was invalid because Louetta Bennett was more than one-eighth Negro and thus prohibited by the state's anti-miscegenation law from marrying Franklin or any other white man. Virginia wanted to invalidate the marriage because, under state law, an individual could will no more than one-quarter of his estate to anyone other than his spouse. If it could be established that the marriage was invalid, then the woman he had believed to have been his wife would receive no more than one-fourth of his estate, and the remaining three-quarters would thus be made available to his relatives, with Virginia Bennett presumably first in line.

The supreme court of South Carolina rejected Virginia Bennett's arguments. With respect to the claim of incest, the court held that state law made the marriage voidable. Expressing disapproval of marriages between uncles and nieces, South Carolina permitted parties to such marriages to withdraw from them freely. But the state did not disapprove to the extent of declaring such marriages void—that is, devoid of legal legitimacy from the outset regardless of the wishes of the parties. Since neither Franklin nor Louetta Bennett had withdrawn from the marriage prior to Franklin's death, there was no basis, in terms of the claim of incest, to interfere with the marriage.

---

26. See Tindall, *South Carolina Negroes*, 298.
27. For discussion of contemporary problems involving racial classifications, see Ford, "Administering Identity," 1231; Hackman, "The Devil and the One-Drop Rule," 1161; Brynes, "Who Is Black Enough For You?" 205; Wright, "Who's Black, Who's White and Who Cares," 513.
28. 10 S.E.2d 23 (South Carolina Supreme Court, 1940).

The court also rejected Virginia Bennett's racial attack on the marriage. The court appears to have conceded that there was "some negro blood in [Louetta Bennett's] veins."[29] But it concluded that the marriage was nonetheless valid because Virginia had failed to prove that the white-looking Louetta was more than one-eighth Negro. In reaching this conclusion, the supreme court of South Carolina affirmatively quoted the factual findings of the trial judge whose conclusions it affirmed. These findings emphasized Louetta's reputation and her participation in activities that were by law or custom limited exclusively to whites. To the judge, it was significant that

> [u]pon the death of [Louetta's] father and mother, she was first taken into the home of white people; then she was placed in a church orphanage for white children; she was confirmed . . . as a communicant of the holy Communion Church of Charleston, a white church; she was taken from the orphanage and placed in a white home as a member of the family; she married a white man, the marriage being solemnized [in] a white church; she votes in the democratic primaries, both City and State, whose rules bar negroes from voting; her children attend the white public schools . . . ; two of her children attend the white Methodist Sunday School . . . ; the Godfather and Godmother of two of her children are Mr. and Mrs. I. M. Fishburne of Walterboro, he being the president of the Farmer's & Merchants Bank; she is generally accepted as a white person.[30]

The South Carolina supreme court simply recited these facts; it did not explain the rationale that prompted it to interpret the facts in a way favorable to Louetta's legal claim. It is worth noting, though, that in contrast to other inquiries into racial identity that we have seen—recall *McPherson* and *Keith*—the inquiry of the South Carolina supreme court did not focus on the genetic tie connecting Louetta with black ancestors. Rather the court judges focused almost exclusively on whether Louetta had been treated as a white woman by her white neighbors and whether she had acted the part of a white woman.[31]

The likely, albeit unexpressed, reasons for this focus were twofold. One was the belief that, generally speaking, in a contested case of racial identification, those who are closest to the person in question are in the best position to judge. In this case, those closest to Louetta deemed her to be white. A second and related belief was that, despite the "taint" in her bloodline, it would have been intolerably unfair to change her status—revoke her whiteness—insofar as Louetta had been perceived to be a white woman and had apparently seen herself as a white woman throughout her life. In detailing the racial checkpoints that Louetta had successfully passed—the orphanage, church, marriage, and voting booth—the South Carolina supreme court was saying implicitly that Louetta was entitled to her claim to whiteness as a matter of adverse possession. Having enjoyed that status for so long, it would now be cruel to withdraw that status from her.[32]

---

29. Ibid., 25.
30. Ibid., 33.
31. On various methods used by judges to determine a person's race, see Gross, *Litigating Whiteness*, 109.
32. Cf. Harris, "Whiteness As Property," 1707.

Moreover, apart from Louetta's own fate, the judges may have been moved a bit by concern over the fate of others around her. If the court had revoked Louetta's claim to whiteness, it would necessarily have rendered her children bastards and embarrassed the many white people with whom she had forged close and strong bonds, including her pastors and godparents.

Perhaps another reason for the court deciding the case in the way that it did was to avoid anxieties that might have arisen had the court revoked the whiteness of a woman who was so seemingly secure in her racial status as Louetta Bennett. In the aftermath of a contrary holding, any white person in South Carolina might well be prompted to peer into a mirror with new intensity and ask anxiously, "Where will it end?"—after all, countless jokes about "niggers in woodpiles" pay witness to the truth that black forebears are part of the bloodlines of many families that think of themselves as exclusively white.

Knowledge of Racial Identity

A close relative of the case in which a person denied an alleged racial identity was the case in which a person claimed not to have any knowledge of his or his partner's "real" racial identity. Three disputes that raise this issue are *Bell v. State of Texas*,[33] *Locklayer v. Locklayer*,[34] and *Wood v. Commonwealth [of Virginia]*.[35]

Katie Bell, a white woman, and Calvin Bell, a black man, were married in 1891 but had been living together since at least 1880. They had five children. Their relationship apparently attracted little attention until 1893 when they became defendants in a civil lawsuit that had nothing to do with their marriage. During the trial of that suit, however, they testified that they were married to one another. Shortly thereafter, officials prosecuted them for violating the state's anti-miscegenation law.[36] Calvin was tried but acquitted. Katie challenged her conviction on the grounds that the acquittal of her husband ought to have precluded her prosecution. Her theory appears to have been that, with miscegenation, either both defendants are guilty or neither is guilty. The Texas court of criminal appeals disagreed, noting that while "the woman may have known she was white . . . the negro [may] have been ignorant of the fact; one, therefore, may be innocent, and the other guilty."[37] The court implicitly declared, in other words that, at least in Texas, to be guilty of miscegenation, one had to know that one's marriage partner was of a different race.

Locklayer v. Locklayer arose from a petition by a white woman, Nancy Locklayer, who sought to claim as a widow the estate of Jackson Locklayer, her deceased husband, a black man. The executor of the estate, J. R. Locklayer, objected

33. 25 S.W. 769 (Texas Court of Criminal Appeals, 1894).
34. 139 Ala. 354 (1903).
35. 159 Va. 963 (1932).
36. See Robinson, "The Antimiscegenation Conversation," 43–44.
37. *Bell v. State of Texas*, 769.

on the grounds that Alabama law prohibited interracial marriages and therefore that Nancy Locklayer was owed none of the legal benefits bestowed upon widows. Nancy Locklayer responded by maintaining that even if Jackson Locklayer had been a Negro, she believed reasonably and in good faith that he was white on the basis of his appearance and of his representations to her. She argued that as an innocent victim of her husband's misrepresentations she should not be deemed to have violated state law. The Alabama supreme court, however, declined to reverse the trial court's finding of fact that Nancy Locklayer did not really believe her husband to be a white man. After all, she knew that her "husband's" first wife had been, in the court's words, "a negress," and she knew as well that a Negro minister officiated at the ceremony at which she was "married."[38] Given the strict segregation of whites and blacks in Alabama society at that time, these blurrings of the color line would surely have put any reasonable observer on notice that something highly unusual was afoot. After all, no typical Alabama white man in 1903 would have permitted himself to be married by a Negro minister! The court appears to have reasoned that, under the circumstances, it was simply implausible to think that a white woman would sincerely believe that she was entering into a normal—that is, intraracial—marriage.

Ruling against Nancy Locklayer, the Alabama supreme court cleared the way for Jackson's black relatives to inherit his estate. Whites were typically the beneficiaries in private actions enforcing anti-miscegenation statutes. *Locklayer v. Locklayer* shows, however, that black people, too, on occasion made use of the laws that prohibited marriage across the race line.

The intersection of racial classification and marriage was illuminated in a very different light in *Wood v. Commonwealth*, a case of alleged criminal seduction. In 1931 in Rockingham County, Virginia, Leonard H. Wood was convicted and sentenced to two and one-half years in prison far having criminally seduced Dorothy Short. Wood's crime consisted of his having sex with Short ("an unmarried female of previously chaste character") on the basis of his promise to marry her, followed by his refusal to carry through with that promise.

At trial, Leonard sought to defend himself by showing that Short was colored. He argued that since she was colored it was unlawful for him to marry her since Virginia prohibited interracial marriage and that his promise (even if there was one, which he denied) was incapable of being performed. At the urging of the prosecution, the trial judge prevented Woods from delving into Short's racial background.

The Virginia supreme court of appeals ruled that the trial judge committed reversible error. It vacated the conviction and remanded the case for a new trial, holding that the trial court should have permitted the defendant to attempt to ascertain whether Short was *aware* that she was colored. According to the court, proving simply that Short was colored would be an insufficient defense—in the same way that proving that a man was already married would be insufficient to insulate him from a charge of criminal seduction. In both cases there would exist

---

38. *Locklayer v. Locklayer*, 358.

a legal impediment to marrying the seduced woman. In the court's view, however, such impediments would not lessen a man's moral turpitude. On the other hand, if a defendant could show that the woman was aware that marriage was impossible because he was already married or because he was of a different race than she, such a showing would decisively undercut the main impetus for seduction prosecutions—protecting the "pure, innocent, and inexperienced woman who may be led astray from the paths of rectitude and virtue by the arts and wiles of the seducer under promise of marriage."[39] If Short was aware that she was colored and was presumably aware as well that she could not lawfully wed Woods, she could not be said to have been an innocent who relied to her detriment on his false promises. If Short was aware of the legal impediment that the difference in blood created, she was aware that Woods's promise could not be lawfully consummated and was thus incapable of being seduced. If she had knowledge of her Negro blood and sought to marry Woods despite the illegality of that relationship, she would be no less implicated in fraud than he—and certainly not an "innocent" woman whose injury demanded redress by the state's criminal process.

Although the Virginia supreme court of appeals vacated Woods's conviction, the evidentiary rule that the court established favored the prosecution upon retrial. That rule put the burden of persuasion on the defense. Upon retrial, the defendant would have to show that Short was aware that she was of a different race than the alleged seducer. Wood argued that Short should be presumed to have knowledge that her grandfather on her mother's side was colored. But the court concluded that "in this case, the natural and human resolve of the mother of the prosecutrix would be to withhold from her the knowledge of what could only humiliate and distress her"—that is, the knowledge of her colored forebear—in view of evidence indicating conclusively "that she was received and accepted socially by white persons as one of them."[40]

Problems of Comity/Conflict of Laws

A difficulty in enforcing prohibitions against interracial marriage that has resurfaced today in disputes over same-sex marriage involved the following question: Ought a state that prohibited interracial marriages recognize such marriages contracted abroad in states that permitted them? Some states expressly criminalized the knowing evasion of their anti-miscegenation statutes. And a few states that permitted interracial marriages nonetheless withheld recognition from marriages celebrated within their borders by persons seeking solely to evade the marital regulations of their home jurisdictions.

What, though, about couples who genuinely resided in a permissive jurisdiction, got married there, and then moved to states that outlawed interracial matrimony?

---

39. *Commonwealth v. Wright*, 27 S.W. 815 (Kentucky Supreme Court, 1894). For useful discussions of seduction, see Larson, "Women Understand So Little, They Call My Good Nature 'Deceit,' " and Berry, "Judging Morality," 848–853.

40. *Wood v. Commonwealth*, 966–967.

The answer that states gave varied widely. Consider *State [of North Carolina] v. Ross*,[41] *Kinney v. Commonwealth [of Virginia]*,[42] and *Miller v. Lucks*.[43]

The Ross case involved the marriage of a black man, Pink Ross, and a white woman, Sarah Spake. Lawfully married in South Carolina in 1873, Pink and Sarah soon thereafter moved to Charlotte, North Carolina, where they lived for three years before they were charged with fornication and adultery. They raised their marriage as a defense. The trial judge ruled in the couple's favor as did the state Supreme Court. While the justices viewed interracial marriages as "immoral" and "revolting,"[44] they noted that this was not "the common sentiment of the civilized and Christian world" insofar as in both the United States and Europe many governments declined to prohibit interracial marriage.[45] Unlike polygamy, interracial marriage was not universally condemned. That being so, a majority of the North Carolina justices believed that toleration made sense for the sake of interstate comity and for the sake of enhancing uniformity and thus stability in matters touching the all-important area of matrimony. "Upon this question above all others," they remarked, "it is desirable . . . that there should not be one law in Maine and another in Texas, but that the same law shall prevail at least throughout the United States."[46]

Justice Edwin G. Reade strongly disagreed. "If [the interracial marriage] solemnized here between our own people is declared void," he asked, "why should comity require the evil to be imported from another State?"[47] He acknowledged the federal constitution provision under which "[t]he citizens of each State shall be entitled to all privileges and immunities of citizens in the several States." But he contended, with considerable justification, that that provision "does not mean that a citizen of South Carolina removing here [to North Carolina] may bring with him his South Carolina privileges and immunities."[48] All it means, Justice Reade declared, is that "when he comes here he may have the same privileges and immunities which our citizens have. Nothing more and nothing less."[49] Since North Carolina citizens had no right to marry across racial lines, it imposed no abridgment of the federal privileges and immunities clause to prevent people from South Carolina from marrying across racial lines. Venting his anger, Justice Reade declared:

> It is courteous for neighbors to visit and it is handsome to allow the visitor family privileges and even to give him the favorite seat; but if he bring his pet rattlesnake or his pet bear or spitz dog famous for hydrophobia, he must leave them outside the door. And if he bring small pox the door may be shut against him.[50]

41. 76 N.C. 242 (North Carolina Supreme Court, 1877).
42. 71 Va. (30 Gratt.) 858 (1878).
43. 203 Miss. 824 (Mississippi Supreme Court, 1948).
44. *State v. Ross*, 244, 246.
45. Ibid., 246
46. Ibid., 247.
47. Ibid., 249.
48. Ibid., 250.
49. Ibid.
50. Ibid.

The voice of dissent in North Carolina, Justice Reade's sentiments carried the day in other states. In one case, for example, a white man and black woman married in Mississippi, where they then resided and where interracial marriages were, for a brief moment in Reconstruction, permitted. The couple subsequently moved to Tennessee where the man was charged with sexual misconduct. He set forth his marriage as a defense. That defense, however, was rejected by the Tennessee supreme court, which argued that accepting it would lead necessarily to accepting "the father living with his daughter . . . in lawful wedlock" or the Turk lawfully "establish[ing] his harem at the doors of the capitol"—horrible possibilities, yet none "more revolting, more to be avoided, or more—unnatural" than interracial marriages.[51]

Virginia also declined to tolerate interracial married couples within its borders, even if they had married somewhere else with no intent to evade the state's anti-miscegenation statute and even if their marriages had been perfectly proper according to the law of the state where the marriages were performed. Thus, in Augusta County, Virginia, in 1877 Andrew Kinney, a black man, was indicted, convicted, and fined for lewdly associating and cohabiting with Mahala Miller, a white woman. In *Kinney v. Commonwealth* Kinney asserted as his defense his marriage to Miller in the District of Columbia. But the Virginia court of appeals concluded that, for the sake of "public morals," the District of Columbia marriage, though lawful where celebrated, ought not be recognized in Virginia and therefore ought not be available in criminal prosecution as a defense for illicit sexual intimacy:

> The purity of public morals, the moral and physical development of both races, and the highest advancement of our cherished southern civilization . . . all require that [blacks and whites] should be kept distinct and separate and that connections and alliances so unnatural that God and nature seem to forbid them should be prohibited by positive law, and subject to no evasion.[52]

A related but distinct issue arose when interracial couples married in a jurisdiction that permitted such unions and then sought to have their marriages recognized in other locales—not for the purpose of living in those areas but for the purpose of inheriting property or obtaining some other benefit that required the recognition of the marriage. *Miller v. Lucks* posed this problem in an interesting setting. In 1923, Pearl Mitchell and Alex Miller were indicted in Hinds County, Mississippi, for unlawful cohabitation. Pearl Mitchell was black and Alex Miller white. The district attorney agreed to forgo pressing charges on condition that Mitchell leave Mississippi. She did. She moved to Chicago, Illinois, where she was soon joined by Miller. After living together for several years, they got married in 1939. Six years later, Pearl Mitchell died. Her relatives believed that they were entitled to the property she owned in Mississippi and filed a petition seeking a declaration of ownership. One of their claims was that they, not Alex Miller, were

---

51. *State v. Bell*, 66 Tenn. (7 Baxter) 9, 11 (1872).
52. *Kinney v. Commonwealth*, 869.

entitled to the property because Mississippi prohibited interracial marriage and, in their view, ought not recognize, even for purposes of successorship, interracial marriages established in other states.

Mitchell's relatives probably believed that this was one of those rare instances in which a white supremacist law would directly benefit black people. They embraced the proposition that interracial marriage was so repugnant to the public policy of Mississippi that the state's legal system should decline to give such unions any recognition. The consequence of that proposition in this case would have been to make the relatives the sole heirs of Pearl Mitchell's estate in Mississippi.

The relatives convinced the chancellor of the chancery court of Hinds County to rule in their favor. The supreme court of Mississippi, however, ruled against them. According to Chief Justice Sydney Smith, the purpose of Mississippi's anti-miscegenation statute "was to prevent persons of Negro and white blood from living together in [Mississippi] in the relationship of husband and wife."[53] But merely "to permit one of the parties to such a marriage to inherit property . . . from the other does no violence" to the underlying purpose of the state's anti-miscegenation provisions.[54] "What we are requested to do," Justice Smith maintained, "is simply to recognize this marriage to the extent only of permitting one of the parties thereto to inherit from the other party in Mississippi, and to that extent it must and will be recognized. This is in accord with the holdings of courts in other states faced with this Negro problem."[55]

One wonders whether the racial identity of the parties had anything to do with the outcome in *Miller*. It is arrestingly ironic, if nothing else, that in 1948 a thoroughly white supremacist Mississippi supreme court was willing to recognize the legality of an interracial marriage when the consequence of doing so involved enriching a white man at the expense of black folks. Moreover, while Pearl Mitchell bequeathed to her husband her substantial holdings of property in Illinois, she declared in her will that her husband was to "have no other claim, right or title to any other property that I may own in the United States except the property specifically mentioned and described in this will."[56] The property in Mississippi was not specifically mentioned in her will. This suggests that Pearl intended her property in Mississippi to go to her relatives. The Mississippi supreme court does not grapple with this aspect of the case other than to say that this argument, though made to the lower court, had not been made to it. On the other hand, the Mississippi supreme court's decision to offer limited recognition to the out-of-state interracial marriage of the Millers was by no means unique. Virtually all of the states that were fiercely opposed to interracial marriage granted limited recognition for purposes of property inheritance and related matters.[57]

53. *Miller v. Lucks*, 832.
54. Ibid.
55. Ibid.
56. Ibid.
57. See Koppelman, "Same-Sex Marriage, Choice of Law and Public Policy," 961.

Divorce

Anti-miscegenation laws not only affected the terms under which people could marry; they also affected the terms under which people could obtain divorces. By voiding marriages between people of different races, anti-miscegenation laws offered a potentially powerful weapon to disgruntled spouses. Theoretically, if a spouse could show that his marriage partner was of a different race than he, the spouse could leave the marriage free of any obligations since, in the eyes of the law, the parties were never lawfully married in the first place. Joe R. Kirby, for example, obtained an annulment of his eight-year-old marriage to Mayellen Kirby in Arizona in 1922 by convincing a court that the union violated the state's anti-miscegenation law since he was white and she was "a Negress."[58] Often, however, judges displayed a striking solicitude for women from whom white men sought separation on the grounds that the women were colored. Abhorrence of race-mixing in marriage came face-to-face with abhorrence of cads who sought to relieve themselves of matrimonial and parental responsibilities by opportunistically discovering a racial "taint" in their wives' lineage. To a notable degree, when facing this dilemma, judges viewed race-mixing in marriage as the lesser of these two distinct evils. *Dillon v. Dillon*[59] and *Ferrall v. Ferrall*[60] are cases that vividly illustrate these themes.

Near the end of the 1870s, a Mrs. Dillon sought alimony from Mr. Dillon, a man with whom she had lived for many years and by whom she had borne several children. Mr. Dillon responded by denying that Mrs. Dillon was really his wife. He charged that she was a Negro, insofar as she had more than one-eighth African blood in her veins, and that she was therefore incapable of lawfully marrying him, a white man. A jury disagreed over whether Mrs. Dillon was one-eighth of Negro blood or more whereupon a judge decreed that she was the lawful wife of the defendant. The Georgia supreme court affirmed the trial judge, mainly on the grounds that, in a close case, public policy is best served by respecting settled expectations.

The court conceded in *Dillon v. Dillon* that Mrs. Dillon's lineage was "doubtful."[61] For a variety of reasons, though, the Georgia supreme court strongly backed the conclusions reached by the lower court. Because Mrs. Dillon was "not black, but of a complexion approximating that of many white persons of pure blood," this was "not an open, bald case of the intermarriage of an African with a Caucasian."[62] Reading between the lines of the court's opinion, it seems that the justices understood this to be a case of a marriage that joined two people who at least *appeared* to be white, even if, in fact, one of the parties was more colored than the law allowed. Since the marriage outwardly conformed to the racial practices of the state, the justices were willing to credit its legitimacy, especially in

58. *Kirby v. Kirby*, 24 Ariz. 9 (Arizona Supreme Court, 1922).
59. 60 Ga. 204 (Georgia Supreme Court, 1878).
60. 153 N.C. 174 (North Carolina Supreme Court, 1910).
61. 60 Ga. 207 (Georgia Supreme Court, 1878).
62. Ibid.

light of certain additional considerations. Perhaps most important, in 1857 Mr. Dillon successfully petitioned the state legislature to pass a special act entitling Mrs. Dillon to the rights and privileges of a citizen of Georgia. The justices viewed this act as a good indication that Mrs. Dillon was at least white enough for them to recognize her marriage. They viewed it as well as an act, initiated by Mr. Dillon, that should preclude him from disputing the racial character of his wife. The special statute, the justices concluded, "does not make her white, but is conclusive evidence against Mr. Dillon . . . that she is white. He is estopped to controvert it."[63] In other words, the court believed that having successfully petitioned the legislature to declare Mrs. Dillon a citizen of Georgia—a political status that presupposed her status as a white person—Mr. Dillon should be prevented from subsequently challenging her claim to whiteness. Having made his bed, they might have said, he should be forced to sleep in it.

The justices also suggested that, as a matter of basic fairness, Mr. Dillon ought not be permitted to evade his matrimonial and paternal obligations (at least in the context of a marriage to a woman who appears to have been white). In the court's words:

> [C]an the husband (after marrying [a woman], living with her as his wife for many, many years, rearing by her a family of children . . .) institute a narrow search into her pedigree, that he may deny her the full measure of support in her declining years to which, if she is truly and legally his wife, the law entitles her? . . . That is the practical inquiry with which we are at present concerned. We think he cannot evade her claim for support, or the claim of his minor children for support, by such means. In respect to alimony, he is estopped to deny that she is his lawful wife. It militates against no interest of society that we can think of, so to treat him. . . . [Society is] benefitted by closing the mouth of any man against repudiating his family when they come to him for needed support. If he may cast them, they will in many instances, fall a weighty burden on the public. To allow a husband to indulge in scruples about the pedigree of his old wife, when her youth, beauty and strength have all waned, and thus escape responding to her claim for reasonable alimony, would be unwise in policy, unsound in principle.[64]

Similar in outcome is *Ferrall v. Ferrall*, a North Carolina case that arose in 1907 when Frank S. Ferrall sought to end his marriage to Susie Patterson Ferrall on the grounds that she "was and is of negro descent within the third generation," that he was ignorant of that fact when they married in 1904, and that state law prohibited marriages "between a white person and a person of negro descent to the third generation inclusive."[65] Mrs. Ferrall denied that she had Negro forebears, but conceded that there was a strain of Indian or Portuguese blood in her background. She also declared that before they were married she had told her husband that some people in her vicinity insisted that she was part Negro, that

63. Ibid., 208.
64. Ibid., 207–208.
65. *Ferrall v. Ferrall*, 174.

because of those rumors she had hesitated to marry him, and that it was he who, in the end, had insisted upon marriage.

At trial, the evidence disclosed a racial "taint" in Mrs. Ferrall's great-grandfather. The litigation then centered upon the extent to which this great-grandfather was a Negro and the extent to which he had to be Negro in order to render his great-granddaughter ineligible from marrying a white man. The trial judge, supported by the North Carolina supreme court, concluded that in order to deprive Mrs. Ferrall of her claim to whiteness, her husband would have to show that her great-grandfather was "a real negro," by which was meant a Negro "that did not have any white blood in him."[66] The jury concluded, unsurprisingly, that he was not a "real negro" and that therefore, despite the mild racial "taint" that he bequeathed to Mrs. Ferrall, her marriage was in accord with the state's anti-miscegenation statute.

The North Carolina supreme court tried to make it seem as though the narrow definition of a "real negro" was mandated by precedent. A more likely explanation for their decisions is that the North Carolina judges, like the Georgia judges in *Dillon*, abhorred the idea of permitting a man to freely dispose of his white-looking wife and children on the grounds that, unbeknownst to hardly anyone, they were "really" Negroes. Part of this judicial opposition stemmed from anger at husbands who appeared to be behaving as heartless cads. Another part of this judicial opposition may have stemmed from empathy for women and children who stood to lose not simply the financial benefits of alimony and child payments, but more fundamentally, the great and manifold privileges of whiteness in a pigmentocracy dominated by whites.

Both of these sentiments were voiced in a concurring opinion in *Ferrall* by Chief Justice Walter Clark. "It would be difficult," he writes, "to find a case so void of merit":

> The [husband] by earnest solicitation persuaded [Mrs. Ferrall] to become his wife in the days of her youth and beauty. She has borne his children. Now that youth has fled and household drudgery and child-bearing have taken the sparkle from her eyes and deprived her form of its symmetry, he seeks to get rid of her, not only without fault alleged against her, but in a method that will not only deprive her of any support while he lives by alimony, or by dower after his death, but which would consign her to the association of the colored race which he so affects to despise. The law may not permit him thus to bastardize his own innocent children . . . but he would brand them for all time . . . as negroes—a fate which their white skin will make doubly humiliating to them.[67]

Moreover, Chief Justice Clark goes on to opine that even if the husband had found a racial taint in his wife's lineage that would have technically voided their marriage, "justice and generosity [would have] dictated that he keep to himself that of which the public was unaware."[68] Following the lead of Mrs. Ferrall's

66. Ibid., 175.
67. Ibid., 180.
68. Ibid.

attorney, Chief Justice Clark likens Mr. Ferrall to Tom Driscoll, the villain in Mark Twain's *Pudd'nhead Wilson* who sold his own mulatto mother down the river to pay for gambling debts. Chief Justice Clark heaps scorn on "this husband and father who for the sake of a divorce would make negroes of his wife and children."[69] "He deems it perdition for himself to associate with those possessing the slightest suspicion of negro blood," Clark observes, "but strains of every effort to consign the wife of his bosom and the innocent children of his own loins to poverty and the infamy that he depicts."[70]

Clark's concurring opinion displays both generosity and bone-deep racism. It is generous because Clark rules in favor of Mrs. Ferrall despite legal rules that, neutrally interpreted, favored her husband. Clark says that he agrees with the court's factual holding regarding the racial identity of Mrs. Ferrall. This part of his opinion, however, should not be taken at face value. He says this in order to make more palatable what the court is really doing—namely, permitting the continuation of what state law would ordinarily deem an interracial marriage. Clark and his colleagues are making an exception though they do not want openly to acknowledge what they are doing. They are making an exception partly to prevent a bad man from profiting from bad conduct. In all likelihood, they are also making an exception because of their empathy with Mrs. Ferrall—a woman who looks as white as any of them, who was accepted by her neighbors and friends as white, who apparently was unaware of the strain of colored blood in her lineage, and who was accepted by her husband as a white woman in three years of marriage during which she gave birth to two of his children. Unwilling to state openly the real basis of the court's decision, Clark obliquely hints at its motivation when he writes that

> If indeed the plaintiff had discovered any minute strain of colored origin after the youth of his wife had been worn away for his pleasure and in his service, justice and generosity dictated that he keep to himself that of which the public was unaware.[71]

Mr. Ferrall failed to do what "justice and generosity dictated," so Clark and his colleagues stepped into the breach to do that which the husband should have done—namely, ignore the "strain of colored origin" in Mrs. Ferrall.

Here as elsewhere in the jurisprudence of anti-miscegenation law, judges injected on an ad hoc basis bits of decency into a massively indecent regime of racial hierarchy. In *Ferrall*, after all, the chief justice of North Carolina expressly argued that, in certain circumstances, an individual is under a moral duty to evade even a duly enacted and legitimate statute. On the other hand, neither the principal opinion nor Clark's concurrence offered any general criticism of the state's anti-miscegenation law. Nor did any of the justices criticize at all the conditions that made being identified as a Negro such a humiliating, stigmatizing, burdensome fate. The court simply concluded that, under the peculiar circumstances at hand, "justice and generosity" dictated the result reached.

69. Ibid., 181.
70. Ibid.
71. Ibid., 180.

References

Applebaum, Harvey M. "Miscegenation Statutes: A Constitutional and Social Problem." *Georgetown Law Journal* 53 (1964).

Berry, Mary Frances. "Judging Morality: Sexual Behavior and Legal Consequences in the Late Nineteenth-Century South." *Journal of American History* 78 (1991).

Brynes, Leonard. "Who Is Black Enough for You? The Analysis of Northwestern University Law School's Struggle over Minority Faculty Hiring." *Michigan Journal of Race and Law* 2 (1997).

Davis, F. James. *Who Is Black: One Nation's Definition* (University Park: Pennsylvania State University Press, 1991).

Ferber, Edna. *Show Boat* (Garden City, N.Y.: Doubleday, Page, 1926).

Ford, Christopher A. "Administering Identity: The Determination of 'Race' in Race-Conscious Law." *California Law Review* 82 (1994).

Fowler, David H. *Northern Attitudes towards Interracial Marriage: Legislation and Public Opinion in the Middle Atlantic States of the Old Northwest, 1780–1930* (New York: Garland, 1987).

Fredrickson, George M. *White Supremacy: A Comparative Study in American and South African History* (New York: Oxford University Press, 1981).

Greenberg, Jack. *Race Relations and American Law* (New York: Columbia University Press, 1959).

Gross, Ariela. "Litigating Whiteness: Trials of Racial Determination in the Nineteenth Century South." *Yale Law Journal* 108 (1998).

Hackman, Christine B. "The Devil and the One-Drop Rule: Racial Categories, African Americans, and the U.S. Census." *Michigan Law Review* 95 (1997).

Harlan, James. *Congressional Globe*, 42d Cong., 2d sess., 1872, pt. 1: 878.

Harris, Cheryl I. "Whiteness As Property." *Harvard Law Review* 106 (1993).

Hening, William Waller. *The Statutes at Large: Being a Collection of All the Laws of Virginia* (New York, 1819–1823).

Higginbotham, Jr., A. Leon, and Barbara K. Kopytoff. "Racial Purity and Interracial Sex in the Law of Colonial and Antebellum Virginia." *Georgetown Law Journal* 77 (1989).

Hodes, Martha. *White Women, Black Men: Illicit Sex in the Nineteenth-Century South* (New Haven: Yale University Press, 1997).

Hughes, Henry. *Treatise on Sociology, Theoretical and Practical* (Philadelphia: Lippincott, Grambo, 1854).

Koppelman, Andrew. "Same-Sex Marriage, Choice of Law and Public Policy." *Texas Law Review* 76 (1998).

Larson, Jane E. " 'Women Understand So Little, They Call My Good Nature "Deceit" ': A Feminist Rethinking of Seduction." *Columbia Law Review* 93 (1993).

Lombardo, Paul A. "Miscegenation, Eugenics, and Racism: Historical Footnotes to *Loving v. Virginia.*" *University of California at Davis Law Review* 21 (1988).

Mangum, Jr., Charles S. *The Legal Status of the Negro* (Chapel Hill: University of North Carolina Press, 1940).

Martyn, Byron Curti. "Racism in the United States: A History of the Anti-Miscegenation Legislation and Litigation." Ph.D. dissertation (University of Southern California, 1979).

Mills, Gary B. "Miscegenation and the Free Negro in Antebellum 'Anglo' Alabama: A Reexamination of Southern Race Relations." *Journal of American History* 68 (1981).

Pascoe, Peggy. "Miscegenation Law, Court Cases, and Ideologies of 'Race' in Twentieth-Century America." *Journal of American History* 83 (1996).

Robinson II, Charles Frank. "The Antimiscegenation Conversation: Love's Legislated Limits, 1866–1967. Ph.D. dissertation (1998).

Sherman, Richard B. "The Last Stand: The Fight for Racial Integrity in Virginia in the 1920s." *Journal of Southern History* 56 (1988).

Sommerville, Diane Miller. "The Rape Myth in the Old South Reconsidered." *Journal of Southern History* 61 (1995).

Spencer, Jon Michael. *The New Colored People: The Mixed-Race Movement in America* (New York: New York University Press, 1997).

Tindall, George B. *South Carolina Negroes, 1877–1900* (1952; repr. Baton Rouge: Louisiana State University Press, 1966).

Wadlington, Walter. "The *Loving* Case: Virginia's Anti-Miscegenation Statute in Historical Perspective." *Virginia Law Review* 52 (1966).

Wallenstein, Peter. "Race, Marriage and the Law of Freedom: Alabama and Virginia, 1860–1960s." *Chicago-Kent Law Review* 70 (1994).

Weinberger, Andrew. "A Reappraisal of the Constitutionality of Miscegenation Statutes." *Cornell Law Quarterly* 42 (1957).

Williamson, Joel. *After Slavery: The Negro in South Carolina during Reconstruction, 1861–1877* (Chapel Hill: University of North Carolina Press, 1965).

Wright, Luther. "Who's Black, Who's White, and Who Cares: Reconceptualizing the United States's Definition of Race and Racial Classifications." *Vanderbilt Law Review* 48 (1995).

Reading Race, Rhetoric, and the Female Body in the *Rhinelander* Case*

JAMIE L. WACKS

On October 14, 1924, Alice Beatrice Jones and Leonard Kip Rhinelander exchanged marriage vows in a courthouse in Westchester County, New York. Only

---

* This previously unpublished essay is in large part excerpted from Jamie Wacks's fully documented 1995 Harvard University senior honors essay, "Reading Race, Rhetoric, and the Female Body: The Rhinelander Case and 1920s American Culture."

    The court record of the *Rhinelander* case—supposedly lost in a fire—can in fact be found at The Association of the Bar of the City of New York. *Rhinelander v. Rhinelander*, New York Court of

six weeks later, Leonard filed papers to sue Alice for an annulment.[1] He accused her of fraud, claiming that she had deceived him about her racial ancestry.[2] Neither Alice nor Leonard realized then that the story of their courtship and their subsequent courtroom battle would become front-page news in *The New York Times* and in many other newspapers across the country during November and December of 1925.[3] The couple surely never imagined that "[p]ornographic picture books purportedly showing" them together would become "best sellers in the gutter market."[4]

Alice and Leonard had met in Stamford, Connecticut, in 1921, when Alice was twenty-three and Leonard was seventeen. Alice was a maid. Although most Americans identified her as black and Alice's attorney conceded in court that she had black ancestry,[5] there is some hearsay evidence that Alice would have self-

Appeals Records and Briefs 20 (1927), henceforth cited as *Court Record*. Drawing primarily from newspaper accounts and without citing the court record, Mark J. Madigan's rich reading of the *Rhinelander* case, "Miscegenation and the 'Dicta of Race and Class': The Rhinelander Case and Nella Larsen's *Passing*," *Modern Fiction Studies* 36 (winter 1990), 523–29 (henceforth Madigan), is the only scholarly report that I have found. Milton A. Smith's source of information is unclear in his "America's Most Sensational Mixed Marriage," *Tan Confessions* 2 (December 1951) (henceforth Smith). The Howard University Moorland-Spingarn Research Center Rhinelander Clippings Files (henceforth Moorland-Spingarn) is also very helpful.

1. New Rochelle's daily newspaper, *The Standard Star*, broke the news several days before Leonard filed the annulment suit. "Rhinelander's Son Marries Daughter of a Colored Man," *The Standard Star*, 13 November 1924, 1.

2. Some speculated that Leonard's father had pressured Leonard to file the suit, threatening him with disinheritance. One journalist wrote, "Of course, everybody knows that he knew that she was colored, and, no doubt, if his family and friends had not objected, he would not now, under cross-examination, be cutting such a pitiful and miserable figure, trying to pose as the dupe of his wife" ("Opinion of the Leading Colored American Thinkers: The Rhinelander Case," *The Messenger* 7 [1925], 388). J. A. Rogers refers to the *Rhinelander* case as "one of the most sensational marriages in American history, mixed or otherwise" and argues that it was "too much for his family and his social set. Rhinelander was forced into bringing a divorce suit on the ground that his wife had tricked him about her race" (*Sex and Race: A History of White, Negro, and Indian Miscegenation in the Two Americas* 2 [New York: Helga M. Rogers, 1942], 346, 348). For more information on other mixed marriages that were litigated on the grounds of race fraud, see Willard B. Gatewood, Jr., "The Perils of Passing: The McCarys of Omaha," *Nebraska History* 71 (Nebraska State Historical Society, summer 1990), 64; see also *San Francisco Examiner*, 30 December 1924, "Amalgamation," and Tuskegee Institute Clippings File Reel 20.

3. The trial itself began on November 9, 1925, and ended on December 5, 1925. See "Order Appealed From," *Rhinelander v. Rhinelander*, New York Court of Appeals Records and Briefs 20 (1927), 3–4.

4. Smith, 72.

5. In the amended complaint, Leonard alleged, among other things, "IV. On information and belief, that in truth and fact the said Alice Jones, also know as Alice Jones Rhinelander, was colored and with colored blood.... V. On information and belief, that the said defendant, Alice Jones, also known as Alice Jones Rhinelander, had colored blood in her veins" (*Court Record*, 10). Alice's answer to the amended complaint stated, "Second—She denies that she has any knowledge or information sufficient to form a belief as to any of the allegations contained in the paragraphs or subdivisions of said complaint numbered respectively IV and V" (*Court Record*, 11). Thus, Alice initially denied that she was colored and had colored blood (*Court Record*, 1083–84). However,

identified as white.[6] The skin color of Alice's face was sufficiently light for her to "pass" as a white person, and her mother, a native Englishwoman, was white. However, she did not hide her father, a visibly darker New Rochelle taxi driver who was of black and white ancestry, from Leonard.[7]

Leonard was the son of Philip Rhinelander, a member of the extremely wealthy, white, old Huguenot, high-society New York Rhinelander clan. He stuttered.[8] And he fell in love with Alice Jones.

On November 23, 1925, when Lee Parsons Davis, Alice Jones' attorney, staged two of the most revealing events of the *Rhinelander* trial, the battle about Alice Jones' identity shocked the American public twice in one day. That morning, while Davis was cross-examining Leonard, Judge Morschauer cleared the courtroom of women and Davis read aloud two sexually explicit love letters written by Leonard to Alice.[9] Later that same day, over the objection of Leonard's attorney,[10] Alice's attorney requested that Alice take her clothes off to allow the all-white, all-male, all-married jury[11] and Leonard to inspect her skin color. Davis said, "I desire to have Mrs. Rhinelander [Alice Jones] brought in here, and I am going to request that this courtroom be further cleared, because I am going to ask this witness [Leonard] to identify the color of her skin" (693). Davis' argument was that the skin color of Alice's body was darker than that of her face, and since Alice and Leonard had been sexually intimate before they were married, Leonard had to have known that she had black ancestry. In order to resolve the scandal that would become known to Americans across the country as the *Rhinelander* case, the attorneys, Alice's mother, the judge, and the jurors proceeded into the jury's chambers to watch Alice take off most of her clothes. According to the description in the *Court Record*:

The Court, Mr. Mills, Mr. Davis, Mr. Swinburne, the jury, the plaintiff, the defendant, her mother, Mrs. George Jones, and the stenographer left the court-

---

before her attorney delivered his opening address to the jury, Alice's attorney explained that her denial was "a technical legal denial" but that the "defendant's counsel withdraws the denial as to the blood of this defendant and for the purposes of this trial admits that she has some colored blood in her veins" (*Court Record*, 1106).

6. A little over a year after the trial, on January 5, 1927, *The Standard Star* of New Rochelle reported that Alice was beginning "a legal battle to clear her name of the allegation she has negro blood in her veins." If true, this article demonstrates that Alice clung to her belief in her white identity. *The Standard Star*'s suggestion that Alice would have to fight another courtroom battle to gain the right to define her race reveals the limitations that the law and American society had imposed on her.
7. Madigan, 525, writes that Leonard alleged that Alice led him to believe that her father was Cuban. *See also Court Record*, 1428–29.
8. See *The New York Times*, 18 November 1925, 4.
9. *See* Defendant's Exhibit S, entered into evidence at *Court Record*, 501, and reproduced at *Court Record*, 1073, and Defendant's Exhibit N-1, entered into evidence at *Court Record*, 685, and reproduced at *Court Record*, 1076.
10. Leonard's lawyer objected, "The proposition to exhibit the naked body of this girl to this jury is not competent" (*Court Record* 693); see also *Court Record*, 1431.
11. See *The New York Times*, 10 November 1925, 8.

room and entered the jury room. The defendant and Mrs. Jones then withdrew to the lavatory adjoining the jury room and, after a short time, again entered the jury room. The defendant, who was weeping, had on her underwear and a long coat. At Mr. Davis' direction she let down the coat, so that the upper portion of her body, as far down as the breast, was exposed. She then, again at Mr. Davis' direction, covered the upper part of her body and showed to the jury her bare legs, up as far as the knees.

The Court, counsel, the jury and the plaintiff then re-entered the court room. (696)[12]

After this viewing, Davis asked Leonard, "Your wife's body is the same shade as it was when you saw her in the Marie Antoinette with all of her clothing removed?" and Leonard answered, "Yes" (697).[13]

By the end of the three-week trial, Leonard and many other witnesses, including the blackface singer Al Jolson had testified (434–36). Although the jury concluded that Alice had not deceived Leonard,[14] she became a recluse in the quiet neighborhood of New Rochelle, never remarrying.[15] In the words of one journalist,

12. The court permitted the jurors to look at Alice's body only to determine "whether he [Leonard] ought to have known that she was of colored blood and was justified in believing that when he saw her body" (*Court Record*, 694).

13. Alice and Leonard spent several days together at the Hotel Marie Antoinette registered under the names of Mr. and Mrs. Smith of Rye (*Court Record*, 154–55, 545).

14. The judgment in Alice's favor in the annulment suit entered by the trial court was affirmed on appeal. See *Rhinelander v. Rhinelander*, 219 N.Y.S. 548 (1927) (*per curiam*), affirmed with no opinion, 245 N.Y. 510 (1927). In 1929, Alice sued Leonard's father, Philip Rhinelander, for alienation of affections. See *In re Rhinelander's Will*, 36 N.Y.S.2d 105, 107 (1942). Leonard filed for divorce on the "ground of cruelty" in Nevada in August 1929, and a decree that granted the divorce and did not provide for Alice's support and maintenance was entered in December 1929. In February 1930, Alice filed suit for separation in New York. Before the suits that Alice brought in New York were resolved, Leonard and Alice signed a settlement agreement in New York in 1930, and Philip guaranteed the agreement. Before the agreement was delivered, the Nevada divorce decree was modified to incorporate the provisions of the agreement for her support and maintenance. The agreement was then delivered to Alice. The agreement specified that Alice would receive payments of $3,600 or $3,800 per year for her life, if Alice persuaded the Nevada court to reopen the divorce decree and successfully defended the suit; she persuaded the court to reopen the decree and to modify it to provide for her support; or the court refused her request to reopen the decree. In return, Alice agreed to withdraw the suit pending against Leonard and the suit pending against Philip, to release the Rhinelanders of liability in connectioin with her alienation of affections claim, to release her rights to a portion of Leonard's estate, and to "use the name of Rhinelander." After the court modified the decree to provide for Alice's support, she received payments, which continued after Leonard died in 1936 until Philip died in 1940. See *In the Matter of Rhinelander*, 290 N.Y. 31, 33–36 (1943). The executors of Philip's estate wanted to allow Alice's claim for payment, but some of Philip's heirs contested the payments. In 1942, the court ruled that the settlement agreement was illegal. See *In re Rhinelander's Will*, 36 N.Y.S.2d 105 (1942). This decision was reversed; both the settlement agreement and Philip's guarantee were deemed enforceable. I have not found any evidence of whether Alice received payments from the estate.

15. *Los Angeles Tribune*, 24 November 1951. This article noted that Alice Jones was living in "obscure middle age."

Alice Jones had become for a "brief 14-month period . . . the most talked-about, read-about, maligned Negro woman in American history."[16]

The lawyers' rhetoric and trial strategies as evidenced by the *Court Record* illuminate that the connections between race, sexual behavior, and class in the 1920s and the images that conveyed these connections were all on trial for the public as well as the jury to deliver their verdicts. The attorneys' contest to define Alice Jones by explicitly invoking the culturally and historically loaded image of the vamp, implicitly drawing on social images of the wily mulatto and the female slave, and placing Alice Jones' body on display was a battle for control over the image of the black woman, which control bell hooks has recognized is essential to preserving "racial domination."[17] The notion that a lower-class woman like Alice Jones whom society labeled as black could trespass into the world of a wealthy white man like Leonard Rhinelander questioned the boundaries between white and black, rich and poor, and the master male and the submissive female, and suggested the vulnerability of alleged white dominance. However, the image of black women that ultimately emerged from the trial helped to allay fears of passing and of racial mobility. The availability of racial fraud as a ground for an annulment demonstrated how critical race was to identity. The trial rhetoric illuminated the interdependence of race, sexuality, and class in defining an individual's identity. Furthermore, Alice Jones' attorney's ultimate decision to concede that Alice had "colored blood" and had never deceived Leonard rather than to argue that she would not have been lying had she identified herself as white if that is how she may have viewed herself reveals the limitations on racial definition in the 1920s; trying to argue that Alice was white would have been unsuccessful in light of the prevalent belief that one was of "colored blood" if one had "colored blood" ancestry.

More than whether or not Alice Jones had deceived Leonard Kip Rhinelander was at stake. It was not surprising that interested spectators crowded into the courtroom and listened attentively throughout this sensational trial.[18] In the 1920s, some blacks were challenging boundaries by venturing into previously white-dominated fields, some blacks were succeeding financially and socially, and some

16. Smith, 22.
17. bell hooks writes, "From slavery on, white supremacists have recognized that control over images is central to the maintenance of any system of racial domination" (*Black Looks: Race and Representation* [Boston: South End Press, 1992], 2).
18. See the journalist who reported that "by 8 o'clock this morning, two hours before court opened, the room was filled the . . . doors shut." In fact, so many people were in the courtroom that Lavinia Verrill Howe, a woman who wanted to listen to the trial "for a religious magazine and needed to study 'the mental reactions of humanity' " had to send a note to Mr. Davis asking him to help her to find a seat (*Baltimore Sun*, 20 November 1925, 8); *see also The New York Times*, 10 November 1925, 8, which reported, "Men in working clothes rubbed elbows with fashionably dressed women, who drove to the court house in their limousines as all sought seats in the court room"; see also author's original thesis, figure 9, reprinting a newspaper photo captioned, "How They Keep Trying to Get In."

blacks were advocating for black rights.[19] Several Harlem Renaissance writers were placing "passing" at the center of the plots of their novels. One of these works even alludes to the *Rhinelander* case. In *Passing*, Nella Larsen wrote that Irene Redfield, a mulatto character, thought "[t]here was the Rhinelander case" as she contemplated what could happen if the husband of her friend Clare Kendry ever discovered that Clare was passing.[20] The *Rhinelander* case thus put the phenomenon of "passing" itself on trial for all of America to watch. What mattered most was not who Alice Jones really was but rather how she was defined in the context of the cultural images of black women that were already in social circulation.

1. The Black Vamp

To cast Alice Jones in the role of the older sexually aggressive woman who seduced the younger Leonard Kip Rhinelander, Isaac N. Mills, Leonard's attorney, characterized Alice as a "vamp." In large part due to Theda Bara, a silent movie actress who portrayed a sexually aggressive woman who preyed on eligible bachelors, the term "vamp," which was slang for a vampire, came to signify a woman who aggressively seduced men.[21] The declaration of Eubie Blake, a black jazz musician in 1924—"If you've never been vamped by a brown skin you have never been vamped at all"[22]—implies that the term "vamp" was sometimes used to define "colored" women. Leonard's attorney's promise to the jurors in his opening address that he would present evidence to show that Alice designed a second and third "line of attack" as part of her "four stages of her fastening upon" Leonard immediately cast Alice as the aggressor (1100).[23] According to Mills in his closing argument, "the high art" of Alice's "management" was her ability to fool Leonard to believe that he was "acting the ordinary male's part, taking the lead" (1358). Mills' description of Alice's plan which "she prosecuted, month after month" as "diabolical" also suggested that malintent fueled her alleged seduction of the young Leonard (1298).

Mills suggested that because Alice Jones was black, she was hypersexual. Alice's race-induced sexuality rendered her guilty of fraud. From Mills' perspective, play-

19. See Marci Knopf, "Introduction," *The Sleeper Wakes: Harlem Renaissance Stories by Women*, ed. Marcy Knopf (New Brunswick, NJ: Rutgers University Press, 1993).
20. Nella Larsen, *Passing* (1929; reprint, Salem, NH: Ayer, 1990), 187. See Madigan.
21. The term *vamp* has been defined as "seductive or sexually aggressive woman; one who entices men; an attractive woman with a strong come-on," in Harold Wentworth and Stuart Berg Flexner, eds. *Dictionary of American Slang—Second Supplemented Edition* (New York: Thomas Y. Crowell Company, 1975), 564. As a verb, *to vamp* meant to "seduce or influence a man through sexual appeal." *See also* the entry for *vamp* which reads, "woman that makes it her habit or business to captivate men by an unscrupulous display of her sexual charm," in Eric Partridge, *A Dictionary of Slang and Unconventional English, Seventh Edition* (London: Routledge and Kegan Paul, 1973), 930. The verb *to vamp* meant "to attract (men) by one's female charms; to attempt so to attract (them)."
22. Quoted in a lecture by Albert Murray in 1982, recorded by Werner Sollors.
23. *The New York Times* quoted Mills' representation of Alice's and Leonard's relationship as if it were a series of "stages" of attack (10 November 1925, 8).

ing the vamp was natural for Alice. According to Mills, "because of her difference of race [she was] much older, relatively" (1353). This statement implied that Alice's "blackness" made her more sexually manipulative than even a white vamp could be because her race made her sexually mature beyond her twenty-three years. Alice's heightened sexuality entranced—perhaps as a vampire might—Leonard, impairing his ability to discern black from white so that he was duped about Alice's race. Leonard's attorney said, "She had him so, as I said in my opening [address], that he did not know black from white, that he did not know or have control of himself" (1350). Thus, Alice's blackness, manifested in part as hypersexuality, was the very thing that made Leonard unable to determine that she was black. Leonard's attorney implied that it was the jurors' duty to rule against Alice Jones the vamp before she had the opportunity to victimize other men. Justifying his trial strategy, Mills warned the twelve jurors that a verdict in favor of Alice Jones would "tell . . . every vampire that she may work her trade beyond the possibility of justice being meted out to her or for her victim" (1298). His use of the culturally available image of the hypersexual vamp thus played into the anxieties in the 1920s about changes in sexual behavior. Although the term "vamp" had been used in other contexts to describe black women before 1925,[24] Mills' decision to define Alice Jones as a vamp in the *Rhinelander* trial brought to the fore of the American imagination the black woman's alleged dangerous potential to use her sexuality to challenge white racial and financial superiority.

2. The Wily Mulatto Who Makes Men into Her "Slaves"

The link between the vamp's moral darkness and racial blackness was a logical one, for the image of the wily mulatto—the extrasensual, loose black woman who, in the days of slavery, had seduced her white master—was also prominent in the American imagination during the 1920s. Although the institution of slavery no longer existed in 1925, the idea persisted that black women were hypersexual.[25] At the turn of the century, the "dominant culture's definition of black women" was "all-sexual" and the "alleged sexual promiscuity of black women" posed serious problems for black women.[26] The wily mulatto was reputed to try to use her sexual hold on white men as leverage to advance the black race as a whole by vying for the inheritance of white male power. In the silent film *The Birth of a*

24. For example, Cécily in Eugène Sue, *Les mystères de Paris* (1842) is called *vampire*.
25. Because of the prevalence of this image, as Elizabeth Ammons notes, "For black women at the turn of the century, defending themselves against the racist charge of sexual immorality . . . represented an essential part of their life-and-death struggle *as women* against lynching in the United States" (Ammon's emphasis, "Breaking Silence, *Iola Leroy*," *Conflicting Stories American Women Writers at the Turn into the Twentieth Century* [New York: Oxford University Press, 1991], 25). *See also* bell hooks, who discusses "that mythic black female in slavery who supposedly 'vamped' and seduced virtuous white male slave owners" (*Black Looks*, 68).
26. Ammons, 24. In fact, some racists even argued that black men raped white women because of the "wantonness of the women of his own [black] race" (Ammons, 25).

Nation (1915), through his characterization of Lydia, a mulatto servant who is played by a woman whose skin color is almost white, as both sexually promiscuous and deceptive with a demonic glimmer in her eye, D. W. Griffith suggested that mulatto women would use their sexuality to persuade white men to collaborate with other mulattos to enslave whites. This image of Lydia the sexual mulatto probably still may have been present ten years later in the minds of the white jurors, courtroom spectators, and newspaper readers of the *Rhinelander* case.

The depiction of Alice Jones as a vamp against the cultural backdrop of the image of the wily mulatto thus produced an iniquitous image of the black woman who threatened to cross the boundaries of black and white and to invert the roles of the slave and the master. In his opening statement, Mills said that Leonard "was an utter slave in her [Alice's] hands" (1100) and that "he was her slave, body and soul" (1101). In his closing argument, Mills repeatedly exploited the idea of Alice as Leonard's master; he said that "she owned him body and soul" (1417) and referred to Leonard as "her slave" (1417) and as "her captive" (1417).[27] She "had the boy a slave at her feet," Mills commented (1350). Referencing "that abhorrent practice" (1349) described in the first sexually explicit love letter that Davis submitted into evidence, Mills asserted, "That was not a white man's act. That was an act of the black-and-tan. That is not a white man's act. That shows beyond all argument, all question, that he was her slave, that he was reduced to the very depths of the most bottomless degradation of which you can conceive" (1349–50).

It was one matter for Alice to seduce Leonard with her sexuality. In the days of slavery, many white men slept with their black female slaves. However, after intercourse, the white slavemaster usually was still the master. When he was finished with the slave, he could send her back to the fields, and she was still his slave. The description of Alice not only as Leonard's seductress, but also as his master who maintained power over him after the initial seduction thus may have been frightening to many whites. In this way, the rhetorical exploitation of the racial and sexual connotations of the vamp image worked well with the image of the wily mulatto to challenge racial and sexual boundaries.

3. Naming Alice as a Woman of Colored Blood and a Member of Womankind

Confronted with these characterizations of Alice, Mr. Davis, Alice's attorney, had to create an image of Alice as a black lower-class woman who was not a vamp, a wily mulatto, or a master—in other words, who was not deceitful and who was easily controlled by the white patriarchy. Just as Mills used the images of the vamp and the wily mulatto to define Alice Jones, Davis refuted these images by trying to create a new image for Alice. Davis said in his closing argument,

27. For picture accompanying caption "Blue-Blood Called Love-Slave," see *The Philadelphia Inquirer*, 11 November 1925, in Moorland-Spingarn.

> We have . . . conceded that she has some colored blood. We haven't made any concession that she is a negress. We have made the concession that she has some colored blood flowing through her veins. . . . I am not branding her as a full-blooded negress, but, understand, our concession is that she has some colored blood. (1181–83)

The semantic nuance between a full-blooded negress and a woman of colored blood was crucial because it created the possibility that Alice could have black ancestry without exhibiting the alleged black female trait of sexual promiscuity. However, to ultimately refute the stereotype of the sexually manipulative wily mulatto, who was also a woman of colored blood, Davis would have to resort to more drastic measures.

One of Davis' tactics was to use Alice's gender to transcend her race. In order to communicate with the male jurors, Alice's attorney appealed to a male bond that was based on common knowledge about women's ways. He justified Alice's alleged lack of forthrightness about her age by attributing such deceit to the character of women, white or black. He said,

> If we were to lock up every woman or girl who told a falsehood about their ages, this would be an awful rotten world for we men to live in, because—God bless the girls and women of our country—they bring sunshine into our lives, and they would all be locked up. . . . A woman who marries a man, when she happens to be older, she doesn't want the fellow to know about it. Now isn't that human nature in women? Bless them for it! (1167–68)

Davis also said, "Girls have a funny way, they say, of trying to make the chap they love jealous. . . . Isn't that human? Why on earth should she be blamed for that? It is a natural course of conduct" (1177). The use of the phrase "human nature in women" implicitly included Alice Jones, a woman who was "colored," in the same category as white women. Davis' rhetoric was risky because it challenged a popular notion that white women were a group apart from and better than black women by suggesting a sisterhood stemming from common behavior toward men. Together with Mills' exclusion of Alice from the category of "woman" by asserting that Alice's sexual behavior was a "challenge . . . to the womanhood of this country" (1349), the trial rhetoric thus suggested both the possibility of and the resistance to the proposal that "woman" might be redefined to include women of black as well as white ancestry.

4. White and Black Fears of Race Mixing

With all of these images circulating in the courtroom, at times the *Rhinelander* case lent support to the fears of many whites that racial intermarriage would lead to what was called "race suicide," or the demise of the white race.[28] Al-

---

28. *See* Tom Lutz, *American Nervousness 1903: An Anecdotal History* (Ithaca: Cornell University Press, 1991), 10. The worry about the "impending extinction" of the white race that Lutz discusses in relation to Theodore Roosevelt persisted into the 1920s.

though New York had no statute at this time outlawing intermarriage between blacks and whites (1182), the anti-miscegenation laws in several other states and the peak in the Ku Klux Klan's membership[29] attest to anxieties about race.[30] In his closing argument, Mills tried to appeal to some white people's revulsion to intermarriage:

> There isn't a father among you who would not rather see his son in his casket than to see him wedded to a mulatto woman. . . . (1287)

> There is not a mother among your wives who would not rather see her daughter with her white hands crossed above her shroud than to see her locked in the embraces of a mulatto husband. And everyone of you gentlemen knows that in this respect I speak unto you the words of truth and soberness. (1288)[31]

The image of Alice as a vamp also reinforced the suggestion that like a vampire, Alice would drain from Leonard some of his whiteness. Mills' rhetoric was thus well-suited to engage the fears of many whites that racial miscegenation was further polluting the already allegedly weakening white race.

Some black commentators voiced their own anxieties about the race mixing that held the center stage of the *Rhinelander* case. In one comment on the *Rhinelander* case, *The Amsterdam News*, New York's leading black newspaper, wrote, "NEGROES, generally, look with as much disfavor upon interracial marriage as white people—possibly more."[32] On the same day, another individual cited the *Rhinelander* case amidst his call for an end to miscegenation.[33] Marcus Garvey referred to the *Rhinelander* case as an example of the "Miscegenation [that] will lead to the moral destruction of both races"[34] and which made it difficult to tell whites from non-whites.[35] Thus, while some whites may have read Alice Jones as a

29. See "An Impression of Utopia by One Who Has Never Been There," *Life* (December 1925), 33. Attesting to racial tensions, this cartoon includes a sketch of a man wearing a KKK hood and robe offering to a frightened black man, "Carry yo' bag, sah?" inside of an enclosed area that has a notice on its gate which reads, "Notice Discard all creeds, prejudices, intolerance, race hatred, hypocrisy, pomp, war propaganda, armament and other nuisances here" and has an arrow pointing to a heap outside of the enclosed area. The Ku Klux Klan restarted as a response to what whites perceived as the "unhealthy" sexual relations between white women and non-white men that were becoming more common in the United States.

30. See, e.g., the Virginia "Act to Preserve Racial Integrity" (1924). [See above, pp. 23–24. —Ed.]

31. Madigan, 526, quoting "Rhinelander's Suit," *Opportunity* 4 (1926), 4.

32. "Rising Above Prejudice," *Amsterdam News*, 9 December 1925, editorial page.

33. Edgar M. Grey, "What the Rhinelander Case Means to Negroes," *Amsterdam News*, 9 December 1925, editorial page. "Now the time has come when we must insist upon a standard which yields more than mere 'good looks' in our progeny and the scorn and contempt of the white race to ourselves. When the leaders of a race have no better advice to offer to the rank and file of that race than the familiar, 'Get white and good-looking, when, where and how you can,' it is time that the race hide its head in shame."

34. Marcus Garvey, "Essays on Racial Purity: Atlanta Penitentiary, ca. July 1925," in *The Marcus Garvey and Universal Negro Improvement Association Papers, Vol. 6, September 1924 to December 1927*, ed. Robert A. Hill (Los Angeles: University of California Press, 1989), 216.

35. Ibid., 217.

symbol of the threat of their own racial suicide, some blacks may have feared that Alice Jones was a race traitor.

5. The Power of the Moneyed Class

In anticipation of Mills' references to the "visions" that Alice supposedly had "of these piles upon piles of brand new ten-dollar bills" (1398), Davis argued that after ensnaring Alice with their wealth, the Rhinelanders used their power to further exploit her. Davis noted, "They [the Rhinelanders] have spent their money freely in order to shatter the Jones home, to shatter their daughters . . . and to shatter everybody else in sight that shows the slightest disposition to oppose them" (1204). Even if Alice was greedy, Davis argued, Leonard had an upbringing that should have equipped him to exercise restraint:

> I do not criticize any family's good name but I say this, that no man or boy liv-ing has a right to hide behind a smokescreen of a long family name. . . . One who has . . . been surrounded by wealth, has less excuse than a boy who is born in a hovel and has not a long family name behind him. So much for the Huguenots. (1190)

Davis turned the privilege of wealth on its head, arguing that Alice's age and the alleged sophistication that accompanied it were no match for Leonard's privileged upbringing:

> Look at the difference in age and . . . look at the difference in opportunities. Look at the difference in setting. Why, this boy is beyond his years. His face shows it. This young woman, the evidence shows it, was brought up in a humble home. This young woman had to work at an early age. . . . she did not have the oppor-tunity to educate herself as you and I have had the opportunity. . . . you have Rhinelander . . . surrounded and given every opportunity in life. . . . That is what counteracts . . . the disparity in ages. . . . here is a woman who had no opportu-nity, and here is a man who did. (1192)

Transforming the traditional association between white and cleanliness, Davis also implied that whiteness alone was not sufficient to ensure moral "cleanliness." Using the Rhinelanders, who "do like filth" (1263), as a case in point, he suggested that upperclassness had the potential to make even white people dirty.

As long as the nonthreatening image of Alice as a poor woman who could not "pass" overshadowed the descriptions of her as a sexual, money-hungry manip-ulator, Alice could win her case. The public could read the *Rhinelander* case as a confirmation that the surreptitious transgression of race, sex, and class divisions was impossible. However, the ease with which the attorneys reimaged Alice's character at the trial suggested that perhaps black women could no longer be defined so simply. To secure Alice's victory, Davis would have to prove that Alice was physically incapable of passing.

6. The Denouement

In the 1920s, some individuals still believed that certain physical characteristics identified individuals as racially black or white.[36] In the *Rhinelander* trial, Mills, Leonard's attorney, asserted that Alice, a mulatto, could have passed for white[37] because, like her father, a mulatto, Alice had "white" features. Mills said about Alice's father,

> What I say in regard to his [Alice's father's] face is that every feature of his face is distinctly Caucasian except the color. I say if by some miracle you could change the color of his skin as he sits there he would pass anywhere for a white man. Let us see. He has got the nose of a white man. His nose is far more aquiline than mine. He has got the same nostrils as a white man; thinner than mine. He has got the high cheekbones which do not belong to the African race. He has got a narrow face. He has got the long face, not the round face of colored blood. I repeat, that if the color of Mr. Jones' skin could be changed by some miracle, all the blackness taken out of it, there is not one of you would ever think that he was a person of colored blood. (1429)

As this quote reveals, Mills tried to argue that the combination of Alice's father's "white" facial features and colored skin blurred racial distinctions. As for Alice, the likelihood of passing was even greater. Mills said,

> To look at her she [Alice] inherits from her father. She has got the same features largely that the father has. Long face. Aquiline nose. The other features of the Caucasian. Her lips are not different from the father's lips. The father's lips are as thin as my lips. That is her facial appearance. You have seen her color. (1431)

Arguing that Alice's facial features were not decidedly "black" and, unlike her father's, her skin color was sufficiently light to pass for white, Mills posited that Leonard could not have known merely by looking at Alice that she had "colored" blood. Mills argued that the apparent "whiteness" of Alice's facial skin and features rendered her physically capable of deception. Her inherently deceptive face was thus an unreliable racial indicator and provided powerful evidence that Alice had misled Leonard. Combined with the testimony from several witnesses that Alice verbally had lied about her race,[38] it would have been somewhat convincing

---

36. For a discussion of the fingernails as a racial signifier, see Werner Sollors, "Fingernails as a Racial Sign," *Neither Black Nor White Yet Both: Thematic Explorations of Interracial Literature* (New York: Oxford University Press, 1997).

37. J. A. Rogers, *Sex and Race* 3:71, writes: "Often these women are not so fair as they seem. An ordinary observer will note that their faces are sometimes several shades lighter than their arms or neck due to powder and bleaching compounds. This fact was strikingly brought out in the Rhinelander case. Alice Rhinelander's body, when she stripped for the jury, was found to be much darker than her face."

38. In response to Davis' question, "You claim that Alice made representations to you that she was white on four or five occasions?" Leonard testified, "Yes" (*Court Record*, 637). Leonard also agreed with the assertion that Alice "volunteered the fact that she was white" (*Court Record*, 620).

that if her face lied, so did she. Mills even argued that it made sense that the skin color of Alice's body was lighter than that of her face.[39]

To prove that Alice was physically incapable of passing, Davis presented Alice's body as the definitive evidence of her race.[40] Whereas Leonard's attorney read Alice's body as falsely creating a "white" appearance, Alice's attorney had to show that it was obviously, undeniably, and unfalsifiably black. To do so, he implicitly relied on a popular belief that anyone who had black ancestry, but who could "pass" for white based on the skin color of the parts of her body that were normally within the public's view, would be revealed as black upon close scrutiny of other body parts.[41] Since Leonard "had unlimited opportunities to look" (1199) and he even admitted that he bathed Alice's "entire body" (649),[42] Leonard could not have been deceived. In his closing argument, Alice's attorney emphasized that Alice's body disclosed her race:

> I let you gentlemen look at a portion of what he [Leonard] saw. You saw Alice's back above the bust. You saw her breast. You saw a portion of her upper leg. He saw all of her body. And you are going to tell me that he never suspected that she had colored blood! . . . You saw that with your own eyes. A boy of twelve would have known that colored blood was coursing through her veins. You saw it in a good light. Am I wrong in saying to you that it practically approached the color of her father's face? (1242)

The use of Alice's semi-naked body as evidence together with the reading of explicit love letters probably also accomplished what one commentator would claim more than twenty years later, that "[e]very white man who ever wanted a Negro woman had one vicariously through [Leonard] Kip [Rhinelander] because everything, real or made-up, that ever happened to them was common knowledge."[43] Mills' objection that Alice's removal of her clothing was "calculated to unduly influence the jury" (694) was thus on target.

---

39. Mills argued, "Every one of you knows that the portions of the body which are covered up of a person who is light at all are lighter than the portions that are exposed to the sun and to the elements" (*Court Record*, 1431).

40. The jurors had already seen Alice's father, who was visibly dark, stand up in court (693), and Davis had also argued that Leonard had spent a great deal of time around Alice's father while visiting her at her parents' house. Davis had already asked Alice to hold her hands up so that Leonard and the jurors could examine her skin color (*Court Record*, 511). Dr. Ceasar P. McClendon, a witness called by the defendant, answered affirmatively that when he examined Alice in 1922, her body was "approximately as dark as" his own face, which according to Mills was darker than Mr. Jones' face (869). Dr. McClendon identified himself as a "colored man" when asked (868).

41. Smith, 24, wrote that Alice's "clothes were removed because in those days whites thought that a Negro woman had certain ineradicable marks of race on their bodies and dark half-moons in their fingernails."

42. In his cross-examination of Leonard, Davis established that Leonard had bathed Alice while they were at the Marie Antoinette (*Court Record*, 649).

43. Smith, 72.

7. Yet Alice Wept

The depiction of the partially naked Alice as a weeping yet arousing victim probably also counteracted the description of Leonard as Alice's slave and of Alice as the vamp. This part of the trial, to use bell hooks' phraseology, facilitated the "recreat[ing of] the imperial gaze—the look that seeks to dominate, subjugate, and colonize."[44] Images of white men, such as Harriet Beecher Stowe's Simon Legree, humiliating black slave women probably still had a powerful hold on the American imagination even though slavery was abolished. Thus, while the jurors may have enjoyed fantasizing about Alice Jones as a sexually available "slave," watching her humiliated in this way to prove her innocence also probably evoked the jurors' pity.[45]

Alice's weeping without speaking suggested that perhaps Leonard was a slavemaster who ruthlessly abused Alice as if she were his helpless slave. This "performance" (693)[46] implied that Leonard's and the Rhinelander family's victimization of Alice compelled her to expose everything about herself, including her flesh, to vindicate herself. Davis said that he hoped Leonard would not "force" him to speak of Leonard's relations with Alice in a way that was not "delicate" (452). Thus, Davis' subsequent resort to reading sexually explicit language from love letters strongly suggested that Leonard forced Davis to humiliate his own client. Davis' depiction of Leonard as abusing his power was probably disturbing, but it still represented Leonard, the white male, in the position of power over Alice, the black woman. Thus, the jurors could rule against Leonard's abuse of his power but reap comfort in the belief that Alice had never usurped that power.

One newspaper referred to Davis' decision not to call Alice to the witness stand as "one of the most dramatic surprises of the always surprising trial of Leonard Kip Rhinelander's suit against his wife."[47] However, in this way, Alice's attorney could try to discount as hearsay Mills' allegations and other people's testimony that Alice deliberately hid her black ancestry. Perhaps Davis did not ask Alice to speak because after her humiliation, which he had implied was Leonard's fault, he wanted to "spare Alice [the] ordeal [of speaking] on [the] witness stand."[48] Had Mills cross-examined Alice, she might have sabotaged her case by trying to

---

44. bell hooks, 7.

45. In the January 1926 issue of *The Crisis*, the official publication of the National Association for the Advancement of Colored People, editor W. E. B. Du Bois focused on the pornographic nature of Alice's removal of her clothes, interpreting the Rhinelander story as one of violation. He wrote that Alice Jones was "strip[ped] naked, soul and body" and she was "defenseless" ("Opinion: Rhinelander," 112).

46. Mills used this word.

47. *Moorland-Spingarn*, 30 November 1925. *See also Rhinelander v. Rhinelander*, 219 N.Y.S. 548 (1927) (*per curiam*) (rejecting Leonard's challenge to judge's jury instructions in connection with Alice's failure to testify).

48. *Brooklyn Daily Eagle, Moorland-Spingarn. See also* the journalist who reports that even though it was Davis who requested that Alice remove her clothes, Davis says he will not have Alice testify because, "we are determined that this girl shall no longer be dragged in the mire by the slanders this man Jacobs [one of Leonard's attorneys] has gathered together, and which he has threatened to use in an effort to tear to pieces what little reputation this poor girl still possessed . . . haven't

establish that she thought of herself as a white person even though she had colored blood. Alice's silence also furthered the theory of her case: just as the jury could determine that it was obvious from her body that she was black regardless of her words, Leonard would have been able to do the same regardless of what she may have said to him.

Alice's silence enabled Leonard's attorney to set forth his own reading of Alice's mind from her love letters just as the jury could read her character from her body. Leonard's attorney asserted that he could represent "her [Alice's] mind, the way it works" (1333). He repeatedly claimed to know what Alice knew (1368, 1400). Reconstructing her thoughts, he said, "She must have had in mind" (1399).

While Alice's silence was strategically sensible, the price was that she did not have the opportunity to define herself in the terms that she might have chosen. Even some black papers asserted Alice's membership in a race which she might have rejected. The front page of *The Amsterdam News*, New York's leading black newspaper, read: "Harlem was for Alice without caring anything personally for Alice. It was for Alice because she stood as a symbol to Negro womanhood throughout the world."[49] And the *Amsterdam News* editorial "Rising Above Prejudice" interpreted Alice's legal victory as a declaration that the law would finally hold white men accountable for sexually exploiting black women:

> [W]e believe the Rhinelander jurors have rendered a great service to womanhood in general and Negro womanhood in particular. . . . [The Rhinelander case proves that] the law will not uphold them [white men] in their promiscuous folly with colored women.[50]

Edgar M. Grey of the *Amsterdam News* suggested in a separate editorial that the case was about whether a white man could "indulge in sexual relationship with a Negro woman and seek the protection of the law against her social and legal claims growing out of this relationship."[51] These journalists heralded Alice as a hero of the black race even though she may not have regarded this gesture as an honor, overlooking that Alice may not have identified herself as black, and thus devalued the importance of her own definition of her self, whatever that was.

In the *Rhinelander* trial, Alice Jones' "whole life had been bared" (1158)[52] and her image had become that of an easily remoldable piece of clay. The jury's verdict in favor of Alice was a declaration that she not only *did not* deceive Leonard about her race, but that she *could not* have deceived him. Using carefully crafted rhetoric, the attorneys and the press described Alice as whomever they wanted her to be.

---

we the right not to subject this woman to any more cruelty than has been heaped upon her? She has been dragged in the sewer and in filth for weeks and we will no longer permit them to do it" (*The New York Times*, 1 December 1925, 12); see also *Court Record*, 1158–59.

49. Mark Whitmark, "Rhinelander's Verdict Meets Harlem's Approval, *The Amsterdam News*, 9 December 1925, 1.
50. "Rising Above Prejudice," *The Amsterdam News*, 9 December 1925, editorial and feature page.
51. Edgar M. Grey, "What the Rhinelander Case Means to Negroes," *The Amsterdam News*, 9 December 1925, editorial page.
52. These are Davis' words.

Although the *Rhinelander* verdict permitted the American public to believe that passing could not go undetected because it was physically impossible, the *Rhinelander* courtroom rhetoric strongly foreshadowed that the very concept of "passing" was becoming inappropriate because the categories between which individuals were said to pass were becoming blurrier with time. Distinctions between black and white, lower class and upper class, the woman as sexual slave and the man as sexual master, were being challenged, suggesting that these distinctions were becoming indefensible in the 1920s—if they were not unfounded from the beginning.

Nonetheless, the *Rhinelander* court's admission of Alice Jones' semi-naked body as evidence and the existence of the cause of action of fraud based on racial deception lent legitimacy to reducing a black woman's character to her body and to defining identity by skin color. The court's tolerance of Leonard's attorney's appeal to race, sex, and class prejudices by invoking derogatory images such as that of the vamp suggests that the courts were not actively monitoring racist representations of black women.

The *Rhinelander* trial demonstrates how deeply rooted race, gender, and class images are in the American consciousness and how difficult it is to separate these elements of identity. It may have been true that the "fierce fires of love had blinded both [Alice and Leonard] to the dicta of race and class,"[53] but this was not the case for the rest of American society in the 1920s. As Mark Madigan writes, "Acquitted of racial deception by law, Alice was persecuted nonetheless as her marriage was ruined and she was forced to endure a long, humiliating annulment trial."[54] More than three-quarters of a century after the *Rhinelander* case, the many questions that it raised, including the role of the law in defining individual identity,[55] continue to pervade public discourse.

Perhaps a diary[56] of Alice Beatrice Jones will someday surface. Then Alice's version of the case will be told, and *she* will reveal who the real Alice Jones was. Because the story of Alice Jones and Leonard Rhinelander unsettled many Americans' sensibilities about race, class, and sexual behavior,[57] the *Rhinelander* trial was a critical moment in the history of America's self-definition and the individual's struggle for self-definition in the twentieth century.

53. "Rhinelander's Suit," *Opportunity* 4 (1926), 4.
54. Madigan, 528.
55. In reference to the *Rhinelander* case, the editors of one black newspaper argued, "Obviously this was an affair that ought to have been settled out of court. . . . The emotions which underlie the whole affair are altogether too obscure and too complex for the coarse processes of any legal system. The realities of the affair lie in a realm of feeling of which the actors themselves were hardly aware, which the wisest doctor and the most discerning priest would need years to explore before they could understand it. . . . The tragedy of the affair is that here was no one mature enough and large-minded enough to take the whole case in hand, and quietly, privately, patently unravel it" ("Lawyers," *Afro-American* 5 [December 1925], in Moorland-Spingarn).
56. One newspaper ran a headline that alleged that Alice kept a diary. See *New York Journal*, 16 November 1925 (Moorland Spingarn).
57. The editors of *The Messenger* wrote: "The Nordics pretend to believe that the purity of their race has been outraged. For this reason, the case transcends in importance the fate of Mr. and Mrs. Kip Rhinelander. What matter though he did deceive her or she deceived him? That's nothing new. It's going on every day" (*Messenger* 7 [December 1925], 388).

Miscegenation Law, Court Cases, and Ideologies of "Race" in Twentieth-Century America*

PEGGY PASCOE

On March 21, 1921, Joe Kirby took his wife, Mayellen, to court. The Kirbys had been married for seven years, and Joe wanted out. Ignoring the usual option of divorce, he asked for an annulment, charging that his marriage had been invalid from its very beginning because Arizona law prohibited marriages between "persons of Caucasian blood, or their descendants" and "negroes, Mongolians or Indians, and their descendants." Joe Kirby claimed that while he was "a person of the Caucasian blood," his wife, Mayellen, was "a person of negro blood."[1]

Although Joe Kirby's charges were rooted in a well-established—and tragic— tradition of American miscegenation law, his court case quickly disintegrated into a definitional dispute that bordered on the ridiculous. The first witness in the case was Joe's mother, Tula Kirby, who gave her testimony in Spanish through an interpreter. Joe's lawyer laid out the case by asking Tula Kirby a few seemingly simple questions:

Joe's lawyer: To what race do you belong?

Tula Kirby: Mexican.

Joe's lawyer: Are you white or have you Indian blood?

Kirby: I have no Indian blood.

. . . .

Joe's lawyer: Do you know the defendant [Mayellen] Kirby?

Kirby: Yes.

Joe's lawyer: To what race does she belong?

Kirby: Negro.

Then the cross-examination began.

Mayellen's lawyer: Who was your father?

Kirby: Jose Romero.

Mayellen's lawyer: Was he a Spaniard?

Kirby: Yes, a Mexican.

Mayellen's lawyer: Was he born in Spain?

---

* From Peggy Pascoe, "Miscegenation Law, Court Cases, and Ideologies of 'Race' in Twentieth-Century America." *Journal of American History* 83.1 (June 1996): 44–69.
1. Ariz. Rev. Stat. Ann. sec. 3837 (1913); "Appellant's Abstract of Record," Aug. 8, 1921, pp. 1–2, *Kirby v. Kirby*, docket 1970 (microfilm: file 36.1.134), Arizona Supreme Court Civil Cases (Arizona State Law Library, Phoenix).

Kirby: No, he was born in Sonora.

Mayellen's lawyer: And who was your mother?

Kirby: Also in Sonora.

Mayellen's lawyer: Was she a Spaniard?

Kirby: She was on her father's side.

Mayellen's lawyer: And what on her mother's side?

Kirby: Mexican.

Mayellen's lawyer: What do you mean by Mexican, Indian, a native [?]

Kirby: I don't know what is meant by Mexican.

Mayellen's lawyer: A native of Mexico?

Kirby: Yes, Sonora, all of us.

Mayellen's lawyer: Who was your grandfather on your father's side?

Kirby: He was a Spaniard.

Mayellen's lawyer: Who was he?

Kirby: His name was Ignacio Quevas.

Mayellen's lawyer: Where was he born?

Kirby: That I don't know. He was my grandfather.

Mayellen's lawyer: How do you know he was a [S]paniard then?

Kirby: Because he told me ever since I had knowledge that he was a Spaniard.

Next the questioning turned to Tula's opinion about Mayellen Kirby's racial identity.

Mayellen's lawyer: You said Mrs. [Mayellen] Kirby was a negress. What do you know about Mrs. Kirby's family?

Kirby: I distinguish her by her color and the hair; that is all I do know.[2]

The second witness in the trial was Joe Kirby, and by the time he took the stand, the people in the courtroom knew they were in murky waters. When Joe's lawyer opened with the question "What race do *you* belong to?," Joe answered "Well . . . ," and paused, while Mayellen's lawyer objected to the question on the ground that it called for a conclusion by the witness. "Oh, no," said the judge, "it is a matter of pedigree." Eventually allowed to answer the question, Joe said, "I belong to the white race I suppose." Under cross-examination, he described his father as having been of the "Irish race," although he admitted, "I never knew any one of his people."[3]

Stopping at the brink of this morass, Joe's lawyer rested his case. He told the judge he had established that Joe was "Caucasian." Mayellen's lawyer scoffed, claiming that Joe had "failed utterly to prove his case" and arguing that "[Joe's]

2. "Appellant's Abstract of Record," 12–13, 13–15, 15, *Kirby v. Kirby.*
3. *Ibid.*, 16–18.

mother has admitted that. She has [testified] that she only claims a quarter Spanish blood; the rest of it is native blood." At this point the court intervened. "I know," said the judge, "but that does not signify anything."[4]

From the Decline and Fall of Scientific Racism to an Understanding of Modernist Racial Ideology

The Kirbys' case offers a fine illustration of Evelyn Brooks Higginbotham's observation that, although most Americans are sure they know "race" when they see it, very few can offer a definition of the term. Partly for this reason, the questions of what "race" signifies and what signifies "race" are as important for scholars today as they were for the participants in *Kirby v. Kirby* seventy-five years ago.[5] Historians have a long—and recently a distinguished—record of exploring this question.[6] Beginning in the 1960s, one notable group charted the rise and fall of scientific racism among American intellectuals. Today, their successors, more likely to be schooled in social than intellectual history, trace the social construction of racial ideologies, including the idea of "whiteness," in a steadily expanding range of contexts.[7]

4. *Ibid.*, 19.
5. Evelyn Brooks Higginbotham, "African-American Women's History and the Metalanguage of Race," *Signs*, 17 (Winter 1992), 253. See Michael Omi and Howard Winant, *Racial Formation in the United States: From the 1960s to the 1990s* (New York, 1994); David Theo Goldberg, ed., *Anatomy of Racism* (Minneapolis, 1990); Henry Louis Gates Jr., ed., *"Race," Writing, and Difference* (Chicago, 1986); Dominick LaCapra, ed., *The Bounds of Race: Perspectives on Hegemony and Resistance* (Ithaca, 1991); F. James Davis, *Who Is Black? One Nation's Definition* (University Park, 1991); Sandra Harding, ed., *The "Racial" Economy of Science: Toward a Democratic Future* (Bloomington, 1993); Maria P. P. Root, ed., *Racially Mixed People in America* (Newbury Park, 1992); and Ruth Frankenberg, *White Women, Race Matters: The Social Construction of Whiteness* (Minneapolis, 1993).
6. Among the most provocative recent works are Higginbotham, "African-American Women's History"; Barbara J. Fields, "Ideology and Race in American History," in *Region, Race, and Reconstruction: Essays in Honor of C. Vann Woodward*, ed. J. Morgan Kousser and James M. McPherson (New York, 1982), 143–78; Thomas C. Holt, "Marking: Race, Race-Making, and the Writing of History," *American Historical Review*, 100 (Feb. 1995), 1–20; and David R. Roediger, *Towards the Abolition of Whiteness: Essays on Race, Politics, and Working Class History* (London, 1994).
7. On scientific racism, see Thomas F. Gossett, *Race: The History of an Idea in America* (Dallas, 1963); George W. Stocking Jr., *Race, Culture, and Evolution: Essays in the History of Anthropology* (1968; Chicago, 1982); John S. Haller Jr., *Outcaste from Evolution: Scientific Attitudes to Racial Inferiority, 1859–1900* (Urbana, 1971); George M. Fredrickson, *The Black Image in the White Mind: The Debate on Afro-American Character and Destiny, 1817–1914* (New York, 1971); Thomas G. Dyer, *Theodore Roosevelt and the Idea of Race* (Baton Rouge, 1980); Carl N. Degler, *In Search of Human Nature: The Decline and Revival of Darwinism in American Social Thought* (New York, 1991); and Elazar Barkan, *Retreat of Scientific Racism: Changing Concepts of Race in Britain and the United States between the World Wars* (Cambridge, Eng., 1992). On the social construction of racial ideologies, see the works cited in footnote 6, above, and Ronald T. Takaki, *Iron Cages: Race and Culture in Nineteenth-Century America* (New York, 1979); Reginald Horsman, *Race and Manifest Destiny: The Origins of American Racial Anglo-Saxonism* (Cambridge, Mass., 1981); Alexander Saxton, *The Rise and Fall of the White Republic: Class Politics and Mass Culture in Nineteenth-Century America* (London, 1990); David R. Roediger, *The Wages of Whiteness: Race and the Making of the American*

Their work has taught us a great deal about racial thinking in American history. We can trace the growth of racism among antebellum immigrant workers and free-soil northern Republicans; we can measure its breadth in late-nineteenth-century segregation and the immigration policies of the 1920s. We can follow the rise of Anglo-Saxonism from Manifest Destiny through the Spanish-American War and expose the appeals to white supremacy in woman suffrage speeches. We can relate all these developments (and more) to the growth and elaboration of scientific racist attempts to use biological characteristics to scout for racial hierarchies in social life, levels of civilization, even language.

Yet the range and richness of these studies all but end with the 1920s. In contrast to historians of the nineteenth- and early-twentieth-century United States, historians of the nation in the mid- to late twentieth century seem to focus on racial ideologies only when they are advanced by the far Right (as in the Ku Klux Klan) or by racialized groups themselves (as in the Harlem Renaissance or black nationalist movements). To the extent that there is a framework for surveying mainstream twentieth-century American racial ideologies, it is inherited from the classic histories that tell of the post-1920s decline and fall of scientific racism. Their final pages link the demise of scientific racism to the rise of a vanguard of social scientists led by the cultural anthropologist Franz Boas: when modern social science emerges, racism runs out of intellectual steam. In the absence of any other narrative, this forms the basis for a commonly held but rarely examined intellectual trickle-down theory in which the attack on scientific racism emerges in universities in the 1920s and eventually, if belatedly, spreads to courts in the 1940s and 1950s and to government policy in the 1960s and 1970s.

A close look at such incidents as the *Kirby* case, however, suggests a rather different historical trajectory, one that recognizes that the legal system does more than just reflect social or scientific ideas about race; it also produces and reproduces them.[8] By following a trail marked by four miscegenation cases—the seemingly ordinary *Kirby v. Kirby* (1922) and *Estate of Monks* (1941) and the path-breaking *Perez v. Lippold* (1948) and *Loving v. Virginia* (1967)—this article will examine the relation between modern social science, miscegenation law, and twentieth-century American racial ideologies, focusing less on the decline of scientific racism and more on the emergence of new racial ideologies.

In exploring these issues, it helps to understand that the range of nineteenth-century racial ideologies was much broader than scientific racism. Accordingly, I have chosen to use the term *racialism* to designate an ideological complex that other historians often describe with the terms "race" or "racist." I intend the

---

Working Class (London, 1991); Audrey Smedley, *Race in North America: Origin and Evolution of a Worldview* (Boulder, 1993); and Tomas Almaguer, *Racial Fault Lines: The Historical Origins of White Supremacy in California* (Berkeley, 1994).

8. On law as a producer of racial ideologies, see Barbara J. Fields, "Slavery, Race, and Ideology in the United States of America," *New Left Review*, 181 (May–June 1990), 7; Eva Saks, "Representing Miscegenation Law," *Raritan*, 8 (Fall 1988), 56–60 [in this volume, pp. 61–81. —Ed.]; and Collette Guillaumin, "Race and Nature: The System of Marks," *Feminist Issues*, 8 (Fall 1988), 25–44.

term *racialism* to be broad enough to cover a wide range of nineteenth-century ideas, from the biologically marked categories scientific racists employed to the more amorphous ideas George M. Fredrickson has so aptly called "romantic racialism."[9] Used in this way, "racialism" helps counter the tendency of twentieth-century observers to perceive nineteenth-century ideas as biologically "determinist" in some simple sense. To racialists (including scientific racists), the important point was not that biology determined culture (indeed, the split between the two was only dimly perceived), but that race, understood as an indivisible essence that included not only biology but also culture, morality, and intelligence, was a compellingly significant factor in history and society.

My argument is this: During the 1920s, American racialism was challenged by several emerging ideologies, all of which depended on a modern split between biology and culture. Between the 1920s and the 1960s, those competing ideologies were winnowed down to the single, powerfully persuasive belief that the eradication of racism depends on the deliberate nonrecognition of race. I will call that belief *modernist racial ideology* to echo the self-conscious "modernism" of social scientists, writers, artists, and cultural rebels of the early twentieth century. When historians mention this phenomenon, they usually label it "antiracist" or "egalitarian" and describe it as in stark contrast to the "racism" of its predecessors. But in the new legal scholarship called critical race theory, this same ideology, usually referred to as "color blindness," is criticized by those who recognize that it, like other racial ideologies, can be turned to the service of oppression.[10]

Modernist racial ideology has been widely accepted; indeed, it compels nearly as much adherence in the late-twentieth-century United States as racialism did in the late nineteenth century. It is therefore important to see it not as what it claims to be—the nonideological end of racism—but as a racial ideology of its own, whose history shapes many of today's arguments about the meaning of race in American society.

The Legacy of Racialism and the *Kirby* Case

Although it is probably less familiar to historians than, say, school segregation law, miscegenation law is an ideal place to study both the legacy of nineteenth-century racialism and the emergence of modern racial ideologies.[11] Miscegenation

9. See especially Fredrickson, *Black Image in the White Mind.*
10. For intriguing attempts to define American modernism, see Daniel J. Singal, ed., *Modernist Culture in America* (Belmont, 1991); and Dorothy Ross, ed., *Modernist Impulses in the Human Sciences, 1870–1930* (Baltimore, 1994). For the view from critical race theory, see Brian K. Fair, "Foreword: Rethinking the Colorblindness Model," *National Black Law Journal,* 13 (Spring 1993), 1–82; Neil Gotanda, "A Critique of 'Our Constitution Is Color-Blind,' " *Stanford Law Review,* 44 (Nov. 1991), 1–68; Gary Peller, "Race Consciousness," *Duke Law Journal* (Sept. 1990), 758–847; and Peter Fitzpatrick, "Racism and the Innocence of Law," in *Anatomy of Racism,* ed. Goldberg, 247–62.
11. Many scholars avoid using the word *miscegenation,* which dates to the 1860s, means race mixing, and has, to twentieth-century minds, embarrassingly biological connotations; they speak of laws against "interracial" or "cross-cultural" relationships. Contemporaries usually referred to "anti-

laws, in force from the 1660s through the 1960s, were among the longest lasting of American racial restrictions. They both reflected and produced significant shifts in American racial thinking. Although the first miscegenation laws had been passed in the colonial period, it was not until after the demise of slavery that they began to function as the ultimate sanction of the American system of white supremacy. They burgeoned along with the rise of segregation and the early-twentieth-century devotion to "white purity." At one time or another, 41 American colonies and states enacted them; they blanketed western as well as southern states.[12]

By the early twentieth century, miscegenation laws were so widespread that they formed a virtual road map to American legal conceptions of race. Laws that had originally prohibited marriages between whites and African Americans (and, very occasionally, American Indians) were extended to cover a much wider range of groups. Eventually, 12 states targeted American Indians, 14 Asian Americans (Chinese, Japanese, and Koreans), and 9 "Malays" (or Filipinos). In Arizona, the *Kirby* case was decided under categories first adopted in a 1901 law that prohibited whites from marrying "negroes, Mongolians or Indians"; in 1931, "Malays" and "Hindus" were added to this list.[13]

---

miscegenation" laws. Neither alternative seems satisfactory, since the first avoids naming the ugliness that was so much a part of the laws and the second implies that "miscegenation" was a distinct racial phenomenon rather than a categorization imposed on certain relationships. I retain the term *miscegenation* when speaking of the laws and court cases that relied on the concept, but not when speaking of people or particular relationships. On the emergence of the term, see Sidney Kaplan, "The Miscegenation Issue in the Election of 1864," *Journal of Negro History*, 24 (July 1949), 274–343 [included in this volume, pp. 219–265. —Ed.].

12. Most histories of interracial sex and marriage in America focus on demographic patterns, rather than legal constraints. See, for example, Joel Williamson, *New People: Miscegenation and Mulattoes in the United States* (New York, 1980); Paul R. Spickard, *Mixed Blood: Intermarriage and Ethnic Identity in Twentieth-Century America* (Madison, 1989); and Deborah Lynn Kitchen, "Interracial Marriage in the United States, 1900–1980" (Ph.D. diss., University of Minnesota, 1993). The only historical overview is Byron Curti Martyn, "Racism in the United States: A History of the Anti-Miscegenation Legislation and Litigation" (Ph.D. diss., University of Southern California, 1979). On the colonial period, see A. Leon Higginbotham Jr. and Barbara K. Kopytoff, "Racial Purity and Interracial Sex in the Law of Colonial and Antebellum Virginia," *Georgetown Law Journal*, 77 (Aug. 1989), 1967–2029 [in this volume, pp. 81–139. —Ed.]; George M. Fredrickson, *White Supremacy: A Comparative Study in American and South African History* (New York, 1981), 99–108; and James Hugo Johnston, *Race Relations in Virginia & Miscegenation in the South, 1776–1860* (Amherst, 1970), 165–90. For later periods, see Peter Bardaglio, "Families, Sex, and the Law: The Legal Transformation of the Nineteenth-Century Southern Household" (Ph.D. diss., Stanford University, 1987), 37–106, 345–49; Peter Wallenstein, "Race, Marriage, and the Law of Freedom: Alabama and Virginia, 1860s–1960s," *Chicago-Kent Law Review*, 70 (no. 2, 1994), 371–437; David H. Fowler, *Northern Attitudes towards Interracial Marriage: Legislation and Public Opinion in the Middle Atlantic and the States of the Old Northwest, 1780–1930* (New York, 1987); Megumi Dick Osumi, "Asians and California's Anti-Miscegenation Laws," in *Asian and Pacific American Experiences: Women's Perspectives*, ed. Nobuya Tsuchida (Minneapolis, 1982), 2–8; and Peggy Pascoe, "Race, Gender, and Intercultural Relations: The Case of Interracial Marriage," *Frontiers*, 12 (no. 1, 1991), 5–18. The count of states is from the most complete list in Fowler, *Northern Attitudes*, 336–439.

13. Ariz. Rev. Stat. Ann. sec. 3092 (1901); 1931 Ariz. Sess. Laws ch. 17. Arizona, Idaho, Maine, Massachusetts, Nevada, North Carolina, Oregon, Rhode Island, South Carolina, Tennessee, Vir-

Although many historians assume that miscegenation laws enforced American taboos against interracial sex, marriage, more than sex, was the legal focus.[14] Some states did forbid both interracial sex and interracial marriage, but nearly twice as many targeted only marriage. Because marriage carried with it social respectability and economic benefits that were routinely denied to couples engaged in illicit sex, appeals courts adjudicated the legal issue of miscegenation at least as frequently in civil cases about marriage and divorce, inheritance, or child legitimacy as in criminal cases about sexual misconduct.[15]

---

ginia, and Washington passed laws that mentioned American Indians. Arizona, California, Georgia, Idaho, Mississippi, Missouri, Montana, Nebraska, Nevada, Oregon, South Dakota, Utah, Virginia, and Wyoming passed laws that mentioned Asian Americans. Arizona, California, Georgia, Maryland, Nevada, South Dakota, Utah, Virginia, and Wyoming passed laws that mentioned "Malays." In addition, Oregon law targeted "Kanakas" (native Hawaiians), Virginia "Asiatic Indians," and Georgia both "Asiatic Indians" and "West Indians." See Fowler, *Northern Attitudes*, 336–439; 1924 Va. Acts ch. 371; 1927 Ga. Laws no. 317; 1931 Ariz. Sess. Laws ch. 17; 1933 Cal. Stat. ch. 104; 1935 Md. Laws ch. 60; and 1939 Utah Laws ch. 50.

14. The most insightful social and legal histories have focused on sexual relations rather than marriage. See, for example, Higginbotham and Kopytoff, "Racial Purity and Interracial Sex"; Karen Getman, "Sexual Control in the Slaveholding South: The Implementation and Maintenance of a Racial Caste System," *Harvard Women's Law Journal*, 7 (Spring 1984), 125–34; Martha Hodes, "Sex across the Color Line: White Women and Black Men in the Nineteenth-Century American South" (Ph.D. diss., Princeton University, 1991); and Martha Hodes, "The Sexualization of Reconstruction Politics: White Women and Black Men in the South after the Civil War," in *American Sexual Politics: Sex, Gender, and Race since the Civil War*, ed. John C. Fout and Maura Shaw Tantillo (Chicago, 1993), 59–74; Robyn Weigman, "The Anatomy of Lynching," *ibid.*, 223–45; Jacquelyn Dowd Hall, " 'The Mind That Burns in Each Body': Women, Rape, and Racial Violence," in *Powers of Desire: The Politics of Sexuality*, ed. Ann Snitow, Christine Stansell, and Sharon Thompson (New York, 1983), 328–49; Kenneth James Lay, "Sexual Racism: A Legacy of Slavery," *National Black Law Journal*, 13 (Spring 1993), 165–83; and Kevin J. Mumford, "From Vice to Vogue: Black/White Sexuality and the 1920s" (Ph.D. diss., Stanford University, 1993). One of the first works to note the predominance of marriage in miscegenation laws was Mary Frances Berry, "Judging Morality: Sexual Behavior and Legal Consequences in the Late Nineteenth-Century South," *Journal of American History*, 78 (Dec. 1991), 838–39. On the historical connections among race, marriage, property, and the state, see Saks, "Representing Miscegenation Law," 39–69; Nancy F. Cott, "Giving Character to Our Whole Civil Polity: Marriage and the Public Order in the Late Nineteenth Century," in *U.S. History as Women's History: New Feminist Essays*, ed. Linda K. Kerber, Alice Kessler-Harris, and Kathryn Kish Sklar (Chapel Hill, 1995), 107–21; Ramon A. Gutierrez, *When Jesus Came, the Corn Mothers Went Away: Marriage, Sexuality, and Power in New Mexico, 1500–1846* (Stanford, 1991); Verena Martinez-Alier, *Marriage, Class, and Colour in Nineteenth-Century Cuba: A Study of Racial Attitudes and Sexual Values in a Slave Society* (Ann Arbor, 1989); Patricia J. Williams, "Fetal Fictions: An Exploration of Property Archetypes in Racial and Gendered Contexts," in *Race in America: The Struggle for Equality*, ed. Herbert Hill and James E. Jones Jr. (Madison, 1993), 425–37; and Virginia R. Domínguez, *White by Definition: Social Classification in Creole Louisiana* (New Brunswick, 1986).

15. Of the 41 colonies and states that prohibited interracial marriage, 22 also prohibited some form of interracial sex. One additional jurisdiction (New York) prohibited interracial sex but not interracial marriage; it is not clear how long this 1638 statute was in effect. See Fowler, *Northern Attitudes*, 336–439. My database consists of every appeals court case I could identify in which miscegenation law played a role: 227 cases heard between 1850 and 1970, 132 civil and 95 criminal.

By the time the *Kirby* case was heard, lawyers and judges approached misceg- enation cases with working assumptions built on decades of experience. There had been a flurry of challenges to the laws during Reconstruction, but courts quickly fended off arguments that miscegenation laws violated the Fourteenth Amendment guarantee of "equal protection." Beginning in the late 1870s, judges declared that the laws were constitutional because they covered all racial groups "equally."[16] Judicial justifications reflected the momentum toward racial catego- rization built into the nineteenth-century legal system and buttressed by the ra- cialist conviction that everything from culture, morality, and intelligence to heredity could be understood in terms of race.

From the 1880s until the 1920s, lawyers whose clients had been caught in the snare of miscegenation laws knew better than to challenge the constitutionality of the laws or to dispute the perceived necessity for racial categorization; these were all but guaranteed to be losing arguments. A defender's best bet was to do what Mayellen Kirby's lawyer tried to do: to persuade a judge (or jury) that one par- ticular individual's racial classification was in error. Lawyers who defined their task in these limited terms occasionally succeeded, but even then the deck was stacked against them. Wielded by judges and juries who believed that setting racial boundaries was crucial to the maintenance of ordered society, the criteria used to determine who fit in which category were more notable for their malleability than for their logical consistency. Genealogy, appearance, claims to identity, or that mystical quality, "blood"—any of these would do.[17]

Although cases that reach appeals courts are by definition atypical, they are significant because the decisions reached in them set policies later followed in more routine cases and because the texts of the decisions hint at how judges conceptualized particular legal problems. I have relied on them because of these interpretive advantages and for two more practical reasons. First, because appeals court decisions are published and indexed, it is possible to compile a comprehensive list of them. Second, because making an appeal requires the preservation of documents that might otherwise be discarded (such as legal briefs and court reporters' trial notes), they permit the historian to go beyond the judge's decision.

16. Decisions striking down the laws include *Burns v. State*, 48 Ala. 195 (1872); *Bonds v. Foster*, 36 Tex. 68 (1871–1872); *Honey v. Clark*, 37 Tex. 686 (1873); *Hart v. Hoss*, 26 La. Ann. 90 (1874); *State v. Webb*, 4 Cent. L. J. 588 (1877); and *Ex parte Brown*, 5 Cent. L. J. 149 (1877). Decisions upholding the laws include *Scott v. State*, 39 Ga. 321 (1869); *State v. Hairston*, 63 N.C. 451 (1869); *State v. Reinhardt*, 63 N.C. 547 (1869); *In re Hobbs*, 12 F. Cas. 262 (1871) (No. 6550); *Lonas v. State*, 50 Tenn. 287 (1871); *State v. Gibson*, 36 Ind. 389 (1871); *Ford v. State*, 53 Ala. 150 (1875); *Green v. State*, 58 Ala. 190 (1877); *Frasher v. State*, 3 Tex. Ct. App. R. 263 1877); *Ex Parte Kinney*, 14 F. Cas. 602 (1879) (No. 7825); *Ex parte Francois*, 9 Fed. Cas. 699 (1879) (No. 5047); *Francois v. State*, 9 Tex. Ct. App. R. 144 (1880); *Pace v. State*, 69 Ala. 231 (1881); *Pace v. Alabama*, 106 U.S. 583 (1882); *State v. Jackson*, 80 Mo. 175 (1883); *State v. Tutty*, 41 F. 753 (1890); *Dodson v. State*, 31 S.W. 977 (1895); *Strauss v. State*, 173 S.W. 663 (1915); *State v. Daniel*, 75 So. 836 (1917); *Succession of Mingo*, 78 So. 565 (1917–18); and *In re Paquet's Estate*, 200 P. 911 (1921).

17. Individual racial classifications were successfully challenged in *Moore v. State*, 7 Tex. Ct. App. R. 608 (1880); *Jones v. Commonwealth*, 80 Va. 213 (1884); *Jones v. Commonwealth*, 80 Va. 538 (1885); *State v. Treadaway*, 52 So. 500 (1910); *Flores v. State*, 129 S.W. 1111 (1910); *Ferrall v. Ferrall*,

In Arizona, Judge Samuel L. Pattee demonstrated that malleability in deciding the *Kirby* case. Although Mayellen Kirby's lawyer maintained that Joe Kirby "appeared" to be an Indian, the judge insisted that parentage, not appearance, was the key to Joe's racial classification:

> Mexicans are classed as of the Caucasian Race. They are descendants, supposed to be, at least of the Spanish conquerors of that country, and unless it can be shown that they are mixed up with some other races, why the presumption is that they are descendants of the Caucasian race.[18]

While the judge decided that ancestry determined that Joe Kirby was "Caucasian," he simply assumed that Mayellen Kirby was "Negro." Mayellen Kirby sat silent through the entire trial; she was spoken about and spoken for but never allowed to speak herself. There was no testimony about her ancestry; her race was assumed to rest in her visible physical characteristics. Neither of the lawyers bothered to argue over Mayellen's racial designation. As Joe's lawyer later explained,

> The learned and discriminating judge . . . had the opportunity to gaze upon the dusky countenance of the appellant [Mayellen Kirby] and could not and did not fail to observe the distinguishing characteristics of the African race and blood.[19]

In the end, the judge accepted the claim that Joe Kirby was "Caucasian" and Mayellen Kirby "Negro" and held that the marriage violated Arizona miscegenation law; he granted Joe Kirby his annulment. In so doing, the judge resolved the miscegenation drama by adding a patriarchal moral to the white supremacist plot. As long as miscegenation laws regulated marriage more than sex, it proved easy for white men involved with women of color to avoid the social and economic responsibilities they would have carried in legally sanctioned marriages with white women. By granting Joe Kirby an annulment, rather than a divorce, the judge not only denied the validity of the marriage while it had lasted but also in effect excused Joe Kirby from his obligation to provide economic support to a divorced wife.[20]

For her part, Mayellen Kirby had nothing left to lose. She and her lawyer appealed to the Arizona Supreme Court. This time they threw caution to the winds. Taking a first step toward the development of modern racial ideologies, they moved beyond their carefully limited argument about Joe's individual racial

---

69 S.E. 60 (1910); *Marre v. Marre*, 168 S.W. 636 (1914); *Neuberger v. Gueldner*, 72 So. 220 (1916); and *Reed v. State*, 92 So. 511 (1922).
18. "Appellant's Abstract of Record," 19, *Kirby v. Kirby*.
19. "Appellee's Brief," Oct. 3, 1921, p. 6. *ibid.*
20. On the theoretical problems involved in exploring how miscegenation laws were gendered, see Pascoe, "Race, Gender, and Intercultural Relations"; and Peggy Pascoe, "Race, Gender, and the Privileges of Property: On the Significance of Miscegenation Law in United States History," in *New Viewpoints in Women's History: Working Papers from the Schlesinger Library 50th Anniversary Conference, March 4–5, 1994*, ed. Susan Ware (Cambridge, Mass., 1994), 99–122. For an excellent account of the gendering of early miscegenation laws, see Kathleen M. Brown, *Good Wives and Nasty Wenches: Gender, Race, and Power in Colonial Virginia* (Chapel Hill, 1996).

classification to challenge the entire racial logic of miscegenation law. The Arizona statute provided a tempting target for their attack, for under its "descendants" provision, a person of "mixed blood" could not legally marry anyone. Pointing this out, Mayellen Kirby's lawyer argued that the law must therefore be unconstitutional. He failed to convince the court. The appeals court judge brushed aside such objections. The argument that the law was unconstitutional, the judge held:

> is an attack . . . [Mayellen Kirby] is not entitled to make for the reason that there is no evidence that she is other than of the black race. . . . It will be time enough to pass on the question she raises . . . when it is presented by some one whose rights are involved or affected.[21]

The Culturalist Challenge to Racialism

By the 1920s, refusals to recognize the rights of African American women had become conventional in American law. So had refusals to recognize obvious inconsistencies in legal racial classification schemes. Minions of racialism, judges, juries, and experts sometimes quarreled over specifics, but they agreed on the overriding importance of making and enforcing racial classifications.

Lawyers in miscegenation cases therefore neither needed nor received much courtroom assistance from experts. In another legal arena, citizenship and naturalization law, the use of experts, nearly all of whom advocated some version of scientific racism, was much more common. Ever since the 1870s, naturalization lawyers had relied on scientific racists to help them decide which racial and ethnic groups met the United States naturalization requirement of being "white" persons. But in a series of cases heard in the first two decades of the twentieth century, this strategy backfired. When judges found themselves drawn into a heated scientific debate on the question of whether "Caucasian" was the same as "white," the United States Supreme Court settled the question by discarding the experts and reverting to what the justices called the opinion of the "common man."[22]

In both naturalization and miscegenation cases, judges relied on the basic agreement between popular and expert (scientific racist) versions of the racialism that permeated turn-of-the-century American society. But even as judges promulgated the common sense of racialism, the ground was shifting beneath their feet. By

21. "Appellant's Brief," Sept. 8, 1921, *Kirby v. Kirby; Kirby v. Kirby*, 206 P. 405, 406 (1922). On *Kirby*, see Roger Hardaway, "Unlawful Love: A History of Arizona's Miscegenation Law," *Journal of Arizona History*, 27 (Winter 1986), 377–90.
22. For examples of reliance on experts, see *In re Ah Yup*, 1 F. Cas. 223 (1878) (No. 104); *In re Kanaka Nian*, 21 P. 993 (1889); *In re Saito*, 62 F. 126 (1894). On these cases, see Ian F. Haney Lopez, *White by Law: The Legal Construction of Race* (New York, forthcoming). For reliance on the "common man," see *U.S. v. Bhagat Singh Thind*, 261 U.S. 204 (1923). On *Thind*, see Sucheta Mazumdar, "Racist Responses to Racism: The Aryan Myth and South Asians in the United States," *South Asia Bulletin*, 9 (no. 1, 1989), 47–55; Joan M. Jensen, *Passage from India: Asian Indian Immigrants in North America* (New Haven, 1988), 247–69; and Roediger, *Towards the Abolition of Whiteness*, 181–84.

the 1920s, lawyers in miscegenation cases were beginning to glimpse the court-room potential of arguments put forth by a pioneering group of self-consciously "modern" social scientists willing to challenge racialism head on.

Led by cultural anthropologist Franz Boas, these emerging experts have long stood as the heroes of histories of the decline of scientific racism (which is often taken to stand for racism as a whole). But for modern social scientists, the attack on racialism was not so much an end in itself as a function of the larger goal of establishing "culture" as a central social science paradigm. Intellectually and in-stitutionally, Boas and his followers staked their claim to academic authority on their conviction that human difference and human history were best explained by culture. Because they interpreted character, morality, and social organization as cultural, rather than racial, phenomena and because they were determined to explore, name, and claim the field of cultural analysis for social scientists, partic-ularly cultural anthropologists, sociologists, and social psychologists, they are per-haps best described as culturalists.[23]

To consolidate their power, culturalists had to challenge the scientific racist paradigms they hoped to displace. Two of the arguments they made were of particular significance for the emergence of modern racial ideologies. The first was the argument that the key notion of racialism—race—made no biological sense. This argument allowed culturalists to take aim at a very vulnerable target. For most of the nineteenth century, scientific racists had solved disputes about who fit into which racial categories by subdividing the categories. As a result, the number of scientifically recognized races had increased so steadily that by 1911, when the anthropologist Daniel Folkmar compiled the intentionally definitive *Dictionary of Races and Peoples,* he recognized "45 races or peoples among im-migrants coming to the United States." Folkmar's was only one of several com-peting schemes, and culturalists delighted in pointing out the discrepancies be-tween them, showing that scientific racists could not agree on such seemingly simple matters as how many races there were or what criteria—blood, skin color, hair type—best indicated race.[24]

23. The rise of Boasian anthropology has attracted much attention among intellectual historians, most of whom seem to agree with the 1963 comment that "it is possible that Boas did more to combat race prejudice than any other person in history"; see Gossett, *Race,* 418. In addition to the works cited in footnote 7, see I. A. Newby, *Jim Crow's Defense: Anti-Negro Thought in America, 1900–1930* (Baton Rouge, 1965), 21; and John S. Gilkeson Jr., "The Domestication of 'Culture' in Interwar America, 1919–1941," in *The Estate of Social Knowledge,* ed. JoAnne Brown and David K. van Keuren (Baltimore, 1991), 153–74. For more critical appraisals, see Robert Proctor, "Eu-genics among the Social Sciences: Hereditarian Thought in Germany and the United States," *ibid.,* 175–208; Hamilton Cravens, *The Triumph of Evolution: The Heredity-Environment Contro-versy, 1900–1941* (Baltimore, 1988); and Donna Haraway, *Primate Visions: Gender, Race, and Na-ture in the World of Modern Science* (New York, 1989), 127–203. The classic—and still the best—account of the rise of cultural anthropology is Stocking, *Race, Culture, and Evolution.* See also George W. Stocking Jr., *Victorian Anthropology* (New York, 1987), 284–320.

24. U.S. Immigration Commission, *Dictionary of Races or Peoples* (Washington, 1911), 2. For other scientific racist classification schemes, see *Encyclopaedia Britannica,* 11th ed., s.v. "Anthropology";

In their most dramatic mode, culturalists went so far as to insist that physical characteristics were completely unreliable indicators of race; in biological terms, they insisted, race must be considered indeterminable. Thus, in an influential encyclopedia article on "race" published in the early thirties, Boas insisted that "it is not possible to assign with certainty any one individual to a definite group." Perhaps the strongest statement of this kind came from Julian Huxley and A. C. Haddon, British scientists who maintained that "the term *race* as applied to human groups should be dropped from the vocabulary of science." Since Huxley was one of the first culturalists trained as a biologist, his credentials added luster to his opinion. In this and other forms, the culturalist argument that race was biologically indeterminable captured the attention of both contemporaries and later historians.[25]

Historians have paid much less attention to a second and apparently incompatible argument put forth by culturalists. It started from the other end of the spectrum, maintaining, not that there was no such thing as biological race, but that race was nothing more than biology. Since culturalists considered biology of remarkably little importance, consigning race to the realm of biology pushed it out of the picture. Thus Boas ended his article on race by concluding that although it remained "likely" enough that scientific study of the "anatomical differences between the races" might reveal biological influence on the formation of personality, "the study of cultural forms shows that such differences are altogether irrelevant as compared with the powerful influence of the cultural environment in which the group lives."[26]

Following this logic, the contrast between important and wide-reaching culture and unimportant (but biological) race stood as the cornerstone of many culturalist arguments. Thus the cultural anthropologist Ruth Benedict began her influential 1940 book, *Race: Science and Politics*, with an analysis of "what race is *not*," including language, customs, intelligence, character, and civilization. In a 1943 pamphlet co-authored with Gene Weltfish and addressed to the general public, she explained that real "racial differences" occurred only in "nonessentials such as texture of head hair, amount of body hair, shape of the nose or head, or color of the eyes and the skin." Drawing on these distinctions, Benedict argued that race was a scientific "fact," but that racism, which she defined as "the dogma that the hope of civilization depends upon eliminating some races and keeping others pure," was no more than a "modern superstition."[27]

---

and *Encyclopedia Americana: A Library of Universal Knowledge* (New York, 1923), s.v. "Ethnography" and "Ethnology."

25. Franz Boas, "Race," in *Encyclopaedia of the Social Sciences,* ed. Edwin R. A. Seligman (15 vols., New York, 1930–1935), XIII, 27; Julian S. Huxley and A. C. Haddon, *We Europeans: A Survey of "Racial" Problems* (London, 1935), 107.

26. Boas, "Race," 34. For one of the few instances when a historian has noted this argument, see Smedley, *Race in North America,* 275–82.

27. Ruth Benedict, *Race: Science and Politics* (New York, 1940), 12; Ruth Benedict and Gene Weltfish, *The Races of Mankind* (Washington, 1943), 5; Benedict, *Race,* 12.

Culturalists set these two seemingly contradictory depictions of race—the argument that biological race was nonsense and the argument that race was merely biology—right beside each other. The contradiction mattered little to them. Both arguments effectively contracted the range of racialist thinking, and both helped break conceptual links between race and character, morality, psychology, and language. By showing that one after another of these phenomena depended more on environment and training than on biology, culturalists moved each one out of the realm of race and into the province of culture, widening the modern split between culture and biology. Boas opened his article on race by staking out this position. "The term race is often used loosely to indicate groups of men differing in appearance, language, or culture," he wrote, but in his analysis, it would apply "solely to the biological grouping of human types."[28]

In adopting this position, culturalist intellectuals took a giant step away from popular common sense on the issue of race. Recognizing—even at times celebrating—this gap between themselves and the public, they devoted much of their work to dislodging popular racial assumptions. They saw the public as lamentably behind the times and sadly prone to race "prejudice," and they used their academic credentials to insist that racial categories not only did not rest on common sense, but made little sense at all.[29]

The *Monks* Case and the Making of Modern Racial Ideologies

This, of course, was just what lawyers challenging miscegenation laws wanted to hear. Because culturalist social scientists could offer their arguments with an air of scientific and academic authority that might persuade judges, attorneys began to invite them to appear as expert witnesses. But when culturalists appeared in court, they entered an arena where their argument for the biological indeterminacy of race was shaped in ways neither they nor the lawyers who recruited them could control.

Take, for example, the seemingly curious trial of Marie Antoinette Monks of San Diego, California, decided in the Superior Court of San Diego County in 1939. By all accounts, Marie Antoinette Monks was a woman with a clear eye for her main chance. In the early 1930s, she had entranced and married a man named Allan Monks, potential heir to a Boston fortune. Shortly after the marriage, which took place in Arizona, Allan Monks declined into insanity. Whether his mental condition resulted from injuries he had suffered in a motorcycle crash or from drugs administered under the undue influence of Marie Antoinette, the court would debate at great length. Allan Monks died. He left two wills: an old one in

---

28. Boas, "Race," 25–26.
29. See, for example, Huxley and Haddon, *We Europeans*, 107, 269–73; Benedict and Weltfish, *Races of Mankind*; Benedict, *Race*; and Gunnar Myrdal, *An American Dilemma: The Negro Problem and Modern Democracy* (New York, 1944), 91–115.

favor of a friend named Ida Lee and a newer one in favor of his wife, Marie Antoinette. Ida Lee submitted her version of the will for probate, Marie Antoinette challenged her claim, and Lee fought back. Lee's lawyers contended that the Monks marriage was illegal. They charged that Marie Antoinette Monks, who had told her husband she was a "French" countess, was actually "a Negro" and therefore prohibited by Arizona law from marrying Allan Monks, whom the court presumed to be Caucasian.[30]

Much of the ensuing six-week-long trial was devoted to determining the "race" of Marie Antoinette Monks. To prove that she was "a Negro," her opponents called five people to the witness stand: a disgruntled friend of her husband, a local labor commissioner, and three expert witnesses, all of whom offered arguments that emphasized biological indicators of race. The first so-called expert, Monks's hairdresser, claimed that she could tell that Monks was of mixed blood from looking at the size of the moons of her fingernails, the color of the "ring" around the palms of her hands, and the "kink" in her hair. The second, a physical anthropologist from the nearby San Diego Museum, claimed to be able to tell that Monks was "at least one-eighth negroid" from the shape of her face, the color of her hands, and her "protruding heels," all of which he had observed casually while a spectator in the courtroom. The third expert witness, a surgeon, had grown up and practiced medicine in the South and later served at a Southern Baptist mission in Africa. Having once walked alongside Monks when entering the courthouse (at which time he tried, he said, to make a close observation of her), he testified that he could tell that she was of "one-eighth negro blood" from the contour of her calves and heels, from the "peculiar pallor" on the back of her neck, from the shape of her face, and from the wave of her hair.[31]

To defend Monks, her lawyers called a friend, a relative, and two expert witnesses of their own, an anthropologist and a biologist. The experts both started out by testifying to the culturalist position that it was impossible to tell a person's race from physical characteristics, especially if that person was, as they put it, "of mixed blood." This was the argument culturalists used whenever they were cornered into talking about biology, a phenomenon they tended to regard as so insignificant a factor in social life that they preferred to avoid talking about it at all.

But because this argument replaced certainty with uncertainty, it did not play very well in the *Monks* courtroom. Seeking to find the definitiveness they needed to offset the experts who had already testified, the lawyers for Monks paraded their own client in front of the witness stand, asking her to show the anthropologist her fingernails and to remove her shoes so that he could see her heels. They lingered over the biologist's testimony that Monks's physical features resembled

30. The Monks trial can be followed in *Estate of Monks*, 4 Civ. 2835, Records of California Court of Appeals, Fourth District (California State Archives, Roseville); and *Gunn v. Giraudo*, 4 Civ. 2832, *ibid.* (Gunn represented another claimant to the estate.) The two cases were tried together. For the 7-volume "Reporter's Transcript," see *Estate of Monks*, 4 Civ. 2835, *ibid.*

31. "Reporter's Transcript," vol. 2, pp. 660–67, vol. 3, pp. 965–76, 976–98, *Estate of Monks*.

those of the people of southern France. In the end, Monks's lawyers backed both experts into a corner; when pressed repeatedly for a definite answer, both reluctantly admitted that it was their opinion that Monks was a "white" woman.[32]

The experts' dilemma reveals the limitations of the argument for racial indeterminacy in the courtroom. Faced with a conflict between culturalist experts, who offered uncertainty and indeterminacy, and their opponents, who offered concrete biological answers to racial questions, judges were predisposed to favor the latter. To judges, culturalists appeared frustratingly vague and uncooperative (in other words, lousy witnesses), while their opponents seemed to be good witnesses willing to answer direct questions.

In the *Monks* case, the judge admitted that his own "inexpert" opinion—that Marie Antoinette "did have many characteristics that I would say . . . [showed] mixed negro and some other blood"—was not enough to justify a ruling. Turning to the experts before him, he dismissed the hairdresser (whose experience he was willing to grant, but whose scientific credentials he considered dubious); he passed over the biologist (whose testimony, he thought, could go either way); and he dismissed the two anthropologists, whose testimonies, he said, more or less canceled each other out. The only expert the judge was willing to rely on was the surgeon, because the surgeon "seemed . . . to hold a very unique and peculiar position as an expert on the question involved from his work in life."[33]

Relying on the surgeon's testimony, the judge declared that Marie Antoinette Monks was "the descendant of a negro" who had "one-eighth negro blood . . . and 7/8 caucasian blood"; he said that her "race" prohibited her from marrying Allan Monks and from inheriting his estate. The racial categorization served to invalidate the marriage in two overlapping ways. First, as a "negro," Marie Antoinette could not marry a white under Arizona miscegenation law; and second, by telling her husband-to-be that she was "French," Marie Antoinette had committed a "fraud" serious enough to render the marriage legally void. The court's decision that she had also exerted "undue influence" over Monks was hardly necessary to the outcome.[34]

As the *Monks* case suggests, we should be careful not to overestimate the influence culturalists had on the legal system. And, while in courtrooms culturalist experts were trying—and failing—to convince judges that biological racial questions were unanswerable, outside the courts their contention that biological racial answers were insignificant was faring little better. During the first three decades of the twentieth century, scientists on the "racial" side of the split between race and culture reconstituted themselves into a rough alliance of their own. Mirroring the modern dividing line between biology and culture, its ranks swelled with those

---

32. *Ibid.*, vol. 5, pp. 1501–49, vol. 6, pp. 1889–1923.
33. *Ibid.*, vol. 7, pp. 2543–2548.
34. "Findings of Fact and Conclusions of Law," in "Clerk's Transcript," Dec. 2, 1940, *Gunn v. Giraudo*, 4 Civ. 2832, p. 81. One intriguing aspect of the *Monks* case is that the seeming exactness was unnecessary. The status of the marriage hinged on the Arizona miscegenation law, which would have denied validity to the marriage whether the proportion of "blood" in question was "one-eighth" or "one drop."

who claimed special expertise on biological questions. There were biologists and physicians; leftover racialists such as physical anthropologists, increasingly shorn of their claims to expertise in every arena *except* that of physical characteristics; and, finally, the newly emerging eugenicists.[35]

Eugenicists provided the glue that held this coalition together. Narrowing the sweep of nineteenth-century racialist thought to focus on biology, these modern biological experts then expanded their range by offering physical characteristics, heredity, and reproductive imperatives as variations on the biological theme. They were particularly drawn to arenas in which all these biological motifs came into play; accordingly, they placed special emphasis on reforming marriage laws. Perhaps the best-known American eugenicist, Charles B. Davenport of the Eugenics Record Office, financed by the Carnegie Institution, outlined their position in a 1913 pamphlet, *State Laws Limiting Marriage Selection Examined in the Light of Eugenics,* which proposed strengthening state control over the marriages of the physically and racially unfit. Davenport's plan was no mere pipe dream. According to the historian Michael Grossberg, by the 1930s, 41 states used eugenic categories to restrict the marriage of "lunatics," "imbeciles," "idiots," and the "feeble-minded"; 26 states restricted the marriages of those infected with syphilis and gonorrhea; and 27 states passed sterilization laws. By midcentury, blood tests had become a standard legal prerequisite for marriage.[36]

Historians have rather quickly passed over the racial aspects of American eugenics, seeing its proponents as advocates of outmoded ideas soon to be beached by the culturalist sea change. Yet until at least World War II, eugenicists reproduced a modern racism that was biological in a particularly virulent sense. For them, unlike their racialist predecessors (who tended to regard biology as an indicator of a much more expansive racial phenomenon), biology really was the essence of race. And unlike nineteenth-century scientific racists (whose belief in discrete racial dividing lines was rarely shaken by evidence of racial intermixture), twentieth-century eugenicists and culturalists alike seemed obsessed with the subject of mixed-race individuals.[37]

35. For descriptions of those interested in biological aspects of race, see Stocking, *Race, Culture, and Evolution,* 271–307; I. A. Newby, *Challenge to the Court: Social Scientists and the Defense of Segregation, 1954–1966* (Baton Rouge, 1969); and Cravens, *Triumph of Evolution,* 15–55. On eugenics, see Proctor, "Eugenics among the Social Sciences," 175–208; Daniel J. Kevles, *In the Name of Eugenics: Genetics and the Uses of Human Heredity* (New York, 1985); Mark H. Haller, *Eugenics: Hereditarian Attitudes in American Thought* (New Brunswick, 1963); and William H. Tucker, *The Science and Politics of Racial Research* (Urbana, 1994), 54–137.

36. Charles B. Davenport, *Eugenics Record Office Bulletin No. 9: State Laws Limiting Marriage Selection Examined in the Light of Eugenics* (Cold Spring Harbor, 1913); Michael Grossberg, "Guarding the Altar: Physiological Restrictions and the Rise of State Intervention in Matrimony," *American Journal of Legal History,* 26 (July 1982), 221–24.

37. See, for example, C[harles] B[enedict] Davenport and Morris Steggerda, *Race Crossing in Jamaica* (1929; Westport, 1970); Edward Byron Reuter, *Race Mixture: Studies in Intermarriage and Miscegenation* (New York, 1931); and Emory S. Bogardus, "What Race Are Filipinos?," *Sociology and Social Research,* 16 (1931–1932), 274–79.

In their determination to protect "white purity," eugenicists believed that even the tightest definitions of race by blood proportion were too loose. Setting their sights on Virginia, in 1924 they secured passage of the most draconian miscegenation law in American history. The act, entitled "an Act to preserve racial integrity," replaced the legal provision that a person must have one-sixteenth of "negro blood" to fall within the state's definition of "colored" with a provision that:

> It shall hereafter be unlawful for any white person in this State to marry any save a white person, or a person with no other admixture of blood than white and American Indian. For the purpose of this act, the term "white person" shall apply only to the person who has no trace whatsoever of any blood other than Caucasian; but persons who have one-sixteenth or less of the blood of the American Indian and have no other non-Caucasic blood shall be deemed to be white persons.

Another section of the Virginia law (which provided for the issuance of supposedly voluntary racial registration certificates for Virginia citizens) spelled out the "races" the legislature had in mind. The list, which specified "Caucasian, Negro, Mongolian, American Indian, Asiatic Indian, Malay, or any mixture thereof, or any other non-Caucasic strains," showed the lengths to which lawmakers would go to pin down racial categories. Within the decade, the Virginia law was copied by Georgia and echoed in Alabama. Thereafter, while supporters worked without much success to extend such laws to other states, defenders of miscegenation statutes added eugenic arguments to their rhetorical arsenal.[38]

Having been pinned to the modern biological wall and labeled as "mixed race," Marie Antoinette Monks would seem to have been in the perfect position to challenge the constitutionality of the widely drawn Arizona miscegenation law. She took her case to the California Court of Appeals, Fourth District, where she made an argument that echoed that of Mayellen Kirby two decades earlier. Reminding the court of the wording of the Arizona statute, her lawyers pointed out that "on the set of facts found by the trial judge, [Marie Antoinette Monks] is concededly of Caucasian blood as well as negro blood, and therefore a descendant of a Caucasian." Spelling it out, they explained:

> As such, she is prohibited from marrying a negro or any descendant of a negro, a Mongolian or an Indian, a Malay or a Hindu, or any of the descendants of any of them. Likewise . . . as a descendant of a negro she is prohibited from marrying a Caucasian or descendant of a Caucasian, which of course would include any person who had any degree of Caucasian blood in them.

---

38. 1924 Va. Acts ch. 371; 1927 Ga. Laws no. 317; 1927 Ala. Acts no. 626. The 1924 Virginia act replaced 1910 Va. Acts ch. 357, which classified as "colored" persons with 1/16 or more "negro blood." The retention of an allowance for American Indian "blood" in persons classed as white was forced on the bill's sponsors by Virginia aristocrats who traced their ancestry to Pocahontas and John Rolfe. See Paul A. Lombardo, "Miscegenation, Eugenics, and Racism: Historical Footnotes to *Loving v. Virginia*," *U.C. Davis Law Review*, 21 (Winter 1988), 431–52; and Richard B. Sherman, "The Last Stand: The Fight for Racial Integrity in Virginia in the 1920s," *Journal of Southern History*, 54 (Feb. 1988), 69–92.

Because this meant that she was "absolutely prohibited from contracting valid marriages in Arizona," her lawyers argued that the Arizona law was an unconstitutional constraint on her liberty.[39]

The court, however, dismissed this argument as "interesting but in our opinion not tenable." In a choice that speaks volumes about the depth of attachment to racial categories, the court narrowed the force to the argument by asserting that "the constitutional problem would be squarely presented" only if one mixed-race person were seeking to marry another mixed-race person, then used this constructed hypothetical to dodge the issue:

> While it is true that there was evidence that appellant [Marie Antoinette Monks] is a descendant of the Caucasian race, as well as of the Negro race, the other contracting party [Allan Monks] was of unmixed blood and therefore the hypothetical situation involving an attempted alliance between two persons of mixed blood is no more present in the instant case than in the Kirby case. . . . The situations conjured up by respondent are not here involved. . . . Under the facts presented the appellant does not have the benefit of assailing the validity of the statute.

This decision was taken as authoritative. Both the United States Supreme Court and the Supreme Judicial Court of Massachusetts (in which Monks had also filed suit) refused to reopen the issue.[40]

Perhaps the most interesting thing about the Monks case is that there is no reason to believe that the public found it either remarkable or objectionable. Local reporters who covered the trial in 1939 played up the themes of forgery, drugs, and insanity; their summaries of the racial categories of the Arizona law and the opinions of the expert witnesses were largely matter-of-fact.[41]

In this seeming acceptability to the public lies a clue to the development of modern racial ideologies. Even as judges narrowed their conception of race, transforming an all-encompassing phenomenon into a simple fact to be determined, they remained bound by the provisions of miscegenation law to determine who fit in which racial categories. For this purpose, the second culturalist argument, that race was merely biology, had far more to offer than the first, that race was biologically indeterminable. The conception of race as merely biological seemed consonant with the racial categories built into the laws, seemed supportable by clear and unequivocal expert testimony, and fit comfortably within popular notions of race.

39. "Appellant's Opening Brief," *Gunn v. Giraudo*, 12–13. This brief appears to have been prepared for the California Supreme Court but used in the California Court of Appeals, Fourth District. On February 14, 1942, the California Supreme Court refused to review the Court of Appeals decision. See *Estate of Monks*, 48 C.A. 2d 603, 621 (1941).
40. *Estate of Monks*, 48 C.A. 2d 603, 612–15 (1941); *Monks v. Lee*, 317 U.S. 590 (*appeal dismissed*, 1942), 711 (*reh'g denied*, 1942); *Lee v. Monks*, 62 N.E. 2d 657 (1945); *Lee v. Monks*, 326 U.S. 696 (*cert. denied*, 1946).
41. On the case, see *San Diego Union*, July 21, 1939–Jan. 6, 1940. On the testimony of expert witnesses on race, see *ibid.*, Sept. 21, 1939, p. 4A; *ibid.*, Sept. 29, 1939, p. 10A; and *ibid.*, Oct. 5, 1939, p. 8A.

The Distillation of Modernist Racial Ideology:
From *Perez* to *Loving*

In the *Monks* case we can see several modern racial ideologies—ranging from the argument that race was biological nonsense to the reply that race was essentially biological to the possibility that race was merely biology—all grounded in the split between culture and biology. To distill these variants into a unified modernist racial ideology, another element had to be added to the mix, the remarkable (in American law, nearly unprecedented) proposal that the legal system abandon its traditional responsibility for determining and defining racial categories. In miscegenation law, this possibility emerged in a case that also, and not coincidentally, featured the culturalist argument for biological racial indeterminacy.

The case was *Perez v. Lippold*. It involved a young Los Angeles couple, Andrea Perez and Sylvester Davis, who sought a marriage license. Turned down by the Los Angeles County clerk, they challenged the constitutionality of the California miscegenation law directly to the California Supreme Court, which heard their case in October 1947.[42]

It was not immediately apparent that the *Perez* case would play a role in the development of modernist racial ideology. Perhaps because both sides agreed that Perez was "a white female" and Davis "a Negro male," the lawyer who defended the couple, Daniel Marshall, did not initially see the case as turning on race categorization. In 1947, Marshall had few civil rights decisions to build on, so he tried an end-run strategy: he based his challenge to miscegenation laws on the argument that because both Perez and Davis were Catholics and the Catholic Church did not prohibit interracial marriage, California miscegenation law was an arbitrary and unreasonable restraint on their freedom of religion.

The freedom-of-religion argument made some strategic sense, since several courts had held that states had to meet a high standard to justify restrictions on religious expression. Accordingly, Marshall laid out the religion argument in a lengthy petition to the California Supreme Court. In response, the state offered an even lengthier defense of miscegenation laws. The state's lawyers had at their fingertips a long list of precedents upholding such laws, including the *Kirby* and *Monks* cases. They added eugenic arguments about racial biology, including evidence of declining birth rates among "hybrids" and statistics that showed high mortality, short life expectancies, and particular diseases among African Americans. They polished off their case with the comments of a seemingly sympathetic Roman Catholic priest.[43]

---

42. *Perez v. Lippold*, L.A. 20305, Supreme Court Case Files (California State Archives). The case was also known as *Perez v. Moroney* and *Perez v. Sharp* (the names reflect changes of personnel in the Los Angeles County clerk's office). I have used the title given in the *Pacific Law Reporter*, the most easily available version of the final decision: *Perez v. Lippold*, 198 P. 2d 17 (1948).

43. "Petition for Writ of Mandamus, Memorandum of Points and Authorities and Proof of Service," Aug. 8, 1947, *Perez v. Lippold;* "Points and Authorities in Opposition to Issuance of Alternative Writ of Mandate," Aug. 13, 1947, *ibid.*; "Return by Way of Demurrer," Oct. 6, 1947, *ibid.*; "Return by Way of Answer," Oct. 6, 1947, *ibid.*; "Respondent's Brief in Opposition to Writ of Mandate," Oct. 6, 1947, *ibid.*

Here the matter stood until the California Supreme Court heard oral arguments in the case. At that session, the court listened in silence to Marshall's opening sally that miscegenation laws were based on prejudice and to his argument that they violated constitutional guarantees of freedom of religion. But as soon as the state's lawyer began to challenge the religious freedom argument, one of the court's associate justices, Roger Traynor, impatiently interrupted the proceedings. "What," he asked, "about equal protection of the law?"

Mr. Justice Traynor: . . . it might help to explain the statute, what it means. What is a negro?

Mr. Stanley: We have not the benefit of any judicial interpretation. The statute states that a negro [Stanley evidently meant to say, as the law did, "a white"] cannot marry a negro, which can be construed to mean a full-blooded negro, since the statute also says mulatto, Mongolian, or Malay.

Mr. Justice Traynor: What is a mulatto? One-sixteenth blood?

Mr. Stanley: Certainly certain states have seen fit to state what a mulatto is.

Mr. Justice Traynor: If there is 1/8 blood, can they marry? If you can marry with 1/8, why not with 1/16, 1/32, 1/64? And then don't you get in the ridiculous position where a negro cannot marry anybody? If he is white, he cannot marry black, or if he is black, he cannot marry white.

Mr. Stanley: I agree that it would be better for the Legislature to lay down an exact amount of blood, but I do not think that the statute should be declared unconstitutional as indefinite on this ground.

Mr. Justice Traynor: That is something anthropologists have not been able to furnish, although they say generally that there is no such thing as race.

Mr. Stanley: I would not say that anthropologists have said that generally, except such statements for sensational purposes.

Mr. Justice Traynor: Would you say that Professor Wooten of Harvard was a sensationalist? The crucial question is how can a county clerk determine who are negroes and who are whites.[44]

Although he addressed his questions to the lawyers for the state, Justice Traynor had given Marshall a gift no lawyer had ever before received in a miscegenation case: judicial willingness to believe in the biological indeterminacy of race. It was no accident that this argument came from Roger Traynor. A former professor at Boalt Hall, the law school of the University of California, Berkeley, Traynor had been appointed to the court for his academic expertise rather than his legal experience; unlike his more pragmatic colleagues, he kept up with developments in modern social science.[45]

Marshall responded to the opening Traynor had provided by making sure that his next brief included the culturalist argument that race was biological nonsense. In it, he asserted that experts had determined that "race, as popularly understood,

44. "[Oral Argument] On Behalf of Respondent," Oct. 6, 1947, pp. 3–4, *ibid.*
45. Stanley Mosk, "A Retrospective," *California Law Review*, 71 (July 1983), 1045; Peter Anderson, "A Remembrance," *ibid.*, 1066–71.

is a myth"; he played on the gap between expert opinion and laws based on irrational "prejudice" rooted in "myth, folk belief, and superstition"; and he dismissed his opponents' reliance on the "grotesque reasoning of eugenicists" by comparing their statements to excerpts from Adolf Hitler's *Mein Kampf*.[46]

Marshall won his case. The 1948 decision in the *Perez* case was remarkable for many reasons. It marked the first time since Reconstruction that a state court had declared a state miscegenation law unconstitutional. It went far beyond existing appeals cases in that the California Supreme Court had taken the very step the judges in the *Kirby* and *Monks* cases had avoided—going beyond the issue of the race of an individual to consider the issue of racial classification in general. Even more remarkable, the court did so in a case in which neither side had challenged the racial classification of the parties. But despite these accomplishments, the *Perez* case was no victory for the culturalist argument about the biological indeterminacy of race. Only the outcome of the case—that California's miscegenation law was unconstitutional—was clear. The rationale for this outcome was a matter of considerable dispute.

Four justices condemned the law and three supported it; altogether, they issued four separate opinions. A four-justice majority agreed that the law should be declared unconstitutional but disagreed about why. Two justices, led by Traynor, issued a lengthy opinion that pointed out the irrationality of racial categories, citing as authorities a virtual who's who of culturalist social scientists, from Boas, Huxley, and Haddon to Gunnar Myrdal. A third justice issued a concurring opinion that pointedly ignored the rationality or irrationality of race classifications to criticize miscegenation laws on equality grounds, contending that laws based on "race, color, or creed" were—and always had been—contrary to the Declaration of Independence, the Constitution, and the Fourteenth Amendment; as this justice saw it, the Constitution was color-blind. A fourth justice, who reported that he wanted his decision to "rest upon a broader ground than that the challenged statutes are discriminatory and irrational," based his decision solely on the religious freedom issue that had been the basis of Marshall's original argument.[47]

In contrast, a three-justice minority argued that the law should be upheld. They cited legal precedent, offered biological arguments about racial categories, and mentioned a handful of social policy considerations. Although the decision went against them, their agreement with each other ironically formed the closest thing to a majority in the case. In sum, although the *Perez* decision foreshadowed the day when American courts would abandon their defense of racial categories, its variety of judicial rationales tells us more about the range of modern racial ideologies than it does about the power of any one of them.[48]

Between the *Perez* case in 1948 and the next milestone miscegenation case, *Loving v. Virginia*, decided in 1967, judges would search for a common denominator among this contentious variety, trying to find a position of principled de-

---

46. "Petitioners' Reply Brief," Nov. 8, 1947, pp. 4, 44, 23–24, *Perez v. Lippold*.
47. *Perez v. Lippold*, 198 P. 2d at 17–35, esp. 29, 34.
48. *Ibid.*, 35–47.

cisiveness persuasive enough to mold both public and expert opinion. One way to do this was to back away from the culturalist argument that race made no biological sense, adopting the other culturalist argument that race was biological fact and thus shifting the debate to the question of how much biological race should matter in determining social and legal policy.

In such a debate, white supremacists tried to extend the reach of biological race as far as possible. Thus one scientist bolstered his devotion to white supremacy by calling Boas "that appalling disaster to American social anthropology whose influence in the end has divorced the social studies of man from their scientific base in physical biology."[49] Following the lead of eugenicists, he and his sympathizers tried to place every social and legal superstructure on a biological racial base.

In contrast, their egalitarian opponents set limits. In their minds, biological race (or "skin color," as they often called it), was significant only because its visibility made it easy for racists to identify those they subjected to racial oppression. As Myrdal, the best-known of the mid-twentieth-century culturalist social scientists, noted in 1944 in his monumental work, *An American Dilemma:*

> In spite of all heterogeneity, the average white man's unmistakable observation is that *most Negroes in America have dark skin and woolly hair,* and he is, of course, right. . . . [The African American's] African ancestry and physical characteristics are fixed to his person much more ineffaceably than the yellow star is fixed to the Jew during the Nazi regime in Germany.[50]

To Myrdal's generation of egalitarians, the translation of visible physical characteristics into social hierarchies formed the tragic foundation of American racism.

The egalitarians won this debate, and their victory paved the way for the emergence of a modernist racial ideology persuasive enough to command the kind of widespread adherence once commanded by late-nineteenth-century racialism. Such a position was formulated by the United States Supreme Court in 1967 in *Loving v. Virginia,* the most important miscegenation case ever heard and the only one now widely remembered.

The *Loving* case involved what was, even for miscegenation law, an extreme example. Richard Perry Loving and Mildred Delores Jeter were residents of the small town of Central Point, Virginia, and family friends who had dated each other since he was seventeen and she was eleven. When they learned that their plans to marry were illegal in Virginia, they traveled to Washington, D.C., which did not have a miscegenation law, for the ceremony, returning in June 1958 with a marriage license, which they framed and placed proudly on their wall. In July 1958, they were awakened in the middle of the night by the county sheriff and two deputies, who had walked through their unlocked front door and right into their bedroom to arrest them for violating Virginia's miscegenation law. Under

49. For the characterization of Franz Boas, by Robert Gayres, editor of the Scottish journal *Mankind Quarterly,* see Newby, *Challenge to the Court,* 323. On *Mankind Quarterly* and on mid-twentieth-century white supremacist scientists, see Tucker, *Science and Politics of Racial Research.*
50. Myrdal, *American Dilemma,* 116–17.

that law, an amalgam of criminal provisions enacted in 1878 and Virginia's 1924 "Act to preserve racial integrity," the Lovings, who were identified in court records as a "white" man and a "colored" woman, pleaded guilty and were promptly convicted and sentenced to a year in jail. The judge suspended their sentence on the condition that "both accused leave . . . the state of Virginia at once and do not return together or at the same time to said county and state for a period of twenty-five years."[51]

In 1963, the Lovings, then the parents of three children, grew tired of living with relatives in Washington, D.C., and decided to appeal this judgment. Their first attempts ended in defeat. In 1965, the judge who heard their original case not only refused to reconsider his decision but raised the rhetorical stakes by opining:

> Almighty God created the races white, black, yellow, malay and red, and he placed them on separate continents. And but for the interference with his arrangement there would be no cause for such marriages. The fact that he separated the races shows that he did not intend for the races to mix.

But by the time their argument had been processed by the Supreme Court of Appeals of Virginia (which invalidated the original sentence but upheld the miscegenation law), the case had attracted enough attention that the United States Supreme Court, which had previously avoided taking miscegenation cases, agreed to hear an appeal.[52]

On the side of the Lovings stood not only their own attorneys, but also the National Association for the Advancement of Colored People (NAACP), the NAACP Legal Defense and Education Fund, the Japanese American Citizens League (JACL), and a coalition of Catholic bishops. The briefs they submitted

---

51. *Loving v. Commonwealth*, 147 S.E. 2d 78, 79 (1966). For the *Loving* briefs and oral arguments, see Philip B. Kurland and Gerhard Casper, eds., *Landmark Briefs and Arguments of the Supreme Court of the United States: Constitutional Law*, vol. LXIV (Arlington, 1975), 687–1007. Edited cassette tapes of the oral argument are included with Peter Irons and Stephanie Guitton, ed., *May It Please the Court: The Most Significant Oral Arguments Made before the Supreme Court since 1955* (New York, 1993). For scholarly assessments, see Wallenstein, "Race, Marriage, and the Law of Freedom"; Walter Wadlington, "The Loving Case: Virginia's Antimiscegenation Statute in Historical Perspective," in *Race Relations and the Law in American History: Major Historical Interpretations*, ed. Kermit L. Hall (New York, 1987), 600–34; and Robert J. Sickels, *Race, Marriage, and the Law* (Albuquerque, 1972).

52. *Loving v. Virginia*, 388 U.S. 1, 3 (1967); Wallenstein, "Race, Marriage, and the Law of Freedom," 423–25, esp. 424; *New York Times*, June 12, 1992, p. B7. By the mid-1960s some legal scholars had questioned the constitutionality of miscegenation laws, including C. D. Shokes, "The Serbonian Bog of Miscegenation," *Rocky Mountain Law Review*, 21 (1948–1949), 425–33; Wayne A. Melton, "Constitutionality of State Anti-Miscegenation Statutes," *Southwestern Law Journal*, 5 (1951), 451–61; Andrew D. Weinberger, "A Reappraisal of the Constitutionality of Miscegenation Statutes," *Cornell Law Quarterly*, 42 (Winter 1957), 208–22; Jerold D. Cummins and John L. Kane Jr., "Miscegenation, the Constitution, and Science," *Dicta*, 38 (Jan.–Feb. 1961), 24–54; William D. Zabel, "Interracial Marriage and the Law," *Atlantic Monthly*, 216 (Oct. 1965), 75–79 [included in this volume, pp. 54–61. —Ed.]; and Cyrus E. Phillips IV, "Miscegenation: The Courts and the Constitution," *William and Mary Law Review*, 8 (Fall 1966), 133–42.

offered the whole arsenal of arguments developed in previous miscegenation cases. The bishops offered the religious freedom argument that had been the original basis of the *Perez* case. The NAACP and the JACL stood on the opinions of culturalist experts, whose numbers now reached beyond social scientists well into the ranks of biologists. Offering both versions of the culturalist line on race, NAACP lawyers argued on one page, "The idea of 'pure' racial groups, either past or present, has long been abandoned by modern biological and social sciences," and on another, "Race, in its scientific dimension, refers only to the biogenetic and physical attributes manifest by a specified population. It does not, under any circumstances, refer to culture (learned behavior), language, nationality, or religion." The Lovings' lawyers emphasized two central points: Miscegenation laws violated both the constitutional guarantee of equal protection under the laws and the constitutional protection of the fundamental right to marry.[53]

In response, the lawyers for the state of Virginia tried hard to find some ground on which to stand. Their string of court precedents upholding miscegenation laws had been broken by the *Perez* decision. Their argument that Congress never intended the Fourteenth Amendment to apply to interracial marriage was offset by the Supreme Court's stated position that congressional intentions were inconclusive. In an attempt to distance the state from the "white purity" aspects of Virginia's 1924 law, Virginia's lawyers argued that since the Lovings admitted that they were a "white" person and a "colored" person and had been tried under a section of the law that mentioned only those categories, the elaborate definition of "white" offered in other sections of Virginia law was irrelevant.[54]

On only one point did the lawyers for both parties and the Court seem to agree: None of them wanted to let expert opinion determine the outcome. The lawyers for Virginia knew only too well that during the twentieth century, the scientific foundations of the eugenic biological argument in favor of miscegenation laws had crumbled, so they tried to warn the Court away by predicting that experts would mire the Court in "a veritable Serbonian bog of conflicting scientific opinion." Yet the Lovings' lawyers, who seemed to have the experts on their side, agreed that "the Court should not go into the morass of sociological evidence that is available on both sides of the question." "We strongly urge," they told the justices, "that it is not necessary." And the Court, still reeling from widespread criticism that its decision in the famous 1954 case *Brown v. Board of Education* was illegitimate "sociological jurisprudence," was not about to offer its opponents any more of such ammunition.[55]

The decision the Court issued was, in fact, carefully shorn of all reference to expert opinion; it spoke in language that both reflected and contributed to a new popular common sense on the issue of race. Recycling earlier pronouncements that "distinctions between citizens solely because of their ancestry" were "odious to a free people whose institutions are founded upon the doctrine of equality"

53. Kurland and Casper, eds., *Landmark Briefs*, 741–88, 847–950, 960–72, esp. 898–99, 901.
54. *Ibid.*, 789–845, 976–1003.
55. *Ibid.*, 834, 1007.

and that the Court "cannot conceive of a valid legislative purpose . . . which makes the color of a person's skin the test of whether his conduct is a criminal offense," the justices reached a new and broader conclusion. Claiming (quite inaccurately) that "We have consistently denied the constitutionality of measures which restrict the rights of citizens on account of race," the Court concluded that the racial classifications embedded in Virginia miscegenation laws were "so directly subversive of the principle of equality at the heart of the Fourteenth Amendment" that they were "unsupportable." Proclaiming that it violated both the equal protection and the due process clauses of the Fourteenth Amendment, the Court declared the Virginia miscegenation law unconstitutional.[56]

Legacies of Modernist Racial Ideology

The decision in the *Loving* case shows the distance twentieth-century American courts had traveled. The accumulated effect of several decades of culturalist attacks on racialism certainly shaped their thinking. The justices were no longer willing to accept the notion that race was the all-encompassing phenomenon nineteenth-century racialist thinkers had assumed it to be; they accepted the divisions between culture and biology and culture and race established by modern social scientists. But neither were they willing to declare popular identification of race with physical characteristics (like "the color of a person's skin") a figment of the imagination. In their minds, the scope of the term "race" had shrunk to a point where biology was all that was left; "race" referred to visible physical characteristics significant only because racists used them to erect spurious racial hierarchies. The Virginia miscegenation law was a case in point; the Court recognized and condemned it as a statute clearly "designed to maintain White Supremacy."[57]

Given the dependence of miscegenation laws on legal categories of race, the Court concluded that ending white supremacy required abandoning the categories. In de-emphasizing racial categories, they joined mainstream mid–twentieth-century social scientists, who argued that because culture, rather than race, shaped meaningful human difference, race was nothing more than a subdivision of the broader phenomenon of ethnicity. In a society newly determined to be "color-blind," granting public recognition to racial categories seemed to be synonymous with racism itself.[58]

---

56. *Loving v. Virginia*, 388 U.S. at 12.

57. *Ibid.*, 11.

58. The notion that American courts should be "color-blind" is usually traced to Supreme Court Justice John Harlan. Dissenting from the Court's endorsement of the principle of "separate but equal" in *Plessy v. Ferguson*, Harlan insisted that "Our Constitution is color-blind, and neither knows nor tolerates classes among citizens." *Plessy v. Ferguson*, 163 U.S. 537, 559 (1896). But only after *Brown v. Board of Education*, widely interpreted as a belated endorsement of Harlan's position, did courts begin to adopt color blindness as a goal. *Brown v. Board of Education*, 347 U.S. 483 (1954). On the history of the color-blindness ideal, see Andrew Kull, *The Color-Blind Constitution* (Cambridge, Mass., 1992). On developments in social science, see Omi and Winant, *Racial Formation in the United States*, 14–23.

And so the Supreme Court promulgated a modernist racial ideology that maintained that the best way to eradicate racism was the deliberate nonrecognition of race. Its effects reached well beyond miscegenation law. Elements of modernist racial ideology marked many of the major mid-twentieth-century Supreme Court decisions, including *Brown v. Board of Education*. Its effects on state law codes were equally substantial; during the 1960s and 1970s, most American states repealed statutes that had defined "race" (usually by blood proportion) and set out to erase racial terminology from their laws.[59]

Perhaps the best indication of the pervasiveness of modernist racial ideology is how quickly late-twentieth-century conservatives learned to shape their arguments to fit its contours. Attaching themselves to the modernist narrowing of the definition of race to biology and biology alone, conservative thinkers began to contend that, unless their ideas rested solely and explicitly on a belief in biological inferiority, they should not be considered racist. They began to advance "cultural" arguments of their very own, insisting that their proposals were based on factors such as social analysis, business practicality, or merit—on anything, in other words, except biological race. In their hands, modernist racial ideology supports an Alice-in-Wonderland interpretation of racism in which even those who argue for racially oppressive policies can adamantly deny being racists.

This conservative turnabout is perhaps the most striking, but not the only, indication of the contradictions inherent in modernist racial ideology. Others run the gamut from administrative law to popular culture. So while the United States Supreme Court tries to hold to its twentieth-century legacy of limiting, when it cannot eradicate, racial categories, United States government policies remain deeply dependent on them. In the absence of statutory definitions of race, racial categories are now set by the United States Office of Management and Budget, which in 1977 issued a "Statistical Directive" that divided Americans into five major groups—American Indian or Alaskan Native, Asian or Pacific Islander, Black, White, and Hispanic. The statistics derived from these categories help determine everything from census counts to eligibility for inclusion in affirmative action programs to the drawing of voting districts.[60] Meanwhile, in one popular culture flash-point after another—from the Anita Hill/Clarence Thomas hearings

---

59. *Brown v. Board of Education*, 347 U.S. 483 (1954). The Court declared distinctions based "solely on ancestry" "odious" even while upholding curfews imposed on Japanese Americans during World War II; see *Hirabayashi v. United States*, 320 U.S. 81 (1943). It declared race a "suspect" legal category while upholding the internment of Japanese Americans; see *Korematsu v. United States*, 323 U.S. 214 (1944). By 1983, no American state had a formal race-definition statute still on its books. See Chris Ballentine, " 'Who Is a Negro?' Revisited: Determining Individual Racial Status for Purposes of Affirmative Action," *University of Florida Law Review*, 35 (Fall 1983), 692. The repeal of state race-definition statutes often accompanied repeal of miscegenation laws. See, for example, 1953 Mont. Laws ch. 4; 1959 Or. Laws ch. 531; 1965 Ind. Acts ch. 15; 1969 Fla. Laws 69–195; and 1979 Ga. Laws no. 543.

60. The fifth of these categories, "Hispanic," is sometimes described as "ethnic," rather than "racial." For very different views of the current debates, see Lawrence Wright, "One Drop of Blood," *New Yorker*, July 25, 1994, pp. 46–55; and Michael Lind, *The Next American Nation: The New Nationalism and the Fourth American Revolution* (New York, 1995), 97–137.

to the *O. J. Simpson* case, mainstream commentators insist that "race" should not be a consideration even as they explore detail after detail that reveals its social pervasiveness.[61]

These gaps between the (very narrow) modernist conception of race and the (very wide) range of racial identities and racial oppressions bedevil today's egalitarians. In the political arena, some radicals have begun to argue that the legal system's deliberate nonrecognition of race erodes the ability to recognize and name racism and to argue for such policies as affirmative action, which rely on racial categories to overturn rather than to enforce oppression. Meanwhile, in the universities, a growing chorus of scholars is revitalizing the argument for the biological indeterminacy of race and using that argument to explore the myriad of ways in which socially constructed notions of race remain powerfully salient. Both groups hope to do better than their culturalist predecessors at eradicating racism.[62]

Attaining that goal may depend on how well we understand the tortured history of mid-twentieth-century American ideologies of race.

61. *People v. O. J. Simpson*, Case no. BA 097211, California Superior Court, L.A. County (1994).
62. See, for example, Kimberle Williams Crenshaw, "Race, Reform, and Retrenchment: Transformation and Legitimation in Antidiscrimination Law," *Harvard Law Review*, 101 (May 1988), 1331–87; Dana Y. Takagi, *The Retreat from Race: Asian-American Admissions and Racial Politics* (New Brunswick, 1992), 181–94; and Girardeau A. Spann, *Race against the Court: The Supreme Court and Minorities in Contemporary America* (New York, 1993), 119–49. See footnote 5, above. On recent work in the humanities, see Tessie Liu, "Race," in *A Companion to American Thought*, ed. Richard Wightman Fox and James T. Kloppenberg (Cambridge, Mass., 1995), 564–67. On legal studies, see Richard Delgado and Jean Stefancic, "Critical Race Theory: An Annotated Bibliography," *Virginia Law Review*, 79 (March 1993), 461–516.

PART II

Literature

This part opens with "A Miscegenation Vocabulary and the Coining of an Americanism," definitions of "Miscegenation," "Mulatto," "Quadroon," "Octoroon," and "Hybrid" that were taken from the *Oxford English Dictionary;* and Sidney Kaplan's "The Miscegenation Issue in the Election of 1864," an unsurpassed account of the history of the *Miscegenation* pamphlet that coined the word. The second section, "The 'Tragic Mulatto' and Other Themes of Interracial Literature," presents pioneering scholarship in the field, starting with philosopher Alain Locke's 1926 essay on "American Literary Tradition and the Negro," an early scholarly work that emphasizes the significance of the theme of "the mulatto house servant concubine and her children" for antislavery literature. (Locke argues against Francis Pendleton Gaines who, in his account of "the plantation tradition," had "discreetly ignored" such figures.) Locke also presents the reemergence of interracial themes in American literature from Reconstruction to the 1920s. His essay covers African American authors, white antislavery radicals, liberals, and "flagrantly derogatory" authors like Thomas Dixon. While Locke's perceptive essay is not cited very often, Sterling A. Brown's pathbreaking "Negro Character as Seen by White Authors" (1933) has informed many discussions of mixed-race figures, even by critics who may not directly quote him. In the two sections included here, Brown names the interracial rapist figure (in what Locke called "derogatory" works) "The Brute Negro," a term not often used in criticism today, and calls the stereotypical portraiture of many interracial characters and situations "The Tragic Mulatto," a term that may have its widest currency now. Just as Locke had offered a critical corrective to Gaines, so Brown wrote in opposition to John Herbert Nelson. But Brown holds up to greatest ridicule his contemporary writers who tried to translate racist theories of divided bloodlines into characters—"nonsense," he calls their work. Penelope Bullock's "The Mulatto in American Fiction" (1945) is the published summary of her 1944 Atlanta University thesis, one of the first comprehensive studies of the topic; the brief essay presents the major literature from George Washington Cable and Mark Twain to Charles Chesnutt, and also treats little-known authors. Two decades later, Jules Zanger, in his often-cited essay "The 'Tragic Octoroon' in Pre–Civil War Fiction" (1966), expanded the list of thematically relevant works. In the essay he offers a corrective to Sterling Brown's "Tragic Mulatto" while delineating the sharpest extant picture of stereotypical views of female mixed-blood characters. William Bedford Clark, "The Serpent of Lust in the Southern Garden" (1974), sees the theme as central to Southern literature from Joel Chandler Harris's "Where's Duncan?" to Robert Penn Warren's *Band of Angels*. Clark pursues common literary themes: the denial of family ties, the pattern of guilt and retribution, and the mulatto figure's identity and dual role as victim and avenger. The last essay of this section, William L. Andrews's "Miscegenation in the Late Nineteenth-Century Novel" (1979), presents concise readings of representative novels including Rebecca Harding Davis's *Waiting for the Verdict*, Cable's *Grandissimes*, and works by Albion Tourgée, Chesnutt, Howells, Mark Twain, Thomas Dixon, and Sutton Griggs.

"Case Studies and Close Readings" are brought together in the third section of part II. Arthur P. Davis's "The Tragic Mulatto Theme in Six Works of Langston Hughes" (1955) examines the different treatment Hughes gave to the theme in his poetry, prose, and drama, and is written with a biographical focus. An extraordinarily suggestive, little-known, and rarely cited essay by Langston Hughes on Mark Twain's *Pudd'nhead Wilson* follows. Simone Vauthier's "Of African Queens and Afro-American Princes and Princesses: Miscegenation in *Old Hepsy*" takes a careful and judicious close reading of Mary Denison's fantastic 1858 novel *Old Hepsy* (worth reprinting today) as the occasion for reflections on the general significance of themes of interracial couples (here also of a white woman and a black man) and their descendants for family romance and gender politics. The historian Tilden Edelstein's survey of the strange fate of "*Othello* in America: The Drama of Racial Intermarriage" (1982) reveals how the history of the play's reception and of theatrical adaptations in the United States can be viewed as a forum of American racial attitudes, citing how *Othello* "enacted what was least practiced and most feared: the legal marriage of a black man and a white woman." The last essay in this section, George Hutchinson's "Jean Toomer and American Racial Discourse" (1993), presents a close reading of Toomer's *Cane* by contrasting Toomer's resistance to American racial discourse with his pervasive reception within that discourse.

The fourth section of part II highlights "Literature in Contexts." Glenn Cannon Arbery draws on René Girard's analysis of scapegoating in *Violence and the Sacred*. Arbery argues that the absence of difference marks the victim status of mixed-race characters. His analysis centers on Faulkner's *Absalom, Absalom!* and *Go Down, Moses,* and also includes suggestive comments on Allen Tate's *The Fathers,* Cable's "Madame Delphine," Longfellow's poem "The Quadroon Girl," and Harriet Beecher Stowe's *Uncle Tom's Cabin.* Karen Sánchez-Eppler's widely cited "Bodily Bonds: The Intersecting Rhetorics of Feminism and Abolition" (1988) is a substantive examination of abolitionist literature from Lydia Maria Child to Harriet Beecher Stowe that offers new possibilities for that literature's fascination with miscegenation and extends and complicates Zanger's approach. Eduardo González's imaginative essay "American Theriomorphia: The Presence of *Mulatez* in Cirilo Villaverde and Beyond" constitutes a "hemispheric" approach to the topic and is informed not only by the semantic difference between Spanish "mulatto" and English "mulatto," between Villaverde's *Cecilia Valdez* and Faulkner's *Light in August,* or Cable's *Grandissimes,* but also by a broader, allusively constituted, comparative perspective on U.S. idiosyncrasies.

A MISCEGENATION VOCABULARY AND
THE COINING OF AN AMERICANISM

Terms from the
Oxford English Dictionary

Miscegenation

miscegenation mi:si d3i ne i.S<e>n. [irreg. f. L; *misce-re* to mix + *gen-us* race + -ation.] Mixture of races; esp. the sexual union of whites with Negroes.

- **1864** (*title*) Miscegenation: The Theory of the Blending of the Races, applied to the American White Man and Negro. Reprinted from the New York Edition.
- **1878** Stanley *Dark Cont.* I. 44 By this process of miscegenation, the Arabs are already rapidly losing their rich colour.
- **1889** *Boston* (Mass.) *Jrnl.* 27 Feb. 4/4 Miscegenation in Kentucky . . . The penalty for miscegenation is three years' imprisonment.
- **1902** *Pilot* 27 Dec. 540/2 The danger of 'miscegenation' . . . ought to warn us against introducing Oriental settlers into South Africa.
- **1927** M. M. Bennett *Christison* ii. 29 'Miscegenation' being official jargon for what Governor Bourke called 'detaining black women by force'.
- **1971** *Sunday Times* 20 June 29/6 [He] must inaugurate 'creative miscegenation' by marrying a Chinese girl.
- **1865** E. Burritt *Walk to Land's End* 64 It is an . . . effort to engraft Christian ideas upon the heathen stock of Grecian mythology. . . . In beautiful . . . contrast with this ostentatious group of Christian and pagan miscegenation is [etc.].
- **1884** J. Hawthorne *N. Hawthorne & Wife* II. 178 The lower regions of palaces come to strange uses in Rome; a cobbler or a tinker perhaps exercises his craft under the archway; a work-shop may be established in one of the apartments; and similar miscegenations.

So (mostly nonce-wds.) **'miscegen** back-formation = miscegenate; **'miscegenate** sb. see-ate2 3, the issue of a union between people of different races; **'miscegenate** v., to produce miscegenation; **'miscegenated** ppl. a., produced by miscegenation; **misce'genesis** (in quot. misci-) = miscegenation; **misce'netic, misce'genic** adjs., pertaining to or involving miscegenation; **'miscege'nationist, 'miscegenator, mi'scegenist**, one who favours miscegenation; also, one who contracts a union with one of another race; **mi'scegeny**, miscegenation.

- **1864** [Croly, etc.] *Miscegenation* 7 To *miscegenate*; i.e. to mingle persons of different races.
- **1864** [Croly, etc.] *Miscegenation* ii. 19 The Griquas, or Griqua Hottentots, are a miscegenated race.
- **1864** [Croly, etc.] *Miscegenation* v. 28 A miscegenetic community.
- **1864** [Croly, etc.] *Miscegenation* vii. 34 The purest miscegen will be brown, with reddish cheeks.
- **1865** *Reader* 20 May 561/2 (art. Emancipation). There are philogynists as fanatical as any 'miscegenists'.

- **1865** S. S. Cox *Eight Yrs. Congress* 354 A very sprightly suffragan of the miscegen stamp.
- **1865** S. S. Cox *Eight Yrs. Congress* 354 The result would be an average miscegen and a superior patriot.
- **1872** Schele de Vere *Americanisms* 289 A Miscegenationist, named Williams, was tarred and feathered, and dumped into the river at Grenada, Mississippi.
- **1880** Winchell *Preadamites* vi. 81 The policy of North American miscegenesis, which has been recommended . . . as an . . . expedient for obviating race collisions.
- **1881** Sala *Amer. Revis.* 316 Two such 'Miscegenators' have been hanged by the mob in Virginia.
- **1898** C. F. Adams *Imperialism* 10 It has saved the Anglo-Saxon stock from being a nation of half-breeds-miscegenates.
- **1941** R. West *Black Lamb* I. 527 It was a fusion, lovely but miscegenic, of the Byzantine and the baroque styles.
- **1935** *Punch* 14 Aug. 176/1 Since miscegeny is not a bad British trouble, *Shanghai* is a film that is more likely to interest America than ourselves.

Mulatto

mulatto mi*u* læ;t*o*, sb. and a. Forms: 6 mulatow, 7 malato, mallatto, melotto, molata, -o, mol(l)otto, mulata, -o, muletto, mullato, 7–8 molatto, -etto, mullatto, 8 malotto, melatto, moletta, 9 mulattoe, 7- mulatto. [a. Sp. (and Pg.) *mulato* young mule, hence one of mixed race, a mulatto, obscurely derived from *mulo* <u>mule</u> sb. 1; hence Fr. *mulâtre* (with assimilation of suffix to -*âtre* = -<u>aster</u>), Ital. *mulatto*.]

A. sb.

1. One who is the offspring of a European and a Black; also used loosely for anyone of mixed race resembling a mulatto.

- **1595** *Drake's Voy.* (Hakl. Soc.) 22 By meanes of a Mulatow and an Indian, we had, this night, forty bundles of dried beife.
- **1613** Purchas *Pilgrimage* vi. xiv. 545 Why then are the Portugalls Children and Generations White, or Mulatos at most.
- **1657** R. Ligon *Barbadoes* 10 A great fat man . . . his face not so black as to be counted a Mollotto.
- **1697** Dampier *Voy.* (1699) 199 The Mulata, because he said he was in the Fireship . . . was immediately hanged.
- **1713** C'tess of Winchilsea *Misc. Poems* 209 Grinning Malottos in true Ermin stare.
- **1727–41** Chambers Cycl., *Mulatto*, a name given, in the Indies, to those who are begotten by a negro man on an Indian woman; or an Indian man on a negro woman.
- **1854** Thackeray *Newcomes* I. 31 Two wooly-headed poor little mulattos.
- **1885** R. L. & F; Stevenson *Dynamiter* xi, That hag of a mulatto was no less a person than my wife.

[obsolete sense]
2. (See quot.) Obs.

- **1664** Jer. Taylor *Dissuas. Popery* i. i. Sect. 3 Purgatory, which is a device to make men be Mulata's as the Spaniard calls half-Christians.

3. Geol. The greenstone of Northern Ireland.

- **1816** Conybeare in *Trans. Geol. Soc.* III. 130 Mulattoe, an arenaceous stone, with a calcareous cement of a speckled appearance (whence its name).
- **1843** Portlock *Geol.* 110 the chalk . . . rests on . . . indurated greensand or (as it has been called) mulatto stone.

4. attrib. and Comb., as

mulatto-like adj.; **mulatto-clay** U.S., a dark-coloured clay; **mulatto jack**, a term for *yellow fever* (Syd. Soc. Lex. 1891); **mulatto land, -soil** U.S., a dark coloured fertile kind of soil; **mulatto loam, mould** = mulattoland; **mulatto prairie**, a prairie of mulatto-soil; **mulatto tree** (see quot.).

- **1788** T. Jefferson *Tour of Amsterdam* in *Writings* (1854) IX. 386 It has a southern aspect, the soil a barren *mulatto clay, mixed with a good deal of stone, and some slate.
- **1741** in *Amer. Speech* (1940) XV. 287/2 A Tract of rich *Mulattoe Land, lying in that County.
- **1794** Morse *Amer. Geog.* 556 The mulatto lands [of Georgia] are generally strong.
- **1883** E. A. Smith *Rep. Geol. Survey Alabama 1881–82* 435 The red or mulatto lands are much the best for cotton.
- **1719** De Foe *Crusoe* i. 177 As for my Face, the Colour of it was really not so *Moletta like, as one might expect.
- **1837** J. L. Williams *Territory of Florida* 82 The surface is covered with a *mulatto or chocolate colored loam.
- **1838** *Jeffersonian* (Albany) 28 Apr. 88 (Th.) The *mulatto mould of the Colorado does not surpass in fatness the alluvial soil of Red River.
- **1869** *Overland Monthly* III. 130 Then there is the 'chocolate' prairie, and the '*mulatto', and the 'mezquite'.
- **1794** Morse *Amer. Geog.* 556 The *mulatto soil [of Georgia], consisting of a black mould and red earth.
- **1819** E. Dana *Geogr. Sk. Western Country* 190 Next to this is very often found a skirt of rich pine land, dark mulatto soil with hickory . . . characteristic of good land.
- **1861** *Trans. Illinois Agric. Soc.* IV. 112 He . . . would not choose the dark prairie mold, but that kind of soil best known in the west as the 'mulatto soil'.
- **1876** *Encycl. Brit.* IV. 97/1 The *Mulatto tree (*Eukylista Spruceana*), one of the Cinchonaceæ.

B. adj.
1. Belonging to the class of mulattos.

- **1677** *Rec. Court of New Castle on Delaware* (1904) 91 The upholding & detayning of this p[laintiff]'s molatto servant in Maryland;

- **1704** T. Brown *Walk round Lond., Tavern* Wks. 1709 III. iii. 9, I shall observe your Caution, says my Moletto Comrade [an Indian].
- **1837** Ht. Martineau *Soc. Amer.* II. 156 She was asked whether she thought of doing anything for her two mulatto children.
- **1900** Deniker *Races of Man* xiii. 542 A Mulatto woman, the offspring of a Spaniard and a negress, may give birth to a Morisco by uniting with a Spaniard.

2. Of the colour of a mulatto; tawny.

- **1622** Mabbe tr. *Aleman's Guzman d'Alf.* ii. 328, I sweare and vow vnto thee by this my Mulata face, that [etc.].
- **1826** Prichard *Res. Phys. Hist. Man.* (ed. 2) I. 151 A man, who . . . was of a mulatto complexion.
- **1870** W. M. Baker *New Timothy* 84 (Cent.) Women of all shades of color, from deepest jet up to light mulatto.

Quadroon

quadroon kwo(hook)dr*u* .n. Forms: α. 8 quarteron, (9 -oon), quatron, 8–9 -eron, 9 -roon. β. 8 quaderoon, 9 quadroon. [ad. Sp; *cuarteron* (hence Fr. *quarteron*), f. *cuarto* fourth, quarter; the mod. form may be due to assoc. with other words in *quadr-*.]

1.

a. One who is the offspring of a white person and a mulatto; one who has a quarter of Negro blood.

b. *rarely* One who is fourth in descent from a Negro, one of the parents in each generation being white.

   In early Sp. use chiefly applied to the offspring of a white and a mestizo, or half-breed Indian. When it is used to denote one who is fourth in descent from a Negro, the previous stage is called a *terceron*: see the transl. of Juan and Ulloa's *Voyage* (1772) I. 30, and cf. quintroon.

   α

- **1707** Sloane *Jamaica* I. p. xlvi, The inhabitants of Jamaica are for the most part Europeans . . . who are the Masters, and Indians, Negros, Mulatos, Alcatrazes, Mestises, Quarterons, &c. who are the Slaves;
- **1793** Jefferson *Writ.* (1859) IV. 98 Castaing is described as a small dark mulatto, and La Chaise as a Quateron.
- **1819** W. Lawrence *Lect. Physiol. Zool.* 295 Europeans and Tercerons produce Quarterons or Quadroons.
- **1837** Carlyle *Fr. Rev.* II. v. iv, Your pale-white Creoles . . . and your yellow Quarteroons.
- **1840** R. H. Dana *Bef. Mast* xiii. 29 The least drop of Spanish blood, if it be only of quatroon or octoon.

   β

- **1796** Stedman *Surinam* I. 296 The Samboe dark, and the Mulatto brown, The Mæsti fair, the well-limbed Quaderoon;

- **1819** [see α];
- **1833** Marryat P. *Simple* (1863) 228 The progeny of a white and a negro is a mulatto, or half and half—of a white and mulatto, a quadroon, or one quarter black.
- **1880** Ouida *Moths* I. 178 That brute goes with a quadroon to a restaurant.

Comb.

- **1860** O. W. Holmes *Elsie V.* xxi. (1891) 292 How could he ever come to fancy such a quadroon-looking thing as that?

c. *transf.* Applied to the offspring resulting from similar admixture of blood in the case of other races, or from crossing in the case of animals or plants.

- **1811** Southey in *Q. Rev.* VI. 346 Whether a man were a half-new Christian, or a quateron, or a half-quateron . . . the Hebrew leaven was in the blood.
- **1879** tr. *De Quatrefages Hum. Spec.* 72 Koelreuter artificially fertilised hybrid flowers . . . and thus obtained a vegetable quadroon.
- **1892** *Daily News* 17 June 5/3 The offspring of these crosses [of rabbits] did not in any instance produce a 'quadroon'.

2. *attrib.* or as *adj.*
quadroon ball;
quadroon black, the offspring of a pure Negro and a quadroon (*Syd. Soc. Lex.* 1897).

- **1748** *Earthquake Peru* iii. 240 Quatron Indians, born of Whites and Mestizos.
- **1748** *Earthquake Peru* iii. 240 Quatron Negroes, born of Whites and Mulattos.
- **1796** Stedman *Surinam* I. vi. 126 A young and beautiful Quadroon girl.
- **1796** Stedman *Surinam* II. xviii. 56 A female quaderoon slave.
- **1805** J. F. Watson in *Amer. Pioneer* (1843) II. 236 These colored women have . . . their weekly balls, (called quartroon balls) at which none but white gentlemen attend.
- **1849** Macaulay *Hist. Eng.* I. i. 14 A marriage between a white planter and a quadroon girl.
- **1880** G. W. Cable *Grandissimes* iii. 19, I saw the same old man, at a quadroon ball a few years ago.
- **1893** F. C. Selous *Trav. S.E. Africa* 60 A pretty . . . mulatto, or rather quadroon girl.
- **1948** *Chicago Tribune* (Grafic Mag.) 8 Feb. 18/3 Most notorious of the carnival affairs, was the Quadroon ball, given by the young men of the town for their mistresses and friends.

Octoroon

octoroon *o(hook)* ktor*u* .n. [A non-etymological formation from L. *octo* eight, after *quadroon* (in which the suffix is -*oon*).] A person having one-eighth Negro blood; the offspring of a quadroon and a white; sometimes used of other mixed races.

- **1861** D. Boucicault (*title*) The Octoroon.
- **1862** J. E. Cairnes *Revol. Amer.* 17 The mulattoes, quadroons and octoroons ... who now form so large a proportion of the whole enslaved population of the South.
- **1864** Webster, *Octaroon*, see *Octoroon*.
- **1891** *Times* 8 Jan. 9/3 The mulatto, the quadroon, and the octoroon are chiefly products of the slavery period.

Hybrid

hybrid h<e>i.brid, hi;brid, , sb. and a. Also 7 hi-, hybride. [f. L. *hybrida*, more correctly *hibrida* (*ibrida*), offspring of a tame sow and wild boar; hence, of human parents of different races, half-breed. Cf. Fr. *hybride* (1798 in Hatz.-Darm.). A few examples of this word occur early in 17th c.; but it was scarcely in use till the 19th. The only member of the group given by Johnson is hybridous a.; Ash and Todd have also *hybrid* adj., to which Webster 1828 adds *hybrid* sb. As to the ultimate etym. of L. *hybrida* see Prof. Minton Warren in Amer. *Jrnl Philol.* V. No. 4.]
A. sb.
1. The offspring of two animals or plants of different species, or (less strictly) varieties; a half-breed, cross-breed, or mongrel.

reciprocal hybrids, hybrids produced from the same two species A and B, where in the one case A is male and B female, in the other B is male and A female, *e.g.* the mule and the hinny.

a. of animals. (In 17th c. only as in original L.)

- **1601** Holland *Pliny* II. 231 There is no creature ingenders so soon with wild of the kind, as doth swine: and verily such hogs in old time they called Hybrides, as a man would say, halfe wild.
- **1623** Cockeram, *Hibride*, a Hog ingendred betweene a wilde Boare and a tame Sow.
- **1828** Webster, *Hybrid*, a mongrel or mule; an animal or plant, produced from the mixture of two species.
- **1851** D. Wilson *Preh. Ann.* (1863) II. iv. ii. 232 Grotesque hybrids, half-bird, half-beast.
- **1859** Darwin *Orig. Spec.* i. 26 The hybrids or mongrels from between all the breeds of the pigeon are perfectly fertile.
- **1862** Huxley *Lect. Wrkg. Men* 112 There is a great difference between 'Mongrels' which are crosses between distinct races and 'hybrids' which are crosses between distinct species.

b. of human beings.

- **1630** B. Jonson *New Inn* ii. ii, She's a wild Irish born, sir, and a hybride.
- **1861** J. Crawfurd in *Trans. Ethnol. Soc.* (N.S.) I. 357 At the best we [English] are but hybrids, yet, probably, not the worse for that.

- 1878 Bosw. Smith *Carthage* 434 Negroes from the Soudan, not such sickly . . . hybrids as you see in Oxford Street . . . but real down-right Negroes halfnaked, black as ebony.

c. of plants.

- 1788 J. Lee *Introd. Bot.* (ed. 4) Gloss., *Hybrida*, a Bastard, a monstrous Production of two Plants of different Species.
- 1828 [see a].
- 1845 Lindley *Sch. Bot.* x. (1858) 167 No hybrids but such as are of a woody perennial character can be perpetuated with certainty.
- 1846 J. Baxter *Libr. Pract. Agric.* (ed. 4) II. 358 Swedes are generally sown first. Hybrids . . . are usually sown next, and white turnips the last.
- 1867 Darwin in *Life & Lett;* (1887) III. 306 The common Oxlip found everywhere . . . in England, is certainly a hybrid between the primrose and cowslip.

2. transf. and fig.
a. Anything derived from heterogeneous sources, or composed of different or incongruous elements; in Philol. a composite word formed of elements belonging to different languages.

- 1850 H. Rogers *Ess.* II.iv.213 A free resort to grotesque compounds . . . favours the multiplication of yet more grotesque hybrids.
- 1860 Darwin in *Life & Lett.* (1887) II. 338, I will tell you what you are, a hybrid, a complex cross of lawyer, poet, naturalist, and theologian!
- 1874 Lisle Carr *Jud. Gwynne* II. vii. 163 A remarkable hybrid between a frank . . . bumpkin, and a used up exquisite.
- 1879 Morris *Eng. Accid.* 39 Sometimes we find English and Romance elements compounded. These are termed *Hybrids*.
- 1895 F. Hall *Two Trifles* 28 The ancient Romans would not have endured *scientistes* or *scientista*, as a new type of hybrid.

B. adj.
1.

a. Produced by the inter-breeding of two different species or varieties of animals or plants; mongrel, cross-bred, half-bred.

- 1775 Ash, *Hybrid*, begotten between animals of different species, produced from plants of different kinds.
- 1789 E. Darwin *Bot. Gard.* 149 *note*, Many hybrid plants described.
- 1823 J. Badcock *Dom. Amusem.* 47 These hybrid, or mule productions.
- 1857 Darwin in *Life & Lett;* (1887) II. 96, I think there is rather better evidence on the sterility of hybrid animals than you seem to admit.
- 1865 Palgrave *Arabia* II. 211 The town inhabitants . . . are at present a very hybrid race, yet fused into a general . . . type.

So
[obsolete sense]
'hybridal,

[obsolete sense]
'**hybridan** adjs. = <u>hybrid</u> a.

- **1623** Cockeram, *Hybridan*, whose parents are of diuers and sundry Nations.
- **1801** T. Jefferson *Writ.* (ed. Ford) VIII. 16, I am persuaded the squash . . . is a hybridal plant.

Inter-

4. Prefixed to adjs. (originally, and most frequently, of Latin origin), in prepositional relation to the sb. implied (as inter-acinous, 'that is inter acinos, between the acini': cf. anti- 3, infra- 1), or sometimes to a phrase consisting of the adj. + a sb. (as inter-accessory 'between accessory processes').
c. Denoting 'Subsisting, carried on, taking place, or forming a communication, between . . . '; hence, sometimes, 'Belonging in common to, or composed of elements derived from, different things (of the kind indicated by the second element)': as in

Inter-racial

- **1888** *Scot. Leader* 20 Aug. 5 *Interracial conflict in Louisiana. Twenty niggers slain.
- **1892** Stevenson & L; *Osbourne Wrecker* viii. 123 Chinatown . . . drew and held me; I could never have enough of its ambiguous, interracial atmosphere.
- **1905** *Athenæum* 30 Sept. 430/1 Inter-racial cordiality.
- **1953** E. H. Brookes *S. Afr. in Changing World* v. 105 Thus the services of Americans to South Africa in the interracial field are spanned across a century.
- **1960** *Spectator* 22 July 128 There is a large, brand-new 'inter-racial' hotel.
- **1968** *Blues Unlimited* Dec. 12 The local interracial Dirty Blues Band.
- **1972** *Publishers Weekly* 7 Feb. 37 (Advt.), Grace Halsell . . . describes what happens to interracial couples when they are joined in a love affair or marriage.
- **1964** *Punch* 26 Aug. 290/1 Anger . . . fomented internally and directed *interracially.
- **1972** *Publishers Weekly* 14 Aug. 40/2 He hustled a basketball scholarship, lost it for dating interracially.
- **1931** *Amer. Speech* VII. 78 A writer in the *Congregationalist* says '*Interracialism, like love, service, and brotherhood, is a splendid word which has been cheapened by overuse.' How many acquaintances have you whose diction suffers from over-use of the word interracialism?

Multi-racial

multiracial, a. Of, pertaining to, or comprising several races, peoples, or ethnic groups; characterized by the coexistence or co-operation of individual members of such groups on amicable and equal terms. Also fig. So **multi-'racially** adv.

- **1923** *Overseas* Sept. 45 The interests of modern civilisation and, I think, Christian ethics, are better expressed in large, bi-racial or multi-racial States . . . where racialism is accounted a public curse rather than a civic virtue.
- **1933** E. B. Reuter in E. S. Bogardus *Social Probl. & Social Processes* 96 The type of accommodation made is of course an individual matter, but the forms that it takes are . . . those familiar in other bi-racial or multi-racial political areas.
- **1947** *Forum* (Johannesburg) X. i. 25/1 We, as a multi-racial society, have had our differences, while sharp antagonisms unfortunately exist today.
- **1957** L. F. R. Williams *State of Israel* 209 The unifying influence which this hostility is exerting upon Israel's multiracial population.
- **1957** *Economist* 19 Oct. 204/2 He triumphantly created the first multiracial government in Africa at the height of Mau Mau.
- **1958** *Times Lit. Suppl.* 10 Jan. 21/2 One feels the pleasant relief of a man living a multi-racial life away from the colour bar.
- **1959** *New Statesman* 28 Feb. 300/1 But it is his attack on the multi-racial clothing industry—involving the dismissal and replacement of 35,000 non-whites—that has frightened the coloured people especially.
- **1963** *Economist* 30 Nov. 887/3 Such a multi-racially-run world.
- **1966** *Listener* 6 Oct. 499/3 Closer contact between . . . the university worker and the industrial scientist, to make a truly 'multi-racial' commonwealth of scholarship.
- **1972** T. Lilley *K Section* ix. 40 The Dock Labourers' Union was one of the biggest. . . . Multi-racial, it owed allegiance only to itself.

The Miscegenation Issue in the Election of 1864[*]

SIDNEY KAPLAN

"Early in 1943," wrote Helen Fuller in a recent issue of the *New Republic*, "Governor Sam Jones of Louisiana and Frank Dixon of Alabama invited the Conference of Southern Governors to join them in the formation of a new Southern Democratic Party, dedicated to 'State's Rights and White Supremacy.' " The plan failed—but was not abandoned. The day after Roosevelt was elected to his fourth term, one Charles Wallace Collins, a constitutional lawyer practicing in Washington, D.C., retired from active practice and "settled down in his Washington Press Building office to write a book stating the case for a return to the rule of the South by a small minority of well-to-do whites, qualified by 'superior birth and intelligence' to decide" what was best for everyone. In December 1947, "just as the more foresighted of the Southern Republocrats were beginning to think about what kind of 'revolt' they should plan for 1948," his book *Whither Solid South?*, was published by the obscure Pelican Press of New Orleans. This

* From Sidney Kaplan, "The Miscegenation Issue in the Election of 1864." *Journal of Negro History* 34.3 (July 1949): 274–343.

"second-rate book" was intended by its "unknown author" to become "the 'Mein Kampf' of a new movement."

Collins, to be sure, fancied himself "the John C. Calhoun of a new Secession," and in his book dwelt "at length on the historical and ethnic bases of white supremacy, the illegality of the Fourteenth Amendment, the moral and religious case for continuing segregation," winding up with a proposal for "a forty-ninth state in Africa." What is of interest here is the technique suggested for accomplishing these things. For, according to Collins, it was entirely within the realm of possibility in 1948 for the conservatives within the Republican and Democratic Parties to combine harmoniously to form what would be the strongest party in the country "*provided* the issue of Negro equality was left to the sponsorship of a new Liberal Party."[1] This was the line the late, unlamented States Rights party tried to follow. "The convention ended with a burst of shouts, cheers and rebel yells, as well as countless parades on the convention floor with a portrait of Gen. Robert E. Lee held high"—thus the *New York Times* of July 18, 1948, described the demonstrations at the Birmingham convention of the Dixiecrats, which followed numerous speeches denouncing Truman and his civil rights program as "threats to make Southerners into a mongrel, inferior race by forced intermingling with Negroes."

It was, of course, a hoary tune. Alexander Stephens and Clement Vallandigham had played it earlier and better. Yet the issue—a sign of our times—cannot be thrust aside as too inane for gentle people to discuss. Collins and his cronies are no doubt even now examining the mistakes of their campaign. The issue will crop up again and again, and will have to be met with forthrightness and understanding. For those who ponder the meaning of the thirty-eight electoral ballots cast for the Dixiecrats in the recent election, an analysis of the "miscegenation" phase of the war-election of 1864 will be of more than specialist or antiquarian interest.

This rather nasty story begins almost a year before the election which returned Lincoln to the White House for a second term. His victory was an impressive one. Yet, as is well known, the summer of 1864 was a time of gloom in the Republican camp; indeed, as November approached, the President recorded his secret and humorless belief that it seemed "exceedingly probable" he would not be re-elected. Why this deep pessimism in August on the eve of victory? There were reasons enough: Sherman was not yet in Atlanta and Fremont's hat was still in the presidential ring—while dissension ruled within cabinet and party.

More intangible yet no less real a source of irritation was the unbridled arrogance of the Copperhead publicists, to whom the Emancipation Proclamation had providentially furnished "a real issue of principle." The war, they noisomely argued, had been declared to save the Union; now it had been transformed by Lincoln and the charlatans in power into a "nigger crusade"—compulsory intermarriage of white and black had finally become the main plank in the Republican

---

1. "The New Confederacy," *New Republic* (Nov. 1, 1948), 10–14.

platform! "May the blessings of Emancipation extend throughout our unhappy lands," ran a "Black Republican Prayer" distributed by the Democrats in 1863,

and the illustrious, sweet-scented Sambo nestle in the bosom of every Abolition woman, that she may be quickened by the pure blood of the majestic African, and the Spirit of amalgamation shine forth in all its splendor and glory, that we may become a regenerated nation of half-breeds and mongrels, and the distinction of color be forever consigned to oblivion, and that we may live in bonds of fraternal love, union and equality with the Almighty Nigger, henceforward, now and forever. Amen.

From January to November 1864 the Democratic press would tear this "issue" to tatters. But could McClellan win on so frantic an issue? To Lincoln, thumbing through reports of vast conspiracies afoot and remembering the sickening draft riots of the previous summer, it was not an altogether bogus optimism exuded by the journals of the Democracy.[2]

In reality the optimism was false and the arrogance born of desperation, for the more knowledgeable politicians and generals of the South had by this time read the handwriting on the wall. Although armies in gray were still powerfully in the field, the most vital front of the war had already shifted to the "peace" press of the North; the keystone of Confederate strategy was now defeat of Lincoln at the polls. The war must go on, counseled Jefferson Davis, "until Mr. Lincoln's time was out," and then the North "might compromise."[3]

It was precisely at this time—a little before Christmas of 1863—that there appeared for sale on newsstands in New York City a seventy-two-page pamphlet, costing a quarter and bearing the enigmatic title *Miscegenation: The Theory of the Blending of the Races, Applied to the American White Man and Negro.*[4] This pamphlet, a curious hash of quarter-truths and pseudo-learned oddities, was to give a new word to the language and a refurbished issue to the Democratic Party— although its anonymous author, for good reason perhaps, never came forward to claim his honors. In the welter of leaflets, brochures, cards, tracts and cartoons struck off by all parties during the Civil War, it stands out as centrally significant.

Miscegenation is a disorganized piece of work, difficult to summarize briefly.[5] With a flourish of scholarship on his very first page the pamphleteer defines the "new words" he finds necessary to coin in order to present his argument. The first is *miscegenation* (from the Latin *miscere*, to mix, and *genus*, race) with its derivatives, *miscegen, miscegenate* and *miscegenetic*; the second—a more precise neologism—is *melaleukation* (from the Greek *melas*, black, and *leukos*, white) with its derivatives, *melaleukon* and *melaleuketic*, "to express the idea of the union of the white and black races."[6]

2. Edward Chase Kirkland, *The Peacemakers of 1864* (New York, 1927), 11–12, 28–29; Carl Sandburg, *Abraham Lincoln, The War Years* (New York, 1939), III, 267.
3. George Fort Milton, *Abraham Lincoln and the Fifth Column* (New York, 1942), 210.
4. New York, 1863; hereinafter referred to as *Miscegenation.*
5. The quotations in the summary that follows are taken *passim* from the pamphlet.
6. The current expression, *amalgamation*, was, according to the author, a "poor word" since it properly

Having disposed of his definitions, the author gets his argument rapidly under way. Science and Christianity have proved beyond doubt "that all the tribes which inhabit the earth were originally derived from one type." Dr. Draper of New York University, Camper of Gröningen, Aristotle, Galen, Dr. Pritchard and Baron Larrey have established the "physiological equality of the white and colored races." Furthermore, if "any fact is well established in history, it is that the miscegenetic or mixed races are much superior, mentally, physically, and morally, to those pure or unmixed." Don Felix De Azara, Pallas, Moodie, Laurence, Dr. Hancock, Dallas and Walker have confirmed this fact. The English are great because they are composite; the French—who invented divorce—were originally a blend; they intermarried and decayed; thus the two most brilliant writers France can boast of are "the melaleukon, Dumas, and his son, a quadroon." The peoples of Sicily and Naples have inbred, and are therefore "probably the lowest people, except the Irish, in the scale of civilization in Europe . . . brutal, ignorant and barbarous," while the "most promising nation in Europe is the Russian, and its future will be glorious, only because its people represents a greater variety of race than any other in Europe." American vitality comes "not from its Anglo-Saxon progenitors, but from all the different nationalities" of the melting-pot. "All that is needed to make us the finest race on earth is to engraft upon our stock the negro element; the blood of the negro is the most precious because it is the most unlike any other that enters into the composition of our national life."

The truth is that "no race can long endure without commingling of its blood with that of other races." Human progress itself depends on miscegenation and "Providence has kindly placed on the American soil . . . four millions of colored

---

referred to the "union of metals with quick-silver, and was, in fact, only borrowed for an emergency, and should now be returned to its proper signification." Said the London *Morning Herald* of November 1, 1864: "Whatever good or evil the authors of 'Miscegenation' may have done in a political way, they have achieved a sort of reflected fame on the coining of two or three new words— at least one of which is destined to be incorporated into the language. Speakers and writers of English will gladly accept the word 'Miscegenation' in the place of the word amalgamation. . . ." *A Dictionary of American English* makes a curious typographic error in one of the historical citations attached to its definition of *miscegenation*. The citation—an excerpt from M. Schele De Vere's *Americanisms* (1872), 288–289—is printed in the *DAE* as follows: "I was one . . . who first publicly used the illshapen word miscegenation, and openly dared to advocate the expediency of favoring, by every agency of State and Church, the mingling of the black and white races." Can this mean that De Vere (Professor of Modern Languages at the University of Virginia in 1872) was a mis-cegenationist?—a startling thought, since a reading of his book reveals him as an unreconciled champion of the Confederacy. The matter is clarified by an examination of De Vere's text, where, following a partisan definition of scalawags as the "evidently dishonest among the Southerners, who went over to the dominant party, and unblushingly lived on their conquered friends and neighbors," the citation in question appears as follows: "It was one of this class, rather than the eloquent advocate of Women's Rights [Wendell Phillips] often charged with the crime, who first publicly used the illshapen word miscegenation, and openly dared to advocate the expediency of favoring, by every agency of State and Church, the mingling of the black and white races." De Vere, of course, was wrong. *Miscegenation* originated in the pamphlet of that title in 1863, as is recognized by the *New English Dictionary*; its brother word, *melaleukation*, did not "take" from the start.

people" for that purpose. It will be "our noble prerogative to set the example of this rich blending of blood."

It is idle to maintain that this present war is not a war for the negro . . . it is a war, if you please, of amalgamation . . . a war looking, as its final fruit, to the blending of the white and black. . . . Let the war go on . . . Until church, and state, and society recognize not only the propriety but the necessity of the fusion of the white and black—in short, until the great truth shall be declared in our public documents and announced in the messages of our Presidents, that it is desirable the white man should marry the black woman and the white woman the black man—that the race should become melaleuketic before it becomes miscegenetic.

The next step is to open California to the swarming millions of eastern Asia. The patience and skill of the Japanese and Chinese in the mechanic arts must be blended into "the composite race which will hereafter rule this continent."

The Indian has shown—and the physiologists have affirmed—that copper is the permanent American skin-color; indeed, the "white race which settled New England will be unable to maintain its vitality as a blonde people." The proof is that tuberculosis in "our Eastern States is mainly confined to the yellow-haired and thin-blooded blondes." Ultimately, black will absorb white; it is a truth of nature. The conquest of Britain by Rome illustrates the fact that all the "noted ancient and modern wars of Europe may be traced to the yearning of the brunette and blonde to mingle." Americans must become "a yellow-skinned, black-haired people—in fine . . . miscegens."

How solve the mystery of the Pyramids? What answer give to the question of the Sphinx? It is the "principle of Miscegenation in ancient Egypt"; civilization, science and art are the creations of "the miscegenetic mind developed upon the banks of the Nile, by Asiatics and Africans." The Jews themselves "were partly of Abyssinian or negro origin." The conclusion is clear: "Let us then embrace our black brother" in America. Perfect religion and perfect mankind will be the results, for "the ideal or type man of the future will blend in himself all that is passionate and emotional in the darker races, all that is imaginative and spiritual in the Asiatic races, and all that is intellectual and perceptive in the white races." He will be "brown, with reddish cheeks, curly and waving hair, dark eyes, and a fullness and suppleness of form not now dreamed of by any individual people." Adam and Christ were type-men, or miscegens, red or yellow.

Furthermore, the mutual love of black and white is based on the natural law of the attraction of opposites. For example, the "sympathy Mr. Greeley feels for the negro is the love which the blonde bears for the black . . . stronger than the love they bear to women." The Abolitionist leaders furnish additional examples: his complexion "reddish and sanguine," Wendell Phillips is one of the "sharpest possible contrasts to the pure negro." Theodore Tilton, "the eloquent young editor of the Independent, who has already achieved immortality by advocating enthusiastically the doctrine of miscegenation, is a very pure specimen of the blonde." That black loves blonde is shown also by the number of "rape cases in the courts and by the experience of Southern plantations." The only remedy is "legitimate melaleuketic marriage." Give nature a free course and men and women, "whether anti-slavery or pro-slavery, conservative or radical, democratic or republican, will marry the most perfect specimens of the colored race." This natural passion is "the secret of the strange infatuation of the Southern woman with the hideous barbarism of slavery. Freedom, she knows, would separate her forever from the colored man. . . . It is idle for Southern woman to deny it; she loves the black man, and the raiment she clothes herself with is to please him."

All this is only preparation. For it is with the specific relationship of the Irish working-people and the Negro—the New York draft riots of the previous summer were fresh in the memory of the country—that the pamphleteer is especially concerned. "Notwithstanding the apparent antagonism which exists between the Irish and negroes on this continent"

> there are the strongest reasons for believing that the first movement towards a melaleuketic union will take place between these two races. Indeed, in very many instances it has already occurred. Wherever there is a poor community of Irish in the North they naturally herd with the poor negroes . . . connubial relations are formed between the black men and white Irish women . . . pleasant to both parties, and were it not for the unhappy prejudice which exists, such unions would be very much more frequent. The white Irishwoman loves the black man, and in the old country . . . the negro is sure of the handsomest among the poor white females. . . . The fusion, whenever it takes place, will be of infinite service to the Irish. They are a more brutal race and lower in civilization than the negro . . . coarse-grained, revengeful, unintellectual . . . below the level of the most degraded negro. Take an equal number of negroes and Irish from among the lowest communities of the city of New York, and the former will be found far superior to the latter in cleanliness, education, moral feelings, beauty of form and feature, and natural sense.

The "prognathous skull, the projecting mouth, the flat and open nostril" are characteristic of the "inhabitants of Sligo and Mayo." With education "and an intermingling with the superior black, the Irish may be lifted up to something like the dignity of their ancestors, the Milesians." There is only one correct course: the Irish should put aside prejudice toward their "dark-skinned fellow-laborers and friends and proclaim intermarriage with the Negro as a solution to their problem."

Do the Irish object to this prognosis? They ought not. Observe the noblemen produced by nature in the Southern aristocracy. Yet the "truth may as well be understood, that the superiority of the slaveholding classes of the South arises from their intimate communication, from birth to death, with the colored race." It is notorious that, "for three generations back, the wealthy, educated, governing class of the South have mingled their blood with the enslaved race." The "emotional power, fervid oratory and intensity which distinguishes all thoroughbred slaveholders is due to their intimate association with the most charming and intelligent of their slave girls." In fact, "legal melaleukation will be first openly adopted in the slave States." The large cities of the South, New Orleans especially, even now swarm with mulattoes, quadroons and octoroons, and the "unions producing these mixtures will be continued under the sanctions of public opinion, law, and religion."

His preamble completed, the pamphleteer is now ready for his main point. What is the meaning, he asks, of all these "scientific" and "historical" data for 1864, the fateful year in which the North must choose a new president? Only this—emancipation means amalgamation; the party of Abolition is "the party of miscegenation." True, the "people do not yet understand" the point and the "party as a whole" will not admit it. But there is still hope that opinion will change, for the "leaders of Progress"—among them Phillips and Tilton—"urge miscegenetic reform" and the "people are ripe to receive the truth." What must be recognized is that the Republican Party "will not perform its whole mission till it throws aloft the standard of Miscegenation."

Yet examine the platform of the Chicago Convention—how meager it is on this vital subject. Nowhere does it acknowledge the fact that "miscegenation reform should enter into the approaching presidential contest." Is it, however, too late to add the miscegenation plank to the platform? Not at all, maintains the pamphleteer in a grand finale: let Abraham Lincoln candidly proclaim that "the solution of the negro problem will not have been reached in this country until public opinion sanctions a union of the two races . . . that in the millenial future, the most perfect and highest type of manhood will not be white or black but brown, or colored, and that whoever helps to unite the various races of man, helps to make the human family the sooner realize its great destiny." And although the Democrats attempt "to divert discussion to senseless side issues, such as peace, free speech, and personal and constitutional rights," let the motto of "the great progressive party of this country be Freedom, Political and Social Equality; Universal Brotherhood."

Excerpts from "amalgamationist" speeches delivered by Theodore Tilton and Wendell Phillips in May and July of 1863, a few lines from a book review of Wilson's *Pre-historic Man*, a selection from an article in the *Independent* on the "intermingling of Colors and Sexes at Oberlin University," and a quotation from Harriet Beecher Stowe's novel *Dred*—a description of Harry and Lisette under the title of "Pen-Portrait of a Miscegenetic Woman and Man"—bring the pamphlet to a close.

So much for the pamphlet itself. The author, apparently an impassioned—even learned—Abolitionist, preferred to remain anonymous. Yet he was proud of his work. So, on Christmas Day, 1863, he mailed out complimentary copies of his little tract to a number of prominent anti-slavery leaders throughout the country. Tucked into each copy was a warm and friendly letter which, after noting that the doctrine of miscegenation might be "in advance of the times," asked the distinguished recipient for an opinion of its merits. There was nothing unusual in the practice; so Emerson had discovered Whitman. Replies were to be addressed to the "Author of 'Miscegenation,' " in care of his Nassau Street publishers.

Now the curious thing about this ostensibly Abolitionist tract was that it was *not* written by an Abolitionist at all. As a matter of fact it was conceived by two clever journalists in the offices of Manton Marble's violently anti-Abolitionist New

York *World*—a newspaper which, in the words of the historian Rhodes, was "the ablest and most influential Democratic journal in the country, the organ of the high-toned Democrats of New York City and State."[7] David Goodman Croly, managing editor of this quasi-Copperhead sheet, and his young friend, George Wakeman, a reporter on its staff, were the joint, forever unconfessed, authors of the pamphlet, *Miscegenation*. Croly himself footed the printing bill.[8]

Of George Wakeman's life or opinions little is known. He had come from Connecticut to New York in 1858 to work on the *Ledger* and had contributed to the *Galaxy, Appleton's Journal* and other periodicals while his steady job was on the *World*. He was a lad of twenty-two, "a clever young journalist" just "discovered" by Croly when he collaborated on the pamphlet.[9]

There is a bit more to be discovered about David Goodman Croly. A dozen years older than Wakeman, he had come from Ireland to New York as a youngster, had served as apprentice to a Manhattan silversmith, reporter on the New York *Evening Post* when Bryant was editor, and head of the city intelligence department of the *Herald* under Frederick Hudson. A year after his marriage to Jane Cunningham, one of the country's pioneer female journalists, he had travelled west to Illinois. In the town of Rockford, the Crolys had purchased the *Democratic Standard*, a weekly newspaper then owned by a relative of Mrs. Croly's, which re-blossomed under their editorship as the Rockford *Daily News*, "Neutral in Politics—Independent in Everything." When the editor of the *Register*, a rival Republican newspaper, had charged that the *News*'s "political stripe" was proslavery Democrat, Croly had denied it. "So Mr. Douglas and the whole proslavery north," the *Register* had commented, "call it a mis-statement when they are termed pro-slavery democrats. But by their fruits are they known." The *News* failed, although Rocklanders offered to refinance it, and Croly returned to New York to become city editor of the *World* just before the war. On its staff at this time were James K. Spalding, Richard Grant White, Ivory Chamberlain and Manton Marble. When the *World* went bankrupt in 1862, Marble, backed reportedly by August Belmont—took it over as a Democratic organ and Croly became its managing editor.[10]

7. James Ford Rhodes, *History of the United States* (New York, 1906), IV, 471. In its editorial box, the *World* described itself as "a sound Democratic newspaper" with 100,000 subscribers and half a million readers.

8. *The Dictionary of American Biography*, Sabin's *Dictionary* and the Library of Congress catalogue err in listing one E. C. Howell as a third author. Howell (whose correct initials are S. C.) was city editor of the *World* while Croly was managing editor but probably took no part in writing the pamphlet. (*Real Estate Record & Builders Guide*, XLIII [May 4, 1889], 613–614). "The little brochure was the joint work of Mr. D. G. Croly, my husband, and a very clever young journalist, Mr. George Wakeman," stated Mrs. David Goodman Croly in 1900. "No other person than the two mentioned had anything at all to do with the production." (MS letter of Mrs. Croly, Dec. 15, 1900, in Boston Athenaeum).

9. *Dictionary of American Biography* (Boston, 1872); *Real Estate Record & Builders Guide*, XLIII, 613–614.

10. *Real Estate Record & Builders Guide*, XLIII, 613–614. *Dictionary of American Biography*; M. James Bolquerin, *An Investigation of the Contributions of David, Jane, and Herbert Croly to American Life—*

Were Wakeman and Croly scalawags among Copperheads, fifth-columnists among the Butternuts? The history of *Miscegenation* will perhaps clarify the motives of its authors.

On Christmas Day Croly and Wakeman had mailed out *Miscegenation* to sundry prominent Abolitionists. By mid-January half-a-dozen replies were in their hands—from Lucretia Mott, Dr. James McCune Smith, the Grimké sisters, Parker Pillsbury and Albert Brisbane. The opinions of the Abolitionists were all rendered in good faith; admiration for the courage of the pamphleteers runs through their letters. But it is an admiration tempered with cautious enthusiasm both for the substance of the pamphlet and for the timeliness of its publication. Was it perhaps a harebrained fellow they were dealing with? Were one's most vociferous friends sometimes one's most confounded enemies?

From Lucretia Mott, the Quaker leader of the American Anti-Slavery Society, came the most cautious reply of all. She had submitted the pamphlet to her "anti-slavery friends"; and while they were not "sufficiently familiar with physiological facts and theories" to render final judgment, they felt that the author's conclusions were scientifically untenable. Most "questionable" was the opinion that the "distinguished advocates" of the slave had been drawn to their task by "the natural love of opposites." As for the idea of putting a miscegenation plank into the anti-slavery platform, while it was true that the Massachusetts Anti-Slavery Society had fought to repeal the evil law making inter-racial marriage a crime, the abolitionists had "never thought it expedient to advocate such unions" and had only sought "to remove all civil and social disabilities from this prescribed class, leaving nature and human affections to take care of themselves." Nevertheless, although it was "not *yet* deemed *expedient* by the anti-slavery reformers to agitate the matrimonial question," they continued to circulate Theodore Tilton's discourse on the Negro. *Miscegenation,* she concluded noncommitally, would "doubtless find readers."[11]

The replies of the Grimké sisters of South Carolina were of the same pattern: joy in the essential liberality of the doctrine, disagreement with some of the flamboyant reasoning, grave doubt concerning the expediency of making miscegenation an issue in Abolitionist politics. Sarah Grimké felt that the author had spoken "extravagantly" in stating "that the first heart experience of nearly every Southern maiden is associated with the sad dream of some bondman lover." That such things had happened she had no doubt; but she knew of only one instance where the passion was consummated and "the lady died at the birth of her child, without revealing the name of her lover." Since the event "excited great horror and indignation," she curiously reasoned, "it could not be common." Since also "the immense distance between a slave and his young mistress would render such things very rare," the statement required "great modification." Angelina Grimké (Mrs. Weld) had found the pamphlet "interesting and instructive." She and her

---

With Emphasis on the Influence of the Father on the Son, unpublished master's thesis (School of Journalism, University of Missouri, July 1948), 16, 17, 26, 36; Sandburg, *op. cit.,* II, 581.

11. New York *World* (Weekly Edition), November 24, 1864.

sister were "wholly at one" with the author—"We have tried the caste system long enough to learn . . . that our safety in future is equality." Would it aid the cause, however, to publish the pamphlet?

> We confess ourselves doubtful on this point, because we fear it may retard that work of justice which has been begun by the nation toward the negro, by warning it or foretelling the ultimate consequence to us as a nationality. There is a laudable desire now to arm the negro, and efforts are being made to place him on an equal footing with white men in the army. The work of promotion for merit, too, has begun in Robert Small[s] and Caesar Hall. We must not despise the day of small things. . . . Will not the subject of amalgamation, so detestable to many minds, if now so prominently advocated, *have a tendency to retard the preparatory work of justice and equality which is so silently, but surely, opening the way for a full recognition of fraternity and miscegenation?*[12]

Dr. James M'Cune Smith, editor of the New York *Anglo-African Review*, was less cautious. He had read the "bold *brochure* with great interest," and unlike Miss Mott, felt that it was marked by "acuteness, vigor, and learning." Its tenth chapter on "The Mistake of All Religions and Systems of Education was worthy of special attention to all who love human kind." Like the Quakeress, however, Dr. Smith saw no "necessity of inscribing 'Miscegenation' on the banner of a political party." His reasons, however, differed from Miss Mott's: first "Such parties always crush any moral cause which they embrace"; second, "when it is remembered that almost every slave state delegalized marriage between white and blacks, we have some testimony that such marriages are bound to occur where such indecent laws are abolished."[13]

---

12. *Ibid.* The idea of "miscegenation," wrote Angelina Grimké in this letter, "was first born into our minds by what was, at that time, a very startling remark of my brother Thomas S. Grimké, of Charleston, South Carolina. We then lived in Philadelphia; and in 1834, just previous to his death, he came there to see us. In a conversation with him on the anti-slavery excitement, then in its infancy, he remarked, although he favored the Colonization society, it was only as a temporary and collateral expedient for the elevation of the colored race, as he well knew that it never could remedy slavery; in fact, said he, 'Emancipation must come in some form or other and amalgamation will be the salvation of our country.' "

13. New York *World* (Weekly Edition), November 24, 1864. Wrote William Wells Brown of Dr. Smith: "Unable to get justice done him in the educational institutions of his native country, James M'Cune Smith turned his face towards a foreign land. He graduated with distinguished honors at the University of Glasgow, Scotland, where he received his diploma of M.D. For the last twenty-five years he has been a practitioner in the city of New York, where he stands at the head of his profession. . . . He has justly been esteemed among the leading men of his race on the American continent. When the natural ability of the negro was assailed, some years ago, in New York, Dr. Smith came forward as the representative of the black man, and his essays on the comparative anatomy and physiology of the races, read in the discussion, completely indicated the character of the negro, and placed the author among the most logical and scientific writers in the country. The doctor has contributed many valuable papers to the different journals published by colored men during the last quarter of a century. The New York dailies have also received aid from him during the same period. History, antiquity, bibliography, translation, criticism, political economy, statistics,—almost every department of knowledge,—receive emblazon from his able, ready, versatile, and unwearied pen" (*The Black Man: His Antecedents, His Genius, and His Achievements* [Boston, 1863], 205–207).

Parker Pillsbury, editor of the *National Anti-Slavery Standard,* writing from New Hampshire, was all enthusiasm with little reservation as to expediency. Although Pillsbury felt that his testimony could render small help to the author, and indeed, "publicly known, might do . . . more harm than good," the pamphlet had "cheered and gladdened a winter morning" which began "in cloud and shadow." He had long been confident of the correctness of the author's philosophy. Indeed he would gladly see the divorce laws "*so modified that new marriages among the American races might even now take place* where unfruitful, or unhappy unions (or disunions) are recognized."

It may not be time to say this aloud; but it will yet be said, and I think not too soon. All the mysteries of the wonderful apocalypse now unfolding in our country, are not even dreamed of yet; and I hail your work as a true prophesy.

"You are on the right track," concluded Pillsbury; "pursue it; and the good God speed you."

Albert Brisbane, the Utopian socialist, writing from Buffalo, while indulging on his own hook in some abstruse Fourierist eugenics on the fusing of "extreme," "central" and "superior" races, was skeptical about the validity of the author's science and logic concerning the "perfect race." Thorough "treatises on the subject" were needed, for men did not "as yet possess the *data* necessary to the forming of an opinion as to *what* races should be crossed, and how or in what proportions, in order to produce good results. . . ." His opinion on the subject of "improving the human race"—which was "still in a purely speculative state, or what Auguste Comte would call the Metaphysical phases"—was "*worth nothing.*" Indeed, raising the question at the moment was putting the cart before the horse; the effort was premature. Before miscegenation could become an issue, "the social organization must first be improved. . . . Women must be placed in a position to regulate the work of procreation . . . and Negro labor must be organized." A "new social order" of "universal association" had first to be established upon the earth; then great "industrial armies, composed of persons from all regions of the earth, would aid the work of a scientific and universal system of miscegenation." Clues would be furnished by the work of Fourier, "the great sociologist." What would happen then was difficult to say. Perhaps "sentiment aroused for the black race" might continue; it might "go even as far as has been dreamed of by some of the most radical abolitionists in the past—namely, amalgamation." He looked upon the pamphlet "*as a sign of the times,* rather than *a solution of a great problem.*"[14] He was curious to see how the work would be received. "If it excites interest," concluded Brisbane skeptically, "you will have touched an important chord; if not, then it will have proved that the public mind is not ready for the discussion of such subjects."[15]

14. Fourier held that a certain portion of Negro blood was necessary to attain a perfectly blended race.
15. New York *World* (Weekly Edition), November 24, 1864.

Thus in good faith the Abolitionists replied to the unknown author, presumably a well-wisher of the Republican left, who, in his zeal for a doctrine that contained more than a modicum of social truth, gave that doctrine so eccentric a twist that it threatened to raise new difficulties in the fight to free the slave.[16]

Croly and Wakeman did not heed this combined counsel of caution. By the first week in February the brochure had been listed as a pamphlet received for review in Theodore Tilton's *Independent* and was being advertised provocatively in the principal Abolitionist papers of the country as available for purchase at newsstands or at the publisher's office. In the *National Anti-Slavery Standard*, the advertisement appeared side by side with an announcement of the publication of William Wells Brown's *The Black Man.*[17]

The pamphlet did not have to wait long for notice and from the Abolitionist press it received its first reviews. On January 23, the *Anglo-African Review*, whose editor, Dr. Smith, had already written the anonymous author a fortnight before, hailed it glowingly.

The word—nay the deed—miscegenation, the same in substance with the word amalgamation, the terror of our abolition friends twenty years ago, and of many of them to-day—miscegenation, which means intermarriage between whites and

16. Wendell Phillips evidently did not reply, although the pamphlet was sent him (as probably to others who did not reply) and he is prominently mentioned and quoted in it. His copy is in the Boston Public Library. Lorenzo Sears, one of his biographers, says briefly: "About this time a great miscegenation outcry had been raised out of sundry 'amalgamation-of-the-races' remarks by Phillips on the 4th of July 1863. . . . The whole matter was best disposed of by the Boston Journal's remark, that it knew of no abolitionists who advocated it, but it was widely practiced in that portion of the Union where an abolitionist, if caught, would be hung to the nearest tree." In this speech, delivered at Framingham, Massachusetts, and quoted in part in the appendix to *Miscegenation*, Phillips had declared: "Now, I am going to say something that will make *The New York Herald* use its small capitals and notes of admiration (Laughter), and yet, no well-informed man this side of China, but believes it in the very core of his heart. That is, 'amalgamation'— . . . Remember this, the youngest of you: that on the 4th day of July, 1863, you heard a man say, that in the light of all history, in virtue of every page he ever read, he was an amalgamationist to the utmost extent. (Applause). I have no hope for the future . . . but in that sublime mingling of races, which is God's own method of civilizing and elevating the world." Phillips' other biographers— Beecher, Russell, Austin, Sears, Martyn, Sherwin—make no mention of his part in the miscegenation controversy.

The great Abolitionist agitator's practical attitude towards the problem in no way contradicted his impassioned platform utterance. To J. Miller McKim on February 8, 1858, he wrote: "A physician has just waited on me and says a merchant living in North Carolina, a patient of his, has fallen in love with a slave-girl—valued at $2,000—he can't afford to redeem her. Is there any person in Philadelphia whom he can . . . communicate with. . . . You see, I know nothing of the man or case. The Doctor is a republican, but his correspondent may be honest or wishing to get someone into a scrape. Can you name anyone in Philadelphia who would aid if he proved honest in his effort? Answer immediately." (Oscar Sherwin, *Prophet of Liberty: A Biography of Wendell Phillips*, unpublished doctoral dissertation [New York University, April 1940], 168.)

Others to whom the pamphlet had been sent were Sumner, Seward and Abby Kelly Foster. (*London Morning Herald*, November 1, 1864.)

17. *Independent*, January 28, February 4, 1864; *National Anti-Slavery Standard*, January 16, 30, 1864; *Liberator*, February 5, 1864.

blacks—"miscegenation," which means the absolute practical brotherhood or social intermingling of blacks and whites, he would have inscribed on the banner
of the Republican Party, and held up as the watchword of the next presidential
platform![18]

It was too late, in the opinion of the *Anglo-African*, "to begin with infant and
Sunday Schooling," for, at birth, children had "the bent of their parents," which
perhaps could be slightly altered but not radically changed. The process of "education and improvement should begin with the marriage of parties who, instead
of strong resemblance, should have contrasts which are complementary each of
the other." It was "disgraceful to our modern civilization," concluded the reviewer, that there existed societies for improving the breed of sheep, horses, and
pigs, while the human race was left to grow up "without scientific culture."

A week later the *National Anti-Slavery Standard* minced no words in greeting
Miscegenation. Although it felt that no new vocabulary was needed to discuss the
subject, the pamphlet itself came "directly and fearlessly to the advocacy of an
idea of which the American people" were "more afraid than any other."

> Through the whole thirty-three years of anti-slavery discussion, no statement has
> been repeated with greater pertinacity, no accusation has been more effective in
> stirring up the rancor of editors and the brutality of mobs, than the charge against
> Abolitionists of advocating "amalgamation." . . . Now the idea thus charged Ab-
> olitionists, individually and collectively, *of preference* for black people as partners
> in marriage, is the very idea seriously advocated and urged in the pamphlet.

Perhaps, thought the reviewer, the theory of attraction of opposites was "a true
one." At any rate, it received "strong presumptive confirmation from the constant
sexual intermingling" of the races in the South. On the question as to whether
the Republican Party should embody the theory in its platform, the *Standard*
expressed no opinion. God's laws would "assuredly fulfill and vindicate themselves." It was "in the highest degree improbable" that He had placed "a national
repugnance between any two families of His Children."

> If He has done so, that decree will execute itself, and these two will never seek
> intimate companionship together. If, on the contrary, He has made no such bar-
> rier, no such one is needful or desirable, and every attempt to restrain these parties
> from exercising their natural choice is in contravention of His will, and is an
> unjust exercise of power. The future must decide how far black and white are
> disposed to seek each other in marriage. The probability is that there will be
> progressive intermingling and that the nation will be benefited by it.

"We are sure," declared the *Standard*, "that many will agree with us in finding
the pamphlet interesting and instructive, and in thanking the unknown author for
it."[19]

---

18. These quotations are taken from S. S. Cox's speech in the House of February 17, 1864 [discussed
    in full later in this selection—Ed.]. They are quotations out of context, excerpted for Cox's
    purpose. Because no copies of the *Anglo-African Review* for 1864 are extant, Cox's quotations
    must be relied on.
19. *National Anti-Slavery Standard*, January 30, 1864. The *Standard* concurred naively with certain

So far Croly's *World* had scrupulously avoided notice of the pamphlet; nowhere in its columns up to this point is the controversial new word to be found. Meanwhile, the fame of *Miscegenation* had crossed the Atlantic. On February 5, the New York correspondent of the pro-Southern London *Times* informed his English readers that a new doctrine had been discovered by "the advanced spirits" of the Republican Party: the Negro was "in many important respects the superior of the whites," and if the latter did not "forget their pride of race and blood and colour, and amalgamate with the purer and richer blood of the blacks," they would die out of America.

The first to give tongue to the new doctrine was the Rev. Theodore Tilton, the coadjutor of the Rev. Henry Ward Beecher in the editorship of the Independent, who a few months ago declared in an assemblage composed of women—possibly all of the strong-minded order—that it was good for white women to marry black men, and that the "passional" and "emotional" nature of the blacks was needed to improve the white race.[20] Mr. Wendell Phillips has often hinted the same thing.

A little tract called *Miscegenation* had recently been circulated, continued the correspondent to his British readers, in which the whole subject was discussed "for the study of such Yankee girls as have exhausted the sensational novels." It had been distributed at a meeting addressed by the famous Miss Dickinson, who perhaps was its author, although it was "highly probable that the author himself" was "one of the lean, gaunt, bloodless Yankees whom he so eloquently describes, and that, failing to find a wife among the strong-minded ladies of whom Miss Anna Dickinson and Mrs. Beecher Stowe" were the types, he longed for "a more congenial partner from the Southern plantations. The unction of this 'new Ana-

---

aspects of the pamphlet's chauvinism: "It is agreed that the strongest, ablest, most intellectual, most practically effective race in the world is the Anglo-Saxon; the product of a mixture, or rather of many mixtures."

20. In this speech, delivered to the American Anti-Slavery Society at Cooper Institute in New York on May 12, 1863, and quoted in part in the appendix to *Miscegenation*, Tilton had said: "The history of the world's civilization is written in one word—which many are afraid to speak—and this is Amalgamation. . . . It is not . . . a philosophical statement to say . . . that the negro race is being absorbed by the white. On the contrary, the negro race is receiving and absorbing part of the white. A large fraction of the white race of the South is melting away into the black. . . . I am not advocating the union of whites and blacks. This is taking place without advocacy. . . . I am often asked, 'Would you marry a black woman?' I reply, 'I have a wife already, and therefore will not.' I am asked, 'Do you think that a white man ought to marry a black woman?' I reply, 'When a man and woman want to be married it is *their* business, not mine, nor anybody's else.' Is not that plain sense? But to read what some newspapers say of the 'monstrous doctrine of amalgamation,' one would think it consisted in stationing a provost-marshal at street corners, to seize first a white man and then a black woman, and to marry them on the spot, against their will, for a testimony to human equality. But I will venture to advance the opinion . . . that a slave-woman's master, who makes himself the father of her children, is in honor bound to make himself her husband. So far from denouncing the marriage of blacks and whites, I would be glad if the banns of a hundred thousand such marriages could be published next Sunday. . . . But whether in marriage or in shame, the fact grows broader every day, that the whites and the blacks of this country, are coalescing; or to use the more horrible word, amalgamating. In Slavery, this amalgamation proceeds rapidly; in Freedom slowly."

charsis Clootz' might almost make one suspect him of being a *mauvais farceur.*"
If this was done "in the green leaf, what shall be done in the dry?"[21]

On February 17, *Miscegenation* broke into Congress. While the House was arguing the establishment of a Bureau of Freedmen's Affairs, Samuel Sullivan
Cox—Vallandigham's mouthpiece—rose from his seat to use the pamphlet as a
bludgeon against the Republican members.[22] This development was, of course, to
be expected; for the pamphlet by this time was notorious public property and
bound to come to his attention. Unexpected, however, was the fact that the personal letters of the Abolitionists anent it—the private property of the apparently
Abolitionist pamphleteer—had been placed in the hands of the Copperhead member from Ohio. So "Sunset" Cox crowed to the House:

> The more philosophical and apostolic of the abolition fraternity have fully decided
> upon the adoption of this amalgamation platform. I am informed that the doc-
> trines are already indorsed by such lights as Parker Pillsbury, Lucretia Mott,
> Albert Brisbane, William Wells Brown,[23] Dr. McCune Smith (half and half-
> miscegen), Angelina Grimke, Theodore Weld and wife and others.

Cox, with a certain grisly Copperhead humor, flayed the pamphlet in thorough
racist manner, sneering at Greeley, that "Warwick of Republicanism," and blasting Phillips, whose golden-lipped eloquence could make "miscegenation as attractive to the ear as it is to the other senses."[24] Holding the author's eloquence
to be "better than his science," he advanced his own scientific refutation of the
miscegenationist doctrine: "The physiologist will tell the Gentleman that the mulatto does not live; he does not recreate his kind; he is a monster. Such hybrid
races by a law of Providence scarcely survive beyond one generation." Moreover,
the irrepressible conflict was not "between slavery and freedom, but between black
and white; and as De Tocqueville prophesied, the black will perish."

On the main point, however—how to make miscegenation a campaign issue—
Cox kept his eye.

> . . . There is a doctrine now being advertised and urged by the leading lights of the
> Abolition party, toward which the Republican party will and must advance. . . .
> They used to deny, whenever it was charged, that they favored black citizenship;

---

21. London *Times*, February 8, 1864; in Palmer's *Index to the Times*, the article is listed as "the Clootz's
    Plan for Improving the White Race." (London, 1887), II, 263–264.
22. Cox was one of the most foully articulate of white chauvinists in Congress. On January 10, five
    weeks prior to his miscegenation speech, the Washington correspondent of the *National Anti-
    Slavery Standard* wrote of him: "Mr. Cox, as usual, moved to strike out the appropriation for the
    Haytian mission, and hung a mean little anti-negro speech upon his motion. . . . Mr. Cox is fond
    occasionally of ventilating his brutal prejudices." On this occasion, Thaddeus Stevens thoroughly
    chastised him. (*National Anti-Slavery Standard*, January 16, 1864.)
23. There is no record extant of a reply from William Wells Brown. Apparently Cox was referring
    to a statement of Brown's on the subject in another place.
24. "Has he forgotten his fine-spun theories upon miscegenation and the grand mulatto species which
    is to result from them?" asked the New York *Herald* the following day in an editorial on a
    reconstruction speech by Phillips. "Is he going to retract his former declaration that amalgamation
    is the only way to save the nation?"

yet now they are favoring free black suffrage in the District of Columbia, and will favor it wherever in the South they need it for their purposes. . . . The Senate of the United States is discussing African equality in street cars. All these things . . . culminating in this grand plunder scheme of a department of freedmen, ought to convince us that that party is moving steadily forward to perfect social equality of black and white, and can only end in this detestable doctrine of—Miscegenation!

Cox spoke at length, but it was by no means all smooth sailing. Kelley of Pennsylvania, Eliot of Massachusetts and Washburne of Illinois heckled and rebutted him effectively. And the *Anglo-African Review* of February 27, commenting on the tirade, noted that although the country needed patriots, a "cross" between Cox and Vallandigham would fail to produce one "for the simple and obvious reason that in both the blood" ran the other way; but, "per contra, if we should get up a 'cross' between Hon. S. S. Cox and Capt. Robert Small[s]," continued the *Review*, "the result would be an average miscegen and a superior patriot."[25]

25. Samuel S. Cox, *Eight Years in Congress, from 1857 to 1865* (New York, 1865), 354. "Another remarkable phase of this discussion," says Cox in his memoirs, "was the queries propounded by Robert Dale Owen, Dr. S. G. Howe, and Col. McKaye, Commissioners on the Freedman, as to the capacity and condition of the mulatto, his offspring, and their tendency to bodily and mental decay. The 'Anglo-African' of the 20th of February, 1864, retorted very pungently upon these querists, and informed them that as the two publishers and one editor of 'The Anglo-African' had had born to them in lawful wedlock no less than twenty-nine children, of whom twenty are now living—some married and budding—they could not help regarding the queries as in a measure personal and impertinent." The *Anglo-African Review* tolerated no nonsense on this subject. Since the issues of this important journal are not extant for 1864, it is necessary to reconstruct its pages from other sources, frequently hostile to it. Such a source is the anti-Negro *New York Freeman's Journal & Catholic Register* from whose issue of April 16, 1864 the following editorial is quoted in full:

Under the teachings of the *Tribune*, the colored people are beginning to "put on airs." In the *Anglo-African* of this week we find a sharp attack upon Elizur Wright, a Boston Abolitionist, because he presumed to say that the negro has not as much virility as the whites. The editor goes on to show that the colored race in this country doubles every two years, while it takes thirty years for the whites, even with the aid of emigration, to double their numbers. But hear how this darky editor talks:

No friend Wright, you need not disturb yourself about the black man in these United States; he has a good standing color, and an abundance of endurance; just brush some of those knotty cobwebs from your brain and look at him; tall, brawny, well-limbed, sound-brained, as God made him, a man and brother. You sharp nosed, hatch faced, black haired people, aided by science and the "hub," have vainly tried to crush the manhood out of him, and failed; do give up; you cannot lie him out of his manhood He is a better man, a better citizen than your race "ever dare to be," under any circumstances, in all climates; if not, why do you cut down his equal chances? Why shut your eyes to facts? Bluff Ben Butler, the other day, started on a forced march of some two or three days. He had two white and two black regiments of infantry. It was in a climate, moreover, favorable to whites. How was it when they arrived there? One half the white soldiers had straggled, exhausted, on the road, every black soldier answered to his name at roll call. Pshaw! Don't fool any longer. If you want this rebellion wiped out, take three hundred thousand of our blacks; give us Ben Butler, or let us go alone, and in sixty days the South shall be wiped out.

For a bankrupt party, however, Cox's speech was urgently needed political capital.[26] Edited and reprinted in Washington, D.C., at the office of *The Constitutional
Union*, a "Democratic Conservative Union Newspaper," Cox's speech was to have
a wide circulation in the Democratic press of the country.

"... No one in Congress," wrote Cox in his memoirs a year later, "thought of
questioning the genuineness and seriousness of the document."[27] The statement
is not entirely true. "The little book upon 'miscegenation' has very generally been
regarded here as a burlesque, or satire," observed the Washington correspondent
of the *National Anti-Slavery Standard* in his dispatch of February 28. "It is said
that Mr. Sumner, upon first glancing over its pages, was inclined to think the
writer was in jest.... Nobody here *advocates* amalgamation, though doubtless
there are very many who believe that in time the two races *will* amalgamate. So
far the Democrats have gained nothing by the debate on this subject."[28]

From Croly's *World*, the fugleman of the Democratic press, the word was still
mum—not even a report of Cox's speech appeared in its columns. On February
18, in a short filler, a jokester observed that it was an error to look on a miscegen

---

This is decidedly rich. These darkies now claim, it seems, to be of a healthier, sounder,
brighter race than their New England admirers.... Negro equality is no longer the doctrine:
it is now negro superiority. What next, we wonder?

26. *Miscegenation or Amalgamation. Fate of the Freedman. Speech of Hon. Samuel S. Cox of Ohio delivered in the House of Representatives, February 17, 1864.* (Washington, D.C., 1864), 5, 10. The Washington correspondent of the *National Anti-Slavery Standard* in the issue of February 27 reported
some of the heckling in detail: "The book on *Miscegenation*, which has been noticed in the leading
papers of the country, came in for an elaborate 'notice' from Mr. Cox.... Mr. Cox, as a matter of
course, found men in the House who would laugh at his coarse wit upon 'miscegenation,' but he
was compelled to hear the House laugh on the other side of the question. Mr. Washburne of Illinois
got the floor as soon as Mr. Cox sat down, and proceeded to refresh the Ohio member with extracts
from one of his own books written several years ago.... I must quote ... 'I desire to show the
House what the Gentleman from Ohio has written in regard to the "African," in a book entitled
"A Buckeye Abroad: or Wanderings in Europe and in the Orient. By S. S. Cox." He is describing
St. Peter's, and says: "In the meantime seraphic music from the Pope's select choir ravishes the
ear, while the incense titilates the nose. Soon there arises in the chamber of theatrical glitter"—
what?—"a plain unquestioned African!" (laughter), "and he utters the sermon in facile Latinity,
with graceful manner. His dark hands gestured harmoniously with the rotund periods, and his
swart visage beamed with a high order of intelligence." (laughter) What was he? Let the Gentleman
from Ohio answer: "He was an Abyssinian. What a commentary upon our American prejudices!
The head of the great Catholic Church surrounded by the ripest scholars of the age, listening to
the eloquence"—of whom?—"of the despised negro; and thereby illustrating to the world the
common bond of brotherhood which binds the human race" (roars of laughter).... "History records that from the time of the revival of letters the influence of the Church of Rome had been
generally favorable to science, to civilization, and to good government. Why?" ... Let the Gentleman answer: "Because her system held then, as it holds now, all distinctions of caste as odious."
(great laughter.) This is the third time that this book has been read upon Mr. Cox by way of reply,
but it was never before done quite so well as Mr. Washburne did it."

27. Cox, *op. cit.*, 354.

28. *National Anti-Slavery Standard*, March 5, 1864. Sumner had been one of the abolitionists to whom
Croly and Wakeman had sent a copy. (*London Morning Herald*, November 1, 1864.)

as a "new light"—he was "Half *light* at best." But that was all. And meanwhile, in the political press from Copperhead right to Abolitionist left, the battle of words continued to rage on the issue of miscegenation.

Egged on by Cox's diatribe, on February 25 the *Independent*—"the leading family newspaper of religious cast in the country"[29]—gave a long column to a consideration of the pamphlet in which its editors had been so copiously quoted and praised. "As some of our contemporaries, who make no scruple of misrepresenting us, have challenged us for an opinion on this subject, we give it today, in the absence of a more pressing topic." The little brochure, carrying "as a figurehead the new and strange word Miscegenation" had "lately launched into a sudden tempest of criticism." For style, not quite good or bad—"clever, in-elaborate, and ill-considered"—it had had "a many-voiced condemnation into fame." On such a topic, John Milton himself would be speared, knived and tomahawked.

Its authorship, continued the *Independent,* was "a well-kept secret"; at least it was unknown to the editors. Nor were they convinced that the writer was in earnest. Their first and remaining impression was that "the work was meant as a piece of pleasantry—a burlesque upon what are popularly called the extreme and fanatical notions of certain radical men named therein." It was in turn sober, absurd and extravagant; if written in earnest, it was not thorough enough to be satisfactory; if in jest, "Sydney Smith—or McClellan's Report" was to be preferred.

The *Independent* was not to be booby-trapped. While its editors candidly agreed with some ideas presented in the pamphlet, they disagreed heartily with much also. The Irishman was not a "July rioter by nature"; he was made so "by Democracy and grog." Nor was it any part of the duty of anti-slavery men, or anybody else, "to advise people whom they should marry, or not marry." Marriage was an affair between bride and bridegroom, "with, perhaps, a mother-in-law's advice thrown in." If black and white intermarried, it was "nobody's business but their own." Further than this, "before a white-skinned slave-master becomes the father of a black woman's child, he ought to be her lawful, wedded husband." The thesis about the perfect brown man of the millennial future was absurd. The rebellion itself did not arise from color prejudice, "for if the slaves were white, instead of black, their masters" would have been no less unwilling to give them up.

As to the main point—here the *Independent* was acute—that the next Presidential campaign, as suggested by the pamphleteer, "turn upon the advocacy of marriage between any two classes of our community—Saxons with Celts, fair faces with dark, Northerners with Southerners, Down-East Yankees with Californians"—this was so absurd as to furnish another reason for thinking these "piquant pages" were "a snare to catch some good folk in, for a laugh at them afterward." The conclusion was clear: "the next Presidential election, nor any succeeding, should have nothing to do with Miscegenation."[30]

---

29. Sandburg, *op. cit.*, II, 577.
30. Wrote the Washington correspondent of the *National Anti-Slavery Standard* in the issue of March 5, 1864: "I think Mr. Tilton's article in the last *Independent* expresses the views of most of the

On February 27, Cox's speech was attacked by the Copperheads as not going far enough. Cox had done the heinous thing of paying lip-service to the idea of abolishing slavery. Dr. J. H. Van Evrie, the rabid editor of the *New York Weekly Day-Book (Caucasian)* would have none of this. Give the Negro freedom and miscegenation would result: "the mixing of blood follows mixing of 'freedom' . . . where numbers approximate and white men are so degraded and wicked as to get down to a level with negrodom. Every man, therefore, opposed to 'slavery' is of necessity in favor of amalgamating with negroes." Thus, in opposing slavery, Cox "necessarily" fostered the idea of amalgamation—at least he was "for forcing it on others, if not liking it exactly for himself." When Cox took umbrage at Van Evrie's impolitic attack—after all they both stood on the Vallandigham platform— the *Day-Book* backed water: "Mr. Cox is about the last man, among the public men of the day, we would do an injustice to, for, with all his errors in respect to putting down 'rebels,' etc., we doubt not he really means to be a Democrat."[31]

"The question of the crossing of races, or as the newly invented sacramental word says, of *miscegenation,* agitates the press and some would-be *savants* in Congress," wrote Count Adam Gurowski, a Washington observer, in his diary a month after Cox's speech.[32] By the middle of March, Greeley was forced to enter the lists. "We notice a tolerably warm discussion going on in the newspapers and elsewhere," editorialized the *New York Tribune,* "concerning what used to be called 'amalgamation,' and is now more sensibly styled 'miscegenation'—a word tolerably accurate, although a little too long for popular and daily use." The mere mention of the word filled "many minds with an unspeakable wrath," and "long-harbored prejudices" obscured the truth; yet it was a question that had to be "considered well, and decided, not by an appeal to old notions, but by experience." Physiologist, ethnologist, historian, theologian and economist were needed to answer accurately the questions inevitably raised. It was a shame that those

---

intelligent Republicans in Congress upon the subject." Tilton's article was reprinted in full in this issue of the *Standard.*

31. *New York Weekly Day-Book,* March 12, 1864.

32. Adam Gurowski, *Diary: 1863–'64–'65* (Washington, D.C., 1866), 140–141. Gurowski's opinion is worthy of note: "The worshippers of darkness and of ignorance, as are the worshippers and defenders of slavery all over the world, but principally in America, are in their element when they utter falsehoods and lies, or when in the most approved democratic manner they back their bad faith by the grossest ignorance. But the other side, the so-called defenders of the negro or African, pitch into the contest as empty-headed as their antagonists; and by high-sounding generalities and phraseology try to make up for their thorough want of scientific information. Neither the one nor the other know in the least anything whatever of the scientific researches and discoveries of the last forty years; and thus neither the one nor the other know how far the ancient continent in Europe and Asia was once occupied by the physiological negro; nor do they know where in Asia are still to be found living remains of the primitive negro race. Oh, these lecturers, these leading editors of dailies, weeklies, monthlies, etc! . . . Oh, these empty-headed rhetors and sham scholars and legislators. . . . Science in hand, how easily it could have been shown to those swarthy-haired and black-souled Seymours, Marbles, Saulsburys, etc., that the difference is only in quantity and not quality of the *melanine* which blacks their eyes, hair, etc., and blacks the whole African! And perhaps, if dissected, their *cerebella* would be found to have less convolutions than those of the negro."

who professed "to be the leaders and informers of the public thought" permitted themselves "blindly to be led by those who are still blinder into a ditch of *ipse dixits* and noisome assumption."

The prejudice against the Negro—"the result of a cruel and systematic degradation"—was by no means a novelty. "All Christians in the middle age supposed that Jews exhaled a bad odor from their bodies, and the marriage of a Jew and Christian at that period would have been far more likely to provoke a mob in any civilized city than the marriage of a white man and a black woman would be now." In spite of religious professions, "we do not dwell together as brethren"; in spite of our Bibles, we do not believe that "God has made all men of one blood." That is the simple fact despite "the whole Copperhead power of wriggle."

If a white man pleased to marry a black woman no one had a right to interfere.

We do not say such union would be wise, but we do distinctly assert that society has nothing to do with the wisdom of matches, and that we shall have to the end of the chapter a great many foolish ones which laws are powerless to prevent. We do not say that such matches would be moral, but we do declare that they would be infinitely more so than the promiscuous concubinage which has so long shamelessly prevailed upon the Southern plantation.

Concluded the *Tribune:* "We are not in favor of any law compelling a Copperhead to marry a negress, unless under circumstances which might compel him to marry a white woman or go to prison; but we insist that if the Copperhead or anybody else is anxious to enter into such union it is not for the Legislature to forbid him, or his fellow creatures to pronounce him a violator of nature and of God."[33]

At Greeley's stand the anti-Lincoln press threw up its hands in horror. "Pursuing the natural course of radicalism," sneered the *New York Journal of Commerce,* "the editors of several of the abolitionist sheets have recently been seized with a strong desire for the introduction of amalgamation into social and domestic life of their and other radical families."[34] "The fact is—and the *Tribune* cannot disguise it," ranted Bennett's *Herald,* "that the radical party wants a war cry. They tried free-love and it failed. Then they tried abolitionism, and it served their purpose for many a long year. But now the war has deprived them of that shiboleth." Disgustedly the *Herald* cited a news item in the *Anglo-African Review* concerning "a colored man, named Joseph H. Card . . . joined in the holy bonds of matrimony to a 'white lady from London'; almost frantically it described the 'Practical Progress of Miscegenation in South Carolina.' "[35] To the racist tirade of the *Express,* the *Tribune* replied that when "Richard M. Johnson married a negro, and raised a large family by her, no Democratic stomach was revolted." For the *Express,* the "horrible consequences of white and black mixture" were

33. *New York Tribune,* March 16, 1864. Greeley's eccentric position—or lack of position—may be seen in a sentence from this editorial: "If a man can so far conquer his repugnance to a black woman as to make her the mother of his children, we ask in the name of the divine law and of decency, why he should not marry her."
34. Reprinted in *Liberator,* April 8, 1864.
35. *New York Herald,* March 26, 1864.

fearful—in the North; "but down in Dixie no such qualms exist; there the breeding of a brawny and salable mulatto boy, or of a saddle-colored girl, for the brothels of New Orleans, is something to brag of."

We have among us in this city at this very time the mulatto daughter of Brigadier-Gen. Huger and the mulatto son of Brigadier-Gen. Withers, both the fathers being now in important commands in the Rebel army—the mothers undoubtedly in slavery or the grave.

"We have also recently had slave children here," concluded the *Tribune*, "much whiter than the editors of *The Express*—fair, blue-eyed children, with bills of sale in their pockets."[36]

Two days later the *Tribune* followed up its demand for a scientific approach to the matter of miscegenation with a London report on a lecture by Professor T. J. Huxley.

Prof. Huxley . . . read extensive extracts from Dr. James Hunt's pamphlet, entitled "On the Negro's place in Nature." Some paragraphs in the dedication of that pamphlet, taken from the letter of a Confederate lady to the author, were read, and excited great laughter among the eminent gentlemen present . . . in which the lecturer joined. When the great laughter . . . had ceased, Prof. Huxley said that he felt it his duty to protest against such baseless and ridiculous assertions, which might be conceived in the spirit of party, but were certainly not in that of science.[37]

In the maelstrom of controversy, the *New York Times* occupied an anomalous position. The *Herald*, frothing at the mouth, under the title "The Beastly Doctrine of Miscegenation and Its High Priests," had charged it with being "a bright mulatto on the subject of miscegenation." Raymond in turn had accused the *Tribune* of "advocating miscegenation" and Greeley had indignantly denied it.[38] Charges and countercharges filled the columns as March petered out—while the identity of the pamphleteer continued to intrigue the combatants.[39] "Holmes or Wise Greeley have coined the new word," sang one Horace Otis of Watertown, New York, in a hundred-line poem in the *Day-Book:*

> Beautiful word, and more beautiful thought!
> None but the wise have its origin sought; . . .
> Fill with mulattoes and mongrels the nation,
> THIS IS THE MEANING OF MISCEGENATION.[40]

36. *New York Daily Tribune*, March 17, 1864; *New York Herald*, March 17, 1864.
37. Hunt's pamphlet, *The Negro's Place in History* was published by Van Evrie in the United States. The *National Anti-Slavery Standard* of March 26, 1864 reprinted an attack on the pamphlet from *The Christian Ambassador*.
38. Reprinted in *National Anti-Slavery Standard*, March 26, 1864.
39. And still does. Cedric Dover, in his eloquent *Know This of Race* (London, 1939), 96, is taken in much as some of the Abolitionists were. After a short discussion of this "anonymous pamphlet issued in 1864," he remarks that its "unsurpassed wisdom" makes him wish he "knew the author's name. He deserves the praise of posterity."
40. *New York Day-Book*, April 16, 1864.

Was it perhaps Wendell Phillips[41] or Theodore Tilton who had penned the tract? The *Herald* played with the idea that the mysterious author was none other than twenty-year-old Anna Dickinson, who had been fired from her job in the Phila-delphia mint three years before for accusing McClellan of treason. Miss Dickinson had since become one of the more popular Abolition orators—her sex, youth and fiery eloquence combining to draw large crowds. In mid-January she had ad-dressed the House of Representatives—Lincoln came down to hear her speech—and had been roundly applauded. A fortnight later she was scheduled to repeat her address at Cooper Institute. "She was somewhat late in making her appearance on the platform," wrote the New York correspondent of the London *Times*, re-tailing Democratic gossip to the British public, "and to pacify her audience (mostly composed of women)," advertisements of *Miscegenation* "were handed round for their perusal—a circumstance which suggested to many that the lecturer was either author of the book or peculiarly interested in its sale."[42]

By the middle of March, Petroleum Vesuvius Nasby, Paster at the Church uv the Noo Dispensashun—of whom Lincoln would say, "For the genius to write like Nasby, I would gladly give up my office"[43]—had commented on the misceg-enation issue. "Alluz preech agin the nigger," he counseled a Democratic student of the ministry, "a youth uv much promise who votid twict for Bookannon. It's soothin to a ginooine, constooshnel Southern-rites Dimekrat to be constantly told that ther is a race uv men meaner than he is. . . . Preech agin amalgamashen at

---

41. Phillips was probably a logical guess to some who remembered his yeoman service in behalf of the Irish fight for freedom and his successful effort to enlist Daniel O'Connell and Father Mathew in the abolition struggle. (See Oscar Sherwin's excellent discussion of this phase of Phillips' career in his unpublished doctoral dissertation, cited above.)

42. Who actually distributed these leaflets it is impossible to determine. Possibly Croly and Wakeman arranged it. Miss Dickinson was later the author of several tracts and a novel, *What Answer?*, in 1864, concerning the tragic love of a quadroon, Francesca Ercildowne for a white man, Will Surrey. The main theme of the novel is summarized by a fictional news item appearing in the Civil War press: "MISCEGENATION, DISGRACEFUL FREAK IN HIGH LIFE. FRUIT OF AN ABOLITION WAR.—We are credibly informed that a young man belonging to one of the first families in the city, Mr. W.A.S.,—we spare his name for the sake of his relatives,—who has been engaged since its outset in this fratricidal war, has just given evidence of its legitimate effect by taking to his bosom a nigger wench *as his wife*. Of course he is disowned by his family, and spurned by his friends, even radical fanaticism not being yet ready for such a dose as this." (Anna E. Dickinson, *What Answer?* [Boston, 1868], 190.) Van Evrie's *Day-Book* of February 27, 1864, carried the following notice: "A Reply to Miss Dickinson.—We understand that Miss Emma Webb, a talented and accomplished young lady, who has traveled extensively in the West India Islands, and knows practically the evil effects of Abolitionism, will reply to Miss Anna Dickinson at the Athenaeum, in Brooklyn, on Friday evening, March 4th."

43. *Divers Views, Opinions, and Prophecies of Yoors truly Petroleum V. Nasby* (Cincinnati, 1867), 182–186. F. B. Carpenter, who painted Lincoln, relates that just previous to the capture of Richmond, Lincoln said to him: "I am going to write 'Petroleum' to come down here, and I intend to tell him if he will communicate his talent to me, I will swap places with him!" (*Ibid.*, ix). At the close of the war, George S. Boutwell, Commissioner of Internal Revenue and later Secretary of Trea-sury, said that crushing the Rebellion could be credited to three forces: the army, the navy and the Nasby letters. (Jack Clifford Hayes, "David Ross Locke, Civil War Propagandist," *Northwest Ohio Quarterly*, XX [January, 1948], 5.)

leest 4 Sundays per munth. A man uv straw that yoo set up yerself is the eesiest nockt down, pertikelerly if you set him up with a view uv nockin uv him down . . . Lern to spell and pronownce Missenegenegenashun. It's a good word."[44]

So far the *World* had not uttered a word on this controversial subject of its own creation, although Croly and Wakeman had inserted an advertisement in the *Liberator* of March 4, quoting Wendell Phillips and stressing the fact that their pamphlet treated of "the relations of the Irish and the Negro." Now a strange thing happened. On March 24, the newspaper whose managing editor had been the principal author of *Miscegenation*, unabashedly made a full-length editorial attack on it. "Some time since there was published, in this city," blandly began the *World*, "a curious anonymous pamphlet, entitled 'Miscegenation: the Theory of the Blending of the Races, applied to the American White Man and Negro'. . . . A writer who seriously advocates the intermarriage and cohabitation of white men with negresses, and white women with negroes, has little claim to notice, on his own account, by journals which make it their chief business to mark and interpret the current indications of public sentiment." What can be the motive of such a writer? Why his anonymity? The answer is given in curious, carefully constructed circumlocutions.

Any man who chooses can write and cause to be printed whatever freak may come into his head; the existence of the production is evidence of nothing but the idiosyncrasy of the writer. If he gives his name, pride of singularity or fanatical devotion to a strange whim may afford a ready explanation of his course; if he publishes anonymously, he is probably feeling the public pulse, if serious, or expecting a profitable market for a piquant oddity, if he has not at heart the cause he ostensibly advocates.

Why bother then to give valuable space to a "piquant oddity"? "In either case, or in any case," continued the editorial, "he deserves only the passing attention due to contributors of public amusement, *unless* the interest awakened by his publication, and the indorsement it receives from some portion of the community, shall rescue him from the charge of singularity, and prove that he is the exponent of a widely-diffused sentiment, or at least the occasion of its manifestation." The endorsement the pamphlet receives "or the opposition it excites . . . makes it an index of public sentiment."

Furthermore, stated the *World*, the *Tribune* article was indicative of the favor the new doctrine was meeting in Abolition quarters. "It is so extensively sanctioned by the leading negrophilists of the country, and by the prominent organs through which their views find expression, that we feel bound to call attention,

44. D. R. Locke, *The Moral History of America's Life-Struggle* (Boston, 1874), 15. At Columbus, Ohio, in 1859, where Lincoln in a speech had gone "out of his way to affirm his support of the law of Illinois forbidding the intermarriage of whites and Negroes," Locke "asked him if such a denial was worth while." Lincoln replied: "The law means nothing. I shall never marry a Nigger, but I have no objection to any one else doing so. If a white man wants to marry a Negro woman, let him do so,—if the Negro woman can stand it." (Cyril Clemens, *Petroleum Vesuvius Nasby* [Webster Groves, Missouri, 1936], 27.)

not to the pamphlet (which is of little account taken by itself), but to the strongly developed tendencies of abolition public opinion which the pamphlet has brought out in bold relief." The *World* did "not propose to enter the lists with the *Tribune*, or any other advocate" of miscegenation. To the contention of the *Tribune* that the subject could only be treated by physiologist, ethnologist, historian, theologian or economist, the *World* replied that by that doctrine not even incest could be discussed until citizens should have "mastered half the sciences in the encyclopedia." If marriage is recommended for a white man with a black woman begetting his children—then precisely the same solution "might be asked in relation to incest, or any other abomination which the *progressists* have not yet dubbed with a euphemistic name." Opinions of this sort were "the logical outgrowth of the extravagant negrophilism" which had "its carnival of blood in this cruel civil war." "We cannot discuss these abominations," piously concluded the *World*. "We merely record and call attention to the *fact* that the leading Republican journal of the country is the unblushing advocate of 'miscegenation,' which it ranks with the highest questions of social and political philosophy."

The *World*, indeed, through Croly and Wakeman, had done its work—and well. Miscegenation, without doubt, had become a central campaign issue—a darling issue for the Copperhead Democracy. Throughout the land, in sharp polemic, right up to the November balloting—although the *World* alone among the Democratic sheets would speak in whispers on the subject—the national press would bandy word and issue about in an unending saturnalia of editorial, caricature and verse.[45]

By May, the miscegenation controversy had travelled north, south and west of New York City. In March, the New Hampshire *Patriot*, under the title of "Sixty-four Miscegenation," had concocted the obscenity that sixty-four Abolitionist school-mistresses of New England, teaching at Port Royal, had given birth to mulatto babies. Democratic newspapers far and wide spread the story and the Republican press was kept busy exposing the "atrocious calumny" as a "Copperhead slander."[46] In early April, Garrison's *Liberator* devoted its entire first

---

45. In May, during Grant's Wilderness campaign, the *World* went through a crisis which perhaps helped to produce its comparative silence. "A few hours of dejection, leaving their effect behind," wrote James Ford Rhodes, "were caused by the publication, May 18, of a proclamation purporting to come from the President, which, admitting by implication the failure of Grant's campaign, appointed a solemn day of fasting, humiliation, and prayer, and called for 400,000 men. It was a cleverly conceived and executed forgery, intended for stock-jobbing purposes, and only by certain happy accidents did it fail to appear in nearly all of the journals in New York City connected with the associated press. It was printed in the New York *World* and New York *Journal of Commerce*, Democratic newspapers, which had assailed the administration with virulence. Their editors strove earnestly to correct the error into which they had fallen innocently, and made adequate and apparently satisfactory explanations to Dix, the commanding general of the department, but before these were transmitted to Washington, the President had ordered their arrest and imprisonment and the suppression of their journals. A lieutenant with a file of soldiers seized their offices, and held possession of them for several days, but the order of personal arrest was rescinded." (*History of the United States* [New York, 1906], IV, 467–468.)

46. *National Anti-Slavery Standard*, March 26, 1864. This is not an isolated instance of Copperhead fraud. The *Sunday Mercury*, rival on weekends of Bennett's *Herald*, pursued the campaign in its

page to editorial excerpts on the subject from the nation's press and a month later inveighed against a "certain class of people, seeking to bring opprobrium upon Republicans and Union men" by accusing them of "advocating what is termed 'miscegenation.' " The Boston *Journal* traded brickbats with the *Courier* and the sound of battle echoed in the towns. The *Cape Cod Republican* warred with the *Barnstable Patriot*—while the nearby *Yarmouth Register* observed that Bennett and his fellow Copperheads had at last found something "sufficiently *smutty*" for their tastes" in a "dull pamphlet on the old theme" thrown together by some fool in New York.[47]

"Amalgamation has nothing to do with emancipation," protested the Philadelphia *Press* in March. "Those who are so loudly opposing it are wasting their trouble upon a cause which has no advocates." Naive brother Republicans were not helping matters: "We can only wonder at the folly of the few anti-slavery journals that have permitted themselves to be used by such mischief makers as the *Herald*."

> The new word miscegenation is not more strange to our ears than is the idea it embodies to our creed. It remains to say that the colored men who are entitled to speak for their own race, have never advocated amalgamation as a thing to be expected or desired.

"It is no time for political miscegenation," observed the St. Louis *Union*, arguing against the anti-Lincolnism of the radical Republican wing. "We need not be at all surprised to see an amalgamation ticket made up with Fremont for President, and Vallandigham for Vice-President."[48] The Pennsylvania Democratic press went at *Miscegenation* hammer and tongs, the *Philadelphia Age* crowing coarsely over a fulsome article that had appeared in the Detroit *Free Press* under the title of "Miscegenation in Detroit," while the *Washington* (Pa.) *Examiner* noted that the "celebrated anonymous work" was "remarkably consistent for an Abolition publication," although the effeminate consumptives" to whom it pleaded did not realize that miscegenation meant physical, mental and moral ruin.[49] According to

---

own way by means of forgeries. In its columns for March 18 appeared two personal notices, one of which reads

> Attention All Ladies—"Hunky Boy," every inch of a soldier, and alive and full of fun and miscegenation . . . solicits correspondence of all unmarried ladies between the ages of sixteen and sixty.

The names signed to the notices are Albert E. Dunwoodie, Sergeant, and Oscar D. Leonard, both of Company B, 55th Massachusetts (Coloured) Volunteers, Folly Island, South Carolina. The letters are fabrications. The rolls of the 55th do not carry these names either in Company B or in any other company. (*Record of the Service of the Fifty-Fifth Regiment of Massachusetts Volunteer Infantry* [Cambridge, 1868].)

47. *Liberator*, April 8, 1864, May 13, 1864.
48. *Liberator*, April 8, 1864.
49. Ray H. Abrams, "The Copperhead Newspapers and the Negro," *Journal of Negro History*, XX (April 1935), 131–152. The *Examiner* acknowledged its indebtedness to Van Evrie's *Negroes and Negro "Slavery"* in preparing the editorial, and Van Evrie reciprocated by reprinting the notice in the *Day-Book* for May 14, 1864.

the West Chester *Jeffersonian,* the Emancipation Proclamation was "a thorough-going program for 'miscegenation' "—a word which the editor began to cherish.[50] "Boston will, we do not doubt, furnish forth a devoted band of zealous misce-genators," ranted the Cincinnati *Enquirer* in a long lascivious editorial. "Those reverend clergymen who have given their sanction to the plan, and who see the movings of the divine spirit in the suggestion will not hesitate to put their hands to the miscegenation plow, and beget seals to their ministry."[51] In the guberna-torial election that spring in Ohio, Clement R. Vallandigham ran from Canada. At campaign rallies throughout the Buckeye State, "a popular feature was a pro-cession of young women bearing placards inscribed, 'Fathers, Save Us from Negro Equality.' "[52]

By June, *Miscegenation* had been reprinted in London and in July the *West-minster Review* commented seriously on it.[53] "Much has been said of late," wrote the Abolitionist Reverend Dr. Moncure D. Conway in an anti-slavery volume published in England in July, "concerning the old horror of the amalgamation of the blacks and whites as it comes in the new dress of *Miscegenation . . .* let me remind the English reader, that nobody in the Northern States has proposed that the blacks and whites shall be *compelled* to intermarry. The proposition is simply that the laws against such marriages which yet remain in some of the Northern States shall be removed. Consequently, that portion of the English press which has been so distressed on this subject may calm itself with the reflection that, were the theory of the wildest miscegenist adopted tomorrow, the relation between the blacks and whites in respect to marriage would be simply conformed to what it is in England and France to-day."[54]

By midsummer also, the noisome Dr. J. H. Van Evrie, to the right even of Vallandigham in his uncompromising Calhounism, had brought out anonymously,

50. Roy H. Abrams, " 'The Jeffersonian,' Copperhead Newspaper," *Pennsylvania Magazine of History and Biography*, LVII (July 1933), 260–283.
51. Reprinted in *New York Freeman's Journal and Catholic Register*, April 9, 1864. Philip S. Foner states that this paper was "for a time the official organ of the Archbishop of New York and had a wide circulation among Irish-American workers." (*History of the Labor Movement in the United States from Colonial Times to the Founding of the American Federation of Labor* [New York, 1947], 269.)
52. Wood Gray, *The Hidden Civil War, The Story of the Copperheads.* (New York, 1942), 150.
53. New Series, XXVI, 223–224. The "anonymous author of a very curious book, entitled 'Misceg-enation,' originally published in New York and now reprinted in London, is of a very different opinion from Dr. Broca; he holds that crossing, or miscegenation as he terms it, is necessary for the production of a perfect type of man, and declares that the future American of the United States is to be a eugenic hybrid between the white and the black."
54. M. D. Conway, A Native of Virginia, *Testimonies Concerning Slavery*, 2nd ed. (London, 1865), 75. Conway went on to say: "Moreover, it is well to remember that 'Miscegenation' is already the irreversible fact of Southern Society in every thing but the recognition of it. . . . No, the trouble is entirely in the political caste of that Negro blood. . . . 'But,' it is said, 'the Abolitionists them-selves are not willing to marry, or have their children marry, Negroes.' No one wishes to marry, or to have a son or daughter to marry, an *unfortunate* person—and such the American Negro is. Moreover, he is often uncultivated. But, apart from this, the majority of Abolitionists would not object to such an alliance."

as a counterpoise to *Miscegenation,* a refurbished edition of one of his old books. Its title was *Subgenation: The Theory of the Normal Relation of the Races;* its subtitle—*An Answer to "Miscegenation."*[55] The invented word *Miscegenation,* in the opinion of Van Evrie, was accurate as applied to "persons of the *same* race" but a misnomer as applied to the different races of American society. As a matter of fact slavery could only exist as a relationship within a single race or between equal races and the word was misapplied when used to denote a relationship of servitude between a *superior* and *inferior* race. "The simple truth is—There is no slavery in this country; there are no slaves in the Southern States."[56] To capture that truth linguistically, Van Evrie aped Croly in inventing a new word—*subgenation,* "from *sub,* lower, and *generatus* and *genus,* a race born or created lower than another; *i.e.,* the natural or normal relation of an inferior to a superior race." For Croly and Wakeman's half-truths and loose generalizations, Van Evrie substituted his own. "The author of 'Miscegenation,' in his vile aspersions against the white women of the South, has won for his name an immortality of infamy—should it ever come to light,—far beyond that achieved by any human being."

> *The equality of all whom God has created equal (white men), and the inequality of those He has made unequal (negroes and other inferior races), are the corner-stone of American democracy, and the vital principle of American civilization and of human progress....* Then, in the face of the world, we should announce that the grand humanitarian policy of progressive and civilized America is to restore subgenation all over the American Continent.

Van Evrie had his political point to make also. Thousands of Democrats in the North believed in the doctrine of subgenation—Vallandigham, Seymour, Wood, Cox among them—but had "not the courage to say it." "Miscegenation is Monarchy; Subgenation is Democracy.... When Lincoln issued his Miscegenation Proclamation he proclaimed a monarchy." The real question before the country was "Subgenation *vs.* Miscegenation." Indeed, the "Peace men must rouse themselves, sweep away the War leaders of the Democracy, nominate a candidate for President who shall bear upon his banner Peace and Subgenation" and usher in *"the adoption by the North of the Confederate Constitution!"*[57]

---

55. Its New York publication was announced in the *Day-Book* of July 16, 1864.
56. In 1856, *DeBow's Review* had criticized *Webster's Dictionary* because it defined a slave as "a person subject to the will of another, a drudge." (F. Garvin Davenport, *Cultural Life in Nashville on the Eve of the Civil War* [Chapel Hill, 1941], 178.)
57. *Subgenation,* 51, 56, 65. Van Evrie quotes Agassiz against Pritchard to demolish the "great luminary of the single-race theory" and pretends to be very rationalistic in attacking the Bible as an authority on scientific questions, citing Galileo and Hugh Miller (the American geologist) in his arguments. Later in the book, however, he drags in the stock-in-trade Biblical arguments for slavery. Professor Draper's physiology is attacked, and the downfall of the Carthaginians, "the Yankees of the Mediterranean," is given as an example of racial corruption. "In Boston the number of births among the negro and mongrel population is not equal to deaths." Mexico, country of "the degenerate miscegen," was conquered "by a few brave Frenchmen." The United States committed an unpardonable sin in not holding Mexico "and restoring subgenation there, prepare it gradually for a Democracy."

Why Van Evrie chose to remain anonymous in this volume may be understood
from its treatment by General Lew Wallace, Provost Marshal of Baltimore, who,

---

That Van Evrie's views have by no means perished is painfully obvious. Suffice to cite a few
passages from a "scientific" work of thirty years ago by Edward M. East and Donald F. Jones,
which reiterates the biological doctrine of *Subgenation:* "The world faces two types of racial
combination: one in which the races are so far apart as to make hybridization a real breaking-
down of the inherent characteristics of each; the other, where fewer differences present only the
possibility of a somewhat greater variability as a desirable basis for selection. Roughly, the former
is the color-line problem; the latter is that of the White Melting Pot, faced particularly by Europe,
North America and Australia. The genetics of these two kinds of racial intermixture is as follows:
Consider first a cross between two extremes, typical members of the white and of the black race.
. . . The real result of such a wide racial cross, therefore is to break apart those compatible physical
and mental qualities which have established a smoothly operating whole in each race by hundreds
of generations of natural selection. If the two races possessed equivalent physical characteristics
and mental capacities, there would still be this valid genetical objection to crossing, as one may
readily see. But in reality the negro is inferior to the white. This is not a hypothesis or supposition;
it is a crude statement of actual fact. The negro has given the world no original contribution of
high merit. By his own initiative in his original habitat, he has never risen. Transplanted to a new
environment, as in the case of Haiti, he has done no better. In competition with the white race,
he has failed to approach its standard. But because he has failed to equal the white man's ability,
his natural increase is low in comparison. The native population of Africa is increasing very slowly,
if at all. In the best environment to which he has been subjected, the United States, his ratio in
the general population is decreasing. His only chance for an extended survival is amalgamation.
. . . It seems an unnecessary accompaniment to humane treatment, an illogical extension of altru-
ism, however, to seek to elevate the black race at the cost of lowering the white. . . . Our first
conclusion may be said to be a decision against the union of races having markedly different
characteristics—particularly when one is decidedly the inferior. . . . Our second thesis is seemingly
paradoxical. It asserts that the foundation stocks of races which have impressed civilization most
deeply have been produced by intermingling peoples who through one cause or other became
genetically *somewhat* unlike." (*Interbreeding and Outbreeding: Their Genetic and Sociological Significance* [Philadelphia 1919], 252–255.)
    John H. Van Evrie deserves a going-over in his own right. He was born in 1814 (died in 1896)
and received a medical degree somewhere. Whether he practiced is problematical; most of his time
seems to have been spent as a pseudo-scientific, screwball propagandist of Copperheadism in New
York. He was co-publisher (Van Evrie, Horton & Co.) of the *New York Day-Book (Caucasian)*
which, advertising itself as "The White Man's Paper," had been denied mailing privileges in 1862.
His *magnum opus* was a 400 page book titled *Negroes and Negro Slavery; the first, an inferior race—
the latter, its normal condition,* published simultaneously in Baltimore and Washington, D.C. and
reprinted in 1854 and in 1861 in New York by his own publishing firm. The edition of 1864,
with its title changed to *Subgenation* is basically the old text with specific argument re Croly
thrown in. Anonymity was protection from charge of treason. The volume was republished in
1866 with the *Subgenation* title; then, since the word had not caught on as *miscegenation* had, in
1867 and 1870 the original text came out with a title better adapted to Secessionist needs in the
Reconstruction period: "*White Supremacy and Negro Subordination or, Negroes A Subordinate Race,
and Slavery Its Normal Condition.* In this text neither the word miscegenation nor subgenation is
used. In 1868, Hinton Rowan Helper, in his revolting *The Negroes in Negroland; The Negroes in
America; and Negroes Generally* cited Van Evrie as an authority. In 1863, Van Evrie, Horton &
Company published S. S. Cox's "Puritanism in Politics."
    Rushmore G. Horton, Van Evrie's partner, was another particularly venomous Copperhead. In
1866, he wrote and published *A Youth's History of the Great Civil War in the United States from
1861 to 1865,* which repeated in primer style all the "arguments" of *Subgenation.* Horton's *History*
quickly ran through a few editions and is still popular in certain quarters. In 1925 a revised edition

according to the Copperhead press, closed a bookshop selling the pamphlet and summoned the proprietor to explain. "It was for the heinous and inexplicable crime of selling a pamphlet called 'Subgenation,' in answer to the beastly *brochure* on 'Miscegenation,' which so disgusted all decent people, except the philanthropical elect, some months ago," howled the *Day-Book*.[58]

Van Evrie schemed tirelessly to turn "miscegenation" to Copperhead use. On July 9 in the *Day-Book* appeared an advertisement for "Political Caricature No. 2," titled "Miscegenation, or The Millennium of Abolitionism," at 25c per copy and cheaper in quantity—"a capital hit upon the new plank in the Republican platform," representing "society as it is to be in the era of 'Equality and Fraternity.' "

> Sumner is introducing a strapping "colored lady" to the President. A young woman (white) is being kissed by a big buck nigger, while a lady lecturer supposed to be "The Inspired Maid" [Miss Anna Dickinson] sits upon the knee of a sable brother urging him to come to her lectures, while Greeley, in the very height of ecstatic enjoyment, is eating ice-cream with a female African of monstrous physique, declaring that society at last had reached absolute perfection. In the background is a carriage, negroes inside, with white drivers and footmen; a white servant girl drawing a nigger baby, and a newly arrived German surveying the whole scene exclaiming, "Mine Got, vot a guntry! Vot a beeples!"

"It ought to be circulated far and wide as a campaign document," concluded the advertisement. Newspapers that copied the blurb and sent in a marked copy would receive four copies of the picture by mail.[59]

Thus through this summer of gloom for the Northern cause the Copperhead press kept up its attack on the "miscegenation" front. The concentration point for the attack—especially as Election Day approached—was New York, a decisive

---

was edited and published by Lloyd T. Everett and Mary D. Carter, dedicated "to those friends of Freedom, the Copperheads of the North—both of earlier and later times."

58. October 15, 1864.

59. This caricature was put out by J. Bromley and Company of New York. Other elements of the caricature emphasize its insidious intent. A "white servant girl" remarks, "and is it to drag nagur babies that I left old Ireland? Bad luck to me." A Negro suitor implores a demure white lass, "Lubly Julia Anna, name de day, when Brodder Beecher shall make us one?" To a "strapping 'colored lady' " being introduced to him by Sumner, Lincoln says: "I shall be proud to number among my intimate friends any member of the Squash family, especially the little Squashes"; to which she replies, "I'se 'quainted wid Missus Linkum, I is, washed for her 'fore de hebenly Miscegenation times was cum. Dont do nuffin now but gallevant 'round wid de white gem'men! he-ah! he-ah! he-ah!" On October 22, 1864, the *Day-Book* advertised another political caricature put out by Browley: "The Greatest Hit Yet—The Miscegenation Ball At the Headquarters of the Lincoln Campaign Club, corner of Broadway and 23d st., N.Y. on the evening of Sept. 21, 1864." In "mazy dance," so goes the description of the picture, "with fat, black wenches, in silks and satins, are dignified, grave, white politicians on the sofas, squeezing and ogling thick-lipped Phillises." The Republican Party answered promptly with the aid of Currier and Ives. In a cartoon on the Chicago convention of the Democrats, the nominees McClellan and Pendleton are portrayed as "The . . . Political Siamese Twins, The Offspring of Chicago Miscegenation," spurned by two Union soldiers.

city in a decisive state. In New York had occurred the draft riots of the previous July;[60] in New York, *Miscegenation*, with its deliberately provocative clap-trap on the necessary and inevitable amalgamation of Negro and Irish, had been born. Correctly manipulated, figured the sachems of Tammany and Mozart Hall, the miscegenation issue could not fail to win the labor and Irish vote for "little Mac."[61]

When in May, Lincoln, recalling these riots, counseled a workingmen's group that "the strongest bond of human sympathy outside the family relation should be the one uniting all working people, of all nations, tongues and kindreds," the Democratic press was not slow to give his words an anti-labor, anti-Irish twist. "Mr. Abraham Lincoln has deliberately insulted the white working classes of the Unites States," ranted the *Jeffersonian*. "He classes labouring white men with negroes. . . . In this brief sentence we have the new doctrine of 'miscegenation' or amalgamation officially announced."

> The most advanced school of Abolitionists now take the position that our citizens of Irish birth are inferior to the negro, and that they could be vastly improved by the intermixture with the negro. The "working people" to whom Mr. Lincoln refers, are, of course, the Irish, for it was upon them the responsibility of the riot was thrown. . . . It is the direct tendency of Abolitionism to reduce the white laboring classes of the country to negro equality and amalgamation.

"We did not expect, however," concluded the *Jeffersonian*, "to find Mr. Lincoln come out and openly advocate this monstrous doctrine."[62] The climax had been reached, according to the *New York Freeman's Journal & Catholic Register:* the "beastly doctrine of the intermarriage of black men with white women" was now "openly and publicly avowed and indorsed and encouraged by the President of the United States. . . . Filthy black niggers, greasy, sweaty, and disgusting, now jostle white people and even ladies everywhere, even at the President's levees." What next would happen in "this cruel, Abolition, miscegenation war?" asked a Philadelphia correspondent of the *Register*. "But a few years ago, Henry Winter Davis was having Irish Catholics murdered in the streets of Baltimore."[63]

---

60. "The Democratic press never tired of stressing the labor competition to be anticipated by white laborers from free Negroes." (Gray, *op. cit.,* 90). Also see Foner, *op. cit.,* 269–270, 320–324, which ably summarizes the monographic material on the subject.

61. A year before, in August 1862, a Brooklyn mob had attacked a factory in which Negroes were working and had tried to fire it. The *New York Evening Post* hit the nail on the head in its comment: "In every case Irish laborers have been incited to take part in these lawless attempts; and the cunning ringleaders and originators of these mutinies, who are not Irishmen, have thus sought to kill two birds with one stone—to excite a strong popular prejudice against the Irish, while they used them to wreak their spite against the blacks." (Allan Nevins, *The Evening Post—A Century of Journalism* [New York, 1922], 305.) According to the census of 1860, there were in New York City 203,000 persons of Irish birth out of a total population of 813,000.

62. Quoted in *New York Freeman's Journal & Catholic Register*, May 21, 1864, under title of "Abe's Philanthropy."

63. *New York Freeman's Journal & Catholic Register*, April 23, 30, 1864. When this newspaper ran out of original invective, it simply reprinted excerpts from *Miscegenation* with appropriate headings, as in the issue of June 11, 1864.

It is not strange, therefore, that during the last days of September as election-eering grew hotter and hotter, the Central Campaign Committee of the Democratic Party circulated a long leaflet titled "Miscegenation and the Republican Party," the main argument of which was directed to the workingclass of New York City.[64] The leaflet, an ambitious and comprehensive attempt to make political capital of "the publication, in the early part of 1864, of a very curious pamphlet, entitled 'Miscegenation,' " reprinted the replies of the Abolitionists to Croly and Wakeman's letter, together with extensive quotations from the national anti-slavery press. After damning Sumner, Phillips, Tilton, Stowe, Emerson, Beecher and others, the leaflet went on to lambaste the women-folk of the Union League of New York for sending off the Twentieth U.S. Colored Regiment with a message of "love and honor from the daughters of this great metropolis to their brave champions in the field." This was "a practical example of miscegenation"![65] Its main shot, however, was aimed against the President, who "in his turgid and awkward way," acknowledging the support of the Working Men's Democratic Republican Association of New York, had advised the laboring classes to "beware of prejudices, working disunion and hostility among themselves." Before this "bogus association," stated Campaign Document No. 11 with horror, "Mr. Lincoln took especial pains to place working negroes and white men on an equality."[66]

64. *Weekly World*, September 29, October 27, 1864. This leaflet, later advertised as "Miscegenation Indorsed by the Republican Party" and printed as "Campaign Document No. 11," was sold at "all Democratic Newspaper Offices at $1. per 1000 pages."

65. On April 30, 1864, the New York *Tribune* printed a letter to the editor, signed *T*, in which the writer discussed "the only case of practical miscegenation" he had ever known. Near Oluscatee, Florida, in 1858, he had entered the residence of a large plantation. Its mistress, an "unmistakeable mulatto woman," age about 40, stout, comfortable-looking and "exhibiting evidences of considerable cultivation in her manner and conversation" had received him. A small child was with her; the other children were at Northern schools. The husband entered—"coarse, brutish"—treated them civilly but coldly, taking no notice of his wife. She was the child of a Jamaica planter. Her husband, a sailor, had agreed to marry her for ten or twenty thousand dollars. The plantation was a prosperous one. The light complexions of the children enabled them to "pass" in the North. "Thus, it seems," concluded *T*, "that in the most Southern of Southern states, miscegenation has been tolerated for 20 years, and that it has been considered proper not only for whites to buy and sell blacks, and their own mulatto children, but even to sell themselves into domestic servitude for a sufficient consideration."

On July 23, 1864, the *National Anti-Slavery Standard*, under the title of "The 'Patriarchal' System, 'Miscegenation' in Perfection," carried a letter from a soldier of the 140th Pennsylvania Volunteers stationed near Richmond, Virginia. The soldier had visited a plantation and had spoken with many of its ex-slaves who were the children of the planter. One woman, a mother, had confessed to being the planter's child. Her moronic son stood nearby. "I asked the mother of this boy if Mr. Scott was his father. . . . The incestuous old beast! *This idiot son—the child of his own daughter and grandfather to his own children!* . . . Do you know how these skin aristocrats rave over the new theory of miscegenation. . . . [here] was the very worst form of incestuous amalgamation."

66. To bolster its argument, Campaign Document No. 11 cited a request of Henry Clay in 1848 to his biographer, the Rev. Walter Colton, to write a pamphlet showing that the "ultras go for abolition and amalgamation, and their object is to unite in marriage the laboring white man and the black woman, and to reduce the white laboring man to the despised and degraded condition of the black man." During the campaign, the Democratic Party also circulated reprints of political addresses made by some of its prominent members. One of these, a speech by Supreme Court

For the ultra-Copperhead Van Evrie, Campaign Document No. 11 was not enough. With the election a month off, there was no time "to read long speeches and pamphlets." What was "put before the people should be short, pithy and pointed"—and Van Evrie proposed to do just that. The *Day-Book*, carrying notices and reports of union meetings as one of its regular features, had for long oriented itself to the special problem of winning New York's workers to Copperheadism. And in this field its demagogy was confusing and clever. "The banker, lawyer, preacher, or other non-producing classes," it continually explained to its workingclass readers,

> need not fear ruin from the "abolition of slavery," but the producing classes, the mechanic, laborer, etc., had better cut the throats of their children at once than hand them to "impartial freedom," degradation and amalgamation with negroes.

To clinch this argument, in the last crucial days of the campaign Van Evrie decided to bring out his own "Campaign Broadside No. 1—The Miscegenation Record of the Republican Party," aimed more specifically than the official Campaign Document No. 11 at the strategic workingclass of New York and its Irish core.[67] After exhuming from *Miscegenation* one of its key provocations—

> The fusion between Negro and Irish *will be of infinite service to the Irish.* They are *a more brutal* race and lower in civilization than the Negro. . . . Of course we speak of the laboring Irish.

—the hydrophobic doctor flew at Lincoln's throat. The President had insulted "every white workingman by including him in the category of negroes, or, in other words, calling him a nigger!" By ignoring "all distinctions of color among the laboring classes," by calling them all "working people," Lincoln had recommended "amalgamation of the white working classes with negroes! In other words, white workingmen should love a negro *better than anyone except a relative!*" The need of the moment was to ram this idea into the heads of wavering people.[68]

Justice Jeremiah S. Black, delivered at the Keystone Club in Philadelphia on October 24, 1864, contained the following passage: "It happens, by the permission of God's providence, that two distinct races of human beings have been thrown together on this continent. All the mental characteristics as well as the physical features and color of one race, make it lower in the scale of creation than the other. . . . The Abolitionists look upon all this with perfect horror. They assert everywhere, in season and out of season, the natural right of the negro to political, legal and social equality. Their theories of miscegenation are too disgusting to be mentioned."

67. *Day-Book,* October 1, 1864. These leaflets were for sale at $1. per hundred. For the *New York Freeman's Journal & Catholic Register,* which evidently oriented itself to the more backward members of the Irish-Catholic workingclass of New York City, "the real secret, aim and object of Abolitionism" was an "instinctive effort . . . to destroy the natural order of society . . . by poisoning the masses with negro equality." (May 21, 1864, reprinted from the *Jeffersonian.*)

68. It must be admitted that the attitudes of certain Abolitionist and labor leaders towards emerging workingclass militancy provided fertile ground for Copperhead seed. Writes Foner: "The Abolitionists did little to overcome the fears of the workingclass regarding the so-called dangers of Negro emancipation. In fact they did a good deal to convince many workers that they were concerned only with the welfare of the Negro slaves and considered the problems of free labor as insignificant. In the first issue of the *Liberator* William Lloyd Garrison denounced the trade union

"Millions of these little documents ought to be distributed at once," urged Van Evrie. "Democratic Clubs, Committees, etc., should order at once."

Nor was Van Evrie alone during the concluding weeks of the campaign in his desire to reach the Irish-Catholic workingmen with this rabid message. "What is a 'Mis-ce-ge-na-tor'?" began a forty-eight-page Copperhead pamphlet by George Francis Train. He is an

... Abolitionist (altered Democrat), Black Republican ... Sneers at Catholics, and calls naturalized citizens d————d Irishmen.

The "campaign cry of Copperhead" was "white Man on the Brain, to distinguish its class from Mis-ce-ge-na-tor, or Nigger on the Brain." The platform of the Republicans was

Subjugation.

Emancipation.

Confiscation.

Domination.

Annihilation.

Destruction, in order to produce

Miscegenation![69]

"Who is Thad Stephen [sic]?" asked another Copperhead pamphlet entitled *The Lincoln Catechism*—and answered: "An amalgamationist from Pennsylvania, who honestly practices what he preaches."[70]

---

movement as an organized conspiracy 'to inflame the minds of our working classes against the more opulent.' " In 1847 the *National Anti-Slavery Standard*, official organ of the American Anti-Slavery Society, stated that no true Abolitionist could have any sympathy for those who denounced wage-slavery as an evil. Even Wendell Phillips in 1847 saw no need for unions. Although Phillips changed his views and Frederick Douglass supported unions, this trend of indifference to wage-workers' problems continued in the Abolitionist movement. Thus Horace Greeley denounced Abolitionists who refused to treat workers decently and turned down an invitation to an anti-slavery convention because of the indifference of many of the delegates to problems of the Northern workers. Sarah Bagley, although ardently anti-slavery, felt herself forced to denounce some Abolitionist leaders for a similar indifference. The fact that in the election of 1860, the Republican Party had widely circulated Helper's *The Impending Crisis*—which attacked Irish-Americans as supporters of slavery—helped to provide a susceptible audience for the Democratic propaganda of 1864. (*Op. cit.*, 270–271, 295). In 1863, facing English audiences, Henry Ward Beecher "laid all blame for the New York draft riots on the Irish Catholics, as though to say that America had the same Irish problem as England" (Sandburg, *op. cit.*, II, 515).

69. Anon. [George Francis Train], *A Voice From the Pit* (Washington, D.C. [?] 1864), 3, 4, 5.

70. Anon., *The Lincoln Catechism Wherein the Eccentricities & Beauties of Despotism Are Fully Set Forth. A Guide to the Presidential Election of 1864* (New York, 1864), 24. On the next page the catechism asked, "Who is Anna Dickinson?" and answered, "Ask Ben. Butler and William D. Kelly." The Republicans replied in a *Copperhead Catechism* by "Fernando the Gothamite," which was copyrighted and perhaps written by Montgomery Wilson. (Joseph Sabin, *A Dictionary of Books relating to America* [New York, 1869–1936], IV, 529.)

Croly and Wakeman did not wait long to take advantage of the new opportunity offered by the President's address to the New York workingmen. They were now to play their last card. On September 29, a copy of *Miscegenation* was dispatched to the White House, accompanying it a letter to Abraham Lincoln. "I hereby transmit a copy of my work on 'Miscegenation,' " began the anonymous author, "in the hope that after you have perused it, you will graciously permit me to dedicate to you another work on a kindred subject, viz: 'Melaleukation.' "

> In the one work I discuss the mingling of all the races which go to form the human family. My object in the new publication is to set forth the advantage of blending of the black and white races on this continent. From the favor with which "Miscegenation" has been received—a great many thousand copies having been sold, and its leading ideas having been warmly indorsed by the progressive men of the country—I am led to believe that this new work will excite even greater interest.

So much for preamble; the main point follows: "I am tempted to make this request from the various measures of your administration looking to the recognition of the great doctrine of human brotherhood, and from your speech to the New-York workingmen, in which you recognize the social and political equality of the white and colored laborer." Allow me, concluded the gracious writer,

> to express the hope that, as the first four years of your administration have been distinguished by the emancipation of four millions of human beings, the next four years may find them freemen raised to the condition of social equality, and becoming an element of the future American race.[71]

One can imagine how Croly's mouth watered as he watched the mails for a reply. But Lincoln did not rise to the bait. Nevertheless, in a ceaseless torrent of invective right up to the November balloting, the President's message to the New York workingmen was twisted and befouled by the defeat-sensing Democratic journals, as they strove to keep the miscegenation issue in the fore of the campaign. At a pro-McClellan mass meeting, the *World* reported a speech by one Colonel Max Langenschwarz, who urged the Republicans to "add to emancipation, to confiscation, and to miscegenation, a policy of polygamy," so that "a man could have a yellow wife from China, a brown wife from India, a black wife from Africa, and a white wife from his own country, and so have a variegated family and put a sign over the door: 'United Matrimonial Paint Shop.' "[72] About nine in the evening of Election Day, wrote the New York correspondent of the pro-Northern London *Daily News*, "I went to Tammany Hall"—

> The hall was densely packed by a most unsavoury crowd . . . a large proportion evidently Irish. . . . "Captain" Rynders, a mob leader of great reputation and influence . . . was engaged in accusing the republican party of an intention to persecute the catholics as soon as they had subjugated the slaveholders.

---

71. MS in Library of Congress.
72. Sandburg, *op. cit.*, II, 581.

This was the same Rynders whose gang some years before had driven the daunt-less Phillips from a New York lecture platform.

> From this he passed rapidly to abuse of the negro. . . . Anything so ribald and disgusting I have never heard in a public assemblage. He rang the changes for twenty minutes on the smell of the negroes, and on their lips, nose, and "wool," and interspersed it with denunciations of the "miscegenators," recurring inces-santly to the passion which he ascribed to the republican leaders for "nigger wenches."[73]

Thus the Democracy hammered at the miscegenation "issue" up to the very last minutes of the campaign. Yet the ugly crusade was destined to fail. The with-drawal of Fremont from the presidential race, together with the bright news from Sherman in Atlanta and Farragut in Mobile Bay, reversed what had seemed to Lincoln in August a terribly ominous trend. True enough, in New York City the Copperhead campaign was something of a success. In 1860, Lincoln had received 33,000 votes to his opponent's 62,000, while now he received only 36,000 to McClellan's 78,000.[74] Nevertheless in the country at large Lincoln received all but twenty-one of the electoral votes, while "Sunset" Cox of Ohio, the chief Congressional accomplice of Croly and Wakeman, lost his seat to the Republican, Samuel Shellabarger.

That the celebrated pamphlet on *Miscegenation* was a colossal hoax was not first revealed in America. In mid-October, a fortnight before the election, the New York correspondent of the pro-Southern London *Morning Herald* mailed off a dispatch that would be printed as a feature article in its issue of November 1.[75] "As this letter will not return in printed form to the United States before the presidential election will have taken place," it began, "it will do no harm where harm might otherwise possibly be done, to give the history of one of the most extraordinary hoaxes that ever agitated the literary world."

> In the beginning of the spring of the present year, a pamphlet was published in this city, bearing the novel and rather barbarous, as far as pronunciation goes, title of "Miscegenation." . . . It was gravely put forth as embodying the only practical solution of that *questio vexata*, the disposal of the negro. Although the theme discussed with such apparent solemnity is not a savory one, the book was very cleverly written, and was full of scientific facts and learned quotations which gave it an air of great plausibility. Several very large editions of the work were sold in the United States; and eventually it found its way across the water, was reprinted by Trubner & Company, and received prominent comment in several English literary journals. Among others, the *Westminster Review* noticed the book with a great deal of gravity, and spoke of it as being a very curious work.

---

73. London *Daily News*, November 26, 1864.
74. Lincoln's majority in New York State was uncomfortably small—7,000 votes. On the other hand, Seymour, who had been elected Democratic governor in 1862, was defeated by the Republican, Fenton, in 1864.
75. Headlines for the article were: "THE GREAT HOAX OF THE DAY! The Great Miscegenation Pam-phlet Exposed—The 'Moon Hoax' in the Shade—Who Wrote the Book—How it Came into Notice—Letters of Indorsement from Leading Progressives."

The fact is, continued the dispatch, the pamphlet "was written by two young gentlemen connected with the newspaper press of New York, both of whom are obstinate Democrats in politics, and was got up solely with the view of committing, if possible, the orators and essayists of the Republican party to the principle it enunciated, that of the complete social equality, by marriage, of the white and black races." No one suspected that it had been written by "people who abhor the doctrine it sets forth." It had "swindled" everybody. The authors of *Miscegenation,* "employing the arguments of the Republicans," had "dextrously managed to make it appear that an amalgamation or miscegenation of the two races was not only desirable but inevitable." To familiarize themselves with the subject, these two "obstinate Democrats" had "crammed" their subject at the Astor Library.[76] They had quoted "Pritchard, Draper, and other learned authorities." But their "true object" was to bring "the Republican party into conflict with the strong anti-negro prejudice existing in the North." Of course, it had been "an admirable weapon to use against the Republicans and the Democrats were not slow to avail themselves of it."

The machinery employed to get the hoax into circulation was very ingenious. Before it was issued, proof copies were sent to all leading abolitionists, male and female, of the country, from Senator Sumner and Secretary Seward down to Abby Kelly Foster, the crinolined abolition ranter. Many of the hare-brained spir-

76. At the Astor Library, Croly and Wakeman might have come across the following passage in William J. Grayson's *The Hireling and the Slave, Chicora, and Other Poems* (Charleston, S.C., 1856), 71, which could have furnished pointed suggestions in the elaboration of their theme:

> Not such his fate Philanthropy replies,
> His horoscope is drawn from happier skies;
> Bonds soon shall cease to be the Negro's lot,
> Mere race-distinctions shall be all forgot,
> And white and black amalgamating, prove
> The charms that Stone admires, of mongrel love,
> Erase the lines that erring nature draws
> To severe race, and rescind her laws;
> Reverse the rule that stupid farmers heed,
> And mend the higher by the coarser breed;
> Or prove the world's long history false, and find
> Wit, wisdom, genius in the Negro mind;
> If not intended thus, in time to blend
> In one bronze-colored breed, what then the end?

In June 1864, the right-of-Copperhead New York *Old Guard* (136–137), reviewing Grayson's poem for the second time, deplored the fact that the "crowd" ran after "that hyena in woman's clothes, Anna Dickinson," while *The Hireling and the Slave* had not "been once named by a northern newspaper." (Brother Basil Leo Lee, *Discontent in New York City* [Washington, D.C., 1943], 146–147.) In 1863, the *Old Guard*'s editor, C. Chauncey Burr, predicted that after March 4, 1865 drawings and paintings would be put on exhibition in Washington, including one of a "white man embracing a Negro wench. An immodest picture, dedicated to Charles Sumner." Burr alluded frequently to "Negro-blooded" Republican leaders. "A western author has issued a pamphlet adducing evidence to show that Old Abe is part negro," he wrote; ". . . Hamlin and Sumner, to the scientific eye, show the presence of Negro blood." (Sandburg, *op. cit.,* II, 135–137.)

itual mediums of the land—and there are a score or more of these ethereal individuals in every northern village—were furnished with advance sheets of the
work, and all "mediums" and more material-minded abolitionists were requested
to furnish their views upon the subject to the author.

"The bait was swallowed with avidity," observed the *Morning Herald*'s correspondent, gleefully enumerating the replies of Pillsbury, a "brilliant of the abolition clique" and of the rest. Through "the dextrous manipulation of the authors," the pamphlet had been "introduced in Congress," where Cox had made
"a brilliant and forcible speech against the theory."

Nor were the abolitionists the only ones deceived. Even S. R. Fiske, one of the
editors of the New York *Herald*—which greatly prided itself upon its sharpness—
had penned a four-column refutation, which was reprinted by the *Leader*. Indeed,
it had been "a decided hit." Although Mr. Charles Congdon, "one of the cleverest
writers on the editorial staff of the New York *Tribune*, had squinted at it very
strongly, so impressed" had he been with the theory that he had written two or
three articles on it. Yet the plot had not been altogether a success. Although the
Anti-Slavery Standard and the *Independent* had espoused the ideas of *Miscegenation*, the "bulk of the Republican party, however, composed as it is of very shrewd
politicians, constantly on the alert for traps of that sort, whether innocently set
by their own radical brethren or by the wicked 'Copperheads,' " had realized that
"whether the book was to be viewed with distrust or not, and however consistent
its doctrines might be with their record and character, its public endorsement
would kill them politically, and so they wisely said very little about the matter."

"Miscegenation," according to the *Morning Herald*, threw the "Moon Hoax,"
perpetrated by J. Locke immediately after the completion of Lord Ross's great
telescope, into the shade. Moreover, it was "very likely that the writers of the
book will never be discovered, but like the author of the world-famous 'Junius's
Letters,' will remain unknown to fame, a puzzle to American bibliographers as
the 'Letters' have been and are to the shrewdest minds of England." *Miscegenation*
had constituted "one of the most amusing chapters of the present political campaign," and the *Westminster Review* and other journals "must own up, as a Yankee
would say, to being very decidedly 'sold.' " Indeed the effect of the pamphlet
would not "die with the mystery of its origin."

The conclusion of the dispatch was bloodthirsty, in the Van Evrie style. There
were "but two solutions" to the problem:

> Either we must have a war of races, which would inevitably result in the extir-
> pation of the negroes; or we must incorporate them with ourselves, in the suc-
> ceeding generations by marriage. Either horn of this dilemma is frightful. . . . No
> sane man supposes that our people will ever marry the negroes out of existence;
> there remains, then, war to the knife, and the knife to the helt, till every vestige
> of the African race disappears from the continent.

Thus would the abolitionists be punished for "their mad attack upon the patriarchal system of the South."[77]

---

77. This section of the *Herald* exposé was expurgated from the *World* reprint. Possibly the tone was

That Croly was in cahoots with the correspondent of the *Morning Herald* may be seen by the latter's dispatch of a week later. "The authors of 'Miscegenation'— the literary, or rather politico-literary hoax of which I have given you a full description—have asked, in a letter, the permission of the President to dedicate their book to him. This 'dodge' will hardly succeed; for Mr. Lincoln is shrewd enough to say nothing on the unsavoury subject."[78] Meanwhile he awaited with interest the exposure of the fraud in the States. Indeed, "the wrathful denunci-ation of the Republican journals and politicians who have endorsed the doctrines of the book, and whose letters and articles are in the possession of the authors, will be amusing."[79]

"When this exposé reaches the United States," the *Morning Herald* had stated, "it will be the first that will have been made regarding the matter." Two weeks after Lincoln had been returned to the White House, the *World,* in all its inno-cence, spread the story of the "Miscegenation Hoax" prominently over its pages. Its technique, as always, was clever. No confession was made of its own conniv-ance in the fraud. The London *Morning Herald* article was reprinted (with the deletion noted above) accompanied by an editorial stating that a New York cor-respondent of the London *Morning Herald* had "just revealed the fact that the 'Essay on Miscegenation,' which excited so much attention, sympathetic and an-tipathetic in this country during the recent election, was simply a clever Demo-

---

so personal and vindictive that not only might it have been impolitic to print it after Lincoln's smashing victory, but also it might have revealed, for those who cared to investigate, the fact that the *World* was originally responsible for the hoax.

78. Andrew Jackson in his campaign of 1828 had to contend with the problem in a more personal way. In a letter to General R. K. Call on August 16, 1828, he wrote: "The whole object of the coalition is to calumniate me, cart loads of coffin hand-bills, forgeries, & pamphlets of the most base calumnies are circulated by the franking privilege of Members of Congress, & Mr. Clay. Even Mrs. J. is not spared, & who, from her cradle to her death, had not a speck upon her character, has been dragged forth by Hammond & held to public scorn as a prostitute who inter-married with a Negro, & my eldest brother sold as a Slave in Carolina. This Hammond does not publish in his vile press, but keeps the statement purporting to be sworn to, a *forgery* & spreads it secretly . . . was not my hands tied, & my mouth closed, I would soon put an end to their slanders" (*Virginia Magazine of History and Biography*, XXIX [April 1921], 191).

79. London *Morning Herald*, November 9, 1864. The English press, of course, fought the American Civil War, on its side of the water. "The *Standard* [owned by the same party as the *Morning Herald*] gained much in circulation in the early 'sixties through the popularity of slashing letters by a Copperhead correspondent in New York." (Henry D. Jordan, "The Daily and Weekly Press of England in 1861," *South Atlantic Quarterly*, XXVIII [July 1929], 308.) On the other hand, pro-Northern English newspapers were at times vigorously critical of the American Copperhead press. For instance, the New York correspondent of the London *Daily News*, discussing the McClellan-Lincoln campaign wrote: "His [Lincoln's] fondness for comic anecdotes, some of them rather coarse . . . furnishes a constant theme for vituperation to some of the foul-mouthed publications in existence, such as the *World*, which has probably no equal in the newspaper press of any country for scurrility." (London *Daily News*, September 27, 1864). Compare with this the opinion of a recent biographer of Joseph Pulitzer: "The hysteria of Greeley, the ferocity of the abolitionists and the horrors of reconstruction are well visualized against the cooler, conservative and, at this distance, sensible attitude of the *World*." (Don C. Seitz, *Joseph Pulitzer, His Life and Letters* [New York, 1924], 118.)

cratic quiz perpetrated upon the owlish leaders of the abolitionists!" The editors of the *World* treated the whole affair drolly—but revealed unwittingly that they had all along known who the perpetrators were: " 'Scared by the sound themselves had made,' the wicked wags, its authors, left events to their natural course; and from their anonymous castle of safety watched with delight the almost divine honors paid to their Abbot of Misrule."

The *Herald*, the *Leader* and other Democratic journals had "gravely assailed the abominable doctrines of 'Miscegenation,' " observed the *World* (omitting to mention that it too, in complete hypocrisy, had done likewise), and the "gospel of miscegenation" had been "glad tidings of great joy" to the "intellectual voluptuaries of fanaticism." The "doctrine of 'Miscegenation,' conceived as a satire," had been "received as a sermon."

> . . . the barbaric character of the compound word "miscegenation" was gladly overlooked even by Boston purists and the *Westminster Review*. . . . The name will doubtless die out by virtue of its inherent malformation. We have bastard and hump-backed words enough already in our verbal army corps.

Miscegenation had "passed into history," concluded the *World*. "The hoax and the hoaxed, the quiz and the quizzed, will live forever in the grateful midriff of a nation."[80]

The correspondent of the London *Morning Herald* had looked forward with amusement to the exposé of the hoax in the United States. The rout of the Copperheads however robbed him of his amusement. Nevertheless the *Herald* had to save face. "The exposure . . . of the miscegenation hoax, with which two young Democrats humbugged the political world here, has created no little excitement in literary circles throughout the Northern States. The *Herald*'s exposure, republished in the *World* newspaper of this city, has been copied everywhere, and the victims of the joke are compelled to bear a great deal of chaffing."[81] This was merely pap for the *Herald*'s readers. As a matter of fact, in the excitement created by Lincoln's decisive triumph, the Republicans in their joy and the Copperheads in their chagrin paid little attention to the exposure of the fraud.[82] "Any one of

80. Compare this fulsome glee with the righteous wrath of the *Weekly World* in its issue of September 15, 1864, under title of "Beware of Republican Forgeries": "Violent articles from the Charleston *Mercury*, and papers of that sort, abusing northern laborers, and ridiculing and insulting northern Democrats, were copied here by Republican papers as representing the true sentiments of the southern people."

81. London *Morning Herald*, December 6, 1864.

82. *Boston Journal* (Evening Edition), November 21, 1864. The London *Morning Herald*'s correspondent, however, continued to grind the axe. In the issue of December 13, 1864, which printed a plug for Mrs. Croly's (Jennie June's) *Talks on Women's Topics*, he spoke scornfully of a jubilee gathering of young colored girls, celebrating Lincoln's victory: "What with the contrast produced by the light dresses, coal black countenances, and irrepressibly curly wool, the unmiscegenetic spectator found it difficult to control the muscles of his face."

   S. S. Cox, in his memoirs, recalling his "Miscegenation" speech of February 17, 1864, confessed that he was duped by the pamphlet which "afterwards turned out to be apocryphal. It was written by two young men connected with the New York press. So congenial were its sentiments with

ordinary shrewdness," commented the editor of the Republican *Boston Journal* a few days after the exposé, "might have divined" that it was "a political pasquinade." He was "surprised to find in the columns" of some of his contemporaries "labored attempts to combat arguments and illustrations which should have been treated only with ridicule." Although it had to be "confessed that the cunning authors . . . succeeded in obtaining for its doctrines a wide notoriety," the book had done little harm. "The fact is that the doctrine of miscegenation is not a practical question here at the North, and the public wisely concluded that it was safe to leave the matter with the Southerners who have been trying the experiment and testing the theory upon a large scale for a number of years."[83]

There were some Copperhead diehards. One curious item of the aftermath was an illiterate and uncouth eight-page pamphlet that appeared in New York City shortly after the election bearing the title *What Miscegenation Is! and What We Are to Expect Now that Mr. Lincoln Is Re-elected,* authored by one L. Seaman, L.L.D. and dedicated sarcastically to Henry Ward Beecher. This pamphlet, chock-full of misinformation, was probably published immediately after the election but before the *World* had exposed its own hoax. Miscegenation—a "word not recognized by Webster, Johnson, or Worcester, and yet in general use"—was, according to Seaman, "coined in New England, and for the times." *Amalgamation* had "done very well for a time as a hobby but it soon lost its effect, and something new was needed to take its place. Accordingly the agitators got their heads together and invented the word 'miscegenation' as best suited to refine their cause, and at once declared themselves 'Miscegenationists.' "

A large and flourishing society soon sprang up under the appropriate title of the "Modern Order of Miscegenationist." The first society being formed in Boston, others sprang up rapidly throughout the State of Massachusetts, and from thence the contagion spread throughout all New England . . . was wafted from Maine to Oregon. . . .

Thus, "not only New England but many of the Western and North Western States" had stood "in solid phalanx for Miscegenation, and with Lincoln trium-

---

those of the leading Abolitionists, and so ingeniously was its irony disguised, that it was not only indorsed by the fanatical leaders all over the land, but no one in Congress thought of questioning the genuineness and seriousness of the document." Cox goes on to compare the pamphlet to Archbishop Whately's *Historic Doubts Concerning Napoleon.* (*Eight Years in Congress,* 352.) He was probably trying to lie his way out of connivance with Croly and Wakeman.

83. A few days later Wendell Phillips, in a lecture at Portland, Maine, said: "Again, no nation ever became great which was born of one blood. It is like the intermarriage of cousins. Spain is an unmixed nation, and she has sunk to a third-rate power. France blends a dozen races, and she leads the van. We should look therefore upon the colored race as we look upon the Irish and the Germans. . . . My goal is a homogeneous nationality which shall weld Boston and New Orleans, New York and Charleston into one thunderbolt, and make us able to control the continent. Then the nations of Europe will respect us." (*Portland* (Me.) *Transcript,* November 26, 1864, reprinted in *National Anti-Slavery Standard,* December 10, 1864.) This is not Phillips at his best. Uncritical acceptance of quack "science" and of "manifest destiny" sometimes blurred his usually clear vision.

phantly re-elected the 'ladies of Washington' " had "commenced to friz their hair."[84]

David Ross Locke, whose abolitionism carried over into the Reconstruction period, continued to poke fun at the straw-man of miscegenation. In a pamphlet of 1866 describing Johnson's swing-around-the-circle, Petroleum Vesuvius Nasby, now "A Dimmicrat of Thirty Years Standing," again climbed into the ring to comment publicly on our "noble President" . . . insulted by a bloody and brutal Radical and Miscegenationist."[85] A little later in the year Nasby returned to the theme in a dispatch from "Confedrit X Roads (wich is in the Stait of Kentucky)":

"Mrs. P.," sed this Illinoiy store-keeper, which his name it wuz Pollock, "do yoo object to miscegenation?"

"Missee——— what?" replied she, struck all uv a heap at the word.

"Miscegenation—amalgamation—marrying whites with niggers."[86]

Throughout 1867 and 1868 postmaster Nasby continued his reports to the nation. "My brethren," preached one Bigler to the unreconstructed Democratic laity,

I'd advise yoo all to abjoor Dimocrisy. Up North, the minit the nigger gits a vote, you are forced to legal missegenashun; down South, the affinity Dimocrisy hez for niggers hez bleached out the race to the color uv molasses. There's no hope for you, save in Ablishinism, which hez the happy fakulty uv doin justis to em without marrying em!

"It didn't make no difference," concluded Nasby———

They didn't know what he wuz talkin about. The word "missegenashen" struck em with amazement, from wich they didn't recover till we left. In speakin to such aujences, men must be keerful uv the words they youse.[87]

In the presidential election of 1868, Locke supported Grant. In the South, Sister Sallie's *The Color Line* had succeeded the Reverend Josiah Priest's ante-bellum *Bible Defence of Slavery*. Widely circulated in the Gulf States during the entire period of Reconstruction, the new "White Line Bible" thundered again at "the doctrine of the abolitionists, the free-lovers, the amalgamationists, the miscegen-

---

84. The Democratic papers did not give up their "miscegenation" harangues after Lincoln's election; thus the *Manchester* (N.H.) *Daily Union* on July 1, 1865, in correspondence from Concord: "The intelligent contraband is already on the way to New England. . . . Last evening, a colored man hailing from Carolina, with some gift of the gab, and big lungs, addressed a large crowd near the corner of Park and Main Streets. The Abolitionists were delighted. . . . He advocated miscege-nation, and intimated that a mixture of the white and black races would make a most splendid race for this country. Finally, several soldiers pitched into him, and bade him 'dry up.' "

85. *Swinging Round the Circle; or, Andy's Trip to the West. Together With A Life of its Hero* (New York, 1866), no pagination.

86. D. R. Locke, *The Moral History of America's Life Struggle* (Boston, 1874), 261.

87. Petroleum V. Nasby, *Ekkoes from Kentucky Bein a Perfect Record Uv the Ups, Downs, and Experiences uv the Dimocrisy, Doorin The Eventful Year 1867 Ez Seen by a Naturalized Kentuckian* (Boston, 1868), 278–279. This Nasby pamphlet was illustrated by Thomas Nast.

ationists and the pseudo-philanthropists," who believed that "all mankind of every blood and color on the habitable globe, are of Adam's race, and are *brothers and sisters nationally*."[88] "The Dimokrasy never hed afore it sich brilliant prospecks," observed Nasby, "or the promise uv a victory so easily won. We hev an abundance uv material to draw from. Ther is waitin to fall into our ranks all uv the followin classes." Foremost in the North were "All them wich dont want ther dawters to marry niggers, and wich demand a law to pertect em agin em."[89]

Neither Wakeman nor Croly ever admitted having a hand in writing the *Miscegenation* pamphlet.

Wakeman, indeed, only lived a half dozen years after its appearance. In 1868 he was appointed stenographer to the New York Senate and in July of that year served as official reporter of the National Democratic Convention held in New York City.[90] The first inkling of his connivance in the pamphlet was given in his obituary printed in the paper which had abetted the fraud. "His humor on paper," noted the New York *World* of March 21, 1870, "was conspicuous in the celebrated Miscegenation hoax, of which he was part author." Did Croly write the obituary?

Croly's part in the *Miscegenation* hoax—evidently the principal one—has remained a kind of well-kept secret to the present day. And this is rather curious and significant, for he was a well-known figure in his time—prominent newspaperman, magazine owner and editor, contributor to periodicals, author of books and a pioneer founder of American positivism.[91] One wonders how his sleazy role in the affair was kept quiet. He himself had coined the new word which had given a label to the issue. "I think Mr. Croly was responsible for the invention of the name," wrote his wife nine years after his death; he claimed it "added a new, distinctive, and needed word to our vocabulary."[92] So it did; but Croly never came forward to claim the honor of invention. Moreover, neither in obituary, wherein his numerous works were usually listed, nor in biography written before or immediately after his death, was *Miscegenation* ever mentioned.[93] The *Dictionary of American Biography* lists him as the principal author of *Miscegenation*

88. Sister Sallie, *The Color Line, Devoted to the Restoration of Good Government, Putting An End to Negro Authority and Misrule, And Establishing A White Man's Government in the White Man's Country by Organizing the White People of the South* (n.p., n.d.), 60. The copy of this pamphlet in the Boston Public Library has been marked by James Redpath (1833–1891), publisher of W. W. Brown's *The Black Man* and author of *Echoes of Harper's Ferry* (1860), "By Rev. Thompson."
89. Petroleum V. Nasby, *The Impendin Crisis uv the Dimocracy* (New York, 1868), 17.
90. *Official Proceedings of the National Democratic Convention Held at New York, July 4–9, 1868.* (Boston, 1868.)
91. "His journalistic career of thirty-five years covered the whole period of the Civil War, and at all times was of the busiest kind." (New York *World*, May 1, 1889.) He was "one of the best known journalists in this country." (*New York Times*, May 1, 1889.)
92. MS letter from Mrs. Croly, Dec. 15, 1900, in Boston Athenaeum.
93. New York *Times*, New York *Daily Tribune*, New York *World*, May 1, 1889; *General Alumni Catalogue of New York University, 1883–1905* (New York, 1906).

but is unaware of the fact that the pamphlet was a hoax—labels him uncritically as an independent, fearless, unorthodox, iconoclast and reformer.[94]

While he lived, no one—with the exception of the bibliographer Sabin—ever accused him of authoring the pamphlet, and to his dying day, 25 years later, Croly never admitted authorship or mentioned the word miscegenation in any of his voluminous writings. The word had entered the language for good, and others were employing it; he himself, dabbling in the Noyesian theory of stirpiculture and continually discussing subjects in which it might conveniently have been employed, always used the old term he had condemned—amalgamation. The shameful secret was hugged close; Mrs. Croly, who, in an obituary on her husband's death had not disclosed it, later discussed the matter feebly and defensively, and, at that, only when forced to it. "Tho' it [the pamphlet] was written partly in the spirit of joke [farce?]," she wrote years later at the turn of the century, "it was not a hoax, and was not palmed off upon the public eye as one. . . . I remember the episode perfectly, and the half joking, half earnest spirit in which the pamphlet was written."[95] Her apology is pitiful and guilty; for the facts challenge it.[96]

Croly's career after 1864 was a varied one. His whole life, linked up as it was with many important aspects of the American scene in the second half of the nineteenth century—the Civil War, the growth of American sensational and graphic journalism, the history of American philosophy, the development of the New York City real estate interest—deserves a book of its own. What few sketchy facts are given now are only designed to complete the picture of the "miscegenation" phase of his career.

Following the election of Grant to the presidency, the relationship of managing editor Croly to owner-editor Marble of the New York *World* became one of running feud—if not in principle, then in circulation-building tactic. When the *Times* fought Tweed, Croly begged Marble either to follow suit or to be neutral, but the *World* supported Tweed. When Marble supported Greeley against Grant for a second term—and Greeley was defeated—Croly handed in his resignation.

Meanwhile he had been busy. In 1867, with C. W. Sweet, he had founded the *Real Estate Record & Builders Guide*, a weekly paper dedicated to the real estate interest, which for the next six years he owned and managed with his friend.[97] By 1868, having gained a reputation as a party stalwart, he wrote the campaign biography of Seymour and Blair for the Democratic Party. Typical campaign hack-work it is, on its first pages striking a note reminiscent of the writer's earlier unsigned effort for the Democracy: "The contest has opened very bitterly. Nor

---

94. Brother Basil Leo Lee mentions the pamphlet in passing and evidently accepts it as *bona fide*. (*op. cit.*, 163).

95. MS letter in Boston Athenaeum from Mrs. Croly, dated Dec. 15, 1900.

96. In an obituary on Mrs. Croly's death in 1901, St. Clair McKelway wrote: "Their union was not made any less congenial by marked dissimilarity of convictions on cardinal subjects." The language here is equivocal. According to one interpretation it might explain Mrs. Croly's reticence on the *Miscegenation* question. (*Memories of Jane Cunningham Croly* [New York, 1904], 215).

97. *Real Estate Record & Builders Guide*, XLIII (May 4, 1889), 613–614.

is this surprising. There are vast material interests at stake. A question of race-superiority is involved. . . ."[98] During these years he was also an occasional contributor to the periodical press,[99] and in 1870 founded and edited a typographically bizarre magazine called *The Modern Thinker,* in which he indulged his predilection for anonymity by writing articles under various inverted pseudonyms and initials. It is worthy of note that one of the contributors to this magazine—which gave up the ghost after its second issue—was none other than the duped Abolitionist, Albert Brisbane. Although the "new thought" and positivist articles that filled its pages discussed stirpiculture, eugenic socialism and Noyesism, the word miscegenation never appeared.

By this time, Croly had become an enthusiastic partisan of Auguste Comte's positivist religion of humanity and together with T. B. Wakeman (father of George, the collaborator of *Miscegenation*) was actively organizing Comtean churches in New York City. In 1871, under the name of C. G. David, he published in New York a handbook for the new movement titled *A Positivist Primer,* a collection of "Familiar Conversations on the Religion of Humanity."

A year after his resignation from the *World,* Croly helped to found the illustrated New York *Daily Graphic,* where he served as editor-in-chief until 1878, resigning in that year because of interference by the owners. He had severed connections with the *Real Estate Record* in 1873 upon taking up his job with the *Graphic* and now after a two year lay-off from journalism and despite poor health he resumed his work with his friend Sweet. For the next nine years, up to a week before his death, he was the *Real Estate Record*'s chief editorial writer.

During these years Croly conducted a column for the *Record* under the heading of *Our Prophetic Department* and in 1872 attained a small-scale fame by predicting the crisis of the following year and naming Jay Cooke and Company and the Northern Pacific as the first victims.[100] In 1888, shortly before his death, most of these columns, edited and expanded, he collected into a book entitled *Glimpses of the Future.*[101] It is an interesting, if not greatly important book, and treats of everything under the sun in the author's typical pseudo-logical, hare-brained style.[102] On its opening pages Croly states that the "most serious difficulty in speculating as to the future is the liability to imagine Utopias. From the 'Republic' of Plato down to Edward Bellamy's 'Looking Backward,' all writers have indulged

98. D. G. Croly, *Campaign Lives of Seymour and Blair* (New York, 1868). The biography begins as follows: "In the compilation of this work I have had the following aims in view: . . . To deal honestly by my readers, making no unfair appeals to passion or prejudice, giving currency to no doubtful statements merely because they might damage the Republican party or its Candidates."

99. *Northern Monthly,* February 1868; *Galaxy,* November 1869.

100. John Howard Brown, ed., *Lamb's Biographical Dictionary of the United States* (Boston, 1900), II, 259.

101. David Goodman Croly, *Glimpses of the Future, Suggestions as to the Drift of Things* (New York, 1888).

102. It might be included as one of the flood of prophetic and Utopian volumes of the period. See Vernon Louis Parrington, Jr., *American Dreams, A Study of American Utopias* (Providence, 1947), which, however, neither discusses the volume nor lists it in the bibliography.

their fancy for ideal social states."[103] Some of the ideas promulgated in the dialogues of this book (with new anti-Semitic ideas thrown in) establish links with the racism of the *Miscegenation* hoax.[104]

103. *Glimpses of the Future*, 5.
104. In 1863 Croly had written: "The time is coming when Russian dominion will stretch to the Atlantic Ocean. Nor should such an event be dreaded. What the barbarians did for demoralized and degenerate Rome, the Russians will do for the effete and worn-out populations of Western Europe. These will be conquered. Their civilization, such as it is, will be overthrown; but the new infusion of a young and composite blood will regenerate the life of Europe, will give it a new and better civilization, because the German, French, Italian, Spanish, and English will be mixed with a miscegenetic and progressive people." (*Miscegenation*, 10) Twenty-four years later in *Glimpses of the Future* the same kind of prediction was made: "A great source of strength to the Russian power is its ability to absorb and assimilate the races it conquers. . . . The blending of races, which has been going on in Russia for three hundred years or longer, is something remarkable." (p. 35) That this is not the only traceable link may be seen by a few other racist quotations from *Glimpses*, which are here subjoined:

. . . We can absorb the Dominion . . . for the Canadians are of our own race . . . but Mexico, Central America, the Sandwich Islands, and the West India Islands will involve governments which cannot be democratic. We will never confer the right of suffrage upon the blacks, the mongrels of Mexico or Central America, or the Hawaiians." (pp. 22, 23.)
    The census of 1880 showing the disproportionate large increase of the blacks was a surprise, for the whites had the advantage of increase by foreign immigration, and it was supposed that the freed slaves would show a heavy mortality, in view of their habits and indifference to the well-being of their offspring. . . . I presume the race of mulatoes is dying out. Some few will intermingle with whites, but the bulk of them will become darker in hue as each generation passes by, for the irregular alliances between blacks and whites are not by any means as frequent under freedom as during slavery. Hence the dividing line between the two races will yearly become more marked. If the blacks left to themselves become as degraded as in the West India Islands, the time may come when they will be treated as badly as the Chinese and Red Indians are now, even to the extent of depriving them of their political privileges. Practically this is the case to-day over a large section of the South. The white race is dominant and will keep their position, no matter how numerous the negroes may become. (pp. 23, 24.)
    Mr. Newlight— . . . the doctrine of human rights applied to the whole human family does not work. Free institutions are only fitted for the Caucasian race, and have not proved workable, except among the English-speaking races.
    Sir Oracle— . . . The negro to-day is the same as he was at the time of Sesostris. He makes no progress except under the tutelage of the white. Left to himself he sinks back into barbarism, as witness Hayti.
    Mr. Newlight— . . . Froude shows that the West Indies are becoming barbarized; that any change which permits the blacks to dominate over the whites will end in the destruction of all civilization. . . . (pp. 133–134.)
    . . . There ought to be some agreement for organizing a system that will compel the savages of Africa to do some regular work. . . . Africa will never be redeemed, except in two ways: either the natives must be forced to work, or they must be killed off to give place for the races who will work. (p. 135.)
    . . . Cuba, Jamaica, and Hayti ought, in the fulness of time, to belong to the United States. But our people will not be willing to hand them over to the tender mercies of the degraded colored people in those islands. Universal suffrage is a farce when exercised by savages. . . . Everything is going to the dogs in those beautiful and fertile islands because

Croly's was the sensational type of journalistic mind that liked to claim "firsts." He boasted of "discovering" George Wakeman, G. A. Townsend, J. B. Stillson, A. C. Wheeler (Nym Crinkle), Clinton Stuart, H. E. Sweetser and St. Clair McKelway. He claimed to be one of the first to "bring before the American people prominently the matter of minority representation," on the basis developed by Hare and Mill, in his *Galaxy* article. He was proud of being one of the founders of the Real Estate Exchange, which displayed its flag at half-mast in his memory.[105] But he never boasted of his most lasting discovery—the word *miscegenation*.

The assessments of his mind and character made by his friends and relatives a few weeks after his death are interesting. The eulogia always contain reservations. "His faults were those of a nervous temperament, combined with great intellectual force, and a strength of feeling which in some directions and under certain circumstances became prejudices," wrote his wife, whose pen-name, Jennie June, had become a household word in the country and who had achieved an ampler fame of her own as a pioneer of the women's club movement in America.[106] "Mr. Croly won an honorable position in New York journalism," observed his brother-in-law, the Reverend John Cunningham. "He was a conservative democrat of the strictest sort, a radical in religion, and had but little appreciation of the deeper forces at work in society and in national life.[107]

Although Edmund C. Stedman praised him unqualifiedly, the memorial notices of many of Croly's former colleagues of the press were full of cutting reservations. Mr. Croly was "brought up in an atmosphere of politics," noted J. D. Bell. "His culture failed of being broad enough fully to tolerate differences of opinion. . . . In his utterances he was often very radical, but in his practice he was always thoroughly conservative. . . . All the arrangements that Mr. Croly made were thoroughly practical—suited to the time and occasion. He made the most of his opportunities." Croly had a "tendency to make one think of principles as a device rather than as a duty, of reforms as a hobby rather than as a mission, of opinions as assets in a schedule," observed St. Clair McKelway, who had joined the *World* in 1866 and later became editor of the Brooklyn *Daily Eagle*. "The man lived monogamy, voted Democracy, and believed Positivism."[108]

Yes, Croly believed positivism—and Copperhead racism, too. Eight years after his *Miscegenation* hoax, he dedicated his *Positivist Primer* to the "only supreme

of the progressive degradation of the free negroes. . . . So far as industry and civilization are concerned, the emancipation of the slaves in the West India Islands has proved disastrous in every way. (p. 137.)

105. *Real Estate Record & Builders Guide,* XLIII (May 4, 1889), 615–616.
106. *Real Estate Record & Builders Guide, Supplement,* XLIII (May 18, 1889), *passim.*
107. John Cunningham, D.D., "A Brother's Memories," in *Memories of Jane Cunningham Croly* (New York, 1904), 7.
108. *Real Estate Record & Builders Guide, Supplement,* XLIII (May 18, 1889), 702.

being man can ever know, The Great But Imperfect God, HUMANITY, In whose image all other Gods were made, And for whose service all other Gods exist, And to whom all the children of men owe Labor, Love, and Worship." Evidently, Comtean positivism, Croly's religion of humanity, was not broad enough to admit the Negro as equal.

THE "TRAGIC MULATTO" AND OTHER
THEMES OF INTERRACIAL LITERATURE

American Literary Tradition
and the Negro*

ALAIN LOCKE

I doubt if there exists any more valuable record for the study of the social history of the Negro in America than the naïve reflection of American social attitudes and their changes in the literary treatment of Negro life and character. More sensitively, and more truly than the conscious conventions of journalism and public debate, do these relatively unconscious values trace the fundamental attitudes of the American mind. Indeed, very often public professions are at utter variance with actual social practices, and in the matter of the Negro this variance is notably paradoxical. The statement that the North loves the Negro and dislikes Negroes, while the South hates the Negro but loves Negroes, is a crude generalization of the paradox, with just enough truth in it, however, to give us an interesting cue for further analysis. What this essay attempts must necessarily be a cursory preliminary survey: detailed intensive study of American social attitudes toward the Negro, using the changes of the literary tradition as clues, must be seriously undertaken later.

For a cursory survey, a tracing of the attitude toward the Negro as reflected in American letters gives us seven stages or phases, supplying not only an interesting cycle of shifts in public taste and interest, but a rather significant curve for social history. And more interesting perhaps than the attitudes themselves are the underlying issues and reactions of class attitudes and relationships which have been basically responsible for these attitudes. Moreover, instead of a single fixed attitude, sectionally divided and opposed, as the popular presumption goes, it will be seen that American attitudes toward the Negro have changed radically and often, with dramatic turns and with a curious reversal of rôle between the North and the South according to the class consciousness and interests dominant at any given time. With allowances for generalization, so far as literature records it, Negro life has run a gamut of seven notes,—heroics, sentiment, melodrama, comedy, farce, problem-discussion and æsthetic interest—as, in their respective turns, strangeness, domestic familiarity, moral controversy, pity, hatred, bewilderment, and curiosity, have dominated the public mind. Naturally, very few of these attitudes have been favorable to anything approaching adequate or even artistic portrayal; the Negro has been shunted from one stereotype into the other, but in this respect has been no more the sufferer than any other subject class, the particular brunt of whose servitude has always seemed to me to consist in the

* From Alain Locke, "American Literary Tradition and the Negro." *Modern Quarterly* 3.3 (May–July 1916): 215–222.

fate of having their psychological traits dictated to them. Of course, the Negro has been a particularly apt social mimic, and has assumed protective coloration with almost every change—thereby hangs the secret of his rather unusual survival. But of course a price has been paid, and that is that the Negro, after three hundred years of residence and association, even to himself, is falsely known and little understood. It becomes all the more interesting, now that we are verging for the first time on conditions admitting anything like true portraiture and self-portrayal to review in retrospect the conditions which have made the Negro traditionally in turn a dreaded primitive, a domestic pet, a moral issue, a ward, a scapegoat, a bogey and pariah, and finally what he has been all along, could he have been seen that way, a flesh and blood human, with nature's chronic but unpatented varieties.

Largely because Negro portraiture has rarely if ever run afoul of literary genius, these changes have rather automatically followed the trend of popular feeling, and fall almost into historical period stages, with very little overlapping. Roughly we may outline them as a Colonial period attitude (1760–1820), a pre-Abolition period (1820–45), the Abolitionist period (1845–65), the Early Reconstruction period (1870–85), the late Reconstruction period (1885–95), the Industrial period (1895–1920), and the Contemporary period since 1920. The constant occurrence and recurrence of the Negro, even as a minor figure, throughout this wide range is in itself an indication of the importance of the Negro as a social issue in American life, and of the fact that his values are not to be read by intrinsic but by extrinsic coefficients. He has dramatized constantly two aspects of white psychology in a projected and naïvely divorced shape—first, the white man's wish for self-justification, whether he be at any given time anti-Negro or pro-Negro, and, second, more subtly registered, an avoidance of the particular type that would raise an embarrassing question for the social conscience of the period; as, for example, the black slave rebel at the time when all efforts were being made after the abatement of the slave trade to domesticate the Negro; or the defeatist fiction types of 1895–1920, when the curve of Negro material progress took such a sharp upward rise. There is no insinuation that much of this sort of reflection has been as conscious or deliberately propagandist as is often charged and believed; it is really more significant as an expression of "unconscious social wish," for whenever there has been direct and avowed propaganda there has always been awakened a reaction in public attitude and a swift counter-tendency. Except in a few outstanding instances, literature has merely registered rather than moulded public sentiment on this question.

Through the Colonial days and extending as late as 1820, Negro life was treated as strange and distant. The isolated instances treat the Negro almost heroically, with an exotic curiosity that quite gaudily romanticized him. At that time, as in the more familiar romantic treatment of the American Indian, there was registered in the emphasis upon "savage traits" and strange ways a revulsion to his social assimilation. The typical figure of the period is a pure blood, often represented as a "noble captive," a type neither fully domesticated nor understood, and shows that far from being a familiar the Negro was rather a dreaded curiosity. Incidentally, this undoubtedly was a period of close association between the more domesticated Indian tribes and the Negroes—an almost forgotten chapter in the history of race relations in America which the heavy admixture of Indian blood in the Negro strain silently attests; so the association of the two in the public mind may have had more than casual grounds. Two of the most interesting features of this period are the frank concession of ancestry and lineage to the Negro at a time before the serious onset of miscegenation, and the hectic insistence upon Christian virtues and qualities in the Negro at a time when the Negro masses could not have been the model Christians they were represented to be, and which they did in fact become later. As James Oneal has pointed out in an earlier article, the notion of the boon of Christianity placated the bad conscience of the slave traders, and additionally at that time there was reason at least in the feeling of insecurity to sense that it was good social insurance to stress it.

By 1820 or 1825 the Negro was completely domesticated, and patriarchal relations had set in. The strange savage had become a sentimentally humored peasant. The South was beginning to develop its "aristocratic tradition," and the slave figure was the necessary foil of its romanticism. According to F. P. Gaines, "the plantation makes its first important appearance in American literature in John Pendleton Kennedy's *Swallow Barn* (1832) and William Carruther's *The Cavaliers of Virginia* (1834)." As one would expect, the really important figures of the régime are discreetly ignored,—the mulatto house servant concubine and her children; the faithful male body-servant, paradoxically enough, came in for a compensating publicity. In fact, the South was rapidly developing feudal intricacies and their strange, oft-repeated loyalties, and was actually on the verge of a golden age of romance when the shadow of scandal from Northern criticism darkened the high-lights of the whole régime and put the South on the defensive. It is a very significant fact that between 1845 and 1855 there should have appeared nearly a score of plays and novels on the subject of the quadroon girl and her tragic mystery, culminating in William Wells Brown's bold exposé *Clotel; or, The President's Daughter* (1853), as the caption of the unexpurgated English edition of this black Abolitionist's novel read. Southern romance was chilled to the marrow, and did not resume the genial sentimental approach to race characters for over a generation.

With the political issues of slave and free territory looming, and the moral issues of the Abolitionist controversy coming on, Negro life took on in literature the aspects of melodrama. The portraiture which had started was hastily dropped for exaggerated types representing polemical issues. The exaggerated tone was oddly enough set by the Negro himself, for long before *Uncle Tom's Cabin* (1852) the lurid slave narratives had set the pattern of Job-like suffering and melodramatic incident. Apart from its detailed dependence on Josiah Henson's actual story, Mrs. Stowe's novel simply capitalized a pattern of story and character already definitely outlined 1845–50, and in some exceptional anticipations ten years previous. Of course, with this period the vital portrayal of the Negro passed temporarily out of the hands of the South and became dominantly an expression of Northern interest and sentiment. In its controversial literature, naturally the South responded vehemently to the Abolitionist's challenge with the other side of the melodramatic picture,—the Negro as a brute and villain. But the formal retaliations of Reconstruction fiction were notably absent; except for a slight shift to the more docile type of Negro and peasant life further removed from the life of the "big house," G. P. James and others continued the mildly propagandist fiction of the patriarchal tradition,—an interesting indication of how the impending danger of the slave régime was minimized in the mass mind of the South. *Uncle Tom's Cabin*, of course, passes as the acme of the literature of the Abolitionist period, and it is in relation to its influence upon the issues involved. But as far as literary values go, *Clotel* by Wells Brown and *The Garies and Their Friends* by Frank J. Webb were closer studies both of Negro character and of the Negro situation. Their daring realism required them to be published abroad, and they are to be reckoned like the Paris school of Russian fiction as the forerunners of the native work of several generations later. Especially Webb's book, with its narrative of a sophisticated and cultured group of free Negroes, was in its day a bold departure from prevailing conventions. Either of these books would have been greater still had it consciously protested against the melodramatic stereotypes then in public favor; but the temptation to cater to the vogue of *Uncle Tom's Cabin* was perhaps too great. The sensational popularity of the latter, and its influence upon the public mind, is only another instance of the effect of a great social issue to sustain melodrama as classic as long as the issue lives. The artistic costs of all revolutions and moral reforms is high.

The Early Reconstruction period supplied the inevitable sentimental reaction to the tension of the war period. The change to sentimental genre is quite understandable. If the South could have resumed the portrayal of its life at the point where controversy had broken in, there would be a notable Southern literature today. But the South was especially prone to sugar-coat the slave régime in a protective reaction against the exposures of the Abolitionist literature. Northern fiction in works like the novels of Albion Tourgee continued its incriminations, and Southern literature became more and more propagandist. At first it was only in a secondary sense derogatory of the Negro; the primary aim was self-justification and romantic day-dreaming about the past. In the effort to glorify the lost tradition and balm the South's inferiority complex after the defeat, Uncle Tom was borrowed back as counter-propaganda, refurbished as the devoted, dependent, happy, care-free Negro, whom the South had always loved and protected, and whom it knew "better than he knew himself." The protective devices of this fiction, the accumulative hysteria of self-delusion associated with its promulgation, as well as the comparatively universal acceptance of so obvious a myth, form one of the most interesting chapters in the entire history of social mind. There is no denying the effectiveness of the Page-Cable school of fiction as Southern propaganda. In terms of popular feeling it almost recouped the reverses of the war. The North, having been fed only on stereotypes, came to ignore the Negro in any intimate or critical way through the deceptive influence of those very stereotypes. At least, these figures Southern fiction painted were more convincingly human and real, which in my judgment accounted in large part for the extraordinary ease with which the Southern version of the Negro came to be accepted by the Northern reading public, along with the dictum that the South knows the Negro.

But the false values in the situation spoiled the whole otherwise promising school—Chandler Harris excepted—as a contrast of the later work of Cable or Page with their earlier work will convincingly show. Beginning with good genre drawing that had the promise of something, they ended in mediocre chromographic romanticism. Though the genteel tradition never fully curdled into hatred, more and more hostilely it focussed upon the Negro as the scapegoat of the situation. And then came a flood of flagrantly derogatory literature as the sudden rise of figures like Thomas Dixon, paralleling the Vardamans and Tillmans of political life, marked the assumption of the master-class tradition by the mass psychology of the "poor-whites." Reconstruction fiction thus completed the swing made quite inevitable by the extreme arc of Abolitionist literature: the crudities and animus of the one merely countered the bathos and bias of the other. In both periods the treatment of Negro life was artistically unsatisfactory, and subject to the distortions of sentiment, propaganda, and controversy. The heavy artillery of this late Reconstruction attack has shambled its own guns; but the lighter fusillade of farce still holds out and still harasses those who stand guard over the old controversial issues. But the advance front of creative effort and attack has moved two stages further on.

As a result of the discussion of the Late Reconstruction period "White Supremacy" had become more than a slogan of the Southern chauvinists; it became a mild general social hysteria, which gave an almost biological significance to the race problem. It is interesting to note how suddenly the "problem of miscegenation" became important at a time when there was less of it than at any period within a century and a quarter, and how the mulatto, the skeleton in the family closet, suddenly was trotted out for attention and scrutiny. From 1895 or so on, this problem was for over a decade a veritable obsession; and from William Dean Howells' *Imperative Duty* to Stribling's *Birthright* the typical and dominant figure of literary interest is the mulatto as a symbol of social encroachment, and the fear of some "atavism of blood" through him wreaking vengeance for slavery. While serious literature was discussing the mulatto and his problem, less serious literature was in a sub-conscious way no less seriously occupied with the negative side of the same problem;—namely, extolling the unambitious, servile, and "racially characteristic" Negro who in addition to presenting diverting humor represented no serious social competition or encroachment. The public mind of the whole period was concentrated on the Negro "in" and "out of his place"; and the pseudo-scientific popularizations of evolutionism added their belabored corollaries. But the real basic proposition underlying it all was the sensing for the first time of the serious competition and rivalry of the Negro's social effort and the failure of his social handicaps to effectively thwart it.

Many will be speculating shortly upon the reasons for the literary and artistic emancipation of the Negro, at a time when his theme seemed most hopelessly in the double grip of social prejudice and moral Victorianism. Of course, realism had its share in the matter; the general reaction away from types was bound to reach even the stock Negro stereotypes. Again, the local color fad and the naturally exotic tendencies of conscious æstheticism gave the untouched field of Negro life

an attractive lure. The gradual assertion of Negro artists trying at first to coun-
teract the false drawing and values of popular writers, but eventually in the few
finer talents motivated by the more truly artistic motives of self-expression, played
its additional part. But in my judgment the really basic factor in the sharp and
astonishing break in the literary tradition and attitude toward the Negro came in
the revolt against Puritanism. This seems to me to explain why current literature
and art are for the moment so preoccupied with the primitive and pagan and
emotional aspects of Negro life and character; and why suddenly something almost
amounting to infatuation has invested the Negro subject with interest and fascination. The release which almost everyone had thought must come about through
a change in moral evaluation, a reform of opinion, has actually and suddenly come
about merely as a shift of interest, a revolution of taste. From it there looms the
imminent possibility not only of a true literature of the Negro but of a Negro
Literature as such. It becomes especially interesting to watch whether the artistic
possibilities of these are to be realized, since thrice before this social issues have
scotched the artistic potentialities of Negro life, and American literature is thereby
poorer in the fields of the historical romance, the period novel, and great problem-
drama than it should be. But the work of Waldo Frank, Jean Toomer, Walter
White, Rudolph Fisher, and Du Bose Heyward promises greatly; and if we call
up the most analogous case as a basis of forecast,—the tortuous way by which
the peasant came into Russian literature and the brilliant sudden transformation
his advent eventually effected, we may predict, for both subject and its creative
exponents, the Great Age of this particular section of American life and strand
in the American experience.

From "Negro Character as Seen by White Authors"*

STERLING A. BROWN

The Brute Negro

> *All Scientific Investigation of the Subject Proves the Negro
> to Be An Ape."*
>
> Chas. Carroll, *The Negro a Beast*

Because the pro-slavery authors were anxious to prove that slavery had been a
benefit to the Negro in removing him from savagery to Christianity, the stereotype
of the "brute Negro" was relatively insignificant in antebellum days. There were
references to vicious criminal Negroes in fiction (vicious and criminal being syn-

* From Sterling A. Brown, "Negro Character as Seen by White Authors." *Journal of Negro Education*
2 (1933): 179–203; here 191–196.

onymous to discontented and refractory), but these were considered as exceptional cases of half-wits led astray by abolitionists. *The Bible Defence of Slavery*, however, in which the Rev. Priest in a most unclerical manner waxes wrathful at abolitionists, sets forth with a great array of theological argument and as much ridiculousness, proofs of the Negro's extreme lewdness. Sodom and Gomorrah were destroyed because these were strongholds of *Negro* vice. The book of Leviticus proved that *Negroes*

> outraged all order and decency of human society. Lewdness of the most hideous description was the crime of which they were guilty, blended with idolatry in their adoration of the gods, who were carved out of wood, painted and otherwise made, so as to represent the wild passions of lascivious desires. . . . The baleful fire of unchaste amour rages through the negro's blood more fiercely than in the blood of any other people . . . on which account they are a people who are suspected of being but little acquainted with the virtue of chastity, and of regarding very little the marriage oath.[1]

H. R. Helper, foe of slavery, was no friend of the Negro, writing, in 1867, *Nojoque*, a lurid condemnation of the Negro, setting up black and beastly as exact synonyms. Van Evrie's *White Supremacy and Negro Subordination, or Negroes A Subordinate Race, and (so-called) Slavery Its Normal Condition* gave "anthropological" support to the figment of the "beastly Negro," and *The Negro A Beast* (1900) gave theological support. The title page of this book runs:

> The Reasoner of the Age, the Revelator of the Century! The Bible As It Is! The Negro and his Relation to the Human Family! The Negro a beast, but created with articulate speech, and hands, that he may be of service to his master—the White Man . . . by Chas. Carroll, who has spent 15 years of his life and $20,000.00 in its compilation.

Who could ask for anything more?

Authors stressing the mutual affection between the races looked upon the Negro as a docile mastiff. In the Reconstruction this mastiff turned into a mad dog. "Damyanks," carpetbaggers, scalawags, and New England schoolmarms affected him with the rabies. The works of Thomas Nelson Page are good examples of this metamorphosis. When his Negro characters are in their place, loyally serving and worshipping ole Marse, they are admirable creatures, but in freedom they are beasts, as his novel *Red Rock* attests. *The Negro: The Southerner's Problem* says that the state of the Negro since emancipation is one of minimum progress and maximum regress.

> [This] is borne out by the increase of crime among them, by the increase of superstition, with its black trail of unnamable immorality and vice; by the homicides and murders, and by the outbreak and growth of that brutal crime which has chiefly brought about the frightful crime of lynching which stains the *good name of the South* and has spread northward with the spread of the ravisher. . . . The crime of rape . . . is the fatal product of new conditions. . . . The

---

1. Josiah Priest, *Bible Defence of Slavery*, Glasgow, Ky.: W. S. Brown, 1851, eighth section.

Negro's passion, always his controlling force, is now, since the new teaching, for the white woman. [Lynching is justifiable] for it has its root deep in the basic passions of humanity; the determination to put an end to the *ravishing of their women by an inferior race*, or by any race, no matter what the consequence. . . . A crusade has been preached against lynching, even as far as England; but none has been attempted against the ravishing and tearing to pieces of white women and children.[2]

The best known author of Ku Klux Klan fiction after Page is Thomas Dixon. Such works as *The Clansman*, and *The Leopard's Spots*, because of their sensationalism and chapter titles (e.g., "The Black Peril," "The Unspoken Terror," "A Thousand Legged Beast," "The Hunt for the Animal"), seemed just made for the mentality of Hollywood, where D. W. Griffith's in *The Birth of a Nation* made for Thomas Dixon a dubious sort of immortality, and finally fixed the stereotype in the mass-mind. The stock Negro in Dixon's books, unless the shuffling hat-in-hand servitor, is a gorilla-like imbecile, who "springs like a tiger" and has the "black claws of a beast." In both books there is a terrible rape, and a glorious ride of the Knights on a Holy Crusade to avenge Southern civilization. Dixon enables his white geniuses to discover the identity of the rapist by using "a microscope of sufficient power [to] reveal on the retina of the dead eyes the image of this devil as if etched there by fire." . . . The doctor sees "The bestial figure of a negro—his huge black hand plainly defined. . . . It was Gus." Will the wonders of science never cease? But, perhaps, after all, Negroes have been convicted on even flimsier evidence. Fortunately for the self-respect of American authors, this kind of writing is in abeyance today. Perhaps it fell because of the weight of its own absurdity. But it would be unwise to underestimate this stereotype. It is probably of great potency in certain benighted sections where Dixon, if he could be read, would be applauded—and it certainly serves as a convenient self-justification for a mob about to uphold white supremacy by a lynching.

The Tragic Mulatto

> *The gods bestow on me*
> *A life of hate,*
> *The white man's gift to see*
> *A nigger's fate.*
>
> "The Mulatto Addresses his Savior
> on Christmas Morning,"
> Seymour Gordden Link

Stereotyping was by no means the monopoly of pro-slavery authors defending their type of commerce, or justifying their ancestors. Anti-slavery authors, too,

---

2. Thomas Nelson Page, *The Negro: The Southerner's Problem*. New York: Chas. Scribners' Sons, 1904. (Italics mine).

fell into the easy habit, but with a striking difference. Where pro-slavery authors had predicated a different set of characteristics for the Negroes, a distinctive sub-human nature, and had stereotyped in accordance with such a comforting hypothesis, anti-slavery authors insisted that the Negro had a common humanity with the whites, that in given circumstances a typically human type of response was to be expected, unless certain other powerful influences were present. The stereotyping in abolitionary literature, therefore, is not stereotyping of *character*, but of *situation*. Since the novels were propagandistic, they concentrated upon abuses: floggings, the slave mart, the domestic slave trade, forced concubinage, runaways, slave hunts, and persecuted freemen—all of these were frequently repeated. Stereotyped or not, heightened if you will, the anti-slavery novel has been supported by the verdict of history—whether recorded by Southern or Northern historians. Facts, after all, are abolitionist. Especially the fact that the Colonel's lady and old Aunt Dinah are sisters under the skin.

Anti-slavery authors did at times help to perpetuate certain pro-slavery stereotypes. Probably the novelists knew that harping upon the gruesome, to the exclusion of all else, would repel readers, who—like their present-day descendants—yearn for happy endings and do not wish their quick consciences to be harrowed. At any rate, comic relief, kindly masters (in contrast to the many brutes), loyal and submissive slaves (to accentuate the wrongs inflicted upon them) were scattered throughout the books. Such tempering of the attacks was turned to pro-slavery uses. Thus, Harris writes:

> It seems to me to be impossible for any unprejudiced person to read Mrs. Stowe's book and fail to see in it a defence of American slavery as she found it in Kentucky. . . . The real moral that Mrs. Stowe's book teaches is that the possibilities of slavery . . . are shocking to the imagination, while the realities, under the best and happiest conditions, possess a romantic beauty and a tenderness all their own.[3]

Anti-slavery fiction did proffer one stereotype, doomed to unfortunate longevity. This is the tragic mulatto. Pro-slavery apologists had almost entirely omitted (with so many other omissions) mention of concubinage. If anti-slavery authors, in accordance with Victorian gentility, were wary of illustrating the practice, they made great use nevertheless of the offspring of illicit unions. Generally the heroes and heroines of their books are near-whites. These are the intransigent, the resentful, the mentally alert, the proofs of the Negro's possibilities. John Herbert Nelson says with some point:

> Abolitionists tried, by making many of their characters almost white, to work on racial feeling as well. This was a curious piece of inconsistency on their part, an indirect admission that a white man in chains was more pitiful to behold than the African similarly placed. Their most impassioned plea was in behalf of a person little resembling their swarthy protegés, the quadroon or octoroon.[4]

3. Julia Collier Harris, *Joel Chandler Harris, Editor and Essayist,* Chapel Hill: University of North Carolina Press, 1931, p. 117.
4. John Herbert Nelson, *The Negro Character in American Literature,* Lawrence, Kan.: Department of Journalism Press, 1926, p. 84.

Nelson himself, however, shows similar inconsistency, as he infers that the "true African—essentially gay, happy-go-lucky, rarely ambitious or idealistic, the eternal child of the present moment, able to leave trouble behind—is unsuited for such portrayal. . . . Only the mulattoes and others of mixed blood have, so far, furnished us with material for convincing tragedy."[5]

The tragic mulatto appears in both of Mrs. Stowe's abolitionary novels. In *Uncle Tom's Cabin*, the fugitives Liza and George Harris and the rebellious Cassy are mulattoes. Uncle Tom, the pure black, remains the paragon of Christian submissiveness. In *Dred*, Harry Gordon and his wife are nearly white. Harry is an excellent manager, and a proud, unsubmissive type:

> Mr. Jekyl, that humbug don't go down with me! I'm no more of the race of Ham than you are! I'm Colonel Gordon's oldest son—as white as my brother, who you say owns me! Look at my eyes, and my hair, and say if any of the rules about Ham pertain to me.[6]

The implication that there are "rules about Ham" that do pertain to blacks is to be found in other works. Richard Hildreth's *Archy Moore, or The White Slave*, has as its leading character a fearless, educated mulatto, indistinguishable from whites; Boucicault's *The Octoroon* sentimentalizes the hardships of a slave girl; both make the mixed blood the chief victim of slavery.

Cable, in the *Grandissimes*, shows a Creole mulatto educated beyond his means, and suffering ignominy, but he likewise shows in the character of Bras-Coupè that he does not consider intrepidity and vindictiveness the monopoly of mixed-bloods. In *Old Creole Days*, however, he discusses the beautiful octoroons, whose best fortune in life was to become the mistress of some New Orleans dandy. He shows the tragedy of their lives, but undoubtedly contributed to the modern stereotype that the greatest yearning of the girl of mixed life is for a white lover. Harriet Martineau, giving a contemporary portrait of old New Orleans, wrote:

> The quadroon girls . . . are brought up by their mothers to be what they have been; the mistresses of white gentlemen. The boys are some of them sent to France; some placed on land in the back of the State. . . . The women of their own color object to them, *"ils sont si degoutants!"*[7]

Lyle Saxon says that "the free men of color are always in the background; to use the Southern phrase, 'they know their place.' "

The novelists have kept them in the background. Many recent novels show this: *White Girl, The No-Nation Girl, A Study in Bronze, Gulf Stream, Dark Lustre*— all of these show luridly the melodrama of the lovely octoroon girl. Indeed "octoroon" has come to be a feminine noun in popular usage.

The stereotype that demands attention, however, is the notion of mulatto character, whether shown in male or female. This character works itself out with mathematical symmetry. The older theses ran: First, the mulatto inherits the vices

5. *Ibid.* p. 136.
6. Harriet Beecher Stowe, *Nina Gordon or Dred.* Boston: Houghton, Mifflin and Co., 1881, p. 142.
7. Quoted in Lyle Saxon, *Fabulous New Orleans.* New York: The Century Co., 1928, p. 182.

of both races and none of the virtues; second, any achievement of a Negro is to be attributed to the white blood in his veins. The logic runs that even inheriting the worst from whites is sufficient for achieving among Negroes. The present theses are based upon these: The mulatto is a victim of a divided inheritance; from his white blood come his intellectual strivings, his unwillingness to be a slave; from his Negro blood come his baser emotional urges, his indolence, his savagery.

Thus, in *The No-Nation Girl*, Evans Wall writes of his tragic heroine, Précieuse:

> Her dual nature had not developed its points of difference. The warring qualities, her double inheritance of Caucasian and black mingled in her blood, had not yet begun to disturb, and torture, and set her apart from either race. . . .
>
> [As a child,] Précieuse had learned to dance as soon as she could toddle about on her shapely little legs; half-savage little steps with strange movements of her body, exotic gestures and movements that had originated among the remote ancestors of her mother's people in some hot African jungle.
>
> . . . The wailing cry of the guitar was as primitive and disturbing as the beat of a tom-tom to dusky savages gathered for an orgy of dancing and passion in some moon-flooded jungle. . . . Self-control reached its limit. The girl's half-heritage of savagery rose in a flood that washed away all trace of her father's people except the supersensitiveness imparted to her taut nerves. She must dance or scream to relieve the rising torrent of response to the wild, monotonous rhythm.

It is not long before the girl is unable to repress, what Wall calls, the lust inherited from her mother's people; the environment of debauchery, violence, and rapine is exchanged for concubinage with a white paragon, which ends, of course, in the inevitable tragedy. The girl "had no right to be born."

Dark Lustre, by Geoffrey Barnes, transfers the main essentials of the foregoing plot to Harlem. Aline, of the darkly lustrous body, thus analyzes herself in accordance with the old clichés: "The black half of me is ashamed of itself for being there, and every now and then crawls back into itself and tries to let the white go ahead and pass." Says the author: "There was too much of the nigger in her to let her follow a line of reasoning when the black cloud of her emotions settled over it." Half-white equals reason; half-black equals emotion. She too finds her ideal knight in a white man, and death comes again to the tragic octoroon who should never have been born. *White Girl, Gulf Stream, A Study in Bronze* are in substance very similar to these.

Roark Bradford in *This Side of Jordan* gives an unconscious *reductio ad absurdum* of this stereotype.

> The blade of a razor flashed through the air. Scrap has concealed it in the folds of her dress. Her Negro blood sent it unerringly between two ribs. Her Indian blood sent it back for an unnecessary second and third slash.

It might be advanced that Esquimaux blood probably would have kept her from being chilled with horror. The strangest items are attributed to different racial strains: In *No-Nation Girl* a woman cries out in childbirth because of her Negro expressiveness; from the back of Précieuse's "ankles down to her heels, the flesh was slightly thicker"—due to her Negro blood; Lessie in Welbourn Kelley's *In-chin' Along* "strongly felt the urge to see people, to talk to people. . . . That was the white in her maybe. Or maybe it was the mixture of white and black."

This kind of writing should be discredited by its patent absurdity. It is generalizing of the wildest sort, without support from scientific authorities. And yet it has set these *idées fixes* in the mob mind: The Negro of unmixed blood is no theme for tragedy; rebellion and vindictiveness are to be expected only from the mulatto; the mulatto is victim of a divided inheritance and therefore miserable; he is a "man without a race" worshipping the whites and despised by them, despising and despised by Negroes, perplexed by his struggle to unite a white intellect with black sensuousness. The fate of the octoroon girl is intensified—the whole desire of her life is to find a white lover, and then go down, accompanied by slow music, to a tragic end. Her fate is so severe that in some works disclosure of "the single drop of midnight" in her veins makes her commit suicide.

The stereotype is very flattering to a race which, for all its self-assurance, seems to stand in great need of flattery. But merely looking at one of its particulars—that white blood means asceticism and Negro blood means unbridled lust—will reveal how flimsy the whole structure is. It is ingenious that mathematical computation of the amount of white blood in a mulatto's veins will explain his character. And it is a widely held belief. But it is nonsense, all the same.

The Mulatto in American Fiction*

PENELOPE BULLOCK

In its heterogenous population and the individualistic traits of its various inhabitants the United States possesses a reservoir teeming with literary potentiality. Throughout the years, the American writer has tapped these natural resources to bring forth products of value and interest. Even though the characters whom he has depicted are not always lasting literary creations, they are significant in that they are social and sociological indices. Wrought from American life, they reflect the temper of the times and the actualities and the attitudes surrounding their prototypes in life. One of these characters is the mulatto. In this study[1] the portrayal of the mulatto by the nineteenth-century American fictionist is presented.

Who and what is the mulatto? According to Webster, he is, in the strictly generic sense, ". . . the first generation offspring of a pure negro and a white." The popular, general conception is that he is a Negro with a very obvious admixture of white blood. (In this study the persons considered as mulattoes are selected as such on the basis of this definition.) But the sociologist more adequately describes the mulatto as a cultural hybrid, as a stranded personality living

* From Penelope Bullock. "The Mulatto in American Fiction." *Phylon* 6 (1945): 78–82.

1. This article is a summary of "The Treatment of the Mulatto in American Fiction from 1826 to 1902." Unpublished Master's thesis, Department of English, Atlanta University, 1944.

in the margin of fixed status. He is a normal biological occurrence but a sociological problem in the United States. In the brief span of one life he is faced with the predicament of somehow resolving within himself the struggle between two cultures and two "races" which over a period of three hundred years have not yet become completely compatible in American life.

Two hundred years after the Negro-white offspring became a member of the population of the United States he made his advent into the American novel. How was he portrayed by the nineteenth-century writer?

The treatment accorded the mulatto in fiction was conditioned to a very large extent by the social and historical background out of which the authors wrote. The majority of them wrote as propagandists defending an institution or pleading for justice for an oppressed group. In depicting their characters, these writers very seldom approached them as a sociologist, or a realist, or a literary artist. They wrote only as partisans in national political issues. They wrote as propagandists: they distorted facts and clothed them in sentiment; they did not attempt to perceive and present the truth impartially. The persons of mixed blood pictured by these authors appealed to the emotional, prejudiced masses. But they are not truthful re-creations of life and of living people. Only a minor number of nineteenth-century writers were concerned with the actual, personal problems which the mulatto had to face because of the circumstances of his social environment.

The first group of propagandists to portray the mixed-blood in fiction were the Abolitionist writers. Outstanding among them were Richard Hildreth; Harriet Beecher Stowe; the Negro author, William Wells Brown; W. W. Smith; J. T. Trowbridge; and H. L. Hosmer. Playing upon the race pride and sentiments of the Caucasian group, these novelists placed in the forefront the near-white victim of slavery and asked their readers: Can an institution which literally enslaves the sons and daughters of the dominant race be tolerated?

From their novels emerges in bold, simple outline a major, stereotyped figure. He is the son or daughter of a Southern white aristocratic gentleman and one of his favorite slave mistresses. From his father he has inherited mental capacities and physical beauty [of the] supposedly superior . . . white race. Yet despite such an endowment, or rather because of it, his life is fraught with tragedy. What privileges and opportunities he may enjoy are short-lived; for he is inevitably a slave. Suffering the degrading hardships of bondage, he becomes miserable and bitter. The indomitable spirit of his father rises up within him, and he rebels. If he is successful in escaping to freedom he becomes a happy, prosperous, and reputable citizen in his community. But even if his revolt against slavery fails, he meets his tragic death nobly and defiantly.

Following Emancipation, the era of Reconstruction brought the conflict between the Negro's assumption of rights which were legally his and the white man's continued monopoly of privileges. Here again was opportunity for the propagandist to take up his pen. And he did. This time, however, there were two groups of such writers, one representing each side of the issue. The pro-slavery writer had been silent concerning the mulatto, for miscegenation was a thrust at Southern society (although it was a phase of Northern life as well). But the white

Southerner now felt impelled to protect the lily-white South from the encroachment of the freed black man.

Representing the South in fiction were Thomas Nelson Page and Thomas Dixon, who pictured the mulatto as a dangerous element among the freedmen. Their sensational caricatures presented him as the despoiler of white womanhood, the corrupter of the white gentleman, and the usurper of political power. In *The Leopard's Spots* (1902) and *The Clansman* (1905), Dixon portrays three significant persons of mixed blood. Through George Harris, a Harvard graduate who wished to woo a white woman; Lydia Brown, the housekeeper and mistress of a radical Reconstruction leader in Congress, whose sinister influence over him threatens to ruin the nation; and Silas Lynch, a bestial brute, he exhorts the South to preserve its racial integrity and prevent future America from being mulatto.

On the other hand, the cause of the freedman was pleaded by such Negro novelists as Mrs. Frances E. W. Harper, Sutton E. Griggs, George L. Pryor, and Mrs. Pauline E. Hopkins. They were at variance in their portrayal of the mulatto. But they did agree that his duty is to ally himself with the Negro group and sincerely and unselfishly aid in the fight for race betterment. In Mrs. Harper's novel, *Iola Leroy; or Shadows Uplifted* (1892), every significant Negro is a mixed-blood who, indistinguishable from white, is confronted with the question: To pass or not to pass? Each is eventually identified as a Negro, thereby upholding the thesis of the novel, which is: the mulatto is a tragic person only because and only so long as he fails to cast his lot with the minority group. But once the shadows are uplifted, once he proudly admits that he is a Negro, he rises above his tragedy and dedicates himself to the cause of the dark American.

Paul Laurence Dunbar, a contemporary of the Negro authors named above, was an outstanding writer in his brief life; but his contribution to the depiction of the mulatto was negligible. His stories of Negro life show only fleeting glimpses of persons of mixed blood.

A facetious yet significant portrayal of the mulatto is given by Samuel L. Clemens in *Pudd'nhead Wilson* (1894). In this story a mulatto slave and a white boy are exchanged in their cradles and grow up in reversed positions without their real identity being detected. Clemens demonstrates that social environment can discount parentage and legal edict in determining one's "racial allegiance." If in his formative years a mulatto has innocently lived as a white person, the discovery of his mixed blood cannot suddenly transform him into a Negro.

Such truth-penetrating analysis of the mulatto character as that by Clemens is rare in nineteenth-century fiction. The authors generally utilized him as an instrument for a cause—the abolition of slavery, a lily-white South, an equality of opportunity and rights for Negro and white citizen alike. There were, however, exceptions to the rule. There were writers to whom the mulatto himself was the cause. They were concerned with him as a human being living in a complex and paradoxical environment. These writers were A. W. Tourgee, a white Northerner; George W. Cable, a white Southerner; and Charles W. Chesnutt, a Northern Negro. In their approach to the mixed-blood they brought keen analysis, sympathetic interpretation, and sometimes literary artistry.

Tourgee portrayed the mulatto in two of his novels, *The Royal Gentleman* (1881) and *Pactolus Prime* (1890). Indicative of the understanding which he shows in his depiction of his subject is an incident described in the latter novel. A young girl lives as a white person until, on the eve of her father's death, she learns that he is a Negro. Realizing her situation, she cries out in agony to her father's lawyer. The lawyer is deeply moved by her reaction:

> It was the first time that he had ever realized the process through which the intelligent young colored American must always go, before our Christian civilization reduces him finally to his proper level of "essential inferiority."[2]

Here Tourgee shows that he is aware of a fundamental truth: the problem of the mulatto is to a very large degree but the problem of all Negroes—the desire for full and unqualified membership and participation in American society and culture.

Cable's convincing delineation of the *gens de couleur* of Louisiana and their peculiar juxtaposition in society was guided by intimate acquaintance with his subject and a sympathy that was neither gushingly sentimental nor politically partisan. Madame Delphine in the short story of the same name and Palmyre and Honore Grandissime, free man of color, in *The Grandissimes* (1880) are tragic mulattoes. Cable, however, took his characters not from the stereotypes of previous literature but from life; and he developed them into three-dimensional characters. As Pattee says, "They are true to the fundamentals of human life, they are alive, they satisfy, and they are presented ever with an exquisite art." Cable's sympathetic attitude toward the mixed-blood is expressed through one of the white characters in *The Grandissimes* (pp. 184–85):

> Emancipation before the law . . . is to them [mixed-bloods] little more than a mockery until they achieve emancipation in the minds and good will of all . . . the ruling class.[3]

Chesnutt was the outstanding delineator of the Negro-white offspring at the turn of the century. Exhibiting an obvious predilection for the mulatto character, Chesnutt gives him a prominent place in most of his short stories and novels. In *The House Behind the Cedars* (1900), the psychological analysis of the reactions of John and Rena to their situations as mixed-bloods indistinguishable from white probes deeply into the minds of these characters and lays bare the thoughts which were fermenting there. Rena believes that it is wrong to live under a veil of concealment when such an important issue as marriage is involved and finally decides that it is her duty to dedicate her life to the uplift of the downtrodden Negro. John's attitude is in direct contrast:

> Once persuaded that he had certain rights or ought to have them, by virtue of the laws of nature, in defiance of the customs of mankind, he had promptly sought

---

2. A. W. Tourgee, *Pactolus Prime* (New York, 1890), p. 206.

3. "The Short Story," *Cambridge History of American Literature*. Edited by W. P. Trent and others (New York, 1933), II, 384.

to enjoy them. This he had been able to do by simply concealing his antecedents and making the most of his opportunities, with no troublesome qualms of conscience whatever.[4]

Himself a near-white, Chesnutt was keenly sensitive to the position of the mulatto in American life and creates characters convincing in their realism.

The portrayals of the mixed-blood by Cable and Chesnutt are the outstanding delineations of this character in nineteenth-century American fiction. To his disadvantage the mulatto entered fiction, at the pen of the advocate of Abolition, as an instrument of propaganda. Unfortunately, the majority of his succeeding portrayers were also zealous partisans of some cause, in whom were lacking the tempering and subtly interpretive attributes of the sociologist and the literary artist. Thus a series of types emerged—such as the beautiful but ill-fated victim of injustice and the extremely race-conscious leader of the minority group—and these patterns of portrayal developed into stereotypes. In the treatment of the mixed-blood the broad outline of actuality was sketched, but seldom was reality re-created. Rarely did the nineteenth-century writer probe beneath the surface to ascertain the truth underlying the fact and the cause effecting the result.

With the literary production of Chesnutt, however, the portrayal of the mulatto in the nineteenth century ends on a redemptive note and gives hope for a promising characterization in twentieth-century literature. Since 1900, inter-racial attitudes have become more intelligent and tolerant, and those members of American society who may be maladjusted have been given more humane consideration. The American fictionist has brought forth a quality of writing dealing with the mixed-blood during this period. The quality of the treatment thus accorded this character remains to be appraised.

The "Tragic Octoroon" in Pre–Civil War Fiction*

JULES ZANGER

One of the most important characters of pre–Civil War Abolitionist fiction was the "tragic octoroon." Presented first in the earliest antislavery novel, *The Slave* (1836), the character appeared in more than a dozen other works.[1] By the time

---

4. C. W. Chesnutt, *The House Behind the Cedars* (Boston, 1900), p. 78.

* From Jules Zanger, "The Tragic Octoroon' in Pre–Civil War Fiction." *American Quarterly* 18 (1966): 63–70.

1. Among the most readily available of these works are R. Hildreth, *The Slave* (1836); J. H. Ingraham, *Quadroone* (1840); H. W. Longfellow, *The Quadroon Girl* (1842); Mrs. E. D. E. N. Southworth, *Retribution* (1840); E. C. Pierson, *Cousin Franck's Household* (1842); H. B. Stowe, *Uncle Tom's Cabin* (1852); W. W. Brown, *Clotel, or the President's Daughter* (1853); Mary Langdon, *Ida May* (1855); W. W. Smith, *The Planter's Victim* (1855); J. T. Trowbridge, *Neighbor Jackwood* (1856); H. B. Stowe, *Dred, A Tale of the Dismal Swamp* (1856); Mayne Reid, *The Quadroon* (1856); J. S. Peacocke,

the most important of these works—*Uncle Tom's Cabin* and *The Octoroon*—were written, the character had acquired certain stereotypic qualities and had come to appear in certain stereotypic situations.

Briefly summarized, the "tragic octoroon" is a beautiful young girl who possesses only the slightest evidences of Negro blood, who speaks with no trace of dialect, who was raised and educated as a white child and as a lady in the household of her father, and who on her paternal side is descended from "some of the best blood in the 'Old Dominion.' " In her sensibility and her vulnerability she resembles, of course, the conventional ingenue "victim" of sentimental romance. Her condition is radically changed when, at her father's unexpected death, it is revealed that he has failed to free her properly. She discovers that she is a slave; her person is attached as property by her father's creditors. Sold into slavery, she is victimized, usually by a lower-class, dialect-speaking slave dealer or overseer—often, especially after the Fugitive Slave Act, a Yankee—who attempts to violate her; she is loved by a high-born young Northerner or European who wishes to marry her. Occasionally she escapes with her lover; more often, she dies a suicide, or dies of shame, or dies protecting her young gentleman.

Although the melodramatic and titillating aspects of this plot are evident, it is specifically the implied or articulated criticism of the institution of slavery that makes the "tragic octoroon" situation so interesting. The octoroon, by her beauty, by her gentility and by her particular vulnerability to sexual outrage, offered to pre–Civil War Northern audiences, accustomed to idealized and sentimentalized heroines, a perfect object for tearful sympathy combined with moral indignation.

To twentieth-century literary historians, the attack on slavery directed by the creators of the "tragic octoroon" appears thin, unrealistic and irrelevant. Modern critics point out that the octoroon situation, while possible, was hardly general and that, while enforced concubinage was a Southern reality, it was hardly the paramount evil of slavery. Further, the tendency of antislavery authors to see the plight of the slave in terms of the octoroon rather than in terms of the full-blooded black has been seen as an indication of racial prejudice.

Bone, for example, writes, "Such novels . . . contain mulatto characters for whom the reader's sympathies are aroused less because they are colored than because they are nearly white." Gloster describes the anti-slavery writers as "sympathetic toward the Negro-white hybrid because of his possession of Caucasian blood, which they often consider a factor that automatically made this character the superior of the darker Negro and therefore a more pitiable individual." Sterling Brown describes the octoroon as "a concession, unconscious perhaps, to race snobbishness even among abolitionists."[2]

The Creole Orphans (1856); V. B. Denslow, *Owned and Disowned* (1857); D. Boucicault, *The Octoroon* (1859); H. S. Hosmer, *Adela the Octoroon* (1860); M. V. Victor, *Maum Guinea's Children* (1861).

2. Robert A. Bone, *The Negro Novel in America* (New Haven, 1958), pp. 22–23; Hugh M. Gloster, *Negro Voices in American Fiction* (Chapel Hill, N.C., 1948), pp. 12, 17; Sterling Brown, *The Negro in American Fiction* (Washington, D.C., 1937), p. 45.

Certainly, the strategy of the octoroon plot was to win sympathy for the anti-slavery cause by displaying a cultivated, "white" sensibility threatened by, and responding to, a "black" situation. It was the octoroon's "white" characteristics which made her pathetic to the white audience—and, consequently, the writers of "tragic octoroon" stories have generally been accused of making their attack not on the institution of Negro slavery, but only on certain particular and incidental injustices arising from the institution of slavery.

Southern apologists have interpreted the "tragic octoroon" figure as corroborating their own theories of white superiority, insisting that only slaves of mixed blood were ever unhappy and that the unhappiness of these was due solely to their white blood. Even such an indefatigable romanticizer of slavery as Mrs. E. D. E. N. Southworth was able to present the pathos of the "tragic octoroon" in Henny of *Retribution*. The tactic of the Southern apologists has been to concede the possibility of the octoroon situation, but to dismiss the octoroon figure, whether female and tragic or male and heroic, as being unrepresentative of "the happy-go-lucky, ignorant, coon-hunting, fun-loving field hand who, more than any other class of slave, typified the great mass of black men throughout the South."[3]

The tendency of modern pro-Negro commentators has been to judge the writers of "tragic octoroon" stories on the grounds of the validity or comprehensiveness of the picture they painted of the Negro in slavery; on these grounds, naturally, the octoroon plot has been found wanting. This judgment, though a just one as far as it goes, has had one unfortunate result: the effectiveness of the conventional octoroon as part of the antislavery arsenal has been belittled. In reaction to the Southern reading of the "tragic octoroon" as a corroboration of Southern race theories, Northern critics have dismissed her and have accused her creators of being racist snobs. It is interesting that when Sterling Brown, a Negro critic, attacks the tragic octoroon as evidence of racial snobbery, he writes: "As one critic says: 'This was an indirect admission that a white man in chains was more pitiful to behold than the African similarly placed. Their most impassioned plea was in behalf of a person little resembling their swarthy proteges.' "[4] The "one critic" he is quoting is J. H. Nelson, an extreme Southern apologist, and the quotation comes from the same book as does the "fun-loving, coon-hunting" passage quoted above.

The charge—that the abolitionist author's motive amounts to no more than a concession to racism—fails to take into account the overriding and avowed purpose of the abolitionist author, the propagandistic intention. What is particularly interesting about the "tragic octoroon" plot is that it revealed the point at which the imagination and sympathy of the pre–Civil War Northern public could be won for the antislavery cause; this is precisely what has been obscured by the oversimplified and unfair view that the octoroon's appeal was based purely upon racial hypocrisy in author and audience.

3. J. H. Nelson, *The Negro Character in American Fiction* (Lawrence, Kans., 1926), pp. 83–84.
4. Brown, p. 45.

Specifically, it should be recognized that the appeal of the "tragic octoroon" situation was not based primarily upon a racially snobbish feeling that a white person in chains was more pathetic than a black one. Rather, the plight of the octoroon evoked a number of widely differing, though related, responses from Northern audiences.

First, the "tragic octoroon" situation flattered the Northern audience in its sense of self-righteousness, confirming its belief in the moral inferiority of the South. The octoroon, to the North, represented not merely the product of the incidental sin of the individual sinner, but rather what might be called the result of cumulative institutional sin, since the octoroon was the product of four [*sic*] generations of illicit, enforced miscegenation made possible by the slavery system. The very existence of the octoroon convicted the slaveholder of prostituting his slaves and of selling his own children for profit. Thus, the choice of the octoroon rather than of the full-blooded black to dramatize the suffering of the slave not only emphasized the pathos of the slave's condition but, more importantly, emphasized the repeated pattern of guilt of the Southern slaveholder. The whiter the slave, the more undeniably was the slaveholder guilty of violating the terms of the stewardship which apologists postulated in justifying slavery. The octoroon became the visible sign of an incremental sin, the roots of which could be seen by Northern audiences as particularly and pervasively Southern. If the "tragic octoroon" plot passed lightly over the suffering of the black field hand, it nevertheless made up for this deficiency by the intensity of its condemnation of his white master. Seen in this light, it might be said that the pre–Civil War popularity of the "tragic octoroon" foreshadowed the North's post–Civil War eagerness to punish the former slaveholder and its relative reluctance to help the former slave.

The accusations against the Southern slaveholder implicit in the plot of the "tragic octoroon" were of major significance in the propaganda war carried on between abolitionist and proslavery writers. Proslavery writers, finding the Yankee assumption of moral superiority unbearable, replied to abolitionist pictures of the horrors of life in the field hands' quarters with pictures of the horrors of life in Northern mill towns. While such "you're another!" arguments are hardly acceptable as defenses of slavery on the rational level, they might have been a more valuable counter-propaganda device if it were not for the availability to the abolitionists of the purely Southern "tragic octoroon" situation.

Certainly, one of the strong motives to which the abolitionists appealed in their attempt to win converts was the motive of self-righteousness. In the octoroon, the antislavery propagandists had an appeal to this Northern sense of superior morality that could not so easily be met by an admonition to "put thine own house in order." While little children up in the Northern cotton mills might slave themselves into pathetically early graves, the Northern mill owner never sold his own daughters into a life of shame, as was clearly the custom down in the Southern cotton fields. The charge of sexual looseness was a serious one in that period; not only in fiction, but in their pamphlets and exhortations, the abolitionists brought that charge again and again—and every light-skinned slave was tangible evidence for the prosecution. Wendell Phillips, for example, called the South "One great brothel, where half a million women are flogged to prostitution," and George

Bourne spoke of the South as a "vast harem where men-stealers may prowl, corrupt, and destroy."

Another particular appeal, apart from the moral, made by the "tragic octoroon" results from the way in which the octoroon situation imaginatively involves the audience in the tragedy of the heroine. Central to the stereotyped plot is the element of reversal whereby the heroine is suddenly reduced, by a legalism, against all evidence of the senses, from aristocratic, pampered white heiress to Negro slave—from riches to worse than rags. This, of course, is the stuff of nightmare, but a nightmare with particular significance for the nineteenth-century American whose own family history might very likely be so obscured by immigration and migration, by settlement and resettlement, that any detailed knowledge of the blood lines of great-grandparents could well be unavailable.

The presentation of the perils faced by the octoroon can be seen, then, on the very simplest and most naive level, as a sort of scare tactic: how do you know they won't be coming after *you* next?

Even in those stories which cannot be said to make this simple appeal, stories in which the octoroon is already aware of her mixed blood, the element of reversal served to involve the audience in the tragedy of the heroine. On the imaginative level, at least, each witness to the octoroon's tragedy was threatened by a similar fate, by the sudden reversal of fortune that was so much a part of the American experience, and the ironic underside of the American dream. The particular discovery which precipitates the fall of the helpless young female, with her fine and tasteful clothes, her cultured speech, her garden full of flowers, was still the same sort of discovery which threatened to destroy the middle-class young white lady of the audience: her father is suddenly bankrupt; her father has died, leaving mountainous debts. In an age when women of the middle class were nearly as dependent upon the head of the household as the poor octoroon was upon her master-father, the antislavery propagandist could draw upon the audience's own dread of the life they would face if the bank failed, the tariff were defeated, the speculation fizzled.

Expressed this way, it becomes clear that the octoroon permits the audience to identify with her, not merely on the superficial level of her color, but more profoundly in terms of the radical reversal of fortune she has suffered—both modes of identification denied, in any case, to the more representative, but less imaginatively available figure of the black slave.

Another relatively constant element in the octoroon situation is the relationship of the octoroon to the major villain of the plot, her lustful pursuer. Though occasionally identified as a gentleman, most often he is an overseer, a slave trader or a parvenu plantation owner. Typically, he is coarse, ill-bred and crudely-spoken. Most interesting, he is often a Yankee. This character first appeared as Jonathan Snapdragon in Hildreth's *The Slave* (1836), the novel in which the "tragic octoroon" made her first appearance. A particularly popular version of the character was McCloskey in Dion Boucicault's very successful play, *The Octoroon*, but he achieved his apotheosis, of course, as Simon Legree in *Uncle Tom's Cabin*.

This character has been critically perceived as a sop to Southern audiences, intended to mitigate the severity of the indictment made of the Southern slave owner by the octoroon situation. The Yankee becomes the sadistic and lecherous agent of evil, while the aristocrat is often presented as entirely innocent of the gross acts perpetrated in his name by the brutal New Englander. Certainly, there is truth in this interpretation of the Yankee overseer, since many of the antislavery writers were, as late as the 1850s, still hoping for a reconciliation between North and South, and to make the overseer explicitly a Yankee is to acknowledge that the guilt of exploiting slaves was not exclusively Southern.

However, while the use of the Yankee overseer may have been intended, in part, to soothe the Southern reader, it cannot be dismissed merely as a detail which had no propaganda effect on the Northern audience. On the very simplest level, to identify the meanest, most immoral, most black-hearted sinner in the whole book as a Yankee is to say that the moral superiority of Northerners is shared only by antislavery Northerners: a Yankee who condones and collaborates with Southern slavery is even worse than a slave owner; he is a regular Simon Legree.

On another level, the conventional overseer, Yankee or not, functions to present the evils of slavery as resulting from the excesses of an individual, unlike the octoroon herself, who functions to represent the sins of slavery as particularly institutional. To understand this apparent contradiction in motives between the function of the overseer and that of the octoroon, we must first recognize that popular audiences in the 1840s and 1850s enjoyed and were accustomed to aristocratic and sentimentalized heroes and heroines, and the conventional Southern Gentleman and his Lady of popular fiction were probably the closest native approximations we had to that ideal. Further, many of the writers of antislavery fiction were themselves sentimentally wedded to the romantic image of the old South by emotions not very different from those which prompted their sympathy for the Negro slave.

The point of the introduction of the villainous overseer was to show that even the happy slave of the kindly master, or worse, the idealized octoroon daughter of an honorable (if sinful) father, can overnight be betrayed into the clutches of a McCloskey. The popular image of the Southern Gentleman as a sentimentalized, aristocratic figure was used by the proslavery side in its defense against abolitionist charges; the documented charges of ill-usage of slaves brought by abolitionists were dismissed as wholly unrepresentative excesses of a few uncouth individuals. The effect of the overseer figure in the octoroon plot, then, is to point out that so long as slaves are property which can be sold or attached for debt, even the stereotypic noble, kindly master of pro-Southern literature would be powerless to protect his slaves—even his slave daughters—from suddenly falling into the hands of the worst slave-driver. The image of the overseer serves to permit the American public to retain its beau ideal, while at the same time it demonstrates that this beau ideal is irrelevant to the moral question of the institution of slavery.

Another aspect of the overseer-octoroon relationship not critically commented upon is that in addition to representing a racial conflict, it represents in certain works a conflict of class and regional attitudes. The conflict, of course, is not merely between the overseer and the octoroon, but between parvenu and aristocrat, between commoner and landed gentleman, between efficiency expert and dreamer. The octoroon is merely the prize for which they struggle. That she was prized, it is suggested, was because of her seven-eighths white aristocratic blood which had made her unattainable until she became a slave at the death of her father. It was the single drop of black blood that made the tragic octoroon available; it was the seven drops of blue blood that made her desirable. Thus, in the fiction of the tragic octoroon, the Yankee figure gloats over the possession of his intended victim as a victory over her father. By possessing the aristocrat's daughter, the Yankee achieves a triumph to which her beauty and his lust seem almost irrelevant.

Seen as an expression of regional conflict, the Legree-McCloskey figure is much more complicated and contradictory than is suggested by the conventional reading of him as a concession to the South. On one hand, it must have seemed to Northern audiences that the Yankee overseer embodied many of the characteristics that such audiences valued. He was keen, assertive, a go-getter. He was in the South to put on a sound basis an economic establishment the Southerner himself was unable to make pay. E. J. Stearns, himself a transplanted Yankee and violent defender of slavery, says in *Notes on Uncle Tom's Cabin:*

> Mrs. Stowe has no good opinion of this class of persons [Yankee Overseers], for she tells us . . . that they are "proverbially, the hardest masters of slaves." This is, no doubt, true; but it does not follow that they are, therefore, "renegade sons" . . . of New England. On the contrary, it is because they are *genuine* Yankees, that they are so hard masters: they have been accustomed to see men do a day's work,—they have done it themselves—and they cannot understand how the negro can do only a half or a third of one.[5]

In comparison with the Southern plantation lord, the Yankee stood for democratic, that is to say native, institutions, while the Southerner represented an aristocratic and European ideal. Further, the Yankee, in his efficiency, stood for the nineteenth century and progress, while the Southerner represented some feudal, Sir Walter Scott past.

On the other hand, the Yankee overseer must have uncomfortably suggested the hard-handed, pushy, shrewd-dealing Yankee entrepreneur who by the mid-century was breaking down many of the old barriers of the genteel past and establishing in the North an illiberal, vulgar and powerful commercial class. Regarded in this light, the Yankee in the South appears as a sinister precursor of Mark Twain's *Connecticut Yankee in King Arthur's Court.*

This double vision of the Yankee reveals itself most fully in Boucicault's *Octoroon,* where we have the evil Yankee, McCloskey, opposed by the heroic Yankee, Salem Scudder, who loves Zoe and wishes to marry her and who, in the best literary tradition, tinkers with new-fangled gadgets, one of which, the camera, providentially proves McCloskey guilty of murder. It may be said that the issue that divides the villainous Yankee from the heroic and benevolent one is the fate each proposes for the tragic octoroon.

---

5. E. J. Stearns, *Notes on Uncle Tom's Cabin* (1853), pp. 141–42.

To sum up, then, the popularity of the tragic octoroon character in pre–Civil War antislavery fiction cannot be explained by suggesting she was simply the nearest thing to a Negro that Northern authors and audiences could wax sentimental about. The attack on the slavery system mounted by the creators of the tragic octoroon was specifically directed toward certain sins implicit in that institution, was particularly appropriate to the audience which it was intended to move and was firmly based on the regional attitudes and moral values of that audience.

The Serpent of Lust in
the Southern Garden*

WILLIAM BEDFORD CLARK

In the minds of many Americans, there are two *Souths*. There is, on the one hand, that South conceived of as an idyllic land of plenty, blessed with a temperate climate and a rich fecundity of soil and inhabited by a happy and hospitable people for whom life is pleasure and pleasure a way of life. The persistent hold this view of the South exercises over the collective American imagination is attested to perhaps most readily by the willingness with which outlanders continue to surrender to the Old South nostalgia of the plantation tradition in both fiction and cinema. On the other hand, however, there is that other South, a kind of nightmare world of torrid and stifling heat in which uncontrollable passions and senseless acts of violence become the outward manifestations of a blighting inner corruption, a secret sin poisoning the very mainstreams of southern life. It was no accident that Faulkner's first commercial success was *Sanctuary* and the reading public's interest in lurid accounts of southern depravity remains strong, as any trip to the corner newsstand suffices to prove. Nevertheless, these two seemingly irreconcilable images of the South manage to merge into a rather shaky synthesis in the national consciousness so that to many Americans the South becomes a thing at once attractive and repulsive, a land simultaneously blessed and cursed. Metaphor is one way of expressing such a paradoxical state of emotional affairs, and one of the oldest and most compelling metaphors for expressing the ambivalence of American attitudes toward the region has been the image of the South as a corrupted garden, or, expressed in Biblical terms, Eden after the Fall.

Charles W. Coleman, in an 1887 *Harper's* article, "The Recent Movement in Southern Literature," provides us with an interesting early example of this metaphor. In discussing the fiction of George Washington Cable, he remarks that Cable writes of an "enchanted, semitropical realm, beautiful with flowers, yet marked by the trail of the serpent." Coleman's observation is a perceptive one, for Cable himself, a southerner whose own ambivalence toward his native region was par-

* From William Bedford Clark, "The Serpent of Lust in the Southern Garden." *The Southern Review* 10.4 (October 1974): 805–822.

ticularly acute, implicitly evokes this same image in an address entitled "What the Negro Must Learn," delivered before the American Missionary Society in 1890. Cable catalogues the many ways in which the South has been blessed: "Natural beauty, military defensibility, harbors, navigation, mineral treasures, forests, fertility of soil, water supply from spring and cloud, equable climate, abundant room." However, he is quick to add that in spite of all these advantages of a natural paradise, there is still "something wrong" in the South, something deeply wrong. For Cable, that "something wrong," the serpent in the southern garden, so to speak, can be traced back to the burden of evil resulting from the white man's injustices toward the black, and in this connection it is interesting to compare Cable's view of his region with that of Isaac McCaslin, the youthful protagonist of Faulkner's "The Bear."

Isaac also pictures the South in terms of a kind of paradisiacal garden, a natural Eden nevertheless cursed as the result of a regional sin inextricably bound up with the institution of slavery. That "sin" is dramatized for him when he learns that his grandfather had been guilty of miscegenation and of subsequently committing incest with a mulatto daughter. Quite significantly, in certain of Cable's works as well, notably *The Grandissimes*, the specific sin of miscegenation becomes a convenient fictional symbol for expressing the South's broader guilt over the whole question of bondage and the racial wrongs arising from it.

It is hardly a coincidence, however, that Cable and Faulkner, widely separated as they are by time, background, and temperament, should both have placed so great a stress on the theme of miscegenation in their respective fiction, working with it in such a way that the traditional serpent of illicit and tabooed lust comes to represent that greater and multiheaded serpent, slavery. Rather, these two writers can be seen as working within a lengthy and easily discernible tradition to which virtually every significant southern novelist since the Civil War has contributed, a tradition which has its emotional genesis in the sexual guilt and repressed self-condemnation of the southern psyche and its literary roots in the abolitionist rhetoric, antislavery fiction, and fugitive slave narratives of the antebellum period. It is a highly fertile tradition, vital and broad enough to include writers of such violently antithetical viewpoints as the humane reformer Cable and the wildly Negrophobic Thomas Dixon, Jr., a tradition to which works as diverse in form and substance as Shirley Ann Grau's *The Keepers of the House* and Carson McCullers' *Clock Without Hands* can both be said to belong.

In a broader sense, of course, the problem of miscegenation is by no means purely the concern of southern writers. The question of mixed blood has long fascinated both the literary and public imaginations of the nation as a whole and has been touched upon by figures like Cooper and Howells, as well as by scores of pulp writers over the years. It intrudes upon the popular imagination by way of a musical like *Showboat* and by way of countless Hollywood productions. As Francis P. Gaines remarked in his classic study *The Southern Plantation*, to call the roll of works in which the issue of racial intermixture is raised would be tedious. Yet quite significantly, it is in the works of white southerners that the theme receives the most persistent attention and takes on the greatest sense of urgency, and although numerous critics have taken note of the theme as it appears in the fiction of authors like Twain, Cable, and Faulkner and some effort has been made to trace its recurrence in nineteenth-century antislavery novels, there has been no satisfactory attempt to account for the question of miscegenation both in terms of the peculiar fascination it holds for the southern novelist and its immense literary potential, a potential that enables the theme, in the hands of more gifted writers, to transcend specifically regional concerns and take on universal implications. Accordingly, the present essay is an attempt at a partial remedy.

Prior to speculating on the origins of what might honestly be termed the "myth" of miscegenation as it is recurs throughout post–Civil War southern writing, it is perhaps useful at this point to examine in some detail a fictional text that serves ideally as a kind of working paradigm of the way in which the southern writer characteristically handles the theme of miscegenation in his fiction. The text in question is that of a little-known short story by Joel Chandler Harris, a story in which that author reaches a level of technical sophistication and a depth of seriousness that far exceed that to be found in his more familiar pieces.

The story is entitled "Where's Duncan?" and its dramatic context is established at the very outset. An aged narrator, a white southerner presumably of the upper class, feels himself compelled to relate to a second party (most likely the author himself in his actual role as journalist) a "happening" out of his youth, a series of events which has, he confesses, "pestered me at times when I ought to have been in my bed and sound asleep." The narrator senses that the story he is about to tell is one of considerable importance, but he insists—in a spirit of naïve objectivity maintained throughout the narrative—that he lacks the skill necessary to tell it as it should be told. For this reason he is entrusting it to his silent listener, hoping that the latter will be better able to articulate the significance behind the events themselves. The story as we have it is the seemingly unedited version as the speaker himself delivers it, and the fact that Harris allows the hidden meaning of the story to emerge implicitly, rather than explicitly sermonizing over it, contributes forcefully to the work's final effectiveness.

The story is a tale of initiation on two levels. It begins with the speaker as a boy taking on his first position of adult responsibility and ends with his growing awareness of an evil at the very core of southern life. As the narrative begins, the boy is entrusted with taking a wagonload of cotton to market. On the road, he encounters a "thick-set, dark-featured, black-bearded" stranger, a man who is to remain nameless throughout most of the rest of the story and who finally hides behind an alias. The stranger agrees to accompany the boy on his difficult trip until the caravan in which they travel reaches that point toward which he is bound. At one stage along the way, the stranger tells the boy a story in the form of a "riddle." It concerns a certain man who sold his own son to the "nigger traders." The narrator's youth and innocence prevent his understanding what the stranger is getting at, but he nevertheless senses the tragic implications which surround such a tale: "I could not unriddle the riddle, but it seemed to hint at such villainy as I had read about in the books in my father's library. Here was a man who had sold his own son; that was enough for me. It gave me matter to dream on."

At last, the caravan reaches the stranger's destination, a white plantation house set in the midst of a grove of beautiful trees, a fitting symbol of the plantation ideal. As the party prepares to camp for the night, an aged, though still handsome, mulatto woman arrives upon the scene and invites them to supper at the big house, hinting at the same time of her master's severe parsimony. The stranger greets this woman with the question "Where's Duncan?" and reiterates it several times. His question drives the woman into a frenzy, and she retires to the house. Shortly thereafter, the stranger disappears.

That night the narrator is awakened from his sleep to find that the big house is on fire. As he and his friends approach the scene, they catch a glimpse of the mulatto woman struggling insanely with her master in the midst of the flames. She finally plunges a knife into him, and seconds later the entire house collapses. This culminating scene is presented with a kind of nightmarish realism which gives it a peculiarly Kafkaesque intensity. Through the juxtaposition of various images—the raging fire, the mulatto woman screaming "Where's Duncan?" at her terrified master, the final collapse of the fiery house on its occupants—the narrator is able to achieve a vividly horrifying climax. Afterward, he learns from one of the Negroes present that the stranger, too, was in the house when it collapsed, rocking away in a corner, seemingly pleased by the hellish spectacle being played out before him.

What we have here is clearly a prototypal "southern" tale, as Leslie Fiedler has conceived of that subgenre, a Gothic "series of bloody events, sexual by impli-cation at least, played out . . . against a background of miasmal swamps, live oak, Spanish moss, and the decaying house." It is a fable in which, as Fiedler also says of the "southern," is figured forth the "deepest guilts and fears of trans-planted Europeans . . . in a community which remembers having sent its sons to die in a vain effort to sustain slavery." While Harris' narrator refuses to speculate aloud on the inner significance of the events he relates, that significance is quite clear to the student of contemporary southern literature. Here is a story con-structed around a mythical pattern of guilt and retribution, a pattern which will arise time and again, in whole or in part, in the works of subsequent writers. It is a story in which miscegenation and the "unnatural" treatment of biracial off-spring conveniently stand for the South's real sins: the prostitution of an entire race of black bodies for the gratification of the white man's "lust" for wealth and power and the resultant violation of those "family ties" traditionally associated with the Christian notion of the brotherhood of man. As such, it prefigures re-markably in terms of basic outline a later work like Faulkner's *Absalom, Absalom!*, with Harris' stranger as a prototype of Faulkner's victim-avenger Charles Bon and both stories ending significantly with a conflagration that reduces a great plantation house—the physical realization of the antebellum dream—to smolder-ing ashes. Indeed, in the person of Harris' narrator himself, with his conscience troubled by a vague, unarticulated, and illogical sense of complicity in the events he relates, it is tempting to see a type of the major narrator in *Absalom, Absalom!*—the neurotic and history-haunted Quentin Compson, who, in struggling to un-derstand the human truths contained in the concrete events of the past, in turn prefigures, as Louis D. Rubin, Jr. suggests in *The Writer in the South,* the contemporary southern writer himself.

Viewed in this way, as a paradigm of the basic myth of miscegenation as it recurs throughout the course of postbellum southern fiction, Harris' short story can be broken down into four thematic motifs that are to play a significant role in works of other writers; these are: (1) the archetypal pattern of guilt and retribution noted above; (2) the tendency to identify the specific sin of miscegenation with the "sin" of slavery and caste as a whole; (3) the dual role of the mulatto figure as both victim and avenger; and, (4) the implicit, yet nevertheless important, question of the mulatto's identity. In Harris' story, as in works like Cable's *The Grandissimes,* Twain's *Pudd'nhead Wilson,* and Faulkner's *Absalom, Absalom!* and *Go Down, Moses,* each of these elements naturally complements the others so that they finally tend to coalesce to form a single, potent fictional structure. Speculation as to the origins of each of these aspects of the broader theme of mixed blood is useful; and although such speculation remains by its very nature hypothetical, it helps to account logically for the peculiar fascination the question of miscegenation continues to exercise over the southern literary imagination.

The first of these four motifs, the theme of guilt and punishment, is the most basic element of our total thematic structure. It is most basic because it contains within itself the seeds of a narrative sequence involving one of the oldest of Western mythical constructs, a theme of immense significance within the framework of the Judeo-Christian tradition. While this basic pattern of human transgression and divine punishment is applicable to cases of individual culpability, it is most powerful when conceived of in collective terms, as it is embodied in the rhetoric of the Old Testament prophets who saw in historical adversity the wrath of a righteous God angered into punitive action by the collective sins of Israel. This same Old Testament stress on the societal species of sin was introduced into this country quite early via New England Calvinism. Indeed, as Perry Miller has pointed out, the Puritan jeremiad, taking its name from the most virulent of Hebrew prophets, Jeremiah, was to become a characteristic form of sermon in which the divine punishments visited upon the Children of Israel were viewed as a type of those calamities the New World Israelites might expect should they refuse to humble themselves through acts of communal penance.

In view of the extent to which antislavery thought in America has so often been an outgrowth of religious sentiment, it is natural enough that early abolitionists tended to conceive of slavery within a religious frame of reference. Viewing the institution as the South's regional sin, they warned slaveholders of the impending wrath of God. The Quaker visionary John Woolman wrote, following a 1746 tour of the southern colonies, that Negro bondage was a "dark gloominess hanging over the land," and he prophesied that "the future consequences will be grievous to prosperity." With the consolidation of abolitionist feelings after 1830, this tendency to identify slavery as a curse and a communal evil became even more overt. Article Two of the *Constitution of the American Anti-Slavery Society* (1833) expressly defined slavery as "a heinous crime in the sight of God." William Ellery Channing warned in 1841 that slavery was a sin that Christians could not afford to ignore, "a guilt which the justice of God cannot wink at, and on which insulted humanity, religion, and freedom call down fearful retribution." Theodore Parker, waxing apocalyptic, likewise foresaw an inevitable "Fire of Vengeance" sweeping the South, and the Reverend George B. Cheever warned the southerner in *God Against Slavery* that "The slave holds, under God's hand, a note against you, with compound interest for the crime committed against his father." In William Lloyd Garrison's definition of slavery as "an earthquake rumbling under our feet—a mine accumulating materials for a national catastrophe," the same concept of collective guilt and divine retribution, stripped of biblical rhetoric, is nevertheless implicit.

The popularity of such prophetic attacks upon the institution of slavery is evidenced by the fact that poets of an antislavery persuasion were quick to echo the warnings of the prose propagandists. In Barlow's *Columbiad* (1807), that early attempt to Virgilize the past, present, and future of America, the figure Atlas prophesies that the course of human events holds for the slaveholder "A vengeance that shall shake the world's deep frame, / That heaven abhors, and hell might shrink to name." And Longfellow, too, threatened catastrophic consequences in his poem "The Warning," in which the Negro race is compared to a "poor, blind Samson" who, "in some grim revel," will "shake the pillars of this Commonweal, / Till the vast temple of our liberties / A shapeless mass of wreck and rubbish lies."

Such rhetoric was soon to be translated into the actual events of history. On his way to a Virginia gallows, John Brown, assuming his self-professed role as latter-day prophet, ventured one last warning to slaveholders: "Without the shedding of blood, there is no remission of sins." And to many contemporary witnesses, Brown must indeed have seemed prophetic when, as Edmund Wilson reminds us in *Patriotic Gore,* northern armies marched South singing Mrs. Howe's celebration of their divinely-ordained crusade to wreak the wrath of God on the enslavers of the Negro.

It should be noted that southerners themselves were not altogether insensitive to charges that slavery was an institutionalized evil. Prior to the 1830s, abolitionist sentiment seems to have been particularly strong among certain of the evangelical sects in the region. The fiery Kentuckian Cassius Clay called slavery "our great national sin" and warned that it "must be destroyed or we are lost." As Robert Penn Warren has suggested in *The Legacy of the Civil War,* the very fact that there was considerable Confederate feeling in favor of banning the slave trade was a tacit confession that not all southerners believed that slavery was the absolute good that proslavery apologists like Thomas Roderick Dew, for example, insisted.

Early in the National Period, Thomas Jefferson, himself the uneasy owner of slaves, had written in his *Notes on Virginia* (1785), "I tremble for my country when I reflect that God is just," and he went on to note that divine justice "cannot sleep forever," and that the perpetuation of slavery meant certain disaster. Jefferson's fears suggest the possibility of a slave revolt in which the black man would rise up and smite his white tormentors, and from the vast amount of evidence we have of the South's obsessive fear of slave insurrections, it is tempting to surmise that such a terror was, in part, the result of the white southerner's secret sense of guilt *vis à vis* the black race. As Tocqueville remarked, the "danger of a conflict between the white and black inhabitants of the Southern States," a conflict the French observer saw as inevitable, haunted the American imagination like an obsessive nightmare. There is a terrible irony in the inconsistency between the antebellum South's rational insistence that slavery benefited all concerned and its irrational phobia over the possibility of slaves rising up to demand bloody vengeance for past wrongs, an irony that even emerges forcefully from a reading of U. B. Phillips' *American Negro Slavery*, but one which that historian's biases enable him to overlook. These hidden feelings of guilt on the part of pre–Civil War southerners provide some clues to the South's hysterical overreaction to an event like the 1831 Southampton Insurrection of Nat Turner who, after all, claimed to have spoken with God and to have been the instrument of divine punishment.

With the conclusion of the war, the South, its own theology largely Calvinistic in orientation, seemed clearly convicted of collective sin by the inexorable, but nevertheless righteous, workings of a providential history. The visitation of wrath threatened in the writings of the abolitionists seemed an accomplished fact. Defeat and widespread destruction were its unmistakable outward signs. Richard M. Weaver points out in *The Southern Tradition at Bay* that the northern victory caused many southerners to feel religious guilt, and no doubt many silently agreed with the young South Carolinian who told John T. Trowbridge in 1866, "I think it was in the decrees of God Almighty that slavery was to be abolished in this way; and I don't murmur. . . . We brought it all on ourselves."

Despite the viewpoint of historians like Eugene Genovese, then, it seems fair to state that there was indeed a sense of guilt over slavery present in the antebellum South, and this guilt was intensified by the South's defeat in the Civil War and its humiliation during the Reconstruction experience. The novelist Thomas Nelson Page attempted to mitigate this sense of guilt by arguing that slavery was a tragic necessity of history, forced upon his region by northern slave traders and the dictates of climate. Still, Page regarded it as the "curse of the fair land where it flourished." There is a defensiveness about Page's apology that is a far cry from the positive arguments of antebellum proslavery propagandists, though the seeds of this historical excuse for slavery can also be found in John C. Calhoun's last speech to the Senate a decade before the war. This very defensiveness is itself implicit evidence to the extent of the South's uneasiness of conscience. In our own century, the young Carson McCullers put it well when she observed that southerners suffer from a special kind of guilt, "a consciousness of guilt not fully knowable, or communicable." It is precisely this kind of guilt that compels the narrator of Harris' "Where's Duncan?" to tell his story, a secret agony of conscience that provides the vital impetus for the tradition of fiction under consideration here. But why should the southern writer's sense of his region's collective historical sin express itself so often in terms of the more-or-less private sin of miscegenation? The answer is logical enough.

In the Old South the slave was property and was meant to be used, and the female slave, particularly if she were "blessed" with physical charms, possessed an added dimension of usefulness. The fact of illicit sexual relations between the white master class and black women, a fact incontrovertibly attested to by an ever-increasing number of light-skinned Negroes both on the plantations and in the cities, was to become the single most vulnerable chink in the South's moral defense of slavery. While the conscientious slaveholder might argue divine sanction for slavery in view of its presence in the Old Testament and assert, along with George Fitzhugh and William J. Grayson, its virtues in contrast to the vices of wage-slave capitalism, he could not escape from charges that the unsanctified sexual liaisons which stemmed naturally from slavery constituted an indefensible evil. Fornication, in and of itself, had long been considered one of the most reprehensible of sins, and an extra portion of sinfulness attached itself to the concept of miscegenation, growing out of a sense of the violation of ancient taboos and the breaking of those natural laws of which the *philosophes* had written. Winthrop Jordan, among others, has noted the traditional loathing of Anglo-Saxons toward darker races, an antipathy that evolves out of an archetypal polarization of light and dark, white and black. Couple this irrational aversion with the fact that the mulatto offspring of white masters were legal property and could thus be bought and sold, and it is easy to see how the question of miscegenation became so effective a weapon for self-righteous assault on the slave system as a whole, a weapon peculiarly equipped to prick southern consciences. As might be expected, antislavery polemicists were quick to use it to indict the South in general. "The South," wrote Wendell Phillips, "is one great brothel."

As early as Colonial times, Samuel Sewall, in *The Selling of Joseph* (1700), had singled out for special condemnation those who sought to *"connive at the Fornication of their Slaves."* Yet connive they did, as travelers in the South took a particular relish in pointing out. Ann Royall, the author of that interesting relic of the 1820s, *Sketches of History, Life, and Manners in the United States*, reported that she was moved to "feelings of horror and disgust" by the large number of persons of mixed ancestry she encountered on her tour of the slave states, and the practice of holding one's mulatto children as chattel moved her to vehement rage. Any man who would doom his own children to bondage was, she insisted, "not only . . . void of virtue; but guilty of the most indignant crime." C. G. Parsons, a northern physician, records similar sentiments in his *Inside View of Slavery* (1855). He also relates the story of how a formerly apathetic Boston merchant was converted to the antislavery cause after seeing a "fancy girl" up for auction, thus illustrating the power of the miscegenation issue in shaping northern opinion on slavery. Even a British visitor like Henry A. Murry, who tended to view American institutions with a good-natured condescension, expressed shock over the selling of mulatto children in his *Lands of the Slave and the Free:* "Can anything be imagined more horrible than a free nation trafficking in the blood of its co-citizens? Is it not a diabolical premium on inequity, that the fruit of the sin can be sold for the benefit of the sinner?"

Perhaps the most valuable of all antebellum travelogues is that of Frederick L. Olmsted, whose unusual objectivity and conscientiousness make his *The Cotton Kingdom* a central source of information about conditions in the Old South. The problem of mixed blood, to be sure, does not go unnoticed by him. While visiting in Virginia, Olmsted reports that he was "surprised" by the number of "nearly white-coloured" slaves he saw there. Furthermore, the prevalence of mulattos in New Orleans, and the elaborate system of concubinage responsible for many of them, is a point of particular interest for him, and he spends a considerable number of pages in reviewing the plight of the quadroon caste. While sexual relations between the races were practiced unabashedly in New Orleans, Olmsted is also aware that they were practiced elsewhere on an equally widespread, albeit covert basis. One southerner tells him that there is not a "likely-looking black girl in this State that is not the concubine of a white man. There is not an old plantation in which the grandchildren of the owner are not whipped in the fields by his overseer."

In a passage of remarkable interest, Olmsted writes of traveling on a Red River steamboat on which copies of Mrs. Stowe's *Uncle Tom's Cabin* are being sold and of a conversation with a native of that region who complained of a lack of verisimilitude in the Red River sections of the novel. The southerner explains that "no coloured woman would be likely to offer any resistance, if a white man should want to seduce her." It requires little imagination to reconstruct the righteous indignation such a statement would have stirred up among readers in the North. There is little wonder that, in many northern eyes, the South was, as Earl E. Thorpe suggests, the ID personified.

Poets sympathetic to the abolitionist cause were also quick to focus their attacks on what they viewed as the prevailing debauchery of the South. In Longfellow's "The Quadroon Girl," a planter sells his daughter to the white man who lusts after her. And in "The Farewell of a Virginia Slave Mother to her Daughters sold into Southern Bondage," Whittier stresses the fate that awaits young slave women sold down the river: "Toiling through the weary day, / And at night the spoiler's prey." Mrs. Frances E. W. Harper, the Negro abolitionist-poet, reiterates this same theme when she writes of "young girls from their mother's arms, / Bartered and sold for their youthful charms." Likewise, antislavery novelists were fond of concentrating their attention on the more lurid and sensationalistic aspects of the question of mixed blood. In Richard Hildreth's *The White Slave*, a work written with the avowed purpose of teaching the slaveholder's conscience "how to torture him with the picture of himself" by invoking "the dark and dread images of his own misdeeds," the horror attendant upon the theme of miscegenation is intensified by the introduction of the theme of incest. So popular was the theme of mixed blood with abolitionist writers that a whole tradition of fiction grew up around the vicissitudes of the "tragic mulatto," usually a beautiful young woman with only the slightest trace of Negro blood who is subjected to a lengthy series of torments and temptations designed to illustrate the wide range of evils nurtured by slavery. As students of this tradition note, the fact that the slave protagonist in such novels was to all appearances white and shared the characteristics of the typical white heroine of melodramatic romance helped stress the arbitrary nature of racial distinctions in general and therefore short-circuited whatever racial biases the northern audience itself maintained.

One of the most typical of these novels is William Wells Brown's *Clotel*, which is particularly interesting because it is the work of this nation's first black novelist, a man who was himself a mulatto fugitive slave. *Clotel* wastes no time in introducing the main thrust of its indictment of the peculiar institution: "With the growing population of the Southern States, the increase of mulattos has been very great. Society does not frown upon the man who sits with his half-breed child upon his knee whilst the mother stands, a slave, behind his chair." For Brown, miscegenation is symptomatic of the degrading influence of slavery upon all it touches, and the author stresses the fact that since no inducement is "held out to slave women to be pure and chaste . . . immorality and vice pervade the cities and towns of the South to an extent unknown in the Northern States."

Charges of this sort, while appealing to self-righteous sentiment in the North, could not help but have a devastating effect upon the conscience of the Bible-reading South. Questions of sexual morality aside, the very presence of anti-amalgamation statutes on the books served to convict many southerners of hypocrisy at the least; nor were all fathers of illegitimate slave children devoid of basic paternal instincts. Many planters freed their mulatto offspring, but manumission became increasingly difficult in the years preceding the Civil War, and sometimes they waited too late. Tocqueville provides an interesting case in point:

> I happened to meet an old man . . . who had lived in illicit intercourse with one of his Negresses and had had several children by her. . . . He had . . . thought of bequeathing to them . . . their liberty; but years elapsed before he could surmount the legal obstacles to their emancipation, and meanwhile his old age had come and he was about to die. He pictured to himself his sons dragged from market to market . . . until these horrid anticipations worked his imagination into a frenzy. When I saw him, he was a prey to all the anguish of despair; and I then understood how awful was the retribution of Nature upon those who have broken her laws.

As is generally recognized, southern women were in a position to feel particularly wronged by widespread miscegenation, and they were not always content to remain silent. Olmsted cites a letter from such a woman, a Virginia lady sent to prison for teaching slaves to read and write. A portion of that letter is of particular interest in view of the way in which it magnifies the "curse" of miscegenation to an extent previously reserved for the institution of slavery itself:

> There is one great evil hanging over the Southern Slave States, destroying domestic happiness and the peace of thousands. It is summed up in the single word—*amalgamation*. This, and this only, causes the vast extent of ignorance, degradation, and crime that lies like a black cloud over the whole South. And the practice is more general than . . . the Southerners are willing to allow.

Once this identification of miscegenation with the South's regional "black cloud" has been made, miscegenation quite naturally becomes emblematic of the sins of slavery as a whole. Feelings of sexual guilt on the part of southerners may well have preceded feelings of institutional guilt, as Earl E. Thorpe and others suggest, but in much southern writing since the Civil War the two kinds of guilt tend to become for all practical purposes inseparable.

If illicit biracial sex and the selling of mulatto children can be said to represent the South's sins writ small, and, as we have seen, sins bring on inevitable retribution, it is not difficult to understand the unique role of the mulatto character within the tradition of fiction with which we are concerned. After all, given the racial stratification of southern society, the very presence of a person of mixed blood constitutes an embarrassment at the least. As Frederick Douglass, himself perhaps the son of a white planter, noted in *My Bondage and My Freedom* (1855), "the mulatto child's face is a standing accusation against him who is master and father to the child." The mulatto, then, functions as a living symbol of sin; and, as a fictional character, he oftentimes becomes quite literally the physical realization of the white southerner's violation of his slaves' humanity. Jules Zanger puts it well in his perceptive article, "The 'Tragic Octoroon' in Pre–Civil War Fiction" (*American Quarterly*, 18, 63–70 [in this volume, p. 287. —Ed.]):

> The octoroon . . . represented not merely the product of the incidental sin of the individual sinner, but . . . the result of cumulative institutional sin, since the octoroon was the product of four generations of illicit, enforced miscegenation made possible by the slavery system. The very existence of the octoroon convicted the slaveholder of prostituting his slaves and of selling his own children for profit.

By imaginative extension, this living symbol and constant reminder of the South's historical guilt over slavery became the fitting instrument through which the eternally-just workings of Providence would be likely to exact vengeance for past wrongs. In this way, the pathetic victim of the "tragic mulatto" tradition was gradually transformed into the figure of the righteous avenger.

The seeds of this characterization of the person of mixed blood were already present in the antislavery fiction of the antebellum period. While heroines of mixed race were portrayed, with few exceptions, as hapless and passive victims of the slave system, the male mulatto protagonist was frequently pictured as an indignant rebel. He felt intensely the demeaning role placed upon him by the institution of slavery. A fierce spirit of freedom, attributed by writers like Hildreth to the mulatto's white blood, burned within him, and his resentment over the wrongs perpetrated against him by white society threatened continually to express itself in violence. Hildreth's Archy Moore, wronged continuously by his white father, is precisely such a character, as is Harry Gordon, the protagonist of Mrs. Stowe's *Dred*, who is the victim of his white half-brother's unnatural cruelties. George Harris, the husband of Eliza in *Uncle Tom's Cabin*, is perhaps the best known of these figures, and he finally vows to endure the abuses of his master no longer and becomes a runaway like his historical counterparts William Wells Brown and Frederick Douglass, two mulattos who made their grievances against slavery manifest through the active roles they assumed in the antislavery struggle. Indeed, it is interesting to note how history and literature tended to reinforce one another in this regard. There is an inescapable and highly appropriate irony in the fact that the sins of the slaveholders often returned to plague them in the persons of their illegitimate offspring and further irony in the fact that many of the most significant black leaders during Reconstruction were also of mixed ancestry. Behind such irony there is this implicit formula: *miscegenation is a sin, and like all sin it involves punishment; there can be no more fitting agent of that punishment than the living embodiment of the sin itself, the haunting figure of the wronged mulatto.*

There appears to be a clear literary bond, then, connecting a character like the vengeful stranger in Harris' "Where's Duncan?" with mulatto characters like Honoré Grandissime and Palmyre Philosophe in Cable's *The Grandissimes*, for example, or Tom Driscoll in Twain's *Pudd'nhead Wilson*. Yet it is perhaps more significant to note that the mulatto avenger appears at his most threatening in the Reconstruction novels of the two southern apologists Thomas Nelson Page and Thomas Dixon, Jr. In Page's *Red Rock*, the animal-like "yaller nigger" rabble-rouser, Moses, is a constant thorn in the side of the war-and-defeat-stricken white community until he pushes his new-found liberty too far and attempts the rape of the local belle. He subsequently flees the vicinity with a band of chivalrous vigilantes at his heels. In Dixon's *The Klansman*, the radical Republican leader, Stoneman, is persuaded to crush out southern civilization at the sly prompting of his mulatto mistress, and another mulatto, the scurrilous Silas Lynch, becomes Stoneman's chief agent in humiliating the prostrate South. Lynch repays his benefactor's trust by making advances toward his daughter. Dixon's lesson to Negrophiles is clear. Fortunately, in Dixon's view at least, the Ku Klux Klan almost always saves the day, although this is not the case in *The Sins of the Father*, Dixon's most elaborate treatment of the theme of miscegenation. In that work, the author admits that mixed blood "is not merely a thing of to-day . . . but the heritage of two hundred years of sin and sorrow." Nevertheless, he insists that the real fault lies with the sensuous and amoral mulatto women of the South who prey upon the virility of the southern gentleman. Dixon's Cleo is pictured as a violent, catlike creature who, when spurned by her white lover, succeeds in systematically bringing ruin to a proud old North Carolina family.

The mulatto avenger makes notable appearances in many of the novels of the southern renaissance as well. A special case in point is the pitiful yet terrifying figure of Yellow Jim in Allen Tate's wrongly neglected novel *The Fathers*. Strictly in accordance with our paradigm, an inevitable curse is visited upon the House of Posey when young Mr. George violates his half-brother's humanity by trading him for a race horse. Charles Bon in Faulkner's *Absalom, Absalom!* is perhaps the best known of all mulatto avengers, and *Absalom, Absalom!* itself stands in many ways as the artistic culmination of the tradition with which we have been dealing here. Faulkner's portrayal of Lucas Beauchamp in *Intruder in the Dust* brings to bear an interesting variation on the role of mulatto as victim-avenger, for it is through passive resistance, rather than violent action, that Lucas becomes "tyrant over the whole country's white conscience." Works like Tate's novel and Faulkner's *Absalom, Absalom!*, *Go Down, Moses*, and *Intruder in the Dust* are a far cry from Harris' "Where's Duncan?" Yet they testify forcefully to the emotional power of the "myth" with which the earlier writer was working and stand as vivid realizations of the fictional potential inherent within it.

Thus far, we have dealt with three aspects of the paradigm emerging from Harris' story: the motif of guilt and retribution; the identification of miscegenation with the sin of slavery and racial caste itself; and the role of the person of mixed blood as both victim and avenger. One element remains to be considered—the question of the mulatto character's ambiguous identity. Although Harris touches upon the possibilities of this issue only in the most implicit and superficial way, contenting himself with surrounding his dark stranger's real identity with thinly veiled mysteriousness, other writers explore the problem of the mulatto character's twofold racial nature and its resultant psychological effect upon his personality in greater depth. When, in a famous comic episode in *Uncle Tom's Cabin*, the St. Clares' cook reminds a group of light-skinned slaves that they are "niggers" as much as she is, she is quite right of course in one sense, for given the sharp line of demarcation separating the races in southern society, one drop of black blood is sufficient to preclude a person from qualifying as a member of the dominant race. But the question of racial identity was no doubt hardly so simple a matter for the mulatto himself, however. If we are to trust the testimony of a long line of historians, as well as fictionists, the problem of self-definition was troublesome to slaves in general, and it is only natural that the person of mixed ancestry should have suffered a particularly acute crisis of identity, for he was caught quite literally between the two irreconcilable polarities of southern life. Writers of fiction seem to have sensed the essential pathos of the mulatto's ambiguous plight from the beginning so that the alienation and self-uncertainties of the mixed-blood became a standard aspect of the "tragic mulatto" tradition.

Even a basically unsympathetic novelist like Dixon is capable of handling this side of the mulatto's character with sympathy. In *The Leopard's Spots*, he traces the career of George Harris, Jr., the son of Mrs. Stowe's Eliza and George. The young Harris is cultured, educated, and nearly white. He is the protégé of the northern philanthropist Lowell who tells him that all men are created equal. George takes his sponsor at his word and asks him for the hand of his daughter, only to learn that Lowell is unprepared to practice what he preaches. In bitter disillusionment, the mulatto tries to make his own way in the world, but he finds that he cannot fit into either white or black society. Finally, he takes a bizarre and irrational pilgrimage throughout the nation, visiting one by one the heaps of ashes that mark the places where Negroes have been lynched by white mobs. Ironically, it is Dixon, the rabid Negrophobe, who has left us with one of the most memorable and haunting early images of the mixed-blood character's faltering search for Self.

In a real sense, however, it is the Afro-American writer who is the legitimate heir to this element of our paradigmatic theme of miscegenation, for black writers have been especially drawn to the fictional possibilities surrounding the person of mixed race and his need to establish for himself a stable sense of identity. The result has been a considerable "literature of 'passing' " in which the protagonist wavers between living as a white or embracing his *Negritude* (in the broader sense of that term). From Rena Walden in Charles W. Chesnutt's *The House Behind the Cedars*, who devotes herself to educating her own people after she has been betrayed by her white fiancé, and James Weldon Johnson's hero of *The Autobiography of an Ex-Coloured Man*, who passes for white only to feel that he has lost something of value in his Negro heritage, to the heroines of Jessie Fauset and Nella Larsen, the mulatto in search of his racial identity appears and reappears in the works of black Americans. The way in which Afro-American novelists utilize this theme and the way in which their use of it prefigures the black man's own quest for identity within American life and institutions is a question worthy of a full-length study in its own right, but it lies beyond the scope of this consideration.

Rather, this essay must be content to close with suggesting the way in which the fictional mulatto's search for self-definition parallels the plight which increasingly confronts "modern" man in general, the man who finds himself in a world in which the sense of selfhood both personal and social, is an elusive entity. In the hands of a southern writer whose literary temper is akin to that of his Continental contemporaries like Sartre and Camus, the essentially parochial dilemma of the person of mixed racial background can become a convenient emblem for the situation facing the "existential" hero himself. Fictional materials indigenous to the regional tradition we have been examining thus take on more universal implications.

This is certainly the case with Faulkner's treatment of Joe Christmas in *Light in August*, as numerous critics have pointed out. And the pathos of Christmas' schizoid existence is intensified by the fact that his "mixed blood" may well be a figment of his own imagination entirely. The heroine of Robert Penn Warren's *Band of Angels*, Amantha Starr, is yet another remarkable case in point. Critics who have been quick to attack *Band of Angels* for its obvious melodrama and its reliance upon nineteenth-century fictional conventions have largely missed the point. Warren is indeed retelling the old story of the mulatto heroine sold into slavery after her father's untimely death, but he pushes his narrative beyond the level of cliché, or, more properly, penetrates to the mythic core behind the cliché, so that Amantha's story becomes an account of man's attempt to free himself through self-knowledge. The novel opens quite literally with Amantha's question, "Oh, who am I?," and ties her hopes for personal liberation to her quest for a successful answer. Paradoxically, it is Amantha's fall from grace into slavery that sets her out on her search for the truth about herself, the truth that alone will set her free. *Band of Angels* is a triumphant example of Warren's ability to ground his philosophical statements about man and his place in history and the cosmos within the specifics of a regional tradition. In works like *Light in August* and *Band of Angels*, the southern writer's perennial concern with the issue of mixed blood lends itself to the exploration of much broader concerns.

The theme of miscegenation has played an important role in American writing, particularly in the South, for over a century now. The possibility for irony implicit within it has furnished ample materials ranging from the tragic to the satiric. The importance of the theme can be measured not only in terms of the sheer number of works in which it asserts itself, but also in terms of the lasting value of a handful of the works which it informs. With the increasing homogeneity of American culture as a whole and the inevitable decline in specifically regional consciousness, the vital impulse behind the literary tradition with which we have been concerned here will no doubt begin to dissipate. Perhaps it is fair to see this tendency already at work in the treatment the problem of miscegenation receives in the novels of Faulkner and Warren. But the tradition is by no means fully exhausted. It reasserts itself effectively in a story like "Bloodline" by the black southerner Ernest J. Gaines, and it may well give rise to significant fiction in the future. If not, it has already given us *Absalom, Absalom!* and *Go Down, Moses,* and has therefore served American literature well.

Miscegenation in the Late Nineteenth-Century American Novel*

WILLIAM L. ANDREWS

In the writing of Charles W. Chesnutt, an Afro-American whose "color line" fiction achieved unprecedented notoriety at the turn of the twentieth century, the problem of miscegenation, its history, its causes, and its moral and social effects, became the unifying theme of an author's entire *oeuvre* for the first time in American literature. In all three of Chesnutt's published novels, the complex social and political problems which are treated appear against the background of suppressed or tragically resolved interracial love and miscegenation.[1] It is important to remember, however, that the possibility of miscegenation as a consequence of the new post–Civil War racial "equality" in America was a question which a great many literary people, white and black, felt obliged to address in fiction. Many of these writers tried their hands at the novel of miscegenation, not merely out of an impulse to concoct a popular romance of forbidden interracial love or to engage in ritual pity for the "tragic mulatto"; directly or indirectly, their novels reflected and influenced most of the positions taken in the national debate over the moral, social, and political ramifications of black assimilation into the mainstream of white American life.

Perhaps the key question facing America after emancipation was to what extent the newly-freed slaves could and should be assimilated into American society. Though many felt the granting of civil and political rights in the abstract through passage of the Fourteenth and Fifteenth Amendments was sufficient aid to the black man in his upward struggle, others argued that greater vigilance was required to see that the black man could exercise his rights in fact as well as theory. Among these supporters of Afro-American equality was George W. Cable, whose "Freedman's Case in Equity" (1885)[2] spoke forthrightly of the need for the South to end its color caste system and change its institutions, educational and penal,

---

* From William L. Andrews, "Miscegenation in the Late Nineteenth-Century American Novel." *Southern Humanities Review* 13.1 (Winter 1979): 13–24.

1. *The House Behind the Cedars* (Boston: Houghton, Mifflin, 1900) dramatizes the private effects of proscribed interracial love before the Civil War on the fates of two individuals living during the Reconstruction era. In the widened focus of *The Marrow of Tradition* (Boston: Houghton, Mifflin, 1901) and *The Colonel's Dream* (New York: Doubleday, Page, 1905), the fates of two representative Southern towns emerging into the twentieth century are jeopardized by reactionary social, political, and economic forces spawned in part by the sexual sins of the antebellum fathers.
2. "The Freedman's Case in Equity" is reprinted in George W. Cable. *The Negro Question,* ed. Arlin Turner (Garden City, New York: Doubleday, 1958).

so that the freedman could occupy a truly free status. The response of nine Southern newspapers to Cable's plea was that "intermarriage, social ruin, and racial warfare would result if his views were followed."[3] Cable answered in "The Silent South" (1885) with an argument which faced squarely the prevalent Southern opinion that the pursuit of civil rights for blacks led inevitably to "social equality" and "amalgamation" of the races. Denying that "The Freedman's Case in Equity" offered a brief for social equality between the races, Cable went further to repudiate those who wished "to suppress a question of civil right by simply miscalling it 'social intermingling'."[4] Yet despite his assurance that his call for a national spirit of brotherhood did not necessitate "fusion of bloods," Cable was ostracized by his region, while his political position regarding blacks was distorted by his most vocal critics into one advocating the "africanization" of the South.

Cable's treatment at the hands of leading Southern apologists of his day reveals a pattern of argument and defense which dominated Southern discussion of the race question in America throughout the latter part of the nineteenth century. The expostulation for black civil rights regularly provoked the standard reply affirming the need for maintaining white supremacy in the South at all costs. Henry W. Grady, perhaps the most persuasive of the apologists for the "New South," considered racial "integrity and dominance of the Anglo-Saxon blood" as the very foundation of the Southern social system.[5] The ultimate purpose of segregation was to preserve those "natural" barriers between the races, without which miscegenation would inevitably occur. To countenance miscegenation or the relaxation of political, economic, or social barriers to it was to threaten the principle of racial purity on which not only Southern race pride but social and political order in the post-war South were based. The "Negro Problem," therefore, could not be discussed as simply a political, economic, or social matter. For, as Thomas Nelson Page, a later Southern "moderate" who replaced Grady as a popular Southern spokesman at the turn of the century, reminded his readers, the source of "the problem" stems from "the very foundation of race preservation."[6] How could the white race and its culture be preserved when the black man's passion, "always his controlling force," according to Page, was "now, since the new teaching, for the white women"? Page's answer was familiar—to proscribe all political and civil rights which might connote in the mind of the "ignorant and brutal young Negro" "the opportunity to enjoy, equally with white men, the privilege of cohabiting with white women." Thus, interpreting the black man's political and civil agitation as simply pretexts for eventual aggression toward Southern Woman (the living embodiment of the cult of Anglo-Saxon race pride[7]), Southern apologists understood post-war political, social, and economic upheavals on the racial front in the simplest of terms. Reconstruction could be seen as a

3. Arlin Turner, *George W. Cable, A Biography* (Baton Rouge: Louisiana State Univ. Press, 1966), p. 197.
4. *The Negro Question*, p. 85.
5. Henry W. Grady, "In Plain Black and White," *Century*, 29 (1885), p. 911.
6. *The Negro: The Southerner's Problem* (New York: Scribner's, 1904), p. 34.
7. W. J. Cash, *The Mind of the South* (New York: Knopf, 1941), pp. 115–116.

kind of attempted rape of the South in various literal and figurative ways. White supremacy as a political and social system had to be retained to combat (1) the threat of the black man not merely as political opponent or economic competitor, but ultimately as sexual rival, and (2) the threat of the black woman as dusky temptress.[8] In fine, the issue of black rights did not come down to a matter of abstract politics but rather of sexual politics in which miscegenation became the ultimate political act of triumph for blacks over the restraints of Southern civilization. Small wonder, then, that Thomas Pearce Bailey concluded with this remark his analysis of the race question as the average Southerner of the early twentieth century saw it: "For say what we will, may not all the equalities be ultimately based on potential social equality, and that in turn on intermarriage? Here we reach the real *crux* of the question."[9] Here also we reach the crux of the significance of the novel of miscegenation in post–Civil War America.

In light of the interpretation of miscegenation informing the views of such Southern spokesmen as Grady, Page, and Bailey, it should not be surprising to find that miscegenation as a literary topic in post–Civil War America did not remain for long in the hands of the historical romancers or the sentimentalists of the occasional "exceptional case" of race mixing. Cable had capitalized on the theme of miscegenation in *The Grandissimes* (1880) and had constructed one of his best novellas, *Madame Delphine* (1881), around the idea of passing. But both of these stories were distanced from the modern age and its problems by several decades and by the strangeness of antebellum Creole culture. Similarly, many popular writers of the day exploited the miscegenation theme after Cable, but their concern was with the isolated instance of the "tragic mulatto" who usually dies conveniently or departs when his or her presence creates embarrassing complications.[10] Several important white and black novelists of this period broke with this trend, however, refusing to limit their studies of miscegenation to the teary injunctions and grave warnings against racial assimilation which were the usual literary accouterments of the tragic mulatto theme in American fiction. From Rebecca Harding Davis to Thomas Dixon among the white and from Frances E. W. Harper to Sutton Griggs among the black novelists of this period, the novel of miscegenation dramatized and tried to resolve in differing ways a fundamental question on which much of the country's racial adjustment seemed to depend, the question of the effect of miscegenation on the American social structure.

8. For an extreme statement of this fear of the black woman see Charles Carroll's *The Tempter of Eve* (St. Louis: Adamic, 1902), in which the betrayer of the human race is revealed to be a Negro woman.

9. Thomas Pearce Bailey, *Race Orthodoxy in the South* (1914; rpt. New York: AMS, 1972), p. 42.

10. A representative selection of "tragic mulatto" stories might include Matt Crim's "Was It An Exceptional Case?" in *In Beaver Cove and Elsewhere* (New York: C. L. Webster, 1892), pp. 194–236; Richard Malcolm Johnston's "Ishmael," *Lippincott's*, 52 (1893), pp. 359–366; Grace King's "The Little Convent Girl," *Balcony Stories* (New York: Century, 1892), pp. 141–162; and Joel Chandler Harris's "Where's Duncan?" in *Balaam and His Master* (Boston: Houghton, Mifflin, 1891), pp. 149–169.

A dominant figure in post–Civil War Afro-American fiction, the mulatto was employed in the service of protest against American racial prejudice much more often than were blacks of darker complexions and less mixed racial ancestry. Unlike many white writers of this period, who may have viewed mulattoes as "the superior of the darker Negro" because of their white blood,[11] most black writers depicted mulattoes respectfully because they seemed the best advertisement the race could show to a skeptical America. As representatives of the Afro-American "Talented Tenth," this educated and comparatively affluent elite was portrayed in fiction as it seemed in fact—as the vanguard which would take the lead in the race's general advancement. Nevertheless, white sentiment remained suspicious of the mixed-blood. His upward mobility alone seemed to identify him as the chief racial troublemaker.[12] The increasing numbers of mulattoes, evidencing the obvious relaxation of the fundamental social taboos against racial intermixture, seemed to portend assaults on the status quo in a number of civil, economic, and social spheres. In a period when the average black man was most often presumed by the public to be, and depicted by America's white writers as, satisfied with or reconciled to a segregated status, America's racial problem, it could be concluded, stemmed from the more specific "problem of the mulatto."[13]

In response to America's fear of the mulatto as a racial subversive, much post–Civil War race fiction placed mulattoes in situations in which assimilation into white society is possible but is high-mindedly refused. In Rebecca Harding Davis's *Waiting for the Verdict* (1867), a mulatto doctor who has passed for white for many years eventually affirms his obligation to the newly-freed blacks and puts aside a prosperous medical practice to lead a black regiment in the Civil War. The father of the white woman whose love Dr. Broderip has sacrificed in order to do his duty to his "own people" states the anti-passing position which would be invoked frequently in later novels. " 'I think this sacrifice for his people'll bring out the man in him more'n any selfish love for a wife or home would have done. He was half beast before, in his own notion; but, curiously enough, it's through his negro blood that humanity's got hold of him. He's one with his kind.' "[14] Thus the refusal to pass into the white world becomes for Davis the evidence of the mulatto's "true humanity," his badge of moral legitimacy.

The implications of a novel like *Waiting for the Verdict* would have been comforting to an American audience which might consider the mulatto's fluid position along the color line a threat to American racial harmony and purity. Rarely, however, did fiction dealing with passing and miscegenation take up the partic-

11. Hugh M. Gloster, *Negro Voices in American Fiction* (Chapel Hill: Univ. of North Carolina Press, 1948), p. 12.

12. See Guion G. Johnson, "The Ideology of White Supremacy, 1876–1910," *Essays in Southern History*, ed. Fletcher Melvin Green (Chapel Hill: Univ. of North Carolina Press, 1949), p. 152.

13. One conclusion of Edward Byron Reuter in his early study of *The Mulatto in the United States* (Boston: Richard G. Badger, 1918) is summarized in the title of his fourth chapter—"The Mulatto: The Key to the Race Problem."

14. Rebecca Harding Davis, *Waiting For The Verdict* (1867; rpt. Ridgewood. N.J.: Gregg, 1968); pp. 326–327.

ularly sensitive issue of a "black" *man*'s passing into the white world via inter-marriage with a white woman. Usually writers liked to picture the mulatto's penchant for renouncing "social equality" through the actions of women, like Eva Prime in Albion Tourgée's *Pactolus Prime* (1890) or Beatrice La Scalla in Alice I. Jones's *Beatrice of Bayou Teche* (1895). Both of these beautiful mulattoes readily practice self-segregation from American society, content to pursue private humanitarian and educational goals rather than confront society with its unfairness toward their social, marital, or professional hopes. The subplot of Gertrude Atherton's *Senator North* (1900) reinforces the decisions of these characters by supplying an object lesson in the futility of efforts to integrate the mixed-blood into the American mainstream. There is a fatalistic conspiracy of circumstance in this novel and others like it[15] which governs racial intermixing and guarantees its ultimate impossibility. *Senator North* declares the article of faith on which such novels as Atherton's are founded: " 'For all the women of the accursed cross of black and white there is absolutely no hope—so long as they live in this country, at all events.' "[16]

In Frances E. W. Harper's *Iola Leroy* (1892), an apology in fiction for the Talented Tenth, the mulatto's preference for "duty" instead of personal worldly success obviates his being sent out of the country, into a convent, or into his grave, as most white novelists were prone to do with him, in order to resolve the problem of his disquieting presence in American life. Instead, Harper shows the upward bound mulattoes of her novel devoted to the advancement of the blacks in the South, as Rebecca Harding Davis had done. A spokeswoman for the idea of racial solidarity and self-help which, by the time of the publication of her novel was beginning to attract a large segment of the black American population,[17] Harper attacks racial assimilationism in *Iola Leroy* by picturing it as a selfish, unchristian betrayal of the black race. Her mulatto heroes spurn the chance to pass for white or otherwise to merge their professional, social, and economic interests with those of the white world. They prefer to lead "their" race "to higher planes of thought and action" rather than "to open the gates of material prosperity" for themselves.[18] The sort of "thought and action" toward which Harper's idealistic young mixed-bloods might lead the masses is left vague in the novel, but it is clearly not "social equality"—which is repudiated in one conversation with whites—nor is it political rights—of which nothing is said in the novel. The mulatto thus represents a conservative attitude toward social and political agitation for entry into the white man's world, an attitude anticipating Booker T. Washington's position. Far from being a threat to the body politic, his particular disavowal of passing, miscegenation, and other forms of "social equal-

15. The Fates prohibit interracial marriage in Margaret Holmes's *The Chamber Over The Gate* (Indianapolis: Charles A. Bates, 1886).
16. Gertrude Atherton, *Senator North* (1900; rpt. Ridgewood, N.J.: Gregg, 1967), p. 246.
17. See August Meier, *Negro Thought in America 1880–1915* (Ann Arbor: Univ. of Michigan Press, 1966), p. 166.
18. Frances E. W. Harper, *Iola Leroy, or Shadows Uplifted* (2nd ed., 1892; rpt. College Park, Md.: McGrath, 1969), p. 219.

ity" shows him to be racially orthodox on the central issue which so many Americans worried about.

A more liberal group of novelists were unwilling to view the mulatto as so altruistic as the Davis-Harper contingent did, nor did this group take such a moralistic and uniformly condemnatory view of passing for white. Albion Tourgée, for example, in both *A Royal Gentleman* (1881) and *Pactolus Prime* depicts with understanding and sympathy the plight of mixed-bloods whose superior abilities and achievements are spurned by white society. Toinette, the heroine of *A Royal Gentleman*, asserts her dignity when she refuses the offer of her former master and lover to live with him after the war as she had done previous to it. Her subsequent decision to go North and "*be* what she seemed—a lady," so that her son "should never be humbled and broken with the stigma of ignoble birth,"[19] is not presented as duplicitous or immoral. Far from the self-denying mulatto heroines of much "tragic mulatto" fiction, "she did not care to devote herself to the elevation of the freed people. She loved the good things of life, her own enjoyments, light, love, music, pleasant and agreeable surroundings." In the end Tourgée seems tacitly to endorse Toinette's self-regarding decision; he grants his heroine the financial support of a white female benefactor in the novel.

Though *Pactolus Prime* contains the self-sacrificial Eva Prime, the novel also contains several sympathetic references to passing for white. An officer in the Union Army encourages Eva's father, the novel's title character, to conceal his racial heritage after escaping from slavery. Prime's lawyer, the executor of his will, refuses to reveal the whereabouts of a young mulatto who has followed Prime's advice to pass for white. Through the lawyer's urbane rhetorical question, " 'Would it not be better to leave him to work out his own destiny?' "[20] Tourgée counsels tolerance and noninterference even in such explosive matters as passing for white and miscegenation. With Eva opposed to passing and miscegenation on moral grounds and her father and his protégé both in favor of it on practical grounds, Tourgée leaves the issue to the individual reader. But in light of the injustice of American racial attitudes, particularly as they touch the mixed-blood, Tourgée seems to regard passing into white society as an understandable option for those who can take advantage of it.[21]

Perhaps the most famous writer to take a realistic and unconventional look at the miscegenation-passing issue at this time was W. D. Howells. In *An Imperative Duty* (1892), Howells took the unprecedented step of allowing a near-white woman to marry a suitor who urges her to choose their happiness over what she at one point conceives as her "imperative duty" to devote herself to humanitarian work among black people. Howells seems to have chosen deliberately the stock "exceptional case" plot, in which a young white woman predictably rejects her lover

19. Albion Tourgée, *A Royal Gentleman* (Boston: Fords, Howard, & Hulbert, 1881), pp. 433–434.
20. Albion Tourgée, *Pactolus Prime* (New York: Cassell, 1890), p. 358.
21. Although a character in *A Royal Gentleman* speculates on the eventuality of race-mixing in America, nothing in the novel matches the boldness of *Toinette* (1875), as earlier, pseudonymously published version of *A Royal Gentleman*, in which Toinette and her master marry at the end of the novel.

after making the shocking discovery of her own mixed ancestry, so that he could ridicule the idea of masochistic renunciation on which so many novels of miscegenation turned. The resolute rationalism of Dr. Olney, the suitor in question, demands that Rhoda Aldgate recognize the unhappy consequences which her decision to do her supposed "duty" would have on everyone concerned. Olney's bemused, good-natured responses to Rhoda's near-hysterical revelation of her antecedents enable Howells to mock the sense of taboo and tragedy which dominated American opinion regarding miscegenation, while also burlesquing the melodrama which represented and exploited such feelings in American fiction.

Among the liberal thinkers on the miscegenation issue, Howells was one of the first prominent white men of his day to suggest that wholesale amalgamation of the races could be the final solution to America's race problem.[22] Yet the outcome of *An Imperative Duty* depicts Rhoda and Olney settling in Italy after marriage, where Rhoda's concealment of her past will be easier. This avoidance of the problem of whether mixed marriages can or should exist on American soil marks Howells's novel as more an evaluation of the abstract reasonableness of Rhoda's "dutiolatry" than a representative study of the moral and social problems of miscegenation in America. The novel's racial implications, while significant, do not compellingly suggest Howells as a leader in trying to redirect American opinion concerning the efficaciousness of racial assimilation on a broad scale.

The novel of miscegenation was also a satiric tool in Mark Twain's *Pudd'nhead Wilson* (1894), a book like *An Imperative Duty* designed more to attack misbegotten social prejudices than to deal with the contemporary problems of passing and intermarriage. Set in the ante-bellum South, *Pudd'nhead Wilson* explores American racial attitudes via the presentation of yet another "exceptional case." The villain of the novel is Tom Driscoll, a mulatto who passes for white, murders his supposed white father, and betrays his mother, Roxy, to almost certain death in the New Orleans slave pens before his criminal campaign is finally halted. Driscoll is perhaps the most reprehensible mulatto figure created in American fiction of Mark Twain's day, and his unscrupulous behavior may very well have reinforced many popular fears concerning the mulatto as racial subversive. Yet if Driscoll is dehumanized in the novel, the reason lies more in Mark Twain's larger satiric purpose than in any view of the consequences of miscegenation which he may have been trying to perpetrate through the novel. The chief function of the mulatto in *Pudd'nhead Wilson* is as "the instrument of an avenging destiny which has overtaken Dawson's Landing" for its sins, particularly the sin of hypocrisy.[23] Behind the myth of white supremacy lurks the mulatto in *Pudd'nhead Wilson* controlling the fortunes of many Southern aristocrats supposedly his superiors. Behind their professions of aristocratic honor and racial purity, the mulatto stands as testimony

22. " 'I've been more and more struck with the fact that sooner or later our race must absorb the colored race; and I believe that it will obliterate not only its color, but its qualities.' " *An Imperative Duty*, ed. Edwin H. Cady (New York: Twayne, 1962), p. 161.

23. James M. Cox, "*Pudd'nhead Wilson:* The End of Mark Twain's American Dream," *South Atlantic Quarterly*, 58 (1959), p. 353.

to the falsehood of such claims. Driscoll himself is not interesting to Mark Twain; rather, what Driscoll signifies and what he may be used to expose concerns Twain.

Although *Pudd'nhead Wilson* concerns the miscegenation problem and pictures the career of a mixed-blood passing for white, the novel sidesteps direct comment on the morality of these issues. Although Roxy believes her son's baseness is attributable to "the nigger in him," Twain suggests that Tom's training and his perilous situation, not his racial background determine his acts. Thus the whole issue of the morality of racial assimilation as a voluntarily chosen means of securing denied rights and opportunities is not broached in *Pudd'nhead Wilson*, so powerful is the theme of circumstantial determinism in the novel. The story is designed to obliterate the pretensions of the Old South myth on which New South white supremacy and anti-assimilationism were based. Nevertheless, while *Pudd'nhead Wilson* is as effective a satire of Cavalier race pride as *An Imperative Duty* is of Puritan dutiolatry, neither novel, as a novel of miscegenation, confronts directly the question of the potential threat of racial assimilation to the American social system of the late nineteenth century.

The two novelists who did most to suggest the threat of miscegenation to turn-of-the-century American society were one-time preachers: Thomas Dixon, the Negrophobic sensationalist, and Sutton E. Griggs, whose fiction was written in part to counter Dixon's race-baiting novels. Dixon made his literary fame and a considerable fortune on *The Leopard's Spots* (1902), a best-seller which defended the rise of white supremacy in post-war Dixie as the only bulwark against the rape of Southern rights and Southern women by hordes of acquisitive, bestial blacks. Dixon's "Romance of the White Man's Burden, 1865–1900"[24] was the first widely-selling American novel to dramatize and exploit the fear of the black man's supposed sexual aggressiveness which underlay much of the argument for white supremacy and segregation in the South. The appearance of the Ku Klux Klan, the rise of Jim Crow legislation, the disfranchisement of the blacks, and the establishment of white political domination of the South are all the necessary and justifiable result of the South's resolution of a question which to Dixon was more vital than other political issues, was "larger than the South, or even the nation, and held in its solution the brightest hopes of the progress of the human race."[25] The question was " '*Shall the future American be an Anglo-Saxon or a Mulatto?*' "

Dixon's interpretation of Southern history after the Civil War follows a predictable pattern; he depicts black political and civil advancement leading irrevocably to an assault on fundamental Southern social institutions. The only act of a mixed legislature which Dixon notes is an act proposing the abolition of white marriages. The black leaders in the novel are categorized as uniformly dangerous to the virtue of white women and the sanctity of the family. Even the most passionate promoter of black civil rights in *The Leopard's Spots*, a well-meaning New England politician named Everett Lowell, recoils at the proposal of George Harris, an educated and capable young mulatto, for the hand of his daughter.

24. This is the subtitle to *The Leopard's Spots* (New York: Doubleday, Page, 1902).
25. *Ibid.*, p. 159.

" 'One drop of your blood in my family could push it backward three thousand years in history.' " Lowell thunders to Harris. To prevent such an eventuality, any methods of restricting black power were acceptable; according to Dixon, the monstrous prospect of a "mulatto America," the outcome of Afro-American political, social, and sexual equality, dwarfed the enormity of his restrictive methods.

The Leopard's Spots occupies an extreme position in the literature of social debate concerning miscegenation. While most novelists posed the question of the social effects of miscegenation in genteel terms, using exceptional cases of possible intermarriage between refined whites and near-whites, Dixon blatantly posed the issue of a "Mulatto America" in the most hysterical terms. He was not concerned with the isolated case of passing, nor did the romance and tragedy of the mulatto in America hold any fascination for him, as it did for so many novelists who wrote in this vein. In Dixon's hands, the problem of miscegenation assumed the cataclysmic social and political dimensions which earlier novelists, social thinkers, and politicians had only intimated. Spurred by the rise of anti-black sentiment at the turn of the century, Dixon used rape as his metaphor for black political, economic, and social advancement, thus playing on the deep-seated fears which Thomas Pearce Bailey would later summarize as the "crux" of the American race problem.

Sutton Griggs, a less prominent but more prolific contemporary of Charles Chesnutt's, took up the Dixon challenge most explicitly in fiction. In one of his early novels, *Overshadowed* (1900), Griggs took a strict separatist line. He warned against "social equality" and miscegenation by citing several cases of white seducers whose blandishments lure upstanding mulatto girls to their shame. But Griggs's most straightforward denunciation of Dixon's view of the black man as subverter of American family institutions and socio-political order is written into a later novel, *The Hindered Hand* (1905). Again, Griggs shows black women victimized by lustful whites while one of his heroes, in a discussion of *The Leopard's Spots*, maintains that black men are neither sexually licentious in general nor passionately attracted to white women in particular. Rejecting the likelihood or the wisdom of George Harris's proposal in Dixon's novel, Griggs emphasizes that intermarriage can only be politically counterproductive as well as personally harmful. He backs up his contention with an allusion to "the spiritual alienation" that Frederick Douglass was never able to overcome after his marriage to a white woman.[26] Furthermore, Griggs has a beautiful octoroon expose the plan of her mother to form a sort of mulatto fifth-column movement in the South, "composed of cultured men and women that could readily pass for white, who were to shake the Southern system to its very foundation."[27] Ultimately, *The Hindered Hand* proposes a solution to the Southern race problem in the formation of "an Eclectic party" of whites and blacks bent on the achievement of political equality through conventional means without recourse to deception or the kind of racial assimilation which many whites feared. The upshot of Griggs's novel, therefore, was to re-

26. Sutton E. Griggs, *The Hindered Hand* (1905; rpt. Miami; Mnemosyne, 1969), p. 212. Douglass's second wife, whom he married in 1884, was white.
27. *Ibid.*, p. 236.

affirm the difference between the pursuit of political and civil equality and the pursuit of "social equality." With George W. Cable, Rebecca Harding Davis, Frances E. W. Harper, and most of his other predecessors in the novel of miscegenation, Griggs repudiated passing as "unnatural" and intermarriage as ill-considered, even spiritually damaging. Opposing black-white assimilation in areas other than politics and civil action, Griggs argued the speciousness of Dixon's racial paranoia by employing the novel of miscegenation and passing in a conventional way to calm the fears aroused by the prospect of unbridled racial assimilation—Dixon's "Mulatto America"—while encouraging sympathy and understanding toward the Afro-American's legitimate political and civil agitation.

Though ostensibly a form of romance,[28] the novel of miscegenation in late nineteenth-century America was a potent tool in the hands of social commentators and racial propagandists on both sides of the color line. To early black fictionists, the novel of miscegenation could be tailored to counter adverse racial stereotypes by stressing the integrity and social responsibility of the mulatto-dominated Talented Tenth. It could focus public attention on the critical, legitimate demands of the race by labeling the red herring of "social equality" as a spurious issue. It could also represent in fictional form the ideals of race pride and solidarity which by the 1880s and 1890s were beginning to draw followers away from the assimilationism of earlier race leaders.

Similarly, in the hands of white novelists, the novel of miscegenation could be used to titillate the sensibilities and tug at the heartstrings of American readers while at the same time reinforcing prevailing social norms against intermarriage. With the notable exception of Thomas Dixon, white writers used the novel of miscegenation to suggest the mulattoes were more sinned against than sinning, while soothing their readers' consciences with ample evidence that extensive assimilation, "social equality," and intermarriage were for the most part no more desired by self-respecting blacks and mulattoes than by whites. Special cases of passing and miscegenation might be entertained so long as they did not portend a socio-political trend. But usually white novelists who dealt with miscegenation obliquely assured their readers that, as a political and social entity, the mulatto, like his darker brother, was "not going to do anything dynamitic to the structure of society. He is going to take things as he finds it, and make the best of his rather poor chances in it. In his heart is no bitterness." Thus opined W. D. Howells in a review of the work of late nineteenth-century America's most "exemplary" Afro-American, Booker T. Washington,[29] a man of mixed blood whose conservative, unaggressive, socio-political philosophy epitomized the view of racial assimilation which so many Americans wanted to find and found in the novel of miscegenation.

28. "The relations between a subject and a dominant race are always fruitful of romance," Albion Tourgée observed in the Preface to *A Royal Gentleman*.

29. W. D. Howells, "An Exemplary Citizen," *North American Review*, 173 (1900), p. 285.

CASE STUDIES AND CLOSE READINGS

The Tragic Mulatto Theme in
Six Works of Langston Hughes*

ARTHUR P. DAVIS

The Weary Blues (1925), the first publication of Langston Hughes contained a provocative twelve-line poem entitled "Cross," which dealt with the tragic mulatto theme. Two years later when Mr. Hughes brought out *Fine Clothes to the Jew* (1927), he included another poem on racial intermixture which he named "Mulatto." During the summer of 1928 when Hughes was working with the Hedgerow Theatre at Moylan Rose Valley, Pennsylvania, he completed a full-length drama on the tragic mulatto theme, which he also called *Mulatto*. This play was produced on Broadway in 1935 where it ran for a full year, followed by an eight month's tour across the nation. From the play, the poet composed a short story, "Father and Son," which though written later than the play, appeared in *The Ways of White Folks* (1934), a year before the drama was produced. Returning once more to the theme, Hughes in 1949 reworked the play *Mulatto* into an opera, *The Barrier*, the music for which was written by the modern composer Jan Meyerowitz. The opera was first produced at Columbia University in 1950. And finally in 1952, Hughes published another short story on the tragic mulatto theme entitled "African Morning." This sketch appears in *Laughing to Keep from Crying*, a second collection of short stories. In short, for over a quarter of a century, the author has been concerned with this theme; returning to it again and again, he has presented the thesis in four different genres, in treatments varying in length from a twelve-line poem to a full-length Broadway play.[1]

Before discussing Mr. Hughes' several presentations of the theme, however, let us understand the term "tragic mulatto." As commonly used in American fiction and drama, it denotes a light-colored, mixed-blood character (possessing in most cases a white father and a colored mother), who suffers because of difficulties arising from his bi-racial background. In our literature there are, of course, valid and convincing portrayals of this type; but as it is a character which easily lends itself to sensational exaggeration and distortion, there are also many stereotypes of the tragic mulatto to be found. And these stereotypes, as Professor Brown has

* From Arthur P. Davis, "The Tragic Mulatto Theme in Six Works of Langston Hughes." *Phylon* 16 (1955): 195–204.

1. I must point out that the six works chosen for this study are not the only ones by Hughes treating the subject. These six, however, are the most typical and therefore serve my purpose best. See "Red Headed Baby" (*The Ways of White Folks*) and "New Cabaret Girl" (*Fine Clothes to the Jew*) for other examples of Hughes' concern with the problem of mixed blood.

so ably pointed out, are not only marked by "exaggeration and omission";[2] they often embody racial myths and shibboleths. In them "the mulatto is a victim of divided inheritance; from his white blood come his intellectual strivings, his unwillingness to be a slave; from his Negro blood come his baser emotional urges, his indolence, his savagery."[3] Whether any given character is a true flesh and blood portrait or a stereotype depends, of course, upon the knowledge, the skill, and the integrity of the artist; and this is true whether the author be Negro or white. But it would not be unfair to state that though both are guilty, the white writer tends to use the stereotype more often than the Negro.

Regardless of the approach, however—valid portrayal or stereotype—the tragic mulatto, because of our racial situation, has been popular with the American writer from the very beginnings of our literature. In fiction and in drama, we have a long line of tragic mixed-blood characters, extending from Cooper's Cora Munro (*Last of the Mohicans*) and Boucicault's Zoe (*The Octoroon*) down to the present-day creations of William Faulkner and Fannie Hurst. Considering its popularity, we are not surprised that Langston Hughes has made use of the theme, but we are intrigued by the persistency with which he has clung to it over the years.

Why then has he been so deeply concerned with the tragic mulatto? Has he given us a deeper and more realistic analysis of the mixed-blood character? Are his central figures different from the stereotypes created by other writers? Or, does Hughes, perhaps unconsciously, employ the theme of the tragic mulatto to express vicariously and symbolically some basic inner conflict in his own personality? It will be the purpose of this paper to seek an answer to these questions through an analysis of six of Mr. Hughes' works.

Let us turn first to "Cross," the original statement of the theme and the "germ-idea" from which the Mulatto group was derived. Surprisingly stark and unadorned, the poem begins with ballad-like abruptness:

My old man's a white old man
And my old mother's black.
If ever I cursed my white old man
I take my curses back.

If I ever cursed my black old mother
And wished she were in hell,
I am sorry for that evil wish
And now I wish her well.

My old man died in a fine big house,
My ma died in a shack,
I wonder where I'm gonna die,
Being neither white nor black?

---

2. Sterling A. Brown, "Negro Character as Seen by White Authors," *Journal of Negro Education, II*, No. 2 (1933), 179ff. This is a full and excellent discussion of the Negro stereotype in American fiction. [Included in this volume, pp. 274–280. —Ed.]

3. *Ibid.*, 194–5 [in this volume, p. 279. —Ed.].

Through suggestion and implication rather than by direct narrative, the poet has given us in three quatrains the whole tragic story of a mulatto's bitter resentment against his "mixed" background and his failure in life which he seems to attribute to that background. We are told specifically that the mulatto at first blamed both parents for his plight; that subsequently, for some unstated reason, he forgives his father and mother; and finally that he pities himself because of a sense of not-belonging. These are the stated facts of the piece, but a close reading of the poem suggests other implications as important as the facts themselves.

There is first of all the idea of desertion on the part of the white father indicated in the two separate death places—one in "a fine big house," the other in a shack. There is also rejection implied in that we assume the mulatto lived with his mother. We therefore detect a hint of envy and regret when he speaks of his father's inaccessible fine big house. Perhaps there is a bit of fondness on the part of the mulatto unconsciously expressed in the phrase "my old man." We know that he forgave his father, and we sense a feeling of regret on his part even for the death of a parent who had rejected him and whom he could not know. In the final analysis, the poem boils down to a fruitless search for a father and a home, and it is this pattern which Langston Hughes has followed in all of the subsequent works on the tragic mulatto theme.

In contrast to the classic restraint and economy of phrase we find in "Cross," Mr. Hughes in "Mulatto"[4] writes with an exuberance which is almost hysterical in quality. We feel immediately the passion and violence, and we somehow get the impression that all of the speakers in the poem (it is a dramatic dialogue) are either shouting or screaming. The clash between white father and rejected son is driven home from the very first line:

> *I am your son, white man!*
>
> Georgia dusk
> And the turpentine woods.
> One of the pillars of the temple fell.
>
> > *You are my son!*
> > *Like hell!*
>
> The moon over the turpentine woods.
> The Southern night
> Full of stars,
> Great big yellow stars.
> > What's a body but a toy?
> > > Juicy bodies
> > > Of nigger wenches
> > > Blue black
> > > Against black fences.
> > > O, you little bastard boy,
> > What's a body but a toy?
> The scent of pine wood stings the soft night air.

---

4. In the following version of "Mulatto," I have omitted several lines because of limited space.

> *What's the body of your mother?*
> Silver moonlight everywhere.
> *What's the body of your mother?*
> Sharp pine scent in the evening air.
> A nigger night,
> A nigger joy,
> A little yellow
> Bastard boy.
>
> *Naw, you ain't my brother.*
> *Niggers ain't my brother.*
> *Not ever.*
> *Niggers ain't my brother.*
> . . . .
> *Git on back there in the night,*
> *You ain't white.*
> . . . . . .
> *I am your son, white man!*

We note at once that the rejection theme so vaguely suggested in "Cross" has become the central theme of this poem. All other issues are subordinate to it; and all of the images, symbols, incidents, and background scenery serve but to accentuate and dramatize the basic thesis of rejection. For example, Hughes intensifies the denial of kinship by making it now into a two-generation refusal: both half-brother and father brutally rebuff the mulatto. The poem also makes use of ironic contrast to degrade the mulatto's circumstances of birth. Stressing the stinging scent of the pine wood— a smell associated with cleanliness, purity, and idyllic lovemaking—he creates of it an inverted and distorted symbol of the sordid act of copulation between "blue black" nigger wenches and fallen white pillars of the temple. The idea of ironic contrast is further implied when he associates the clean and crystal-like brilliance of the innumerable "great big yellow stars" with the many "yellow bastards" so carelessly conceived beneath their sparkling splendor. The slurring reference on the part of the whites to this kind of evening's fun as "nigger joy" and the whole barbecue-like abandon of the scene both stress and dramatize the irresponsible casualness of this type of frolicking in the Negro section "against black fences." The use of the preposition "against" heightens the insult. All of these things serve not only to highlight the rejection of the mulatto but in effect to furnish a rationale for it.

The most insulting of these slurring expressions in the mouths of the white speakers is the line thrice repeated in the poem: "What's the body of your mother?" This slur, the rankest form of "the dozens," degrades the rejection of the yellow bastard past all hope of reconcilement. Hence there is no hint of fondness or forgiveness here. The mulatto, no longer a vaguely unhappy misfit as in "Cross," has become in the eyes of the whites a pariah, a mongrel cur who can never be "recognized." The rejection here is sadistically final and decisive.

We note one curious approach in "Mulatto." Hughes seems to place no blame at all on the dusky women who take part in these "nigger nights." He seems to ignore entirely their burden of guilt. All of his castigation is aimed at the white pillars of the temple who can indulge in such orgies and then callously reject the issue of their evening's pleasure. Is the poet suggesting that the black women are helpless victims? That would be too unrealistic. What he probably implies here is simply this: that the nocturnal inter-racial love-making itself is not the essential evil. It is the rejection of parenthood on the part of the father which is the unforgivable crime. And in other works on this theme, as we shall see later, he recognizes the economic pressures which motivate these black-white liaisons.

The next three versions of the tragic mulatto theme—the play, *Mulatto*, the short story, "Father and Son," and the opera libretto, *The Barrier*—may be treated together because they are one story presented in three different forms. Although there are minor differences among the three—differences occasioned largely by the nature of the form used—it is surprising how closely each follows the other. Unfortunately, the only one of the three published in English is "Father and Son" (there is an Italian version of *Mulatto* in print). My quotations from the play and the opera, therefore, will come from manuscript copies of these works. (May I say in passing that the opera libretto is artistically the most finished version of the story. Much of the violence and sensationalism of the original play is toned down in the poetry of the libretto. I know that it is impossible to evaluate an opera apart from its music, but the libretto of *The Barrier* stands well alone as poetic drama.) Since the play *Mulatto* is the original version of the three, I shall use that as a point of departure, quoting from "Father and Son" and *The Barrier* whenever necessary.

Mulatto tells the story of Colonel Thomas Norwood, a Georgia plantation owner, and his bastard son, Bert, a mulatto who insisted on being not just another "yard-nigger," but Colonel Norwood's son. The child of Cora Lewis, Norwood's colored mistress, Bert, unlike the other children of this alliance, looks like his father, has his father's eyes and height, and above all else, possesses the colonel's fiery spirit. When the story opens, we find that Bert has returned home for the summer. For the past six years he had been kept in school in Atlanta and is back now only because of his mother's pleading. At home Bert refuses to work as a field hand, ignores the colonel's rule about Negroes using his front door, talks back to white folks in the town, and violates in every way the mores of the community. Most shocking of all, Bert publicly announces that he is not "all-nigger," that he is Colonel Norwood's son and heir. Appalled by this conduct, Norwood calls Bert in and brutally attempts to make him "see his place." A violent scene between father and son takes place. Taunted by insults to his and to his mother's status, Bert in anger—and really something deeper than anger—kills his father and then commits suicide symbolically in his father's house before the mob can get him. This in barest of outlines is the plot of all three versions of the story. Let us look now at several pertinent details.

Again as in the poem "Mulatto," the central theme here is violent rejection. As a little tot, Bert used to trail at the colonel's heels, and the latter seemed to like this mark of affection until one day Bert made the mistake of calling Norwood "papa" in front of white visitors. The child received a vicious slap from his father for this *faux pas*. That was the first denial, and it left an indelible impression on the boy. In the last violent scene with Norwood, Bert tells the old man: "I used to like you, when I first knew you were my father . . . before that time you beat me under the feet of your horses." (Slowly) "I liked you until then."

The second denial came when Bert returned from school that summer. In utter forgetfulness of Southern custom, he had attempted to shake his white father's hand and had been cruelly rebuffed. In the third encounter between the two, Norwood raises his cane to strike the boy but is restrained by the latter's unflinching belligerency. And in the final tragic meeting of the two, we have the supreme rejection: Colonel Norwood denying, not the physical but the spiritual kinship between the two:

> *Norwood:* . . . Now, I'm going to let you talk to me, but I want you to talk right.
> *Bert* (still standing): What do you mean, 'talk right'?
> *Norwood:* I mean talk like a nigger should to a white man.
> *Bert:* Oh! But I'm not a nigger, Colonel Tom. I'm your son.
> *Norwood* (testily): You're Cora's boy.
> *Bert:* Women don't have children by themselves.
> *Norwood:* Nigger women don't know the fathers. You're a bastard.

After this taunting and degrading denial, Bert loses all control. Screaming hysterically, "Why don't you shoot?" he wrests a gun from the old man's hands and then chokes him to death. The fact that his father wanted to kill him is too much for the young boy's strained emotions. He cannot get the old man's intention out of his mind. "Why didn't he shoot, mama?" he asks wildly. "He didn't want *me* to live, why didn't he shoot?" The subsequent suicide is not only a way of cheating the mob. We sense that with the death of the colonel, the bottom has really dropped out of Bert's world, and he kills himself proudly.

One notes that throughout the play Bert seems to feel no shame for being a bastard; on the contrary, he seems almost proud that he is Norwood's son. On one occasion he tells his mother: "I'm no nigger anyhow, am I, ma? I'm half-white. The colonel's my father—the richest man in the country—and I am not going to take a lot of stuff from nobody."

It was not that Bert was living unhappily between two worlds—he had made an excellent adjustment in Atlanta Negro society. Nor did he want to be white. Bert simply wanted a home and a father; and with the unprejudiced viewpoint of youth, he could not understand why the colonel would not accept him as a son. His mother tries to reason with him on the matter (and I use here a quotation from *The Barrier*):

> *Cora:* You don't seem to know that here in Georgia
> You are not your father's son.
> *Bert:* Mama, I love you . . .
> But I can't understand now
> What you're saying.
> All I know is I am his son—
> And not in Georgia, nor anywhere else,
> Should a man deny his son.

This is Bert's position; it is also that of Langston Hughes. In spite of racial background and regional traditions, the problem, looked at objectively, is a personal one: the rejection of his son by a father.

Before we leave these three versions of the Bert–Colonel Norwood story, let us consider Cora. Again as in the poems, Hughes attaches no blame or condemnation to Cora's status as a white man's mistress. Except for the troubles which Bert caused—troubles which she understands better than anyone else in the play—Cora leads a fairly happy life; and more significant, she considers herself a good woman. Note her reaction when the tragedy comes to her loved ones:

> I lived right, Lawd!
> I tried to live right!
> Lawd! Lawd!
> And this is what you give me!
> What is the matter, Lawd,
> Ain't you with me?

There is no feeling of guilt here because Cora, motivated by economic pressures, had taken honest advantage of a relationship which gave her and her family a fuller and more secure life. Note again the position she takes in Act II (Scene 2) of *Mulatto* as she recalls hysterically her first affair with the Colonel:

> . . . then I cried and cried and told my mother about it, but she didn't take it hard like I thought she'd take it. She said fine white mens like de young Colonel always take good care of their colored womens. She said it was better than marryin' some black field hand and workin' all your life in the cotton and cane.

The last version of the tragic mulatto theme in Langston Hughes' works is found in "African Morning," a short story appearing in *Laughing to Keep from Crying* (1952). The scene of this little sketch is laid in the delta country of the River Niger. The story depicts a day in the life of Maurai, a lonely, twelve-year-old, half-white, half-native boy, the only mixed-blood person in his seaport village. Son of the English local bank president and his native mistress, Maurai had been reared inside the European enclosure in the home of his father. Having lost his mother, Maurai had been rejected by her people and left with his father's new African mistress. He was also rejected by his father who tolerated him, used him for running errands, but who wasted no love or affection on the little half-caste child. For example, when white visitors came, the father made Maurai eat in the kitchen with the black mistress.

When the story opens we find Maurai changing from his native to European dress in order to go on an errand for his father. (Note that even in dress he has no fixed world.) Going to the bank, he walked into his father's office where whites were counting gold. "Wait outside, Maurai," said his father sharply, covering the gold with his hands. Natives were not allowed to possess gold; it was the white man's jealously-guarded prerogative to do so, and because of this proscription gold became a symbol of the whites' power and control. "Maybe that's why the black people hate me," Maurai mused, "because I am the color of gold." (Langston Hughes here and elsewhere uses "yellow" as a symbol for the degradation and unhappiness which supposedly come from mixed-blood situations.)

After delivering his father's message to a sea captain, Maurai is taken for a native "guide boy" by one of the white sailors; but as soon as he reaches the docks he is taunted and beaten by the native black boys and the black women because of his color and his European clothes. He runs to the jungle with the sound of their "yellow bastard" ringing in his ears. In a jungle lagoon, he finds solace for both bruised body and lacerated spirit. Maurai was not afraid of the jungle or of the crocodiles or snakes that could be in the lagoon. Maurai was afraid of only three things: "white people and black people—and gold." As he floated in the pool, he began to pity himself and his sad lot: "Suppose I were to stay here forever," he thought, "in the dark at the bottom of the pool." But Maurai was only twelve, and these morbid thoughts soon passed. He got out of the pool, dressed, and returned to his home inside the European enclosure. As lonely as his present existence was, he realized that it would be much worse when his father returned to England, "leaving him in Africa where nobody wanted him."

Artistically, "African Morning" ranks with *The Barrier*. Probably because of its African background, it seems more convincing than the other versions of the tragic mulatto theme. It is also more touching because it concerns a defenseless child. All in all "African Morning" is a restrained, finished, and effectively-written sketch. Possessing none of the sensationalism of the Mulatto-trio, it nevertheless tells once more the same basic story—that of a mixed-blood boy, hungry for recognition, being rejected by a father.

On the surface, Langston Hughes' tragic mulattoes do not seem to be essentially different from the stereotypes of other writers. Their violence, as in the case of Bert, their loneliness, their divided loyalty, their frustrations, their maladjustments, and their tendency to destroy themselves—all of these characteristics, typical of the stereotype, are found (or suggested) in Hughes' central figures. But there are at least two vital differences in the latter's approach. In the first place, many—not all—but many white writers state or imply that the effect of mixed blood per se has something to do with the mulatto's supposedly confused personality; note, for example, the following passage from Paul Green's *In Abraham's Bosom:*

> *Bud:* White and black make bad mixtry.
>
> *Lije:* Do dat. (Thumping his chest) Nigger down heah. (Thumping his head) White mens up here. Heart say do one thing, head say 'nudder. Bad, bad.

As a Negro, Hughes is never guilty of this kind of nonsense. Knowing, as do all intelligent persons, that heredity works along individual rather than racial patterns, he has avoided this aspect of the stereotype, and that in itself is a difference of some importance.

The outstanding contribution, however, which Hughes has made in his delineation of the tragic mulatto, it seems to me, is to point out that at bottom the problem of the mixed-blood character is basically a personal problem. Bert and

Maurai, for example, would have been satisfied just to have the recognition of their respective fathers. They were apparently not interested in the larger sociological aspects of divided inheritance. They were not trying to create racial issues. They wanted two very simple but fundamental things: a home and a father. In short, Hughes reduces his tragic mulatto problem to a father and son conflict, and for him the single all-important and transcending issue is rejection—personal rejection on the part of the father.

I am convinced that Langston Hughes felt very keenly on this whole matter of rejection, and I believe that a most revealing postscript to this discussion of father-son relationships may be found in his autobiography, *The Big Sea* (1940). In this work there is a chapter entitled simply "Father," in which Hughes has accounted for, it seems to me, several of the attitudes he portrays in his tragic mulattoes.

Coming from a split home, Langston Hughes did not get to know his father until he was seventeen, the latter having moved to Mexico after the family break-up. During all of his early years of frequent removals and hand-to-mouth living with his mother and other relatives, Hughes came to look upon his father, living "permanently" in Mexico, as the "one stable factor" in his life. "He at least stayed put," and to the young Langston this was an impressive achievement. Although his mother had told him that the senior Hughes was a "devil on wheels," he did not believe her. On the contrary, he created in his mind a heroic image of his father, picturing him as a "strong bronze cowboy in a big Mexican hat," living free in a country where there was no race prejudice.

And then at seventeen, Hughes met his father and went to live with him in Mexico. Disillusionment came quickly, followed by a reaction far more serious. He found that the elder Hughes was neither kind nor understanding. "As weeks went by," he writes, "I could think of less and less to say to my father. His whole way of living was so different from mine." For the first time, the boy began to understand why his mother had left her husband; he wondered why she had married him in the first place; and most important of all he wondered why they had chosen to have him. "Now at seventeen," Langston Hughes tells us, "I began to be very sorry for myself. . . . I began to wish that I had never been born—not under such circumstances."

And then this unhappy, seventeen-year-old boy, like Maurai in "African Morning," contemplated suicide: "One day, when there was no one in the house but me," he writes, "I put the pistol to my head and held it there, loaded, a long time, and wondered if I would be any happier if I were to pull the trigger."

Subsequently, during a spell of serious illness, Langston Hughes' dislike of his father crystallized into something dangerously approaching fixation. "And when I thought of my father," he tells us, "I got sicker and sicker. I hated my father."

That last short sentence helps to explain for me Hughes' persistent concern with the tragic mulatto theme. In his handling of the theme he has found an opportunity to write out of his system, as it were, the deep feelings of disappointment and resentment that he himself felt as a "rejected" son.

Mark Twain's *Pudd'nhead Wilson**

LANGSTON HUGHES

Mark Twain's ironic little novel, *Pudd'nhead Wilson*, is laid on the banks of the Mississippi in the first half of the 1800s. It concerns itself with, among other things, the use of fingerprinting to solve the mystery of a murder. But *Pudd'nhead Wilson* is not a mystery novel. The reader knows from the beginning who committed the murder and has more than an inkling of how it will be solved. The circumstances of the denouement, however, possessed in its time great novelty, for fingerprinting had not then come into official use in crime detection in the United States. Even a man who fooled around with it as a hobby was thought to be a simpleton, a puddenhead. Such was the reputation acquired by Wilson, the young would-be lawyer in the Missouri frontier town of Dawson's Landing. But Wilson eventually made his detractors appear as puddenheads themselves.

Although introduced early, it is not until near the end of the book that Wilson becomes a major figure in the tale. The novel is rather the story of another young man's mistaken identity—a young man who thinks he is white but is in reality colored; who is heir to wealth without knowing his claim is false; who lives as a free man, but is legally a slave; and who, when he learns the true facts about himself, comes to ruin not through the temporarily shattering knowledge of his physical status, but because of weaknesses common to white or colored, slave or free. The young man thinks his name is Thomas à Becket Driscoll, but it is really Valet de Chambre—a name used for twenty-three years by another who is held as a slave in his stead, but who, unknown to himself, is white—and therefore legally free.

Puddn'head Wilson is the man, who, in the end, sets things to rights. But for whom? Seemingly for spectators only, not for the principals involved, for by that time to them right is wrong, wrong is right, and happiness has gone by the board. The slave system has taken its toll of all three concerned—mother, mammy, ward and child—for the mother and mammy, Roxana, matriarch and slave are one. Roxy is a puppet whose at first successful deceits cause her to think herself a free agent. She is undone at the climax by the former laughing stock of the town, Pudd'nhead Wilson, whose long interest in the little swirls at the ends of the fingers finally pays off.

Years before he published *Pudd'nhead Wilson* Mark Twain had been hailed as America's greatest humorist. From *The Celebrated Jumping Frog of Calaveras County* in 1865 to *The Adventures of Huckleberry Finn* in 1884, most of his fiction— and his spoken words on the lecture platform—had been sure sources of laughter. But in this work of his middle years (Twain was 59) he did not write a humorous novel. Except for a few hilarious village scenes, and a phonetic description of a baby's tantrums, the out-loud laughs to be found in *Tom Sawyer* or *Huckleberry*

* From Langston Hughes, "Introduction" to Mark Twain's *Pudd'nhead Wilson* (New York: Bantam Books, 1962), vii–xiii.

Finn are not a part of *Pudd'nhead*. In this book the basic theme is slavery, seriously treated, and its main thread concerns the absurdity of man-made differentials, whether of caste or "race." The word *race* might properly be placed in quotes for both of Mark Twain's central Negroes are largely white in blood and physiognomy, slaves only by circumstance, and each only "by a fiction of law and custom, a Negro." The white boy who is mistakenly raised as a slave in the end finds himself "rich and free, but in a most embarrassing situation. He could neither read nor write, and his speech was the basest dialect of the Negro quarter. His gait, his attitudes, his gestures, his bearing, his laugh—all were vulgar and uncouth; his manners were the manners of a slave. Money and fine clothes could not mend these defects or cover them up, they only made them the more glaring and pathetic. The poor fellow could not endure the terrors of the white man's parlour, and felt at home and at peace nowhere but in the kitchen."

On the other hand, the young dandy who thought his name was Thomas à Becket, studied at Yale. He then came home to Dawson's Landing bedecked in Eastern finery to lord it over black and white alike. As Pudd'nhead Wilson, who had the habit of penning little musings beneath the dates in his calendar, wrote, "Training is everything. The peach was once a bitter almond; cauliflower is nothing but cabbage with a college education." It took a foreigner with no regard for frontier aristocracy of Old Virginia lineage to kick Thomas à Becket right square in his sit-downer at a public meeting. In the ensuing free-for-all that breaks out, the hall is set afire. Here the sparkle of Twain's traditional humor bursts into hilarious flame, too, as the members of the nearby fire department—"who never stirred officially in unofficial costume"—donned their uniforms to drench the hall with enough water to "annihilate forty times as much fire as there was there; for a village fire company does not often get a chance to show off." Twain wryly concludes, "Citizens of that village . . . did not insure against fire; they insured against the fire-company."

Against fire and water in the slave states there was insurance, but none against the devious dangers of slavery itself. Not even a fine old gentleman like Judge Driscoll "of the best blood of the Old Dominion" could find insurance against the self-protective schemes of his brother's bond servant, Roxy, who did not like being a slave, but was willing to be one for her son's sake. Roxy was also willing to commit a grievous sin for her son's sake, palliating her conscience a little by saying, "white folks has done it." With "an unfair show in the battle of life," as Twain puts it, Roxy, as an "heir of two centuries of unatoned insult and outrage," is yet not of an evil nature. Her crimes grow out of the greater crimes of the slave system. "The man in whose favor no laws of property exist," Thomas Jefferson wrote in his *Notes on Virginia*, "feels himself less bound to respect those made in favor of others."

Roxy's fear of eventually receiving the same punishment as that threatened other servants for the thieving of a few dollars from their master, Percy Driscoll, was enough to start a chain of thought in her mind that led eventually to disaster. Even though her master was "a fairly humane man towards slaves and other animals," was he not a thief himself? Certainly he was, to one in bondage, "the man who daily robbed him of an inestimable treasury—his liberty." Out of the structure of slave society itself is fashioned a noose of doom. In *Pudd'nhead Wilson* Mark Twain wrote what at a later period might have been called in the finest sense of the term, "a novel of social significance." Had Twain been a contemporary of Harriet Beecher Stowe, and this novel published before the War between the States, it might have been a minor *Uncle Tom's Cabin*. Twain minces no words in describing the unfortunate effects of slavery upon the behavior of both Negroes and whites, even upon children. The little master, Thomas, and the little slave, Chambers, were both born on the same day and grew up together. But even in "babyhood Tom cuffed and banged and scratched Chambers unrebuked, and Chambers early learned that between meekly bearing it and resenting it, the advantage all lay with the former policy. The few times his persecutions had moved him beyond control and made him fight back had cost him . . . three such convincing canings from the man who was his father and didn't know it, that he took Tom's cruelties in all humility after that, and made no more experiments. Outside of the house the two boys were together all through their boyhood. . . . Tom staked him with marbles to play 'keeps' with, and then took all the winnings away from him. In the winter season Chambers was on hand, in Tom's worn-out clothes . . . to drag a sled up the hill for Tom, warmly clad, to ride down on; but he never got a ride himself. He built snow men and snow fortifications under Tom's directions. He was Tom's patient target when Tom wanted to do some snowballing, but the target couldn't fire back. Chambers carried Tom's skates to the river and strapped them on him, then trotted around after him on the ice, so as to be on hand when wanted; but he wasn't ever asked to try the skates himself."

Mark Twain, in his presentation of Negroes as human beings, stands head and shoulders above the other Southern writers of his times, even such distinguished ones as Joel Chandler Harris, F. Hopkins Smith, and Thomas Nelson Page. It was a period when most writers who included Negro characters in their work at all, were given to presenting the slave as ignorant and happy, the freed men of color as ignorant and miserable, and all Negroes as either comic servants on the one hand or dangerous brutes on the other. That Mark Twain's characters in *Pudd'nhead Wilson* fall into none of these categories is a tribute to his discernment. And that he makes them neither heroes nor villains is a tribute to his understanding of human character. "Color is only skin deep." In this novel Twain shows how more than anything else environment shapes the man. Yet in his day behavioristic psychology was in its infancy. Likewise the science of fingerprinting. In 1894 *Pudd'nhead Wilson* was a "modern" novel indeed. And it still may be so classified.

Although knowledge of fingerprinting dates back some two thousand years, and fingerprints are found as signatures on ancient Chinese tablets and Babylonian records, it was not until 1880 that the first treatise on the possible use of fingerprinting in criminal identification appeared in English. And it was sixteen years later (two years after the appearance of *Pudd'nhead Wilson*) before the International Association of Chiefs of Police meeting in Chicago in 1896 decided to set up a Bureau of Criminal Identification and, as a part of its program, study ways and means whereby fingerprinting might supplement or perhaps supplant the Bertillon system of bodily measurements as a means of identifying criminals. So Mark

Twain was well ahead of the international keepers of law and order when he devoted several pages in his novel to a description of how fingerprints might be used for the positive identification of a criminal who has neglected to put on gloves before committing a crime.

"Every human being," Twain has Pudd'nhead Wilson inform the court, "carries with him from his cradle to his grave certain physical marks which do not change their character, and by which he can always be identified—and that without shade of doubt or question. These marks are his signature, his physiological autograph, so to speak, and this autography cannot be counterfeited, nor can he disguise it or hide it away, nor can it become illegible by the wear and the mutations of time. . . . This autograph consists of the delicate lines or corrugations with which Nature marks the insides of the hands and the soles of the feet. If you will look at the balls of your fingers—you that have very sharp eyesight—you will observe that these dainty curving lines lie close together, like those that indicate the borders of oceans in maps, and that they form various clearly defined patterns, such as arches, circles, long curves, whorls, etc., and that these patterns differ on the different fingers."

Curiously enough, as modern as *Pudd'nhead Wilson* is, its format is that of an old-fashioned melodrama, as if its structure were borrowed from the plays performed on the riverboat theatres of that period. Perhaps deliberately, Twain selected this popular formula in which to tell a very serious story. Moving from climax to climax, every chapter ends with a teaser that makes the reader wonder what is coming next while, as in Greek tragedy, the fates keep closing in on the central protagonists. And here the fates have no regard whatsoever for color lines. It is this treatment of race that makes *Pudd'nhead Wilson* as contemporary as Little Rock, and Mark Twain as modern as Faulkner, although Twain died when Faulkner was in knee pants.

The first motion picture was made in the year in which Twain wrote *Pudd'nhead Wilson*. As if looking ahead to the heyday of this medium, the author begins his story with a sweeping panorama of the river and Dawson's Landing, then briefly poses by name the cast of characters against it. Thereafter, he continues his tale in a series of visualizations, most of them growing logically one from another, but some quite coincidentally. A common dictum in Hollywood is, "Simply picture it on the screen, and the audience will believe it—because *there it is*." The advent of two handsome Italian twins in Dawson's Landing is pictured so vividly that the reader believes the men are there, and only briefly wonders *why*—although these two fellows immediately begin to figure prominently in the frightful march of events leading toward the novel's climax. But, to tell the truth, we do not need to know exactly why these ebullient twins came to Dawson's Landing. And they do brighten up the story considerably.

Additional, and what seem at first to be extraneous flashes of amusing brilliance in the novel (and at other times sober or ironic comment) are the excerpts that serve as chapter headings from *Pudd'nhead Wilson's Calendar*. "Few things are harder to put up with than the annoyance of a good example." And another: "It is often the case that the man who can't tell a lie thinks he is the best judge of one." And an observation that would have almost surely, had there been a Mc-

Carthy Committee in Twain's day, caused the author to be subpoenaed before it: "*October 12—The Discovery*—It was wonderful to find America, but it would have been more wonderful to miss it." And a final admonition that might almost be Mark Twain himself concerned with the tight and astringent style of this smallest of his novels: "As to the Adjective: when in doubt, strike it out." *Pudd'nhead Wilson* marches along much too rapidly to be bothered with a plethora of adjectives.

Of African Queens and Afro-American Princes and Princesses: Miscegenation in *Old Hepsy**

SIMONE VAUTHIER

By 1858, when Mrs. C. W. Denison published *Old Hepsy*,[1] the antislavery novel was a well-established sub-genre. It had its stock characters and its archetypes; especially when written by women, it tended to be firmly centered in the family circle[2] and to exploit tear-jerking situations, thus overlapping the "domestic and sentimental novel"; and insofar as it often depicted a tragic octoroon girl, persecuted by a lecherous master who was as likely as not bloodkin to her in the setting of an isolated plantation, it blended motifs and figures inherited both from Rich-

---

* From Simone Vauthier, "Textualité et stéréotypes: Of African Queens and Afro-American Princes and Princesses: Miscegenation in *Old Hepsy*." In *Regards sur la littérature noire américaine*, ed. Michel Fabre (Paris: Publications du conseil scientifique de la Sorbonne Nouvelle—Paris III, 1980), 65–107.

1. Mrs. C. W. Denison, *Old Hepsy*, N.Y., A. Burdick, 1858, p. 459. Parenthetical page references are to this edition. Mary Andrews Denison was born in Cambridge, Mass., in 1826 and died in 1911. She married Charles Wheeler Denison, a journalist and clergyman, who was the first editor of *The Emancipator (Appleton's Cyclopaedia)*. Herself the first woman editor of *The Olive Branch*, she was a prolific author, publishing 60 novels of which more than 1,000,000 copies were sold (*National Cyclopaedia of American Biography*, 1926, vol. XIX). Her tales are "mainly of home life, some of them to be classed as Sunday school literature, while others are of a more ambitious character," says O. F. Adams, who does not mention *Old Hepsy* (*A Dictionary of American Authors*, 1904). C. W. Denison (sometimes spelled Dennison) was in relation whith the Weld-Grimké group (*see Letters of Theodore Dwight Weld, Angelina Grimké Weld and Sarah Grimké, 1822–1844*, edited by Gilbert H. Barnes and Dwight L. Dummond, N.Y., 1934, I, 123). This may explain why Mrs. Denison makes Mabel Van Broek a Quakeress and Kenneth a Northerner turned slaveholder in reverse of the Grimkés' evolution. Neither husband nor wife has received much attention from antislavery scholars and information on them is sketchy.

2. The predominance of the familial setting is by no means confined to the fiction of "female scribblers." The family metaphor shapes much of the proslavery debate: see Jenkins *Proslavery Thought in the Old South*, Philip C. Wander, "The Savage Child: The Image of the Negro in the Proslavery Movement," *The Southern Speech Communication Journal*, XXXVII, summer 1872, N° 4, pp. 335–360. Even the authors of slave narratives could on occasion endorse the family stereotype when they told about humane treatment (See John W. Blassingame, *The Slave Community, Plantation Life in the Ante-Bellum South*, N.Y., 1972, p. 193).

ardson and the gothic novel into an updated version of *roman noir* that was peculiarly American in its socially relevant sensationalism. But while largely conforming to the pattern, *Old Hepsy* gives it so novel a slant as probably to explain its fall into oblivion. As readable as the great majority of antislavery novels, if not indeed more so,[3] the work must have proved unpalatable to many contemporary readers and would certainly prove offensive to a whole category of readers today.

A Tale of Lowly Life: The Characters

Most of the black characters[4] in the crowded canvas of the novel are easily recognizable types, even when they are somewhat individualized. To mention but a few, there is "the noble looking black [. . .] a real African king," Joycliffe the blacksmith, as seen by a Northern visitor, or, in a Southern view, "a good sort of fellow and perfectly respectful, knows his place" (p. 141). There is Phillis, a "bright-looking mulatto girl"[5] with "plump and brown" shoulders—the pert lady's maid. And Old Tabby "devotedly pious and trustworthy," and Aunt Esty who knows the ways of the white world. Not even the Christ-like figure is missing: Jack is "a good, faithful, loving heart that, lacerated and torn as it was, could rise to a heroism like that of the thorn-crowned Christ, and with bleeding lips ask that his scourgers might be forgiven—they who had bruised his life out of him, and ground the soul that God breathed into him into the very dust" (pp. 311–12). Nor is Christian meekness the only stance represented. A few of the slaves abjectly accept their condition: Suzan, who is desperate because her husband has been sold away, yet puts on "a look of affected calmness horribly grim," and even agrees with her master that "Sam belong to you" (p. 207). Some take a prudential attitude like Aunt Esty who advises her son not to listen to the antislavery speeches of young Marshall Randolph, a Southerner on the way to Abolitionism: "niggers must always side wid de marjoram, 'cause dey's de strongest power" (p. 230). A good many like Joycliffe do not "concede that superiority to whites accorded them by themselves" (p. 185); while quite a few "think of revolution" (p. 187), and are even ready to take steps to ensure their freedom: as a result of an aborted insurrection, 24 slaves are burned to death on one of Lawyer Kenneth's Kentucky plantations, at the moment when, at Washington Grange, his Maryland home, he says to his dinner guests, " 'I never whipped a slave in my life,' [. . .] smacking his lips at his luxurious table" (p. 104). Perhaps one may discern in

---

3. *Old Hepsy*, indeed, is probably more readable today because it eschews explicit propaganda and embodies most of the antislavery thesis in the action. In spite of the sensational character of its subject, its treatment is quiet and subdued: there are no lurid scenes as in *Uncle Tom's Cabin*, no titillating ones as in the social fiction of a George Lippard.

4. Hereafter, the word "black" will be used to refer to all those people having, as the saying goes, "Negro blood," whatever the admixture. Mrs. Denison calls some of her characters "white slaves," thus setting herself at a distance from those fictional whites who call them "darkey" or "African."

5. Unlike many of her contemporaries the author seems able to see beauty in a black face. See for instance the description of Joycliffe's son, p. 186: "His face was as black as Joycliffe's but even more intelligent and decidedly handsome."

Mrs. Denison's fictional slaves a larger share of black pride than is usually found even in antislavery novels. Hepsy repeatedly boasts of her African origin: "I'se right from ole Afric" (p. 209). Alascus teases Phillis who prides herself on being "none of your common niggers" and claims, "Yah! heah! common niggers is yallow—aristocracy am black. No mean white blood in dese yer veins—good King Pampolo blood—none of yer mixed stuff I r'al pure grained Africum—da's so" (p. 319). And to his master telling him "what a pity you are black," Jupiter answers very pointedly:

> "Laws mars', I's de handsomest color in de world, I is. Don't de ladies wear black gowns—aint dey got black eyes an' black har? Don't mars' 'mire black hat an' black coat an' trowsers? Ky! ebery ting black nice, but nigger. Misse kiss little black dog—bery pretty! bery fine! kiss little black baby—whew! not git taste out ob her mouf more dan a year—ky!" (p. 295)

On the whole the slaves are idealised, as they usually are in the antislavery novel. Mrs. Denison only allows for some pettiness—engendered by the system—among house servants who vie for their mistresses' favour. To balance this there is the solidarity which mulattoes feel towards the blacks: "they seldom disown their kindred, seldom pretend to be superior to them in any ways" (p. 178). Even the hated slavedriver, as exemplified by Jack, is a kind man perverted by a sadistic owner.

In spite of this idealization and beyond her type casting the novelist attempts to give a two-dimensional picture of her characters by juxtaposing appearances and reality. The athletic Joycliffe has brains as well as brawn, although the idea is ludicrous to slaveowners: " 'don't talk of intellect and niggers,' said Maggie in a laughing way" (p. 141) a propos of this man. Under the clowning, the buffoon may be a shrewd man making fun of his white audience (p. 295). Conformance to the master's attitudes may be a way of deriding them. When Jupiter tells his mistress, "Laws, miss, I's ought to be beat, da's a fac'. I's an outrageous nigger" (p. 351), by seeming to accept her values, he in fact deprives her of her victory. Often their preconceived notions prevent the whites from understanding the people around them. Of Keene who is technically though not legally white, Amy Kenneth says:

> "He is the strangest kind of darkey, full of sentiment, quoting poetry, putting on such ridiculous airs—to be sure, he is called as smart as a white man, and he *is* smart in his own way. But then he may thank his white blood for that." (p. 369)

By the time it is introduced, this vision of Keene can clash with the image of him which has been built by the narration. He is a very educated, competent man who is entrusted with his employer's business, as well as a man who genuinely likes literature. He is strange to Amy only because seeing him as her milieu conditions her to see him, i.e. simply as a "darkey," she cannot fit the behaviour and the emotions of the individual into the rigid mould of the social definition. She must therefore resort to the lame explanation of his white blood to account for his being "smart," unaware of the paradox that makes his very real physical whiteness invisible to her eye and yet somehow discernible in an intellectual quality. By such devices, even the minor characters—among which Keene cannot be numbered—acquire a sort of stereoscopic dimension.

Along with the numerous extras, the cast includes four major black characters, two "white slaves," a freeman "without a trace of coloured blood about him" and an old African woman. Of the four, Lucina the octoroon is the most stereotyped. An "exotic-like" beauty, more gifted than Amy Kenneth, her young mistress, she has in fact been raised in the North as a white girl but she has been lured away down South as a result of what she calls "some dreadful plot in operation to disgrace" her, sold as a slave and bought by Mrs. Kenneth. Powerless, she can only appeal to the pity of the people around her, and only women—first Mrs. Kenneth for reasons to be elucidated later, then Mabel Van Broek, Mr. Kenneth's Quaker sister—endeavour to help her. Kenneth, her master, nurses a peculiar hate towards her; and though he does not lust after her himself, he plans to sell her to a notorious rake for the avowed purpose of degrading her. In face of such adversity—to which is added the hostility of Amy Kenneth and of the slave women she has replaced in their mistress's favour, Lucina grows desperate. "She had no motive, no hope and no courage [. . .] She saw before herself only mechanical hopeless slavery. So she obeyed whatever command came first, with a blind unquestioning obedience, but hardly knowing why" (p. 40). A passive victim, she illustrates the crushing power of slavery over body and mind. Moreover, in conformity with the tragic octoroon stereotype, Lucina expresses the feeling that slavery has put an indelible "taint" upon her—an idea which Mabel Van Broek pooh-poohs.

Hollister, as befits a man, does not submit to his fate resignedly. Handsome, with a brow "fairer than that of the man who owned him," he has "manly grace," a "shrewd, intuitively swift" mind and a complex character that endows him with great potentialities for good and perhaps evil:

> His eye, brilliant and commanding, was yet in expression as sweet and gentle as that of a babe. His lips were delicately shaped, Grecian in outline, and like Napoleon's, passing easily from a smile to a menace. (pp. 48–49)

The son of old Hollister and a "beautiful mustee" he is therefore half-brother to his present mistress, Mrs. Kenneth, who has inherited him, and half-uncle to Amy, eight years younger than he is. He deeply resents his condition:

> It had burned in his heart for twelve long years, and still his lot among slaves was an enviable one. His mistress deferred to him, his master consulted with him and often left his business in his hands. (p. 49)

So slavery is a frequent topic in his discussions with his confidant, Fred Keene.[6]

Fred, although fifteen years older, is his half-brother, a Hollister by a different slave mother. But apparently, on gaining his freedom, Fred has chosen a surname

---

6. Most though not all of the antislavery propaganda is carried by discussions between *black* characters. But convincingly, they rarely speak of freedom in abstract terms. Hollister for instance will express his resentment at being obliged to earn money for his master (p. 236). Nor is rebelliousness confined to the octoroons. Among the slaves to be burned for revolting on Mr. Kenneth's plantation in

that would not recall the Hollister family. Both men are "aware of their relation-ship, and never were two brothers closer friends" (p. 77). For a while after his emancipation, Fred lived in the North—where he refused to pass for white—but he has come back to Maryland, partly out of disillusionment at Northern discrim-ination. (The latent racism in the free states comes under criticism. For instance, Randolph Marshall attacks Northern hypocrisy in these terms:

> ". . . they *profess* so much more than we do. . . . They talk about the 'brotherhood of the races' and 'the immateriality of complexion,' and yet will not ride a mile with a black man" [p. 179].)

When the action opens, Keene is the right-hand man of General Randolph, a neighbour of the Kenneths, and tries to alleviate the lot of his master's slaves. More experienced than Hollister, his blood cooled by unknown trials, he encour-ages his younger brother's rebelliousness while preaching patience and cunning. He wants "to destroy this system" and even agrees with Hollister's idea that "we can only be regenerated in blood," understanding his wish to see the oppressors thrown into the flames. "Burn, white fiends. Burn! Burn!" Yet he reminds him that in order to gain power you must learn self-control (p. 243). For his part, he plays the game:

> "They think here that I am wedded to the South, that I believe that my race was doomed from the beginning to bondage: that I hate the North, that in fact, I am a silent advocate for their system." (p. 249)

All the while, however, he plans to help Lucina and Hollister escape, thus hoping to provide the latter with "an opportunity to do more with [his] pen for [their] poor, downtrodden people, than [he] could with cold steel" (p. 249). Both men are educated and find knowledge a solace in their troubles.

> "It is laughable—I couldn't help it—to hear us two 'niggers' as *they* would call us, talking like schoolmasters. Well, well, we *do* know something, Hollister, there's some comfort in that. Lawyer Kenneth couldn't beat us in the grammatical line." (p. 247)

Whereupon he suggests that they read some Shakespeare for entertainment.

On the contrary, old Hepsy is illiterate, though endowed with "a poetic tem-perament" and a ready tongue, and just as articulate in her rejection of slavery. A "tall, venerable, and still queenly African" she has been emancipated long ago, being one hundred and ten when the story begins. Her old master used to say that "he was ten years taming her" but she counters: "Massa say he ten years broking my spirit; didn't do it yet! Sperit made o' somethin' can't be broke—da's so" (p. 209). In virtue of her great age and renowned "powers," she exerts some influence on the community—black and white. "A strange mixture of sim-plicity and shrewdness, was old Hepsy—of religious faith and the most abject

---

Kentucky "some were light and some were ebon black" (p. 103) and seven of the twenty-four were *women*, an unusual sidelight, however fictional, into slave insurrections.

superstition" (p. 53). "An embodiment of old Africa," "powerless to redress its wrongs," she yet takes whatever action is open to her, fostering dissatisfaction and recalcitrance among the slaves, preaching the vengeance of the Lord, laying various curses and spells on Lawyer Kenneth who has sold her children away, and maliciously hinting at the dark secrets she knows about the Hollister family. Clearly Hepsy belongs to a line of fictional African witches—the witnesses of the whites' dark past and the prophetesses of a gloomy future—starting with Bombie, the sorceress of *Koningsmarke* (1823). However, not only is she more fully and realistically treated than Paulding's romantic personage but her function in the story is more integrative. Her reiterated curses, African death wails and magic may not be instrumental in bringing about the destruction of the Kenneth family, as she believes, but they do create uneasiness among the fictional characters, white and black, and evidence the general superstition that pervades Southern life as depicted in the novel.[7] Thus they do not simply contribute to the gothic atmosphere of the story but also to the social criticism. Moreover Hepsy becomes a symbol of both the wrong of slavery and the continuing curse it has entailed on the country. "I'se de wrath ob de lord," she claims, and so she is metaphorically.

While it is hardly necessary to point out that the main black characters are all exceptional, attention must be paid to one of the metaphors that conveys this superiority—the royalty image. Assuredly this image is a cliché of antislavery poetry and fiction, which may be traced back to *Oroonoko*. The appeal of the image lay partly in the complete reversal of fortunes—from the highest to the lowest rank—which made the Royal Slave exemplary, if exceptional. Needless to say, the cliché was modified with each occurrence. And *Old Hepsy* is significant in that it makes a varied use of it. When applied to Joycliffe, it functions in a conventional way to signify downtrodden nobility. The discussion of Hepsy's royal birth, while it indirectly upholds the antislavery ideology, manifests that the slave in real life may have found, like the fictional character, some ego satisfaction in clinging to the now empty title and have had some success in reminding the slave owner of his or her former status. ("I wonder how many queens have come from Africa," queried Mrs. Kenneth quietly. "I do half believe Hepsy, though," said Amy. "There is something so different about her from other Negroes. Was she really smuggled over from Africa?" [p. 73].) On the contrary, when Maggie admiringly calls Hollister "an Americo-Anglo-African prince," his princeliness, divorced from country and lineage, only denotes some quality of manners and character in a man she sees as the product of the unacknowledged American melting-pot, since he is a "blending of nations." And ironical as Kenneth and his

---

7. The theme of superstition, important as it is, cannot be traced here: the following statement by Maggie a Southern girl sums up the idea which many incidents illustrate: "I know it's foolish of me; but remember they [these superstitions] were almost born with me, as you might say; indeed I dare declare that my mother was brought up in just such a fashion. I know she put great faith in dreams and omens. The slaves in that thing are our teachers and masters; they impregnate the whole white population. I don't believe there's a Southern man, woman or child but is always more or less under the influence of superstition" (p. 364). Thus the cultural action of the black community over the white is strongly underlined.

daughter may be when they call Lucina princess, they unwittingly assert what they seek to deny—the superiority she is assumed to feel. The epithet is more than a grace note since Kenneth also sneers at Lucina's name, "Stewart—a royal name, too." While the original cliché is almost lost sight of, the image functions as a projection of the white fictive characters. At the same time it appears as an underlying motif of the total fictional form.

As for the white actors, they might almost seem old acquaintances to the reader of antislavery fiction. Overbearing, drunken Kenneth, old Hollister the dissolute planter with "the bad Hollister blood," General Randolph and his illegitimate offspring, Harry Van Broek the serious-minded Northerner, or even young Marshall Randolph the Southerner with conscientious scruples about slavery, not to mention the remote mistress, Mrs. Kenneth, the arrogant and spoiled Amy, the giddy but kind-hearted Maggie who will also be converted to abolitionism—all of them wear familiar faces.

"The Grange, However, Was a Modern Paradise": The Situations

Similarly, many of the situations through which the action is developed are stock situations which directly or indirectly impugn the myth of an idyllic order—the sales of slaves, the heart-breaking separations, the death of the tortured slave, the Negro dance, the acts of downright cruelty, the callous remarks passed by masters in the presence of those they humiliate, etc. The importance of encounters between black and black, however, deserves special mention: conversations between Hepsy and the gardener, Hepsy and Hollister, and of course between Hollister and Keene provide some interesting scenes and suggest a context of relations among the blacks that go on unobserved by the whites, which indeed the slaves take care to keep hidden from the masters (p. 186).

More important still, familiar situations often become revitalized by a fresh approach, as one example will show. Jack, Hepsy's much abused son, has run away, after repeated floggings, and has come to his mother's to die—not before he has had time to forgive his exploiters—All in the best Uncle Tom tradition. At the burial service, the slaves sing a spiritual "Done an' gone to Glory"—three stanzas of which are quoted[8]—then the white minister who has condescended to officiate because of Hepsy's great age, takes "care to impress the Negroes with the idea that God punished those who ran away from their masters, either with great suffering or with death" (p. 339). Throughout the sermon his audience wordlessly show their rejection of the lesson:

8. Several Negro songs are quoted in *Old Hepsy*, evincing Mrs. Denison's interest in a music that Thomas Wentworth Higginson had not yet helped to popularize. Significantly, too, two of these are sung by Lawyer Kenneth, one more example of the interaction of the black and white worlds (see p. 210, 302, 305, 335, 419). In the fiction of the period, of course, black songs do get mentioned but are often qualified as "rude" or "weird" or "obstreperous."

Hollister's brow grew dark. Keene looked straight at the floor, but his lip took an unconscious and scornful curve. Old Hepsy sat bolt upright, moving mouth and fingers nervously. (p. 340)

And when the minister ends by telling her, "the Lord comfort you," she snaps back: " 'Hopes He will,' said Hepsy, rocking herself faster, 'needs it after such a 'scourse as da'; good Lord knows I does' " (ibid.). To the Uncle Tom saintliness of Jack is, in fact, opposed another sort of faith which is not blind acceptance of the master-approved brand of Christianity and even attempts to interpret the Biblical message to fit the needs of the oppressed, seeking to reconcile the need for vengeance with the divine Law. True, the novel has implied earlier in a narrator's aside that Hepsy's faith lacks something of the evangelical spirit:

> Hepsy enjoyed her religion—shouted as warmly as the rest her amens and hallelujahs,[9] but she could not comprehend the exceeding beauty of the New Testament code, as many of her brothers and sisters in bondage did. (p. 211)

But the point is that the novel only makes passing references to those who have comprehended the beauty of Christian meekness while it focusses on, and draws sympathetic pictures of, people who, like Hepsy, entertain Old Testament notions of retribution, or, like Keene and Hollister, are unable to see in Christianity a lesson of submission to an unjust social order. Thus there is in *Old Hepsy* an attempt, however clumsy and shaped by the author's bias, to investigate the complex relationship of the blacks to the Christian religion.[10]

"A Frightful Feature of Our Domestic Institution": The Major Theme

Given its main antislavery thesis and its family setting, the novel centers around the theme of miscegenation—again a conventional antislavery theme of which

9. Mrs. Denison notes the "shouting" and the fervor of black religious meetings but, it would seem, does not take a condescending view of it. It is on a par with the new convert's zeal of Randolph, as a remark of Esty's suggests. "Jus' be particler and don't 'dorse what mars Randolph say— 'cause proberly he was decited same's your old ma [i.e., herself] when she shout glory down to camp meetin' and don't know wedder she's on she head or heels" (p. 230).

   This piece of humorous self-criticism reflects a basic assumption of the novel that beyond apparent differences blacks and whites are alike. But while the white Negro episodes imply that black can be like white, this restores some balance by suggesting that white can be like black. Of course, in the system of values projected by the novel, neither Randolph's antislavery zeal, however outrageous to his friends and neighbours, nor Esty's fervor, since she is shown as a really pious character, can be really "decited."

10. There are several good Christians among the black characters: Esty, Old Jordan, forgiving on his death bed General Randolph who beat him severely in a drunken fit, and of course, Jack. But the point is that all of them, including Jack, are minor figures.

   On the other hand, those white Christians who participate directly in slavery or wash their hands of the whole business, like the minister who refuses to help Lucina, are satirized with zest. In her fiction, Mrs. Denison may have been settling accounts with people she had met as the wife of a minister with antislavery opinions.

Hildreth had made egregious—though more limited—use in *The Slave, or Memoirs of Archy Moore* (1836). In *Old Hepsy* the overall social significance of amalgamation is exposed discursively in a conversation between Harry Van Broek and Marshall Randolph.[11] The Northerner underlines that the Constitution says "We the people of the United States, not we, the *white* people, nor 'we, the free people' but WE THE PEOPLE" (p. 174). What Marshall finds objectionable is not the abstract statement but its practical consequences. "But the idea of amalgamation! They tell me you Northerners advocate such principles. That is revolting to me; I couldn't go that" (Ibid.). Harry can then point out the paradoxical character of such repugnance:

> "Which do you think carries the principle into *practice* most thoroughly, Mr. Randolph, the North or the South? I have seen, in my short visit, not a few white faces in slave quarters. There's a verse in the Bible that runs thus: 'Can the Ethiopian change his skin?' If *he* can't, I should think that the Southern masters were doing it for him pretty thoroughly." (ibid.)

While granting that "it is a frightful feature of our domestic institution," Randolph (who has bitter knowledge of his own father's habits and his mother's suffering on this account) nevertheless falls back on the notion of "an intuitive repugnance in our very nature," a "peculiar dislike" "implanted within us by God." This argument Harry refutes on theological grounds ("Can God be a partial deity?") and on empiric grounds: the masters easily accept the contact of blacks when they "do any little inferior *service* for them."

> "But if he comes to you as a free man, you feel 'repugnance' then. This seems very strange to me, but only proves conclusively that it is not the color but the condition of the black. His race has been enslaved. Slavery implies abjectness and degradation; and we feel, like the man in the Scripture, to say 'Stand off. I am holier than thou.'" (p. 175)

The idea thus expounded discursively is embodied in the *present* action of the novel as well as illustrated in several narrated stories.

Both Hollister and Keene are silent witnesses to the sexual victimization of the slave woman. Keene's mother, "A French mustee," the daughter of a rich man who had *married* a slave, is despoiled of her father's inheritance, "through some clause" of the will, and sold to old Hollister, to die, not many years later, probably of violent death. Hollister's mother, "formed an attachment with the oldest son of the house" where she was a slave. Soon the young man was dispatched to Europe and she sent back to old Hollister, her legal master. "The old reprobate did as all such devils do, just as they please" (p. 240). After the birth of her son she becomes a raving maniac and is let loose in a wild wood where she lives like an animal. Conventional as the situation is—which detracts nothing from the

---

11. That the fictional argument with its pros and cons embodies widely held ideas of the antebellum period cannot be demonstrated here. Confirmation could be found in any number of scholarly studies, one of the best being George Fredrickson's *The Black Image in the White Mind, the Debate on Afro-American Character and Destiny, 1817–1914*, N.Y., 1971.

odiousness of it—the vitality of *Old Hepsy* lies in its unsentimental approach: it makes no allusion to high-principled virtue and lofty dedication to Christian purity. Indeed the problem is set in terms that suggest the link between antislavery and the genesis of women's rights: as Hollister bitterly meditates, "Had she been a free white woman, *with the control of her own body*, this dreadful thing would never have happened" (p. 251, italics added). Even the madness of the wronged woman is shown not only as precipitated but sustained by the system: a white woman, Hollister thinks, would have been treated and perhaps cured. Thus this madness is not the ineluctable lot of the no longer virtuous, but just as strongly related to the prevailing social conditions as sexual exploitation is.

Besides the impact of the motif is all the greater because the mother's story is narrated from the point of view of the sons, thus setting off faint Freudian ripples.[12] When Keene tells Hollister about his mother's fate, the young man who, believing her dead, had never realized his relation to the crazy creature in the woods, is suddenly maddened. Shedding "blood, blood" seems the only way to revenge her. And since the father is dead, nothing will do but the total destruction of the Father's country: "to see the whole South in ruins—covered with dead bodies—a great funeral pyre, nothing else will satisfy me" (p. 243). Moreover, the fate of his mother is repeatedly linked in Hollister's mind with the thought of Amy Kenneth. The first connection is made by Keene: "My mother was as good as Amy Kenneth, so was yours" (p. 237), the second by Hollister himself: "And you, Amy Kenneth" [Hollister thinks] "*you* are no better than *she* was; not a whit, not one whit. Why should not *your* haughty head be bowed?" (p. 251). To the already great charms of Amy is added one powerful attraction: for the black son, "to bow the head" of the tabooed white girl will make up for the sexual humiliation of the black mother by the white father, Amy's grandfather.

Of Love and Dust

And here, of course, one comes across what is one major deviation from the traditional pattern. In antislavery literature white men could love mulatto girls—nay, on occasion, marry them—witness Lydia Maria Child's "The Quadroons" (1842) or William Wells Brown's *Three Years in Europe, or, Places I Have Seen and People I Have Met* (1852). But for a mulatto man to aspire to a white woman was an altogether different thing. Nor can Hollister by any stretch of the imagination be considered an early version of the black rapist of Reconstruction literature. Simply, Hollister loves Amy with a passion that is all the more human and all the more convincing fictionally for being on occasion tinged with resentment and perhaps hate. Moreover, he can believe that his love is reciprocated:

12. Hildreth also had Archy Moore tell his mother's story and the incest theme is important but sexuality is approached much more intellectually whereas in *Old Hepsy* it is at once more discrete—there is no seduction *scene* such as the scene between Cassy and her own father—and more pervasive.

"Strange . . . that in spite of her cruelty, I can still love her! Strange, strange! Yet there is a consciousness in her face whenever I meet her eye, the blood colors her whole cheek; she turns her glance away like lightning. What! love a slave! Can it be possible? Yes, I wish I were as sure of my salvation as I am that she loves me." (p. 252)

When he affirms to Keene that she loves him but is "prouder than Lucifer," his friend exclaims: "Nonsense, Hollister! You make yourself ridiculous, what a dream!" (p. 250). Nevertheless the reader knows that, in truth, Hollister has some grounds for deluding himself, since the narration has shown him Amy's repeated blushes, and Amy's flirtatiousness with the devoted slave.

This, needless to say, is where *Old Hepsy* innovates most daringly—so daringly indeed that for decades no novelist would tackle the delicate subject which Mrs. Denison approached without squeamishness. Not that the relation between Amy and Hollister is a love relationship. It is both much less and much more. For Amy's feelings towards the slave are strangely ambivalent, a mixture of very conscious contempt and unconscious attraction—which, notwithstanding the novelist's discretion in the matter, seems to the modern reader more physical than emotional. Her behavior towards him never ceases to fluctuate. After coquetting with him as an adolescent, her pride rebels when she realizes that "this chattel possessed affections, and that they were given unreservedly to her," she becomes "suddenly as cold and haughty as she had before been capricious and coquettish" (p. 49). Once, indeed, she strikes him across the face with her crop: "The blow was hot and scorpion-like in his heart and all his great love could not forgive her" (p. 50), so on meeting her later he gives her another glance of defiance, which at first pleases her:

"Insolence," she exclaimed to herself, "I hope he hates me now!" No sooner had she spoken thus than came a secret hope that he would not. Strange to say, that dark look of yesterday, in which a concentrated malice seemed to gather, had in the slightest degree, altered the current of her feelings . . . The face looked terribly grand in its wrath. The more she thought of it, the more its dark beauty impressed her. Yet she shut the emotion—whatever it might be, close down in her heart. (p. 50)

On another occasion, she asks him to play the part of a liveried servant in some *tableaux vivants*. Though a carpenter, he accepts, however reluctantly, to please her—much to the disgust of Keene who would rather kill himself than "have put on any of their symbols of degradation" (p. 288). But Hollister's sad acceptance somehow moves Amy:

There was a strange dizzy feeling in her brain—a singular sensation in her throat, something like a sob; the still, mournful look and manner touched her deeply, and with a hurried "Thank you" she glided from the room. (p. 200)

But she immediately hates herself for "the small modicum of sympathy" she has then felt for a slave. Although "perhaps unconsciously she wished he were free— her equal" (p. 385), she can never forget his condition.

At the climax of the novel, when the drink-crazed Kenneth has banished Amy's mother and locked the girl into her room, Hollister comes in through the window, speaks his love and his dream and offers her elopement and marriage. But she answers scathingly:

> "Insolent, insolent, insulting wretch!" cried Amy, forgetting all caution, "to ask me to unite myself with such a fate! you, my father's slave," she added choking with pride and passion. "How dare you? Do you think I would stoop to look at such as you?" (p. 436)

Taunted by her further scorn, Hollister then reveals to her her mother's secret, upon which she faints, and he revives her with a drink that is poisoned. She soon realizes this and is terrified of death.

> "I can't die *now*! Oh, Hollister, how could you?" she cried in her anguish, *seizing his hands imploringly*, "Tell me it will not harm me!—tell me this pain is nothing—only fright. Tell me you did not poison me, and *I will do whatever you say. I will be your wife! anything to live.* Oh life! life! I cannot die now." (p. 437, italics added)

As she grows weaker, he takes her into his arms, "her head rested against the bosom of the slave." This will be their closest intimacy. He lays her down on a couch, stretches on the carpet and saying, "God knows my love was pure," drinks off the poison.[13] There they remain for a day while the rain lashes through the window, she "with a half sorrowful expression," he with "a strange half-mocking smile" on his face (p. 439).

Dramatic the scene may be, but its sensationalism is subdued, in view at least of the literary tastes of the fifties. Although unexpected, Hollister's act appears likely because it has been carefully led up to by the narration. Above all, the treatment of it is far from conventional. The murder of Amy is by no means a sex murder, in the ordinary sense of the phrase, or a deed of vindictive malevolence: it is a sacrifice which will ensure their reunion in an Other World: "We must meet somewhere as equals," says Hollister in answer to Amy's supplications (p. 436). But the general import of this private crime will be examined later. It is enough to state here that both the young slave and the planter's daughter appear as victims of an environment that perverts human emotions. "And so, in madness and despair, slavery had sent these souls before their Maker" (p. 438). For the unfortunate Amy is not the lily-white sentimental heroine ready to sacrifice her life on the altar of virtue and purity. Her behavior must have been shocking to the gentle reader nurtured on saccharine conventions.

To make things worse, Amy is presented neither as a particularly wicked girl nor as a unique case. Southern belles are keenly aware of the looks of their handsome mulatto slaves—which are even a matter of gossip (cf. pp. 141, 181, 216, 263); and they are not above flirting with them, to keep their hands in, for lack of superior material: Maggie frankly admits:

---

13. Although the issue is miscegenation, the black characters are not invested with above average sexuality and are in fact remarkably self-controlled: the pruriency in the novel is reserved to the whites, though not to all.

"I am mighty proud of [our white slaves], especially when they travel with us. It gives one more consequence to carry around an elegant-looking slave, with perfumed locks, gold chain, and kids. And when there are no beaus, it's somewhat amusing tot pretend to show them a little extra notice, too. I think it's prime fun, because they do often actually like one; and they *are* slaves, indeed. My! We have one at home who will fly if I lift my finger, quicker than any gallant I've got!" (p. 89)

As for the slaves, they hint at even more compromising relations: "White ladies *very* kind to white niggers, oh, Lor'! Yah, yah!" (p. 79).

In truth, a white lady has been very kind to Fred Keene, as the novel slowly divulges, first through indirect suggestions then through hints and finally through a full (and reiterated) revelation of the facts. Before her marriage, Mrs. Kenneth, then Amy Hollister, who was "what was generally called a wild girl," had on coming home from a young ladies' seminary been surprised to find the black playmate of her childhood, whom she had taught his letters, turned into a fine fellow.

She also admired his finely formed figure, his handsome features and intellectual face and mien, and in school-girl fashion, without reflecting upon the consequences that might result by her encouragement of look and word—forgetting also the great distance in their comparative stations—entirely ignorant besides of his near relationship, fell in love with him, as the romantic phrase goes, and allowed herself to think too much of the elegant slave. (p. 453)

Another passage makes it even clearer that *she* played seducer. "In fact she was to blame, not he. Those who knew it said so," says Keene, telling his story anonymously (p. 246). A confirming fact is that both Keene and Hepsy are paid for their silence, the former with his freedom, the latter with money. Married to a young northern lawyer, Mrs. Kenneth never loses touch with the people who, up North, bring up Lucina. At first totally unaware of her past, her husband soon begins to hear vague rumors. Himself a faithful, loyal man with "a great regard for the truth," he feels deeply the cruel deception, "his character gradually change[s]" and he becomes an alcoholic, subject to terrible fits. Meanwhile Mrs. Kenneth also changes, withdrawing more and more from society to devote herself to her much-spoiled daughter, Amy. When Keene comes back to the neighborhood, she endures "acute torments": "always fearful, always desponding, doomed often to see the father of her absent child, her whole life was a series of troubles, agitations and aggravations" (p. 455). Things get even worse when her trust is betrayed and she is obliged to buy Lucina. Unaware at first of their relationship, Kenneth soon suspects and discovers the truth. This accounts for his growing hatred of the girl and his decision to let a rake of the neighborhood buy her, notwithstanding his promise to sell her to his sister who wants to adopt Lucina: for by now the girl has become the unwitting instrument of his cunning vengeance. Both Mrs. Kenneth and Mrs. Van Broek, apart or jointly, try to protect Lucina and plan to free her. But despite many attempts, neither woman can eventually be of help to the girl. Lucina would be sold away into prostitution, if Keene did not succeed in having her escape. At the close of the story, father and daughter live in Pennsylvania where he is editor of an abolitionist paper. "They seem to be happy and contented in the society of each other" and are rarely separated: "At morning, noon and evening, father and child are together. He rarely goes out unless she accompanies him" (p. 458).

In the meantime Kenneth in a mad fit has publicly denounced his wife's sin. She turns for solace and love to Hepsy, who having been revenged and having learnt to be more charitable, embraces her. "A scene, gentlemen, a scene," cries Kenneth. Both husband and wife completely lose their minds when Amy is killed and they die soon after. Nothing remains of the "House of Kenneth," not even good, innocent Mabel whom a lingering disease had taken off some time earlier.

This summary will have shown how much Mrs. Kenneth's fate departs from the norms of genteel fiction.[14] A planter's daughter, she is no conventional Southern Lady, but a warm-blooded woman. She is allowed to survive her fault, and even childbearing; she marries well according to social standards. She even enjoys three years' "unalloyed happiness" though her self-torment increases with time. She is unaware of her husband's suspicions and blindly regards his alienation not as a reaction to the deception she has practiced upon him but as a "special punishment from heaven" for her fault. Only with the advent of Lucina upon the scene and Mr. Kenneth's pointed animosity to the girl does she realize that he knows and, what is more, is intent upon revenging himself on her daughter. Thus the catastrophe usually involved in sexual transgression finally overtakes her but is rather belated. Clearly, though guilty of grave sexual misdemeanor, she is by no means, in the eyes of the author, a "bad" woman. Excuses for her conduct are even propounded. Her flightiness may have been determined by genetical inheritance: since her mother was a permanently ailing woman and her father a dissolute man, she may have been "constitutionally injured." Her behavior was moreover conditioned by a corrupting milieu. It is a propos of Mrs. Kenneth that Marshall Randolph owns to Harry Van Broek, Mabel's stepson,

> "These are the things that make one great brothel of the South. I myself have known in this veιy town slave-owners send their young daughters from home to keep them away from the slaves. It is a system full of abominations. It corrupts the daughter as well as the son—the mistress as well as the master—though the criminals are supposed to be comparatively fewer in the former cases. Still they do occur and no one will attempt to deny it." (p. 419)[15]

This states the central theme of the novel. Slavery was often supposed to wound women's tender souls (witness Mrs. Shelby) or harden their shallow hearts (witness Marie St. Clare) but its influence was restricted to definite areas. *Old Hepsy*,

---

14. Mrs. Denison was not always as unconventional and in *The Master* (Boston, 1862) for instance, she tells the story of a man who raises his orphan niece, but without acknowledging her as such, hence taking the risk of alienating his beloved wife's affection, simply because he mistakenly believes the child to be illegitimate.

15. Marshall Randolph echoes here the famous statement of Wendell Phillips that the South is "one great brothel, where half a million women are flogged to prostitution," quoted by Jules Zanger, "The 'Tragic Octoroon' in Pre–Civil War Fiction," *American Quarterly*, XVIII, Spring 1966, p. 67 [included in this volume, pp. 274–280. —Ed.].

on the contrary, implies the equality of men and women in susceptibility to evil, and the recognition of woman's sexuality, which makes Mrs. Denison's novel a milestone in the history of woman's liberation.[16]

As a result of this unusual frankness, the novel casts a deeply ironic light on the patriarchal legend, and the domestic metaphor. Mrs. Stowe's "sensuous argument from the 'woman nature' " had already "illuminated the contradictions of a patriarchal thesis and the extensions of miscegenation"[17]—and with greater efficiency, it is true. But Mrs. Denison's work, written from hitherto unplumbed depths of "woman nature," while pursuing Mrs. Stowe's line of attack, presses her weapon further home: *Old Hepsy* in effect explodes the family metaphor in two different though related ways. In the first place, the patriarchal legend allowed the slave a role in the family constellation that was fixed and therefore non-threatening. He was to remain a child in relation to the white parental figures of the master and mistress while his or her adult role as genitor or genitrix was confined to the area of the black family. Even when the relations of a planter with a woman slave raised her to the level of an adult partner, this place could present no great threat to the established family structure, insofar as it was only that of a female—hence a dependent on male power. To recognize the male slave as a possible adult was of course much more subversive. In the second place the novel disrupts the remaining stability of the patriarchal order which was located in virtuous Southern womanhood. Its challenge is much more perturbing to the existing order because the planter's wife, like Caesar's, must be above suspicion, not only for the private sexual fears of her husband to be allayed but for miscegenation to be confined within known bounds, out of the inner white family and the dominant "race." The planter may scatter his seed indiscriminately; as long as he refuses to acknowledge his offspring he can keep his bloodline pure and his dynastic order working, if fractured. On the contrary, the very basis of the family as an institution and of white supremacy is threatened when the familiarity generated by the Southern patriarchy leads to liaisons between not-so-black men and white women.[18] Thus, in an even more drastic way than her famous predecessor, Mrs. Denison exposes the familial analogy as both false and truer than the Southerner can afford to think it. On the one hand it is a mere metaphor, since black families within the so-called "family circle" of the plantation[19] can be separated

16. To be held a goddess is of course to be considered unequal. Lillian Smith has in our times denounced the bitter fruits of the idealization of the Southern Woman (*Killers of the Dream*, N.Y., Norton and Co, 1949). But conviction of Woman's moral superiority was not reserved to Southern culture; it was a deeply held tenet of American society at mid-century (William Wasserstrom, *Heiress of All the Ages, Sex and Sentiment in the Genteel Tradition*, Minneapolis, University of Minnesota Press, 1959). In upsetting the Southern Woman's pedestal, Mrs. Denison was going against the American grain.
17. Severn Duvall, "*Uncle Tom's Cabin*; The Sinister Side of the Patriarchy," reprinted in *Images of the Negro in American Literature*, ed. Seymour Gross and John E. Hardy, Chicago, 1966.
18. In a sense, Mrs. Denison avoided dealing frontally with the issue by making Keene and Miss Hollister's child a girl, i.e., some one who in any case would not transmit the patronym to further generations.
19. The expression appears in "Southern Thought Again," *De Bow's Review*, XXIII, 1857, p. 453.

from this and their own smaller unit broken, as numerous cases in *Old Hepsy* illustrate, and since, moreover, in the case of mixed-blood children, the bloodlines and the legal lines of succession are parallels that do not meet. The familial analogy therefore serves the social function of obfuscating the real relationship between black and white, which is that of chattel to owner. On the other hand the metaphor expresses, together with those obvious aspects which *do* assimilate the peculiar institution to a patriarchy, the unrecognized reality of miscegenation. Paradoxically the plantation system providing the setting and the occasion for amalgamation can thus create what it claims to be—a family order—only to disown the new family members, then reduced to making up a loose shadow family. The irony is further compounded when, because of the non-inclusion in the genealogical tree of certain offspring, kindred on the same or different sides of the color line have relations that would otherwise be prohibited. Insofar as the fact of incest is not commented on discursively in *Old Hepsy* and, I believe, the word is not pronounced, the theme is kept muted, perhaps out of literary discretion, perhaps out of a desire to be "realistic": the novel, in fact, dramatizes Southern ignorance of interracial incest while playing on the fascinated horror of incest in the American reader. Nevertheless the theme is strongly marked in the action since Keene is half-brother to Miss Hollister, Hollister half-uncle to Amy, and, in another case related, the man was also the girl's half-brother.[20] The arresting duplication of the incest pattern is also underlined by the curious parallel and crossing of names in the two actions: the consummated union links Amy Hollister to Fred Keene, the unconsummated one Amy Kenneth to Hollister. Furthermore Amy Hollister and Fred Keene were brought up as playmates and even Amy Kenneth's childhood was spent in Hollister's company. The girl remembers Hollister's "handsome childhood when *she hardly knew but he was a brother*—the bright and beautiful face of seventeen with whom she was always trusted, because he was so grave and careful, the maturer age of young manhood when she began to seek the glance of his dark eyes, and acknowledge his admiration—perhaps, without thinking, allot him a share of her own" (p. 278, italics added). The adult tie is in reality the reactivation of a former real, though presumably asexual, bond. It is this passage from infantile complicity in play between siblings to sexual attraction which normally society succeeds in repressing.[21] The failure to do so in this case is again evidence of the extent to which the family, one of whose functions is to enforce certain sexual prohibitions, has been disrupted. As for its function of protection, it plays it so discriminatingly, again excluding black members, that individuals may be unable to exert the responsibilities they are willing to assume towards their black kin. Neither her biological mother nor Mabel, who

---

Of course, the family metaphor can "work" because the word now designates a narrower group comprising only kindred of the same race, now designates metonymically a larger economic unit, with fluid outlines since the chattel can be sold away from it.

20. "In one case, although the woman loved him, and she was a planter's beautiful daughter, he was murdered; and murdered by her father. . . . Yes, and he was that man's son, too; the girl's brother, of course" (p. 246).

21. Luc de Heusch, *Essais sur le Symbolisme de l'Inceste Royal en Afrique*, Bruxelles, 1958, p. 21.

would like to adopt Lucina, can save the heroine, the former because she is hampered by her married woman's status and is caught in the meshes of the slave system,[22] the latter because she is too ignorant of Lucina's history and of Southern mores. Nor is Amy better protected by father or mother against herself and the dangers of exerting a woman's power where she is not allowed to give a woman's love.[23] And let us not mention the anonymous children of Colonel Randolph. Symbolically at the end of the novel the Kenneth family is utterly destroyed but a new family is reconstituted in the North because the black father was able to assume his responsibility towards his child. The salvation of Keene and Lucina indicates that sexual relations between black and white may represent a fall from innocence but do not spell out doom for all involved: in Mrs. Denison's fictional universe, fate does not frown at miscegenation, *per se*.

If the Southern family of Mrs. Denison is considered as a synecdoche for Southern society, then her vision is basically darker, though less lurid than Mrs. Stowe's, both because the dry rot of slavery has spread to the solid core of womanly virtue and because the link between the family unit and the overall social structure is more clearly exposed. The problem, of course, arises of how faithful this fictional picture is to a social reality. A modern historian, James Hugo Johnston, found evidence that supports Mrs. Denison's thesis, including cases in which witnesses established that "the woman encouraged and consented to the act of the Negro."[24] Though granting that it is not possible to "determine the extent of such practices"[25] as affairs between slaves and married or single white women, he writes that an examination of the U.S. census returns for 1830 seems to indicate that there were more cases than is usually suspected[26] and concludes:

> The white man is most responsible for the creation of the mulatto population of the slave days. However, the human passions which motivated the man were also the passions of the woman of the South, and the white woman has a share of responsibility in the existence of the mulatto.[27]

22. This is again a slight deviation from the octoroon pattern. Usually as long as he lives the "good" white father can protect his daughter whose tribulations begin after his death. That neither Mrs. Kenneth nor Mrs. Van Broek can do anything for Lucina might suggest the limits of a woman's power in the slave society.

23. Yet there are indications of how the system works to enforce the taboo that keeps the white woman away from the black man:

> "Hi! nigger git flogging in old mars' Hollister place ef dey *look* in white woman's eye. White woman cry ef nigger look at she—tell ole mars'—he call nigger—'Harry! wha' you dar look at yo' missus for?'
> 'I no look, massa.'
> 'Wha! missus *lie* den, do she? gib him fifty in de calaboose for dat. Whop! gib he 50 in de calaboose for *dat*!' massa Hollister have reason for not want nigger o'look in missees face!"
> (p. 203–4).

24. James Hugo Johnston, *Race Relations in Virginia 1776–1860* and *Miscegenation in the South*, Amherst, 1970, p. 258.

25. Ibid., 263.

26. Ibid., 265.

27. Ibid., 267.

Almost a hundred years before, *Old Hepsy* had suggested exactly the same thing. As Keene comments, "Hollister, the slave-owners, I mean among the men are pretty bad scoundrels, often, but the slave owner's daughter, and the slave-holder's wife, sometimes stoop to folly, as well" (p. 244).

However, Mrs. Denison's novel cannot be regarded simply as documenting a little-known phase of racial relations in the South.[28] It also reveals indirectly something of the position from which the Southern situation is viewed. Granted that the commanding image of the family was provided by the culture under scrutiny, the transformations which it undergoes as the novel develops are created by an altogether different kind of discourse. The most striking feature, in this respect, is undoubtedly the choice of white Negroes as *main* characters (though one must keep in mind that the title heroine, the unreverenced queen, Hepsy, is African). Such a preference was a current feature of the antislavery novel and has consequently been commented on by many critics; it is often explained as a reflection of white narcissism, "a concession," in the words of Sterling Brown, "unconscious perhaps, to race snobbishness even among abolitionists."[29] Jules Zanger has ably demonstrated that the "tragic octoroon" furnished antislavery writers with a powerful weapon, emphasizing "the repeated pattern of guilt of the Southern slaveholder" and permitting identification with the heroine "not merely on the superficial level of her color, but more profoundly in terms of the radical reversal of fortune she has suffered."[30] But the argument could be developed still further.

Important as it is at a certain level, the reversal pattern is however an *added* dramatic twist to a theme which is more central and more inclusive, since it also concerns the male mulatto, and an extension of a metaphor which more profoundly refers to identity and its uncertainties. For the mulatto not only designates the sin, incidental and individual, or cumulative and institutional, that produced him; he also designates the moment of origins, when black and white met on a footing of *sexual equality*,[31] and ultimately the *humanity* of the black partner. Chocolate brown or honey colored, he disproves the myth of two discrete races separated by an "impassable gulf": in the Biblical image of the novel, the white man is doing the impossible, changing the Ethiopian's skin for him. To the believer in the myth, the mulatto has the fascination of *lusus naturae*; for the antislavery propagandist, on the other hand, he has the attraction of a *lusus culturae* which throws light on the disorder underlying the apparent social order, and may, or

28. It is to be noted that Kenneth is a Northerner, "a renegade" who married into the plantation system and is destroyed by it because he does participate in the guilt of the South. Conventional as he may seem at first, with his arrogance and callousness, his portrait acquires some depth as the story progresses since his increasing degradation is seen as a result of his wife's lack of faith.

29. Sterling Brown, *The Negro in American Fiction* (Washington, D.C., 1937, p. 45) and "Negro Character as Seen by White Authors," *Journal of Negro Education*, II, April 1933, 179–203; Penelope Bullock "The Mulatto in American Fiction," *Phylon*, VI, 1945, 78–82; Jules Zanger, "The 'Tragic Octoroon' in Pre–Civil War Fiction," *loc. cit.*

30. Zanger, Ibid., 66–67 [in this volume, p. 287. —Ed.].

31. See Hollister's remark: "I'm her equal, anyway. . . . I'm a man and she's a woman, neither nothing more nor less" (p. 203).

may not,[32] according to the self-image and worldview of individual thinkers, attest to the need for a new, more integrative definition of *Homo Americanus*. More particularly, the white Negro, as the oxymoron used to refer to him manifests, is the incarnation of a non-disjunction and, is, as it were, a walking contradiction. But contrary to what is often thought it is not *merely* his whiteness which makes him of interest to the white imagination, it is the *unidentifiable* remaining blackness in the whiteness. The visibility of Negroid traits is an axiom of the social organization. But if black, which is non-white, can look non-black, nay white, then the opposition white/non-white shows up as problematical. Thus, on the one hand, the social structure insofar as it determines status according to race, i.e., color, is jeopardized. (This is why it became increasingly imperative for the states to define precisely what admixture of black blood makes a person a Negro and why the attempt can have but a *legal* value, for it cannot help displacing the problem, with percentages varying from 1/4th to 1/8th, 1/16th, "one drop of Negro blood," until one comes back full circle to the *imaginary* underlying point; when "any *ascertainable* trace of Negro blood" is enough to define the non-white, one is still left with the boggling uncertainty of the unascertainable trace.) On the other hand, the place of the white individual within the race-based social scheme and hence his very identity are threatened by the mere existence of the white Negro. In order to tell what I am and what is my place in the pecking order I must be able to tell what you are and what is your place. The white Negro raises up fears of indifferentiation as he calls into question the whiteness of the white man.[33] So both the reversal of fortune of the "tragic octoroon" and the rise of the militant octoroon signify, in fact, the destruction of the myth of a God-given

---

32. The *ludus naturae* aspect of the mulatto is, for instance, emphasized in the thinking of ethnologists J. C. Nott and G. R. Gliddon, who considered the mulatto as a hybrid and as such less fertile than the pure-blood, and destined to "die off." "Mulatto humanity seldom, if ever, reaches through subsequent crossings with white men, that grade of dilution which washes out the Negro stain" (*Types of Mankind: or, Ethnological Researches, based upon the Ancient Monuments, Paintings, Sculptures, and Crania of Races* . . . (Phila., Lippincott, 1854, p. 402). But Mrs. Royall, though she was no advocate of slavery, also provides an early example of recoil before the mulatto and the implications of blood mixture:

> Some of these [mulattoes] were about half white, some almost white, *leaving it difficult to distinguish where the one ends and the other begins.* To one unaccustomed to see human nature in this guise, it excites feelings of horror and disgust. It has something in it *so contrary to nature,* something which seems never to have entered into her scheme, to see a man neither black nor white, with blue eyes, and a woolly head, has something in it at which the mind recoils. It appears that these people instead of abolishing slavery, are gradually not only becoming slaves themselves, but *changing color.* (*Sketches of History, Life and Manners in the United States,* New Haven, 1826, p. 101, italics added)

33. That doubt as to one's whiteness was not simply a racist's nightmarish fantasy but may have been a real objective fear is evidenced by a note in which Andrew Jackson protests because his "pious mother" "has been dragged forth by Hammond and held to public scorn, as a prostitute who intermarried with a Negro, and my eldest brother sold as a slave." James H. Johnston who cites this curious document induces it as evidence that "there were elements of the population that might have been led to believe rumors that prominent men were of Negro extraction" (*op. cit.* 205–6).

and/or natural order in which one's place is supposedly fixed by racial differences. Both patterns are an invitation, tendered either in fear of chaos, or in serene acceptance of the new, to reconsider the definition of blackness and whiteness. Concern with the white Negro may therefore imply awareness of the multiracial character of *American* society, which he spectacularly embodies, and when they focus their attention on him, some of the antislavery writers may be groping towards a new assessment of an America in which "there is no unmiscegenation."[34] Symbolically in *Old Hepsy*, Keene and Lucina become influential citizens in the North. And no less symbolically, Hollister is called by a Southern girl, "The Americo-Anglo-African prince," because "there is a blending of nations in the man" (p. 181).

It follows also that interest in the white Negro may be read as an imaginary testing of boundaries. The white Negro represents a *cas limite,* the smallest difference that marks the point where the Other turns into the Same, when the either/or disjunction is no longer operative. Thus Lucina is not only as light as Amy, a *brunette,* but she is indistinguishable from the traditional genteel heroine. In fact she is the only paragon of virtue in the novel. (So great is her purity that Keene will not tell her that the hiding-place he has had Hollister build for her is in the latter's cabin for fear of shocking her "delicacy"!) Lucina's whiteness obviously is not merely due to a failure of creative power or identification since Mrs. Denison draws old Hepsy more fully, but to the desire of projecting a whole spectrum of "color." (At one point, the novelist even satirizes the ready identification of the slave-owner with the white slaves when she has Maggie conclude the really harrowing story of her slave companion, Dinny, with these words, the irony of which is inescapable.

"I never want to like a slave girl again—no never. If Dinny had been just a common black slave, I suppose I shouldn't have cared or thought much of her distress, but she was as white as I am, every whit." [p. 97])

And incidentally, it must be emphasized that the clear-complexioned daughter of Southern aristocracy, the "princess" as Kenneth jeeringly calls her, submits more tamely, in spite of her horror and despair, to the indignities of slavery than the indomitable though enslaved daughter of African kings.[35] In this way, too, the potentialities of the white Negro for "good" and "evil" are carefully balanced: neither Lucina's purity nor Hollister's passion can be taken as typical of their blood mixture.

34. The phrase is Milton Mayer's in "The Issue is Miscegenation" (*White Racism, Its History Pathology and Practice,* Ed. Barry N. Schwartz and Robert Disch, N.Y., 1970, p. 211. W. J. Cash, quoting Herskovits' figure that only a little over 20% American Negroes are unmixed, adds that "everything points to the conclusion that this state of affairs was already largely established by 1860" (*The Mind of the South,* N.Y., 1954, p. 96).

35. Indeed as one analogy suggests, Hepsy may be, for Lucina, an inspiration not to despair. "Still the snow white head of the vengeful negress appeared like a *vivid light in a dark night* directly before her" (p. 110). Hepsy certainly tries to encourage the girl.

Similarly, the emphasis—through redundancy—of the incest motif in *Old Hepsy* may be interpreted as a concern with transgression, that is to say with the breaking of limits. When refusing to acknowledge his slave son, the father fails to transmit with his surname what Jacques Lacan calls the Name-of-the-Father, i.e., the universal Law that prohibits incest.[36] Instead he forbids the White Woman *en masse* thus setting a (fairly) clear but extensive and artificial boundary while discounting the normal universal barrier. This law does not carry the same weight as the Name-of-the-Father and leaves the slave freer—in fancy if not in fact—to combine aspiration to his master's daughter, i.e., his half-sister, and yearning for social justice. In Hollister's speech, quoted above, oedipal fantasies of parricide and the dream of social redress get fused in images of blood and fire which have at the same time psychoanalytic significance and revolutionary relevance. In the affair between Keene and Miss Hollister, incest with the half-sister represents the greatest sexual transgression compatible with the smallest difference. (Incest with the black mother or the black sister could conveniently be ignored by the white father; intercourse with the father's wife, though taboo, would not be incestuous while the father's sister would be further removed genetically from the black partner.) Obviously such exploration of the area of possibilities uses the Southern plantation as a convenient available background. No social group offered a more suitable setting for the staging of "realistic" incestuous dramas, since, if bastardy is a common enough phenomenon, in no modern society has the *silence* of the Father been to the same extent a factor in the development and structuration of the social organism. Sociologically then, preoccupation with the white Negro may betray fear of the chaos that slowly and secretly pervades a society when it excludes a part of its population from onomastic filiation and consequently from the Law, in the psychoanalytic sense of the word. But just as obviously the fascination exerted by this kind of situation proceeds from psychic sources that cannot be called Southern. In other words, *Old Hepsy*, notwithstanding the usual claims it makes to truth,[37] does not so much mirror a reality as it shapes a verbal *image* of life. To this extent, ironical as the phrase is in the *social* context of the novel, Washington Grange is indeed "a modern paradise" at least as a fictional form. Whatever hellish actualities Mrs. Denison may expose under the idyllic agrarian legend, *Old Hepsy* builds up a myth of its own, out of history and of childhood dreams, out of a dark national present and the nostalgia for a private vanished happy time.

For a further examination of this fantasmatic dimension the story of Lucina provides a good starting-point. Lucina, the fruit of an incestuous interracial relation, is doubly emblematic of the unacknowledged American. Her case is indeed atypical in many respects but all the more exemplary. "A poor, dependent little girl cared for by hirelings," she is brought up like a white girl in ignorance of her identity, and without love. But she believes herself to be "Southern born,"

---

36. Jacques Lacan, *Ecrits*, Paris, 1966.
37. The "Preface" consists of the truism: " 'Tis strange but true; for truth is always strange, stranger than fiction."

white of course, and the daughter of "an honored, loving wife" (p. 37). She has to face up the fact that she is both non-white and *a bastard because of her white ascendancy*, there being no question of her mother's marrying her father. Nor does the "loving" mother ever acknowledge the relationship directly to her. Identity is gained at the price of renouncing the dream. Nevertheless it brings about the unexpected boon of reunion with the father. Whereas the archetypical octoroon has both to forgive and forget the slave mother who transmitted the socially despised black genes and the white father who failed adequately to ensure her protection against the lust of his kindred, Lucina has to forgive and forget the *white mother* whose love proved insufficient and inefficient, and the white grandfather who did not acknowledge his son her father; but she can love, and be loved by, the black father. Assuredly her being a paragon of virtue stresses the social significance of her plight and the repeated failure on the part of whites to assume the responsibilities of parenthood. But her experience signifies on another level insofar as it undoubtedly can be regarded as a fictionalized version of what Freud called a "family romance." Lucina indulges in dreaming up a legitimate genealogy when circumstances seem to indicate that she is not legitimate—in reversal of the procedure by which the normal child imagines himself to be a foundling or a bastard.[38] Yet Lucina's dream concerns not the father whose role it is to confirm legitimacy, but the mother, who is in fact the lost object. Furthermore the "bad" mother who has abandoned her child to the indifferent care of hirelings is fantasied as the "good" mother. But Lucina is not a real person and her own "family romance" is only the fictional representation within the narration, as in a mirror, of the more comprehensive family romance which informs the novel and in which as a fictive character she is an important figure. At this level, her story of Foundling turned Bastard reflects the wish to dethrone the mother—the queen sexually guilty of seducing the father—in order to form a "pure," therefore indissoluble couple with the father, who is both innocent and all powerful. Significantly, Lucina trusts Keene almost on sight: "If she did shudder and tremble going up the narrow stairs, she yet *clung confidently to the hand* that guided her. She felt *so secure in his protection*" (p. 388, italics added). And the last vision given of them creates the same impression of an infantile relationship. "Father and *child* are together." To call Lucina a daughter would have endowed her with sexuality: to call her a child is to keep her safe in the perennial paradise of pregenital love.

Needless to say, this is not the place to elaborate a psychoanalytic interpretation of the novel. I simply wish to point out the part which fantasms play in the fable. Two of them are specially worthy of notice because they recur in much fiction dealing with black-and-white relations.

The first one may be called the dream of restoration. Mrs. Kenneth, almost out of her mind with worry about Lucina and herself, turns to old Hepsy to

---

38. Freud's insights can be found in Otto Rank's *The Myth of the Birth of the Hero*, N.Y., 1959. Marthe Robert has developed them into a brilliant analysis of the novel as genre, *Roman des origines et origines du roman*, Paris, 1972.

whom she has in fact come to pay a visit of condolence: "I'm sorry for you Hepsy—I'm sorry for everybody who suffers now" (p. 333). Soon, instead of offering comfort to the bereaved mother, she is asking to be comforted:

> "Oh, Hepsy, *do* comfort me—do!—I'm dying for someone to say a comforting word to me. . . . I'm all alone, Hepsy, all alone—my heart is famishing, perishing! Oh, Hepsy, let me lay my head on your shoulder, as my mother did, and die there." (pp. 333–34)

And Hepsy, softened by Mrs. Kenneth's sorrow and her growing likeness to her mother, the one white who showed the slave woman some kindness, Hepsy, of course, gives her her shoulder, her solace. The scene is *repeated* at the end when Kenneth publicly repudiates his wife, and although she asks whether years of remorse and penance do not atone for her crime, banishes her. "With a wild cry, Mrs. Kenneth stretched forth her hand towards old Hepsy. 'You will not desert me!' she cried brokenly" (p. 418). Again, Hepsy rises up to the occasion:

> "Lord knows I won't, poor lamb. . . . Sure as you live, honey, God deal with he! I knows all about it poor lamb! An' I pities ye, and has pitied ye, eber sence poor Jack die. 'Fore dat time, 'deed I was mighty savage, an' I curse de whole house an' land. Hopes de Lord forgive me." (p. 419)

Later, despite her one hundred-and-ten years, Hepsy will take care of Mrs. Kenneth, who has become mad; and, faithful to the end, her dying words will be to entrust her charge to the new owners of Washington Grange. To find in the embrace of the abused black mother—nay in the arms of the black male, as Leslie Fiedler has shown[39]—ultimate forgiveness for the guilt of the white race is a fantasm that underlies a good many American novels. The motif takes on a special coloration in *Old Hepsy* because Hepsy never fulfilled the role of Mammy before; nor were her relations to Mrs. Kenneth, whom she frightened with sly allusions to her two daughters, particularly friendly. Yet the vengeful old African becomes a mother-substitute who can remit all sins. For indeed, although Mrs. Kenneth's need for pardon betrays on the first occasion an awareness, however dim, of her guilt as slaveowner, what she desires is another kind of absolution. Interestingly, forgiveness for Mrs. Kenneth is to be obtained not from the daughter—whom she most deeply wronged as parent and slaveholder—but from a figure that unites phallic and maternal traits. Only a return to a maternal *imago* can offer the hope to make the sinner and the world whole again. It may not be too far-fetched to see in this situation the fictional representation not so much of a social sense of guilt as of a much more universal desire for reparation in the Kleinian sense. If at the level of the narration, there is no true restoration for Mrs. Kenneth, except in the final regression to madness and death, black Hepsy's willingness and ability to take charge of her gives symbolic assurance that the rejected mother will not be rejecting and will always eventually assume her role.

---

39. Leslie Fiedler, *Love and Death in the American Novel*, N.Y., 1960.

More generally, the characters in *Old Hepsy* evince widespread interest in genealogy. Even a secondary figure like Marshall Randolph speculates on his kinship to the new mulatto child he sees on his return to the paternal plantation. Kenneth suspects Lucina's origins before he can be sure. Amy has her own doubts about the beautiful slave, which she expresses to her mother: "*My* father may be *hers*. If so, I hate her." Although her mother assures that she is wrong, she still feels obscurely jealous of the girl and consequently tries to marry her off to Hollister. The marriage would satisfy her need to humiliate both the feared rival and the presumptuous slave lover. Later she begins "to comprehend that there were motives underlying her father's hostility to this slave which she could not understand" (p. 315). The explanation of the mystery, when given by Hollister, will be such a shock that she faints, which provides Hollister with an opportunity to administer poison to her. In this sense, the secret of the mother's sexual dalliance indirectly brings death to the daughter. As has been seen, Lucina for her part muses upon her birth; and Keene, a father figure, gives Hollister an account of both his own ascendancy and his brother's, thus provoking Hollister to greater boldness towards Amy.

Such concerns are a familiar phase of human development, together with the fantasmatic remodelling of one's known history. *Old Hepsy* weaves in its tapestry the double and contrasting pattern of the "family romance," as analysed by Marthe Robert. We have seen that Lucina incarnates the pre-oedipal fantasies of the Foundling. As befits a fantasmatic Foundling, she lives partly in an imaginary world, seeing "shapes" in clouds, and considering it is "always best to leave something to the imagination" (p. 282). Hence she is ill-equipped to cope with the realities of the outside world which almost crushes her. A passive character, she can only cry, "Oh! save me! save me!" "with chattering teeth" or in desperate moments think of committing suicide, when she becomes the object of the neighbouring planters' lust. She disconsolately awaits redemption from the outside— at the hands of unexpected but in a sense likely parental figures, of Mabel Van Broek, the would-be foster mother of wealth and refinement, and of Keene, the competent father. In contrast, Keene and Hollister who appear later in the story, embody the oedipal romance of the Bastard. Both will try to remold the world; both will affront the Father who denied them, Hollister through intended incest and accomplished murder, Keene through his liaison with his sister, the rescue of Lucina, and *journalistic* work aimed at overthrowing the Father's system. Through their aggressions both Bastards attempt to fill symbolically the place which their "real" father's denial of them has left empty. If Hollister is destroyed—but not vanquished—in his struggle against the patriarchal values, Keene succeeds in escaping both slavery and the death and/or castration that threatens the rebellious potent black. The hope of renewal for Southern and American society as projected in the fable may well lie in this individual who has broken the sexual taboos of his society, defied the Father, and yet survived to prove himself capable of a father's pact.[40]

---

40. Incest with the half-sister is not condemned, and its fruit, Lucina, is worthy of admiration, but that it is not condoned can perhaps be read in the fact that no prolongation of the line, no

The fictional characters, however, are not alone in speculating about their or someone's place in a given family structure. The narration itself places the reader in the characters' situation of curiosity, since the secret of Lucina's parentage is only slowly unveiled. And once disclosed, it is told three times—a repetition which may point less to some awkwardness in the story-telling than to the profound importance of the disclosure itself. Besides, Keene and Hollister, presented sympathetically from the very first, are themselves too exceptional and too mysterious not to raise questions. In each case the knowledge sought for relates to a seduction or a rape. In each case the narration takes little account of the time-element in conquest or generation. Even in the story most developed, that of Miss Hollister, nothing is told of her approaches once she has met again the handsome slave, or naturally of her expecting the baby. The result is that, in spite of, or rather because of, the circumspection of the tale, what is emphasized obliquely is the sexual encounter—the unseen, untold primal scene. And the essential, *under-lying* theme of *Old Hepsy* is that of the quest of origins. The quest—a hidden motif of much art and the very nucleus of myth[41]—is here given fresh impact because of the social structure in which it is dramatized. The intricacy of inter-racial relationships in the slave society, and more precisely the evasions of roles and the displacement of familial positions which the system entails create fairly complex patterns which are used here to mask and unmask the basic symbolic myth. In this context, a crucial example is furnished by Kenneth's remark to Hollister whom he finds busy making a coffin for his mother:

"Your mother?—your mother!" repeated the delirious man. . . . "I didn't know as you fellows ever had mothers; had an idea that you sprung up like mushrooms."
(p. 421)

The taunt originates in Kenneth's reluctance to accept what he knows to be true, the fact of his wife's having borne a mixed-blood child. But it also embodies a phantasm of origins, an infantile theory of generation, so that when Kenneth forbids Hollister to bury his mother in a *coffin*, he is not only refusing him (and her) the sign of a certain social status, he is, in fact, on a symbolic level, endeavouring to deny the birth-to-death, matrix-to-matrix cycle. Above and beyond this, private fantasies depend on and express a social context. The *delirious* man's speech exposes the unconscious wish of the white man to evade the implications of the mulatto's existence by shaping a myth of non-sexual, indeed non-human

grandchild is foreseen in the fictional future. This may symbolize that the prohibition of incest is in fact necessary for the structuration of society.

It must be added that many of the black characters are pictured in parental roles: Esty admonishing her son to keep his ideas to himself, Joycliffe proud of his son's education but despondent at the idea of the severe restrictions imposed on his bright boy's future, Hepsy, giving advice to Phillis, though after the sale of her last child, she "never did think" she'd "care about folks anymore" are but a few examples. Similarly the brotherly love of Hollister and Keene has no parallel in the fiction of the times and the scene when they part, Keene confident because he has given his brother money to run away, Hollister aware of saying adieu is indeed a moving one.

41. See in particular Guy Rosolato, *Essais sur le symbolique*, Paris, 1969.

generation, which serves a social function. But what the myth represses, it cannot of course obliterate. Kenneth's words further goad on Hollister to his act of revenge and the young man evokes his plan (hitherto unknown to the reader) in these terms: "Tomorrow there will be no one to call him father" (p. 426). Deprived of both parents, never allowed the opportunity to insert himself into a family discourse,[42] Hollister in his turn strips Kenneth of his father's role and of his father's place in his daughter's speech, i.e., his daughter's desire. Hollister will however make an attempt—which he knows to be doomed—to establish a significant dialogue with Amy: "I had *a strange dream*," he tells her, "I dreamed that you loved me" (p. 436, italics added). But failing to elicit from the frightened girl anything but standardized epithets (boy, slave, insolent) and the stereotyped speech of caste, he executes his plan. Murder has become the only way for him to assert himself as a man, as a sexual being capable of taking the daughter away from the father, the only way to engage with her in a new relationship—even though it be through immolation. In this manner, "amalgamation" is once more revealed as being far more than the union of two individuals, since in the examples just given, a third party, whether the husband or the father, is vitally though indirectly involved and, through the use of language and the language used, "amalgamation" appears as the insertion in a nexus of relationships, affirmed or denied, imaginary or "real." Thus, too, the novel furnishes a clue to the general appeal of the white Negro *figure* to the white reader. A paradigm of the dark sexual secret of generation and a symbol of the rejected child, his relation both to the very real problems of a specific culture and to the human mystery *par excellence* makes him a meaningful archetype, all the more flexible for being inherently ambivalent.

Insofar as he is a metaphor of the minimal difference that prevents the Other from being the Same, and hence too a metaphor of *desire*—the white Negro in *Old Hepsy* can be seen as a pregnant image of the possibility of human renewal. Possibly Mrs. Denison was not fully aware of the pattern which her web of words was making—though her willingness to let Keene escape with his life and his pride, which could hardly be unconscious, seems highly significant. But intent on destroying the paternalistic Southern legend, she created a fiction that adumbrates a much older myth. Indeed, that she too bluntly laid bare the links in the metaphorico-metonymic chain that leads from "representation" of the "Southern family" to such a myth is proved by the neglect into which the novel has fallen. This same chain, on the contrary, should be incentive enough for today's reader to overlook what is clumsy in her technique, incomplete in her analysis, inconsistent in her attitude and to go straight to the vital meaning of the book. Certainly the African-born queens have long disappeared from the American scene but some of their full-blooded descendants and a majority of "Americo-Anglo-African"

---

42. Following Freud, psychoanalysts have stressed the importance of the "heard" and of the "family discourse" in the development of phantasms: "Mais l'entendu, c'est aussi . . . l'histoire, ou la légende, des parents, des grands-parents, de l'ancêtre : le *dit* ou le *bruit* familial, ce discours parlé ou secret, préalable au sujet, où il doit advenir et se repérer" (Jean Laplanche et J. B. Pontalis, "Fantasme originaire, fantasmes des origines, origines du fantasme," *Les Temps Modernes*, n° 215, Avril 1964, p. 1854).

princes and princesses whom the culture has borne only to deny them full participation in the genealogical line of power are still with us. Nor have the "white Negroes," princely yet still debarred from their high inheritance—exiles in the American mythical homeland—ceased to figure in the fantasmatic dramas which literature stages for the benefit alike of self and society. Whether as Kingsblood Royal in Sinclair Lewis' novel of the same title, or as the sophisticated Charles Bon in Faulkner's *Absalom Absalom!* (whose fate bears some little resemblance to Hollister's) or as Amantha Starr in Robert Penn Warren's *Band of Angels*, to mention but a few, they still haunt the white "city of words," still ask the reader to decipher the riddle of America and the riddle of the sphinx.

Othello in America: The Drama of Racial Intermarriage*

TILDEN G. EDELSTEIN

A recent historian of nineteenth-century race relations claims that pre-Victorian Americans so feared racial intermarriage and amalgamation that they "found it difficult to sit through a performance of *Othello*." Given the history of American race relations such difficulty hardly seems surprising. Paradoxically, despite its racial and sexual elements, *Othello* has been one of the most frequently performed Shakespearean plays in a nation that has watched more Shakespeare than it has the works of any other playwright.[1] Shakespeare encompassed art, culture, and the wisdom of Western civilization; and for American actors and audiences *Othello*'s volatile racial, sexual, and class themes provided drama surpassing the dimensions of the stage. Engrossing drama, exemplified by *Othello*, communicates symbolically, simultaneously presenting the recognizably concrete event with verbal and physical images transcending material reality. Two centuries of American *Othello* performances dramatized some of this country's racial reality and its racial fantasies.

A standard Shakespearean reference source warns that *Othello* was "not intended as a problem of miscegenation American style, because Othello was an aristocrat of royal birth." A writer in the *Shakespeare Quarterly* argues that "it is not important that he happened to be full-blooded, or part-blooded Arab, Moor, Negro, Blackamoor, or whatever. These are just names." Even the distinguished

* From Tilden G. Edelstein, "*Othello* in America: The Drama of Racial Intermarriage." In *Region, Race, and Reconstruction: Essays in Honor of C. Vann Woodward* (New York, Oxford: Oxford University Press, 1982), 179–197.

1. Linda K. Kerber, "Abolitionists and Amalgamators: The New York City Race Riots of 1834," *New York History*, 48 (1967), 28. The popularity of Shakespeare is surveyed in Esther C. Dunn, *Shakespeare in America* (New York, 1939); David Grimsted, *Melodrama Unveiled: American Theater and Culture, 1800–1850* (Chicago, 1968); and Charles H. Shattuck, *Shakespeare on the American Stage: From the Hallams to Edwin Booth* (Washington, D.C., 1976). Also see William B. Carson, *Theatre on the Frontier Stage* (Chicago, 1932).

historian of American culture Louis B. Wright stresses that "Shakespeare was *not* trying . . . to emphasize any racial differences between the hero and the heroine." But Wright concedes that the generations after Shakespeare may have perceived the play in racial terms.[2] Obviously fundamental to perception in the theater is the direct visual sense of the action—you go to *see* a play—and so, regardless of what Shakespeare intended, if *Othello* is perceived in racial terms, this will affect the acting and reception of the play and even its very meaning.

From the eighteenth century to the present, changing American racial, sexual, and class attitudes necessitated the periodical alteration of characterization, costuming, makeup, and even dialogue. These changes, of course, functioned reciprocally: they both reflected and promoted revealing responses to the play from audiences and critics. What is revealed are societal tensions found in pervasive and changing American views about race, sex, and class. Especially important is the conclusion of a recent American theater historian who notes that, particularly in the first half of the nineteenth century, "closeness of audience control made the drama, more than any art form, the theater as much as any social institution, immediately sensitive to public opinion." These audiences, he writes, were a pluralistic mix of classes, colors, and sexes.[3]

The colonists' distrust of the theater, primarily motivated by Puritan moral prescriptions against idleness and frivolity, delayed the first American performance of *Othello* until the mid-eighteenth century. At Newport, Rhode Island, in 1765, it was performed in a tavern and advertised as a "Moral Dialogue in Five Parts," since local law banned both plays and theaters. The playbill didactically noted the moral lessons taught by each character, including the "dreadful passion of jealousy" demonstrated by the "noble and magnanimous Moor." Brabantio's rejection of Desdemona's marriage to black Othello also had a moral: her father "is foolish enough to dislike the noble Moor . . . because his face is not white, forgetting that we all spring from one root. Such prejudices are very numerous and very wrong." The playbill further embellished the racial moral with a couplet:

> Fathers beware what sense and love ye lack.
> 'Tis crime, not color, makes the being black.

But class insubordination was not tolerated. Emilia was a faithful attendant and a good example "to all servants, male and female, and to all persons in subjection." Accepting the prevailing single-origin theory of evolution did not mean conceding class equality. Neither menial servant nor slave, but a black man of royal birth, Othello, in this era, was qualified by class to marry Desdemona. Only the racially prejudiced could disagree.[4]

---

2. Oscar J. Campbell and Edward J. Quinn, *The Reader's Encyclopedia of Shakespeare* (New York, 1966), p. 599; Arthur H. Wilson, "Othello's Racial Identity," *Shakespeare Quarterly*, 4 (April 1953), 209; Louis B. Wright, ed., *General Reader's Shakespeare* (New York, 1957), p. xiv.

3. Grimsted, *Melodrama Unveiled*, p. 62.

4. Hugh F. Rankin, *The Theater in Colonial America* (Chapel Hill, 1960), pp. 2–7; Alfred Westfall, *American Shakespeare Criticism, 1607–1865* (New York, 1939), pp. 56–57; Robert A. Law, "Shakespeare in Puritan Disguises," *Nation*, November 23, 1916, p. 486.

In this production, as in others of the seventeenth and eighteenth centuries, a white actor played Othello wearing heavy black makeup, and the most renowned Othellos toured major American Northern and Southern cities. The white American actor James Quin, a big, black Othello, wore a white wig, an all-white British officer's uniform, and white gloves. As a result of the visual impact of contrasting colors, high drama occurred when Quin peeled off his white gloves to reveal his black hands.[5] Shakespeare, the actor David Garrick argued, had depicted jealous white men before, but in *Othello* he sought to disclose this passion in all its violence and so chose an "African in whose veins circulated fire instead of blood."[6] Men's passions, in the Age of Reason, were a central concern; in *Othello* the passion of jealousy is magnified by the character of the black African. His white British uniform further linked Othello to his white audience, making visible the idea that black was not entirely separate from white.

Similarly, John Adams, writing in 1760, judged the play's moral to be how love turns to hatred and revenge when a man feels betrayed. He quoted Othello: "Arise, black Vengeance, from the hollow Hell."[7] Adams, whose thought was indebted both to the Enlightenment and to Puritan moral didacticism, emphasized human frailty, not distaste for racial intermarriage. Yet by accepting Shakespeare's linking of black with irrational vengeance, and the Newport production's view that crime was "black," Adams's opinion confirms Winthrop Jordan's suggestion that a negative color consciousness emerged before racist theory fully developed.[8] Nevertheless, moral questions rather than racial ones dominated Adams's thought as it did that of other eighteenth-century American intellectuals.

Seeing *Othello* performed in London in 1786, Abigail Adams perceived none of the racial-equality themes stressed by the 1765 Newport production. Her response also contrasted with her husband's observations of 1760. Mrs. Adams's perceptions were too close to the era's racial views to be dismissed as exemplifying only her unique view. Massachusetts, which had abolished slavery in 1783, reenacted its law against racial intermarriage in 1786 while eliminating legal prohibitions against interracial fornication. Abigail Adams admitted that she was disturbed by "the sooty appearance of the Moor. . . . I could not separate the African color from the man, nor prevent that disgust and horror which filled my mind every time I saw him touch the gentle Desdemona; nor did I wonder that Brabantio thought some love potion or some witchcraft had been practiced to make his daughter fall in love with what she scarcely dared to look upon."[9] Here were

5. Marvin Rosenberg, *The Masks of Othello* (Berkeley, 1971), p. 38; John S. Kendall, *The Golden Age of the New Orleans Theater* (Baton Rouge, 1952), pp. 5, 6, 49, 153, 163, 243, 269, 524; R. P. McCutcheon, "Shakespeare in Antebellum Mississippi," *Journal of Mississippi History*, 5 (1943), 28–37.
6. George W. Stone, Jr., "Garrick and *Othello*," *Philological Quarterly*, 45 (1966), 305; the quotation is from Carol Carlisle, *Shakespeare from the Greenroom* (Chapel Hill, 1969), p. 188.
7. John Adams to Josiah Quincy, summer 1759, in Lyman H. Butterfield, ed., *Diary and Autobiography of John Adams*, 4 vols. (Cambridge, Mass., 1961), I, 114.
8. Winthrop Jordan, *White over Black* (Chapel Hill, 1968), pp. 4–11.
9. Abigail Adams to Mrs. Shaw, March 4, 1786, in C. F. Adams, ed., *Letters of Mrs. Adams, the Wife of John Adams* (Boston, 1840), p. 125.

fundamental issues for Mrs. Adams and her contemporaries: the paramount importance of black indelibility and revulsion against physical contact between a black man and a white woman. Her perception that it requires evil black magic for a white woman to succumb to the love for a black man suggests a growing awareness of women's will in relationships with men. Inability to see beyond Othello's blackness obstructed comprehension of any deeper meaning, she admitted: "I lost much of the pleasure of the play." Othello's color did not magnify a human trait like vengeance but compelled her to distinguish him from any white lover of a white woman.

Observing that the renowned Sarah Siddon, who played Desdemona, was pregnant, Mrs. Adams expressed comfort that the actress's brother, John Phillip Kemble, acted Othello "so that both her husband and the virtuous part of the audience can see them in the tenderest scenes without once fearing for their reputation."[10] Obviously, racial intermarriage, *not* any thoughts of incest, caused Mrs. Adams's repugnance for Othello. Knowledge that a white man in black makeup was playing Othello seemed obscured to her in the context of America's struggle to reconcile freedom and slavery, equality and racism. The aristocratic compatibility of Desdemona and Othello would no longer compensate for their racial differences.

Although a Natchez editor called Othello a "dirty Moor" and suggested that had any other playwright "laid such a plot and made such an ill-assorted match it would have damned him," it was not merely reverence for Shakespeare that accounted for antebellum Americans' continuing to attend *Othello* productions— and nowhere more than in the South. Charleston witnessed most performances, and it played as often in New Orleans as in Philadelphia.[11] Fascination with the racial and sexual themes remained, but major adjustments were needed to make the play more acceptable to early-nineteenth-century audiences. For the next 125 years American audiences could not accept the credibility of a "noble Moor" of aristocratic and royal birth whose skin color was black. How, then, to get audiences to feel the tragic power of *Othello?*

Edmund Kean, after having played the part in traditional black makeup, greatly lightened that coloring by 1820 and thus inaugurated the so-called bronze age of *Othello.* Most free blacks in the North and South were mulattoes, who were accorded higher status than blacks.[12] An actor playing Othello now had the advantage, explained a Southern newspaper, of "not being so dark as to obscure the expression of his countenance."[13] Light makeup, it has been argued, was demanded by poor stage illumination and by a new romantic acting style emphasizing facial expressions.[14] Underlying the view that black skin hides expression, however, were the clichés that all black faces looked the same and were expres-

10. Ibid., p. 126.
11. Quoted in James Dormon, *Theater in the Antebellum South, 1815–1861* (Chapel Hill, 1967), p. 276; Grimsted, *Melodrama Unveiled*, p. 252.
12. Carlisle, *Shakespeare from the Greenroom*, pp. 191–92; Joel Williamson, *New People: Miscegenation and Mulattoes in the United States* (New York, 1980), p. 15.
13. Virginia *Herald* [1819], in Harvard University Theatre Collection.
14. Carlisle, *Shakespeare from the Greenroom*, p. 190.

sionless. Such anonymity ill suited the unique personality Shakespeare created and the play's dramatic impact.

The gradual decline of the Enlightenment belief in environmental causes of black character and the growing acceptance by Americans of the theory that blacks were closer in origin to animals than to men made blacks appear inherently unequal to whites and therefore subject to different treatment. In the South, until about 1850, only the mulatto, thanks to some white blood, would be viewed as a black not limited by animal traits.[15] Also contributing to the play's credibility was the nineteenth-century tradition that the actors playing Othello and Iago exchanged roles at different performances. Audiences thus were reminded that *Othello* was a play and not reality.

Samuel Taylor Coleridge is as revealing as Abigail Adams in explaining why makeup changed and how the British, for a time, shared American views. Shakespeare, said Coleridge, was not "so utterly ignorant as to make a barbarous *negro* plead royal birth. . . . It would be something monstrous to conceive this beautiful Venetian girl falling in love with a veritable negro." After seeing the great Edmund Kean playing Othello in light makeup, Coleridge exuberantly concluded that it was "like reading Shakespeare by flashes of lightning."[16]

Further "lightening" of Othello soon occurred in the United States. After Kean's last American performance as Othello in the 1820s, a young Philadelphian, Edwin Forrest, appeared on the New York stage with the makeup of an octoroon. Tragic octoroons, looking white but having a trace of black blood and some telltale Negroid features that condemned them to slavery or prevented their marrying whites, were frequent figures in sentimental antebellum fiction. Until about 1840, Forrest had played a robust Othello, a blinded giant who killed Desdemona by seizing her "with illimitable rage." This characterization, so close to popular fears about animallike free blacks, Forrest distinctly muted by deleting lines dealing with racial amalgamation; and he moved further away from portraying Othello as a black and closer to a "warrior Moor . . . the descendant of a long illustrious line of ancestry."[17] Thus another step had been taken to whiten Othello. An English critic observed that the American actor looked more like a Shawnee or a Mohican than a Moor.[18] To have an Indian, or, even better, a man who only looked like one, marry your daughter was obviously less repulsive to many Americans than the prospect of a black son-in-law.

15. George M. Fredrickson, *The Black Image in the White Mind* (New York, 1971), pp. 1–5, 13, 172–73; William Stanton, *The Leopard's Spots* (Chicago, 1960), pp. 19–22; Williamson, *New People*, pp. 15–19.
16. Quoted in Gino J. Matteo, "Shakespeare's *Othello:* The Study and the Stage, 1604–1904" (Ph.D. diss., University of Toronto, 1968), p. 275; Barbara Alden, "Differences in the Conception of Othello's Character as Seen in the Performances of Three Important Nineteenth-Century Actors on the American Stage" (Ph.D. diss., University of Chicago, 1950), p. 29.
17. Howard H. Furness, *A New Variorum Edition of Shakespeare* (Philadelphia, 1886), VI, 406; Shattuck, *Shakespeare on the American Stage*, p. 79; New York *Dramatic Mirror*, November 26, 1836, October 26, 1889; Jean F. Yellin, *The Intricate Knot* (New York, 1972), pp. 84–85, 171–72; Jules Zanger, "The 'Tragic Octoroon' in Pre–Civil War Fiction," *American Quarterly*, 18 (1966), 63–70 [in this volume, pp. 284–291. —Ed.].
18. Richard Moody, *Edwin Forrest* (New York, 1960), p. 225.

During the Jacksonian era, John Quincy Adams's views about *Othello* reveal the continuing difficulties, despite Forrest's lightening efforts, that color-conscious Americans were having with the play, especially in the 1830s and 1840s, when emerging racist thought was denying human characteristics to blacks or seeing them unequal to whites, and when the number of state laws prohibiting racial intermarriage was increasing.[19] In the very years when Adams was heroically defending slaves who had mutinied aboard the *Amistad* and was fighting the "gag rule" in Congress against antislavery petitions, he wrote in his diary about Desdemona, "whose sensual passion I thought over ardent, so as to reconcile her to a passion for a black man; and although faithful to him, I thought the poet has painted her as a lady of easy virtue."[20] A few years later Adams revealed how much beyond his mother, Abigail Adams, he had traveled in perceiving the play principally in racial and sexual terms and how much more troubled even a thoughtful American had become about racial intermarriage, miscegenation, and female sexuality. Now a published theater critic, John Quincy Adams abandoned the privacy of his diary to publish two articles about *Othello*. Dwelling upon what he interpreted as the wanton character of Desdemona, he wrote:

> . . . she not only violates her duties to her father, her family, her sex and her country, but she makes the first advances. . . . The great moral lesson of *Othello* is that black and white blood cannot be intermingled without a gross outrage upon the law of Nature; and that, in such violations, Nature will vindicate her laws. . . . Upon the stage her fondling of Othello is disgusting. Who, in real life, would have her for a sister, daughter or wife. . . . She is always deficient in delicacy. . . . This character takes from us so much of the sympathetic interest in her sufferings that when Othello smothers her in bed, the terror and the pity subside immediately to the sentiment that she had her just deserts.[21]

Adams noted in another essay, "I must believe that in exhibiting a daughter of a Venetian nobleman of the highest rank eloping in the dead of night to marry a thick-lipped, wool-headed Moor, opening a train of consequences which lead to her own destruction by her husband's hands, and to that of her father by a broken heart, he [Shakespeare] did not intend to present her as an example of the perfection of female virtue."[22] A thick-lipped, wooly-headed Moor hardly was identical to the portrayal of an eighteenth-century aristocratic African king. Yet as disturbing as Othello's race were Desdemona's exaggerated female characteristics, which moved her to make the first advances, elope, and remain a loving wife in alleged defiance of her father, family, sex, country, and class. To Adams, she seemed to have uncontrolled sexual passions instead of feminine warmth; instead

19. Frederickson, *Black Image*, pp. 176–81; David Fowler, "Northern Attitudes towards Interracial Marriage: A Study of Legislation and Public Opinion in the Middle Atlantic States and the States of the Old Northwest" (Ph.D. diss., Yale University, 1963), pp. 155–57, 163–69.
20. November 1831, in Alan Nevins, ed., *The Diary of John Quincy Adams, 1794–1845* (New York, 1928), p. 424; Frederickson, *Black Image*, pp. 46–58, 132.
21. "Misconceptions of Shakespeare upon the Stage," *New England Magazine*, 9 (1835), 252.
22. "The Character of Desdemona," *American Monthly Magazine*, 1 (1836), 151.

of being sweetly innocent she seemed devastatingly gullible; and instead of showing unquestioning filial loyalty she appeared a woman doggedly enslaved to her
black husband. Only by seeing Desdemona as wanton and the play as a lesson
against racial intermarriage could Adams accept the credibility of even a bleached
Othello and a Desdemona who betrays her race and class.

Still another way to make the play plausible to antebellum American audiences
was to cast Desdemona as an innocent blond victim, blondness being the characteristic attribute of the virtuous female until the 1920s, when it began to connote
the very opposite of innocence. Desdemona became a childlike blond who tragically strayed too far from her English teas, domestic needlework, polite music,
and proper dancing. As either a wanton woman or an innocent victim, Desdemona
thus exemplified a view of the play in which the race issue eclipsed not only the
question of jealousy but just about everything else. Only after the subsequent
casting of Edwin Booth as an Othello who bore no resemblance to a black African,
either as African king or thick-lipped wooly-headed Moor, would Desdemona be
characterized as both a virtuous and rational woman.

Booth, who played Othello for the first time in 1849, sought to expunge from
the play any taint of miscegenation by becoming the lightest-skinned Othello ever,
thus eliminating visually any liaison between a black man and a white aristocrat's
daughter. (Even after electricity illuminated the stage in 1878 and the alleged
problem of black makeup hiding facial expressions no longer could be defended,
Booth never became black.)[23] Wearing robes of glittering Oriental splendor, he
was transmogrified into Desdemona's Persian suitor. With studied gestures, such
as holding above his purple-and-gold turban a scimitar forming a crescent, Booth
made his costume, makeup, and manner identify Othello. At times he wore a
long, hanging, Tartar-like mustache to emphasize that Othello was "Arabian, not
African." His confessed purpose was to raise Othello's character above that of a
"brutal blackamoor."[24]

Portraying, moreover, chivalrous love devoid of onstage embraces, Booth presented a genteel Othello. (One critic complained of Booth's acting like a "young
Jesuit student" or like an "elderly schoolboy.") To Ellen Terry, one of his most
famous leading ladies, he vowed: "I shall never make you black." When he touched
her, Booth shielded her fair skin from his tan makeup with his costume. His characterization allowed Desdemona to be cast as "a true woman with a mind of her
own."[25] Once Othello ceased being black, Desdemona no longer had to be viewed as
a wanton woman or an innocent child lured sexually to love a black man.

Booth's Othello was popular throughout much of the post–Civil War era, suggesting the continuity of racial and sexual attitudes from 1850 to 1880 in the

23. Carlisle, *Shakespeare from the Greenroom*, p. 205; Alden, "Othello's Character," pp. 210, 325; New
York *Herald*, September 13, 1869.
24. Edwina Booth Grossman, *Edwin Booth* (New York, 1894), pp. 21–22, 210; Boston *Evening Transcript*, March 6, 1878.
25. Alden, "Othello's Character," pp. 179–80; Shattuck, *Shakespeare on the American Stage*, p. 141;
Booth to Howard H. Furness, May 12, 1885, in Grossman, *Edwin Booth*, pp. 285, 304.

North, as he continued to expunge lines that explicitly emphasized race. American audiences demanded whitewashed Othellos, so it was understandable that Henry Irving, the great English Shakespearean actor, never played the part in any of his eight American tours. Irving had a reputation for acting Othello in black makeup and besmirching his leading ladies with it.[26] American audiences, on the other hand, had the reputation, according to an antebellum critic, of considering "actors as public slaves . . . bound to be obedient victims of their caprice."[27]

Until the 1850s the South welcomed productions of *Othello*. But when the lines separating North and South grew more distinct, Southern cities witnessed a declining number of *Othello* performances. In Macon, Georgia, a Shakespearean company was informed that the play displeased many of the town citizenry and that no actor could portray a black Othello. To avoid a disturbance, said one leading man, "I played him nearly white." As the South moved toward secession and the issue of miscegenation became central to the slavery debate, Joel Williamson has written, another Othello admitted being "afraid of the negro part." The period of Booth's greatest popularity coincided with the strong fear of mulattoes that initially affected the South in the decade before the Civil War, and then spread through all America once emancipation came.[28] Despite the whitening and orientalizing of the main character, that fear of one drop of black blood in the men whom white daughters married continued to haunt and fascinate Americans with the tenacity of a morbid compulsion.

Issues that audiences have difficulty confronting directly are often presented, as we know, by the indirectness of parody. Through satire and ridicule, parodies of *Othello* both evaded and capitalized on miscegenation tensions. In parody the continuing demands for plausibility could be ignored. Of all Shakespearean plays, it was *Othello* that was most frequently parodied in nineteenth-century America, and always the parody assured the audience of the absurdity of racial intermarriage. Among the parodies were *Dars de money, Old Fellow, or the Boor of Vengeance,* and *Desdamonium.* The most popular parody was performed by the Christy Minstrels.[29] Suggesting that Othello married for money, it included this speech by Desdemona:

> For you I've run away from pap,
> But I don't care a snap for that. . . .
> I love you and you love me,
> And all our lives we'll merry be . . .
> With you I'll sport my figure . . .
> Although you are a nigger.

26. Laurence Irving, *Henry Irving* (New York, 1952), pp. 272, 377, 709, 715, 716; Matteo, "Shakespeare's *Othello,*" p. 297.
27. Quoted in Grimsted, *Melodrama Unveiled,* p. 64.
28. Quoted in Dormon, *Theater in the Antebellum South,* p. 276; Frederickson, *Black Image,* p. 49; Williamson, *New People,* pp. 65–100.
29. Ray B. Browne, "Shakespeare in American Vaudeville and Negro Minstrelsy," *American Quarterly,* 12 (1960), 384, 387–88; George W. Griffin, *"Othello": A Burlesque* (New York, 188[?]), p. 4.

One Othello not requiring dark makeup was the New York–born black actor Ira Aldridge. A celebrated Othello in Europe, Aldridge received enthusiastic acclaim for his London performance of 1833. Here at last, said a European drama critic, was an Othello whose complexion did not need "licorice juice or coffee grounds, or steeves of chocolate colored meat. He had the right skin already. . . . Consequently his appearance on the scene was magnificent . . . his eyes half shut as if dazzled by an African sun . . . that easy negro gait which no European can imitate." European audiences watched Aldridge enclose Desdemona's hand in his, but while the Europeans appeared less fearful about racial intermarriage and miscegenation than Americans did, they were not equalitarian in racial thought. Black men, explained a European who saw Aldridge as Othello, believe that black women are licentious and therefore distrust all women.[30]

Aldridge never performed in the United States. Not only was it unprecedented for black actors to appear with whites; Aldridge's life hardly recommended him to Americans. He was married to a white woman while simultaneously fathering children by his Swedish mistress.[31] A black Othello, James Hewlett, had appeared on the New York stage in 1821 but with an all-black cast and audience, and not at a major theater. Only after the Civil War did black actors even perform in minstrel shows; those who looked mulatto wore burnt cork in the tradition set by white minstrels.[32]

Black actors remained excluded from major *Othello* productions, and well into the decades after the Civil War most audiences continued to see light-skinned Othellos. However, in 1873, a touring Italian actor, Tomasso Salvini, brought to America a new conception of the part. Wearing makeup shaded between copper and coffee, Salvini was the darkest Othello Americans had seen since early in the nineteenth century. His acting style also contrasted with Booth's fastidiousness and studied diction and elocution. Salvini spoke only Italian and often performed with a cast of his countrymen. A lurid and terrifying Othello, he "fiercely swept into his swarthy arms the pale loveliness of Desdemona. . . . Passion choked, his gloating eyes burned with the mere lust of the 'sooty Moor' for that white creature of Venice." Emile Zola hailed Salvini as the "champion of modern realism."[33] But one era's realism can be another era's stereotypes. Salvini's Othello was frequently likened to a tiger or a lion.[34] Before he murdered Desdemona he paced back and forth

30. Newspaper clipping, April 1883, Stead Collection, Vivian Beaumont Library Theatre Collection; Rosenberg, *Masks of Othello*, p. 118; Hermann Burmeister, *The Black Man* (New York, 1853), p. 18; *Blackwood's Magazine*, 57 (1850), 484. Also see Christine Bolt, *Victorian Attitudes to Race* (London, 1971), pp. 23, 209, 295.
31. Herbert Marshall and Mildred Stock, *Ira Aldridge: The Negro Tragedian* (New York, 1958), pp. 79, 219, 295.
32. Edith Isaacs, *The Negro in the American Theatre* (New York, 1947), p. 19; George Odell, *Annals of the New York Stage*, 15 vols. (New York, 1927–1949), XII, 305.
33. Boston *Transcript*, May 16, 1861; New York *Dramatic Mirror*, April 17, 1880; Alden, "Othello's Character," p. 428; Zola quoted in ibid., p. 347.
34. Henry James, "Salvini's Othello," *Atlantic Monthly*, 51 (March 1883), 377–86; *Othello* Scrapbooks, Folger Library.

with long strides, like a caged lion, his head sunk upon his breast. . . . Convulsed with fixed and flaming eyes, half-crouched, [he] slowly circled the stage toward her, muttering savagely and inarticulately as she cowered before him. Rising at last to his full height with extended arms, he pounced upon her, lifted her into the air, [and] dashed with her across the stage. . . . You heard a crash as he flung her on the bed, and growls as of a wild beast over his prey.[35]

Of course that savage and inarticulate muttering might simply have been Salvini's speaking Italian to an uncomprehending audience. To murder Desdemona brutally (Booth had acted as if it were a sacrificial religious rite) and then repeatedly hack at his own throat with a short scimitar previously concealed in his belt portrayed the frenzied behavior of a dangerous, lower-class foreigner, not a royal British officer with white gloves. Salvini explained that he had Othello stab himself because it was an African custom. And by adding the epithet "cruel tiger" for Emilia to shout at Othello, Salvini enhanced the animal and jungle imagery. When he acted Othello in the 1880s, accompanied by an English-speaking cast, few actresses were willing to be Desdemona and submit to the physical fury of his attacks.[36]

Salvini exhilarated most critics, and audiences rushed to see him in New York, Boston, Philadelphia, Chicago, and New Orleans. Except for New Orleans, with its long tradition of miscegenation, the South, however, no longer would tolerate performances of *Othello*. At a time when many Americans increasingly feared the social impact of Italian immigration, Salvini's acting reached a tremulous emotional level as the fair Desdemona married not only a black man but one who was Italian. The producer had a great drawing card "in the Anglo-Italian idea," acknowledged one newspaper reporter. While responding favorably to Salvini's performance, Henry James, never one to lose his sense of proportion, concluded: "The pathos is perhaps a little crude." He also conceded: "There is a class of persons to whom Italians and Africans have about equally little to say."[37]

Emma Lazarus, soon to welcome Europe's huddled masses in her poem enshrined on the Statue of Liberty, wrote that Salvini's Othello "won our love, our admiration, our pity, our horror, and in the end our active sympathy." Disagreeing, however, were those who had admired Booth and rejected a lower-class black Othello. One critic commented: "Salvini's Moor excited no sympathy with him. . . . You hate him and are impatient for his death, as you might be for the death of a mad dog let loose in the streets of a crowded city." Even when Salvini eliminated some tiger leaps in response to those who found them un-Shakespearean, the reporting of a Chicago performance reveals the prevailing image of Othello as a barbarian, and the barbarian as a cannibal. Salvini "looks

35. John Ranken Towse, *Sixty Years of the Theater* (New York, 1916), pp. 93, 162–63; Clara Morris, *Stage Confidences: Talks about Players and Play Acting* (Boston, 1902), p. 240.
36. Alden, "Othello's Character," pp. 275, 420; Tomasso Salvini, "My Interpretation of Othello," *Putnam's Magazine*, 3 (October 1900), 27; New York *Dramatic Mirror*, December 4, 1880; Arthur Hornblow, *A History of the Theatre in America* (New York, 1919) II, 229.
37. "Tomasso Salvini," *Century*, 23 (November 1881), 413; *New York Times*, December 14, 1880; New York *Dramatic Mirror*, December 4, 1880; James, "Salvini's Othello," p. 380.

as if he could eat up Booth . . . in a single meal, then go on and play the Moor as if he were hungry for another banquet of light weight tragedians."[38] By contrast with John Quincy Adams's day, when a white Desdemona was blamed for irrationally succumbing to a black man and thus deserved to be murdered, by the 1880s it was the aggressive black man's character as tiger, lion, mad dog, or cannibal that warranted being killed. Worrying less about their daughter's wantonness than about the emancipated slaves' physical aggressiveness, playgoers, in keeping with late-nineteenth-century racial thought, at last found a plausible black Othello—but only if he was deprived of his aristocratic class and the ability to speak the language of his American audiences, as well as being portrayed as a wild beast. The "Noble Moor" had disappeared entirely. In his place was an example of the new realism, of a fascination with repulsive characters and events.

The 1880s saw the height of *Othello*'s popularity in post–Civil War America. An all-black cast performed it in Greenwich Village, ironically having Desdemona played by an octoroon. It was an era when that word was seriously treated in fiction, and also by the 1890 census takers, who sought to count the numbers of octoroons along with blacks, mulattoes, and quadroons in America. A racially integrated performance of *Othello* occurred in 1890 but only because an American Indian played the title part.[39] Subsequent efforts to copy Salvini's style or makeup were not well received. When another Italian actor played Othello, his graphic murder of Desdemona caused several women to leave the theater and the men to hiss. Thomas Kean's attempt to appear Negroid by emphasizing Othello's gleaming teeth moved one critic to comment that he looked as if he were going to bite Desdemona. And when Tomasso Salvini's son, Alexander, played the part in the 1890s he was praised for not being "offensively swarthy." Declaring that his father had been wrong for choosing very dark makeup, the young Salvini said: "Desdemona could not have loved a man of such dark skin, no matter how noble his other qualities, so I resolved to make him as attractive as possible, despite his necessary color."[40]

From 1890 to 1920, during the Jim Crow era, with heightened national fear about "mongrelization" of the white race and about increased miscegenation, the play declined in popularity and was seldom staged. When an all-black cast played it in 1910, a Boston critic called the performance enjoyable although the black cast was "less dextrous with rapiers than members of their race have the reputation of being with other sharp implements of more frequent use." When the same cast, headed by Edward Sterling Wright, performed before a predominantly

38. New York *Dramatic Mirror*, November 4, 1882; Newspaper clipping, October 27, 1885, Harvard University Theatre Collection; New York *Tribune*, April 27, 1886; Boston *Evening Transcript*, May 11, 1886; Chicago *Herald*, January 7, 1890; Alden, "Othello's Character," pp. 439–40.

39. Odell, *Annals of the New York Stage*, XII, 125, and XV, 34; Robert A. Bone, *The Negro Novel in America* (New Haven, 1965), pp. 22–23.

40. Odell, *Annals of the New York Stage*, XV, 325; New York *Dramatic Mirror*, November 5, 1881; Boston *Traveller*, May 19, 1886; Boston *Globe*, May 19, 1886; [May 1886], February 12, 1914, January 27, 1898, Harvard University Theatre Collection: Boston *Evening Transcript*, March 5, 1907.

black audience in New York, a newspaper critic suddenly discovered "proof of an unsuspecting histrionic genius in the colored race."[41]

A record fifty-seven Broadway performances of *Othello* occurred in 1925 with Walter Hampden as the lead, but without any change from the light makeup. Othellos were praised for not being "so black skinned as to be taken as escaped from a minstrel show." As one critic explained, "if we are to believe that Desdemona, the fine spirited daughter of a patrician Venetian household, was a normal woman and not an erotic pervert, only such an Othello could, to twentieth century imaginations, have plausibly won her."[42] Calling a white woman an "erotic pervert" for marrying a black man is different from John Quincy Adams's suggesting that Desdemona revealed "over ardent sensual passions." Yet the degree of difference does not warrant the assertion made by the historian George Frederickson that opposition to miscegenation lacked the sexual tone during the antebellum era that it acquired in the post–Civil War era.[43] The difference might simply have been the addition of the language, lacking in antebellum America, of Krafft-Ebing and Freud.

About the only group in which an Othello in black makeup performed with a white cast in the 1920s was New York City's Yiddish Art Theatre Company, known for exploring the anguish of distorted family relationships. But here the director added a silent character: a young daughter of Emilia and Iago. Her complexion was dusky and her features resembled Othello's.[44] Iago now had compelling conjugal reasons for seeking Othello's destruction.

Paul Robeson made his debut as Othello in London in June 1930. With a fine sense of poetic justice, he acknowledged receiving help in preparing for the part from the daughter of Ira Aldridge, herself named Ira Aldridge. American critics attending Robeson's performance left convinced that "by reason of his race" he had been "able to surmount difficulties" in playing Othello because he belonged to "a race whose characteristic is to keep control of its passions only to a point and after that point to throw control to the winds." Said Robeson in an interview: "I think there is no question that he [Othello] must be of a different race, in order to make his jealousy credible." And now with a black Othello and racially liberal ideas becoming evident, Desdemona seemed a brave pioneer rather than a passive victim. The New York *Tribune*'s drama critic enthusiastically predicted that the production would come to New York during the next season.[45]

Twelve years later Robeson appeared for the first time in the United States as Othello. Cautiously opened during a summer tryout in Cambridge, Massachusetts,

41. Macon *Telegraph*, November 4, 1897; Philadelphia *Public Ledger*, April 5, 1916; newspaper clippings, January 1898, May 9, 1916, Harvard University Theatre Collection; New York *Tribune*, April 24, 1916.
42. Boston *Herald*, September 11, 1944; Boston *Evening Transcript*, March 5, 1907; newspaper clipping, February 12, 1914, and New York *Telegram*, January 3, 1923, Harvard University Theatre Collection.
43. Frederickson, *Black Image*, pp. 276–77.
44. New York *Tribune*, January 26, 1929.
45. Newspaper clipping, June 9, 1930, Harvard University Theatre Collection; Boston *Transcript*, New York *Tribune*, June 29, 1930.

this historic wartime performance ended with the whole cast joining the audience to sing the national anthem. Like those wartime movies which often depicted the ethnic and racial diversity of Americans, here was Robeson's popular *Ballad for Americans* on the Shakespearean stage.

Othello arrived on Broadway in October 1942. American fears about interracial marriage had not vanished. While Robeson obviously relished being Othello, he was very conscious of the likely public response to a black man's marrying and making love to a white woman. "For the first two weeks in every scene I played with Desdemona," he recalled, "that girl couldn't get near me, I was backin' away from her all the time. I was like a plantation hand in the parlor, that clumsy. But the notices were good. I got over it."[46]

Robeson's good notices emphasized the importance of his race: "He convinces you that he is a man of a different race from the woman he marries, a man who, for all his heroic virtues, is set apart by his color and origins from those whose equal he has become through virtue of his personal achievements." Otherwise Othello "swallows a series of preposterous lies and murders his wife on evidence that would not convince an observant child." In contrast to a response to his 1930 performance, Robeson now could not be criticized for being unstately, for walking stooped over, and for appearing too humble and apologetic. In order to stress Othello's heroic virtues he changed the way he played the epileptic scene in London, and the way Salvini had played it, by ceasing to froth at the mouth. Robeson represented the thrust to integration during World War II by the black intelligentsia and sympathetic white liberals. After 400 Broadway performances, he took Othello on an American tour in 1944, but refused to appear in any theater that practiced racial discrimination, sharply reducing the number of places where he could perform. Othello, it was predicted, would unlikely ever be played again by anyone but a Negro.[47]

Subsequently, Earle Hyman, Canada Lee, and James Earl Jones were the leading black actors to cross the racial barrier Robeson had breached as Othello. But it was the English performance of Sir Laurence Olivier, reaching America on film in 1966, that was as revolutionary as Robeson's original American appearance. Olivier reflected the growing American disillusionment with both the image of the innocent and poetic black man and the idealization of interracial marriage. He abandoned a noble and sensitive Othello by transforming him into a dangerous and self-satisfied fool. Olivier's Othello, suggested one American critic, was like some neophyte diplomat representing a new African nation in the United Nations General Assembly. Rather than needing each other, Desdemona and Othello, in a post-Freudian world, were a modern couple needing a psychiatrist.[48] On the

46. Boston *Herald*, August 11, 1942; Edwin P. Hoyt, *Paul Robeson: The American Othello* (Cleveland, 1967), p. 53; *New York Times*, June 6, 1943.
47. Newspaper clipping, May 19, 1930, Harvard University Theatre Collection; *New York Times*, January 16, 1942, October 24, 1943, July 3, 1944; Boston *Herald*, September 26, 1943; *New Yorker*, October 20, 1943, p. 38; New York *Tribune*, October 17, 1943.
48. Boston *Record American*, February 17, 1965; New York *Tribune*, October 14, 1964; *Newsweek*, January 17, 1965, p. 85.

other hand, by wearing makeup that made him look blacker than Robeson, Olivier had returned to the Othello tradition of the seventeenth and eighteenth centuries, a tradition that accepted Othello's deep blackness as an intrinsic part of the play. Abandoned was the more recently developed racial notion that only a man born black was capable of acting Othello successfully.

Throughout its American stage history, *Othello* stimulated actors, directors, and audiences to use the play as a forum for their attitudes about miscegenation and racial intermarriage, to display them from the physical and psychological distance that the theater allowed. Shakespeare's accepted authority as a sage and spokesman of culture required that *Othello*, unlike many other controversial fictional works, not be ignored or dismissed as racially and sexually unpalatable; instead it had to be transformed by actors and directors, and perceived by audiences in ways harmonious with changing racial, sexual, and class attitudes. In the very process of transformation and perception, the play itself probably contributed to shaping the views of performers and audiences.

It remained popular because the real tragedy of America's racial history found a suitable stage on which to be observed and played. Much of the play's power was readily evident, but that power also stemmed from the play's implications, for it avoided what was more common in America, the illicit sexual relationship between a white man and a black woman. Instead, it enacted what was least practiced and most feared: the legal marriage of a black man and a white woman. What Claude Wauthier has said about miscegenation fiction was made even more graphic in the performances of *Othello:* "There are few literary subjects where crime and love, blood and sex are so morbidly interwoven."[49] *Othello*, it appears, helped American audiences define their own racial morality and vicariously experience their own imaginings.

Jean Toomer and American Racial Discourse*

GEORGE HUTCHINSON

The culture which will transcend, and thus unite, East and West, or the Earthlings and the Galactics, is not likely to be one which does equal justice to each, but one which looks back on both with the amused condescension typical of later generations looking back at their ancestors.

Richard Rorty[1]

49. *The Literature and Thought of Modern Africa*, trans. Shirley Kay (New York, 1967), p. 183.
* From George Hutchinson, "Jean Toomer and American Racial Discourse," *Texas Studies in Literature and Language* 35.2 (summer 1993): 226–250.
1. *Consequences of Pragmatism: Essays, 1972–1980* (Minneapolis: U of Minnesota P, 1982), xxx.

> *Knowledge of what cannot be said . . . signals the rock-*
> *bottom shape, the boundaries, of our situation in the world;*
> *it is the ethical, in the classical sense of the term.*
>
> Bruce W. Wilshire[2]

An undated poem kept in a tin box that no one but the author ever saw in his lifetime bears haunting witness to the great lack of Jean Toomer's existence:

> Above my sleep
> Tortured in deprival
> Stripped of the warmth of a name
> My life breaks madly. . . .
> Breaks against world
> Like a pale moth breaking
> Against sun.[3]

In their biography of the poet, *The Lives of Jean Toomer*, Cynthia Kerman and Richard Eldridge discuss the relationship of this poem to Toomer's sense of lacking a permanent and certain name, deriving from the fact that his name had changed during his childhood and that different family members called him by different names. His grandfather, for example (the patriarch with whom he lived to young adulthood and who died, Toomer claimed, the day after he completed the first draft of "Kabnis"), would not acknowledge the name he had been given at birth.[4] "Jean Toomer" itself is a later fabrication of the author.

No doubt it is a fact of the first importance that Toomer was a self-named man. He was also a man who devoted an extraordinary amount of energy to defining himself, authoring some seven autobiographies that never found publishers in his lifetime.[5] In all of his self-definitions, Toomer dwells intensely on his racial identity, which he specifically differentiates from the races now acknowledged and named in the public discourse of the United States. He names his own race, the "American" race, striving to claim the central term of our national discourse to signify an identity which few "Americans" have been willing to acknowledge. If Toomer's family could not agree with each other upon what exactly to call him, thus stripping him of the "warmth" of a name, so far most of those who read his works have equally "de-nominated" and renamed him, conferring on him the denominations "Negro," "Afro-American," "black." The naming has curiously and ironically empowered his voice by fitting it anew within

2. Introduction, *William James: The Essential Writings,* ed. Bruce W. Wilshire (Stony Brook: State U of New York P, 1984), lxiii.
3. Margorie Content Toomer Papers, in the possession of Margery Toomer Latimer, Pineville, PA; qtd. in Cynthia Earl Kerman and Richard Eldridge, *The Lives of Jean Toomer: A Hunger for Wholeness* (Baton Rouge: Louisiana State UP, 1987), 29.
4. "Outline of an Autobiography," 59, box 20, folder 515, Jean Toomer Papers, American Literature Collection, Beinecke Rare Book and Manuscript Library, Yale University. Kerman and Eldridge, 28–30.
5. Kerman and Eldridge, 393–94.

the very "American" racial discourse whose authority he radically, incessantly disputed. Only recently have a very few critics begun to take his racial self-identification seriously. Donald B. Gibson, for example, has argued that *Cane* is "an index of the orientation of its author": "It is difficult to believe that critics who have seen *Cane* as in some sense a revelation of the essential black soul are not talking about something other than Toomer's book."[6] But it is precisely the orientation of the author that comes under Gibson's attack, as an "escapist" philosophical idealism: "Rather than a depiction of black life as it really is, *Cane* turns out instead to be the response of one for whom black life in its social, political, and historical dimension was too much to bear."[7] If *Cane* is not a "black" text, the argument goes, then it is escapist and "inauthentic." The vast majority of teachers and critics, however, have disagreed with Gibson's conclusions and have insisted instead upon the "blackness" of *Cane*, in part by differentiating it from the rest of Toomer's published and unpublished texts. Hence, it has entered the anthologies and literary histories as a seminal work of African American literature. Contrary to this conventional wisdom, I believe that *Cane* is of a piece with the other texts Toomer wrote in the early to mid-1920s. The difficulty of speaking or writing from outside the dominant discourse of race is a pervasive motif throughout *Cane*, and it has been matched by the difficulty of reading the text *against* the boundaries of that discourse.

Toomer's career, the reception of his published texts, and his texts themselves (including *Cane* and contemporaneous works) indicate how the belief in unified, coherent "black" and "white" American "racial" identities depends formally and ethically upon the sacrifice of the identity that is *both* "black" *and* "white," just as American racial discourse depends upon maintaining the emphatic silence of the interracial subject at the heart of Toomer's project. Moreover, the very acts of discursive violence that banish the forbidden terms and thus enable the social fictions by which we live must remain unacknowledged, virtually unconscious gestures—in the case of Toomer scholarship, typically North American "racial" gestures with undertones of the rituals of scapegoating.

1

Most critics who recognize the nature of Toomer's insistence upon a new "American" racial identity nonetheless perceive *Cane* either as falling into a brief period when the author considered himself a "Negro" or as affirming (regardless of the author's identity) an African American vision, as well as revealing African American expressivity as the "true source" of Toomer's creativity.[8] In the most inter-

6. Donald B. Gibson, "Jean Toomer: The Politics of Denial," *The Politics of Literary Expression: A Study of Major Black Writers*, ed. Donald B. Gibson (Westport: Greenwood, 1981), 155.

7. Gibson, 179.

8. Two important exceptions are David Bradley, "Looking Behind *Cane*," *Southern Review* 21 (1985): 682–95; and Alain Solard, "The impossible Unity: Jean Toomer's 'Kabnis,'" *Myth and Ideology in American Culture*, ed. Regis Durand (Villeneuve d'Ascq: U de Lille III, 1976), 175–94. For the more traditional view, see, for example, Robert Bone, *The Negro Novel in America* (1958; rev. ed.,

esting and sophisticated recent interpretation of *Cane,* Henry Louis Gates, Jr., while seeming to accept Toomer's self-identification, tries ingeniously to evade the problem this identification poses not only by separating intentionality and biographical context from textuality but by defining the "multiracial" text as "black." Hence, because of its "double-voiced discourse," *Cane* is "the blackest text of all."[9] Even if we accept the necessity of separating textuality from biography, however, the trap remains the same: a discourse that allows no room for a "biracial" text (except by defining it as "black") is part of the *same discursive system* that denies the identity of the person who defines himself or herself as both black and white (or, in Langston Hughes's phrase, as "neither white nor black"). Critics routinely ignore Toomer's idea that, as "black" is to "white" identity, the "American" identity (in Toomer's sense) is to "black/white" identity. The "American" race in his view "differ[ed] as much from white and black as white and black differ from each other."[10] Toomer dramatizes, that is, *another* threshold of "racial" difference that he considers to be of a "higher level" than the threshold between black and white, and his "multi-voiced" language aims to bring us to that threshold, to give us a glimpse of what lies beyond.

In fending off the disturbing implications of Toomer's racial thought, readers often fall into the yet more disturbing rhetorical gestures of traditional American racial discourse, despite their own avowed resistance to that discourse. For example, Gates charges, "In a curious and perhaps perverse sense, Toomer's was a gesture of racial castration, which, if not silencing his voice literally, then at least transformed his deep black bass into a false soprano."[11] Here, as so often in discussions of the "mulatto," the signifier of interracial mediation is replaced by the trope of a sexual lack (a fact all the more ironic in that Gates himself is often attacked for betraying the "authentic" voice of the "black bas[e]" and too intimately embracing seductive "white" theory).[12] It is not Toomer who is doing the

---

New Haven: Yale UP, 1965), 56, 60, 80–89; S. P. Fullinwider, "Jean Toomer: Lost Generation, or Negro Renaissance?" *Phylon* 27 (1966): 396–403; Clifford Mason, "Jean Toomer's Black Authenticity," *Black World* 20 (1970): 70–76; Darwin T. Turner, *In A Minor Chord: Three Afro-American Writers and Their Search for Identity* (Carbondale: Southern Illinois UP, 1971), 1–59; George W. Kent, *Blackness and the Adventure of Western Culture* (Chicago: Third World, 1972), 26; Bowie Duncan, "Jean Toomer's *Cane:* A Modern Black Oracle," *CLA Journal* 15 (1972): 323–33; Mabel M. Dillard, "Jean Toomer—the Veil Replaced," *CLA Journal* 17 (1974): 468–73; Michael J. Krasny, "Jean Toomer's Life prior to *Cane:* A Brief Sketch of the Emergence of a Black Writer," *Negro American Literature Forum* 9 (1975): 40–41; and Nellie Y. McKay, *Jean Toomer, Artist* (Chapel Hill: U of North Carolina P, 1984).

9. Henry Louis Gates, Jr., *Figures in Black: Words, Signs, and the "Racial" Self* (New York: Oxford UP, 1987), 206.

10. Toomer, "Autobiographical Sketches," unpaginated, box 11, folder 343, Jean Toomer Papers.

11. Gates, 208.

12. See, for example, Joyce A. Joyce, "The Black Canon: Reconstructing Black American Literary Criticism," *New Literary History* 18 (Winter 1986): 335–44, and " 'Who the Cap Fit': Unconsciousness and Unconscionableness in the Literary Criticism of Houston A. Baker, Jr., and Henry Louis Gates, Jr.," *New Literary History* 18 (Autumn 1986): 371–84; Harold Fromm, "Real Life, Literary Criticism, and the Perils of Bourgeoisification," *New Literary History* 20 (Autumn 1988): 49–64; Diana Fuss, " 'Race' under Erasure? Poststructuralist Afro-American Literary Theory,"

castrating. Deeply revealing, Gates's metaphors connect with an old racialist tradition that held male "mulattoes" to be more effeminate, less potent sexually, than either blacks or whites. "Highly ephemeral persons," according to this self-serving white fantasy, mulattoes were "effete . . . both biologically and, ultimately, culturally."[13] Indeed, "mulatto" sexual unions purportedly produced fewer offspring than any other combination, and if black-white unions would only cease, according to many authorities "mulattoes" would entirely die out. Male "mulattoes" were, like mules, effectively *castratos* unless they "back-crossed" with one of the "purer" races—and Southern custom, of course, determined with which of the races "mulattoes" would fuse.[14] This white Southern "muleology" has been curiously transmuted from biological theories of racial inheritance to the analysis of Toomer's texts and to interpretations of *Cane*'s relation to "racial" tradition. Ultimately, it seems that the division between "biographical" and "textual" criticism evaporates when we turn our attention to the positions of both "racial self" and "racial text" in American discourse.

Other revealing metaphors from the critical tradition suggest that Toomer "disappeared" into "white obscurity" or became "invisible."[15] His "visibility," like his potency, is directly connected to his status as a "black" author. One may well ask whether *Cane* would enjoy whatever canonical status it does today—whether, indeed, it would even be in print—had it not been "rediscovered" and valorized in the late 1960s as a "*seminal*" "black" text, comfortably fitting within the North American racial archive. Perhaps the greatest irony of Toomer's career is that at the time modern American racial discourse was taking its most definite shape, "mulattoes"—because they threatened the racial bifurcation—"disappeared" as a group into either the white "race" (through passing) or the black "race" while the "one-drop rule" was defined in increasingly definite terms. The 1920 U.S. census, coinciding with the beginning of the Harlem Renaissance, was the last to count "mulattoes."[16] At the same time, "interracial" mating, and particularly "interracial" marriage, rare as it already was, drastically declined.[17] By 1990 the census forms, despite objections, explicitly instructed that all persons who considered themselves both black *and* white, or biracial, must designate themselves "black."[18]

Essentially Speaking: Feminism, Nature, and Difference (New York: Routledge and Kegan Paul, 1989), 73–96; and R. Baxter Miller, "Forum," *PMLA* 105 (Oct. 1990): 1124–25.

13. Joel Williamson, *New People: Miscegenation and Mulattoes in the United States* (New York: Free P, 1980), 73, 95.

14. Thomas F. Gossett, *Race: The History of an Idea in America* (Dallas: Southern Methodist UP, 1963), 48–59; and Williamson, 114, 73, 95–96.

15. See, for example, Arna Bontemps, "The Negro Renaissance: Jean Toomer and the Harlem of the 1920's," *Anger and Beyond: The Negro Writer in the United States*, ed. Herbert Hill (1966; rpt. New York: Harper and Row, 1968), 24; Barbara Christian, *Black Women Novelists: The Development of a Tradition, 1892–1976* (Westport: Greenwood, 1980), 48; and Gates, 202.

16. Williamson, 114.

17. Williamson, 188–90.

18. The instruction was necessary because a rising number of "biracial" persons objected to being identified as strictly "black" or even "African American." A movement then arose to ignore the

The mutely "tragic," "ghostly" figure of the "mulatto" haunts our racial ideology as its absent center, the scapegoat whose sacrifice both signifies the origin of racialist discourse and sustains it. As René Girard has emphasized, scapegoating purges a community of the threat of "strange mixtures," first instituting and then maintaining the system of differences upon which signification itself depends. Every discursive system, indeed, depends upon some such sacrifice.[19] Thus, as Simone Vauthier has written, the biracial character in the literature of the United States, "designates the moment of origins," exposing and undermining "the myth of two discrete races separated by an impassable gulf."[20] The maintenance of racial boundaries demands the sacrifice of the "mulatto" either through tragedy or by his or her incorporation into one of the "fixed" racial groups.[21] Kenneth Burke's meditations on the relationship between tragedy and scapegoating are relevant here. Viewing tragedy as a secular extension of the "therapeutics" of scapegoating, Burke argues that tragedy reduces to a specific conflict a pervasive, unresolved tension typical of a given social order and, by doing away with the "marked" hero, purges fears of basic ideological contradictions.[22] Little wonder, then, that the "mulatto" is America's most distinctive tragic figure. As Werner Sollors has argued, it is the story of the mulatto that, "against all odds, continued the tragic

---

census instructions and use a new identifying term in common, but it seems that people failed to agree on what name to use! Avowedly, the reluctance to be counted as *only* black derives not (as in an earlier era, perhaps) from shame or "racial self-hatred" but rather from a reluctance to accept a *sacrifice of identity* written into the racial discourse, and to the fact that many of these people's closest family members (mothers or fathers) are white. The debate was partially carried on in the new magazine *Interrace,* which is aimed at interracial families. The editor of the magazine, interestingly, finally suggested a non-English word, *melange*—to put the identification entirely outside of the dominant discourse—but responses to this suggestion apparently have been mostly negative, precisely because it is not "American" enough.

19. On the relation of scapegoating to the origins of communal discourse, see especially René Girard, *Violence and the Sacred,* trans. Patrick Gregory (Baltimore: Johns Hopkins UP, 1977); and Eric Gans, *The Origin of Language: A Formal Theory of Representation* (Berkeley: U of California P, 1981). In a gloss on Girard, Julia Kristeva writes: "Sacrifice designates, precisely, the watershed on the basis of which the social and the symbolic are instituted: the thetic that confines violence to a single place, making it a signifier" (*Revolution in Poetic Language,* trans. Margaret Waller, New York: Columbia UP, 1984, 75).
20. [In this volume, p. 347. —Ed.] Qtd. in Werner Sollors, " 'Never Was Born': The Mulatto, an American Tragedy?" *Massachusetts Review* 27 (1986): 305.
21. According to Judith Berzon, the options open to fictional "mulattoes" in American literature are limited to their becoming African American race leaders, " 'passing,' adopting a white middle-class image and value system, or succumbing to despair" (*Neither White Nor Black: The Mulatto Character in American Fiction,* New York: New York UP, 1978, 14). Even in African American fiction since the Harlem Renaissance, typically the mulatto character either is destroyed (or spiritually diminished) by inner conflicts caused by his or her alienated condition in a racially bifurcated society, or he or she becomes "whole" by becoming wholly "black." The idea of biracial people achieving healthy identities by embracing their multiple ancestry has been virtually unthinkable to writers and critics alike.
22. Kenneth Burke, *"Coriolanus*—and the Delights of Faction," *Language as Symbolic Action* (Berkeley: U of California P, 1968), 81–97.

tradition in the New World" by confronting racial fictions with kinship lines.[23] With Nella Larsen, Toomer has come to be regarded as one of the chief "tragic mulattoes" of American literary history because—like increasing numbers of bi-racial youths today—he insisted upon a self-naming that threatened racialist discourse, along with the rich structures of knowledge, identity, and power to which that discourse is inextricably bound.[24]

In a preface to one of his unpublished autobiographies—appropriately called "Book X"—Toomer regrets that he will have to resort to conventional and distorting terms to get his racial message across, as our very language allows no other means of expressing his sense of identity; he has considered the problem for years and cannot find any adequate solution. "If I have to say 'colored,' 'white,' 'jew,' 'gentile,' and so forth, I will unwittingly do my bit toward reinforcing the limited views of mankind which dismember mankind into mutually repellant factions."[25] Toomer's attempts to explain himself led to a very precise awareness of the connection between language and ideology, the impossibility of developing an entirely "new" discourse that would be independent of the inherited one.[26]

The problem was so severe that for a period he stopped writing, convinced that the more he wrote, the more he reinforced the very ideology he was trying to escape.

This dilemma of the writer happens to strike me with peculiar force. It impresses and sometimes depresses me and makes me beat my brains almost to the point that I voluntarily seal my lips and stop writing. Indeed in the past there was a time when I did become mute, owing to a realization of this very matter which, as I saw then as I see now, involved the entire use of words with reference to any and all aspects of life.[27]

The sense of entrapment in a racialist language founded specifically upon the denial of his own "racial" name precipitated an intense realization of the general inadequacy of language to express "truth." Language, always shaped by oppressive social conventions and more profoundly by what Michel Foucault would later

---

23. Sollors, 296, 309.
24. Larsen, writes Adelaide Cromwell Hill in her 1971 introduction to *Quicksand*, "always wishing to seem apart from her race, to be accepted as a writer, not as a Negro, was permanently weakened as a writer in 1930" before she went to Europe to write a never-finished novel. She returned from Europe, divorced her black husband, and "sank into oblivion by becoming just another nurse. So far as one can ascertain, she neither passed as White nor identified with Blacks—she *merely existed*" (in Nella Larsen, *Quicksand*, New York: Macmillan, 1971, 16; emphasis added). Barbara Christian assents to Hill's view: "Larsen, like Jean Toomer, . . . disappeared into the wide world, to be neither black nor white, but *merely apart*" (48; my emphasis). "Mere" "existence" and "apartness" are here explicitly differentiated from "strong" selfhood and positive identity, which would require submission to the dominant discourse. The "disappearances" of Toomer and Larsen—more accurately, their "silences"—seem to be intimately related. Moreover, the history of the reception of their books reveals many parallels.
25. "Preface no. 3" of "Book X," 10, box 11, folder 359, Jean Toomer Papers.
26. See also "Race Problems and Modern Society," 31–32, box 51, folder 1120, Jean Toomer Papers.
27. "Preface no. 3," 12.

call the "archive" of the "cultural unconscious," was a hindrance to spiritual development and self-redescription. This rather remarkable insight of Toomer's helps us understand why, when he, as most readers would have it, "turned his back on his race"—seeking what countless critics have termed a "raceless" identity but which he considered the only self-consciously "American" one—he simultaneously turned to mysticism, a route to knowledge "beyond words."

The years of silence to which Toomer refers in the autobiography are in fact basically the years following *Cane*, a work that, he wrote in a letter to the editors of *The Liberator*, was "a spiritual fusion analogous to the fact of racial intermingling."[28] The general audience's interpretation of this book, he once said, was "one of the queer misunderstandings" of his life. He later thought it ironic that his writing, which should have made his racial position understood, "was being so presented and interpreted that I was now much more misunderstood in this respect than at any time of my life."[29] Discounting or ignoring such attestations, most critics see *Cane* as falling into a brief period of the author's strong identification with his "true" racial heritage and lament his turn away from "racial" writing toward mysticism, but *Cane* and the works written along with it—the story "Withered Skin of Berries" and the play *Natalie Mann*—show, upon close reading, a strong impetus toward the deconstruction of a traditional American racial ideology and the "birth-pangs" of a new one. To Toomer, the "old" racialism, for whites and blacks alike, had reached a dead end. Together with his contemporaneous works, *Cane* exemplifies the frustrations attendant upon a transformation from one field of "racial" existence to another. The works of the early 1920s are attempts to initiate a new American tradition, to provoke a new "racial" consciousness that would displace the dualistic racial consciousness of "white" and "black" Americans. Although all of *Cane* can be read as initiating such a tradition, in "Kabnis"—the climax of the volume—Toomer achieves the most concentrated and complex articulation of his theme. He dramatizes the tortured "dusk-before-dawn" of a new kind of ethnic subject, the possibility of whose existence was disallowed by both "white" and "black" definitions of "racial" subjectivity.[30]

2

A few comments about significant elements in the first two sections of *Cane* will help to show how the concluding story/play relates to the volume as a whole.

28. Toomer to *The Liberator* 9 Aug. 1922, Jean Toomer Papers. This was in the same letter in which Toomer said that the black folk culture of the South had awakened his artistic impulses, a statement that has been used repeatedly as evidence that he identified himself as "black" while writing *Cane*.
29. "On Being an American," 51, box 20, folder 513, Jean Toomer Papers.
30. Both white and black readers (including Toomer's publisher and some of his closest friends) insisted upon viewing Toomer as "Negro" and considered his objection to this designation a denial of his race. On the other hand, a close black friend, upon hearing him read and explain his poem "The First American," responded disparagingly, "You're white" (see Toomer, "On Being an American," 42, 50, 36).

The first section of the book, which Toomer called a "swan song" for the dying African American folk culture of the South, shows the enormous contradictions inherent in Southern "racial" culture. Behind all the tragedies of the South lies the repression of "natural" desires, repression of life itself by conventions governing all human relations. A chief contradiction (which Toomer's friend and mentor Waldo Frank would also make the basis of his novel *Holiday*) is the desire certain members of each "race" feel for members of the other—and by extension, for incorporation into the "new race"—despite a brutally enforced, "unnatural" segregation. The sexual and racial codes of the South turn this desire into various perverted, stunted, and oppressive manifestations, but interracial desire remains an ineluctable fact.

The text is full of people of "mixed race," episodes revolving around or emanating from interracial liaisons. The "biracial" Fern (Jewish and African American)[31] is an erotic-mystical magnet to black and white alike, for example; but one whom, like a vestal priestess, both black and white men leave alone, sensing something "taboo" about her: "She was not to be approached by anyone."[32] The narrator, indeed, draws male readers of both "races" into her spell: ("[I]t makes no difference if you sit in the Pullman or the Jim Crow as the train crosses her road," 18). The reference to her "weird," mystical eyes as a "common delta," into which both God and the Southern landscape flow, evokes Toomer's consistent trope (from the 1910s through the 1930s) of a river signifying the dissolution of the "old" races into the "New World soul." Moreover, Fern's spiritual "hunger" and frustration as well as her muteness match Toomer's sense of the frustration and inarticulateness of the yet "unawakened" people of his new race.

Interracial desire is denied, thwarted, made a tool of oppression (as in "Blood-Burning Moon"), driven underground, or violently purged throughout section 1 of *Cane*. Manifestations of this desire and denial—this burial, this violence—become sacred, taboo in such pieces as "Becky," "Fern," "Esther," "Blood-Burning Moon," and "Portrait in Georgia." Since women are the objects of a dominating male desire, they often bear the "cross" of this contradiction.

In "Becky," for example, the title character—who has given birth to "mulatto" sons—is ostracized by both black and white communities, each of which "prayed secretly to God who'd put His cross upon her and cast her out" (7). Toomer emphasizes a parallelism in white and black responses to Becky and her unknown lover: "Damn buck nigger, said the white folks' mouths. She wouldnt tell, Common, God-forsaken, insane white shameless wench, said the white folks' mouths. . . . Low-down nigger with no self-respect, said the black folks' mouths. She wouldnt tell. Poor Catholic poor-white crazy woman, said the black folks' mouths" (7). Blacks and whites together have built her a cabin precisely on an "eye-shaped

---

31. Fern has a "semitic" nose, a common Jewish surname, and "cream-colored" skin. On first seeing her, the narrator is reminded of a Jewish cantor's singing. See also Hargis Westerfield, "Jean Toomer's 'Fern': A Mythical Dimension," *CLA Journal* 14 (1971): 274–76, which makes much of Fern's German Jewish surname.
32. Jean Toomer, *Cane*, ed. Darwin T. Turner (New York: Norton, 1988), 16–17; hereafter cited in the text.

piece of ground" between a road and the railroad tracks, and she—who has be-come "invisible"—lives at this boundary line between the white and black sections of town. No one ever sees Becky, and she is utterly silent. Yet people scribble prayers on scraps of paper and throw them toward her house as they pass it, until one day the chimney of her disintegrating cabin caves in and buries her. Returning from church on a Sunday, the narrator and his friend Barlo hear the chimney fall and even enter the home. The narrator thinks he hears a groan, but instead of investigating further and possibly saving her, the two men quickly leave, Barlo throwing his Bible on the mound. Like a true scapegoat, Becky is invested with the sacred aura of the taboo; the food and other objects people leave near her home are distinctly presented as propitiatory offerings for the sign of "pollution," the sacrifice of which sustains racial identities. Even her boys disappear, shouting, "Godam the white folks; Godam the niggers" (8). The mutual decision by blacks and whites to ostracize Becky gives them a commonality: "*We*, who had cast out their mother because of them, could we take them in?" asks the narrator. "They answered black and white folks by shooting up two men and leaving town" (8; emphasis added).

The poem "Portrait in Georgia" is another haunting evocation of the racial boundary, curiously merging the image of a white woman and of a lynched black person—implied to be a man burned to death for "despoiling white womanhood."

> Hair—braided chestnut,
>   coiled like a lyncher's rope,
> Eyes—fagots,
> Lips—old scars, or the first red blisters,
> Breath—the last sweet scent of cane,
> And her slim body, white as the ash
>   of black flesh after flame. (29)

On one level, the white woman becomes a sinister figure, rather like the seductive "White Witch" of a James Weldon Johnson poem of that name, or like Lula in Amiri Baraka's *Dutchman*. But Toomer goes beyond these writers in suggesting an identity between the figures joined in his poem. By superimposing the images of the white woman, the apparatus of lynching, and the burning flesh of the black man, Toomer graphically embodies both a union of black male and white female *and* the terrifying method of exorcising that union to maintain a racial difference the poem linguistically defies.

Other pieces suggest the terrible price to be paid for transgression of the racial divide, or indeed for literally embodying the transgression of that divide as a person of "mixed race" such as Fern and Esther. Edward Waldron has aptly written of the latter: "Caught between two worlds, one which she denies herself—a world of mixed-color reality—and one which is denied *her*—the world of total blackness/Purity, a dream world which can only exist in her desperate mind—Esther finds nothing. She is left in Limbo, with not even a Hell in sight."[33] She

---

33. Edward Waldron, "The Search for Identity in Jean Toomer's 'Esther,' " *Jean Toomer: A Critical Evaluation*, ed. Therman B. O'Daniel (Washington, DC: Howard UP, 1988), 275.

attempts in vain, by seeking Barlo, to embrace a "pure" blackness that will ensure her a sharply defined identity. The story suggests that this proposed solution to her problem of selfhood is delusional.

Toomer's vision of a coming merging of the races makes perfect sense within the framework of the first section of *Cane:* the dystopia of the contemporary South implies a corresponding utopia. Alain Solard's comment on "Blood-Burning Moon" is apt: "To the artist, Bob, Tom, Louisa belong to 'another country' which they feel, but do not know is their own."[34] When desire is freed (as segregation is dismantled), it will cross racial boundaries without violence, embarrassment, or perversion. Those "mixed-race" persons now left in "limbo" will ultimately find home; indeed, the entire country will be transformed in their image. The United States will be a "colored" nation. But at the same time, many elements contributing to the beauty of the South—specifically of the African American folk spirit—will be lost as the conditions of its emergence disappear. "America needs these elements," Toomer wrote in a well-known passage the year he composed *Cane.*

> They are passing. Let us grab and hold them while there is still time. Segregation and laws may retard this solution. But in the end, segregation will either give way, or it will kill. Natural preservations do not come from unnatural laws. . . . A few generations from now, the negro will still be dark, and a portion of his psychology will spring from this fact, but in all else he will be a conformist to the general outlines of American civilization, or of American chaos.[35]

"Race-mixing," in Toomer's view, follows natural laws. If Toomer would hasten the end of racial division and oppression, he would also have to accept the end of that specific sort of folk culture engendered by slavery, a largely preindustrial economy, Jim Crow, and post-Reconstruction peonage. Hence, he is called, in this swan song, to memorialize. "The Negro is in solution," he wrote Waldo Frank.

> As an entity, the race is loosing [sic] its body, and its soul is approaching a common soul. . . . In my own stuff, in those places that come nearest to the old Negro, to the spirit saturate with folk-song: Karintha and Fern, the dominant emotion is a sadness derived from a sense of fading, from a knowledge of my futility to check solution. There is nothing about these pieces of the buoyant expression of a new race. The folk-songs themselves are of the same order.[36]

34. Alain Solard, "Myth and Narrative Fiction in *Cane:* 'Blood-Burning Moon,' " *Callaloo* 8 (Fall 1985): 558.

35. Toomer to Waldo Frank, box 3, folder 84, Jean Toomer Papers. The letter is undated but internal evidence indicates it was written after the fall of 1922 and before the publication of *Cane,* thus placing it sometime in the winter or spring of 1922–1923.

36. Jean Toomer to Waldo Frank (winter or spring 1922–23), box 3, folder 84, Jean Toomer Papers. Contrary to McKay's assertion in *Jean Toomer, Artist* (91) that Toomer attributed the dissipation of the folk culture to racist oppression, Toomer believed that such oppression was a *necessary condition* of that culture (a position that matches Waldo Frank's idea that oppression had fostered the depth and beauty of European and Russian peasant cultures). Writing of Harper's Ferry to Frank, he notes that "[r]acial attitudes, on both sides, are ever so much more tolerant [than in

Toomer implies that if there is nothing in *these* pieces about the "buoyant expression of a new race," the "sense of fading" of the "old races" will be *followed*
by such expression. Indeed, *Cane* presupposes such expression.

Precisely because of the deep "roots" of black culture in Southern soil, because
of what Toomer considered the settled, non-"pioneer" nature of black folk culture, in the South many indispensable elements of a truly aboriginal—though
hybrid—American culture could be found. This is exactly what Toomer's friend
Waldo Frank had failed to consider in his influential book *Our America* (1919).[37]
Moreover, important elements of the folk culture (those developed in urban centers, via jazz, e.g.) were powerful antidotes to "Puritanism" and Anglophilia, as
well as to the acquisitive "pioneer" mentality that had outlived its usefulness. All
of these concerns find their distilled expression in the second section of *Cane*.

In "Seventh Street," Toomer sets the tone for the entire section by opposing
the spirit of "black reddish blood" and the "crude-boned, soft-skinned wedge of
nigger life" to the "white and whitewashed wood of Washington." The wedge of
folk-descended black life (presented in partially phallic sexual images) will "split"
the stale "wood" of the city, scandalizing social conformists. "Blood suckers of
the War would spin in a frenzy of dizziness if they drank your blood. Prohibition
would put a stop to it" (41).[38] The intoxication of its "loafer air, jazz songs and
love, thrusting unconscious rhythms" threatens the sexual as well as racial mores
of proper Washington, black and white. It is even pitted against the authority of
established religion, "Swirling like a blood-red smoke up where the buzzards fly
in heaven." "God would not dare to suck black red blood. A Nigger God! He
would duck his head in shame and call for the Judgment Day" (41). An ungov-
ernable bodily force threatens at once sexual mores, racial purity, and the religious
divisions of "spirit" and "body," heaven and earth.

'Middle Georgia'], even friendly. Oppression and ugly emotions seem nowhere in evidence. And
there are no folk songs. A more stringent grip, I guess, is necessary to force them through" (letter
of Aug. 1922, Jean Toomer Papers).

37. See Toomer's unpublished typescript, "The South in Literature": "The South has a peasantry,
rooted in its soil, such as neither the North nor West possess. Therefore it has a basic adjustment
to its physical environment (in sharp contrast to the restless mal-adjustment of the northern
pioneer) the expression of which the general cultural body stands in sore need of" (1, box 48,
folder 1008, Jean Toomer Papers). In "General Ideas and States to Be Developed," Toomer points
out that writers concerned with the American scene have so far ignored "the peasant-adjustment
rhythm of the Southern Negro. The non-pioneer rhythm of the South" (4, box 48, folder 1002,
Jean Toomer Papers). This was certainly true of *Our America*, which lamented that North America
had no peasantry like Russia's and Europe's; such a peasantry in the Old World carried the deep
potential energy, religious and aesthetic, that feeds great art and empowers movements of revolt.
After his contact with Toomer, while working on *Holiday*, Frank expressed the intention to revise
and expand *Our America* in order to include the Negro. See Toomer to Frank, 25 July 1922, box
3, folder 83, Jean Toomer Papers.

38. Toomer's point here fits with the concepts of the one-time *Seven Arts* group to which he was so
close, connecting fervor for war and false "patriotism" with prohibition, "Puritanism," "Anglophilia," American hypocrisy, and racism.

The lyric opening and closing of the piece also indicates the opposition of the strident jazz spirit to "Puritan" mores embodied in thrift, sexual continence, Prohibition, and taming of modern exuberance:

> Money burns the pocket, pocket hurts,
> Bootleggers in silken shirts,
> Ballooned, zooming Cadillacs,
> Whizzing, whizzing down the street-car
> tracks. (41)

Throughout the second section of *Cane,* one has the impression of bottled-up desire finding brief expression in jazz or dance, occasionally a sort of uncontrolled rage intent on breaking the inhibitions to erotic/"spiritual" satisfaction. (For Toomer, as for his prophet Whitman, the erotic and the spiritual are properly one.)

The section includes a series of vignettes suggesting hunger, thirst, unsatisfied or unacknowledged desires. Characters repeatedly fail to achieve the "fusion" of several important dualities: body and soul, intellect and emotion, blackness and whiteness, manhood and womanhood. The "powerful underground races" (as they are called in "Box Seat") hold the key to breaking the repression that inhibits American self-realization. From deep below ground, a "new world Christ" is coming up. Instinctive desires, the urges of *life,* however, are far in advance of mental and social conditioning. Hence, even whites can be moved by jazz to overcome, provisionally, sexual and racial restraints; but as soon as the music stops, so to speak, they stop dancing and go back to their old ways, as Bona does in "Bona and Paul." Moreover, as "Box Seat" and "Calling Jesus" indicate, the "black bourgeoisie" itself is as adamant as the white in repressing desire and self-knowledge. They have adopted the "pioneer" and "Puritan" mentalities with a vengeance, in self-defensive reaction against white stereotypes of black people.

In the terms of "Harvest Song," people "fear knowledge of [their] hunger" (71). The poem, which Toomer once suggested was the culmination of the "spiritual entity" behind *Cane,* epitomizes the sense of the ending of a cycle that we find throughout the book—whether signified by dusk, autumn, "blood-burning" harvest moon, or fallen leaves. Toomer depicts the ending of one cycle of American history, a "dusk" that must be followed by a dawn—the birthing of his "American" race. In "Bona and Paul," the final piece of the second section (and also set at dusk), the fear of interracial hunger is dramatically evident in Bona's fear of her "hunger" for the mulatto Paul, who tells the black doorman at a nightclub as he leaves with her: "I came back to tell you, brother, that white faces are petals of roses. That dark faces are petals of dusk. That I am going out and gather petals. That I am going out and know her whom I brought with me to these Gardens which are purple like a bed of roses would be at dusk" (80). Predictably, when Paul turns to rejoin Bona, she has been overcome by her sexual/racial fear and deserted him. So ends the final story in section 2 of *Cane,* which Toomer associated with his "spiritual awakening." The importance of the interracial taboo in this story carries over to the intensely autobiographical drama that follows, "Kabnis."

3

It is instructive to read "Kabnis" in relation to the other texts Toomer was working on between 1921 and 1923. In notes for a book he apparently intended to publish just after *Cane,* for example, he outlines the concept of a hero whose consciousness, at the beginning of the novel, is "shredded by surfaces which it cannot relate" and by glimpses of a "scattered humanity" of segregated ethnic groups. The intellect of the hero, like Lewis's and Kabnis's in *Cane,* is not yet related to his "spiritual" and "emotional" "heave." He is, like Kabnis, "tortured for synthesis." This hero has "touched" but not yet "absorbed" the work of the writers associated with *Seven Arts* magazine, such as Waldo Frank's *Our America* (which had had a tremendous impact upon Toomer before he wrote *Cane*). After a psychic breakdown, he leaves New York City for mountain country where he convalesces (as Toomer had done at Harper's Ferry), then returns to New York. "Again shredded. Forces converge and drive the character down South: Washington, first, Georgia."[39] The outline closely follows Jean Toomer's own development up until his trip to Sparta and also connects with the title character of "Kabnis," whose consciousness is similarly "shredded" and "tortured for synthesis," whose intellect is unrelated to his spiritual and emotional energies (*Cane,* 108–09). In the second book, however, Toomer apparently envisioned the hero as emerging from his underworld experience, an articulate embodiment of the "new race"—like Toomer himself—expressing himself in a "classic American prose," a fusion of diversely appropriated idioms.[40]

I argue that Kabnis is a man struggling to create the words adequate to a new ethos, a new and, in Toomer's terms, "inclusive" consciousness—the sort of consciousness exemplified in the works that were at one time intended to appear in yet another volume that was to follow *Cane,* "Withered Skin of Berries" and *Natalie Mann,* the heroes of which would be articulate exemplars of the new American race.[41] In each of these works, significantly, the prophet/hero has written a piece that Toomer would insert in the first section of *Cane*—"Conversion" and "Karintha," respectively.

Most scholars interpret "Kabnis" as if the failure of the hero is caused by his rejection of his "true" African American identity. This interpretation hinges upon particular views of Lewis, Carrie Kate, and Father John, as well as the title character—upon the idea that the black Christian/folk tradition embodied in Fa-

39. Toomer, "Book I," leaf 2, box 48, folder 1002, Jean Toomer Papers.
40. "Esthetic," 2, box 48, folder 1002. These are notes on the form and prose for the work outlined in "General Ideas and States to Be Developed."
41. See Kerman and Eldridge, 100; and Toomer, letter to Waldo Frank, undated (probably summer 1923), box 3, folder 84, Jean Toomer Papers. Nathan Merilh, the hero of *Natalie Mann,* is commonly considered "black" by scholars today, but Toomer pointedly contrasts him with his "New Negro" friend, Brown, who considers him "inimical to the race." Similarly, Merilh's homes in both Washington and New York suggest a fusion of "white" and "black" identities into a new "racial" ideal in which we well know Toomer believed. See *Natalie Mann,* in *The Wayward and the Seeking: A Collection of Writings by Jean Toomer,* ed. Darwin Turner (Washington, DC: Howard UP, 1980), 243–325.

ther John and carried on by those such as Carrie Kate will herald a new dawn of African American peoplehood. Too weak to accept the pain of the African American past, Kabnis, so the argument goes, rejects his "true" "black" identity, and this explains his failure to become "whole." Moreover, because of its strong autobiographical echoes, the story is thought to represent Toomer's brief identification of himself as a "black" author. Indeed, just after finishing the manuscript, he wrote Waldo Frank in an intense letter, "Kabnis is *me*."[42]

The story opens with the haunting lyrics of a song the "night-winds" whisper through cracks in the walls of Kabnis's cabin:

> White-man's land.
> Niggers, sing.
> Burn, bear black children
> Till poor rivers bring
> Rest, and sweet glory
> In Camp Ground (83)

The lines, of course, bring to mind the African American heritage, specifically the spirituals. But Toomer puts a strange spin on familiar phrases. In a letter to Waldo Frank counseling the latter on how to write the introduction to *Cane*, Toomer wrote that such lines as "I want to cross over into camp ground" (from the spiritual "Deep River") not only signified the desire for salvation but could be translated in social terms as meaning, "my position here is transient. I'm going to die, or be absorbed."[43] Indeed, preposterous as it sounds, Toomer interpreted the lines as prophetically anticipating the merging of the "Negro" into the new American race. In "Withered Skin of Berries," the "mulatta" Vera longs to plunge into a river, signifying the merging of black and white races in the "new world soul," intoning, "Lord, I want to cross over into camp ground."[44] She longs for the river to "sweep her under" as she "crosses" over into the "American" identity. Indeed, Toomer frequently uses images of rivers in his work written at this time and later to suggest the current that would dissolve past racial and cultural identities into a new one.[45] He adapted this motif in part from Romain Rolland's *Jean-Christophe*, in which the Rhine acts as a prophetic solvent of French and German identities—the identities Jean-Christophe blends in his music of a new pan-European culture.[46] Jean-Christophe was a modern John the Baptist *and*

---

42. Toomer to Frank, undated (winter or spring 1922–23), box 3, folder 84, Jean Toomer Papers. Significantly, this is the same letter in which he wrote, "[T]he Negro is in solution. . . . As an entity, the race is loosing [sic] its body, and its soul is approaching a common soul."

43. Toomer to Frank, undated (winter or spring 1922–23), box 3, folder 84, Jean Toomer Papers.

44. Toomer, "Withered Skin of Berries," *The Wayward and the Seeking*, 157.

45. The same motif shows up in a Georgia Douglas Johnson poem of this period, "Fusion," which seems to have been inspired by discussions Toomer led at her home, shortly before he went to Georgia in 1921, concerning the "place and condition of the mixed-race group" in the United States. See George B. Hutchinson, "Jean Toomer and the New Negroes of Washington," *American Literature* 63 (1991): 683–92.

46. Toomer's initial ambition as an artist (modeled after Jean-Christophe) was to be a musician—an interest that contributed significantly to his later writing. In *Natalie Mann*, for example, the hero

Christ figure, whose first name Toomer had taken for himself, altering his given name "Eugene" at the time he turned seriously to writing as a vocation.

Kabnis suffers inner conflict in great part because of his denial of the pain of the black past and his connection to it. However, the conflict is exacerbated by his "mixed" racial identity. Like Toomer, Kabnis has straight, thin hair, a "lemon" face, brown eyes, and a mustache of "slim silk" (83). He longs to become "the face of the South." Like Toomer's, his ancestors were "southern blue bloods" as well as the black slaves Lewis will not let him deny. The conflict between these identities is precisely the key to Kabnis's difficulty. Lewis charges: "Can't hold them, can you? Master; slave. Soil; and the overarching heavens. Dusk; dawn. They fight and bastardize you. The sun tint of your cheeks, flame of the great season's multi-colored leaves, tarnished, burned. Split, shredded: easily burned. No use" (108–09).

Whereas, in the work planned to follow *Cane*, the protagonist's consciousness is initially "shredded by surfaces it cannot relate," the metaphor of "multi-colored leaves" also appears prominently in the pre-*Cane* story "Withered Skin of Berries," in which David Teyy (the hero) is the "man of multi-colored leaves"— white, black, and American Indian. Significantly, part of a poem attributed to him shows up in the first section of *Cane* as "Conversion." An "American" prophet, he is obviously a projection of Toomer's ideal image of himself, a reborn Kabnis. The female character, Vera—also of "mixed" race but still thinking of herself as "Negro"—needs him to "fill" her with "dreams": "Dreams of dead leaves, multi-colored leaves. Dreams of leaves decaying for a vernal stalk, phosphorescent in the dusk, flaming in dawn."[47] Each of the main characters in this story—white, black, and "mixed"—has "choked with the sum" of racial identities contributing to the new race. Some instinct toward "amalgamation" has stirred them in a spiritual experience they scarcely dare to credit; all but the hero have repressed the memory. In speaking of her dreams to Art, her black suitor, Vera asks, "[I]n that South from which you come, under its hates and lynchings, have you no lake, no river, no falls to sit beside and dream . . . dream?"[48] (He replies that rather than rivers he has red dust roads—a primary image in *Cane*.)

Ralph Kabnis calls himself a "dream" and regrets that a dream is soft, easily smashed by the "fist" of "square faces." He lacks the "bull-neck" and "heaving body," the strength, to bring his dream to reality. "If I, the dream (not what is weak and afraid in me)," he wonders, "could become the face of the South" (83–84). Lewis, perceiving the difficulty of "holding" the "sum" of his conflicting "racial" origins, precisely indicates the source of Kabnis's problem in achieving

---

Nathan Merilh is a musician combining European and African American forms in his inspired pieces. In a letter to Mae Wright of 15 Aug. 1922 (when *Cane* was still being composed out of scattered pieces), Toomer says Jean-Christophe is "true to me. Many of his trials and problems are or have been or will be mine. To know him is to know the more difficult side of Jean Toomer" (Waldo Frank Correspondence, Special Collections, Van Pelt Library, U of Pennsylvania). See also Charles Scruggs, "Jean Toomer: Fugitive," *American Literature* 47 (Mar. 1975): 84–96.

47. Toomer, "Withered Skin of Berries" 151.
48. Toomer, "Withered Skin of Berries" 151.

an identity and its adequate expression, an expression that would make him "the face of the [white/black] South" that would realize his dream.⁴⁹ In fact, Kabnis longs to achieve an identity by means of verbal expression and is frustrated by his inability to shape the right words, to *name* his reality adequately. Speaking of people of the "expanding type" (i.e., the "new" people), Toomer once wrote, "often they have been so compelled and are now so accustomed to use the dominant, which is to them an alien, language, that they can find no words for even talking to themselves, much less to others."⁵⁰

In striving for an integration of his personality and an adequate expression of his sense of the world, Kabnis is caught between violently antagonistic racial identities, victimized by a history of racial oppression and hatred, a world divided. As a person who physically and culturally embodies the transgression of that division, he is the signifier of "sin," taboo, that which cannot be spoken except in curses—and Kabnis curses profusely. The achievement of "Kabnis," its very language, derives from the sort of tension Kabnis feels—not merely the tension between black and white but, most important, the tension between "black/white" discourse and the dream of an alternative one, a new "American" discourse that would be completely divorced from the old. Toomer came to realize, however, that he would have to borrow terms from the "old" language of race even as he strived to destroy it. This realization is anticipated by the way that Kabnis's violent verbalizations betray the frustrations of a man who hates the very words he speaks.

The most common reading of the story assumes that Father John—a representative of the slave past and African American Christianity—holds the secret that could "cure" Kabnis, but a number of details in the story make this assumption problematic. First of all, it is unclear whether the old preacher is, in Lewis's terms, "a mute John the Baptist of a new religion—or a tongue-tied shadow of an old." Given the close relationship between Kabnis and the old man, it makes sense to interpret the former as a Toomer-like mute prophet of a new religion (unable to shape the words to fit his soul), and the latter as a "tongue-tied shadow of an old." While Kabnis clearly must face the pain of the past and accept his African American heritage, one cannot infer that this acceptance precludes the prophecy of a "new" race that will arise as the older racial identities fade away. Quite the contrary, Toomer associated the rising of the new race with a recognition of the contributions of all past races and of the great suffering endured in the "birthing" of the new race. "Black" culture would be a powerful force in transforming "white" culture, even as both were "absorbed."

The narrator, who rarely speaks, interrupts the dialogue just after Lewis names the old black preacher "Father John": "Slave boy whom some Christian mistress taught to read the Bible. Black man who saw Jesus in the ricefields, and began

49. Notably, Toomer was convinced at this time that the South would be the origin of a new, truly "American" literature. He apparently thought that he and Waldo Frank together were its harbingers.
50. "Race Problems in Modern Society," 31–32, box 51, folder 1120, Jean Toomer Papers.

preaching to his people. Moses- and Christ-words used for songs. Dead blind father of a muted folk who feel their way upward to a life that crushes or absorbs them" (106). The narrator here gives explicit voice to Toomer's own conception of the future of the black folk culture that Father John represents. In the same letter in which he told Waldo Frank that "Kabnis is *me*" as he finished the manuscript, Toomer wrote, "Don't let us fool ourselves, brother: the Negro of the folk-song has all but passed away: the Negro of the emotional church is fading."[51]

Father John's "banal" emphasis upon the "sin" of the white folks in making the Bible lie, as Darwin Turner has suggested, is presented without any clear indication of how it will help lead toward the future.[52] Even Lewis, who perceives Father John's importance as a link to the past, finds the Christian attitude wanting. He parodies Christianity: "Get ready, ye sinners, for the advent of Our Lord. Interesting, eh, Kabnis? but not exactly what we want" (101). Moreover, earlier in the story, the narrator pointedly undercuts the adequacy of a Christian vision for the reality that confronts Kabnis. As the black community gathers for worship, "[t]he church bell tolls. Above its squat tower, a great spiral of buzzards reaches far into the heavens. An ironic comment upon the path that leads into the Christian land" (88).

If Kabnis both resists Father John and fails to achieve self-integration, it is not at all clear that embracing what Father John represents would alone solve his problem. Throughout *Cane* the Christian attack on "sin" is undermined—which is not to say that oppression is accepted or that white America can escape responsibility for its history. The sins of the white masters and the "skeleton stone walls" that survive them as racist custom (as in "Blood-Burning Moon") are precisely what make so difficult a "synthesis" of the past racial identities—even though those sins, in the form of rape and concubinage, for example, have played a part in producing the "germ," so to speak, of the new race. I think we can credit Kabnis's statement that the main sin was not making the Bible lie, but something more far-reaching, the violation of a sacred relation (indeed, a *family* relationship, a relationship of the soul and the flesh) between blacks and whites:

> It was only a preacher's sin they knew in those old days, an that wasn't sin at all. Mind me, th only sin is whats done against the soul. Th whole world is a conspiracy t sin, especially in America, an against me. I'm th victim of their sin. I'm what sin is. Does he [Father John] look like me? Have you ever heard him say th things you've heard me say? He couldn't if he had th Holy Ghost t help him. (116)

Significantly, Carrie Kate has been taught to "hate" sin. In attempting to identify the nature of "sin" in contradistinction to Father John's conception, Kabnis—whose very name is an abbreviated inversion of "sin ba[c]k[wards]"—expresses his racial difference from Father John and his need for a new language to express

51. Toomer to Frank, undated (winter or spring 1922–23), box 3, folder 84, Jean Toomer Papers.
52. Turner, *In a Minor Chord*, 25.

his soul (which is, in effect, the repressed soul of the nation itself). That trans-gressive, "miscegenationist" soul *is* "sin" in America (from the conventional point of view), and at the same time the soul sinned against (in Toomer's view) the tabooed, denied, nearly unspoken spirit of a new conception.

The reality of this conception is cruel; Toomer expresses it in natural images both serene and harsh: "White faces, pain-pollen, settle downward through a cane-sweet mist and touch the ovaries of yellow flowers. Cotton bolls bloom, droop. Black roots twist in a parched red soil beneath a blazing sky" (107). White pollen, black roots, red soil—the associations are consistent with Toomer's system of racial metaphors in contemporaneous works. Whites are mobile, spread across the land like seed (just as white men, often by rape and concubinage, spread their "pain-pollen" and thus, despite their racist beliefs, helped conceive the new race); the Native Americans, aboriginal, are the spirit of the land, red soil; black people, in Toomer's view kept in "place" by slavery, the only American "peasant" group, have struck roots deep in the red southern soil of aboriginal America.

Kabnis, the very embodiment of this harsh and pained new growth, struggles for the words to express his "soul"—that soul that is "what sin is," impure, polluted, an abominable and "tortured" mixture.

> The form thats burned int my soul is some twisted awful thing that crept in from a dream, a godam nightmare, an won't stay still unless I feed it. An it lives on words. Not beautiful words. God Almighty no. Misshapen, split-gut, tortured, twisted words. . . . White folks feed it cause their looks are words. Niggers, black niggars feed it cause theyre evil an their looks are words. Yaller niggers feed it. This whole damn bloated purple country feeds it cause its goin down t hell in a holy avalanche of words. I want t feed the soul—I know what that is; the preach-ers dont—but I've got t feed it. (111)

"Kabnis," the action of which occurs almost entirely at night, ends before its central character achieves what Toomer would call "fusion." Indeed, nowhere in *Cane* do we find fulfillment. Apparently Toomer intended *Cane* as an embodiment of a phase that both he and the United States were about to pass out of, while his projected next book would indicate the future.[53] The controversial closing scene of *Cane* has Kabnis ascending the stairs from "the Hole" with a bucket of dead coals while Carrie Kate, who relies on Christianity and keeps telling Kabnis

---

53. While arranging and polishing *Cane,* Toomer had plans for a second book composed of short pieces (including "Withered Skin of Berries," *Natalie Mann,* and another story or play, perhaps *Balo*), which was to be completed by fall of 1923. Liveright had even taken an option on publishing it before the appearance of *Cane.* Toomer also had in mind a novel about which he was particularly excited. "This whole brown and black world heaving upward against, here and there mixing with the white world. But the mixture being insufficient to absorb the heaving, it but accelerates and fires it. This upward heaving to be symbolic of the proletariat or world upheaval. To be likewise symbolic of the subconscious penetration of the conscious mind" (Letter to Waldo Frank, undated, probably summer 1923, Jean Toomer Papers). Based on other statements in the letter, it is evident that Toomer wrote it when he was preparing "Kabnis" for its initial publication in *Broom.* Kerman and Eldridge (100) mention the proposed novel but mistakenly identify it with the *collection* Toomer had in mind and which he had already largely completed even as he worked on *Cane.*

to go to church to find the answer to his problems, kneels before Father John murmuring, "Jesus, come." "Light streaks through the iron-barred cellar window. Within its soft circle, the figures of Carrie and Father John" (117). It is a serene scene, but, I would argue, one representing the past, a confinement in an oppressive racial (and religious) discourse from which Kabnis has collected his dead coals.[54] Given the attitude to Christianity (even African American Christianity) throughout the story, how can we now believe that Carrie and Father John represent the future?[55] "*Outside*, the sun arises from its cradle in the tree-tops of the forest. Shadows of pines are dreams [Kabnis's "nightmares"?] the sun shakes from its eyes. The sun arises. Gold-glowing child, it steps into the sky and sends a birth-song slanting down gray dust streets and sleepy windows of the southern town" (117; emphasis added). The "gold-glowing child" substitutes for the "golden words" Kabnis would like to utter but cannot because the form burned into his soul is "a twisted awful thing that crept in from a dream, a godam nightmare" (111). Caught in that nightmare, dissipating his energies, as Toomer would later comment, Kabnis does not have the strength to win "a clear way through life" and ends frustrated and defeated, driven to a "passive acceptance" of "white dominance and its implications"—including, most importantly in Toomer's mind, the pervasive racialist discourse of the United States.[56]

4

Many scholars have charged that Toomer, like Kabnis, finally accepted white dominance and its implications. This conclusion follows from the perception that he denied his African ancestry.[57] But, as David Bradley has suggested, he could be charged more accurately with refusing to deny the rest of his ancestry. His growing frustration with the insistence that he be *either* "black" *or* "white" forced him to a tactic of denying association with any race except the "American" race. Thus, ironically, the demand that he accept a "black" identity drove him away from connection with African American culture, a fundamental source of his art.[58]

Toomer once wrote, in reference to the period of his apprenticeship to writing, "I began feeling that I had in my hands the tools for my own creation"—the

---

54. See Turner, *Minor Chord*, 25: "The virgin child prays before a deaf, blind, and senile savior. Meanwhile, Kabnis, who is unfit to be a laborer, carries the ashes of dreams into his apprenticeship for a trade which is soon to be obsolete."

55. Toomer wrote to Frank concerning the religion of the "peasant Negro": "Their theology is a farce (Christ is so immediate); their religious emotion, elemental, and for that reason, very near sublime" (letter of 21 Aug. 1922, Waldo Frank Correspondence). The vision of Carrie Kate and her words, "Jesus come," exemplify such a combination of sublime emotion and (in Toomer's view) an imprisoning religious dogma that *Cane* consistently discredits.

56. Toomer, "The South in Literature," 6.

57. It is true that Toomer finally began implying that he did not know positively of any "Negro blood" in his background, but this was long after *Cane* and after continued frustration in making his racial position understood.

58. Bradley, 692–93.

tools, we might say, to name himself with "golden words."⁵⁹ This brief faith in
the power of self-naming, however, was shattered by the reception of *Cane* and
Toomer's growing awareness of the impossibility of making himself understood.
In the context of the dominant racial discourse, the "American" race could have
no name; in the vision which that discourse bespoke, no visible place. Its invisibility, after all, made possible the defining light and shade of the vision. Hence,
Henry Louis Gates's revealing accusation: "To be a human being . . . Toomer felt
that he had to efface his mask of blackness, the cultural or racial trace of difference, and embrace the utter invisibility of being an American."⁶⁰ Such a statement
precisely misses Toomer's point, in a predictable way. It is representative of a
pervasive repression of Toomer's idea that, rather than erasing all racial "traces
of difference," he envisioned a *new* difference as fundamental—as, indeed, the
only (and the inevitable) route out of America's continuing racial nightmare.
Toomer felt that his "race" was invisible to other Americans because they had
yet to cross the divide in which "black" and "white" could be perceived as elements of the same spiritual, discursive, and social field, a field in which his ideas
could only be considered mad, his "race" invisible.

"New Negro" and not at the same time—North American in the specific conflicts that produce it and in its idiomatic language, its clash of "racial" forms—
as we read it *Cane* can, however, make visible the nature of our assumptions about
"race" and American identity. In its silences—in Kabnis's failure to find the
words to name his soul—it reveals the significant silences of our own deeply
racialized social text, the gaps and absences which critics, in turn, have failed to
make speak.⁶¹ The rules and structures of our racial "archive"—shaped both for
and in reaction against white hegemony, while leaving its foundational discursive
violence intact—operate against any acknowledgment of sanity in Toomer's
speech. There are certain things that we are ideologically forbidden to say.
Toomer's struggle, like Kabnis's, was to break the silence as he brought his "fragments" to "fusion," as he liked to say, a struggle in which he did not, could not,
publicly succeed. He became a "mystical irrationalist"; according to the prevailing
view he "disappeared." Terry Eagleton has well expressed the sort of conundrum
Toomer found himself up against:

[T]he languages and devices a writer finds to hand are already saturated with
certain ideological modes of perception, certain codified ways of interpreting reality; and the extent to which he can modify or remake those languages depends
on more than personal genius. It depends on whether at that point in history,
"ideology" is such that they must and can be changed.⁶²

59. Toomer, "Outline of the Story of an Autobiography," 55, box 20, folder 515, Jean Toomer Papers.
60. Gates, 202.
61. My point here is adapted from Pierre Macherey's argument about the ways in which a text is tied
    to ideology less by what it says than by what it does not and cannot say (see *A Theory of Literary
    Production*, trans. Geoffrey Wall, London: Routledge and Kegan Paul, 1978).
62. Terry Eagleton, *Marxism and Literary Criticism* (London: Verso, 1976), 26–27.

By illuminating what, racially speaking, "cannot be said," Toomer's *Cane*, as the second epigraph to this article would suggest, poses an ethical challenge. It dramatizes in its own thematic focus and form, enacts in its relation to the crisis of Toomer's literary career, and exemplifies in its interpretive history—its "racial" place in the "canon"—the suppression of the "invisible," "transcendental" signifier upon whose sacrifice our racial discourse ultimately depends. Through his "failure" (to create a language, to be called by his own name) and his subsequent "disappearance" from the literary scene, Toomer revealed the shared contradictions in "black" and "white" American racial ideologies, the violate and tabooed space of miscegenation that, like the black and white citizens who at least can agree to ostracize white Becky for her mulatto sons, we mutually repress and unwittingly sanctify to preserve our racial selves.

LITERATURE IN CONTEXTS

Victims of Likeness: Quadroons and Octoroons in Southern Fiction*

GLENN CANNON ARBERY

> *Now he understood what it was she had brought into the tent with her, what old Isham had already told him by sending the youth to bring her in to him—the pale lips, the skin pallid and dead-looking yet not ill, the dark and tragic and foreknowing eyes.* Maybe in a thousand or two thousand years in America, *he thought.* But not now! Not now! *He cried, not loud, in a voice of amazement, pity, and outrage: "You're a nigger!"*
>
> *William Faulkner,* Go Down, Moses

I

At certain junctures since the mid-nineteenth century, American fiction about the antebellum South has explored the relations between the races, especially in matters of equality, by dwelling with fascination and perplexity on the enigmatic figure of the quadroon or the octoroon. The words themselves, now rather arcane, are liable to evoke the image of "a face like a tragic magnolia, the eternal female, the eternal Who-suffers"—Faulkner's description of Charles Bon's mistress in *Absalom, Absalom!* Derived from the Spanish *cuarteron,* "quadroon" denoted a person one-fourth black, that is, with one Negro grandparent; an "octoroon"—a word coined in this country—was one-eighth black, the child of a quadroon and a white parent. To the extent that full equality under the law was simply a matter of being white, it would seem that the more white ancestry a person had, the closer to full equality he would have come. But there was a kind of logical problem in this approximation: the numerator and the denominator of the octoroon's white ancestry could never be equal, never quite resolve into a simple *one.* Unequal in himself, he could never be fully equal to others. The slave system therefore ignored the mathematics of parentage—except insofar as the white blood increased the value of the slave—and treated virtually *any* fractional admixture of Negro blood (as little as one sixty-fourth) as dominant and decisive in the determination of race. The octoroon, who might look no different from a white man or woman and who might be educated in the same way, was no closer to real equality than a full Negro.

* From Glenn Cannon Arbery, "Victims of Likeness: Quadroons and Octoroons in Southern Fiction," *Southern Review* 25.1 (winter 1989): 52–71.

The words quadroon and octoroon signify a reality of transgression that predates the term "miscegenation," an Americanism coined from Latin *miscere*, to mix + *genus*, race. The first use of the term listed by the *Oxford English Dictionary* is from the title of a pamphlet published in New York in 1864, *Miscegenation: The Theory of the Blending of the Races, Applied to the American White Man and Negro*. Part of an "ingenious hoax designed to discredit the Republican Party in the election of 1864," the pamphlet was supposed to convince voters that Republican doctrines would inevitably lead to racial amalgamation. Hoax or not, the term was rapidly adopted, probably because it was understood to mean an *improper* mixture of races, the opening *mis-* being taken in its usual sense as a prefix. With the end of the Civil War, Americans began to consider the mixture of white and black blood in terms of legally equal races (part of the shock value of the hoax), rather than unequal individuals. To make a grammatical analogy, it had not been possible before the Civil War to construct a compound sentence with the Negro and the white as independent clauses; the term "miscegenation" implies the possibility of such a construction. Under slavery, the sentence was always complex or compound-complex, a racial hypotaxis in which one element was always subordinated to another, and no matter how much the subordinate clause contained— no matter if it took on a Jamesian fullness and intellectual subtlety—it could never stand alone as a full unit of meaning because of the subordinating conjunction, blackness.

The octoroon, then, bears the pain of this tantalizing approximation to the cultural definition of completeness: the tragic status of apparent whiteness, near-unity. The abolitionists were the first to use the plight of quadroons and octoroons to expose the problems inherent in treating blackness as the sign of a different *nomos*. In *Uncle Tom's Cabin*, Harriet Beecher Stowe bases her major subplots on the agonies of quadroon women purchased as concubines. In twentieth-century southern novels exploring the propertied, aristocratic southern family, the presence of an octoroon allows the plot to move toward the shocking discovery of black blood in a relative of white appearance. Several of Faulkner's greatest works involve a partially black character who embodies the action's central tensions because of his blood relation to the white family of the novel, Charles Bon being the most striking example. The characteristic feature of these fictional quadroons and octoroons, both in abolitionist novels and in modern southern writing, is their tendency to be forced into the role of victims and to suffer the whole weight of the social difference between the races. But there are major differences between the nineteenth-century abolitionists who wrote about them and twentieth-century southerners such as Faulkner. Although Faulkner's ambivalence toward the South is deep, he sees no hope of achieving equality if it requires the blurring or ignoring of differences. Even more than the abolitionists, Faulkner brings the unresolved "approximate" status of the octoroon to light in its complexity, acknowledging the pain of his position yet refusing to sanction the eradication of the differences that give him pain.

Contrary to what the abolitionists believed, the quadroon never becomes a victim, even in their own fiction, because of his blackness alone. The crime he embodies is a blurring of the difference between races, a blurring for which his white father is responsible; yet since the difference between races has to be kept clear, his father must deny him a full standing in being, and if the quadroon insists that his father is at fault and tries to claim the rights of a child, he must be rejected altogether. In his recent book *The Scapegoat*, René Girard argues that the psychology of victimization has been misconceived:

> In all the vocabulary of tribal or national prejudices hatred is expressed, not for difference, but for its absence. It is not the other *nomos* that is seen in the other, but anomaly, nor is it another norm but abnormality. . . . We hear everywhere that "difference" is persecuted. This is the favorite statement of contemporary pluralism, and it can be somewhat misleading in the present context.
>
> Even in the most closed cultures men believe they are free and open to the universal; their differential character makes the narrowest cultural fields seem inexhaustible from within. Anything that compromises this illusion terrifies us and stirs up the immemorial tendency to persecution. This tendency always takes the same direction, it is embodied by the same stereotypes and it always responds to the same threat. Despite what is said around us persecutors are never obsessed by difference but rather by its unutterable contrary, the lack of difference.

The victim is often the stranger who turns out to be, like Oedipus, the rejected or denied legitimate heir, the one who combines "the marginality of the outsider with the marginality of the insider." The quadroon or octoroon is the white man's nearly white child, rejected as white—a victim who bears "the paradoxical marks of the absence of difference."

As a hidden fraction or a concealed hypotaxis, the quadroon or octoroon can stand as complete—that is, as a white man or woman—until the fact of the concealment appears. But this belated appearance calls into question the crucial differentiating power of the culture, precisely because the blackness on which so many distinctions are based has *not* been apparent in him, and the person exposed immediately takes on the "paradoxical marks" of the victim. In *Absalom, Absalom!*, for instance, Quentin Compson and his friend Shreve imagine a scene in the last days of the Civil War in which Thomas Sutpen tells his son Henry that Charles Bon is not only Henry's brother but that Bon's mother was part Negro. When Bon later perceives that his brother is suddenly acting distant, he recognizes what old Sutpen must have told Henry: "–So it's the miscegenation, not the incest, which you can't bear," Bon says to Henry. For years, Bon has put off marrying his half-sister Judith, who loves him, because he hopes that old Sutpen will stop the marriage and thus acknowledge Bon as his son; now he forces the issue by insisting that he will marry Judith as soon as the war ends. Since Thomas Sutpen will not acknowledge Bon, only Henry can prevent the marriage. Bon gives Henry his pistol and tells him to shoot him now if he wants to stop him:

> Henry looks at the pistol; now he is not only panting, he is trembling; when he speaks now his voice is not even the exhalation, it is the suffused and suffocating inbreath itself.
> —You are my brother.
> —No I'm not. I'm the nigger that's going to sleep with your sister. Unless you stop me, Henry.

One can be elegant and accomplished, admired and imitated, as Bon is by Henry, but the revelation of black blood, regardless of how little of it there is with respect to the whole makeup of the man and despite the physical and cultural invisibility of this "subordinating conjunction," makes him an elegant, accomplished "nigger" who has to be rejected.

Bon cannot be accepted as *really* possessing the same ontological standing as a propertied white man, any more than a subordinate clause can be accepted as an independent clause. For a southerner like Henry Sutpen, propertied whiteness is a system of differences based on the possibility of closing out and subordinating— as the boy Thomas Sutpen was closed out of the rich plantation owner's front door because he was a poor white—and he has to insist that the individual fall within its criteria of completeness to be valid, that is, fully to *be*. He cannot ignore Bon's incompleteness without rejecting the differential system that gives him meaning, yet in killing Bon, he has to cast out the superior older brother who is "subordinate" only in the terms of the system whose illusion he threatens. For a man like Thomas Sutpen, the conventions of race become a paradigm of enlightened modernity because they are based on the desire to establish an ontological hierarchy in which the darker and more complex elements have been given their place in a sub-order; Thomas Jefferson, for instance, actually put his slave quarters at Monticello *underground* so that the view from his windows would not be interrupted by them. These conventions of subordination—or repression—provide Henry with his only meaning as a son and potential heir. As John T. Irwin has pointed out, Bon's blackness plays a large part in his role as Henry's (and Quentin Compson's) double; the double becomes the victim, Girard would argue, because of the "absence of difference." As Bon perceives, Henry does not object to incest; what he cannot tolerate is that Bon, Thomas Sutpen's firstborn son, embodies Sutpen's actual but unacknowledged blurring of the difference that underlies the very possibility of Sutpen's "design" of self-made aristocracy, the difference between owners and the people they enslave. Having already been rejected as a son, Bon cannot become the heir of that design as a son-in-law without canceling out the very possibility of the completeness that Sutpen wants to achieve. Simply by being who he is—older brother, suitor of Judith, and black man—Bon deconstructs the most basic distinctions of Henry's life. Henry must kill him in order to save his family because the "nigger" is not *different enough*.

II

What is true of Bon is more or less true of the quadroon or octoroon in general: to the extent that he forces himself to be recognized for his whiteness, he forces blackness to appear as an abstraction. Since there is no visible difference between his blackness and his whiteness, Bon thus forces himself into the role of victim. But there is another element involved in the quadroon-victim that Bon himself does not fully represent. Bon was conceived in a legal marriage that Sutpen later renounced when he discovered that his wife was "part negro," but in most cases the antebellum quadroon or octoroon represents an instance of the slaveowner or his sons taking sexual advantage of the fact of ownership. In his novel *The Fathers* Allen Tate describes a "half-grown mulatto girl with kinky red hair and muddy green eyes in a pretty, Caucasian face"; when Lacy Buchan asks to whom she and the boy with her belong, she says, giggling, "We b'longs to Marse Henry." The giggle, one suspects, is owing to her recognition that "Marse Henry" is her father, that she "b'longs" to him in more ways than her little brother does. She is the living sign of her mother's concubinage and her owner-father's adultery. The quadroon or octoroon signifies this transgression doubled or tripled; he or she exists as the evidence of sin repeated, brought closer in its results to the likeness of the original transgressor, whose sin thus becomes more obvious to all observers even though it remains officially unacknowledged. Oddly, the slave became a bastard son or daughter, properly speaking, only when he or she had white blood, which bore within it the conceptual possibility of legitimacy; one would not think of the child of two slaves as either "legitimate" or "illegitimate" since slaves had no rights in any case. In the South, even if the slaveowner would not acknowledge his partially white children, the paradoxically legitimizing fact of bastardy was nevertheless implicit in their mixed blood, and the Old Testament injunction against accepting the bastard into the assembly (in this case, the community defined by propertied whiteness) therefore applied doubly to the quadroon or octoroon, who was illegitimate in the second or third generation. The bastard Negro who could pass for white threatened the difference between those within the cultural covenant and those without.

Sabbath Hawks, the preacher's daughter who seduces Hazel Motes in Flannery O'Connor's *Wise Blood*, puts the problem of bastardy neatly when she describes to Haze a letter she once wrote to an advice columnist:

"I says, 'Dear Mary, I am a bastard and a bastard shall not enter the kingdom of heaven as we all know, but I have this personality that makes boys follow me. Do you think I should neck or not? I shall not enter the kingdom of heaven anyway so I don't see what difference it makes.' "

Sabbath's "problem" was one that complicated the already complex relation of propertied white men to mixed-blood women. New Orleans provides the most sophisticated example of the possible permutations of this relation. Attracted by the cultured and carefully reared quadroon or octoroon women of that city, white men saw in them natural concubines, bastard daughters of slaveowners sold and bred for the service of other men's desire, their fraction of blackness the necessary sign that they "shall not enter the kingdom of heaven anyway." In *King Lear* Gloucester introduces his bastard son Edmund to Kent with a frank acknowledgment that "there was good sport at his making"; the men looking at octoroon women could not fail to see in them a history of illegitimate "good sport" implicating their own fathers and grandfathers. The New Orleans octoroon was "taken at childhood, culled and chosen and raised more carefully than any white girl, any nun, than any blooded mare even," as Quentin Compson's father says. She beautifully embodied three generations of transgression, a subtilizing repetition that amounted to an unofficial or shadow-tradition of *eros*. The whiteness of sisters and wives appeared under the sign of blackness, now subordinated even from appearance. In becoming more fully illegitimate, these women were more obviously already damned and more powerfully subject to victimization.

Unlike a Charles Bon, the quadroon or octoroon woman became a victim of sexual ownership, an erotic violence to her will, because of her "paradoxical marks of the absence of difference." The abolitionists who wrote about these women, Harriet Beecher Stowe in particular, misunderstood them as being victimized because of a difference that was almost an abstraction. She portrays them as more or less white in appearance but subject to sale as slaves because of the quarter or the eighth of black blood in them; she wants their very slight difference from white women to make the system of slavery appear as an absurd and brutal denial of equality. But Stowe and the other abolitionists neglect the obvious danger of describing these women as white, then showing them for sale. They are like the opponents of pornography who reproduce what they oppose in order to show how shocking it is. Henry Wadsworth Longfellow and Stowe both seem unaware that their descriptions of quadroons, for instance, might actually force their readers to participate in victimization. For instance, in Longfellow's poem "The Quadroon Girl," a slaver bargains with a planter for a "Quadroon maiden" who stands before them; Longfellow devotes two stanzas to her appearance:

> Her eyes were large, and full of light,
>   Her arms and neck were bare;
> No garment she wore save a kirtle bright,
>   And her own long raven hair.
>
> And on her lips there played a smile
>   As holy, meek, and faint,
> As lights in some cathedral aisle
>   The features of a saint.

The reader sees this saintly beauty in a description as summary as the practiced buyer's glance. Although the planter quarrels with himself because he knows "whose passions gave her life," he needs the money, and he sells his daughter. At the same time that Longfellow makes the reader aware of her as a white girl who is the child of transgression, he presents her as chattel for sale. Her cheek grows "pale as death"—an emphasis on her whiteness crucial to the effect that Longfellow hopes to achieve—and she is led away to become her buyer's "slave and paramour." What Longfellow does, in effect, is to emphasize the girl's white appearance as though it were what made her sale so unthinkable, but in emphasizing it, he forces her blackness to appear as the absence of difference, thus putting her more powerfully in the victim's role. Longfellow unwittingly makes his male readers identify with the slaver (whose name suggests bestial salivation) in what Girard calls "the immemorial tendency to persecution," in this case a sexual one.

Because of their desire to help their readers imagine individuals brought into full equality from a constraining, unchosen history, the abolitionists put their stress on those features of the woman that were most *like* the white ones. Faulkner, who was as subject to the unchosen history of the South as Quentin Compson or Charles Bon, and who was also the benefactor of the twentieth century's greater candor about the psychology of sexual desire, understood that women *like* white women would be more quickly subjected to sexual enslavement, even as images, if they were presented in terms of their appearance. He has Quentin Compson's father imagine Charles Bon's revelation of the quadroon and octoroon slave markets of New Orleans to Henry Sutpen:

> Without his knowing what he saw it was as though to Henry the blank and scaling barrier in dissolving produced and revealed not comprehension to the mind, the intellect which weighs and discards, but striking instead straight and true to some primary blind and mindless foundation of all young male living dream and hope— a row of faces like a bazaar of flowers, the supreme apotheosis of chattelry, of human flesh bred of the two races for that sale—a corridor of doomed and tragic flower faces walled between the grim duenna row of old women and the elegant shapes of young men trim predatory and (at the moment) goatlike.

Longfellow attempts to speak to "the intellect which weighs and discards," but he also speaks, despite himself, to that "primary blind and mindless foundation of young male living dream and hope" that Mr. Compson sees beneath "comprehension."

In *Uncle Tom's Cabin* Harriet Beecher Stowe has several scenes similar to Longfellow's, similar even in the emphases of the physical description. She first describes Emmeline, for example, when the girl is on sale at the slave market in New Orleans. She is sitting nestled against her mother, "a respectably-dressed mulatto woman between forty and fifty." The fact of an already doubled transgression is present in this pair. The older woman would not be a mulatto if her mother had not become pregnant by a white man, and Emmeline would not be a quadroon if the same thing had not been repeated with her mother. Stowe leaves these matters implicit, but the fact of Emmeline's white father "may be seen from her fairer complexion, though her likeness to her mother is quite discernible. She has the same soft, dark eyes, with longer lashes, and her curling hair is of a luxuriant brown. She is also dressed with great neatness, and her white, delicate hands betray very little acquaintance with servile toil." The greater length of her eyelashes and the soft whiteness of her hands advertise that she is *like* a white woman ·vithout being one; she is a simulacrum of white femininity, unsuited for work but extremely valuable as a pure delicacy of sex, for sale, without rights.

Stowe wants the monstrosity of this treatment of her to be evident, as of course it is on one level; for instance, the cruder passions her readers might feel are made repugnant and rejected by being located in the brutally phallic figure of Simon Legree, who buys Emmeline. The problem with Stowe's presentation is that when she has the quadroon submit to the sexual gaze of her potential buyers, her polemical intent—to alert her readers to the horrors done to the delicate feelings of women who are not really any different from white women—requires that she also bring Emmeline blushing voluptuously before the imagination under circumstances that play far too obviously to "young male living dream and hope," thus to persecution. When Emmeline appears on the auctioneer's block, "the blood flushes painfully in her otherwise colorless cheek, her eye has a feverish fire, and her mother groans to see that she looks more beautiful than she ever saw her before. The auctioneer sees his advantage, and expatiates volubly in mingled French and English, and bids rise in rapid succession."

Stowe has Emmeline's mother appeal to her own purchaser to buy Emmeline as well, but he cannot afford her when Legree drives up the price. Of Legree, Stowe writes, "He has got the girl, body and soul, unless God help her!" Faulkner seems to have this passage in mind in the scene, mentioned earlier, when Quentin Compson's father is thinking about Charles Bon and Henry Sutpen with the New Orleans octoroons. Mr. Compson imagines Bon telling Henry why he had bought and "married" an octoroon woman in New Orleans. Speaking for his class of gentlemen, Bon considers the purchase a variety of salvation, and he seems to have in mind Simon Legree: "We do save that one, who but for us would have been sold to any brute who had the price, not sold to him for the night like a white prostitute, but body and soul for life to him who could have used her with more impunity than he would dare to use an animal, heifer or mare." Faulkner is not the same as Mr. Compson by any means, and at this point in *Absalom, Absalom!* Mr. Compson does not know that Charles Bon himself had black blood; from the later perspective of the novel, Bon's "marriage" to one of these octoroons had to be a *conscious* repetition of what Thomas Sutpen had done with Bon's mother, as a kind of self-persecution. Yet Mr. Compson is right, if not complex enough, in recognizing that an even more subtle repetition of the original victimization of black women is to repeat it, on those who seem most white, *as salvation*—the temptation to which Stowe unknowingly leads her readers in making them desire to "save" Emmeline. Part of the explosive appeal of *Uncle Tom's Cabin* in the 1850s was surely that it combined millenarian religion with a potent, unconscious eroticism—unconscious because Stowe did not see quite enough of the quadroon's "marginality of the outsider." Emmeline is not simply another conventionally pretty white girl; what makes her so valuable as a slave and so problematic as a character is her absence of difference without sameness. She is the victim because she is *already* the victim—of erotic transgression, birth to slavery, bastardy. Stowe enhances the quadroon girl's sexual volatility for her reader/buyers (Emmeline as image-chattel) the more she urges Emmeline's whiteness as the index of her unjust treatment. Emmeline's situation will tend to deconstruct any "white" cultural form because of the very things that make her a sexual victim. Without a clear separation of social and spiritual salvation, Stowe risks fostering a fantasy of salvation that remains an immanent, erotic double of the Christian one.

III

Mr. Compson's Bon (the Bon unaware of his own black blood) has a theory of the white motivation that led to the breeding of quadroon and octoroon women. In effect, his theory requires a rethinking of the idea of black subordination. According to him, black women embody a fundamental female principle; although they are bred to be beautiful according to white standards, they are really valued for a quality that does not exist in white women. His is essentially a Dionysian understanding of the delicately prepared octoroon:

> Yes: a sparrow which God himself neglected to mark. Because though men, white men, created her, God did not stop it. He planted the seed which brought her to flower—the white blood to give the shape and pigment of what the white man calls female beauty, to a female principle which existed, queenly and complete, in the hot equatorial groin of the world long before that white one of ours came down from trees and lost its hair and bleached out—a principle apt and docile and instinct with strange and ancient curious pleasures of the flesh (which is all: there is nothing else) which her white sisters of a mushroom yesterday flee from in moral and outraged horror—a principle which, where her white sister must needs try to make an economic matter of it like someone who insists upon installing a counter or a scales or a safe in a store or business for a certain percentage of the profits, reigns, wise supine and all-powerful, from the sunless and silken bed which is her throne.

Faulkner allows Bon (who will later, in Quentin and Shreve's version of him, prove to be black himself) to acknowledge a belief that shadows the writings of the abolitionists without ever being expressed: a belief in the irreducible principle of primordial femaleness inherent in black blood. This principle underlies Stowe's presentation of the male docility of Uncle Tom as much as it does the creation of quadroons and octoroons as an early exercise in eugenics. Implicit in this use of blackness is a Dionysian desire for the destruction of overly rigid order; in being a *willing* female subordination inseparable from ancient pleasures of the flesh, blackness becomes the paradoxically regal subordinator of whiteness. The men who bred these women of mixed blood wanted to re-create white women inside an *explicitly* economic arrangement that released the "wise supine and all-powerful" darkness of female sexuality from what *King Lear*'s Edmund calls the "dull, stale, tired bed" of marital economics. They wanted to create white women who could be bought outright and who were willingly victimized *from within* by the anti-economic pleasures they simultaneously fled, blushing, with "moral and outraged horror"—why else would Emmeline's *blushes* drive up the bids?—women who temporarily destroyed the white order in a *sparagmos* of pleasure, yet who remained legally slaves.

George Washington Cable, the first southern writer to address the problem of mixed race, comes close to making the same kind of identification of the "female principle" as Mr. Compson, but, like the abolitionists, his desire for equality is in fact a desire for the elimination of difference. His description of Olive, an octoroon girl in "Madame Delphine," is so much like those of Longfellow's "Quadroon maiden" and Stowe's characters that one suspects the quadroon of becoming, not an approximation of the ideal, but the ideal itself. Cable speaks of the girl's "abundant hair rolling in dark, rich waves back from her brows and down from her crown, and falling in two heavy plaits beyond her round, broadly girt waist and full to her knees, a few escaping locks eddying lightly on her graceful neck and her temples." This tide of Victorian hair symbolizes an abundant sexual nature, informed by African wildness ("dark" and "rich" are the adjectives consistently applied to both the hair and the eyes of female quadroons in *Uncle Tom's Cabin*), yet conforming to the refined lineaments of European beauty. The girl possesses "large, brown, melting eyes, where the openness of child nature mingled dreamily with the sweet mysteries of maiden thought. We say no color of shell on face or throat; but this was no deficiency, that which took its place being the warm, transparent tint of sculptured ivory." Cable uses ivory as his comparison because its whiteness is the ornamental, artistically reworked aspect of the most massive animal power of Africa; shells, by contrast, are small, washed up, common, and brittle. Cable embeds the "principle apt and docile and instinct with strange and ancient curious pleasures of the flesh" in his Olive, who is also as saintly as Longfellow's quadroon girl.

By law, Olive cannot marry Monsieur Vignevielle, the white pirate she has reformed. Cable has Olive's mother take all the victimization onto herself by denying her maternity and thus freeing Olive from any suspicion that she is tainted by black blood, so that she can marry Vignevielle. In one twist, the history of transgression is negated by a noble lie; Olive becomes the ideal "white" wife, because—as only the reader and Madame Delphine's confessor know—she looks white but actually possesses the "queenly and complete" sexuality symbolized by her ivory complexion. The marriage seems very promising. But some questions arise, especially since the differences between races have been explicitly repressed. Is the marriage not a hushed acceptance of the eugenically prepared octoroon as the best of wives, a subtle introduction of slavery—redeemed slavery, to be sure—into the role of wives? In blurring differences and enlisting the reader's sympathies with Madame Delphine's sacrifice, Cable also blurs the crucial difference between wives and slaves within marriage. Aristotle saw this difference as the decisive one between the Greeks and the Persians, who treated their wives as slaves, and it might be said to be the basis of the Western understanding of political freedom. If Cable did not believe in the powerful "female principle" of blackness, this fictional presentation of repressed difference would not be troubling, because it would simply suggest that Olive can enjoy the freedom of a wife. But Olive was exactly what the "creators" of octoroons, the men who held Nietzsche's view of women as a kind of refreshment and reward for male will, desired: as Mr. Compson's Bon puts it, a woman "raised and trained to fulfill a woman's sole end and purpose: to love, to be beautiful, to divert." Inconspicuously, the Dionysian pleasure that subordinates any amount of whiteness enters the white *nomos*; having been "saved" in an erotic subversion of the laws of New Orleans, Olive begins, unintentionally, the cultural deconstruction for which she has been so carefully bred.

IV

But this is surely excessive. What does it really hurt for Olive to get away with it? The "female principle" of blackness was a nineteenth-century Romantic fantasy. Will the failure to distinguish Olive from white women really dissolve the possibility of social distinctions? At the end of the story, everyone in the story believes that she is white, and Cable clearly wants his readers to be relieved that she has been saved from a kind of limbo existence, that octoroon prophylaxis of reality that Cable himself speaks of as a white man's "Arcadia." Has she *not* been saved? What effect could it possibly have that her difference will go unrecognized?

The problem is not what happens in the world of the story, unfortunately, but what happens in the world that *reads* the story. Cable introduces the real possibility of a repression of differences; he approves, in this instance at least, an instance of miscegenation. No one should be surprised that Cable was violently denounced all across the South. Perhaps there were grains of real wisdom in the southern reaction. The lie about Olive's origin is also a prophylaxis of reality, however socially unjust the consequences of the truth might be, and Cable makes himself party to it. When Allen Tate asks himself for what the poet is responsible, he writes that "he is responsible for the virtue proper to him as poet, for his special *arete* for the mastery of a disciplined language which will not shun the full report of the reality conveyed to him by his awareness: he must hold, in Yeats' great phrase, 'reality and justice in a single glance.'" Has Cable been as true to reality as he should have been in hoping that mercy and sacrifice will fill in what is missing in Olive's whiteness? Is the desire for justice served by a sacrificial subordination of the truth itself?

What is this truth? That Olive is a "nigger"? The category itself reflects a long history of injustice. It seems barbarous to consider the unrecognized octoroon a kind of disease that subtly alters the inner codes of the cultural grammar, marriage among them, and undercuts the standing that *anyone* has in that culture, yet almost every white southerner of the nineteenth century and half of the twentieth would have felt the force of that consideration. Without those distinctions, they would have asked implicitly in their instinctive outrage, how are people in the society, black or white, to understand themselves? How can the historical memory of slavery and the natural difference in appearance simply be repressed because of a desire for justice? *"Maybe in a thousand or two thousand years in America,"* Isaac McCaslin cries to himself in *Go Down, Moses* when he sees the girl—his own relative, the descendant of his grandfather's incestuous miscegenation—bring in the son of his other kinsman, Roth Edmonds, who has repeated ancestral incest and miscegenation without knowing it. Whatever is repressed returns; the difference repressed because of the righteous and guilty idea of "equality" comes back in a substitute who bears "the paradoxical marks of the absence of difference" to be victimized again, perhaps in the willing chattelry of the purchasable image.

What is really being repressed is the knowledge that evil is implicit in the nature of man; the recognized quadroon or octoroon will not let the fact of inherited, unchosen, but binding transgression be forgotten. This transgression, which has no salvation except real transcendence, can be culturally forgotten if poetry itself, in its marriage of differences—reality and justice, reason and "wise supine and all-powerful" creative pleasure—is replaced by stories bred for desire. This danger emerges even in very discerning men. After his first reading of Tate's novel *The Fathers* Donald Davidson wrote him a letter praising his achievement. He had only one reservation: "I was troubled somewhat by the final incident of Yellow

Jim's doings, & what immediately followed. I shall have to read it again to check this. But you do seem here to play into the hands of our Yankee torturers just a little." What bothered Davidson was the "unnecessary blood-kinship of Yellow Jim & his own white folks. And certain other things, possibly—because they will be misunderstood." Early in the novel, George Posey sells his half-brother Yellow Jim and buys a horse with the money; when Jim escapes from his owner after several years and returns home, he beats the horse and, in the scene to which Davidson refers, rapes his half-sister, Jane. The two major acts—the sale of Jim for a horse, the rape of Jane—balance each other as acts eliminating difference. One can only guess which "other things" in the novel Davidson meant; perhaps he was remembering a rather unsavory scene, thematically similar, in which Wink Broadacre nods to the "half-grown mulatto girl" mentioned earlier; she is lying nearby under the pavilion, and Wink callously asks Lacy Buchan, the narrator, if he "wants some of it." This girl, too, is probably kin to her "own white folks," probably, in fact, Wink's half-sister.

Perhaps Davidson worried that the "Yankee torturers," the descendants of the abolitionists, would not notice that the major abuses in the slave system came from slaveowners like George Posey—rationalists disaffected with the *noblesse oblige*, the codes of honor, the manners, and the traditional religion that characterized the South. To men like Posey, slaves were commodities to be sold without regard to kinship or feeling, and even if "all are born Yankees of the race of men / And this, too, now the country of the damned," as Tate puts it in one of his poems, such men were not typical of the antebellum South. All this aside, however, Davidson still did not want to suffer imaginatively the real violence of the novel, the convergence of incest and miscegenation. Tate, on the other hand, was bound by his responsibility as a poet not to "shun the full report of the reality conveyed to him by his awareness," and the kinship of Yellow Jim to George Posey was very much the point of the episode for Tate. In his letter defending the Yellow Jim incident, he replied to Davidson that he had based it on "certain actual circumstances pertaining to a negro in my grandfather's family." Unlike Yellow Jim, Tate wrote, this man had not been "so closely related as half-brother, but he was at least a first cousin of the lady he attacked." Tate insisted that the event in his family past contained "a profound truth of the relation of the races."

Tate seems most like Faulkner in this respect: he habitually comes to terms with the ideas and stances he most abhors by taking them into his family, knowing them, as it were, in his own blood. Looking back on slavery, for which he accepts an ancestral responsibility, he faces its darkest abuses through the intuitive medium of kinship, which will not allow it to be abstracted and disowned. Isaac McCaslin does the same thing in *Go Down, Moses*. He accepts his responsibility for the miscegenation and incest of the past by admitting his kinship with the quadroon and octoroon descendants of his own grandfather. He renounces the property due him by inheritance and gives it to McCaslin Edmonds, but two generations later he nevertheless finds incest and miscegenation repeated in Edmonds' grandson, a tragic repetition he also has to acknowledge as partially his fault. At first, after he recognizes that the girl who has come to the hunting camp with Roth Edmonds' baby is a "nigger," he wants her to take some money and leave as soon as possible. Then it registers on him that she is the granddaughter of James Beauchamp, "Tennie's Jim," who was both the grandson and the great-grandson of Lucius Quintus Carothers McCaslin, Ike's own grandfather. He touches her hand: "He didn't grasp it, he merely touched it—the gnarled, blood-less, bone-light bone-dry old man's fingers touching for a second the smooth young flesh where the strong old blood ran after its long lost journey back to home. 'Tennie's Jim,' he said. 'Tennie's Jim.' " Through her, he touches an intimate past that he can recover only in this substitute who represents the very transgression he has tried all his life to reject. Like the girl, Ike is holding in mind six generations of their mutual blood when he says, harshly, "It's a boy, I reckon. They usually are, except that one that was its own mother too." He means Tomasina, mother of Turl by old McCaslin and daughter of Eunice, also by old McCaslin, who slept with his own mulatto or quadroon daughter, repeating the owner-sin of her begetting with her mother and deepening it with incest.

Significantly, Isaac bestows his sign of recognition on the girl by giving the bastard son of Roth Edmonds old General Compson's hunting horn. It is a gesture both of despair and love. The horn is the sign of wilderness and the possibility of beginning anew, of loving the virgin, of canceling the past by becoming an origin; it is the Biblical symbol of masculine plenitude. Uncle Ike might be saying, with the whole pain of irony, what the narrator in Donald Davidson's "Randall, My Son" says to remind his heir of the rich past:

> Take, what I leave, your own land unforgotten;
> Hear, what I hear, in a far chase new begun
> An old horn's husky music, Randall, my son.

But Ike gives away the horn at the moment he realizes that young originality always moves toward the discovery that it is a repetition. The boy who represents repeated transgression will carry the sign of masculine power to beget, to begin an action. The fact that it was General Compson's horn links the McCaslin story to the whole history of the Compsons, including their relation (as narrators, in-terpreters, witnesses) to the story of the Sutpens. The son of Roth Edmonds is like Charles Bon returning after generations to inherit what has already been irrevocably lost.

Even after he gives away the horn, old Uncle Ike does not know what to do with the recognition of kinship; he continues to think of having to "wait" for the difference between races to become meaningless. His advice to the girl retains a kind of rational obtuseness:

> "You are young, handsome, almost white; you could find a black man who would see in you what it was you saw in him, who would ask nothing of you and expect less and get even less than that, if it's revenge you want. Then you will forget all this, forget it ever happened, that he ever existed—"

Isaac's mistake, like the mistake of Virgil in the *Aeneid*, is the belief that Lethe is in Hell instead of at the top of Purgatory. The girl's correction of him is profound:

> She stood in the gleaming and still dripping slicker, looking quietly down at him from under the sodden hat.
> "Old man," she said, "have you lived so long and forgotten so much that you dont remember anything you ever knew or felt or even heard about love?"

According to an old Empedoclean doctrine, Love and Hate alternate; Love unifies all things, whereas Hate keeps things discrete and separate. If the universe feels Love alone, the differences sustained by Hate are eliminated, and chaos ensues. In his final tragic meditation after the girl leaves, Isaac interprets the girl's love as the victory of this Empedoclean principle of Dionysian *eros*; he reflects that in the Delta where he has sought the last remnant of wilderness, *"usury and mortgage and bankruptcy and measureless wealth, Chinese and African and Aryan and Jew, all breed and spawn together until no man has time to say which one is which nor cares."* His view of a world collapsing inward from its own desire, returning to chaos, reflects his sense of the rejection of the Christian vision, in which love held all things in unity by keeping them distinct, as the Persons of God are different in their simple unity. Everything in the Delta, this final image of the "hot equatorial groin," rushes toward a kind of apocalyptic *in*difference. He does not fail to see the sacrificial significance of the animal killed after the girl's departure. When he asks what it was, Will Legate answers, "Just a deer, Uncle Ike. . . . Nothing extra." Correcting this indifference, Ike symbolically recognizes the departed girl with the old sign of the victim, saying to himself, "It was a doe."

V

Both Faulkner and Tate make essentially the same move with respect to the unrecoverable past, which cannot be known simply through official history: its alien and passive distance becomes comprehensible for them through kinship, which makes blackness (as the ironic obverse symbol of a lost plenitude in being) appear as the excluded quality *within*, written in the blood. This, perhaps, is knowledge carried to the heart: the "marginality of the outsider" that the storyteller brings into the story he tells, trying to find himself in it through his "kinsmen." But what happens when the writer centrally implicated in the being of the cultural story is finally excluded from it? What happens when a society officially committed to the elimination of differences feeds its concomitant hunger for persecution by making men and women into images, images into chattel, until it thinks that all images are subject to its appetite, that none are authoritative? For Tate, the poet in the modern world who tries to bring in the "full report" of reality has taken on certain similarities to the *pharmakos* of ancient Greece. Poetry, says Tate, had an immense future at the end of the nineteenth century:

> It had to be immense because, for men like Arnold, everything else had failed. It was the new religion that was destined to be lost more quickly than the old.

Poetry was to have saved us; it not only hadn't saved us by the end of the fourth decade of this century, it had only continued to be poetry which was little read. It had to be rejected. The primitive Athenians, at the Thargelian festival of Apollo, killed two human beings, burnt them, and cast their ashes into the sea. The men sacrificed were called *pharmakoi:* medicines. We have seen in our time a powerful attempt to purify ourselves of the knowledge of evil in man. Poetry is one of the sources of that knowledge. It is believed by some classical scholars that the savage ritual of the *pharmakoi* was brought to Athens by barbarians. In historical times effigies made of dough were substituted for human beings.

The nineteenth century, one may infer from this brilliantly tacit passage, saw in poetry "the paradoxical marks of the absence of difference" from religion, and it tried to substitute the mimetic story for the sacrificial ritual, believing that sacrifices, with their reminders of violence, were a kind of barbarism. When poetry proved different in its effects from sacrifice, it had to be rejected; in fact, it had to be *sacrificed* so that the avoidance of the knowledge of evil that had led to its original substitution for ritual could be perpetuated. The price of this substitution continued to grow through the 1930s and 1940s, Tate suggests. As the attempt to "purify ourselves of the knowledge of evil" had led to a sense of general cultural contamination, the level of violence and persecution increased. Misunderstanding the causes, modernity insisted even more loudly that there was no difference between people, as if this appeal to "the intellect which weighs and discards" would save those who were victims because they were not different enough.

Jacques Derrida and others have written more recently than Tate about the role of the *pharmakos*, whose name carries the connotations both of poison and of medicine; Derrida writes in "Plato's Pharmacy" that although this victim had to be excluded from the official community of ancient Athens,

> the representative of the outside is nonetheless *constituted*, regularly granted its place by the community, chosen, kept, fed, etc., in the very heart of the inside. ... The ceremony of the *pharmakos* is thus played out on the boundary line between inside and outside, which it has as its function ceaselessly to trace and retrace. *Intra muros/extra muros.* The origin of difference and division, the *pharmakos* represents evil both introjected and projected.

The poet became the *pharmakos* because he became a kind of octoroon in a world where the elimination of differences had become doctrinal; he became unacceptable at the moment he was perceived to threaten the enlightened dream of subordinating darkness. He brought to light the inheritance of transgression— the repeated and binding history known as tradition—as an *absence of difference* from modern society. He stood there, feminized by rejection, like the great-great-granddaughter of the old incestuous transgressor, revealing the repetition in what was supposed to be the radical originality of modern "progress" out of and away from darkness. No wonder the modern world tried to get him out of the tent, crying "not loud, in a voice of amazement, pity, and outrage: 'You're a—!' "

Bodily Bonds: The Intersecting Rhetorics of Feminism and Abolition*

KAREN SÁNCHEZ-EPPLER

As Lydia Maria Child tells it in 1836, the story of the woman and the story of the slave are the same story:

> I have been told of a young physician who went into the far Southern states to settle, and there became in love with a very handsome and modest girl who lived in service. He married her; and about a year after the event a gentleman called at the house and announced himself as Mr. J. of Mobile. He said to Dr. W., "Sir, I have a trifling affair of business to settle with you. You have married a slave of mine." The young physician resented the language; for he had not entertained the slightest suspicion that the girl had any other than white ancestors since the flood. But Mr. J. furnished proofs of his claim.[1]

Convinced, and under the threat of having his wife sold at public auction, the doctor bought her for eight hundred dollars. When he informed her of the purchase, "The poor woman burst into tears and said, 'That as Mr. J. *was her own father*, she had hoped that when he heard she had found an honorable protector he would have left her in peace.'" The horror of the story lies in the perversion of an almost fairytale courtship—complete with a suitor who has traveled far, a modest girl, and love—into an economic transaction, and the perversion of the bonds of paternity into the profits of bondage. It is the collapse of the assumed difference between family and slavery that makes this anecdote so disturbing; in this story the institutions of marriage and of slavery are not merely analogous, they are coextensive and indistinguishable. The passage of the woman from father to husband and of the slave from one master to another form a single event. Not only are the new husband and the new master one man, but he needs only one name, for bourgeois idealizations of marriage and Southern apologies for slavery both consider him an honorable protector.

This merger of slavery and marriage redefines love and protection as terms of ownership, thereby identifying the modest girl, object of this love and honorable protection, as an object of transaction. Significantly, Child places the anecdote within a section of her *Anti-Slavery Catechism* that asserts the difficulty of distinguishing the bodies of slaves from the bodies of free people. Indeed the story concludes a catalogue of bodily features ("nose prominent," "tibia of the leg straight") that do not protect one from enslavement.[2] In this story the composite of bodily traits that identify a girl as marriageable proves misleading, putting into question the presumption that the body can provide reliable information about

* From Karen Sánchez-Eppler, "Bodily Bonds: The Intersecting Rhetorics of Feminism and Abolition," *Representations* 24 (fall 1988): 28–59.

1. Lydia Maria Child, *Anti-Slavery Catechism* (Newburyport, Mass., 1836), 17.
2. Ibid., 16.

the institutional and racial status of the whole person. What matters about the girl for Child's purposes is that a doctor intimately acquainted with her flesh perceives no hint of blackness.[3] If the body is an inescapable sign of identity, it is also an insecure and often illegible sign.

In Child's story the conflation of the figures of woman and slave, and of the institutions of marriage and bondage, results from difficulties in interpreting the human body. I wish to suggest that the problems of having, representing, or interpreting a body structure both feminist and abolitionist discourses, since the rhetorics of the two reforms meet upon the recognition that for both women and blacks it is their physical difference from the cultural norms of white masculinity that obstructs their claim to personhood. Thus the social and political goals of both feminism and abolition depend upon an act of representation, the inscription of black and female bodies into the discourses of personhood. Despite this similarity of aims, I find that the alliance attempted by feminist-abolitionist texts is never particularly easy or equitable. Indeed, I will argue that although the identifications of woman and slave, marriage and slavery, that characterize these texts may occasionally prove mutually empowering, they generally tend toward asymmetry and exploitation. This essay thus interrogates the intersection of feminist and abolitionist discourses through an analysis of the attitudes toward black and female bodies revealed there. The composite term that names this intersection, *feminist-abolitionist*, has come into currency with the writings of twentieth-century historians.[4] Women involved in both the abolitionist and woman's rights movements also tended to advocate temperance, oppose prostitution, and reform

3. That his confidence in her racial purity is expressed in terms of white lineage "since the flood" ridicules the most frequently deployed biblical defense of slavery, which dated the divine sanctioning of racial subjugation from the curse Noah pronounced on Ham's son Canaan (Gen. 9.25). Ham's fault, coincidentally, was the disrespect of looking upon the body of his drunken and naked father. For a discussion of the antebellum debate over the significance of this passage, see Ron Bartour, " 'Cursed be Canaan, a Servant of Servants shall he be unto his Brethren: American Views on 'Biblical Slavery,' 1835–1865, A Comparative Study," *Slavery and Abolition* 4, no. 1 (May 1983): 41–55.

4. On the simple level of events the intersections between antebellum feminism and abolition are legion: the Grimké sisters, antislavery lecturers of the 1830s, were the first women to give public lectures before "mixed" or "promiscuous" audiences, and Angelina Grimké was the first American woman to speak before a legislative body. Censured for such unfeminine activity, they increasingly addressed the issue of woman's rights within their antislavery discourse. In the 1830s and 1840s, Susan B. Anthony and Lucy Stone worked as paid agents of the American Anti-Slavery Society, lecturing both on abolition and woman's rights. Elizabeth Cady Stanton and Lucretia Mott first met at the World's Anti-Slavery Convention of 1840, at which the female delegates were refused seats; legend has it that the idea of a woman's rights convention—not realized until 1848—was first discussed in the London hotel rooms of these excluded women. For varying accounts of the relation between the two movements see Ellen DuBois, "Women's Rights and Abolition: The Nature of the Connection," in Lewis Perry and Michael Fellman, eds., *Antislavery Reconsidered: New Perspectives on the Abolitionists* (Baton Rouge, La., 1979); and DuBois, *Feminism and Suffrage: The Emergence of an Independent Women's Movement in America, 1848–1869* (Ithaca, N.Y., 1978); Blanche Glassman Hersh, *The Slavery of Sex: Feminist-Abolitionists in America* (Urbana, Ill., 1978); and Gerda Lerner, *The Grimké Sisters from South Carolina: Pioneers for Woman's Rights and Abolition* (New York, 1971).

schools, prisons, and diets; they referred to themselves as "universal reformers." My use of the term *feminist-abolitionist* is thus an anachronistic convenience, the hyphen neatly articulating the very connections and distinctions that I intend to explore. I will therefore focus on those writings in which the rhetorical crossings of women and slaves predominate: the political speeches and pamphlets that equate the figure of the woman and the figure of the slave; the sentimental novels and giftbook stories in which antislavery women attempt to represent the slave and more obliquely depict their own fears and desires, so that the racial and the sexual come to displace one another; and the more conservative Sunday-school primers that, in trying to domesticate slavery, recast its oppressions in familial terms, demonstrating the complicity of the two institutions and hence the degree to which domestic and sentimental antislavery writings are implicated in the very oppressions they seek to reform.

Feminists and abolitionists were acutely aware of the dependence of personhood on the condition of the human body since the political and legal subordination of both women and slaves was predicated upon biology. Medical treatises of the period consistently assert that a woman's psyche and intellect are determined by her reproductive organs.[5] Indeed, to the political satirist the leaders of the woman's rights movement are nothing but wombs in constant danger of parturition:

> How funny it would sound in the newspapers, that Lucy Stone, pleading a cause, took suddenly ill in the pains of parturition, and perhaps gave birth to a fine bouncing boy in court; or that Rev. Antonia Brown was arrested in the middle of her sermon in the pulpit from the same cause, and presented a "pledge" to her husband and the congregation. . . . A similar event might happen on the floor of Congress, in a storm at sea, or in the raging tempest of battle, and then what is to become of the woman legislator?[6]

In this lampoon the reproductive function interrupts and replaces women's attempts to speak; their public delivery of arguments, sermons, and service is superseded by delivery of children. The joke betrays male fear of female fertility while fashioning the woman's womb and its relentless fecundity into a silencing gag.

The body of the black was similarly thought to define his role as servant and laborer. Subservience, one Southern doctor explained, was built into the very structure of his bones. The black was made "submissive knee-bender" by the decree of the Almighty, for "in the anatomical conformation of his knees, we see 'genu flexit' written in his physical structure, being more flexed or bent than any

---

5. Carroll Smith-Rosenberg, "Puberty to Menopause: The Cycle of Femininity in Nineteenth-Century America," in *Disorderly Conduct: Visions of Gender in Victorian America* (New York, 1985).

6. Included in Aileen S. Kraditor, *Up from the Pedestal: Selected Writings in the History of American Feminism* (Chicago, 1968), 190–91. This fantasy was published as an editorial in the *Herald*, thus fulfilling its own gleeful wishes.

other kind of man."[7] As God writes "subservience" upon the body of the black, in Latin of course, the doctor reads it; or, more crudely, as the master inscribes his name with hot irons ("He is *branded on the forehead* with the letters A. M. and *on each cheek* with the letters J. G."), or the fact of slavery with scars ("His back shows *lasting impressions of the whip*, and leaves no doubt of his being a *slave*"), the body of the slave attains the status of a text.[8] Thus the bodies of women and slaves were read against them, so that for both the human body was seen to function as the foundation not only of a general subjection but also of a specific exclusion from political discourse. For women and slaves the ability to speak was predicated upon the reinterpretation of their flesh. Feminists and abolitionists share a strategy: to invert patriarchal readings and so reclaim the body. Transformed from a silent site of oppression into a symbol of that oppression, the body becomes within both feminist and abolitionist discourses a means of gaining rhetorical force.

Though the female body, and particularly female sexual desires, as I hope to demonstrate, are at least covertly inscribed within feminist-abolitionist texts, the paradigmatic body reclaimed in these writings is that of the slave. The slave, so explicitly an object to be sold, provides feminism as well as abolition with its most graphic example of the extent to which the human body may designate identity. "The denial of our duty to act [against slavery] is a denial of our right to act," wrote Angelina Grimké in 1837, "and if we have no right to act then may *we* well be termed the 'white slaves of the North' for like our brethren in bonds, we must seal our lips in silence and despair."[9] As I have already suggested, the alliance between black bodies and female bodies achieved by the rhetorical crossing of feminist-abolitionist texts was not necessarily equitable. By identifying with the slave, and by insisting on the muteness of the slave, Grimké asserts her right to act and speak, thus differentiating herself from her brethren in bonds. The bound and silent figure of the slave metaphorically represents the woman's oppression and so grants the white woman an access to political discourse denied the slave,

---

7. The diagnosis is that of Dr. Samuel A. Cartwright in "Diseases and Peculiarities of the Negro Race," *De Bow's Review* (1851), excerpted in James O. Breeden, ed., *Advice Among Masters: The Ideal in Slave Management in the Old South* (Westport, Conn., 1980), 173. Breeden identifies Cartwright as among the "leading scientific spokesmen" of "the campaign to defend the South's sectional interests and to promote southern nationalism" and thus a consciously biased interpreter of anatomy.

8. Lydia Maria Child included these quotations along with many similar items gleaned from the Southern press in *The Patriarchal Institution as Described by Members of Its Own Family* (New York, 1860), 13, 11. She added the italics as a form of commentary. The first quote mentioned here is cited by Child from an advertisement for the runaway slave of Anthony M. Minter [A.M.] in the *Free Press* (Alabama), 18 September 1846. She takes the second from an advertisement posted by John A. Rowland, jailer, to publicize his capture of a presumed runaway, in the Fayetteville, North Carolina, *Observer*, 20 June 1838.

9. Angelina Grimké, *An Appeal to the Women of the Nominally Free States: Issued by an Anti-Slavery Convention of American Women Held by Adjournment from the 9th to the 12th of May 1837* (New York, 1837).

exemplifying the way in which slave labor produces—both literally and meta-phorically—even the most basic of freedom's privileges.[10]

In feminist writings the metaphoric linking of women and slaves proves ubiq-uitous: marriage and property laws, the conventional adoption of a husband's name, or even the length of fashionable skirts are explained and decried by ref-erence to women's "slavery."[11] This strategy serves to emphasize the restrictions of woman's sphere, and, despite luxuries and social civilities, to class the bourgeois woman among the oppressed. Sarah Grimké, beginning her survey of the con-dition of women with ancient history, notes that "the cupidity of man soon led him to regard woman as property, and hence we find them sold to those who wished to marry them," while within marriage, as defined by nineteenth-century laws of coverture, "the very being of a woman, like that of a slave, is absorbed in her master."[12] "A woman," Elizabeth Cady Stanton explains to the Woman's Rights Convention of 1856, "has no name! She is Mrs. John or James, Peter or Paul, just as she changes masters; like the Southern slave, she takes the name of her owner."[13] The image of the slave evoked not simply the loss of "liberty" but the loss of all claims to self-possession. At stake in the feminists' likening of women to slaves is the recognition that personhood can be annihilated and a person owned, absorbed, and un-named. The irony inherent in such comparisons is that the enlightening and empowering motions of identification that connect feminism and abolition come inextricably bound to a process of absorption not unlike the one that they expose. Though the metaphoric linking of women and slaves uses their shared position as bodies to be bought, owned, and designated as a grounds of resistance, it nevertheless obliterates the particularity of black and female experience, making their distinct exploitations appear as one. The difficulty of preventing moments of identification from becoming acts of appropriation con-stitutes the essential dilemma of feminist-abolitionist rhetoric.

The body of the woman and the body of the slave need not, of course, only merge through metaphor, and it is hardly surprising that the figure of the female slave features prominently in both discourses. Yet even in the case of the literally enslaved woman, the combining of feminist and abolitionist concerns supports both reciprocal and appropriative strategies. The difference between the stereo-

10. For a more general analysis of how the idealization of freedom that characterizes Western thought relies upon the historical and factual presence of slavery, see Orlando Patterson, *Slavery and Social Death* (Cambridge, Mass., 1982).

11. See Hersh, *Slavery of Sex*, chaps. 1, 2, and 6 for a summary of the analogies drawn by feminist abolitionists. Examples of the first two follow; a more frivolous example of the analogy can be found in Amelia Bloomer's defense of the short skirts and pantaloons that carry her name: "I suppose in this respect we are more mannish, for we know that in dress as in all things else, we have been and are slaves, while man in dress and all things else is free."

12. Sarah Grimké, *Letters on the Equality of the Sexes and the Condition of Women: Addressed to Mary S. Parker, President of the Boston Female Anti-Slavery Society* (Boston, 1838), 13, 75.

13. Elizabeth Cady Stanton to the National Woman's Rights Convention, Cooper Institute, dated Seneca Falls, New York, 24 November 1856, included in the appendices of *The History of Woman Suffrage*, ed. Elizabeth Cady Stanton, Susan B. Anthony, and Matilda Joslyn Gage, 6 vols. (New York, 1881), 1:860.

typic cultural conceptions of black and female bodies was such that in the crossing of feminist and abolitionist rhetoric the status of the slave and the status of the woman could both be improved by an alliance with the body of the other. Their two sorts of bodies were prisons in different ways, and for each the prison of the other was liberating. So for the female slave, the frail body of the bourgeois lady promised not weakness but the modesty and virtue of a delicacy at once supposed physical and moral. Concern for the roughness and impropriety with which slave women were treated redefined their suffering as feminine, and hence endowed with all the moral value generally attributed to nineteenth-century American womanhood.[14] Conversely, for the nineteenth-century woman there were certain assets to be claimed from the body of the slave. "Those who think the physical circumstances of women would make a part in the affairs of national government unsuitable," Margaret Fuller argues, "are by no means those who think it impossible for Negresses to endure field work even during pregnancy."[15] The strength to plant, and hoe, and pick, and endure is available to the urban middle-class woman insofar as she can be equated with the laboring slave woman, and that equation suggests the possibility of reshaping physical circumstances. Fuller's words provide a perfect example of the chiasmic alignment of abolition and woman's rights, for though embedded within a discussion devoted to feminist concerns this passage achieves a double efficacy, simultaneously declaring the physical strength of the woman and implying the need to protect the exploited slave.[16]

Just as the figure of the female slave served feminist rhetorical purposes, she also proved useful in abolitionist campaigns and was frequently employed to at-

14. See Barbara Welter, "The Cult of True Womanhood, 1820–1860," *American Quarterly* 18, no. 2 (Summer 1966): 151–74; and Barbara J. Berg, "Towards the Woman-Belle Ideal," in *The Remembered Gate: Origins of American Feminism, The Woman and the City, 1800–1860* (New York, 1978), for compendiums of all the virtues a "True Woman" was expected to possess. It is worth noting that one of the charges consistently brought against the Grimké sisters' antislavery lectures was that of indelicacy. In their Pastoral Letter (Boston, 1837), directed at the Grimkés, the Massachusetts Congregationalist clergy "especially deplore the intimate acquaintance and promiscuous conversation of females with regard to things 'which ought not to be mentioned.' " The unmentionables, of course, were the rape and concubinage of slave women, and the nullity of slave marriage. See Kraditor, *Up from the Pedestal*, 51–52; and Sarah Grimké's response to the pastoral letter in the third of her *Letters on the Equality of the Sexes.*

15. Margaret Fuller, "Woman in the Nineteenth Century" (1844), in *The Writings of Margaret Fuller*, ed. Mason Wade (New York, 1941), 123.

16. The most famous instance of this turn is Sojourner Truth's refrain "a'n't I a woman" at the Akron Woman's Rights Convention on 29 May 1851.

"Dat man ober dar say dat womin needs to be helped into carriages, and lifted ober ditches, and to hab de best place everywhar. Nobody eber helps me into carriages, or ober mud-puddles, or gibs me any best place!" And raising herself to her full height, and her voice to a pitch like rolling thunder, she asked, "And a'n't I a woman? Look at me! Look at my arm! (and she bared her right arm to the shoulder, showing her tremendous muscular power)."

For this audience her body makes her argument. "Reminiscences of Frances D. Gage: Sojourner Truth," in Stanton, Anthony, and Gage, *History of Woman Suffrage*, 1:116.

tract women to abolitionist work. William Lloyd Garrison, for example, headed the "Ladies Department" of the *Liberator* with the picture of a black woman on her knees and in chains; beneath it ran the plea, "Am I not a woman and a sister?" Such tactics did not attempt to identify woman's status with that of the slave but rather relied upon the ties of sisterly sympathy, presuming that one woman would be particularly sensitive to the sufferings of another. Indeed such a strategy emphasized the difference between the free woman's condition and the bondage of the slave, since it was this difference that enabled the free woman to work for her sister's emancipation.

The particular horror and appeal of the slave woman lay in the magnitude of her sexual vulnerability, and the Ladies Department admonished its female readers to work for the immediate emancipation of their one million enslaved sisters "exposed to all the violence of lust and passion—and treated with more indelicacy and cruelty than cattle."[17] The sexual exploitation of female slaves served abolitionists as a proof that slave owners laid claim not merely to the slave's time, labor, and obedience—assets purchased, after all, with the wages paid by the Northern industrialist—but to their flesh. The abolitionist comparison of slave and cattle, like the feminist analogy between woman and slave, marks the slip from person to chattel.[18] More startling than the comparison of the slave to a cow, however, is the Ladies Department's equation of "indelicacy" with "cruelty," for set beside the menace of brandings, whippings, beatings, and starvation, rudeness seems an insignificant care. This concern with indelicacy becomes explicable, however, in terms of the overlap of feminist and abolitionist discourses. To the male abolitionist the application of those notions of modesty and purity that governed the world of nineteenth-century ladies to the extremely different situation of the slave must have seemed a useful strategy for gaining female support on an economic, political, and hence unfeminine issue. Viewed from this perspective the language of feminine modesty simply reinforces traditional female roles. Even here, however, the emphasis on sexual exploitation suggests that the abolitionist's easy differentiation between the free woman and the enslaved one may conceal grounds of identification. For in stressing the aspect of slavery that would seem most familiar to a female readership, the abolitionist press implicitly suggests that the Ladies Department's readers may be bound like the slaves they are urged to free.

As the examples of the Grimkés and Stanton demonstrate, feminist-abolitionists emphasize the similarities in the condition of women and slaves; nevertheless, their treatment of the figure of the sexually exploited female slave betrays an opposing desire to deny any share in this vulnerability. The same metaphoric

17. *Liberator*, 7 January 1832, as quoted by Hersh, *Slavery of Sex*, 10–11.
18. Whether Garrison knew it or not, there is no etymological slippage at all, as *cattle* refers not only to the bovine but more generally to "moveable property or wealth," that is, to chattel: both forms derive from *capitale*. *Capital* is accumulated currency, "stock in trade," and the classification of slaves as livestock recognizes that their status as things (however vital) implies exchangeability. The evolving connotations of these words encapsulate centuries of economic history, which my discussion collapses and necessarily simplifies. See the *OED*, s.v. "cattle."

structure that enables the identification of women and slaves also proves capable of serving the antithetical purpose of precluding such identification. Thus in the writings of antislavery women the frequent emphasis on the specifically feminine trial of sexual abuse serves to project the white woman's sexual anxieties onto the sexualized body of the female slave. Concern over the slave woman's sexual victimization displaces the free woman's fear of confronting the sexual elements of her own bodily experience, either as a positive force or as a mechanism of oppression. The prevalence of such fear is illustrated by the caution with which even the most radical feminist thinkers avoid public discussion of "woman's rights in marriage"; it is only in their private correspondence that the leaders of the women's rights movement allude to sexual rights. "It seems to me that we are not ready" to bring this issue before the 1856 convention. Lucy Stone writes to Susan B. Anthony:

> No two of us think alike about it, and yet it is clear to me that question underlies the whole movement and all our little skirmishing for better laws and the right to vote, will yet be swallowed up in the real question viz.: Has woman a right to herself? It is very little to me to have the right to vote, to own property, etc., if I may not keep my body, and its uses, in my absolute right. Not one wife in a thousand can do that now.[19]

The figure of the slave woman, whose inability to keep her body and its uses under her own control is widely and openly recognized, becomes a perfect conduit for the unarticulated and unacknowledged failure of the free woman to own her own body in marriage. In one sense, then, it is the very indelicacy of the slave woman's position that makes her a useful proxy in such indelicate matters.

Garrison's Ladies Department attests to the importance of women to the antislavery movement. In 1832 the Boston Female Anti-Slavery Society was founded as an "auxiliary" to the all male New England Anti-Slavery Society. By 1838 there were forty-one female auxiliary societies in Massachusetts alone.[20] The function of these auxiliaries was to provide support—mostly in the form of fundraising—for the work of the male organizations. Thus the auxiliaries behaved much like other female philanthropic or benevolence societies, and most of the women who worked in them gave no public speeches, wrote no political pamphlets, and did not see their antislavery activities as challenging the traditions of male authority and female domesticity. Nevertheless, in their work against slavery these female societies transformed conventional womanly activities into tools of political persuasion, "presenting," as Angelina Grimké explains, the slave's "kneeling image constantly before the public eye." Toward this end they stitched the pathetic figure of the manacled slave onto bags, pincushions, and pen wipers ("Even the

---

19. Quoted by Hersh, *Slavery of Sex*, 66, from Lucy Stone's letter to Susan B. Anthony dated 11 September 1856.
20. Hersh, *Slavery of Sex*, 16; her figures are taken from the records of the Massachusetts society. Angelina Grimké asserted in 1836 that there were a total of sixty female antislavery societies in the Northern states, though I have found no other evidence to corroborate this figure; *Appeal to the Christian Women of the South* (New York, 1836), 23.

children of the north are inscribing on their handiwork, 'May the points of our needles prick the slaveholders' conscience' "), and wrote virtually all of the sentimental tales that describe the slaves' sufferings.[21]

In many ways, then, the antislavery stories that abolitionist women wrote for Sunday-school primers, juvenile miscellanies, antislavery newspapers, and giftbooks need to be assessed as a variety of female handiwork, refashioned for political, didactic, and pecuniary purposes. The genre is fundamentally feminine: not only were these stories—like virtually all the domestic and sentimental fiction of the period—primarily penned by women, but, beyond this, women largely controlled their production, editing the giftbooks and miscellanies that contained them, and publishing many of these volumes under the auspices of female anti-slavery societies.[22] The most substantial and longest-lived abolitionist publishing endeavor of this type, the Boston Female Anti-Slavery Society's annual giftbook the *Liberty Bell*, provides the most obvious illustration of these practices, and one that subsequent antislavery collections sought to imitate.[23] In their efforts to raise

21. Grimké, *Appeal to the Christian Women of the South,* 23. Her list of antislavery handiwork includes card racks and needle books as well as all those items listed in the text. This fairly conservative portrait of female antislavery societies, though accurate in its depiction of the majority of the women involved in antislavery work, does not necessarily characterize all of the authors whose stories I will be discussing here, just as it does not fit the Grimkés and other public lecturers and political organizers cited above. In particular, Lydia Maria Child and Carolyn Wells Healey Dall saw their fiction writing as a distinctly political, indeed revolutionary, form of action. Nevertheless, women lecturers urged this more conventional form of political activity on their female audiences, and less daring women constituted the major readership for all of these stories as well as the authors of many of them.

22. There has as yet been no systematic study of the history of antislavery stories. Carolyn Karcher postulates that Child's story "The St. Domingo Orphans," published in her *Juvenile Miscellany* for September of 1830, may well initiate the genre. Though antislavery stories appeared in the *Liberator* from 1831 and in many other antislavery papers, the major forum for their publication was provided by giftbooks and collections of literature for children, since these permitted more lengthy narrations than most newspapers could afford. The earliest antislavery giftbook of which I am aware—*Oasis* (1834)—was produced by Child; it contained mostly her own stories, accompanying them with two articles by her husband, David Child, and a handful of disparate pieces by abolitionist friends. Later antislavery giftbooks, and most notably the *Liberty Bell* (1839–58), follow this model of female production and control. Male contributors to such collections, even though they constituted a large percentage of the authors, supplied argumentative pieces and poetry but rarely stories. For example, while two-thirds of the over two hundred contributors to the *Liberty Bell* were men, only two (Edmund Quincy and a presumably male, anonymous "a Southron") wrote stories. Karcher suggests, and my own findings support this, that the antislavery stories written by men generally differ from those by women in thematic terms: men's tend to focus more on slave rebellions than on sexual exploitation, while in women's stories miscegenation, concubinage, rape, and—I would add—the break-up of families predominate, with slave rebellions occupying a more peripheral position. The thematics of escape is shared by both sexes. There are, of course, individual instances that contradict these generalizations. See Carolyn Karcher, "Rape, Murder, and Revenge in 'Slavery's Pleasant Homes': Lydia Maria Child's Antislavery Fiction and the Limits of Genre," *Women's Studies International Forum* 9 (Fall 1986): 323–32.

23. Most obvious among these followers is *Liberty Chimes,* published in 1845 by the Ladies Anti-Slavery Society of Providence, Rhode Island. But also see the somewhat more successful giftbook

funds the Boston auxiliary organized an Anti-Slavery Fair, and it was for the sixth fair, as a further educational and fundraising gesture, that the *Liberty Bell* was published. Under Maria Weston Chapman's skillful editorial hands it appeared at virtually every fair from 1839 to 1858, to be sold alongside the quilts and jams.[24] The minutes of the committee for the tenth Anti-Slavery Fair claimed that the *Liberty Bell* "always doubles the money invested in it." Since the cost of producing the volume was three to four hundred dollars (covered by donations drawn largely from among the contributors), the committee's claim would assess the *Liberty Bell* at slightly less than a fifth of the fair's average proceeds of four thousand dollars a year.[25] One important feature of the tales published in the *Liberty Bell*, then, was that they were considered saleable. The depiction of the slave was thought to have its own market value. The reasons the volumes sold, moreover, appear paradoxically at odds both with each other and with abolitionist beliefs. On the one hand the horrific events narrated in these tales attract precisely to the extent that the buyers of these representations of slavery are fascinated by the abuses they ostensibly oppose. For despite their clear abolitionist stance such stories are fueled by the allure of bondage, an appeal which suggests that the valuation of depictions of slavery may rest upon the same psychic ground as slaveholding itself. On the other hand, the acceptability of these tales depends upon their adherence to a feminine and domestic demeanor that softens the cruelty

---

Autographs of Freedom, edited by Julia Griffith for the Rochester, New York, Ladies Auxiliary in 1853 and 1854; it is unique in containing a number of pieces by exslaves, including Frederick Douglass, and for the closing of each selection with a facsimile of the author's signature—hence the title. Antislavery giftbooks were also occasionally produced by men; for example, Richard Sutton Rost compiled *Freedom's Gift* (Hartford, Conn., 1840) predominantly as a showcase for William Lloyd Garrison; many of the poems and fictional pieces, however, were contributed by women.

24. Before 1846 they were known as the "Massachusetts Anti-Slavery Fair," then from 1847 until their replacement by "soirées" in 1858 they were more grandly entitled the "National Anti-Slavery Bazaar." In 1839, the first *Liberty Bell* was released on 29 October, but the fair and publication were subsequently moved to the more lucrative Christmas season, and later editions are all dated in early December. The only missed years were 1840, 1850, 1854, 1855, and 1857; so a total of fifteen volumes were published, all except the last (which reprinted some earlier selections) consisting entirely of new material. See Ralph Thompson, "The *Liberty Bell* and Other Anti-Slavery Gift-Books," *New England Quarterly* 7, no. 1 (March 1934): 154–68. The relation between the *Liberty Bell* and other sale items is nicely illustrated by "An English Child's Notion of the Inferiority of the Colored Population in America," in which a mother recounts her daughter's explanation of the words this five-year-old had stitched on a sampler she was making for the Boston fair. The child sent her sampler, the mother sent this anecdote—presumably accompanied by her own needlework; *Liberty Bell* 8 (1847): 49.

25. The average of the fair's profits is taken from Jane H. Pease and William H. Pease, "The Boston Bluestocking, Maria Weston Chapman," in *Bound with Them in Chains: A Biographical History of the Anti-Slavery Movement* (Westport, Conn., 1972), 45; and the information on the finances of the *Liberty Bell* from Thompson, "*Liberty Bell* and Other Gift-Books," 158–59. Thompson queries the committee's boast, arguing that many volumes were distributed free of cost and hence at a loss, but even if the committee's figures are inflated there is no reason to believe that the books were not economically successful, especially considering that the cost of each printing was donated.

they describe and makes their political goals more palatable to a less politicized readership. Chapman, explaining the success of the *Liberty Bell*, admits as much, suggestively presenting her giftbook as a mother who treats the public "like children, to whom a medicine is made as pleasant as its nature permits. A childish mind receives a small measure of truth in gilt edges where it would reject it in 'whity-brown.' "[26] Though plain by giftbook standards, the embossed leather and gilded edges of the *Liberty Bell* permitted it to fit without apparent incongruity into any household library. Despite their subject matter, the antislavery stories it contained attempt a similar and uneasy compliance with the conventions that governed nineteenth-century domestic fiction. The contradictory nature of antislavery fiction's appeal thus raises more general questions about what it means to depict slavery, and hence about the politics and power of representation.

Critics have frequently argued that sentimental fiction provides an inappropriate vehicle for the project of educating the public to slavery's real terrors.[27] This criticism, however, simply echoes the authors' own anxieties about the realism of the stories they tell. Almost every antislavery story begins by citing its source: a meeting with the hero or heroine, an account of the events in the newspaper, or most often and simply just having been told.[28] "The truth of incidents" claimed in Harriet Beecher Stowe's preface to *Uncle Tom's Cabin* is documented by her subsequently published *Key* to the novel—the genre's most sustained and impressive attempt to demonstrate its veracity. But her very effort to prove that her novel is "a collection and arrangement of real incidents . . . a mosaic of facts" propounds the difference between her narrative and her key to it, since "slavery, in some of its workings, is too dreadful for the purposes of art. A work which

---

26. Quoted by Pease and Pease, "Maria Weston Chapman," 34–35, from a letter by Chapman dated 27 January 1846.

27. The point, of course, is that the sentimentality required by genre necessarily undermines any aspirations toward realism. For a far more sophisticated and interesting variation on this critique see Walter Benn Michaels, "Romance and Real Estate," in *The American Renaissance Reconsidered: Selected Papers from the English Institute, 1982–83*, ed. Michaels and Donald Pease (Baltimore, 1985), in which he argues that Stowe's claims to realism mask an essentially romantic belief in inalienable property.

28. The examples are endless, but to choose three from the stories discussed in this paper: Frances Green's "The Slave-Wife," in *Liberty Chimes* (Providence, R. I., 1845), is presented as told by a friend who met Laco Ray, the slave husband, after his escape to Canada. Reprinting "Mary French and Susan Easton" anonymously in *The Slave's Friend* (New York, 1836), Lydia Maria Child added this italicized introduction: *"Perhaps some of my little readers may remember seeing, about a year and a half ago, advertisements in the newspapers,"* "Mark and Hasty" by Matilda G. Thompson, in *The Child's Anti-Slavery Book* (New York, 1859) is prefaced with a note that the "facts" of this St. Louis story "were communicated to the author by a friend residing temporarily in that city." Fiction had, of course, long been viewed with suspicion in Puritan America, and the practice of defending tales with the claim that they were "founded on fact" had become, by the eighteenth century, a conventional attribute of all storytelling. Because, however, antislavery stories proposed to alter attitudes and behavior—to change the facts of American slavery—their claims to a factual basis served a double purpose, countering not only the general prejudice against frivolous or decadent fictionality but also the more specific charge that fiction had no bearing on political realities.

should represent it strictly as it is, would be a work which could not be read."[29] The reading of these stories, and therefore both their marketability and their political efficacy, depends upon their success in rearranging the real. The decision to rearrange it into sentimental tales, I will argue, is highly appropriate, not only because of the dominance of the form during the period, nor simply because of its popular appeal and consequent market value, but also because sentimental fiction constitutes an intensely bodily genre. The concern with the human body as site and symbol of the self that links the struggles of feminists and abolitionists also informs the genre in which nineteenth-century women wrote their anti-slavery stories.

The tears of the reader are pledged in these sentimental stories as a means of rescuing the bodies of slaves. Emblematic of this process, Child's story of "Mary French and Susan Easton" relates how the white Mary, kidnapped, stained black, and sold into slavery, is quite literally freed by weeping; her true identity revealed because "where the tears had run down her cheeks, there was a streak whiter than the rest of her face."[30] Her weeping obliterates the differential of color and makes Mary white, thereby asserting the power of sentiment to change the condition of the human body or at least, read symbolically, to alter how that condition is perceived. The ability of sentimental fiction to liberate the bodies of slaves is, moreover, intimately connected to the bodily nature of the genre itself. Sentiment and feeling refer at once to emotion and to physical sensation, and in sentimental fiction these two versions of *sentire* blend as the eyes of readers take in the printed word and blur it with tears. Reading sentimental fiction is thus a bodily act, and the success of a story is gauged, in part, by its ability to translate words into pulse beats and sobs. This physicality of the reading experience radically contracts the distance between narrated events and the moment of their reading, as the feelings in the story are made tangibly present in the flesh of the reader. In particular tears designate a border realm between the story and its reading, since the tears shed by characters initiate an answering moistness in the reader's eye.[31] The as-

29. Harriet Beecher Stowe, *Uncle Tom's Cabin* (New York, 1982), preface, 10; Stowe, *A Key to Uncle Tom's Cabin,* in *The Writings of Harret Beecher Stowe,* 16 vols. (Boston, 1896). 2:255–56. My evocation of Stowe here, and throughout this paper, is admittedly opportunistic, as her position within the contemporary critical canon allows me to assume a familiarity with the problematics of her work obviously lacking for most of the other texts I cite. Thus her more accessible and discussed novels provide a way into the issues confronted in their more obscure precursors, and a means of situating these stories within contemporary critical discourse. An implicit assumption in my work, moreover, is that Stowe's achievement needs to be read and evaluated within a genre of antislavery fiction initiated at least two decades before the success of *Uncle Tom's Cabin.* In adopting this approach I will deemphasize the importance of distinguishing between novel and story, at least for the issues of corporeality and the effort to redefine personhood with which I am here concerned; the anecdotal structure of Stowe's novels, with their focus on repeated and distinct tableaus, diminishes the violence of this critical strategy.

30. Lydia Maria Child, "Mary French and Susan Easton," *Juvenile Miscellany,* 3rd ser., no. 6 (May 1834): 196.

31. In *"Cage aux folles*: Sensation and Gender in Wilkie Collins's *The Woman in White." Represen-tations* 14 (Spring 1986): 107–36, D. A. Miller argues that the nervous sensations that characterize the reading of sensation novels are associated, within the novels themselves, with femininity. This

surance in this fiction that emotion can be attested and measured by physical response makes this conflation possible; the palpability of the character's emotional experience is precisely what allows it to be shared. In sentimental fiction bodily signs are adamantly and repeatedly presented as the preferred and most potent mechanisms both for communicating meaning and for marking the fact of its transmission.[32]

Sentimental narrative functions through stereotypes, so that upon first encountering a character there is no difficulty in ascertaining his or her moral worth. In sentimental writing the self is externally displayed, and the body provides a reliable sign of who one is. Nina Gordon, the heroine of *Dred* (Stowe's other antislavery novel), develops an instinctive goodness more potent than her lover Edward Clayton's principled virtue. In her instantaneous and unproblematic discrimination of good from evil, Nina provides a paradigm for reading the novel that contains her.

> Looking back almost fiercely, a moment, she turned and said to Clayton:
> "I hate that man!"
> "Who is it?" said Clayton.
> "I don't know!" said Nina. "I never saw him before. But I hate him! He is a bad man! I'd as soon have a serpent come near me as that man!"
> "Well, the poor fellow's face isn't prepossessing," said Clayton. "But I should not be prepared for such an anathema. . . . How can you be so positive about a person you've only seen once!" . . .
> "Oh," said Nina, resuming her usual gay tones, "don't you know that girls and dogs, and other inferior creatures, have the gift of seeing what's in people? It doesn't belong to highly cultivated folks like you, but to us poor creatures, who have to trust to our instincts. So, beware!"[33]

Skill in reading the body of the stranger belongs not to the highly cultivated man who talks of what is prepossessing and what an anathema but to girls who hate and will call a man bad. To Nina Mr. Jekyl's face is "very repulsive," and in feeling herself repelled, pushed away by his visage, she weighs the evidence of

---

insight and the implications Miller elaborates from it prove equally suggestive for the similarly gendered weeping that characterizes the reading of sentimental fiction. The gendering of physical response in sentimental and sensation fiction bears, however, somewhat different meanings. For while the feminine nervousness instigated by thrillers produces the confinement and incarceration of femininity, the tears ushered by sentimental fiction flow outward as mechanisms of escape.

32. Analyzing the "power" of *Uncle Tom's Cabin,* Jane Tompkins finds that in sentimental fiction "not words, but the emotions of the heart bespeak a state of grace, and these are known by the sound of a voice, the touch of a hand, but chiefly in moments of greatest importance, by tears." Tompkins is most centrally interested in that "state of grace" expressed by emotions that are themselves spoken through bodily signs. So in her catalogue of scenes marked by weeping Tompkins defends these tears in terms of the message of "salvation, communion, reconciliation" that they suggest; in contrast, I am concerned here less with what the tears may say than with Stowe's recourse to bodily symptoms as the most efficacious means of saying it. Tompkins, "Sentimental Power: *Uncle Tom's Cabin* and the Politics of Literary History," in *Sensational Designs: The Cultural Work of American Fiction, 1790–1860* (New York, 1985), 131–32.

33. Harriet Beecher Stowe, *Dred: A Tale of the Great Dismal Swamp,* in *Writings,* 3:190–91.

his character in the reaction of her body to his body. Jokingly shared with dogs, the girl's capacity to read signs by instinct is as physical as the traits it correctly interprets. The succeeding chapters prove the adequacy of Nina's reaction to Mr. Jekyl, and so endorse her and the sentimental novel's mechanisms of assessment.[34]

Nina Gordon is the ideal reader of all sentimental fiction, not simply of antislavery tales, but her ability to read bodies correctly is more important for antislavery fiction, where the physical vocabulary has been suddenly enlarged to include very different looking bodies, making the interpretative task more difficult. The problem, for the antislavery writer, lies in depicting a black body that can be instantly recognized not only as a loyal or a rebellious servant but as a hero or a heroine. Stowe introduces Dred:

> He was a tall black man, of magnificent stature and proportions. His skin was intensely black, and polished like marble. A loose shirt of red flannel, which opened very wide at the breast, gave a display of a neck and chest of herculean strength. The sleeves of the shirt, rolled up nearly to the shoulders, showed the muscles of a gladiator. The head, which rose with an imperial air from the broad shoulders, was large and massive, and developed with equal force both in the reflective and perceptive department. The perceptive organs jutted like dark ridges over the eyes, while that part of the head which phrenologists attribute to moral and intellectual sentiments rose like an ample dome above them.[35]

A magnificent, herculean, and imperial gladiator—with these words Stowe arrays Dred in the vocabulary of classical heroism. That gladiators were also slaves only strengthens the claims Stowe desires to make for this slave. The density of such terms, however, equally evinces her sense of the difficulty of granting and sustaining Dred's heroic status. She therefore supplements her attempt to fashion Dred into a polished black marble icon of classical heroism with the pseudoscientific language of phrenology. The phrenologist, like the reader of sentimental fiction, reads internal characteristics from the external signs offered by the body. By enlisting the phrenologist in her descriptive task, Stowe garners the authority of study for what she has previously presented as instinctual knowledge. Her need for these multiple buttresses attests to the frailty of this structure. The precariousness of Dred's heroic stature is all the more telling because in Stowe's description the heroic and the phrenological have combined to present him less as a man than as a monument. A structure of magnificent proportions crowned by an ample dome, this massive figure of polished marble achieves a truly architectural splendor. In this description Stowe has not so much described Dred as built his body.

34. *The Slave's Friend*, a penny monthly for children published in New York by the American Anti-Slavery Society from 1836 to 1838, makes its lessons in reading more explicit. The first article of the first number of the 1837 edition follows a picture of two girls—one black and one white—peering together at a large book with three pages of detailed analysis explaining how to interpret the scene. It concludes by pointing to the dog in the lower corner of the print and informing its young readers that "when you see a dog in a picture like this, it is an emblem, or sign of Fidelity" (3). The signs are sure; one need only learn the vocabulary.

35. Stowe, *Dred*, 247–48.

Stowe's difficulty in creating a slave hero is best demonstrated, however, not by the body she constructs him in but by the features she silently omits. For though Stowe describes Dred as having eyes of that "unfathomable blackness and darkness which is often a striking characteristic of the African eye," she avoids detailing the rest of his visage. In "The Slave-Wife," Frances Green, less sensitive to the racism that underlies this dilemma, gives her hero, Laco Ray, a face that exemplifies Stowe's problem:

> Tall, muscular, and every way well-proportioned, he had the large expansion of chest and shoulders that are seen in the best representation of Hercules. He was quite black, the skin soft and glossy; but the features had none of the revolting characteristics which are supposed by some to be inseparable from the African visage. On the contrary they were remarkably fine—the nose aquiline—the mouth even handsome—the forehead singularly high and broad.[36]

Green's Laco Ray inhabits in 1845 virtually the same body Stowe gives to Dred in 1856, confirming the genre's reliance on stereotypes: every hero, even a black one, is simply another in a familiar series of "best representations of Hercules." In making her black Hercules, however, Green registers her need to reject "the revolting characteristics" of nose, mouth, and brow that she criticizes others for supposing "inseparable from the African visage." Her desire to separate them is, obviously, as suspect as the assumption of their inseparability. Her own insecurity about attaining such a separation betrays itself in adverbs as she constantly modifies her description to emphasize its unexpectedness: *remarkably* fine, *even* handsome, *singularly* high and broad; what she finds most exceptional about Laco Ray's features is that they belong to him. Making a black hero involves not only dyeing the traditional figure of the hero to a darker hue but also separating blackness from the configuration of traits that in the bodily grammar of sentimental fiction signals revulsion. In replacing or omitting revolting features, both Green and Stowe remake the black body in order to mold the slave into a hero. These features revolt, moreover, not only because they fail to conform to white criteria for beauty but, more interestingly, because they threaten to overturn sentimental fiction's stable matrix of bodily signs.

The project of depicting the body of the sympathetic black thus becomes a project of racial amalgamation. Child's story of Mary French's transition from white to black and back to white again begins with an idyllic scene in which Mary and her free-black playmate Susan frolic with a white-and-black spotted rabbit. In his alternating patches of color the rabbit presents an ideal of amalgamation that would not blur racial distinctions into mulatto indifferentiation but rather preserve the clarity of difference without the hierarchies of valuation imposed by prejudice. The problem in Child's story, as in Stowe's and Green's, is that this sort of equality-in-difference becomes impossible to maintain. Susan, kidnapped with Mary, cannot prove her right to freedom by bodily traits; her father (afraid of being kidnapped himself) cannot search for her; and Mary's father does nothing

---

36. Green, "Slave-Wife," 82.

to pursue this search once he has redeemed his own daughter. The racial prejudice implicit in her only half happy ending is obviously one of Child's points. Nevertheless her concluding remarks instance such racial hierarchization. "The only difference between Mary French and Susan Easton is," she explains, "that the black color could be rubbed off from Mary's skin, while from Susan's it could not."[37] Despite her clear desire for a different answer, the only solution to racial prejudice Child's story can offer is rubbing off blackness, and though she does not say this, it is impossible to imagine what one could produce by such a purging except whiteness.[38] If Mary's liberating tears offer, as I have argued, a perfect emblem for sentimental fiction's power to emancipate, that emblem includes the recognition that the freedom it offers depends upon the black being washed white.[39] The problem of antislavery fiction is that the very effort to depict goodness in black involves the obliteration of blackness.[40]

Child's story challenges the prevalent bodily vocabulary that interprets dark skin as an unvarying sign of slavery: for Susan, being black and being a slave are not the same thing. Yet whatever Susan's "right to be free," even under antebellum law, the blackness of her body is itself described as a form of enslavement, and one that no act of emancipation can rub off. The painful longing for such an emancipation from one's own skin is explored in Eliza Lee Follen's story "A Melancholy Boy." Throughout most of this story Follen relates a series of anecdotes about the good but inexplicably unhappy Harry, without in any way describing his physical appearance, though the publication of this piece in the *Liberty Bell* would prompt readers to expect that some abolitionist issue is at stake. In the last paragraph of her tale Follen "discover[s] the cause of Harry's melancholy,"

37. Child, "Mary French and Susan Easton," 202.
38. The fantasy of colorlessness in fact amounts to the same thing, for though the pinkish-yellowish-gray of "white" skin is indeed a color, *white* (as defined in the first entry of *Webster's New Collegiate Dictionary*) means "free from color."
39. Child's struggle with this problem can be traced through her revisions of the story as she prepared it for republication in the *Slave's Friend* of 1836. In this later version "the streak whiter than the rest of [Mary's] face" is replaced by a streak that is "lighter": a substitution that masks the problem but does not really avoid it.
40. One source of difficulty is that black and white have traditionally symbolized the basic moral dichotomy between good and evil. For antislavery discourse such symbolism is profoundly troubling, frequently resulting in absurdly paradoxical rhetoric in which the positive valuation of the black man is depicted in terms of whiteness. For example, the vignette of the "Apple and the Chestnut," presents a "white man" taunting a "poor colored man" by comparing his own race to an apple and the black to a chestnut. The black man replies with a witticism that, by inverting the intended insult, ultimately deepens it: "O, Massa, what you say is true. The chestnut has dark skin just like poor black man, but its kernel is all white and sweet. The apple, though it looks so pretty, has many little black grains at the heart." Attempting to explain the moral of this exchange, the narrator only intensifies the contradictions: "Now little boys and girls can't be abolitionists until they get rid of all these black grains in their hearts." Such logic suggests that the ability to liberate the black people would depend upon first expunging blackness; *Slave's Friend* 1 (February 1836): 3.

I was returning from a walk, and saw him at a little brook that ran behind my house, washing his face and hands vehemently, and rubbing them very hard. I then remembered that I had often seen him there doing the same thing. "It seems to me, Harry," I said, "that your face and hands are clean now; and why do you rub your face so violently?" "I am trying," he said, "to wash away this color; I can never be happy till I get rid of this color."[41]

Harry does not name his color, though he does distinguish himself from the other boys: "They are all white." Follen too refrains from naming "this color," so that the story centers upon the absence of the word *black*. Both Harry and Follen attempt to escape his blackness, not only by violent scrubbings but also by suppressing the word that names it. In Harry's hopeless efforts to attain personhood through the denial of his body, antislavery fiction locates the problems of representation established by the encounter between sentimental narration and abolitionist ideals within the psyche of the very entity it wishes to represent.

With its reliance on the body as the privileged structure for communicating meaning, sentimental fiction thus constantly reinscribes the troubling relation between personhood and corporeality that underlies the projects of both abolition and feminism. The issues I have been exploring are not peripheral to feminist concerns, for by responding to the representational problems posed by the black body with a rhetoric of racial amalgamation, the women who wrote these antislavery stories encode the racial problematic within a sexual one. The "rubbing off" of blackness that characterizes antislavery fiction imitates the whitening produced by miscegenation. Moreover, miscegenation provides an essential motif of virtually all antislavery fiction, for even in those stories in which escape, slave rebellion, or the separation of families dominates the plot, its multiple challenges suffuse the text. My identification of the human body as the site at which feminist and abolitionist discourses intersect can be further particularized in the images of the black woman's rape by the white man; or their unsanctioned, unprotected, and unequal love; or the always suppressed possibility of the white woman's desire for the black man; or the black man's never sufficiently castrated attraction to the white woman; or, most of all, in the ubiquitous light-skinned slave whose body attests to the sexual mingling of black and white. Though it marks the intersection of abolitionist and feminist discourses, the body of the light-skinned slave means differently for each of them: the less easily race can be read from his or her flesh, the more clearly the white man's repeated penetrations of the black body are imprinted there. The quadroon's one-fourth blackness represents two generations of miscegenating intercourse, the octoroon's three—their numerical names attesting to society's desire to keep track of an ever less visible black ancestry even at the cost of counting the generations of institutionalized sexual exploitation.

Critical discussions of the mulattos, quadroons, and octoroons who figure in these texts have dealt almost exclusively with the obvious racist allegiances that make a light-skinned hero or heroine more attractive to a white audience, and that presume that the feelings of identification so essential for sentimental fiction

41. Eliza Lee Follen, "A Melancholy Boy," *Liberty Bell* 5 (1844): 94–95.

cannot cross race lines.⁴² I am not interested in attempting to defend either authors or audiences from this charge. My discussion of the rhetoric of amalgamation already has suggested that the light-skinned body is valued in this fiction precisely because of its ability to mask the alien African blackness that the fictional mulatto is nevertheless purported to represent. I would contend, however, that an acknowledgment of this racism ought to inaugurate, not foreclose, discussion of antislavery fiction's fascination with miscegenation. For at stake in the obsession with the fictionalized figure of the mulatto is the essential dilemma of both feminist and abolitionist projects: that the recognition of ownership of one's own body as essential to claiming personhood is matched by the fear of being imprisoned, silenced, deprived of personhood by that same body. The fictional mulatto combines this problematics of corporality and identity for both discourses because miscegenation and the children it produces stand as a bodily challenge to the conventions of reading the body, thus simultaneously insisting that the body is a sign of identity and undermining the assurance with which that sign can be read. Moreover, stories of miscegenation inevitably link the racial and the sexual, demonstrating the asymmetry of abolitionist and feminist concerns—and the by now familiar ways in which, by identifying with her enslaved sister, the free woman comes to betray her.

The form miscegenation usually took in the American South was, of course, the rape and concubinage of slave women by their white masters. Caroline Healey Dall's "Amy," published in the *Liberty Bell* of 1849, tells this story, and records in its telling the interlocking structure of patriarchy's dual systems of racial oppression and sexual exploitation. The story begins with a marriage: "In Southern fashion, Edith was not quite sixteen when she was wooed and won, and borne, a willing captive, to a patriarchal dwelling." Edith's ambiguous role as a willing captive within the patriarchal systems of marriage and slaveholding becomes more sinisterly evident as the story progresses and she eventually proves willing to prostitute her slave and half sister Amy. As Dall explains, "The offspring of a lawless and unrequited affection," Amy "had, nevertheless, unconsciously dedicated her whole being to vestal chastity. But nothing availed." The problem of Amy's ancestry is not, despite prevailing cultural expectations, that as the child of lawless sexuality she has inherited lascivious desires but rather that as the child of sexual exploitation she has inherited the role of being exploited. Her body displays not only a history of past miscegenation but also a promise of future mixings. A friend of Edith's new husband sees Amy, reads both her desirability and her vulnerability on her "graceful form," and reenacts a parodic version (or is it?) of the wooing and winning with which the story begins. The woman Charles

---

42. The only notable exception to this trend is Jules Zanger, "The 'Tragic Octoroon' in Pre–Civil War Fiction," *American Quarterly* 18, no. 1 (Spring 1966): 63–70, which discusses some of the strategic uses this figure is put to in abolitionist writing. His most useful insight for my purposes is that the octoroon "represented not merely the product of the incidental sin of the individual sinner, but rather what might be called the result of cumulative institutional sin, since the octoroon was the product of four [sic] generations of illicit, enforced miscegenation made possible by the slavery system" (66) [in this volume, p. 287. —Ed.].

426   Sánchez-Eppler

Hartley must woo in order to win Amy is, however, not Amy but her mistress, Edith. In this transaction Amy is prostituted as much by the white woman's reluctance to discuss sex as by the white man's desire to indulge in it. For as Charles keeps pressing Edith to procure Amy for him, she comes to see her slave's sexual modesty as a threat to her own delicacy:

> Not only did the whole subject distress her, but to be so besought on such a subject, by one until lately a stranger, was a perpetual wound to her delicacy. She felt herself losing ground in her own self-respect. Her husband regarded it as a desecration, and repeatedly asked whether her own life was to be worn out in defense of Amy.

In the end, concurring with her husband's insistence on the sanctity of her delicacy, Edith signs the "deed of transfer."

In Dall's story the pairing of feminist and abolitionist concerns proves double edged: for if Edith's inability to prevent male desire, or refute male conceptions of feminine purity, allies her to her powerless slaves and names her a captive of patriarchy, she nevertheless remains fully complicitous in Amy's sexual victimization. The role of feminine delicacy that she accepts is paid for not just by her own loss of efficacy but by Amy's destruction. Dall's critique of female delicacy identifies it as an essential prop both for the subordination and demoralization of women and for the exploitation of slaves. The narrative voice in which Dall tells this story, however, conforms to the requirements of the delicacy it condemns. In describing Amy as "dedicated . . . to a vestal chastity," it is the narrator, not Edith's husband, who first equates female purity with the sacred; while in calling the lust that fathered Amy "affection," Dall mitigates the very evil her story was intended to expose. The problem is that traditional notions of female purity attach both to the body—in its vulnerability to rape or enforced concubinage—and to language. The conventions of chastity count speech as a sexual assault; hence Edith can describe Charles's propositions as a "perpetual wound." Dall fears that to name explicitly the obscene events that comprise her plot would be experienced by her readers as the infliction of wounds. The cultural critique voiced by Dall is leveled at her own prose, for in respecting the sensibilities of her readers she adheres to the dictates of a linguistic delicacy that she has demonstrated simultaneously protects against and inflicts physical indecencies.[43]

The sacrifice of Amy's chastity serves not only to defend Edith's delicacy but also, paradoxically, to provide her with a variety of safely mediated sexual experience. After all, it is to Edith that Charles brings his suit for sexual favors, and—after the requisite protestations of lost self-respect—it is Edith who yields. That she can yield Amy's body rather than her own demonstrates the usefulness of the slave woman as a surrogate for the white woman's sexuality, and particularly the usefulness of the mulatta, who in being part white and part black (and in Amy's

---

43. Caroline Wells Healey Dall, "Amy," *Liberty Bell* 10 (1849): 6, 8, 11, and 12. In "The Inalienable Love," *Liberty Bell* 15 (1858), Dall makes this point explicit, asserting that if she were to write her story with the "nervous strength" of the slave's narration, "All the women in the land would tear the pages out of the fair volume" (87).

case, being more explicitly half sibling and half not) simultaneously embodies self and other. Thus through the prostitution of Amy Edith can be perceived as gaining a degree of sexual license normally forbidden the proper bourgeois woman. Edith's husband and her husband's friend, however, fill virtually interchangeable roles in this narrative, both equally involved in demanding Edith's compliance. Her husband's anger over her desecration is directed at her initial defense of Amy's chastity, not at Charles's presumption in bringing the matter up. Consequently, even Edith's passive and unconscious circumvention of sexual prohibitions ultimately functions as a demonstration that the white woman, like her slave, remains a sexual possession of the white man. In these terms fictional depictions of the slave woman's sexual vulnerability may themselves constitute an act of betrayal not unlike Edith's own, for in such stories antislavery rhetoric disguises, and so permits, the white woman's unacknowledgeable feelings of sexual victimization and desire. The insights and emotions granted to the white woman by such conflations of the racial and the sexual remain divorced from her body. If, as Lucy Stone insisted, the ability to control the "uses" of one's own body constitutes the most basic condition of freedom, then for the white woman the strongest proof that she is not owned by the white man lies in the inadmissible possibility of using her body elsewhere—a possibility only granted her, within antislavery fiction, through a vicarious reading of the body of the slave.[44]

In antislavery fiction the story of the white woman's desire for the black man is not told, and his desire for her is constantly reduced to the safer dimensions of a loyal slave's nominally asexual adoration of his good and kind mistress.[45] Child comes closest to giving voice to these desires not in her fiction but in her first abolitionist tract, *An Appeal in Favor of That Class of Americans Called Africans*. While this book established her as an abolitionist leader, it cost her both her popular readership (so many subscriptions to the *Juvenile Miscellany* were canceled by horrified parents that the series was forced to fold), and, with her expulsion from the Atheneum, her position in Boston literary society. Perhaps chief among the *Appeal*'s many challenges to societal norms was Child's call for

---

44. The opposite, and most conservative, pattern of racial and sexual pairings is demarcated by another frequently told story of miscegenation: one that romanticizes the relation between a white man and a darker woman. In its most prevalent form a beautiful, refined quadroon loves a white gentleman only to lose him either through death or marriage, and this loss entails, in addition to the broken heart shared by all ill-fated lovers, a fall from a life of luxury and endearments into one of slavery and sexual exploitation. I would argue, however, that even in these stories, where the power of the white man and the exclusion of the black man seem most absolute, miscegenation works to interrogate white male supremacy. For these are stories about the unequal positions of men and women within a love relation, where the inherent similarities between the nearly white quadroon and the white woman serve to emphasize the ways in which the quadroon's inability to control her fate is only an extreme example of the victimization of all women in a society that considers love a fair exchange for power.

45. The examples of this last passion are myriad; see especially Harry's incestuous worship of his half sister and mistress Nina Gordon in Stowe's *Dred* and Jan's rivalry with both the husband and the son of his beloved mistress Maria in Lydia Maria Child's "Jan and Zaida," *Liberty Bell* 14 (1856): 41–93.

the repeal of anti-miscegenation laws.[46] Although her attack on these discriminatory statutes explicitly distinguishes between society's refusal to sanction interracial marriage and its willingness to condone such liaisons out of wedlock, she
implies that what is at stake in these contradictory attitudes is not miscegenation
per se but rather the patriarchal melding of sexual and racial oppression that
assures the supremacy of the white man, granting only to him the freedom to
choose his sexual partners.

> An unjust law exists in this Commonwealth, by which marriages between persons
> of different color is pronounced illegal. I am perfectly aware of the gross ridicule
> to which I may subject myself by alluding to this particular; but I have lived too
> long, and observed too much, to be disturbed by the world's mockery. . . . Under
> existing circumstances, none but those whose condition in life is too low to be
> much affected by public opinion, will form such alliances; and they, when they
> choose to do so, *will* make such marriages in spite of the law. I know two or
> three instances where women of the laboring class have been united to reputable,
> industrious colored men. These husbands regularly bring home their wages, and
> are kind to their families. If by some odd chances, which not unfrequently occur
> in the world, their wives should become heirs to any property, the children may
> be wronged out of it, because the law pronounces them illegitimate. And while
> this injustice exists with regard to *honest*, industrious individuals, who are merely
> guilty of differing from us in a matter of taste, neither the legislation nor customs
> of slaveholding States exert their influence against *immoral* connexions.

In the next paragraph she discusses the "temporary connexions" made by
"White gentlemen of the first-rank" and New Orleans quadroons.[47] Her examples
of illegal miscegenating marriages pointedly make the woman white and the man
black, while the case of the quadroon concubine pairs race and sex differently.
Child's care in this passage to discriminate her own desires from those she discusses indicates the strength of the taboo against which she writes. For even as
she disclaims any concern for the "world's mockery," Child admits the impossibility, at least under the prevailing social conditions, of any but the very low so
utterly discounting public opinion as to enter into such a union. Child only risks
a defense of this most subversive version of miscegenation once she has placed
the sturdy barrier of class between herself and the women who enact it. By asserting that the female laborers who choose black mates are "merely guilty of
differing from us in a matter of taste," Child insists on the distinction between
tastes and morals, and on the comparative insignificance of the former. But by
using this moment to forge an identification with her readers based on a shared

---

46. See the discussion of the revolutionary force of Child's stand on miscegenation in both Karcher's
article "Rape, Murder, and Revenge" and in her introduction to Lydia Maria Child, *Hobomok
and Other Writings on Indians* (New Brunswick, N.J., 1986). In *Hobomok* as in Catharine Sedgwick's
Hope Leslie, the marriages of white women and Native American men are (somewhat equivocally)
endorsed, suggesting once again the difference in antebellum racial attitudes toward the noble
savage and the slave.

47. Child, *An Appeal in Favor of That Class of Americans Called Africans* (New York, 1836; reprint
ed., New York, 1968), 196–97.

set of tastes she backs away from her argument, suggesting the power of social sanctions to delimit desires. Thus even here, in perhaps the most daring argument in her most daring text, Child refrains from denouncing society's distaste for a form of miscegenation that would threaten and exclude the white man. Instead, as she names herself part of the social "us," her persuasive strategy of identification collapses into a defensive one.

In light of Child's caveats it is hardly surprising that, at least so far as I am aware, no antislavery fiction admits to the possibility of a white woman loving or wedding a black man. Yet I would like to suggest that this forbidden desire constitutes a repressed but never completely obliterated narrative within even the most conventional of these stories. Recalling Stowe's and Green's portraits of their black heroes, it is now evident that one of the tasks implicit in the amalgamating strategies that constructed these Herculeses is the creation of a black man who can be easily assimilated to the white woman's sexual tastes. Once again it is the figure of the mulatta who permits this desire to be inscribed. The light skin of the mulatta names her white, yet her black ancestry keeps her union with the black hero from being labeled miscegenation. Through this figure the love of a white-skinned woman and a black-skinned man can be designated, and even endorsed, without being scandalous. The polysemous body of the fictional mulatta simultaneously expresses the white woman's desires and protects her from them, by marking them safely alien.

Clearly not intended to articulate a feminist position, Frances Green's "The Slave-Wife" tells the familiar abolitionist story of a slave woman's sexual exploitation by her master, despite her—legally null—marriage. But because of her complexion this story encloses another narrative, the tale of a white woman's preference for a black lover. Even hidden under the mask of the mulatta, this story of the inadmissible union of a white woman and a black man is so threatening that it must be dismantled at the very moment it is made, so that the story becomes a sequence of alternating disavowals and contradictions. Laco Ray's description of his wife proffers a double reading of her race: "She was white. At least no one would suspect that she had any African blood in her veins." The modifications that follow cannot erase the clarity of that first adamant assertion of her whiteness. Laco's wife is named Clusy; it is a slave name, unfit for other roles, so that Clusy's name and her body sustain the tension already noted between her African blood and white flesh. Just as Clusy's flesh, ancestry, and name offer conflicting signs to her identity, the story's plot consists of a series of displacements in which Laco Ray and his master alternately claim the trophy that is Clusy. Their competition, like Clusy's ambiguous race, serves to contain the white woman's scandalous desire for the black man; for as master and husband each attempt to claim exclusive sexual rights, the question of the woman's choice and desire is made moot. Laco Ray's narration of this rivalry makes it clear that he sees the price of loss as the distinctly patriarchal threat of castration:

> She was beautiful. She was in her master's power. She was in the power of every white man that chose to possess her, she was no longer mine. She was not my wife.

The question of "The Slave-Wife" is whether or not a black man can possess a woman—particularly a white woman—and from its very title, which simultaneously makes Clusy a wife and yet fetters that role with the contradictory one of slave, the answer remains ambiguous. Despite Laco's sense of dispossession, the white man's power never quite manages to control Clusy. Finally, as Laco reports it, continuing to reject the master's "wishes," "She was bound to the stake; and while cruel and vulgar men mocked her agony, THERE *our babe was born*!" The torture that attempts to make Clusy the white man's sexual property only succeeds in eliciting proof of her sexual intimacy with a black man. Yet once again the message is double, for the child who marks Laco's potency in the face of the master's power is stillborn. Weak from childbirth and beatings Clusy escapes with Laco Ray only to die before reaching Canada. The story ends here with a stalemate. The inconclusiveness of both Laco's and his master's attempts to claim Clusy reflects Green's own incapacity to give the white woman to the black man, even as it attests to her desire to do so.

Laco's final request that his auditor "publish it abroad" recasts the story not as one of male possession, whether white or black, but as one of female desires and female virtue:

> For if any woman can hear [this story] without a wish, a determination to labor with all her might to abolish THE SLAVERY OF WOMAN, I impeach her virtue—she is *not* TRUE —she is NOT PURE.[48]

The passage asserts that sexual virtue consists not of a delicacy that eschews sexual topics but of a purity that opposes sexual exploitation. This definition of sexual virtue as resistance to the slavery of woman makes abolition a question of woman's rights. Laco's phrase "the slavery of woman" carries two meanings, and Clusy's story illustrates the impossibility of separating them. What interests me about this merger of feminist and abolitionist arguments is that, unlike many of the instances discussed above, Green's narrative appears to be oblivious to the connections it nonetheless makes. The rhetoric of "The Slave-Wife" stresses the contradictions inherent in Clusy's double role as chattel and spouse, and it disregards the ways in which the two terms might be identical, and Green's title a tautology. Thus the story defines slavery as a woman's issue at the same time that it writes woman's desire out of woman's rights, denying and hiding the sexual body of the white woman. Yet by depicting Laco Ray and his master as rival claimants for the possession of Clusy, her positions as wife and slave are implicitly presented as analogous: in both cases she is male property; in neither case are her desires, including her subversive preference for her black husband, permitted autonomous expression. From a feminist perspective these implications discredit Laco Ray's desire to have Clusy as his own, and hence to own her, and therefore undermine his sympathetic position in Green's abolitionist argument. That the links between sexual and racial oppression strategically forged by feminist-abolitionists hold, even within narratives whose logic is jeopardized by this coupling, suggests that

---

48. Green, "Slave-Wife," 87, 94, 103, and 107.

these links have become so normative as to be unavoidable. Thus the antislavery stories written by women who appear to have no intention of questioning marital or familial relations constantly employ rhetoric or depict scenarios that jar against their benign assumptions about woman's proper domestic place.

Antislavery fiction's focus on miscegenation evades the difficulties of representing blackness by casting the racial problematics of slavery into the terms of sexual oppression. In defining the question of ownership of one's body as a sexual question, the ideal of liberty and the commercial concept of ownership attain not only an intimately corporeal, but also an explicitly marital or domestic, dimension. This presentation of slavery as a sexual, marital, and domestic abuse thematizes the structure of the genre as a whole, since antislavery stories attempt to describe slave experience within the feminine forms of domestic fiction. As such antislavery stories are constructed on the foundation of a presumed alliance between abolitionist goals and domestic values, an alliance that, it should already be obvious, is fraught with asymmetries and contradictions. The domestic realm of women and children occupies, after all, a paradoxical place in both feminist and abolitionist arguments. For feminists, it constitutes not only the source of woman's power but also, antithetically, the "sphere" in which she finds herself incarcerated. For abolitionists, the domestic values that ostensibly offer a positive alternative to the mores of plantation society simultaneously serve to mask slavery's exploitations behind domesticity's gentle features.

Situated outside of the specifically abolitionist forums provided by antislavery societies, even further detached from the woman's rights movement, and aimed at the most sentimental figure of the domestic scene—the good child—the antislavery stories written for Sunday-school primers baldly exemplify the narrative disjunctions inherent in attempts to domesticate slavery. Julia Coleman and Matilda Thompson's collection of such stories, *The Child's Anti-Slavery Book,* first published by the evangelical American Tract Society in 1859 and then twice reprinted in the "Books for Sunday School" series of a New York publisher, provides a characteristic and fairly popular sample of the genre. The collection constantly inscribes its own domesticity. The introduction, "A Few Words About American Slave Children," begins by describing the loving, happy homes of the American free children who constitute its readership. Such homes are then replicated within the stories themselves. Thus "Aunt Judy's Story" narrates the life of this elderly exslave through a frame in which Mrs. Ford tells her children the tale of their impoverished neighbor, with daughter Cornelia literally "leaning her little curly head against her mother's knee," while they discuss the likelihood of Judy's children having been torn away from her maternal knee. The virtue of the Ford home marks every exchange. If Cornelia is "getting a little impatient," the narrator turns to remind the child reader, who might mistakenly see this moment as condoning such behavior, that it was "only a little, for Cornelia was remarkable for her sweet and placid disposition." Bountiful meals are consumed in every chapter, and neither parent ever lets an opportunity for a moral lesson go to waste, nor does Mrs. Ford ever fail to revel in "every act of kindness to the poor and needy performed by her children." In these Sunday-school stories, lessons in patience or generosity—the everyday virtues of domestic life—inextricably mingle with the teaching of antislavery. The Fords treat Aunt Judy as a site for the moral education of their children, while the promised story of her life serves as a didactic and desirable form of entertainment: "Dear papa, tell us a story with a poor slave in it, won't you?" Cornelia implores.[49]

The subordination of the poor slave to the family who tells her story bespeaks the dominance inherent in the act of representation: the Ford children "profit" from Aunt Judy in a manner more moralistic than, but not sufficiently distinct from, the material profits reaped by the slave owners her story teaches them to condemn. On the other hand the family these children inhabit, and the lessons of patience and selflessness they are taught, reproduce under the benign guise of domesticity a hierarchy structurally quite similar to that of slavery itself.[50] The sentimental and domestic values engaged in the critique of slavery are compromised by the connection, and implicated in the very patterns they are employed

49. Matilda G. Thompson, "Aunt Judy's Story: A Story from Real Life," in *Child's Anti-Slavery Book*, 113, 115, 112, and 117. For a more extended example of this narrative strategy see Jane Elizabeth Jones, *The Young Abolitionists; or, Conversations on Slavery* (Boston, 1848); this juvenile novel begins with a series of conversations between a mother and her three children and then dramatizes these lessons in abolition as the family helps to hide a group of fugitive slaves.

50. I do not mean to deny that abolitionists found the domestication of slavery politically useful but only to suggest that despite its strategic efficacy the practice had costs for women, children, and slaves. For a brilliant analysis of how the strategy worked see Philip Fisher, "Making a Thing into a Man: The Sentimental Novel and Slavery," *Hard Facts: Setting and Form in the American Novel* (New York, 1985). Fisher argues that the domestication of slavery in *Uncle Tom's Cabin*, and particularly the distillation of the horrors of slavery into the recurring image of the separation and destruction of slave families, performs the cultural work of "making a thing into a man" and so proves efficacious in restructuring popular attitudes toward the slave. The notion of the slave as thing, object, property is replaced in domestic antislavery fiction with the imaginative conception of the slave as person because this fiction makes the slave familiar by putting him or her within the ordinary and emotionally accessible realm of the family. Furthermore, Fisher points out that setting the destruction of the black slave family within the context of the white slave-owning family makes "the contradiction between the inevitable sentimental nature of the family and the corrosive institution of slavery . . . the central analytic point of Stowe's novel" (101). While agreeing with Fisher's analysis, I would add that the juxtaposition of the institutions of slavery and family also reveals the corrosive dimension of the family itself.

Gillian Brown's article "Getting in the Kitchen with Dinah: Domestic Politics in *Uncle Tom's Cabin*," *American Quarterly* 36, no. 4 (Fall 1984): 503–23, though prior to the publication of *Hard Facts* and positioned largely in response to Jane Tompkins's evaluation of Stowe's use of domestic values as the source of sentimental power and the ideal replacement for political and commercial power, can also serve as a critique of Fisher on this point, questioning his essentially positive reading of the family. Brown argues that the comparison between slavery and family in *Uncle Tom's Cabin* reveals the economic basis of existing familial relations and that therefore Stowe's utopian vision of a society governed by familial mores is predicated upon a prior restructuring of the family. Stowe, she asserts, "seeks to reform American society not by employing domestic values but by reforming them. . . . Stowe's domestic solution to slavery, then, represents not the strength of sentimental values but a utopian rehabilitation of them, necessitated by their fundamental complicity with the market to which they are ostensibly opposed" (507). The obvious difference between Stowe's work, as Brown interprets it, and that of Coleman and Thompson is that the latter do not self-consciously embrace the feminist project of rehabilitating domesticity, a fact that makes their unwitting display of the similarities between slavery and family all the more disturbing.

to expose. The values of the loving family embodied in the doting mother and the dutiful child look, despite all disclaimers and despite all differences, much like the values of the plantation. But because the domesticity of women and children is glorified in these stories, the fact of subjugation and the disavowal of freedom implicit in domestic values remains masked.

Thompson and Coleman's defensive insistence on the differences between slavery and family suggests that even the most emphatically domestic writers were aware of the danger that their stories might collapse the very distinctions they were designed to uphold. For example, when in "A Few Words About American Slave Children" they attempt to differentiate between the experiences of slave and free children, the similarities between the two haunt their arguments.

> Though born beneath the same sun and on the same soil, with the same natural right to freedom as yourselves, they are nevertheless SLAVES. Alas for them! Their parents cannot train them as they will, for they too have MASTERS.

"They too have masters," the passage explains, and whatever is learned about the powerlessness of slave parents, the notion that all children have masters is equally clear—for who, except the child, stands at the other side of that "too"? This conception of all children as unfree slips between the emphatic insistence (so emphatic because so precarious?) that "Children, you are free and happy. . . . *You are free children!*" Yet the very description of this freedom reveals it to be, at best, deferred.

> When you become men and women you will have full liberty to earn your living, to go, to come, to seek pleasure or profit in any way that you may choose, so long as you do not meddle with the rights of other people.[51]

In short, the liberty described is one projected into the future, not one attainable for the child within familial structures. The male bias of even this deferred freedom is made obvious by a nearly identical passage from another antislavery book for children from the period. This one, *The Child's Book on Slavery; or, Slavery Made Plain*, was published as part of a series "for Sabbath Schools" in Cincinnati.

> When the Child grows to be a man or woman he can go and do for himself, is his own ruler, and can act just as he pleases, if he only does right. He can go and come, he can buy and sell; if he has a wife and children, they cannot be taken away, and he is all his life *free*.[52]

The absurdity of the child grown to be a woman ever having a wife makes it clear that the passage's slide into the singular masculine pronoun, and everything logically attributable to *him*, is not only idiomatically conventional but poignantly symptomatic. Indeed, the ability to have "a wife and children" like the ability to "go and come" or "buy and sell" serves to define freedom, so that the juxtapo-

---

51. Anonymous, "A Few Words About American Slave Children," in *Child's Anti-Slavery Book*, 10 and 9.
52. Anonymous, "The Difference Between a Slave and a Child," in *The Child's Book on Slavery; or, Slavery Made Plain* (Cincinnati, 1857), 31.

sition of these pairs categorizes women and children not as potential free persons but rather as the sign and condition of another's freedom. The freedom so defined in these antislavery books is available to neither child nor woman. The domestic ideology that informs the genre can no more accommodate an actual, corporeal, and present freedom than can the slave ideology itself.

The homological ideologies of the family and of slave society need not imply, antislavery writers insist, that both structures support the same meanings: thus the patriarchal pattern that would signal exploitation and power in the case of a plantation society could mean benevolent protection and love within a familial setting. "The relation between the child and the parent is first and chiefly for the child's good, but the relation between the slave and his master is for the master's pleasure," the anonymous author of *The Child's Book on Slavery* explains. In both cases the less powerful "must obey" the more powerful, but, the author asserts, the good garnered by such obedience accrues differently.[53] Leveled against pro-slavery assurances that bondage is beneficial to the weaker African race, this logic also defends against the specter of parental pleasure in the subservience of the child, and by extension, of patriarchal pleasure in the conventions of domestic hierarchy. The difference between slavery and domestic order is cast as a conflict between selfish hedonism and benevolence; in this Sunday-school primer the critique of pecuniary motives is displaced by a discussion of moral considerations.[54] By situating antislavery discourse within an idealized domestic setting these stories purport to offer moral and emotional standards by which to measure, and through which to correct, the evils of slavery. The problem is that these standards are implicated in the values and structures of authority and profit they seek to criticize. The contradictions inherent in the alliance of abolitionist thought and domestic ideals can be identified, in part, as the conflict between a structural or material and an emotional or moral conception of social reality. Failing to discover tangible and stable grounds on which to distinguish idealized domestic values from the abhorred system of slavery, antislavery writers retreat to the realm of the intangible; once they do so their arguments for the difference between slavery and domesticity reconstruct this opposition in terms of the tension between physical and spiritual ontologies and epistemologies.

Feminist-abolitionist awareness of the need to recognize the links between one's identity and one's body, and of all the difficulties inherent in such a recognition, informs, as I have argued, the problems of representation that characterize antislavery fiction. The domestic and sentimental conventions of this fiction, however,

53. Ibid., 30, 28.
54. Such displacements into the moral realm are quite common in abolitionist discourse. For example see Rev. Charles Beecher's very similar argument in the American Anti-Slavery Society tract *The God of the Bible Against Slavery*. Quoting from a decision by Judge Ruffin that distinguishes between the structures of authority associated with slavery and with the family by reference to the differing "ends" of the two systems ("the happiness of youth" versus "the profits of the master"), Beecher characterizes slavery as "intrinsically and unchangeably selfish" and the parent-child relation as "intrinsically benevolent." Reprinted in *Anti-Slavery Tracts*, series 1, nos. 1–20, *1855–1856* (Westport, Conn., 1970), tract 17, pp. 5–7.

simultaneously subscribe to a moral, emotional, and fundamentally spiritual code that devalues bodily constraints to focus on the soul. As employed in the service of patriarchal authority, the distinction between body and soul traditionally functioned to increase, not decrease, social control over the body. Historically this distinction had buttressed Christian apologies for slavery as it enabled the pious to simultaneously exploit bodies and save souls.[55] Similarly, an emphasis on the special and discrete nature of the spiritual realm permitted women's souls a power that was denied to their bodies. It has been frequently demonstrated that in losing economic and political power with the rise of bourgeois society the American woman increased her value as the moral and spiritual guardian of the nation: her gain in moral status bolstered her exclusion from the political and commercial arenas.[56] The writers of antislavery fiction seem well aware of the oppressive consequences of locating personhood in the soul. The hypocritical minister who defends slavery as a means of converting the heathens of Africa, and levies docility with the threat of hellfire for those who do not follow the biblical injunction "Servants obey your masters," serves as a stock villain of this fiction. Equally familiar is the ineffectual kind mistress who, like Stowe's Mrs. Shelby, is prevented by her husband from participating in economic decisions but is expected to provide enough piety and benevolence for the whole family.[57] Despite these depictions of the ways in which evocations of a spiritual reality can be used as a placebo for women's and slaves' lack of social power, antislavery fiction nevertheless endorses the belief in an alternate spiritual realm where power and efficacy are distributed differently. From this perspective the powerlessness of women and slaves would not matter, because whatever the condition of their bodies their souls could remain blessed and free.

The most famous instance of such recourse to the refuge provided by a separate spiritual reality is, of course, the victory of Tom's faith-filled spiritual power over Simon Legree's physical brutality.

"Did n't I pay down twelve hundred dollars, cash, for all there is inside yer old cussed black shell? An't yer mine, now, body and soul?" he said, giving Tom a violent kick with his heavy boot; "tell me!"

In the very depth of physical suffering, bowed by brutal oppression, this question shot a gleam of joy and triumph through Tom's soul. . . .

55. See David Brion Davis, *The Problem of Slavery in Western Culture* (Ithaca, N.Y., 1966), esp. chaps. 6 and 7, both titled "The Legitimacy of Enslavement and the Ideal of the Christian Servant," and chap. 10, "Religious Sources of Antislavery Thought: Quakers and the Sectarian Tradition."

56. For a discussion of this dynamic in antislavery work see Ronald G. Walters, "Families: The 'Center of Earthly Bliss' and Its Discontents," in *The Antislavery Appeal: American Abolitionism After 1830* (Baltimore, 1976). For a more general discussion see Smith-Rosenberg's introductions to parts 1 and 2 of *Disorderly Conduct*.

57. See for example the minister Laco Ray consults in "The Slave-Wife" or the whole collection of church apologists for slavery in Stowe's *Dred*. Along with Mrs. Shelby from *Uncle Tom's Cabin*, see *The Child's Anti-Slavery Book's* Mrs. Nelson and Mrs. Jennings, who cannot prevent the sale of Mark in "Mark and Hasty"; a less harsh reading of Edith's delicacy might also cast her in this role.

"No! no! no! my soul an't yours, Mas'r! You have n't bought it,—ye can't buy it! It's been bought and paid for, by one that is able to keep it."[58]

In this passage Stowe insists on the oppressive presence of physical reality; the constraints of Tom's position can be weighed and measured; the boot is heavy. The triumph of Tom's soul is thus emphatically presented as rebutting material conceptions of personhood. In response to Legree's threats and abuses Tom insists on the irrelevance of the condition of his body in identifying him not as a thing but as a man.[59] The primacy granted Tom's soul in constituting his identity is the culmination of a process evident throughout the novel, for though Tom's body is explicitly and frequently described by Stowe in the same Herculean terms she would later use in her portrait of Dred, her emphasis on the childlike and feminine character of his soul serves to supplant these physical descriptions so that in most readers' minds, and in George Cruikshank's 1852 illustrations, Tom appears effeminate and physically weak. Thus her celebration of Tom's soul serves to erase his flesh. Equally telling is Stowe's failure to imagine an America in which blacks could be recognized as persons. Perhaps the most disturbing insight of her novel is that the utopian freedom she constructs is predicated upon the absence of black bodies: Tom's "victory" wins him the freedom of heaven; George, Eliza, and the rest find theirs only in Liberia.

The Christian and sentimental vision of noncorporeal freedom and personhood obfuscates the conception of the corporeality of the self with which I credit feminist-abolitionist discourse. Yet I would argue that antislavery fiction's recourse to the obliteration of black bodies as the only solution to the problem of slavery actually confirms the ways in which feminist-abolitionist projects of liberation forced a recognition of the bodiliness of personhood. Antislavery writers' tendency to do away with bodies stands as a testimony to their terrified sense that the body is inescapable. Thus, graphically extending the ways in which the freedom praised by domestic fiction excludes women and children, the freedom offered by antislavery fiction regularly depends upon killing off black bodies, defining death as a glorious emancipation from plantation slavery. "A Thought upon Emancipation" in the *Liberty Chimes* offers this vision of immediate abolition:

Even, now, the slave himself need no longer be a slave. Has he the heroism to prefer death to slavery and the system is at an end.

Let the terrible determination go forth through all Slavedom, that the slave *will not*—work—*will not* eat—*will not* rise up or lie down at the bidding of an

58. Stowe, *Uncle Tom's Cabin*, 415.
59. Tom's soul, however, is not completely disentangled from the commercial realm, for in responding to Legree's taunts, Tom engrafts the New Testament vocabulary of redemption based upon Christ's sacrificial payment onto Legree's assertion that the money he paid for Tom establishes his ownership. In claiming God as his purchaser, Tom excludes himself from the conflict and recasts it as a dispute between masters. See Walter Benn Michaels's discussion of the ways in which Stowe found that both the body and, even, the soul "could not be guaranteed against capitalistic appropriation"; "Romance and Real Estate," 176.

owner and will be free or *die*, and it is done. Tomorrow's sun beholds a notion of freedom indeed.[60]

What is done, terminated, in this fantasy is not only slavery but all slaves. The apocalyptic tone of the piece does provide the radical reinterpretation of freedom it promises. Antislavery writing responds to slavery's annihilation of personhood with its own act of annihilation.

The obliteration of the body thus stands as the pain-filled consequence of recognizing the extent to which the body designates identity. Indeed this glorification of death is but a more extreme example of processes already evident in the domestic, amalgamating, and appropriative strategies that characterize feminist-abolitionist discourse's various attempts to transform the body from a site of oppression into the grounds of resisting that oppression. The discovery that these efforts to liberate the body result in its repression and annihilation attests to the difficulties and resistance inherent in acknowledging the corporeality of personhood. The bodies feminists and abolitionists wish reclaimed, and the bodies they exploit, deny, or obliterate in the attempted rescue, are the same.

American Theriomorphia: The Presence of *Mulatez* in Cirilo Villaverde and Beyond*

EDUARDO GONZÁLEZ

MULO, "macho," 1042. From lat. MULUS . . . Deriv. Mula . . . Mulato, 1525 . . . "young macho," by comparison with the hybrid engendering of the mulatto and the mule; mulata, 1602 . . .

TEZ, 1470, "color and terseness of the surface of things, and principally of the epidermis and the human visage." A word peculiar of Castilian and Portuguese. Probably from the reduction of aptez to atez, "perfección, robustness," derived from lat. APTUS, "perfect," "appropriate," and later on "robust," "healthy."

J. Corominas, Breve diccionario etimológico

---

60. C., "A Thought upon Emancipation," in *Liberty Chimes*, 80. I do not want to discredit the heroic potential of slave suicides. Surely the will to take one's own life may be the last, and in some situations perhaps the only, means of expressing a will at all. What is suspect here is not the slave's suicide but the abolitionist's desire for and glorification of such deaths.

* From Eduardo González, "American Theriomorphia: The Presence of *Mulatez* in Cirilo Villaverde and Beyond." In *Do the Americas Have a Common Literature*, ed. Gustavo Pérez Firmat (Durham, N.C.: Duke University Press, 1990), 177–193.

Pariahs and Priests

Several years ago I traveled on Greyhound from New England to Indiana to attend a rite of passage. Besides the necessary clothes, a toothbrush, and Fredric Jameson's *The Prison House of Language*, the only heavy piece I carried was my freshly typed dissertation bound in black. The driver (he was brown) who assumed command in Philadelphia, and who was to steer our transient lives only up to Toledo, was asked a question regarding St. Louis as a point of passage along someone's trip to California. Thrice he stood firm and rather unhelpful in answering: "Lady, this goes to Toledo and points West!" Obviously, he was neither Hermes the Psychopomp nor an imperial agent; his map was defined by his salary, as mine was by the vague anxieties that litter the academic realm. It must have been beyond Toledo that I fell asleep resting my head on the shoulder of a massive brown woman; when I got up at Indianapolis, she told me not to forget my hat. A few years later this same appendage—bought at an army surplus store— prompted some revelers to call me "rabbi" as I left an elevator at a Holiday Inn in wintry Syracuse, where I had gone to read a paper on Carpentier's "Viaje a la semilla." If I indulge in these colorless memories it is to underscore a point about the intended meaning of *beyond* in my title: that it should imply being away from home but in a new home; being homeless but reasonably happy; discovering home as it may be found, as much within the old as in the new.

"It's not a house, it's a home!" pleads a voice in a Bob Dylan song, referring to a brothel and addressing none other than Jesus himself, the incarnate pilgrim whom every house should welcome as a brother and not just as a client. Indeed, the homeless seek more than shelter, for they are as tired of carrying a makeshift home on their backs as they are of being offered sanctuary by the institutions of charity. A spiritual lesson on exile emerges from their wretched situation: home is always built; whether or not it is covered by a roof, it dwells in the heart and rises outward; home is the only furnishing that must survive wandering. In a comic and stoic sense, exiles should resemble turtles: no matter where they move, a portable, horny canopy should cover them from neck to tail. Likewise, resembling those ancient Chinese turtles known for their hieroglyphic shells, a literature of exile (which consists mostly of readings and recognitions) runs the risk of being surveyed from above by alien eyes; a literature that should remain a pariah among gentiles may fall one way or the other in the hands of priests. Regardless of other distinctions, in certain exile situations pariahs and priests stand apart from each other by the style and substance of their approach to amalgamation: priests are likely to impress their hosts by devising cults based on scriptures and murals; but pariahs, quite romantically, want to scare and seduce them, so they arrive at the party with the old or the native copied on their skin, and with the mixed ink of the new still fresh from the tattoo parlor, where it needled itself into shape in front of a smoking mirror. In this sense at least, our pariah exiles seem like pagans who had to leave home without a chance to regret it, and who flaunt on themselves and others their double birth.

Having said enough about *beyond*, I should simply add that it stands for a condition of the *here* and *now*, and that it *works* or takes effect mainly as it may inspire us into awareness of the sacred and the erotic. Yes, like Coriolanus's *elsewhere, beyond* lies beyond politics and wars; it is rather the crib where the political unconscious must have first hallucinated and dreamed. But, beware: *beyond* is anecdotic, not surreal. Two places in Freud's text need revision in order to adjust us to this old-fashioned site, the *here* and *now* surveyed in exile. In "The Uncanny," the tourist (Freud himself) wanders into a maze-like ghetto of prostitutes, their painted faces framed on windows; he keeps returning to the same spot until regaining the piazza, free from "any further voyages of discovery."[1] Neither epiphanic nor in any real sense demonic, Freud's encounter with the unsavory and vulgar—his slip into remote but neighborly temptation—wraps theory in the garments of biography. But for the one in exile, the biographic as such may not ring a personal note as authentically experienced and recalled as Freud's; the exile's biographic *topoi* have a harder time finding an actual place in ancestral life wherein to dwell: for the exile, every trace of personal memory is already ancestral; he suffers from a Jungian complex. At its best, the exile's biographic spot may lie between any former native habitat or encounter still within reach of his remembrance and some piece of reading; in this case, perhaps a fragment from Herodotus (with a hint of Borges) about a sacred temple or something about sacred prostitution (now it is Georges Bataille who comes to mind) that must have been read after leaving home for good (the hungry nostalgia of having known old Havana while reading Bataille is the spark that sets off biography in this instance). As a pariah, the exile does not know how to separate biography from allegory; Walter Benjamin transformed this pedestrian inability into migratory essays worthy of Montaigne.

The other element from Freud belongs to the much exploited and reworked (by Lacan, Derrida, and so on) *fortda* game in *Beyond the Pleasure Principle*: the child lies adrift in the crib, the mother comes and goes, a toy spool has been left behind by her, only to be transformed into a (here-now-and-then-gone-and-here-again) mobile idol of captivity (or perhaps into the prelude to a Pythagorean siesta). But for the exile of the here and now, little Moses may find himself as if by miracle out of the crib, as the mother comes to him on the cool floor, and beholds him right under the suspended spool, unharmed by theory, gone to sleep in tiny hardness.

The Kitchen as Ghetto

While living in the sugar mill enclave where I grew up, I often ate in the kitchen, where one of my three living mothers cooked, killed chickens, drank an occasional beer (with sugar), and taught me how to play cards. She was brown with a hint of Chinese in her cheekbones. All I have to say about Cuban *mulatez* is curiously tempered by her vivid presence in my mind, and only as such does it become worthy of being something more than sheer fiction. She knew about Cecilia Val-

---

1. Sigmund Freud, "The Uncanny," in *The Standard Edition of the Complete Psychological Works of Sigmund Freud*, ed. James Strachey and Anna Freud (London: Hogarth Press, Institute of Psychoanalysis, 1953–1974), 17:237.

dés, I am certain, only through the overture and songs of Gonzalo Roig's sugary operetta, whose most famous lines ("yo soy Cecilia, Cecilia Valdés") represent our best "Call me Ishmael." How many among well-educated Cubans had read Cirilo Villaverde's novel remains a matter of guessing; the essence of its plot was all that mattered: a white master had a daughter with a light-colored *mulata*, the girl ended up seduced and rejected by her white half brother, who was then killed on the way to his wedding by her frustrated suitor, another mulatto. Even if known by many, the rest of the novel—with its copious account of Cuban society in the 1830s—would probably have nurtured in most readers sentimental visions of colonial life.

As an object of serious study, *Cecilia* found a salient place in the roster of antislavery novels written in Cuba during the nineteenth century: From such a vantage point, it can inspire comparison with any number of abolitionist works and, of course, with *Uncle Tom's Cabin*, with which it has little in common besides its program to expose and condemn slavery. The dominant tendency in *Cecilia* studies has taught us how to appreciate Villaverde's avowed realism, just as much as it has played down or deplored his reliance on romantic melodrama and the incest machinery behind it. If it were up to most critics I know, the whole business of incest would play a minor role in our reflections on the novel, or at least one in which the essentially white ghost of incest would be exposed and punctured, for it may represent just a boogeyman nagging the master's conscience with a measure of intoxicating masochism.[2] What these critics find in *Cecilia* is what they are best trained to explore: evidence of Cuban social and economic history during the age in which the colony approached its first war of independence and acquired everlasting racial tones enslaving and decimating broken nations of African blacks. Under the influence of more or less orthodox Marxism, the best informed critics of *Cecilia* hold in suspicion or rule out most theoretical constructs of the speculative sort. Homegrown materialism weeds out any hybrid forms of interpretation, of mythic or psychoanalytic origin. The argument that such approaches—with their own specular rapport with romantic ideology—should have heuristic value in confronting Villaverde's haunted sensibility would be dismissed by Marxists as being abstruse and in itself ideological. For what is at stake in such criticism is nothing less than the liberation of the novelist from the vestigial hindrances of plot and character stereotyping that he learned, in his own peculiar way, while reading Scott, Cooper, and Manzoni (Villaverde produced but never published a translation of *David Copperfield*). What emerges from such an isolationist project is a rehabilitated *Cecilia Valdés o, la Loma del Angel*, acting as the founding text of Cuban realism and historical fiction. The novel's *mulata* protagonist and her

2. Around the centenary of *Cecilia* in 1982, a whole cycle of critical work appeared, including both reprints and fresh views: see *Acerca de Cirilo Villaverde*, ed. Imeldo Alvarez García (Havana: Editorial Letras Cubanas 1982); as well as Reinaldo González's informed and imaginative *Contradanzas y latigazos* (Havana: Editorial Letras Cubanas, 1983). Since first writing this essay in the fall of 1987, I have read Reinaldo Arenas's *Graveyard of the Angels*, trans. Alfred J. MacAdam (New York: Avon Books, 1987), whose satirical recasting of *Cecilia* as a surreal farce can be seen as a classic example of pariah excess.

rich iconography play a marginal and controlled role in such readings; she becomes a poor sister to Clio, and her fiction is seen sustaining mature interest only if it gives historical testimony above any dalliance with myth.

Such an emphasis on social realism can result in extinguishing the ritual fires in *Cecilia* and obscuring the novel's kinship with ancient forms of melodrama, in which the protagonist remains luxuriously central while playing the role of sacrificial victim. No matter how morally objectionable such a sacrificial covenant with passion might be, its prestige (and the stormy effects of a truly ironic rapport with religious performance) are likely to outlast milder forms of social drama. Restored to the center of dramatic strife, Cecilia would bring back excess, embarrassment, and turbulence; elements whose consensual sublimation most realistic formulas tend to promote. Since it cannot in the end be arrested, sublimation boils down to a question of deferral, of how long it may be held off.

Not far from being Nietzsche's hot *mulata* (he called her his "sirocco incarnate"), Lou Andreas-Salomé wrote the epigraph for what could serve as our understanding of *mulatez* lifted in sublimation: "to sublimate (she says) is to bury an impulse in part and substitute another as different as is resurrection from the grave, the tabooed and the highest values—the sub- and the super-human—are mutually dependent, in fact covertly equivalent, and the grandest transmutations befall those objects or instincts most reviled, which then, when their hour strikes, ride the golden coach like that cloacal heroine Cinderella to a dignity and glory far exceeding their once worthier sisters."[3] The charm and power of this view of sublimation resides in the minor spectacle of folk characters rising and falling. Andreas-Salomé might have agreed that folklore and myth are peculiarly enchanting forms of sublimation in a preanalytic sort of way; and I would press the issue of adopting such older means (like folktale and myth) in order to reenchant the Cuban cult of the *mulata* besides (but not too far away from) its erotic and sexist cant. A vernacular Cuban version of Cinderella would not name its heroine *la Cenicienta* but instead *la Tiznada:* in place of ashes, it would have *smut, grime, soot,* as attributes of the sister who all but spends her whole life in the kitchen.

It took me a while to understand why I disliked and found absurd the word *mulatto,* while at the same time finding useful and caressing the words *mulato* and *mulata.* The extra *t* distracted me into false details: was it that creeping, unfamiliar *r*-sound, as when Mrs. Tulliver thanks God for not putting in her family Maggie's hue: "no more nor a brown skin as makes her look like a mulatter"?[4] But my enthralled reading of *The Mill on the Floss* could only confuse the issue of an ambivalence toward *mulatto* soon running into decent dread. The answer was plain and unliterary: I had known, played, and dealt intimately with—and had in fact slept for years next to—people who gladly accepted the name *mulato* in coy and picaresque fashion. Quite besides the erotic cult of the *mulata* I had lived with and loved common beings of that description. On the other hand, American En-

3. Rudolph Binion, *Frau Lou: Nietzsche's Wayward Disciple* (Princeton, N.J.: Princeton University Press, 1968), 543, 548.
4. George Eliot, *The Mill on the Floss* (Oxford: Oxford Classics, 1983), 13.

glish and polite manners in this country had taught me slowly but surely to regard *all* people of color [*gente de color*] as black. And then, reading deeper into black culture in this country, I thought I learned another, far more interesting fact: the unencumbered richness of hues and colors that blacks have created throughout their history in order to pinpoint their own amalgamation with nonblacks. Racial polemics and white racism prevent this essentially erotic and playful impulse— to name hues and verbally flavor them—from breaking into the open.[5]

As far as I know, Freud left no thoughts of great consequence on the matter of race mixture, but one may venture a guess on the matter in reference to his greatest speculation on reproduction and the survival of organisms. In *Beyond the Pleasure Principle*, the fate of *thanatos* is to unravel and destroy the binding impulses of *eros*; rather than disruptive, sexuality's aim is seen as life-enhancing. It is hard to imagine a better example of Freud's dualistic norm than the one offered by a race or ethnic group that controls or prevents its own reproductive mixture with other such groups, and which most often would enforce cross-racial taboos on chosen (and tacitly on all) females of its own kind. In Freud's grand scheme the distinction between primitive, unicellular, asexual organisms and more developed or sexually reproductive ones plays a dominant role; in this regard, sexual reproduction would seem to imply an inherent tendency to procreate mixtures and to insure adaptation through the proliferation of somatic differences. Finally, it should not pass unnoticed that, in harboring eggs, the female within sexual reproduction might bring into Freud's biologistic fantasy an archaic tendency on the part of the organism's regressive capabilities to forgo sexual reproduction in favor of self-induced engendering. Were sex to disappear in its present bisexual form, the last race to vanish before the onset of a universe of mothers would be that made up of connected males—of all colors. A close reading of a racist paranoiac like the Southerner Tom Dixon would tend to confirm that behind the specter of miscegenation lies the threat of male extinction and the incestuous horror of excessive masculine dependence on female ovulation.

In this regard, the racist mytheme derived from mule infertility opens the manual of what I should like to call the art of chasing mulattoes, or the cynegetics so lavishly bestowed on their hybrid breed by friends and foes alike. The motifs of the chase and its taxonomy are of central concern in Mark Twain's *Pudd'nhead Wilson* and Faulkner's *Light in August*, regarded by many as the best novels on black-white crossbreeding in American culture.

In Twain's satire, the cryptic fault opened by the mere arrival of children of mixed race runs parallel to their fingerprinting by amateur detective Wilson. It is as if the two milk-brothers belonged more to dactylography than to their breast-mother, with the novel technique of fingerprinting playing the role of an asexual foster parent. One may recall how the *daktuloi*, or Dactyls of Mount

5. I first became aware of this black polyphony while reading Lawrence Levine, *Black Culture and Black Consciousness: Afro-American Folk Thought from Slavery to Freedom* (New York: Oxford University Press, 1977), one of the few nonfiction books I am fond of rereading (it was while reading Levine that I first bumped into Claude McKay).

Ida in Crete, represent fingertip versions of the Couretes, the ephebic *kouroi* or young men who in various myths undergo initiation, most often in a grand cynegetic affair like the one involving the hunt of the Calydonian boar.[6] Detective Wilson is far from being a sensualist, and therefore lacks one of the features that could qualify him as a racist technician of the flesh and its birthmarks; his business consists in locating minuscule and mintlike traces of difference, so he might not heed the obvious nostalgia that mythic fingertips could feel for the navel, the old *omphalos*. Wilson's addiction to folklore is of the satirical sort, so instead of noting that our primal parents might not have sported a navel, he is quick to remind us of one of their principal advantages: "that they escaped teething." It seems clear that, at least in his *Calendar*, Wilson regards myth and religious folklore with the appetite of a debunking heretic: "Adam was but human. . . . He did not want the apple for the apple's sake; he wanted it only because it was forbidden. The mistake was in not forbidding the Serpent; then he would have eaten the Serpent."[7] Where this leaves Eve is not clear, although Wilson's sense of cannibal instincts in Adam suggests forms of totemic sex between the primal pair worthy of Géza Róheim's psychoanalytic ethnography.[8] Besides Wilson's humor, the lack of a navel (rather than the exemption from teething) has been regarded as a sign of purity in Adam and Eve and their motherless engendering. In his "La creación y P. H. Gosse," Borges begins by reminding us of such a belief,[9] as when Sir Thomas Browne writes: "The man without a Navel yet lives in me" or when Joyce mentions Heva in *Ulysses*: "naked Eve. She had no navel. Gaze. Belly without blemish, bulging big, a buckler of taut vellum, no, whiteheaped corn, orient and immortal, standing from everlasting to everlasting. Womb of sin."[10] Not being a courthouse gnostic, Wilson does not commit the excess of linking the minted identity that he can reveal in the fingertips with the *omphalos*, its inherent place at the center of the garden, its cordlike ties with the mother, and the fanciful notion of her fingers having possibly fashioned that mark in her sons. For it might have been at the navel of some lost garden that the milk-brothers could have found a way to preserve their preracial resemblance as twins, and where they might have kept themselves free from the mythic need of one of them being a criminal. But the hunt exists in order to turn fingers into weapons and brothers into predators and prey. Wilson is the God of the hunt and the labyrinth, he can read the cynegetics of the hands' tenfold name grooved on each finger.

6. Bernard Sergent, *Homosexuality in Greek Myth*, trans. Arthur Goldhammer (Boston: Beacon Press, 1968), 221ff., offers a recent view of this youthful brood of hunters and warriors.
7. Mark Twain, *Pudd'nhead Wilson* (New York: Penguin, 1969), 61, 75.
8. Géza Róheim, *The Eternal Ones of the Dream* (New York: International Universities Press, 1945).
9. Borges remains frustrated by not having been able to find in any library a book called *Omphalos*, on which Gosse based his own speculations on geology and *Genesis*. See his "La creación y P. H. Gosse," in *Otras inquisiciones* (Buenos Aires: Emecé, 1960), 37.
10. James Joyce, *Ulysses* (New York: Random House, 1946), 39. On Adam Kadmon and Joyce, see Don Gifford and Robert J. Seidman, *Notes for Joyce: An Annotation of James Joyce's Ulysses* (New York: Dutton, 1974), 34.

Faulkner's Joe Christmas fits into this mythic framework like a thumb with no print, a sure sign of not having (or ever being) a father. He becomes the object of a chase, a theriomorphic being, and a god of the wild; his tragic and at times grotesquely comic dumbness in human intercourse may suggest that Joe is sacredly sterile. He is more blank than either white or black; Joe is anything but a mulatto: he excels in resembling *no one* in particular, while mulattoes are chased by a culture in which they are forced to resemble someone. Mulattoes are pushed into a racial either/or beyond the boundaries of the properly white. But Faulkner places Joe's tragic presence inside the souls of white folks. In killing only whites, Joe kills that part of himself that whites hate most: themselves. With Joe Christmas, the chase of the mulatto reaches an ontological impasse before the mirror of incest and suicide.

Hamlet and the Sacred Mule

> The negro is the human donkey. You can train him, but
> you can't make of him a horse. Mate him with a horse, you
> lose the horse, and get a large donkey called a mule, inca-
> pable of preserving his species.
>
> Tom Dixon, The Leopard's Spots

> Ese seguro paso del mulo en el abismo suele confundirse con
> los pintados guantes de lo estéril.
> (The mule's steady step over the abyss begs confusion with
> the painted gloves of sterility.)
>
> José Lezama Lima, "Rapsodia para el mulo"

Tom Dixon confuses the blend of black and white with male sterility; and behind his view of blacks as donkeys one can feel him being struck by the fantasy that all blacks are or should be male (one wonders if Dixon ever had a dream in which all men were black, including himself). On his part, Lezama Lima pays poetic homage to the mule, who climbs over the abyss like a beast burdened with sacredness. Such are the extremes of theriomorphia: a formula linking breeder and beast through maleness stands next to a visionary poem in which a beast tremulously climbs the ladder of sacredness. At the very least, the theriomorphic imagination involves two possible acts: the latent crossbreeding of the master with his male beast, and the poet's sublime grasp of transcendent form. The male homoerotic aspect of theriomorphia harks back to those primary processes that were so dear to Melanie Klein, who regarded fantasies as their typical manifestation. In psychoanalytic language, theriomorphia involves the narcissism of the poet, as he shapes forms in his imagination, and the paranoia of the breeder, as he copulates with some ultimate shape of punishing phallicism.[11] Theriomorphia in-

---

11. Klein's understanding and explorations of archaic fantasies should be applied to any thorough account of theriomorphia. See Phyllis Grosskurth, *Melanie Klein: Her World and Work* (New York: Knopf, 1986), 59*n*, 169–70, 317–20, 322–23. Skeptics about the value of psychoanalytic

cludes two central characters: a narcissist and a masochist. So reduced, the man-animal bonding between metamorphosis and racial mixture can indeed imply that the poet sublimates twice: he lifts breeding into voice and vision, and he transforms the aberrant desire to copulate with himself in beastly form into multiple uplifted figures in his unbound imagination. Such might be the case, in a blunt speculative sense.

In any event, the question of *mulatez* enters history and biography embedded in a racist complex whose deepest sources in fantasy are difficult to fathom without practicing a form of parasitic and erotic racism. In literary fictions, racial mixture and incest go hand in hand; their kinship forces the interpreter into the role of son or Oedipal detective, who repeats in analytic language the destruction of paternal maleness (in both father and son) and the desperate foreclosure of the mother's love already witnessed in the plot. The case of Melville's Pierre Glendinning seems exemplary: from the vast figure of the grandfather (who was "a great lover of horses" and who liked to breed himself into them) comes the delirious assumption of incest in his male grandchild, impotently in love with his dark half sister. In the ruins of narcissistic enthusiasm and pantheistic rhetoric lie both the Glendinning family and Pierre's extinct life as an artist.[12]

Before addressing the place of women in this scenario, I should review it as follows: mulatto theriomorphia is *sexist* (colored by sex) and *homoerotic* (it recognizes in sex the exclusive rule of one gender); the actions of its imaginary characters include the poet's implied but sublimated fusion with the breeder's hated and enviable potency, and the poet's incestuous and hateful kinship with the master's beastly management of reproduction. These ambivalent mergers and intermixtures would also include the woman (she too might be an artist, a *soul*) and her conception of a similar fantasy of rampant maleness; a maleness dominant in what should be (but almost never is) her own untramelled approach to fe-male *mulatez*. Reflected in the mirror of *mulatez*, the *womansheartist* (to echo Faulkner's savage use of "womanshenegro" in *Light in August*) can play several roles: she may cast herself specularly as her own sexual adversary, or as her potential female lover, and also she might engage in the male-exclusive revelry of phallic theriomorphia. Phallocentric? Yes, for, as *mulatas* well know, Phaedra has always been the most feared goddess in the plantation.

perspectives on the racist mind should read the historical account of Tom Dixon, his work, and family history given by Joel Williamson in *The Crucible of Race; Black-White Relations in the American South Since Emancipation* (New York: Oxford University Press, 1984), 140–79.

12. Carolyn L. Karcher writes: "In Saddle Meadows, where 'man and horse are both hereditary,' the descendants of General Glendinning's horse are 'a sort of family cousins to Pierre . . . ' like the illegitimate mulatto children fathered by slaveholders" (see *Shadow Over the Promised Land: Slavery, Race, and Violence in Melville's America* [Baton Rouge: Louisiana State University Press, 1980], 101). Some recent important interpretations of *Pierre* include: Michael Paul Rogin, *Subversive Genealogy: The Politics and Art of Herman Melville* (Berkeley: University of California Press, 1979), 155–86; Eric Sundquist, *Home as Found: Authority and Genealogy in Nineteenth-Century American Literature* (Baltimore: Johns Hopkins University Press, 1979), 143–85; and Myra Jehlen, *American Incarnation: The Individual, the Nation, and the Continent* (Cambridge: Harvard University Press, 1986), 185–226.

Even before reading Reinaldo Arenas's *Graveyard of the Angels*, I thought that Villaverde's understanding of *mulatez* gave direct access to a full theriomorphic scenario. Arenas's satirical reading confirmed my sense of the *daimonic*, of the pagan element in *Cecilia* and the need to translate it in terms of certain outlandish forms of romantic transcendentalism, wholly lacking on the surface of Cuban prose fiction perhaps until Lezama Lima's orphic digressions. When Martín Morúa Delgado deplores the absence in *Cecilia* of "un personaje simpático," or of someone "truly understanding," he might be unwittingly calling for a strong representative of romantic self-love and of the self's own pantheistic beauty. Most critics think that Morúa Delgado's readings of *Cecilia* are resentful and naive, but these critics are mainly interested in building Cuban literature around Villaverde's maturing and belated revisions and expansions of the novel and the purging of his own romantic sensibility; they want Villaverde as a full-fledged social realist.[13] Morúa Delgado rejects what he sees as Villaverde's imprisonment in moralistic romanticism; he wants a more naturalistic novelist, or the kind of writer capable of creating *Sofía*, which became his own answer to the question of the mulatto in *Cecilia*. Unlike Morúa Delgado, I look for evidence of a genuine romantic crisis which Villaverde never quite managed to re-create in his fiction. What I deplore is the absence in Cuba of the artistic and religious ferment that informs the writings of Hawthorne and Melville. (No one has yet explained why Carpentier should have used an epigraph from a Melville letter to Hawthorne near the end of *La consagración de la primavera* [*The Rites of Spring*]; the possibility that Carpentier might have felt a void in Cuba's lack of transcendentalist and romantic anxieties should be explored.) Cuban culture in the 1830s and 1840s experienced crisis in resisting colonial despotism and in dealing with the political economy of slavery. In religious matters nothing took place at the time but a shuffling of scholastic formulas. One gets the feeling that our writers were on the run, and that, like a certain fellow in Kierkegaard, just as they were about to be born, they climbed back into the womb nagged by the feeling of having forgotten something. Some of them, like Plácido, were put to death in barbaric fashion; others, like Heredia, Villaverde, and eventually Martí, fled into exile. There was little opportunity in Cuba to create and then to revise and assault an agonistic sense of national consciousness, one freed from harsh political demands; nor was there a well-established philistine class, with its fiction, poems, and temples, capable of driving some imaginations into the sort of domestic alienation from which Hawthorne and Melville began writing. (The epigraph quoted by Carpentier expresses just such alienation; I will quote it only in Spanish in order to preserve its freshness and current urgency in Cuban terms: "¿Cuándo acabaremos de acontecer? Mientras nos quede algo por hacer, nada hemos hecho.") In the end, to appreciate a writer like Villaverde within and without his national boundaries, we ought to imagine him at least in part as a woman writer. In dedicating *Cecilia* from exile

---

13. Martín Morúa Delgado, "Las novelas del señor Villaverde," in *Acerca de Cirilo Villaverde*, 64–97. Reinaldo González offers a tolerant if condescending Marxist reading of Villaverde's romantic burdens; see his *Contradanzas*.

to Cuban women, he hoped that they represented those persons most eager to read such a book; but he thought that they should form a group, rather than just a collection of much-worshipped individuals who nonetheless remained an unfulfilled and hidden community.

The absence of a person of sympathy (perhaps a woman) noted by Morúa Delgado should be reinterpreted as the apparent lack of answerable pathos, or of the crucial romantic element of centeredness in *Cecilia*. The invention of such a center of personal depth in Villaverde's melodrama requires a dramatic strategy. The lure of strong feelings that turns sympathy into a call to come inside and to partake of the person's inner turmoil should take effect, paradoxically, as a denial of depth, as an affirmation that the melodramatic unconscious lies outside each major character, and that the soul is on stage, on parade. A drama (or a film) becomes imaginable when based on the notion that one literary work can serve as the concrete unconscious of another. For instance, Melville's Pierre Glendinning could become the full archetype of Leonardo Gamboa, or perhaps his melodramatic antitype. Leonardo's shallowness and frivolity make a travesty of incest; he remains his mother's surrogate, her ambassador to a land of romance whose very existence she denies. But, in assessing this relationship in *Cecilia*, one should think of Pierre, whose ardor to become a writer and to purge evil from his family overwhelms the very notion of any sexual decorum: if incest did not exist, Pierre would invent it. For him, incest represents an artifice, a climate that one can dare to create until it breaks loose and wreaks havoc in the manor. This suicidal assumption is what Pierre's archetype as a ruined artist reveals to Gamboa's indolent sexuality. Critics are both right and wrong when they see an idealist distraction in *Cecilia*'s preoccupation with incest. They are right in seeing its seductiveness, its tokenism of darkness, and its descent from the religion of poets in love with themselves. But the critics are wrong when they fail to see in incest a mode of defense against impersonality and against the absence of an organic community, inside and outside the family. It is fitting then that mulattoes should crop up at the heart of incest fear, but not as their presence is commonly understood. Mulattoes in novels like *Cecilia* should have no part of incest; to begin with, they have all but been deserted by their fathers, and in order to fall into incest, as conceived in these novels, one must have a father. This much might be learned from Pierre: it does not matter whether or not your dark half sister is your father's daughter; in her alluring hues, she incarnates the mother, the *womanity*, the universal and yet particular human being in whom we are all by turn engendered. And Pierre sees in this woman as transcendent object a sort of maleness transfigured, a mishmash that haunts every self-conscious mulatto as well as everyone who, like Pierre, would translate *mulatez*, rather accurately, as *maleness* sublime.

Leonardo Gamboa's dubious sister signifies among other things the real and symbolic exclusion of black and mulatto males from the engendering of *mulatez*. Cecilia is a *sister* by virtue of her nonblack breeder; she is a *daughter* by virtue of her rank within a genealogy of breeding mothers in whom the regressive force of blackness continues to implant sex and predatory mating. These mothers and daughters have something truly sororal about them, as if they represented the elementary structures of the harem. Consider these words: "My great-grandmama told my grandmama the part she lived through that my grandmama didn't live through and my grandmama told me what they all lived through and my mama told me what they all lived through and we're suppose to pass it down like that from generation to generation so we'd never forget."[14] The female voice of *mulatez* speaks here in a way not found and yet implicit in *Cecilia*. Actually, this utterance of single-gender lineage can become an instance of reunion, if and when someone like Cecilia Valdés meets a mother like María de Regla, the breast-feeder who sets in motion the daughter-relation in the plot; she also speaks about the dispersal of children and of brothers and sisters in the wake of a rupture in black kinship. Through María de Regla's presence, the two severed sisters in the novel come face to face: Cecilia and her look-alike Adela Gamboa, Leonardo's youngest sister. Sisterhood remains split as long as the father retains his power over these women and keeps them as perennial daughters, whom he one day might seduce. In the role of specular sisters, Cecilia and Adela look at themselves in a mirror held by their father. As their resemblance shifts from portrait into action, their father's features change registers: an allegory of mythic sisterhood replaces any realistic emphasis on the mere facts of crossbreeding.

Adela's portrait at the Gamboa dinner table enhances the father's coinage of her: "There was between father and daughter something more than what is generally regarded as a family resemblance; the same physiognomic expression, the same spirit in her carriage, impressed on her face the seal of her progeny."[15] A second affinity is soon noted between Adela and her father's only son: an *ángel*, a love messenger binds them together; they would love each other like "the most celebrated lovers ever known," if they were not "hermanos carnales" (57). Leonardo inhabits a love triangle drawn by the father and his two daughters. But we should listen to Nemesia, Cecilia's mulatto understudy, who tells her brother José Dolores Pimienta, who is Cecilia's frustrated suitor, that the Gamboa "father and son are in love with Cecilia up to the tip of their hair" (94). Nemesia's words are well-founded: with the Gamboa pair, breeding comes like a one-man tribe in which a single male plays both father and son. In this regard, Leonardo's rapacious loneliness (his being an only son and his lack of a brother) has its own tribal resonance. His mother sends him to Cecilia as to a whore; she knows better than to think of incest regarding this matter; she is in her own ways a better father than her husband. With her blessings, Leonardo enjoys something of the forbidden mother in Cecilia. What arouses the avenging angel in José Dolores Pimienta is the cynical and exclusive use of the *mulata*, as both mother and daughter, on the part of the conspiring white predators; that is why Pimienta plays the Oedipus role that Leonardo has the luxury of avoiding, as long as he can continue to trick Cecilia behind his and her father's back; a father who neither of them really has

14. Gayl Jones, *Corregidora* (New York: Random House, 1975), quoted in Mary V. Dearborn, *Pocahontas's Daughters: Gender and Ethnicity in American Culture* (New York: Oxford University Press, 1986), 131.

15. Cirilo Villaverde, *Cecilia Valdés: novela de costumbres cubanas*, ed. Raymundo Lazo (Mexico City: Porrúa, 1979), 96. Subsequent references are cited in the text (all translations are my own).

beyond the rhetoric of breeding. With his vanity nourished by a paternalistic mother and his manhood sought after by one of the father's madwoman creations, Leonardo Gamboa is killed by the excluded mulatto who, unlike him, cannot afford to regard females as objects of leisure; his murder at the hands of Pimienta includes the death of the father as a parasite of the paternal order.

Euripides in Havana

As a matter of theme and technique, incest had already been tried by Villaverde before he undertook writing the first version of *Cecilia*. But he never quite made it out of stories like "El ave muerta" ("The Dead Bird") (1837). Reading it, one struggles with Villaverde to corner incest and to let it fly over the churchyard wall; one tries in vain to awake the brother and the sister as they become narcoleptic; as such, their spiritual ruin turns into a replica of the writer's own failure to produce a successful story. The relative artistic success of the final 1882 *Cecilia* can be attributed to Villaverde's escape from a similar plot and to his attainment of a broad vision of Cuban society. It can equally be said, however, that in his youthful exploitation of romantic themes he failed to translate inspired incest into a theme nimble enough to animate an entire novel. Maybe *Cecilia* was held for too long in the hands of its slowly maturing author, far too long after what might have been its romantic release point.

A partial view of a more romantic *Cecilia* can be obtained by imagining a movie version of it. With a big budget, I would add New Orleans and Rome to the Cuban locations, using as decor George Washington Cable's *The Grandissimes* and Hawthorne's *The Marble Faun*. Imagined in its bare essentials, the film could begin at the dinner table, with a close-up study of resemblances focused on Adela and her father, in preparation to a flashback about the birth of Cecilia, the internment of her mother, and the young nymph's street-urchin life in Havana. This flashback would be narrated from inside a jail cell by José Dolores Pimienta, the closest thing to my protagonist, who would be played by Terence Trent D'Arby, somewhat disfigured by makeup, and cast also, in shameful splendor, in the role of Cecilia as a teenager. In my film, the elder Gamboa will be colored olive brown; he should possess the strong genius of an upstart mulatto, acquired as if by mimicry in his dealings with *negreros*; but in his visits to various octoroon women, he will resemble a properly white Victorian gentleman. Leonardo should be like his mother, both being white and incongruous, speaking and acting like a yuppie couple on holiday from Miami. Finally, Cecilia's grandmother, María de Regla, and Dolores Santa Cruz should be strictly barred from taking any part in the action; they would live in Rome, where the director comes to interview them at intervals that should create a certain choral tone, with the old but quite spirited women risking offhand, nostalgic, but bawdy comments on the entire story.

My present surmise comes to rest on two scenes. Adela is getting down from a carriage, when the snake-bitten Pimienta pulls her hair loose and creates a bronze maiden. Frightened and confused, Adela will dream that, sometime in the near future, a young, beautiful brown woman whom she seems to know by the name of Cecilia finds herself in the same situation. Instead of the unknown man who took away her shell comb, however, it is Leonardo, who in the company of his fiancé looks just like Adela herself, as he gets insulted by this other Cecilia, who somehow seems to look like not only Adela and Isabel but Leonardo as well! As the dream unfolds and gets scary, the insulting maiden begins to look like a harpy, uncannily resembling the dreamer herself, although crude and awesome, like a black Medusa.

My film is becoming too much like a mere dream. Also, I do not know yet how to get to New Orleans, and the trick of bringing that city to Havana seems too literary, in the worst postmodernist style. So I may have to settle for a soap, being content with seeing the same drama changing somewhat with each serial, or from movie to movie. There could always be surprises in this method. For instance, in *The Grandissimes*, Cecilia could become a neo-African princess named Palmyre Philosophe; she would descend from "high Latin ancestry" and be colored with "Jaloff African" tints, and have a "barbaric and magnetic beauty," and be endowed with "mental acuteness, conversational adroitness, concealed cunning, and noiseless but visible strength of will," and have, finally, "that rarest of gifts in one of her tincture, the purity of true womanhood."[16] But this threatens to become a museum piece unless it travels the road of myth. So, as "a little quadroon slave-mate," Palmyre may grow up as the sole playmate of the fair Aurore Nancanou. They are sisters, just like, in a certain way, Cecilia and Adela are, in spite of everything else. But wait, Palmyre and Aurore get separated (for "Aurore had to become a lady and her playmate a lady's maid; but not *her* maid, because the maid had become, of the two, the ruling spirit"). This is just how Adela and Cecilia might separate in order to become heraldic sisters with a third presence ruling over them, the same force of female sacredness that causes Palmyre to be rushed away from Aurore. . . .

Euripides is blamed for inventing melodrama. Perhaps plays like his seriocomic *Ion* should serve as mediators between the unfinished romanticism of *Cecilia* and the mythic coloration of *The Grandissimes*. I think of *Ion* because of the richness of its treatment of Athenian beliefs in racial purity and all the tough questions of birthright, because of its earnest interest in the suffering of women, and because of its ironic reverence for mothers.[17] Besides, *Ion* includes the story of Pallas's slaying of her playmate, the Gorgon, in which I see an archaic instance of the

16. George Washington Cable, *The Grandissimes* (New York: C. Scribner's Sons, 1908), 80. The quotation that follows appears on p. 60. The novel first appeared in book form in 1880. For an excellent discussion of the author and his work see Louis D. Rubin, Jr., *George Washington Cable: The Life and Times of a Southern Heretic* (New York: Pegasus, 1969). A new edition has just appeared in the Penguin Classics: see *The Grandissimes*, ed. Michael Kreyling (New York: Penguin Classics, 1988).

17. *Ion by Euripides: A Translation with Commentary*, ed. and trans. Anne Pippin Burnett (Englewood Cliffs, N.J.: Prentice-Hall, 1970). For a view of *Ion* as comedy, see Bernard Knox, "Euripidean Comedy," in his *Word and Action* (Baltimore: Johns Hopkins University Press, 1979), 250–74. On questions of race, see Arlene W. Saxonhouse, "Myths and the Origins of Cities: Reflections on the Autochthony Theme in Euripides' *Ion*," in *Greek Tragedy and Political Theory*, ed. J. Peter Euben (Berkeley and Los Angeles: University of California Press, 1986), 252–73; and George B. Walsh, "The Rhetoric of Birthright and Race in Euripides *Ion*," *Hermes* 106, 2 (1978): 301–15.

specular themes that inform the relationship among females discussed thus far. Palmyre Philosophe could easily embody Pallas's wisdom and masculinity plus the Gorgon's threat to each of these endowments; but she may also represent the tragic sublation, the simultaneous adoption and banishment of the killing female by the domestic and xenophobic rules of kinship. Thus, Palmyre gives, as Euripides seems to have intended, an ironic view of mythic recognition and, in our terms, of a certain romantic covenant with archaic religion as the ultimate social unconscious. Recessive and gorgonic, Palmyre turns sisterhood into a mirror of surrounding cruelties; the Gorgon becomes an effect rather than just a personified character as she fades into a trauma and then flashes into sudden view and becomes archaic only by virtue of her blunt and at times horrifying recurrence. The Gorgon happens: upon being captured and tortured, a fugitive slave kills himself by swallowing his tongue. Villaverde's close-up description of the black face (eyes bulging out, warrior scars running from eyelids to chin, teeth filed, jaws clenched withholding tongue inside the throat) evokes a bizarre quotation of the Gorgon's apotropaic display; the unseen tongue, swallowed rather than hanging, transfers the grotesque ornamental value of the Gorgon into unspeakable wretchedness. It might seem frivolous to plaster the iconography of a magic toy on a scene of witnessed suffering (Villaverde actually saw what he narrates); but that is precisely the point. At the most graphic moment of its testimonial realism, *Cecilia* comes out of the novelistic frame; and to pretend that nowadays the slave's face would be available to most readers outside of their film memories and expectations, I find ridiculous. After all, films of whatever genre tend to survive within memory in expressionistic fragments, much like myths do in Euripides' melodramatic repertoire.

Roman Revelers

> *The idea of the modern Faun . . . loses all the poetry and*
> *beauty which the Author fancied in it, and becomes nothing*
> *better than a grotesque absurdity, if we bring it into the ac-*
> *tual light of day. He had hoped to mystify this anomalous*
> *creature between the Real and the Fantastic, in such a*
> *manner that the reader's sympathies might be excited to a*
> *certain pleasurable degree, without impelling him to ask how*
> *Cuvier would have classified poor Donatello, or to insist*
> *upon being told, in so many words, whether he had furry*
> *ears or no. As respects all who ask such questions, the book*
> *is to that extent, a failure.*
>   *Nathaniel Hawthorne (to a reader),* The Marble Faun;
>   The Centenary Edition

In the absence of Calvinism and of any subsequent awakenings, the romantic sublime in Cuba could only grow by internalizing and purging other codes, other disciplines of the self not directly influenced by a powerful current of religious egoism.[18] The approach to the sublime in Cuba, as in Villaverde's case, led to the exorcism of the demons of race. Carpentier approached it from the other end, or by celebrating what he once called our *"fecundos mestizajes."* He included his own version of *Cecilia* in Cuba's greatest work of romantic apprenticeship and disenchantment, *El siglo de las luces* (*Explosion in the Cathedral*). Like Melville's Pierre, Esteban represents Leonardo Gamboa's antitype and, in purely fictional terms, he is Leonardo's precursor. Esteban is the son of a gross merchant, a primitive accumulator who might have died while having sex with a mulatta. In Sofía, Esteban found his incestuous horizons, his literature, and the template of revolt against despotism (those who read *El siglo* as a companion piece to Castro's revolution are only kidding themselves). Esteban is learning to be Stendhal, but he is not quite there yet. At the end of *El siglo*, he seems to have fallen from the pages of one of Ann Radcliffe's romances and into a private diary in which he cannibalizes Chateaubriand's incestuous American pastorals with all the greed of a cultural pariah. Earlier, he relives on a Caribbean beach a Jungian version of Wordsworth's unrevised *Prelude*; and in fact, Esteban and the pilgrim protagonist of that poem visit revolutionary Paris almost at the same time: the main difference in their subsequent political disenchantment lies in Esteban's slow ascent to an ascetic form of eroticism warmed by the savage feminism of mother Sofía.

Had they survived the third of May, 1808, in the turbulent Madrid of Goya, Esteban and Sofía, in their wanderings through Europe, might have run into the young, hauntingly dark and charismatic Simón Bolívar. Esteban would have had to prevent Sofía from running away with this new and improved version of Victor Hughes. Perhaps escaping from him, they would have moved to Italy, and with a stolen treasure bought a villa in the heart of Etruria. I think that their next avatar, or the only way for them to return to America without leaving Europe, is found in late Hawthorne; for it is with him that the theme of transcendental incest reaches a peculiar impasse, in a shift from the myths of poets and revolutionaries to those fashioned by a cultural elite.

In a recent study of *The Marble Faun*, Richard Brodhead argues that Hawthorne wrote it "in full awareness of the contemporary reorganization of the literary sphere"; thus, Hilda becomes "the exponent of the canonical attitude, the attitude that identifies art with an exclusive group of transcendent makers."[19] Earlier in his career, Hawthorne's artist types worked somewhat like pariahs, at the margins of community; like Hester, they were branded with the stigma of sacred pollution.

---

18. Certainly not in any pedestrian sense, but as a cardinal virtue, I admire the theological egoism of the great and the anonymous among the Puritans. Ann Douglas has written that "Calvinism was a great faith, with great limitations: it was repressive, authoritarian, dogmatic, patriarchal to an extreme. Its demise was inevitable, and in some real sense welcome"; but she adds that "it de-served, and elsewhere and at other times found, great opponents," and that one "could argue that the logical antagonist of Calvinism was a fully humanistic, historically minded romanticism," of which she regards Melville and Margaret Fuller as rare examples; see her *The Feminization of American Culture* (New York: Knopf, 1977), 12–13.

19. Richard H. Brodhead, *The School of Hawthorne* (New York: Oxford University Press, 1986), 73. Subsequent references are cited in the text.

But, in Brodhead's view, Hilda "imagines, in extraordinary precise detail [a coun-
terpart of Hester's eroticism of embroidery?], the mid-nineteenth-century development in which the freshly segregated sphere of secular high art became sacral-
ized, made a new locus for the sacred" (74). Through Hilda, "Hawthorne reads
the advent of a canonical model of art as one phase of a more general objectifi-
cation of authority in his culture, the artistic yield of a process whose products
also include the intensification of the superego's abstracting legalism and the compulsory etherialization of erotic life" (75). These are high charges against those
who, as cultural tourists, became beacons of moral reference and deserted a haz-
ardous encounter with the spirit of place, or with the sublime and uncanny.

By means of its archeological obsessions with mythic mixtures and the primal
breeding of an aristocratic family, *The Marble Faun* elevates the theme of miscegenation to the artistic context of the *Kulturroman* and its inherent cosmopoli-
tanism. A Southern plantation is brought to the ancient navel of Etruria at Monte
Beni, but well within reach of Rome. On the other side of Brodhead's view of
the elite, I see a portrait of an upper-crust group of unfulfilled bohemians, a
troupe of future celebrities and entertainers, of filmmakers. There is a strong hint
of publicity, of the search for the right angle and exposure, as if these characters
were making a documentary or a television drama on the life of Gibson, for
instance, with his "colored Venuses," so pruriently tainted or "stained" with
"tobacco juice"; or his Cleopatra, with "full, Nubian lips," inspected and almost
professorially flavored by Kenyon. And then of course we have Miriam to contend
with: the padded mystery of a celebrity, "the offspring of a Southern American
planter," with "the one burning drop of African blood" that drove her into exile.
Allegory has a hard time finding unpolluted luster in Rome, where everything
exudes a measure of lust; it is no wonder that Hilda has moved up into a tower.

It should be remembered that with the 1860 publication of his romance in
Germany, under the title of *The Transformation*, Hawthorne became one of the
first American authors to "weave daguerreotypy into his fiction."[20] Since photo-
lithography had not yet been developed, the two volumes were sold with an
optional set of original photographs pasted at places deemed appropriate along
the narrative. The photograph of Praxiteles' Faun stands out as a kind of unique
photogenic object ideal for the delights of theriomorphia; all the generic amalgams
in the textures of *The Marble Faun* find quiet resolution in this simple study of
ephebic beauty. Seeing it, one can better appreciate the exertions of the allegorical
work ethic evident in Hawthorne's descriptions of paintings. The spiritual sweat-
ing implied in the enhancement of such artwork evokes the combustive aura generated by lovers during sex. But the painted scene concerns the mixture of eroticism and race. With her own history of amalgamation, Miriam is about to ruin
the beatitude of Guido's Archangel subduing Satan: "Just fancy," she tells Kenyon, "a smoke-blackened, fiery-eyed demon, bestriding that nice young angel,

---

20. Carol Shloss, "Nathaniel Hawthorne and Daguerreotypy: Disinterested Vision," in her *In Visible
Light: Photography and the American Writer, 1840–1940* (New York: Oxford University Press,
1987), 25–50.

clutching his white throat with one of his hinder claws; and giving a triumphant whisk of his scaly tail, with a poisonous dart at the end of it!" This is, she concludes, "what they risk, poor souls, who do battle with Michael's enemy."[21] Such a blasting of Guido's balanced forces creates pollution by mixture; Miriam's fantasy of a painting that she dreads to actually copy may imply that her own mixture of the angelic and the demonic puts her, by turn, in both of the contending and heavily eroticized positions that she awakens in the painting. I see Miriam and Donatello in a transparency: holding them up like a slide, I can see the teenage Cecilia, her theriomorphic image split in two from a vanishing point. On one retina is Donatello, on the other Miriam; and on the retina's target either Praxiteles' Faun or Cecilia herself.

Amid the pastoral accretions of Monte Beni, two bachelors sojourn as they delay what could never be a single wedding. Miriam enters the scene in the role of intruder already patented by the predatory Model when he haunted her and Donatello. She complains to Kenyon about his curious abrogation of Donatello's interest in her: "You are taking him from me . . . and putting yourself, and all manner of living interest, into the place that I ought to fill" (284–85). Kenyon abides, perhaps fearing that the scene could turn into one of Miriam's hideous mental paintings: he does not "pretend to be the guide that Donatello needs"; he is a man, "and between man and man, there is always an insuperable gulf. They can never quite grasp each other's hands; and therefore man never derives any intimate help, any heart-sustenance, from his brother man, but from woman— his mother, his sister, or his wife" (285). I ask: what sort of masochism has taken possession of Kenyon? If his words are meant as premarital wisdom, they border on the perverse. For, in proving that she is fit to marry Donatello, Miriam has had to involve him (and herself) in the violent and contaminating ordeal that should prove that she can become a chaste bride, by showing that she was never a criminal on the occasion of her own outrage—that of being raped by her father. Yet the proof of female innocence obtained by Donatello, the murderous manner in which he grasps and releases it, and the need to have Miriam's vision ravished by the sight of his liberating crime, make her more than ever a suspect in the former perpetration of her own defilement. Here, reenacting the crime means blaming its victim. In not being able (in masochistic fashion) to see this shameful transfer of guilt onto a daughter, Kenyon becomes an impotent sadist toward women, and a potent ally of those females in whose invulnerable chasteness eroticism has died. There is then a dire need for the Etruscan sanctuary in which perennial bachelors (like Kenyon) and ancestral love-objects (like Donatello) can sublimate their sensuousness while embowered in a rustic landscape of immense pictorial femininity, a virtual womb of projected eroticism forbidden to men.

In one of her many celebrations of what she called *protonarcissism*, Lou Andreas-Salomé once noted "that huge, simple fact that there is nothing to which we are

21. Nathaniel Hawthorne, *The Marble Faun; or, The Romance of Monte Beni*. The Centenary Edition (Columbus, Ohio: Merill, 1969), 23. Subsequent references are cited in the text.

not native."[22] It seems to me that Hawthorne loved and feared this crude form of pantheism, and that in writing *The Marble Faun*, he found no cure for this ambiguity; if anything, his pantheistic horizons are reached through exhaustion and the wreckage of romance. In *Concierto barroco*, Carpentier took a Cuban African named Filemón all the way to the Venice of Longhi and Vivaldi; I cannot see why Cecilia should not, in similar fashion, migrate to the Rome of Miriam and Donatello, and into a carnival in which she could even play Baubo with all the cunning of a black Athena. I surely would like to find some traces of her there, if I ever reach Rome. I would avoid the Faun out of a certain romantic fear; or as if, upon seeing it, I could suddenly feel very old, incapable of finishing all my readings. But I would go in search of a narrow alley like those in Havana's old colonial center; and there, in front of some suitable effigy, I would utter some words of prayer to our Lady of the Anal Sublime. I would say something in little Italian, like: "Io sono Cecilia, Cecilia Valdés . . ."

22. Binion, *Frau Lou*, 343.

PART III

Social Theory and Analysis

The last part begins with recent "Statistics of Black-White Intermarriage Rates in the United States." The six essays that follow offer heterogeneous theoretical perspectives on interracialism, and all have strong practical implications or advance explicit proposals. W. E. B. Du Bois finished the essay "Miscegenation" in early 1935 for an encyclopedia in which it was ultimately not included: it is informed by a global historical perspective on the pervasiveness of race mixing and on new theoretical approaches to "race" that help clarify an antiracist position. The essay "Intermarriage and the Social Structure: Fact and Theory" (1941) by the eminent sociologist Robert K. Merton offers clear, sharply drawn models for interpreting interracial sexual and marital patterns within the social structure. Hannah Arendt's "Reflections on Little Rock" (1959) greatly provoked readers when it was first published because Arendt implies that integrationists may have been ignoring the important issue of interracial marriage in their focus on education and service. The emergence of sexual topics and revulsion of previous racial laws indicates the changing mood of Americans. William H. Turner, in "Black Men–White Women: A Philosophical View" (1973), calls attention to mental structures and clichéd notions of interracial love in opposition to intraracial relations, making only the latter appear "natural." Joel Perlmann proposes, in "Reflecting the Changing Face of America: Multiracials, Racial Classification, and American Intermarriage" (1997), a reconsideration of current Census practices which inhibit interracial counting and self-description of American citizens.

Statistics of Black–White Intermarriage Rates in the United States[*]

Married Couples of Same or Mixed Races and Origins: 1980 to 1996
[In thousands. As of March. Persons 15 years old and over. Persons of Hispanic origin may be of any race. Except as noted, based on Current Population Survey.]

Race and Origin of Spouses	1980	1990	1995	1996
Married couples, total	49,714	53,256	54,937	54,664
RACE				
Same race couples	48,264	50,889	51,733	51,616
White/White	44,910	47,202	48,030	48,056
Black/Black	3,354	3,687	3,703	3,560
Interracial couples	651	964	1,392	1,260
Black/White	167	211	328	337
Black husband/White wife	122	150	206	220
White husband/Black wife	45	61	122	117
White/other race[1]	450	720	988	884
Black/other race[1]	34	33	76	39
All other couples[1]	799	1,401	1,811	1,789
HISPANIC ORIGIN				
Hispanic/Hispanic	1,906	3,085	3,857	3,888
Hispanic/other origin (not Hispanic)	891	1,193	1,434	1,464
All other couples (not of Hispanic origin)	46,917	48,979	49,646	49,312

[1] Excluding White and Black.

Source: U.S. Bureau of the Census, *Current Population Reports,* P20–488, and earlier reports; and unpublished data.

Miscegenation[†]

W. E. B. DU BOIS

The truth as to the mixture of races is difficult to study because of the opinions and desires of people and of their deep-seated prejudices. The leading European

[*] From U.S. Bureau of the Census, *Current Population Reports,* no. 62.
[†] From W. E. B. Du Bois, "Miscegenation" (January 1935), published in *Against Racism: Unpublished Essays, Papers, Addresses, 1887–1961, by W. E. B. Du Bois,* ed. Herbert Aptheker (Amherst: University of Massachusetts Press, 1985), 90–102.

nations of today, being generally convinced of their superiority to other types of men, are opposed in theory to racial inter-mingling as tending to degrade their stock. Beneath this, and supporting the conviction, are decided economic advantages based on the use of colored labor as an exploited caste, held in place by imperial military and naval expansion.

When back of all this one seeks scientific reasons, the path is singularly difficult. First of all, there is the basic question: What is a race? Usually we think of three main races, but Blumenbach found 5, Agassiz 8, Huxley 11, Haeckel 12, Topinard 18, Crawford 60, and Gliddon 150.

The matter is not really of great importance. As von Luschan says:

> The question of the number of human races has quite lost its raison d'etre, and has become a subject rather of philosophical speculation than of scientific research. It is of no more importance now to know how many human races there are than to know how many angels can dance on the point of a needle. Our aim now is to find out how ancient and primitive races developed from others, and how races have changed or evolved through migration and interbreeding. (Professor Felix Von Luschan in "Anthropological View of Race," *Inter-Racial Problems*, 1911, pp. 16, 21, 22)

Taking the conventional divisions of mankind into black, yellow and white, we can place no hard and fast dividing line between them. They fade insensibly into each other; and when we take into account other characteristics, such as head-form, bony structure, hair form and bodily measurements, the confusion is almost complete. The inevitable conclusion is as Ratzel says: "There is only one species of man, the variations are numerous, but do not go deep." Deniker adds: "Where the genus homo is concerned, one can neither speak of the species and variety nor the race in the sense usually contributed to these others in zoology."

Broadly speaking, we mean by Race today, not a clearly defined and scientifically measured group, but rather "a great division of mankind, the members of which, though individually varying, are characterized as a group by a certain combination of morphological and metrical features, principally non-adaptive, which have been derived from their common descent" (p. 397, Hooton, *Up from the Ape*).

It is conceded that the present main races and their numerous subdivisions also often called races, arose from the intermingling of more primitive groups. Reuter says:

> . . . Ever since the existing human species diverged into its four or five existing varieties or sub-species, there has been a constant opposite movement at work to unify the type. Whites have returned southwards and mingled with Australoids, Australoids have united with Negroids, and produced Melanesians, and Papuans; and these, again, have mixed with proto-Caucasians or with Mongols to form the Polynesian. The earliest types of white man have mingled with the primitive Mongol, or directly with the primitive Negro. There is an ancient Negroid strain underlying the populations of Southern and Western France, Italy, Sicily, Corsica, Sardinia, Spain, Portugal, Ireland, Wales and Scotland. Evidences of the former existence of those Negroid people are not only to be found in the features of their mixed descendants at the present day, but the fact is attested by skulls, skeletons, and works of art of more or less great antiquity in France, Italy, etc.

... There are few Negro peoples at the present day—perhaps only the Bushmen, the Congo-Pigmies, and a few tribes of forest Negroes—which can be said to be without more or less trace of ancient white inter-mixture. (p. 15, *The Mulatto in the United States,* Reuter)

The modern problem of race intermixture arises when the intermingling of racial groups, as they are at present constituted, is considered. These groups are in no case pure races. They have been built up through indiscriminate interbreeding throughout past ages, and as Haddon says: "A racial type is after all but an artificial concept." Whatever the origin of these races may be, nevertheless today mankind is obviously divided into various groups widely different in appearance and degree of culture. How far are these groups at present intermingling, what is the future of such cross-breeding, and what will be the physical and cultural results? First, it must be remembered that even at present racial types are not static but are growing and developing entities.

Modern Italians, Frenchmen, Englishmen and Germans are composites of the broken fragments of different racial groups or sub-groups. Interbreeding has broken up ancient races and interaction and imitation have created types with uniformities in manners, languages and behavior. World-wide communication has tended to miscegenation on a broad scale.

What has been the result in modern times? Can we look upon this intermingling as the unfortunate meeting of superior and inferior stocks? Von Luschan, as quoted above, says:

Fair and dark races, long and short-haired, intelligent and primitive, all come from one stock. Favorable circumstances and surroundings, especially a good environment, a favorable geographical population, trade and traffic, cause one group to advance more quickly than another, while some groups have remained in a very primitive state of development; but all are adapted to their surroundings according to the law of the survival of the fittest. One type may be more refined, another type may be coarser, but if both are thorough-bred, or what we call good types, however they may differ, one is not necessarily inferior to the other.

This question of innate racial differences is a difficult one. Ratzel says:

It may be safely asserted that the study of comparative ethnology in recent years has tended to diminish the weight of traditionally accepted views of anthropologists, as to racial distinctions, and that in any case, they afford no support to the view which sees in the so-called lower races of mankind a transition stage from beast to man.

Spiller says:

It is not legitimate to argue from differences in physical characteristics to differences in mental characteristics. The physical and mental characteristics in a particular race are not either permanent or modifiable only through ages of environmental pressure, but rather marked changes in education, public sentiment, and general environment, even apart from inter-marriage, materially transform physical and mental characteristics in a generation or two. The status of a race at any particular moment or time offers no index to its innate and inherited capacities.

It is important to recognize that civilizations are meteoric in nature, bursting out of obscurity only to plunge back into it. (*Inter-Racial Problems*, G. Spiller, pp. 35, 36, 38)

Boas, speaking particularly of the alleged inferiority of Negroes, says:

An unbiased estimate of the anthropological evidence so far brought forward does not permit us to countenance the belief in a racial inferiority which would unfit an individual of the Negro race to take his part in modern civilization. We do not know of any demand made on the human body or mind in modern life that anatomical or ethnological evidence would prove to be beyond the powers of the Negro. . . .
    In short, there is every reason to believe that the Negro, when given facility and opportunity, will be perfectly able to fulfill the duties of citizenship as well as his white neighbor. It may be that he will not produce as many great men as the white race, and that his average achievement will not quite reach the level of the average achievement of the white race; but there will be endless numbers who will be able to out run their white competitors, and who will do better than the defectives who we permit to drag down and to retard the healthy children of our public schools. (Franz Boas, *The Mind of Primitive Man*, pp. 272, 273)

Scientific opinion at present tends to admit that the Negro is not inferior in any essential character of mind; and is approximately equal to other races in his ability to acquire culture.

Hankins almost alone of current anthropologists tries to prove that physical differences must mean mental differences. But even he acknowledges that racial differences are of degree and not of kind, and that races may be inferior to others, in some respects, and superior in other respects (F. H. Hankins, *The Racial Basis of Civilization*, p. 322).

The average reader, particularly since the advent of Hitler, will be tempted to agree with Hooton:

"So much nonsense has been talked about 'race' that many pessimists are inclined to regard it as little more than a slogan of mass snobbery bellowed by propagandists or piped by anemic pleaders for an aristocratic regime long obsolete and vanished" (Hooton, *Up From the Ape*, p. 501).

What has been the cultural result of racial intermingling? The effect of the growth of national consciousness and imperial rivalries has been an attempt to prove that all modern culture derives from an Aryan or Nordic race and that degeneration and relapses from cultural standards have been the result of racial mixture. This theory was first stated in its extreme form by Count Joseph A. Gobineau in the middle of the 19th century; and his thesis has been expanded and continued by H. S. Chamberlain in Germany, and Grant, Gould, Stoddard and McDougall in America. Recently, the theory has received singular emphasis on the part of Hitler and his Nazis.

Historical criticism, however, and anthropological research, do not support this thesis. It has been shown, for instance, that race mixture among the Romans was more frequent in earlier Roman history than later, and that Nordics like the golden-haired Commodus and the blue-eyed Nero were much more despicable than Trajan and Hadrian, whose descent was doubtful. The decline of Rome was certainly social and economic, rather than racial. Indeed, it is a tenable thesis to declare with Schneider, that at least some race mixture is a prerequisite to the greatest cultural development. Egypt, Babylon, and all Western Asia show great race mixture. Mayo-Smith says "that there has never been a state whose population was not made of heterogeneous ethnical elements," and von Luschan says:

> We all know that a certain mixture of blood has always been of great advantage to a nation. England, France and Germany are equally distinguished for the great variety of their racial elements. In the case of Italy, we know that in ancient times and at the Renaissance Northern "Barbarians" were the leaven in the great advance of art and civilization; and even Slavic immigration has certainly not been without effect on this movement.

In Spain, there was great mixture of blood: Venetians, Carthaginians, Romans, Visigoths, Vandals, Jews, Arabs and Moors. With the Moors came a considerable infusion of Negro blood. The mixture of Danes and Eskimos has made a superior race of mixed bloods. The population of South America is composed of Indians, whites and Negroes with a large class of persons of mixed blood from all three elements in varying proportions.

Lacerda says of the half-breeds of Brazil that they have given birth down to our time to poets, painters, sculptors, distinguished musicians, magistrates, lawyers, eloquent orators, remarkable writers, medical men and engineers, who have been unrivaled in their technical skill and professional ability.

> The co-operation of the mulattoes in the advance of Brazil is notorious and far from inconsiderable. They played the chief part during many years in Brazil in the campaign for the abolition of slavery. I could quote celebrated names of more than one of these mulattoes who put themselves at the head of the literary movement. . . .
> It was owing to their support that the Republic was erected on the ruins of the empire. (p. 381, *Inter-Racial Problems*, G. Spiller)

In modern European history there have been many instances of distinguished mulattoes, such as Pushkin of Russia, and the Dumas of France. Also, among the mixed European Asiatic group in India and Java, there have been several artists and men of distinction.

While the general effect of inter-mixture of blood is fairly manifest, and exceptional mulattoes and other mixed bloods are well-known, there is little in the line of actual scientific study and measurement of mixed-bloods upon which to base conclusions. Von Luschan says: "We are especially ignorant as to the moral and intellectual qualities of half-castes."

There have been few thorough-going studies of mulatto groups. Two outstanding studies are by Professor Eugen Fischer and Carolyn Bond Day. The study by Fischer is of the Reheboth community of south-west Africa (*Die Rehobother Bastards und das Bastardierungsproblem beim Menschen*, Jena, 1913). This consists of the descendants, some 150 in number, through five or more generations, of the hybrid offspring of a group of trek Boers and Hottentot women, and includes the offspring of a number of unions with members of the parent races. Professor Fischer finds these people a strong, healthy and fruitful people, taller than either parent race, i.e., they show a common indication of hybrid vigour. Physically there is no predominance of heritage from either race, but the inheritance of facial characters and colour is described as alternate, and in spite of the three groups there is no special tendency for the inheritance of facial characters and colour is described as alternate. Psychologically, the most important observation is that the Hottentot mentality predominates; there is neither European energy nor steadfastness of will.

Carolyn Bond Day's excellent study of 2,537 mulattoes shows a healthy, moral and virile group, fully a part of their modern cultural environment. The Editor, E. A. Hooton, says: "I cannot see that these data afford any comfort to those who contend that miscegenation between Negroes and whites produces anthropologically inferior types." There is no adequate study of crime, disease and delinquency among any large group of mixed bloods.

The bitterest protest and deepest resentment in the matter of inter-breeding has arisen from the fact that the same white race which today resents race mixture in theory has been chiefly responsible for the systematic misuse and degradation of darker women the world over, and has literally fathered millions of half-castes in Asia, Africa and America. At the same time, whites have stigmatized and sneered at their own children, and in most cases, refused to recognize or support them; nor has this system been wholly the sexual incontinence of the dreg of white society which so often represents the advanced nations in their contact with backward nations. In a large number of instances, the best blood of the upper-class whites has been also widely represented.

Today, the moral and physical problems of race mixture are tense and of present interest chiefly in Germany, South Africa and the United States. In West Africa, the West Indies and South America, the racial mixture which is going on does not disturb the community and is not, therefore, a social problem. In Germany, Hitler's renaissance of anti-Semitism is simply a part of the general resentment and suffering in Germany because of the results of the war, and of the Treaty of Versailles. Of the great gift made by Jews to German culture during the last thousand years, there can be absolutely no dispute. On the other hand, it is also indisputable that present economic rivalry and racial jealousy give Hitler and his followers a whip today to drive the German people into clannish and cruel opposition to their Jewish fellow citizens.

In South Africa, the intermingling of races went on until the ascendency of the Boers stiffened racial solidarity and built a wall against the advance of the natives. The colored group in Cape Colony and Southwest Africa form an isolated and suppressed mass without full political freedom or fair economic opportunity.

In the United States, the question of racial inter-mixture is one that has caused the most intense feeling and controversy. And yet, singularly enough, it has been given a minimum of scientific study. Franz Boas says:

> I think we have reason to be ashamed to confess that the scientific study of these questions has never received the support either of our government or of any of our great scientific institutions, and it is hard to understand why we are so indifferent toward a question which is of paramount importance to the welfare of our nation. The anatomy of the American Negro is not well-known; and, not-

withstanding the oft-repeated assertions regarding the hereditary inferiority of the mulatto, we know hardly anything on this subject. If his vitality is lower than that of the full-blooded Negro, this may be as much due to social causes as to hereditary causes. Owing to the very large number of mulattoes in our country, it would not be a difficult matter to investigate the biological aspects of this question thoroughly. The importance of researchers on this subject cannot be too strongly urged, since the desirability or undesirability of race-mixture should be known. Looking into a distant future, it seems reasonably certain that with the increasing mobility of the Negro, the number of full-bloods will rapidly decrease; and since there is no introduction of new Negro blood, there cannot be the slightest doubt that the ultimate effect of the contact between the two races must necessarily be a continued increase of the amount of white blood in the Negro community. (Franz Boas, *The Mind of Primitive Man*, pp. 274, 275)

As is usual in such cases, the greater our ignorance of the facts the more intense has been the dogmatism of the discussion. Indeed, the question of the extent to which whites and blacks in the United States have mingled their blood, and the results of this inter-mingling, past, present and future, is, in many respects, the crux of the so-called Negro problem in the United States. In the last analysis most thinking Americans do not hate Negroes or wish to retard their advance. They are glad that slavery has disappeared; but their hesitation now is to how far complete social freedom and full economic opportunity for Negroes is going to result in such racial amalgamation as to make America octoroon in blood. It is the real fear of this result and inherited resentment at its very possibility that keeps the race problem in America so terribly alive.

This, instead of encouraging scientific study of the facts of miscegenation, hinders and makes it difficult. Men hasten to express their opinions on the subject without being willing to study the foundation upon which such opinions are based.

Historically, race mixture in the United States began far back in Colonial days. Many white women of the indentured servant class married slaves or free Negroes. Much confusion arose in the fixing of the legal status of the issue of such marriages and laws began to be passed forbidding the marriages largely because of their economic results. An indentured servant marrying a free Negro legally became free, and the child of a slave by a free white woman was according to American law also free. Travellers, like Branagan, and de Warville, cite several cases involving inter-marriage between Negroes and respectable white people. Bassett says that in North Carolina many of the free Negroes were children of white women by Negro men. On the other hand, the larger part of this inter-mingling naturally resulted from the association of slave owners with their female slaves. Then, as a free Negro and a mulatto class began to multiply, numbers of white men supported mistresses and raised families of mulatto children.

In some parts of the South, especially Louisiana, a type of polygamy arose in institutional form. Negro and mulatto girls became the mistresses of white men by regular arrangement. They were supported and families of mulatto children were reared. If the man married a white woman, the colored mistresses were sometimes deserted. Often, but not always, without provision for their support. In many other cases, the white man supported both a white and a colored family, and two sets of children. The free mulatto girls, from families of wealth and culture, often contracted such unions. Besides this more regularized form, the keeping of Negro mistresses was common in the South.

The attempt to study the size and growth of the mulatto group through the United States Census has not been very successful. In 1930, no compilation was made and there were no figures before 1850. In four censuses, between 1850 and 1890, the mulatto population was counted. No count was made in 1880, and in 1900, the attempt was given up probably because the plan in 1890 to make a distinction between persons of different degrees of white and Negro blood was officially acknowledged to have been a failure. In all the census figures, the method of ascertaining the presence of Negro and white blood is left almost entirely to the judgment of the enumerator. The census of 1920 says:

> Considerable uncertainty necessarily attaches to the classification of Negroes as black and mulatto, since the accuracy of the distinction made depends largely upon the judgment and care employed by the enumerators. Moreover, the fact that the definition of the term "mulatto" adopted at different censuses has not been entirely uniform doubtless affects the comparability of the figures in some degree. At the census of 1920 the instructions were to report as "black" all full-blooded Negroes and as "mulatto" all Negroes having some proportion of white blood. The instructions were substantially the same at the censuses of 1910 and 1870; but the term "black" as employed in 1890 denoted all persons "having three-fourths or more black blood," other persons with any proportion of Negro blood being classed as "mulattoes," "quadroons," or "octoroons." In 1900 and in 1880, no classification of Negroes as black or mulatto was attempted, and at the censuses of 1860 and 1850 the terms "black" and "mulatto" appear not to have been defined.

With these explanations, the figures for mulattoes in the United States, according to the census, are as follows:

Continental United States Negro Population

Census Year	Total Negro	Black	Mulatto	Percent Mulatto
1850	3,638,808	3,233,057	405,751	11.2
1860	4,441,830	3,853,467	588,363	13.2
1870	4,880,009	4,295,960	584,049	12.0
1890	7,488,676	6,337,980	1,132,060	15.2
1910	9,827,763	7,777,077	2,050,686	20.9
1920	10,463,131	8,802,577	1,660,554	15.9

These figures are of doubtful validity. There is, for instance, no reason to think that the mulatto population decreased by 400,000 between 1910 and 1920. I said in 1906: "From local studies in all parts of the United States, covering about 40,000 colored people, I found 17,000 blacks, 15,000 brown, and 6,000 yellow and lighter," and that "I was inclined to think from these specific studies and wide observation throughout the nation that at least one-third of the Negroes of the United States had recognizable traces of white blood." T. Thomas Fortune, earlier than this, estimated that not more than 4,000,000 of the 10,000,000 in the country were of (pure) Negro descent. These estimates have recently been supplemented by the studies of Herskovits. He says that:

"In the American Negro today, we find represented the three principal racial stocks of the world: African, Negroes, Caucasians from Northern and Western Europe, and Mongoloids; that is, American Indians from Southeastern North America and the Caribbean Islands.

"From groups studied at Howard University, in Harlem, New York City, and in a rural community in West Virginia," Herskovits concludes that:

Class	Number of Individuals	Percent of Total
Unmixed Negro	342	22.0%
Negro and Indian	97	6.3%
Negro and White	798	50.8%
Negro, White and Indian	314	20.9%

"When, therefore, we speak of American Negroes, we speak of an amalgam and not of Negro in its biological sense. The American Negro is forming a definite physical type with a variability as low as that of the populations from which it has been derived, and perhaps lower. They are a homogeneous population despite the fact that they are greatly mixed" (M. J. Herskovits, *The American Negro*).

The census estimate of 85% pure Negro is not correct. There is a large infiltration of Indian blood in the Negro race, amounting, perhaps, to 29% (M. J. Herskovits, *Anthropometry of the American Negro*, p. 279).

No other careful studies of mulatto physique have been made, although Atlanta University (Publications No. 11) brought together much interesting data. Most American students have the curious habit of studying Negroes in America indiscriminately without reference to their blood mixture and calling the result a study of the Negro race. This method invalidates much of the anthropological and psychological data collected during the World War. There were some efforts to distinguish between degrees of white blood but usually these were based crudely on mere skin color.

Assuming, then, that most recent measurements and tests of American Negroes are studies mainly of mulattoes with a minority of full-bloods, we have these results: The measurements of physique have been summarized by W. M. Cobb. He declares that the American Negro "is forming a type intermediate between the parent Negro, white and Indian stocks in those superficial traits which are differential race characters. . . .

"In fundamental bodily characters and developmental patterns, the American Negro is identical with other types of modern man" (W. M. Cobb, "The Physical Constitution of the American Negro").

In the psychological tests, results are equally indeterminate. Strong, Phillips, Yerkes and Brigham, are sure that intelligence tests prove the inferiority of the Negro race, while Herskovits, Reuter, and Bagley disagree. Much depends on how the tests are given and by whom. Also, there has been some suppression of results. Louisville, Kentucky, has never published her results of the intelligence tests for white and colored children. The charge comes from responsible circles that the results did not "come out right." One may fairly conclude with M. S. Viteles of the University of Pennsylvania:

"From among these varied conclusions it is possible for anyone interested in the problem of Negro-white differences to choose one which best suits his particular bias. The varied character of the findings themselves and the difficulties of interpretation suggest extreme caution in generalizing on differences between the Negro and the white" (p. 175, *The American Negro*).

With regard to the educational achievements of Negro and mulatto children, Charles H. Thompson of Howard University concludes:

"That the doctrine of an inherent mental inferiority of the Negro is a myth unfounded by the most logical interpretation of the scientific facts on the subject produced to date" (p. 208, *The American Negro*).

There long persisted a legend born of slave propaganda that people of mixed blood were less fertile than the parent stocks. Davenport and others declare that there is no support for this notion. There is no lack of fecundity in Negro-white crosses nor deficit viability. It is not generally true that hybrids between whites and blacks are relatively infertile. Some such hybrids show an especially high fecundity.

So much for our knowledge of the extent of race mixture in the United States, and of its physical results. Its social results are in violent dispute. As a matter of theory, McDougall does not believe in mixing widely different stocks, and makes the general statement that "the soul of the cross-bred is, it would seem, apt to be the scene of perpetual conflict of inharmonious tendencies." Hertz points out that this same argument was used against the inter-mingling of the blood of Roman patricians and plebeians; and of course the real conflict comes in the environment of the mulatto and not in his soul. An illegitimate or even a legitimate child, uncared for and uneducated, in conflict with his surroundings and untrained by his parents, may easily become a degenerate criminal, torn by inner contradiction; but this does not probably arise from his blood and physical descent, but obviously from his environment.

In general, the achievement of American mulattoes has been outstanding, so much so that many writers, like Reuter, have declared that the whole extraordinary accomplishment of the Negro race in America has been due to its mulatto leadership. This is a palpable exaggeration, and overlooks leaders like Sojourner Truth, Dunbar, Roland Hayes and Robert Moton. But certainly the number of outstanding Americans of mulatto blood is considerable, including as it does Frederick Douglass, Booker Washington, Henry O. Tanner, the artist, and Charles W. Chesnutt, the writer.

The real problem of miscegenation in America is not a question of physical possibility. That has been proven by many centuries of inter-mingling. Nor is it a question of its possible cultural results in individual cases, since the mulattoes have not only produced a number of exceptional men, but have in many instances formed normal, progressive groups. Nor is there any doubt but that continued residence of white and black people together in this country over a sufficiently long term of years will inevitably result in complete absorption, unless strong reasons against it, in place of mere prejudice, are adduced. There is, however, a very grave problem as to how fast and under what conditions this amalgamation ought to take place, and equally it may be questioned if separate racial growth over a considerable time may not achieve better results than quick amalgamation. It is here that the nation needs the guidance of careful and unbiased scientific inquiry.

If a poor and ignorant group amalgamates with a large and more intelligent group, quickly and thoughtlessly, the results may easily be harmful. There will be prostitution and disease, much social disorganization, and the inevitable loss of many human values by both groups. The lower group will tend to lose its self-respect and possibility of self-determination in its eagerness to reach the standards of the higher group; and it may disappear as a separate and more or less despised entity. The higher group will tend to lower its standards, will exploit and degrade the lower group, and fall itself into crime and delinquency, because of the ease with which it can use the lower group. It will try to protect itself by caste regulations, and refuse the lower group protection for its women by anti-marriage laws, and in turn lose respect for its own legislation in its fear of the other group. All this will lead on to the dangers of lawless caste, race hatred, and war. On the other hand, if by encouraging mutual respect and evenhanded justice, the two races can possibly readjust their social levels until they attain essential equality in well-being and intelligence, then either amalgamation will take place gradually and quietly by mutual consent, or by equally peaceful methods the groups will seek separate careers or even separate dwelling places, either in the same or different lands.

Bibliography

As has been said, any person with mind made up in regard to miscegenation can find a strong body of literature to support his belief whatever that belief may be. If one believes that miscegenation is wrong and harmful, one may base one's conclusions on these books:

Gobineau, Arthur de. *The Inequality of Human Races.* Translated from the French editions of 1853–55 by A. Collins. London: Heinemann, 1915.

Chamberlain, Houston Stewart. *The Foundations of the Nineteenth Century.* Translated from the German by John Lees. London and New York: John Lane, 1912.

Grant, Madison. *The Passing of the Great Race.* New York: Charles Scribner's Sons, 1916.

Gould, Charles W. *America: A Family Affair.* New York: Charles Scribner's Sons, 1920. Rev. ed., 1922.

McDougall, William. *The Group Mind: A Sketch of the Principles of Collective Psychology, with Some Attempt to Apply Them to the Interpretation of National Life and Character.* New York: G. P. Putnam's Sons, 1920.

Stoddard, Lothrop. *The Rising Tide of Color against White World-Supremacy.* New York: Charles Scribner's Sons, 1920.

Liberal anthropologists and students of race can be studied in the following books:

Haddon, Alfred Cort. *The Races of Man and Their Distribution.* New York: Frederick A. Stokes Co., 1910.

Sergi, Giuseppi. *The Mediterranean Race: A Study of the Origins of European Peoples.* 1901. Reprint. Atlantic Highlands, N.J.: Humanities Press, 1967.

Deniker, Joseph. *The Races of Man: An Outline of Anthropology and Ethnography.* London: Walter Scott Pub. Co., 1901.

Ratzel, Friedrich. *The History of Mankind.* Translated from the German by A. J. Butler. New York: Macmillan Co., 1896.

Fischer, Eugen. *Die Rehobother Bastards und das Bastardierungsproblem beim Menschen.* Jena: Gustav Fischer Verlag, 1913.

Seligman, C. G. "Anthropology." In *Encyclopedia Britannica,* 14th ed. 2:41–50, 1929.

Hankins, Frank H. *The Racial Basis of Civilization: A Critique of the Nordic Doctrine.* New York: Alfred A. Knopf, 1931.

Reuter, Edward Byron. *The Mulatto in the United States; Including a Study of the Role of Mixed-Blood Races throughout the World.* Boston: R. G. Badger, 1918.

———. *Population Problems.* Philadelphia: J. B. Lippincott, 1923.

———. *The American Race Problem: A Study of the Negro.* New York: Thomas Y. Crowell Co., 1927.

Hooton, Earnest A. *Up from the Ape.* New York: Macmillan Co., 1931.

Davenport, Charles Benedict. *Heredity of Skin Color in Negro-White Crosses,* with appendix of field notes chiefly by Florence H. Danielson. Washington, D.C.: Carnegie Institution, 1913.

Viteles, M. S. "The Mental Status of the Negro." *Annals of the Academy of Political and Social Sciences* 140 (November 1928).

The following books will be deemed by some to be unusually favorable to the Negro race, and backward races in general.

Day, Caroline B. *A Study of Some Negro-White Families in the United States,* with foreword and notes by E. A. Hooton. Cambridge, Mass.: Peabody Museum of Harvard University, 1932.

Spiller, G., ed. *Papers on Inter-Racial Problems Communicated to the First Universal Races Congress, London, July 26–29, 1911.* London: P. S. King and Son; Boston: World's Peace Foundation, 1911. New ed., with introduction, by H. Aptheker. New York: Citadel Press, 1970. [Du Bois notes particularly the following contributions from this volume:]

Brajendranath Seal. "Meaning of Race, Tribe, Nation," pp. 1–13.

Felix von Luschan. "Anthropological View of Race," pp. 13–24.

Alfred Fouillée. "Race from the Sociological Standpoint," pp. 24–29.

Gustav Spiller. "The Problem of Race Equality," pp. 29–39.

Earl Finch. "The Effects of Racial Miscegenation," pp. 108–12.

Jean Baptiste de Lacerda. "The *Metis,* or Half-Breeds of Brazil," pp. 377–82.

Herskovits, Melville J. *The American Negro: A Study in Racial Crossing.* New York: Alfred A. Knopf, 1928.

————. *The Anthropometry of the American Negro.* New York: Columbia University Press, 1930.

Finot, Jean. *Race Prejudice.* Translated from the French by Florence Wade-Evans. London: Archibald Constable Co., 1906.

Boas, Franz. *The Mind of Primitive Man.* New York: Macmillan Co., 1911.

Du Bois, W. E. B. *Health and Physique of the Negro-American.* Atlanta University Studies, no. 11 Atlanta, Ga., 1906.

Cobb, W. Montague. "The Physical Constitution of the American Negro." [Du Bois gives no date or other information concerning this article. It is likely that it was a then-unpublished paper by a well-known Black physician who was a friend of Du Bois's. Cobb had an article entitled "Physical Anthropology of the American Negro" published in the June 1942 issue of the *American Journal of Physical Anthropology* and one entitled "Physical Anthropology and the Negro in the Present Crisis" in the September 1942 *Journal of the National Medical Association* (34:181–87).]

Intermarriage and the Social Structure: Fact and Theory[*]

ROBERT K. MERTON

The paradox is now fully established that the utmost abstractions are the true weapon with which to control our thought of concrete fact.

A. N. Whitehead

Intermarriage is a concrete action involving numerous facets, the more dramatic of which have been accorded considerable attention by students of interpersonal relations. The dramatic, however, is not always the theoretically significant; human interest and scientific relevance do not invariably coincide. Among the more prosy aspects of intermarriage is the rôle of the social structure. Rates and patterns of intermarriage are closely related to cultural orientations, standardized distributions of income and symbols of status. The conflicts and accommodations of mates from socially disparate groups are partly understandable in terms of this

* From Robert K. Merton, "Intermarriage and the Social Structure: Fact and Theory." *Psychiatry* 4 (August 1941): 361–374.

environing structure. A provisional theory of structural components in intermarriage, then, can contribute to the analysis of interpersonal relations although, as Sapir has noted, the sociological abstractions refer to consistencies in cultural definitions rather than to the actions of particular persons. The theory of social structure complements the theory of personal interaction; from a functional standpoint, regularities in the two spheres are mutually implicative.

No society lacks a system of marriage. In no society is the selection of a marriage partner unregulated and indiscriminate. The choice, whether by the contractants themselves or by other delegated persons or groups, is subject to regulation by diffuse cultural controls and sometimes by specific social agencies. These regulations vary in many respects: in the degree of control—permission, preference, prescription, proscription; in the social statuses which are thus categorized—for example, kinship, race, class, and religion; in the sanctions attached to the regulations; in the machinery for carrying the rules into effect; in the degree to which the rules are effective. All this can be said with some assurance but there still remains the problem of systematizing these types of variation into some comprehensible order.

To assume that the variations are random is to provide a spurious solution of the problem by abandoning it. The apparent chaos must be shaped into a determinable order. The task of organizing these data has of course long since been taken up. Such concepts as endogamy, exogamy, preferential mating; as caste, class and estate; and a host of interrelated concepts reflect preliminary victories of an attack upon the problem. In this paper we seek to extend these conceptual formulations by suggesting some means for their further integration in the field of intermarriage.

Speaking literally, all marriage is intermarriage in the sense that the contractants derive from different social groups of one sort or another. This follows immediately from the universal incest taboo which forbids marriage at least between members of the same elementary family unit and derivatively restricts marriage to members of different family groups. Marriage contractants invariably[1] come from different elementary family groups; often from different locality, occupational, political, nationality groups; and at times from different religious and linguistic groups, races and castes. Thus, if the term intermarriage is used to denote all marriage between persons of *any* different groups whatsoever, without any

---

1. "Invariably" on the basis of a study of 220 societies by George P. Murdock, *Sex Mores and Social Structure*, an unpublished paper presented at the annual meetings of the American Sociological Society, 29 December 1940. "All societies prohibit sexual intercourse and marriage between mother and son, father and daughter, and brother and sister. Our 220 cases reveal no genuine exception to any of these three universal incest taboos. To be sure, in two instances brother-sister marriages are customary in the royal family, and in one case a paramount chief may marry his own daughter, but in all three societies such incestuous unions are rigorously forbidden to the rest of the population and special factors explain their occurrence among the chosen few of highest status." Linton, Ralph, *The Study of Man*; New York, Appleton-Century, 1936 (ix and 503 pp.); p. 125, holds that "the prohibition of marriage between mother and son is the only one universally present." Whether occasional exceptions to this taboo are 'genuine' or not, the approximation to universality is not questioned.

Rules Governing Choice of Spouse

Practices in Choice of Spouse		In-Group Marriage Prescribed ≡ Out-Group Marriage Proscribed	In-Group Marriage Proscribed ≡ Out-Group Marriage Prescribed
	Conformity to Rule: Agathogamy²	Endogamy	Exogamy
	Deviation from Rule: Cacogamy³	Inter-group mesalliance	Intra-group mesalliance (incestuous marriage)⁴

further specification of the groups involved, it becomes virtually synonymous with the term marriage and may well be eliminated. In other words, differences in group-affiliation of the contractants may occur, but if these affiliations—for example, political, neighborhood, social clubs—are not defined as relevant to the selection of a spouse, then the case is one of marriage, not intermarriage. The fact is, however, that certain types of marriage are sufficiently distinctive with respect to the group-affiliations of the contractants as to mark them off as a special category. Intermarriage, then, will be defined as *marriage of persons deriving from those different in-groups and out-groups other than the family which are culturally conceived as relevant to the choice of a spouse.* Thus, a given marriage may be, within one frame of reference—for example, the caste—in-marriage, and within another frame of reference—for example, social class—intermarriage. The distinction is analytical.

The standardized rules of intermarriage range from prescription, and social approval, to proscription, and social disapproval. These polar extremes give rise to two distinguishable types of intermarriage: the first, representing conformity to the rules, called *exogamy:* the second, involving prohibited deviations from the rules, may be called *cacogamy.* Prescribed marriage with*in* a specified group is, of course, *endogamy.* The combination of *rules* requiring or forbidding in-marriage and of *practices,* which may or may not conform to the rules, thus generates four type-cases of marriage. These are set forth in the above table.

2. *Agathogamy:* marriage which conforms to the norms governing selection of a spouse. From *agathos* = good, virtuous + *gamos* = marriage. At present there is no word to denote that class of marriages which conform to these norms. Agathogamy is intended to fill this gap.

3. *Cacogamy:* marriage which involves tabooed deviations from the norms governing selection of a spouse. From *kakos* = bad + *gamos* = marriage.

4. Incestuous marriages are often termed *inter*-marriage. This would appear to be an instance of the rhetorical fallacy of catachresis, in which one term is wrongly put for another. Its source is possibly the following. In lay language, the term intermarriage commonly denotes those marriages which *deviate* from *endogamous* norms. This attribute of *non-conformity and group disapproval* has come to be the identifying characteristic of intermarriage. Hence, incestuous marriage—surely at the polar extreme from inter- (group) marriage—which is also commonly *condemned,* comes mistakenly to be assimilated to the category of intermarriage, which is interpreted as tabooed marriage. This usage is misleading for analytical purposes and should be dropped from the sociological if not the folk lexicon.

This set of distinctions may help to eliminate that theoretical confusion in interpretations of intermarriage which stems from the failure to distinguish clearly between the two levels of rules and practices. Marriages which are superficially similar should not be classified as though they were significantly alike. Thus, marriages between persons with grandparents of different nationalities are often categorized as internationality marriage even in those cases where there is no consciousness by the contractants or the community of such group "affiliation" and, more importantly, even where there are no norms in the law or mores prescribing, preferring or proscribing such marriages. Cases such as these are not profitably classified as intermarriage since the ultimate group origins of the contractants are not culturally defined as relevant to the choice of a spouse. They are socially and culturally in-marriages, not intermarriages. The failure to discriminate between norms and practices also obscures the necessary distinction between those intermarriages which are approved and those disapproved by the community. Clearly, cacogamous intermarriages which repudiate social norms are not to be classified with exogamous marriages which represent conformity to these norms. The confusion here lies in not discriminating between significantly different types of marriage just as in the previous instance it lies in discriminating between essentially similar types. Our four-fold table provides a ready guide for the avoidance of such errors.[5]

The distinctions between norms and practices of mate-selection is further necessary because practices are influenced not only by the rules but also by certain *conditions* which facilitate or hinder conformity to the rules. In other words, the actual practices are resultants of the norms *and* specifiable conditions of group life. Among the non-normative conditions affecting actual rates of in- and out-marriage are size of groups, sex composition, age composition, and degree of contact between members of different groups. These conditions, it will be noted, are not directly matters of standardized attitudes, sentiment or cultural definitions although they are interdependent with normative factors. Norms may affect the degree and type of social contact; as embodied in immigration laws, for example, they may influence the size of nationality groups and indirectly even their sex and age composition. But the conditions may best be treated as largely independent factors in the selection of mates, quite apart from the cultural norms. As Romanzo Adams has indicated in this connection, "the larger the group the higher the percentage of in-marriage, ir-

---

5. It will be noted, however, that this classification is not exhaustive for it does not distinguish between permissive, preferential and assortative mating. Uniform patterns of mate-selection and the standardized ratings of potential spouses constitute a familiar phenomenon in many societies. Both preferential mating, which occurs in accordance with definite rules setting forth the particular statuses from which the spouse is to be selected, and assortative mating, which involves selection on the basis of more diffuse cultural values, are contained within the foregoing categories. Rules of preferential marriage simply specify in more detail the status attributes of the potential spouse; assortative mating is also usually within the normative framework—that is, agathogamous. A more detailed analysis would follow through the special features of preferential marriage but this problem is not wholly relevant here.

respective of any sentiment relative thereto."[6] Likewise, a radical disproportion in the sex ratio, as in the case of Chinese and Filipinos in this country, exerts a pressure for out-marriage. These pressures may be more than counterbalanced by in-group sentiments but analytically it is necessary to recognize their significance. Comparisons between rates of intermarriage in different populations should take account of the relative numbers of potential in-group mates, as affected by size, sex and age composition, territorial distribution and technologically determined opportunities for contact. Norms and actual frequencies of intermarriage, then, are not to be confused.

When, with a changing social structure, the functional significance of certain norms governing choice of a spouse diminishes, the antagonism toward violations and finally the norms themselves will tend to disappear. When the in- and out-groups are in fact progressing toward social and cultural assimilation; when pathways for group consolidation are established; when a considerable part of the population is alienated from traditional group distinctions; when social mobility is notably high; when physical and cultural marks of group distinction have largely disappeared and group "differences" persist merely as a matter of purely technical definition—as, for example, with the third generation of native-born white Americans—then a state of affairs is reached where the quadrisyllable, "intermarriage," is whittled down to a bisyllable, "marriage." The groups previously defined as severally endogamous become redefined as jointly endogamous; the circle of permissible mates is enlarged and the change in social organization is registered by newly modified norms concerning the selection of marriage partners.

Intermarriage whether permitted or tabooed does not occur at random but according to more or less clearly describable patterns. Two of these patterns may be selected for special attention. The first may be called *hypergamy*, a term which we adapt from its usage in connection with the Hindu caste system to denote institutionalized or non-institutionalized patterns of intermarriage wherein the female marries into a higher social stratum, in a system of caste, class or estate— *Stände*. We may introduce the term *hypogamy* to denote the pattern wherein the female marries into a lower social stratum. *Institutionalized* hypergamy or hypogamy denote those instances where the practice conforms to a norm contained in the law or mores; *non-institutionalized* hypergamy or hypogamy denote statistical uniformities of a hypergamous or hypogamous nature which are not, however, explicitly governed by a norm. Thus, Hindu hypergamy is an institutionalized pattern; American caste-hypogamy, a non-institutionalized pattern or a statistical uniformity but not a normatively prescribed arrangement.

We have now reviewed certain types of regulations and practices in the field of intermarriage. We have distinguished between endogamous and exogamous norms; between prescription, proscription, preference and permission; between agathogamy, or conformity to rules and cacogamy, or nonconformity; between

---

6. Adams, Romanzo, *Interracial Marriage in Hawaii;* New York, Macmillan, 1937 (xvii and 353 pp.); p. 191—Adams has an excellent discussion of the problem of distinguishing between practices and norms in the field of intermarriage.

hypergamy and hypogamy; between institutionalized and non-institutionalized practices. It is suggested that these conceptual distinctions provide a framework for the observation and arrangement of relevant intermarriage data. In other words, one of the more general theses of this paper is that an explicit conceptual outfit, a part of theory, is necessary even for fruitful discoveries of fact. It is our second general thesis that much of the available statistical materials on intermarriage are of relatively little value because the fact-finders, so-called, have not assembled and classified *relevant* facts and that this inadequacy is tied up with their neglect of a coherent theoretical system in terms of which relevance of facts might be determined.[7] Studies of intermarriage which are concerned simply with 'the facts' may incidentally be of some use for the scientific study of the subject but only when they tacitly relate to a system of theory. A science without a matrix of logically inter-related propositions is a contradiction in terms. A canvass of empirical studies of intermarriage suggests that these views need to be labored for the "factual materials" are often discrete, scattered and arranged in what seems to be a wholly private and unusable fashion.

Negro-White Intermarriage

A survey of the scanty statistical materials on Negro-white intermarriage in the United States will illustrate the basis for this judgment. The relations of "fact" and "theory" will be further instanced by setting forth a theoretically oriented taxonomy for the fruitful classification of such data. Accordingly, although our general categories apply to other types of intermarriage as well, the rest of our discussion will be devoted to the caste-class aspects of Negro-white intermarriage in this country. To refer to these cases merely as "interracial marriage" is an insufficiently analytic statement of a complex kind of event. It fails to bring out the fact that such intermarriage involves intercaste, and sometimes interclass, as well as interracial marriage. Furthermore, it does not direct attention to the racial, caste and class origins of each of the marriage contractants. Yet, there are significant sex differentials in the rate of Negro-white intermarriage. These interracial marriages, then, must be resolved into their elements, of which we shall attend to three: the caste, class and sex of each contractant. A classification of these attributes suggests categories in which statistical data on Negro-white intermarriage might profitably be arranged and provides a benchmark for evaluating the available data. The *logically possible* combinations of the three attributes give rise to eight types of Negroes and whites who may enter into marriage.

Racial Caste	Social Class[8]	Sex
A. Negro	lower class	female
B. White	lower class	female

7. In this general connection, reference is made to Parsons, Talcott, The Role of Theory in Social Research. *Amer. Sociological Rev.* (1938) 3:13–20.
8. The evident simplification involved in dealing with only two social classes, loosely termed "upper" and "lower," is not of crucial importance at this point. Consideration of further class differentiation would serve only to multiply the possible types of mates without materially affecting the analysis.

C. Negro	upper class	female
D. White	upper class	female
E. Negro	lower class	male
F. White	lower class	male
G. Negro	upper class	male
H. White	upper class	male

These eight types of potential mates may be arranged into sixteen logically possible marriage pairs, which are readily classifiable into four major categories: those which conform to norms of both caste and class endogamy; those which involve caste endogamy and interclass marriage; those which involve class endogamy and intercaste marriage; those which deviate from norms of both caste and class endogamy.

I
Caste and Class Endogamy

1. AE
2. BF
3. CG
4. DH

II
Caste Endogamy
Interclass Marriage

5. AG—class hypergamy
6. BH—class hypergamy
7. CE—class hypogamy
8. DF—class hypogamy

III
Intercaste Marriage
Class Endogamy

9. AF—caste hypergamy
10. BE—caste hypogamy
11. CH—caste hypergamy
12. DG—caste hypogamy

IV
Intercaste Marriage
Interclass Marriage

13. AH—caste and class hypergamy
14. BG—caste hypogamy; class hypergamy
15. CF—caste hypergamy; class hypogamy
16. DE—caste and class hypogamy

Although these sixteen pairings are logically possible, it is evident that they are not, in fact, equally probable. At this juncture the proper procedure would be, of

This twofold class distinction is advisedly a first approximation designed to indicate the general lines of the classification.

course, to determine the relative frequency with which these possible combinations actually occur in order to test theoretically derived hypotheses concerning the selection of marriage-partners.[9] Significantly, this cannot be done for the available statistical series do not include the necessary data, possibly because the empiricism of "fact-finders" included no canons of theoretical relevance. The statistical data will be briefly reported and the rest of our discussion will be devoted to an interpretation which these data are not altogether adequate to sustain. It should be noted, however, that our hypotheses are such that they are clearly subject to confirmation or refutation when the relevant facts have been assembled.

In view of the fact that Negro-white intermarriage is forbidden by law in thirty states and condemned by the mores throughout the nation, it is scarcely surprising that such marriages seldom occur. Reuter's estimate of "perhaps less than one hundred per year"[10] since the Emancipation may be a slight understatement, but

Negro-White Intermarriage

	Negro males–White females		White males–Negro females		Total	
	Per cent[11]	No.	Per cent[11]	No.	Per cent[11]	No.
New York City, 1908–12 [12]	1.78		.44		1.08	
New York State, 1919–29 [13]	2.92		1.00		1.95	
Rhode Island, 1881–93 [14]		51		7		58
Michigan, 1874–93 [14]		93		18		111
Connecticut, 1883–94 [14]		..		..		75
Boston, 1855–90 [14]		..		..		624
Boston, 1900–07 [15]		203		19		222
Massachusetts, 1900 [16]		43		10		53

9. For the logic of this procedure, consult Lazarsfeld, Paul F., Some Remarks on the Typological Procedure in Social Research. *Zeitschr. f. Sozialforschung* (1937) 6:119–139; Hempel, Carl G., and Oppenheim, Paul, *Der Typusbegriff im Lichte der neuen Logik*; Leiden, A. W. Sijthoff, 1936 (viii and 130 pp.); in particular, pp. 44–101. For other samples of this procedure, consider Merton, Robert K., Social Structure and Anomie. *Amer. Sociological Rev.* (1938) 3:672–682; Menger, Karl, An Exact Theory of Social Groups and Relations. *Amer. J. Sociol.* (1938) 43:790–798; Lundberg, George A., *Foundations of Sociology*; New York, Macmillan, 1939 (556 pp.); pp. 353 and 372–373.
10. Reuter, Edward Byron, *The American Race Problem*; New York, Crowell, 1938 (xiii and 430 pp.); p. 143.
11. These are percentages of "all Negro marriages."
12. Drachsler, Julius, *Intermarriage in New York City*; New York, Columbia University Press, 1921 (204 pp.); p. 50.
13. De Porte, J. V., Marriages in the State of New York with Special Reference to Nativity. *Human Biology* (1931) 3:376–396; in particular, p. 393. These figures are exclusive of New York City.
14. Hoffman, Frederick L., *Race Traits and Tendencies of the American Negro*; New York, Macmillan, 1896 (x and 329 pp.); pp. 198–200.
15. Stephenson, Gilbert T., *Race Distinctions in American Law*; New York and London, D. Appleton, 1910 (xiv and 388 pp.); p. 98. . . . Stone, Alfred H., *Studies in the American Race Problem*; New York, Doubleday Page, 1908 (xxii and 555 pp.); p. 62, reports that 13.6 per cent of all Negro marriages in Boston, 1900–04, were intermarriages with whites. Although Reuter, Edward Byron,

as the scattered statistics in the table [above] indicate, the figure is not appreciably higher. Moreover, there is no tendency for this negligible rate to increase.

This low rate of intermarriage is not particularly problematical; it simply reflects a high degree of conformity to strongly entrenched norms. In view of the vigorous taboos on intercaste marriage, we expect that most marriages in this country will be caste-endogamous—categories I and II. What is problematical, what does require generalized explanation, is the presence of these endogamous norms. Three related problems require consideration. First, what are the structural and functional bases[17] of the current norms governing Negro-white intermarriage? Second, what are the putative sources of deviations from these norms? Finally, how can we account for the prevalently caste-hypogamous pattern of these deviations?

Although the taboos on Negro-white intermarriage are primarily a matter of caste, as distinct from social class, the class affiliations of potential interracial spouses are not altogether irrelevant. In our open-class system, the preferred type of marriage, so far as *both* partners are concerned, is class endogamy. However, this norm is flexible and anything but rigorous for reasons which derive from the class structure itself and from other aspects of the culture. In a mobile social system, it is of course advantageous to marry a person of high class position. Interclass marriage has an acknowledged place as a means of consolidating class-gains within a structure which contains mobility as a primary aspiration. Thus, despite preferential class endogamy, we should expect relatively frequent interclass unions. Paradoxically, this pattern is supported by the prevalent *romantic complex* which emphasizes the dominant importance of "love" rather than utilitarian calculations in choosing a marriage-partner. Romance is presumably blind to class differences. The marriage of the heiress and the chauffeur, the wealthy scion and the shop-girl, when love conquers all, are enshrined in our folklore, our folksongs and drama. The romantic complex is largely but not wholly integrated with preferential class endogamy. Unless closely restricted by the prior importance of class-endogamous preference, romanticism interferes with the smooth functioning of the regulations regarding choice of a spouse; it makes for some instability and lack of consensus in appraising certain interclass marriages which may be disapproved in terms of the endogamous norms but praised in terms of romanticism. Such lack of consensus also derives in part from our *democratic creed* which officially denies strict class lines and thus subverts the effectiveness of preferential class endogamy. These interdependent definitions—preferential class endogamy, on one hand, and romantic and democratic values, on the other—prevent class endogamy from being a stable, unchallenged norm in our society. It is a tendency,

---

The Mulatto in the United States; Boston, Badger, 1918 (417 pp.); p. 136, quotes this percentage, it appears to be implausibly high and Stone's original sources should be rechecked.

16. Reference footnote 15, *Studies in the American Race Problem*, p. 62. This refers to 37 Massachusetts towns and cities.

17. We are primarily concerned with the generalized, not the historical, basis of these norms. A full analysis would deal with the historical or diachronic as well as the structural-functional or synchronic elements involved. The two approaches are readily integrated in this case.

not a strict uniformity. We expect the majority of marriages to occur within a social class, if only for reasons of mutual accessibility and participation in common social groups by members of the same class, but the norm is sufficiently flexible to allow frequent interclass unions. Class endogamy is loosely preferential, not prescriptive.

Insofar as Negro-white intermarriage is a matter of social class, that is, insofar as we may temporarily abstract from other considerations affecting such inter-marriage, a loose class endogamy with some interclass marriage is to be expected. Of course, it is abundantly clear that Negro-white marriage in our society is *not simply* a matter of the class affiliation of the contractants, but this is no reason for assuming that the class-positions of the mates are wholly irrelevant to the prob-ability of certain types of pairing. The class origins of spouses in interracial ca-cogamy are distinctly relevant to patterns of such intermarriage.[18] However, con-siderations of social class are supplemented by the norms of caste which prescribe, not merely prefer, endogamy.

In our racial-caste system,[19] the taboos on intermarriage are not materially coun-teracted by the influences of romanticism and the democratic creed. The romantic complex operates largely with*in* the confines of a caste and, when it fails to do so, it is more than outweighed by caste controls. Moreover, in a racial-caste struc-ture, the criteria of pulchritude are commonly derived from the physical traits characteristic of the dominant caste, so that even in these terms, lower-caste mem-bers will usually be deemed "unattractive." These derived æsthetic criteria thus minimize one possible source of deviation from the endogamous norm. Another such potential source, the democratic creed, has been largely accommodated to the caste structure so that its "subversive" influence with respect to the non-democratic caste system is negligible.[20] In other words, although the caste struc-ture is not integrated with the democratic and romantic values, it persists by being

18. In fact, Miller goes so far as to say that the objection to Negro-white intermarriage is "merely a class objection and strong as it is, it is no stronger than has prevailed between clearly defined classes within the same race." Miller, H. A., Race and Class Parallelism. *The Annals* (1923) 140: 3–4. This view attaches too much weight to class whereas others have completely ignored this element in interracial cacogamy.

19. Kingsley Davis has distinguished between racial castes, non-racial castes and non-caste systems of race relations. He indicates that the differences lead to different types of regulation of intermar-riage. Intermarriage in Caste Societies. *Amer. Anthrop.* (1941) 43:376–395. The nature of my extensive debt to Davis' analysis will be evident to those who consult his excellent paper. Despite some differences in terminology, our substantial agreement on certain independently conceived classifications and interpretation may be held to enhance the cogency of both papers. The con-vergence of independent researches toward common conclusions is, after all, a significant test of reliability. This applies particularly to the following items: conformity to and deviations from norms of mate-selection-agathogamy and cacogamy; ascription to endogamy of the function of making for cultural compatibility of spouses; ascription to the taboo on cacogamy of the function of precluding disruption of the matrix of kinship and other interpersonal relations in which the spouses are embedded; the concept of compensatory intermarriage.

20. Merton, Robert K., Fact and Factitiousness in Ethnic Opinionnaires. *Amer. Sociological Rev.* (1940) 5:13–28; in particular, pp. 23–28.

largely insulated from the application of criteria contained in these value-systems. Conflict arising from this lack of integration is minimized by segmentation of attitudes and rationalization: democratic and romantic criteria are largely restricted to intra-caste evaluations and elaborate explanations account for the necessity, justice and desirability of doing so. Intercaste marriage is not granted even qualified approval as subserving the function of social mobility for mobility is ruled out by the very nature of caste structure. Finally, the contacts between members of different racial-castes are regulated by codes of racial etiquette so that there are few opportunities for relationships not involving considerable social distance. This in turn largely prevents the type of contact which might result in marriage.

Thus, various characteristics of the social and cultural structure support the prevalent code of racial-caste endogamy in the United States. But all this does not account for the existence of such endogamy. What, then, are the structural and functional bases of racial-caste endogamy?

Endogamy is a device which serves to maintain social prerogatives and immunities within a social group.[21] It helps prevent the diffusion of power, authority and preferred status to persons who are not affiliated with a dominant group. It serves further to accentuate and symbolize the "reality" of the group by setting it off against other discriminable social units. Endogamy serves as an isolation[22] and exclusion device, with the function of increasing group solidarity and supporting the social structure by helping to fix social distances which obtain between groups. All this is not meant to imply that endogamy was deliberately instituted for these purposes; this is a description in functional, not necessarily purposive, terms.

Facts which apparently controvert this functional account seem, upon analysis, to lend it further support. Thus, in American society where the class structure involves preferential rather than prescriptive endogamy, interclass marriage acts as a means of social mobility. When groups are relatively permeable, when new class status may be attained through socially recognized achievements, the endogamous norms are sufficiently relaxed to be integrated with mobility. Contrariwise, in a caste system with unbridgeable gaps between strata where individual mobility is the rare exception, the endogamous norms are rigid. This interpretation is consistent with historical changes in endogamous norms. It appears that notable increases in group consciousness and solidarity involve a tightening of endogamous prescriptions. The Nazi taboo on interracial and interreligious marriage is a case in point.

The structural basis for endogamous rules may be seen by examining their bearing upon the conjugal family units themselves. Endogamy ensures to a certain

---

21. Reference footnote 1; Linton, p. 204.
22. [E. T.] Hiller has introduced the useful term, *isolation device*, to denote arrangements and symbols which mark off in-groups from out-groups. His usage may be profitably modified to this extent: *isolation devices* are those employed by subordinate groups for this function; *exclusion devices*, those employed by dominant groups. Hiller, E. T., *Principles of Sociology*; New York, Harpers, 1933 (xix and 661 pp.); pp. 24 and 325.

extent that the marriage contractants will have a rough similarity of cultural background inasmuch as they have been socialized in groups with similar culture.[23] A universe of discourse common to the contractants lessens the likelihood of intrafamilial conflict deriving from different sets of values of the spouses. Moreover, by precluding diverse group loyalties of the mates, the conjugal unit is integrated with the larger social structure. Both class and caste endogamy prevent that familial instability which occurs when children identify themselves with the upper-status parent and condemn the lower-status parent in terms of the cultural values which they have assimilated. This potential split of loyalties becomes especially disruptive within a racial-caste system where the child's animosity may be directed against himself as well as the lower-caste parent who bears the invidious racial marks. This interpretation in terms of the functions of endogamy for the conjugal family unit may account in part for the widespread tendency to conceive of the conjugal unit as involving equality of status in the framework of stratification.[24]

A further structural basis for the taboo on intercaste marriage is found in the effect of such marriage upon the network of social relationships in which the contractants are implicated. Marriage introduces the mates into a new set of kinship relations. Kinship relatives, with exceptions such as mother-in-law avoidances which are not relevant here, are culturally defined as standing in a relation involving ready social accessibility.[25] Cacogamous intercaste marriage introduces an abrupt breach into this network of social relations for with it comes a conflict between the superordinate-subordinate relations deriving from status differences of the new-made kin and the mutual accessibility in terms of equality deriving from the kinship structure. Nor does the conflict cease at this point. Each of the persons in the new kinship group is normally embedded in a matrix of friendships and cliques. Usually, such friendship groupings are, apart from age and sex differences, potentially accessible to one another.[26] Intermarriage between persons of radically different social status thus conflicts with the existing organization of cliques and friendship groups involving the spouses and their kin. Rules of avoidance or social distance and rules of accessibility are brought into open conflict. The taboo on such intermarriage may be construed as a defensive arrangement for restricting the incidence of such conflicts. A cross-caste mésalliance would entail a considerable readjustment of established systems of social relationships which, since they are affectively significant, are most resistant to abrupt and profound alterations. Intercaste marriage is thus seen to involve not only an internally contradictory relationship between the spouses but to influence directly an elab-

23. Kingsley Davis—Reference footnote 19—properly stresses the importance of this fact.
24. Davis, Kingsley, The Forms of Illegitimacy. *Social Forces* (1939) 18:85–87; Parsons, Talcott, An Analytical Approach to the Theory of Social Stratification. *Amer. J. Sociol.* (1940) 45:841–862; in particular, p. 850. These two papers may be profitably read in conjunction with the present study since they all involve the same general theoretical system.
25. Reference footnote 24; Davis, p. 86.
26. To be sure, friendship groupings are often confined to a single sex and a single generation, but this limits rather than eliminates the potential accessibility of friends and kin of members of the group.

orate network of social relations ramifying through the immediate families, the extended kinship group and their friends. Viewed in such a context, the profound emotional resistance to racial-caste intermarriage becomes largely comprehensible. These outbursts of moral indignation are defensive devices which stabilize the existing organization of interpersonal relations and groups.

In a society where certain types of intermarriage are forbidden, several alternative adjustments by cacogamous pairs are possible. The relative frequency of these attempted adjustments depends at least in part on the larger social organization. In any case, the "adjustment" will involve the rupture of some social systems involving the offending pair. In a society such as our own, with its pattern of virtual independence of conjugal groups and with high rates of geographic mobility, ostracism of the offending couple involves a minimum of social readjustment, particularly should the pair leave the immediate community. Such ostracism, when the marriage provoking it is not widely known, *approximates*—though it is not affectively identical with—a recognized cultural pattern in which new conjugal pairs maintain relatively few active relations with their families of orientation and their native community. If the cacogamous pair leaves the local community, the families of orientation are *publicly* little more depleted than if the departure were in response to economic opportunities elsewhere. A highly mobile, segmented society, then, to this extent minimizes the disturbing influences of cacogamy upon the local community and affords somewhat more loopholes for such irregular unions.

In the case of intercaste mésalliances, however, the problem is not solved by such makeshift "escapes" to another community, for here the problem of establishing new social relationships is encountered. This problem becomes almost insuperable in cases of racial-caste intermarriage where ineffaceable physical badges of affiliation with different castes bar the way to a reintegration of the conjugal pair with new social groups. Similarly, when status differences are correlated with marked cultural differences leading to high visibility of another kind, flight from the native community fails to solve the problem. Under these conditions, new relationships can no more satisfactorily be established than the old relationships could be maintained. In cases of intermarriage where both physical and cultural visibility are absent, the temporarily atomized pair may gear into a satisfactory set of new social relationships as a conventional family group. But all such adjustments by the deviant pair which, in the optimum case, may attain some measure of personal success are still at the expense of the social relationships which have been sloughed off by ostracism and mobility. Successful evasions indicate loopholes in the structure of community control, not modifications of the marriage structure. Hence, although a segmented, mobile society may reduce the animus directed toward certain types of cacogamy, it is functionally necessary to maintain such effective antagonism if the going arrangement of social relationships is not to be endangered.[27] Metaphorically, intercaste marriage may be viewed as

27. This functional statement does *not* imply a value-judgment favoring or rejecting the current social arrangements. Only a perversion of functional analysis systematically results in rationalizations of the *status quo* in various areas of social life.

a catalyst which activates and intensifies group consciousness. It symbolizes the repudiation of standardized cultural values which have been defined as sacrosanct and inviolable. A cultural axiom is being challenged. Cultural orientations are, by virtue of this challenge, presumably no longer secure. The response is immediate and familiar. The violation is intensely condemned; the nonconformists are stigmatized; the cultural norms are reaffirmed. All this has little of design, of the predetermined plan. It resembles rather the automatic, the prompt triggerlike response ensured by socialization and rooted in sentiment. The pattern is an integrated arrangement of action, sentiment and reaction serving to order social relationships. It may suggest a premeditated structure but it is more nearly reminiscent of the ordered integration of reflexive behavior. The crisis arouses self-consciousness; in this instance, consciousness of self as a member of the in-group.

The Pattern of Caste Hypogamy

Structural and functional elements, then, would appear to account for the prohibition of racial-caste intermarriage in our society. The taboo appears to be largely supported by the standardized sentiments of both Negroes and whites and, consequently, the rate of intermarriage continues to be low. But what of the intermarriages which do occur, in spite of the taboo? The most striking uniformity in the statistics of Negro-white intermarriage is the non-institutional pattern of caste hypogamy, *i.e.*, marriage between white females and Negro males. In our samples, such pairings are from three to ten times as frequent as the Negro female–white male combination. This uniformity has often been remarked by students of the subject. Even the collection of mixed marriages assembled from cases "personally known" to a group of students consists of 18 caste-hypogamous unions to seven hypergamous unions.[28] What is the basis of this uniformity?

The hypogamous pattern is clearly not attributable to non-normative conditions affecting intermarriage. There is no significantly unbalanced sex ratio among either the Negro or white populations which can be taken to account for this pattern.[29] Similarly, neither the etiquette of race relations nor sheer propinquity would make for more frequent contacts between white females and Negro males than between Negro females and white males.[30] We may entertain the hypothesis

---

28. Baber, Ray E., A Study of 325 Mixed Marriages. *Amer. Sociological Rev.* (1937) 2:705–716. Reference is also made to Baber, Ray E., *Marriage and the Family*; New York, McGraw-Hill, 1939 (656 pp.); pp. 163–173.
29. Consult, for example, relevant data presented by Cox, Oliver C., Sex Ratio and Marital Status Among Negroes. *Amer. Sociological Rev.* (1940) 5:937–947.
30. If at all involved, the contrary is more probable since Negro females and white males are more likely to have sustained contacts than are the complementary pairs, in view of the fact that the ratio of Negro women to Negro men engaged in domestic and personal service is about 4 to 1. [It should be added, however, that this disproportion did not obtain prior to 1910, the period to which all but one of our statistics of Negro-white intermarriage refer. Consult Harris, Abram L., and Spero, Sterling D., Negro Problem, *Encyclopedia of the Social Sciences*; New York, Macmillan, 1937, 11:342; Haynes, Elizabeth R., Negroes in Domestic Service in the United States. *J. Negro History* (1923) 8:384–442; in particular, pp. 386–393.] In any event, such contacts scarcely serve

that hypogamy is understandable in terms of the social structure; a view which is not invariably shared by other students of the subject. Thus, Baber raises the question in these non-structural, individualistic terms: "Surely there is no more stigma attached to the white man who marries a Negro woman than to the white woman who marries a Negro. Is color difference in the mate less repulsive to the white woman than to the white man?"[31] This way of posing the problem illustrates the necessity of systematic theory if empirical data are to be made intelligible. An *ad hoc* common sense hypothesis such as Baber's contains no reference to social structure and ignores the fact that most illicit miscegenation involves Negro women and white men. "Repulsiveness" is not a datum; it is a cultural artifact requiring sociological analysis.

Dealing with this same general question, Park asserts that hypergamy is "one principle which seems to have been everywhere operative in determining the amount of miscegenation." It appears to be true that intercaste sex relations largely involve upper-caste males and lower-caste females, but clearly "hypergamy," which denotes a form of *marriage*, is far from universal. Park further holds that hypergamy "seems to be a principle in human nature . . . which operates spontaneously."[32] A third hypothesis holds that "the disposition of men to go abroad for wives and of women to welcome these roving strangers is probably part of original nature. Human beings are naturally exogamous." Here again, certain abstract characteristics are attributed to human nature as such and, in contrast to Park's usual analytical insight, with no regard for the rôle of social organization. How would one test the hypothesis that exogamy is fixed in original nature? What theoretical or factual basis exists for this hypothesis? In any case, these gratuitous assumptions do not clarify the prevalently hypogamous pattern of Negro-white intermarriage.

Donald Young[33] and Kingsley Davis[19] have severally advanced hypotheses which may be elaborated to account for the relative frequencies of the logically possible pairings of Negroes and whites. Inasmuch as the statistics show a marked predominance of caste-hypogamy, we know that most of the actual intercaste pairings are contained among the following types: Numbers 10 BE; 12 DG; 14 BG; 16 DE. It is suggested that the frequencies of these pairings may be interpreted within the context of the generalized scheme shown on page 372.

Limitations of space and the absence of sufficient concrete data prevent a detailed analysis of the multiple structural factors involved in patterns of interstratum marriage. The general lines of analysis may be briefly illustrated. In our twofold racial-caste and open-class structure, all Negro-white marriages are cacogamous, that is, they deviate from endogamous norms and are attended by the

---

to account for the caste-hypogamous pattern, in view of the social distance deriving from both caste and class differences.

31. Reference footnote 28; A Study of 325 Mixed Marriages, p. 706.
32. Park, Robert E., Race Relations and Certain Frontiers. Reuter, E. B., [ed.], *Race and Culture Contacts;* New York, McGraw-Hill, 1934 (261 pp.); In particular, pp. 80–81. Park's essay contains an excellent summary of comparative materials on interracial marriage.
33. Young, Donald, *American Minority Peoples;* New York, Harpers, 1932 (xv and 621 pp.); p. 409.

sanctions of ostracism and the ascription of lower-caste status to offspring. Within such a context, it is likely that pairing Number 10 will be found among the pariahs of the society, among those persons who have become, as it were, "cultural aliens" denying the legitimacy of much of the social structure in which they occupy disadvantaged positions.[34] Interracial cacogamy is, in this instance, simply a special case of the larger repudiation of cultural means and goals. There is little in the way of mutual socio-economic compensation between the cross-caste mates. This particular pairing, however, would not be expected to occur any more frequently

---

Variables in the Analysis of Intermarriage between Persons from Different Social Strata

I. *The System of Stratification*

    A. Open-class

    B. Estate or *Stände*   these may be combined in concrete social systems: racial caste-and-

    C. Caste   class in United States; estate-and-class in England, Prussia—especially

        1. Racial   18th to 19th centuries

        2. Non-racial

II. *Bases of Ascribed or Achieved Status in the System of Stratification*[35]

    A. Membership in a kinship unit   D. Possessions

    B. Personal qualities—including race   E. Authority

    C. Achievements   F. Power

III. *Types of Intermarriage*

    A. Exogamy—agathoga-   B. Intergroup mésalliance—caco-

       mous intermarriage   gamous intermarriage

        1. Compensatory[36]   1. Compensatory

          a. hypergamy   a. hypergamy

          b. hypogamy   institutionalized or non-   b. hypogamy

        2. Non-compensatory   institutionalized   2. Non-compensatory

          a. hypergamy   a. hypergamy

          b. hypogamy   b. hypogamy

IV. *Status of Children of Cross-Stratum Marriage*

    A. Matrilineal

    B. Patrilineal

    C. Positional (that is, status of either upper-stratum or of lower-stratum parent)

V. *Status of Conjugal Pair*

    A. Same as prior status of husband

    B. Same as prior status of wife

    C. Same as prior status of upper-stratum spouse

    D. Same as prior status of lower-stratum spouse

    E. Status of pariahs, outcaste, déclassé

---

34. For an account of the structural sources of the cultural alien, see Merton, Robert K., Social Structure and Anomie. *Amer. Sociological Rev.* (1938) 3:672–682.

35. For a discussion of these bases of differential valuation, consider Parsons, reference footnote 24.

36. Kohn-Bramstedt, Ernst, *Aristocracy and the Middle-Classes in Germany*; London, P. S. King, 1937 (xii and 362 pp.); p. 244, properly stresses the importance of social or economic compensation in cacogamous intermarriage.

than its complementary hypergamous type, Number 9, involving a lower class Negro female and a lower class white male. Concubinage, rather than marriage, would be the probable type of durable sex relationship in these cases.

Type Number 12, when it occurs, will also not involve mutual compensation with respect to socio-economic position, since here the class positions of the upper-class mates are roughly equal. The relation is asymmetrical inasmuch as the Negro male does not compensate for the upper-caste status of his wife. Such marriages would be expected to occur among "emancipated" persons, so-called radicals, who repudiate legitimacy of caste distinctions. The sole formal difference between types Numbers 10 and 12, then, is that in the former the contractants are disadvantaged persons who relinquish social norms because of the ineffectiveness of their efforts to gear into the social structure and achieve a "respectable" status, whereas in the latter type, the contractants enjoy eminently satisfactory status as judged by conventional standards but have become alienated from the values, institutional ideologies and organization of the caste system.[37]

We should expect pairing Number 14—lower class white woman and upper class Negro man—to occur most frequently for it involves a reciprocal compensatory situation in which the Negro male "exchanges" his higher caste status.[38] This does not at all imply that the 'exchange' is necessarily the result of an explicit utilitarian calculus in which the contractants deliberately weigh the economic and social returns to be gained from the marriage. The event may be experienced by them as simply an affectional relationship, but this psychic reaction is manifestly structured by the social organization. A comparable reciprocity pattern often emerges even more clearly in hypergamous unions in caste or estate systems of stratification. In the Hindu caste system, for example, the bride's family "have to pay for marrying her to a man above her in rank, whilst they also desire to make a show of wealth as a set-off to the bridegroom's social advantages."[39] In an estate-system where titles descend patrilineally, the hypergamous exchange of wealth for noble status is often quite explicit, as in the patterns involving American heiresses and foreign nobles since the middle of the last century. Thus, the marriage settlement between Consuelo Vanderbilt and His Grace the ninth Duke of Marlborough was set forth in an official document in which the Duke was guaranteed for life the income from $2,500,000 of Beech Creek Railway stock.

37. One of the cases reported by Baber appears to fall more or less in this category. The white woman "was very well educated, a member of Phi Beta Kappa, and from a highly respected family." The Negro male, evidently highly mobile within the class system, was a law student who came of a poor family. "They were both radicals." Reference footnote 28; Baber, p. 708. The distinction between the personality types in pairings Numbers 10 and 12 corresponds to those established by Merton as "retreatism" and "rebellion." Reference footnote 34; p. 676.

38. This is the special case of hypogamy with which Kingsley Davis was primarily concerned in which the dual caste-class structure "makes it economically profitable for some white women to marry some Negro males." Reference footnote 19.

39. Blunt, E. A. H., *The Caste System of Northern India;* London, Oxford University Press, 1931 (vii and 374 pp.); p. 70.

Among the hypogamous pairings, type Number 16 would, on our hypothesis, occur least frequently. Here *both* the class and caste positions of the white female are superior to that of the Negro male, and there is no element of social or economic compensation involved. Such a marriage abjures all social and cultural considerations and this compound deviation from class–and–caste standards would be most difficult to find culturally acceptable motivation. It is consistent with our interpretation that the upper class white woman in a union of this sort, reported by Baber, believed that her Negro husband is "the only man who can satisfy her sexually."[40]

This brief canvass of types of caste hypogamy is avowedly hypothetical, but it involves theoretically derived hypotheses which lend themselves to empirical confirmation or refutation. Furthermore, it sets forth the particular attributes which must be included in future statistical and case materials in order to test this interpretation. Baber has apparently made a step in this direction. However, the available data are too unsystematic and fragmentary to provide an adequate test although, so far as they go, they are consistent with our analysis. Thus, Reuter observes that uniformly in intercaste marriages, the Negro "groom is of some importance and the white bride a woman of the lower class."[41]

We have yet to examine the structural bases for the greater frequency of caste-hypogamy as compared to caste-hypergamy in our society. Two aspects of the rôles ascribed to males and females appear to be primarily relevant. The latitude permitted women to seek an occupational career has increased greatly but it does not approximate that accorded men. Moreover, even in the most "emancipated" circles the status of a conjugal unit is primarily that of the male head of the family. The standardized case is one in which the social rank of the female is largely derivative from that of her husband or, prior to social adulthood, her father. In a society where this is the case, intra-familial conflict often occurs when the wife has outdistanced her husband in the occupational sphere since feminine careers are hedged about by conceptions of the impropriety of competition between husband and wife. Occupational achievement is still considered the usual if not the exclusive prerogative of the male, despite the larger participation of women in economic and public life. The male is "the provider," the chief source of economic status. The second difference in sex rôles is contained in the prevalent code of sex morality wherein, despite some slight modifications, the female of the

40. Reference footnote 28; p. 708. "She comes of an excellent family and is well educated, while he is ignorant and of very poor family stock."
41. Reference footnote 15; Reuter, p. 138. Reuter cites Hoffman's study of 57 mixed unions which were predominantly between members of the lower classes of both castes—pairing No. 10—and included a generous proportion of criminals and prostitutes. This again concurs with our analysis but since Hoffman does not indicate the basis on which he selected his cases, his study cannot be accorded much weight. Only 23 of Hoffman's cases were actual marriages. Although Reuter refers to Hoffman's canvass as a "careful investigation," it should be noted that Hoffman gives only the following indication of the source of his information and the basis of selection of cases: "I have been able during a number of years to collect information of a fairly reliable character in regard to 37 mixed relations." Reference footnote 14; p. 204. In view of Hoffman's bias and naiveté in other respects, there is no reason to assume that this sample was representative.

species is more circumscribed in the range of allowable activity. Moreover, it is commonly considered more appropriate that sex relations be initiated by the male; that the male will propose and the female dispose; and that the male will seek out the female, for examples. These definitions are not unchallenged but they exercise a discernible control.

Given these differences in rôle-definitions, then, an upper-caste male, by virtue of his sex rôle, may more properly make advances than an upper-caste female and, secondly, he may more readily flout the caste taboos, by virtue of his upper-caste status than a lower-caste male may dare. In short, the sex morality supports sex advances by the male; the caste morality more easily enables the dominant upper-caste member to initiate cross-caste sexual overtures. Thus, the individuals who incorporate the "male-attribute" and the "upper-caste attribute," that is, white males, may more readily initiate cross-caste sexual relations than either the white female, who lacks the male prerogative, or the Negro male, who lacks the upper-caste prerogative. This enables us to see structural sources of the fact that most intercaste *sex relations*—not marriages—are between white men and Negro women.

It remains to be seen, then, why the durable relationships between white men and Negro women are usually extramarital. Once again, sex rôles and the caste-and-class structure would appear to account for the facts. Given the dominance of the white male with his relative immunity from active retaliation by the lower-caste male, there is no pressure to legitimize his liaison by marriage. Concubinage and transient sex relations are less burdensome and less damaging to his status, since these may be more easily kept secret and, even if discovered, are less subject to violent condemnation by fellow caste-members, since they do not imply equality of the sex partners. Furthermore, as Davis has suggested, the marriage of a lower class white male with a wealthy Negro woman is less likely than the complementary hypogamous pairing in view of the standardized rôle of the male as "economic provider."

We may tentatively conclude that most cross-caste sex relations will be clandestine and illicit. Within a racial-caste structure, the non-institutionalized statistical pattern of the few intermarriages which do occur will be largely hypogamous. In a non-racial caste structure, as in India, the institutionalized pattern of hypergamy may be interpreted as a system manifesting the prerogatives of upper-caste males who thus have *legitimate* access to women of their own caste *and* to women of the immediately inferior subcaste. In a racial-caste structure, the institution of hypergamy is not probable because the ambiguous position of cross-caste offspring would introduce an instability in the caste system by eventually eliminating the identification of race and caste.[42]

The classification and interpretation presented in this paper are highly provisional and rudimentary: the one needing to be further tested for convenience, the other requiring a larger body of systematically collated data than is yet at hand. The random collection of facts will not lead to further understanding of the

42. Consult the article by Davis for a comparative analysis. Reference footnote 19.

phenomenon of intermarriage; the collection of facts in terms of our conceptual framework may do so. Confirmed by whatever relevant facts are available, our interpretation enjoys a measure of plausibility; consistent with a wider body of theory which in turn is supported by systematic empirical inquiry, it may lay claim to a further degree of validity; stated in such terms as to be testable by freshly accumulated facts, it is, at the very least, open to further confirmation or disconfirmation.

Reflections on Little Rock*

HANNAH ARENDT

Preliminary Remarks

This article was written more than a year ago upon the suggestion of one of the editors of *Commentary*. It was a topical article whose publication was delayed for months because of the controversial nature of my reflections which, obviously, were at variance with the magazine's stand on matters of discrimination and seg-regation. Meanwhile, things had quieted down temporarily; I had hopes that my fears concerning the seriousness of the situation might prove exaggerated and no longer wished to publish this article. Recent developments have convinced me that such hopes are futile and that the routine repetition of liberal clichés may be even more dangerous than I thought a year ago. I therefore agreed to let *Dissent* publish the article as it was written—not because I thought that a year-old topical essay could possibly exhaust the subject or even do justice to the many difficult problems involved, but in the hope that even an inadequate attempt might help to break the dangerous routine in which the discussion of these issues is being held from both sides.

There are, however, two points which were brought to my attention after I wrote the article which I would like to mention at least. The first concerns my contention that the marriage laws in 29 of the 49 states constitute a much more flagrant breach of letter and spirit of the Constitution than segregation of schools. To this, Sidney Hook (*New Leader*, April 13), replied that Negroes were "pro-foundly uninterested" in these laws; in their eyes, "the discriminatory ban against intermarriages and miscegenation is last in the order of priorities." I have my doubts about this, especially with respect to the educated strata in the Negro population, but it is of course perfectly true that Negro public opinion and the policies of the NAACP are almost exclusively concerned with discrimination in employment, housing and education. This is understandable; oppressed minorities were never the best judges on the order of priorities in such matters and there are many instances when they preferred to fight for social opportunity rather than for basic human or political rights. But this does not make the marriage laws any

* From Hannah Arendt, "Reflections on Little Rock." *Dissent* 6.1 (winter 1959): 45–56.

more constitutional or any less shameful; the order of priorities in the question of rights is to be determined by the Constitution, and not by public opinion or by majorities.

The second point was mentioned by a friend who rightly observed that my criticism of the Supreme Court's decision did not take into account the role education plays, and has always played, in the political framework of this country. This criticism is entirely just and I would have tried to insert a discussion of this role into the article if I had not meanwhile published a few remarks on the widespread, uncritical acceptance of a Rousseauist ideal in education in another context, i.e. in an article in the Fall 1958 issue of *Partisan Review*, entitled "The Crisis in Education." In order not to repeat myself, I left the article unchanged.

Finally, I should like to remind the reader that I am writing as an outsider. I have never lived in the South and have even avoided occasional trips to Southern states because they would have brought me into a situation that I personally would find unbearable. Like most people of European origin I have difficulty in understanding, let alone sharing, the common prejudices of Americans in this area. Since what I wrote may shock good people and be misused by bad ones, I should like to make it clear that as a Jew I take my sympathy for the cause of the Negroes as for all oppressed or underprivileged peoples for granted and should appreciate it if the reader did likewise.

It is unfortunate and even unjust (though hardly unjustified) that the events at Little Rock should have had such an enormous echo in public opinion throughout the world and have become a major stumbling block to American foreign policy. For unlike other domestic problems which have beset this country since the end of World War II (a security hysteria, a runaway prosperity, and the concomitant transformation of an economy of abundance into a market where sheer superfluity and nonsense almost wash out the essential and the productive), and unlike such long-range difficulties as the problem of mass culture and mass education—both of which are typical of modern society in general and not only of America—the country's attitude to its Negro population is rooted in American tradition and nothing else. The color question was created by the one great crime in America's history and is soluble only within the political and historical framework of the Republic. The fact that this question has also become a major issue in world affairs is sheer coincidence as far as American history and politics are concerned; for the color problem in world politics grew out of the colonialism and imperialism of European nations—that is, the one great crime in which America was never involved. The tragedy is that the unsolved color problem within the United States may cost her the advantages she otherwise would rightly enjoy as a world power.

For historical and other reasons, we are in the habit of identifying the Negro question with the South, but the unsolved problems connected with Negroes living in our midst concern of course the whole country, not the South alone. Like other race questions, it has a special attraction for the mob and is particularly well fitted to serve as the point around which a mob ideology and a mob organization can crystallize. This aspect may one day even prove more explosive in the big Northern urban centers than in the more tradition-bound South, especially if the number of Negroes in Southern cities continues to decline while the Negro population of non-Southern cities increases at the same rate as in recent years. The United States is not a nation-state in the European sense and never was. The principle of its political structure is, and always has been, independent of a homogeneous population and of a common past. This is somewhat less true of the South whose population is more homogeneous and more rooted in the past than that of any other part of the country. When William Faulkner recently declared that in a conflict between the South and Washington he would utimately have to act as a citizen of Mississippi, he sounded more like a member of a European nation-state than a citizen of this Republic. But this difference between North and South, though still marked, is bound to disappear with the growing industrialization of Southern states and plays no role in some of them even today. In all parts of the country, in the East and North with its host of nationalities no less than in the more homogeneous South, the Negroes stand out because of their "visibility." They are not the only "visible minority," but they are the most visible one. In this respect, they somewhat resemble new immigrants, who invariably constitute the most "audible" of all minorities and therefore are always the most likely to arouse xenophobic sentiments. But while audibility is a temporary phenomenon, rarely persisting beyond one generation, the Negroes' visibility is unalterable and permanent. This is not a trivial matter. In the public realm, where nothing counts that cannot make itself seen and heard, visibility and audibility are of prime importance. To argue that they are merely exterior appearances is to beg the question. For it is precisely appearances that "appear" in public, and inner qualities, gifts of heart or mind, are political only to the extent that their owner wishes to expose them in public, to place them in the limelight of the market place.

The American Republic is based on the equality of all citizens, and while equality before the law has become an inalienable principle of all modern constitutional government, equality as such is of greater importance in the political life of a republic than in any other form of government. The point at stake, therefore, is not the well-being of the Negro population alone, but, at least in the long run, the survival of the Republic. Tocqueville saw over a century ago that equality of opportunity and condition, as well as equality of rights, constituted the basic "law" of American democracy, and he predicted that the dilemmas and perplexities inherent in the principle of equality might one day become the most dangerous challenge to the American way of life. In its all-comprehensive, typically American form, equality possesses an enormous power to equalize what by nature and origin is different—and it is only due to this power that the country has been able to retain its fundamental identity against the waves of immigrants who have always flooded its shores. But the principle of equality, even in its American form, is not omnipotent; it cannot equalize natural, physical characteristics. This limit is reached only when inequalities of economic and educational condition have been ironed out, but at that juncture a danger point, well known to students of history, invariably emerges: the more equal people have become in every respect, and the more equality permeates the whole texture of society, the more will differences be resented, the more conspicuous will those become who are visibly and by nature unlike the others.

It is therefore quite possible that the achievement of social, economic, and educational equality for the Negro may sharpen the color problem in this country instead of assuaging it. This, of course, does not have to happen, but it would be only natural if it did, and it would be very surprising if it did not. We have not yet reached the danger point, but we shall reach it in the foreseeable future, and a number of developments have already taken place which clearly point toward it. Awareness of future trouble does not commit one to advocating a reversal of the trend which happily for more than fifteen years now has been greatly in favor of the Negroes. But it does commit one to advocating that government intervention be guided by caution and moderation rather than by impatience and ill-advised measures. Since the Supreme Court decision to enforce desegregation in public schools, the general situation in the South has deteriorated. And while recent events indicate that it will not be possible to avoid Federal enforcement of Negro civil rights in the South altogether, conditions demand that such intervention be restricted to the few instances in which the law of the land and the principle of the Republic are at stake. The question therefore is where this is the case in general, and whether it is the case in public education in particular.

The administration's Civil Rights program covers two altogether different points. It reaffirms the franchise of the Negro population, a matter of course in the North, but not at all in the South. And it also takes up the issue of segregation, which is a matter of fact in the whole country and a matter of discriminatory legislation only in Southern states. The present massive resistance throughout the South is an outcome of enforced desegregation, and not of legal enforcement of the Negroes' right to vote. The results of a public opinion poll in Virginia showing that 92% of the citizens were totally opposed to school integration, that 65% were willing to forgo public education under these conditions, and that 79% denied any obligation to accept the Supreme Court decision as binding, illustrates how serious the situation is. What is frightening here is not the 92% opposed to integration, for the dividing line in the South was never between those who favored and those who opposed segregation—practically speaking, no such opponents existed—but the proportion of people who prefer mob rule to law-abiding citizenship. The so-called liberals and moderates of the South are simply those who are law-abiding, and they have dwindled to a minority of 21%.

No public opinion poll was necessary to reveal this information. The events in Little Rock were quite sufficiently enlightening; and those who wish to blame the disturbances solely on the extraordinary misbehavior of Governor Faubus can set themselves right by listening to the eloquent silence of Arkansas' two liberal Senators. The sorry fact was that the town's law-abiding citizens left the streets to the mob, that neither white nor black citizens felt it their duty to see the Negro children safely to school. That is, even prior to the arrival of Federal troops, law-abiding Southerners had decided that enforcement of the law against mob rule and protection of children against adult mobsters were none of their business. In other words, the arrival of troops did little more than change passive into massive resistance.

It has been said, I think again by Mr. Faulkner, that enforced integration is no better than enforced segregation, and this is perfectly true. The only reason that the Supreme Court was able to address itself to the matter of desegregation in the first place was that segregation has been a legal, and not just a social, issue in the South for many generations. For the crucial point to remember is that it is not the social custom of segregation that is unconstitutional, but its *legal enforcement*. To abolish this legislation is of great and obvious importance and in the case of that part of the Civil Rights bill regarding the right to vote, no Southern state in fact dared to offer strong opposition. Indeed, with respect to unconstitutional legislation, the Civil Rights bill did not go far enough, for it left untouched the most outrageous law of Southern states—the law which makes mixed marriage a criminal offense. The right to marry whoever one wishes is an elementary human right compared to which "the right to attend an integrated school, the right to sit where one pleases on a bus, the right to go into any hotel or recreation area or place of amusement, regardless of one's skin or color or race" are minor indeed. Even political rights, like the right to vote, and nearly all other rights enumerated in the Constitution, are secondary to the inalienable human rights to "life, liberty and the pursuit of happiness" proclaimed in the Declaration of Independence; and to this category the right to home and marriage unquestionably belongs. It would have been much more important if this violation had been brought to the attention of the Supreme Court; yet had the Court ruled the anti-miscegenation laws unconstitutional, it would hardly have felt compelled to encourage, let alone enforce, mixed marriages.

However, the most startling part of the whole business was the Federal decision to start integration in, of all places, the public schools. It certainly did not require too much imagination to see that this was to burden children, black and white, with the working out of a problem which adults for generations have confessed themselves unable to solve. I think no one will find it easy to forget the photograph reproduced in newspapers and magazines throughout the country, showing a Negro girl, accompanied by a white friend of her father, walking away from school, persecuted and followed into bodily proximity by a jeering and grimacing mob of youngsters. The girl, obviously, was asked to be a hero—that is, something neither her absent father nor the equally absent representatives of the NAACP felt called upon to be. It will be hard for the white youngsters, or at least those among them who outgrow their present brutality, to live down this photograph which exposes so mercilessly their juvenile delinquency. The picture looked to me like a fantastic caricature of progressive education which, by abolishing the authority of adults, implicitly denies their responsibility for the world into which they have borne their children and refuses the duty of guiding them into it. Have we now come to the point where it is the children who are being asked to change or improve the world? And do we intend to have our political battles fought out in the school yards?

Segregation is discrimination enforced by law, and desegregation can do no more than abolish the laws enforcing discrimination; it cannot abolish discrimination and force equality upon society, but it can, and indeed must, enforce equality within the body politic. For equality not only has its origin in the body politic; its validity is clearly restricted to the political realm. Only there are we all equals. Under modern conditions, this equality has its most important embodiment in the right to vote, according to which the judgment and opinion of the most exalted citizen are on a par with the judgment and opinion of the hardly literate. Eligibility, the right to be voted into office, is also an inalienable right of every citizen; but here equality is already restricted, and though the necessity for personal distinction in an election arises out of the numerical equality, in which everybody is literally reduced to being one, it is distinction and qualities which count in the winning of votes and not sheer equality.

Yet unlike other differences (for example, professional specialization, occupational qualification, or social and intellectual distinction) the political qualities needed for winning office are so closely connected with being an equal among equals, that one may say that, far from being specialties, they are precisely those distinctions to which all voters equally aspire—not necessarily as human beings, but as citizens and political beings. Thus the qualities of officials in a democracy always depend upon the qualities of the electorate. Eligibility, therefore, is a necessary corollary of the right to vote; it means that everyone is given the opportunity to distinguish himself in those things in which all are equals to begin with. Strictly speaking, the franchise and eligibility for office are the only political rights, and they constitute in a modern democracy the very quintessence of citizenship. In contrast to all other rights, civil or human, they cannot be granted to resident aliens.

What equality is to the body politic—its innermost principle—discrimination is to society. Society is that curious, somewhat hybrid realm between the political and the private in which, since the beginning of the modern age, most men have spent the greater part of their lives. For each time we leave the protective four walls of our private homes and cross over the threshold into the public world, we enter first, not the political realm of equality, but the social sphere. We are driven into this sphere by the need to earn a living or attracted by the desire to follow our vocation or enticed by the pleasure of company, and once we have entered it, we become subject to the old adage of "like attracts like" which controls the whole realm of society in the innumerable variety of its groups and associations. What matters here is not personal distinction but the differences by which people belong to certain groups whose very identifiability demands that they discriminate against other groups in the same domain. In American society, people group together, and therefore discriminate against each other, along lines of profession, income, and ethnic origin, while in Europe the lines run along class origin, education, and manners. From the viewpoint of the human person, none of these discriminatory practices makes sense; but then it is doubtful whether the human person as such ever appears in the social realm. At any rate, without discrimination of some sort, society would simply cease to exist and very important possibilities of free association and group formation would disappear.

Mass society—which blurs lines of discrimination and levels group distinctions—is a danger to society as such, rather than to the integrity of the person, for personal identity has its source beyond the social realm. Conformism, however, is not a characteristic of mass society alone, but of every society insofar as only those are admitted to a given social group who conform to the general traits of difference which keep the group together. The danger of conformism in this country—a danger almost as old as the Republic—is that, because of the extraordinary heterogeneity of its population, social conformism tends to become an absolute and a substitute for national homogeneity. In any event, discrimination is as indispensable a social right as equality is a political right. The question is not how to abolish discrimination, but how to keep it confined within the social sphere, where it is legitimate, and prevent its trespassing on the political and the personal sphere, where it is destructive.

In order to illustrate this distinction between the political and the social, I shall give two examples of discrimination, one in my opinion entirely justified and outside the scope of government intervention, the other scandalously unjustified and positively harmful to the political realm.

It is common knowledge that vacation resorts in this country are frequently "restricted" according to ethnic origin. There are many people who object to this practice; nevertheless it is only an extension of the right to free association. If as a Jew I wish to spend my vacations only in the company of Jews, I cannot see how anyone can reasonably prevent my doing so; just as I see no reason why other resorts should not cater to a clientele that wishes not to see Jews while on a holiday. There cannot be a "right to go into any hotel or recreation area or place of amusement," because many of these are in the realm of the purely social where the right to free association, and therefore to discrimination, has greater validity than the principle of equality. (This does not apply to theaters and museums, where people obviously do not congregate for the purpose of associating with each other.) The fact that the "right" to enter social places is silently granted in most countries and has become highly controversial only in American democracy is due not to the greater tolerance of other countries but in part to the homogeneity of their population and in part to their class system, which operates socially even when its economic foundations have disappeared. Homogeneity and class working together assure a "likeness" of clientele in any given place that even restriction and discrimination cannot achieve in America.

It is, however, another matter altogether when we come to "the right to sit where one pleases in a bus" or a railroad car or station, as well as the right to enter hotels and restaurants in business districts—in short, when we are dealing with services which, whether privately or publicly owned, are in fact public services that everyone needs in order to pursue his business and lead his life. Though not strictly in the political realm, such services are clearly in the public domain where all men are equal; and discrimination in Southern railroads and buses is as scandalous as discrimination in hotels and restaurants throughout the country. Obviously the situation is far worse in the South because segregation in public services is enforced by law and plainly visible to all. It is unfortunate indeed that the first step toward clearing up the segregation situation in the South after so many decades of complete neglect did not begin with its most inhuman and its most conspicuous aspects.

The third realm, finally, in which we move and live together with other people—the realm of privacy—is ruled neither by equality nor by discrimination, but by exclusiveness. Here we choose those with whom we wish to spend our lives, personal friends and those we love; and our choice is guided not by likeness or qualities shared by a group of people—it is not guided, indeed, by any objective standards or rules, but strikes, inexplicably and unerringly, at one person in his uniqueness, his unlikeness to all other people we know. The rules of uniqueness and exclusiveness are, and always will be, in conflict with the standards of society precisely because social discrimination violates the principle, and lacks validity for the conduct, of private life. Thus every mixed marriage constitutes a challenge to society and means that the partners to such a marriage have so far preferred personal happiness to social adjustment that they are willing to bear the burden of discrimination. This is and must remain their private business. The scandal begins only when their challenge to society and prevailing customs, to which every citizen has a right, is interpreted as a criminal offense so that by stepping outside the social realm they find themselves in conflict with the law as well. Social standards are not legal standards and if legislature follows social prejudice, society has become tyrannical.

For reasons too complicated to discuss here, the power of society in our time is greater than it ever was before, and not many people are left who know the rules of and live a private life. But this provides the body politic with no excuse for forgetting the rights of privacy, for failing to understand that the rights of privacy are grossly violated whenever legislation begins to enforce social discrimination. While the government has no right to interfere with the prejudices and discriminatory practices of society, it has not only the right but the duty to make sure that these practices are not legally enforced.

Just as the government has to ensure that social discrimination never curtails political equality, it must also safeguard the rights of every person to do as he pleases within the four walls of his own home. The moment social discrimination is legally enforced, it becomes persecution, and of this crime many Southern states have been guilty. The moment social discrimination is legally abolished, the freedom of society is violated, and the danger is that thoughtless handling of the civil rights issue by the Federal government will result in such a violation. The government can legitimately take no steps against social discrimination because government can act only in the name of equality—a principle which does not obtain in the social sphere. The only public force that can fight social prejudice is the churches, and they can do so in the name of the uniqueness of the person, for it is on the principle of the uniqueness of souls that religion (and especially the Christian faith) is based. The churches are indeed the only communal and public place where appearances do not count, and if discrimination creeps into the houses of worship, this is an infallible sign of their religious failing. They then have become social and are no longer religious institutions.

Another issue involved in the present conflict between Washington and the South is the matter of states' rights. For some time it has been customary among liberals to maintain that no such issue exists at all but is only a ready-made subterfuge of Southern reactionaries who have nothing in their hands except "abstruse arguments and constitutional history." In my opinion, this is a dangerous error. In contradistinction to the classical principle of the European nation-state that power, like sovereignty, is indivisible, the power structure of this country rests on the principle of division of power and on the conviction that the body politic as a whole is strengthened by the division of power. To be sure, this principle is embodied in the system of checks and balances between the three branches of government; but it is no less rooted in the government's Federal structure which demands that there also be a balance and a mutual check between Federal power and the powers of the forty-eight states. If it is true (and I am convinced it is) that unlike force, power generates more power when it is divided, then it follows that every attempt of the Federal government to deprive the states of some of their legislative sovereignty can be justified only on grounds of legal argument and constitutional history. Such arguments are not abstruse; they are based on a principle which indeed was uppermost in the minds of the founders of the Republic.

All this has nothing to do with being a liberal or a conservative, although it may be that where the nature of power is at stake, liberal judgment with its long and honorable history of deep distrust of power in any form can be less trusted than on other questions. Liberals fail to understand that the nature of power is such that the power potential of the Union as a whole will suffer if the regional foundations on which this power rests are undermined. The point is that force can, indeed must, be centralized in order to be effective, but power cannot and must not. If the various sources from which it springs are dried up, the whole structure becomes impotent. And states' rights in this country are among the most authentic sources of power, not only for the promotion of regional interests and diversity, but for the Republic as a whole.

The trouble with the decision to force the issue of desegregation in the field of public education rather than in some other field in the campaign for Negro rights has been that this decision unwittingly touched upon an area in which every one of the different rights and principles we have discussed is involved. It is perfectly true, as Southerners have repeatedly pointed out, that the Constitution is silent on education and that legally as well as traditionally, public education lies in the domain of state legislation. The counter-argument that all public schools today are Federally supported is weak, for Federal subvention is intended in these instances to match and supplement local contributions and does not transform the schools into Federal institutions, like the Federal District courts. It would be very unwise indeed if the Federal government—which now must come to the assistance of more and more enterprises that once were the sole responsibility of the states—were to use its financial support as a means of whipping the states into agreement with positions they would otherwise be slow or altogether unwilling to adopt.

The same overlapping of rights and interests becomes apparent when we examine the issue of education in the light of the three realms of human life—the political, the social, and the private. Children are first of all part of family and home, and this means that they are, or should be, brought up in that atmosphere of idiosyncratic exclusiveness which alone makes a home a home, strong and secure enough to shield its young against the demands of the social and the responsibilities of the political realm. The right of parents to bring up their children as they see fit is a right of privacy, belonging to home and family. Ever since the introduction of compulsory education, this right has been challenged and restricted, but not abolished, by the right of the body politic to prepare children to fulfill their future duties as citizens. The stake of the government in the matter is undeniable—as is the right of the parents. The possibility of private education provides no way out of the dilemma, because it would make the safeguarding of certain private rights dependent upon economic status and consequently underprivilege those who are forced to send their children to public schools.

Parents' rights over their children are legally restricted by compulsory education and nothing else. The state has the unchallengeable right to prescribe minimum requirements for future citizenship and beyond that to further and support the teaching of subjects and professions which are felt to be desirable and necessary to the nation as a whole. All this involves, however, only the content of the child's education, not the context of association and social life which invariably develops out of his attendance at school; otherwise one would have to challenge the right of private schools to exist. For the child himself, school is the first place away from home where he establishes contact with the public world that surrounds him and his family. This public world is not political but social, and the school is to the child what a job is to an adult. The only difference is that the element of free choice which, in a free society, exists at least in principle in the choosing of jobs and the associations connected with them, is not yet at the disposal of the child but rests with his parents.

To force parents to send their children to an integrated school against their will means to deprive them of rights which clearly belong to them in all free societies—the private right over their children and the social right to free association. As for the children, forced integration means a very serious conflict between home and school, between their private and their social life, and while such conflicts are common in adult life, children cannot be expected to handle them and therefore should not be exposed to them. It has often been remarked that man is never so much of a conformer—that is, a purely social being—as in childhood. The reason is that every child instinctively seeks authorities to guide it into the world in which he is still a stranger, in which he cannot orient himself by his own judgment. To the extent that parents and teachers fail him as authorities, the child will conform more strongly to his own group, and under certain conditions the peer group will become his supreme authority. The result can only be a rise of mob and gang rule, as the news photograph we mentioned above so eloquently demonstrate. The conflict between a segregated home and a desegregated school, between family prejudice and school demands, abolishes at one stroke both the teachers' and the parents' authority, replacing it with the rule of public opinion among children who have neither the ability nor the right to establish a public opinion of their own.

Because the many different factors involved in public education can quickly be set to work at cross purposes, government intervention, even at its best, will always be rather controversial. Hence it seems highly questionable whether it was wise to begin enforcement of civil rights in a domain where no basic human and no basic political right is at stake, and where other rights—social and private— whose protection is no less vital, can so easily be hurt.

Black Men–White Women: A Philosophical View*

WILLIAM H. TURNER

Any student familiar with the literature on Black and white sexual relations and intermarriage knows that such offerings have been couched in one or a coupling of the following theses: (1) that sexual freedom and racial intermarriage is for whites the most important aspect of the Black-white caste system; and conversely, for Blacks such matters were of least importance among the various forms of discrimination they had to suffer (Myrdal, 1944); or (2) that the "sanctity" of the white woman and the savage "sexuality" of the Black man made them both the envied ones of the universe (Hernton, 1965). More recently though, a new dimension of the Black male–white female relationship has come to the attention of social scientists. That aspect concerns the political ramifications of such racial/ sexual "freedom" in the wake of the so-called Black revolution in America. This paper focuses on the latter theme; that is, in spite of the classical offerings of Myrdal and Hernton, and void of the common stereotypes about the sexual potency of Black men and the omnipresence of the white woman as a sex symbol, what are some other questions we might raise, which, when clarified, might more profitably help us in understanding the present-day status of such relationships? Among these questions are: (1) What are some of the basic assumptions regarding Black male-white female relationships? (2) In what ways have the assumptions changed over the past few years? (3) Have the social responses (rejections) to Black male-white female relations become biological? and (4) What are the prospects of such relationships in light of the liberation struggle?

Relative to some prior points in the history of Blacks in America, things have improved. The overall climate in this country is, at the present time, such that Blacks can feel relatively free to do whatever they choose. Consequently, a lot of

* From William H. Turner, "Black Man/White Woman: A Philosophical View." In Doris Y. Wilkinson, *Black Male/White Female: Perspectives on Interracial Marriage and Courtship* (Cambridge, Mass.: Schenkman, 1975), 170–175.

Black men have chosen to mingle with and/or marry white women. But, since Black male–white female relationships (at whatever level) cannot exist in a vacuum, certain perceptions and definitions are made of that situation. Assumption one: Black men dating/married to white women are perceived by other members of society (especially other Blacks) as doing "it" at the expense of some other potential mate—his own Black woman. A complementary assumption: white women who engage themselves with Black men are either constitutionally deficient, morally permissive, or simply sexual freaks acting as though the "myth" of Black male sexuality were real.

Such assumptions, which do not pretend to cover the range of things, become exacerbated in the contemporary scheme of sexual politics in America. Politically, one might assume that Black men are presently more enfranchised as "men"; thusly, it should follow that Black men need not masque their manliness in sexual acts which compensate for political and social inequity (Clark, 1965). That is, Black men "ought" now begin to crystallize their role as fathers, male images, providers, etc., and be about the busy work of stabilizing their Black families. This does not exclude Black men who are single or those who are married already to white women; for they too, as long as they associate with white women, are presumably potential heads of Black families. The fact is that where Black men interact more frequently with white females, the likelihood is greater that such Black men are themselves more educated, have higher incomes, and are (ostensibly) the prototypes of Black manhood most capable of bringing the Black family out of the welfare syndrome (Staples, 1966:48). In short, the Black male is the bulwark and cornerstone of a revolutionary mass; and consequently, Black male interaction with white females is defined as politically and socially contradictory. Moreover, the Black man who mingles with white women, *prima facie*, implies his vote of "no confidence" and non-participation in the plight of Black people. Summarily, as Black poet Don L. Lee puts it: "You can't talk Black and sleep white" (1968).

It would seem then that Black men who date or marry white women and who want to avoid the kinds of dilemmas discussed above need only to disengage (and perhaps vocally declare) their non-participation in the so-called "movement." The "talk Black–sleep white" dilemma appears to exclude from criticism that Black man who simply "sleeps quietly." But, since such relationships do not exist in social vacuums, and since Blacks are perceived of and defined as a group (and not as individuals with free choice) then the Black man who simply sleeps and wants to be left alone with his own mate-choice is not above these considerations. He too, no matter how clandestine his relationship with a white woman, is caught in the same fundamental contradiction. What are the bases of that contradiction?

The response to a Black man and a white woman in America *was* a social response. In fact, the situation was defined socially. After hundreds of years in which the image of one has been positively nurtured and that of the other having been deprecated, the response itself has transcended mere social definitions. A dialectic has evolved. And in such a dialectic, Black male–white female relationships become essential biological contradictions rather than manifestations of a social contradiction. The essence of that dialectic is Euro-American thinking and its philosophical system which regards all things as forever isolated from one another and as forever changeless (Tse Tung, 1960:3). Under such an ideological system, it is no wonder that the Black male–white female relationship has become regarded as fundamentally absurd and self-negating. As such, Black men–white women, just like other "inherent contradictions," are defined in light of a vulgar onesideness: an Either/Or kind of antagonism (Dixon and Foster, 1970). Such Euro-American emphasis on Either/Or world views allows for the following kind of thinking: It is raining or it is not raining; things are beautiful or they are not beautiful; people are Black or they are non-Black; people are white or non-white; and, *reductio ad absurdum*, Black men love Black women *or* they love white women. The affirmation of the one reflects the negation of the other. And, since we are examining the political ramifications of such affirmations, it follows that the affirmation of the woman also reflects the affirmation of the race (the opposing values), ". . . to caress white breasts is to hold white civilization in the palms of (Black) hands" (Fanon, 1967:166). In this scheme of things, to date or marry white women becomes for Black men a negation and contradiction of the Black race and the attendant revolutionary value system.

For white females though, such an analysis only skirts her aggressiveness. The onus is always on the Black male. The burden of the myth has depended most often on his sexual prowess as proof of his basic manhood (masculinity). Sexism, in this sense, comes to play. The manhood of Black males has been socially and legally blocked because the dominant culture (and its system of rewards and symbols) kept such "criteria" for manhood as the exclusive domain of white men (Frazier, 1939). At the present time though, the very Black men who are by-and-large "more" rewarded by culturally sanctioned symbols of manhood and masculinity are the very ones blamed for using the "white woman avenue" as proof of their manhood. In this sense, the white woman has outlived her usefulness as a way of proving one's manhood. This suggests that the very Blacks (e.g., white-collar workers, professionals, politicians, the liberal-urbane, athletes, and the militant revolutionist) who are able to compete for their "manhood" with white men are revitalizing the sole avenue (sexual prowess) on which they, presumably, outdistance white men.

A further dimension of this metaphysical view has been discussed by Frantz Fanon (1967). Fanon studied the phenomenology of Black male–white female relationships and he considered the basic constituent of those affairs as "Negrophobia." For him, the response to such relationships by society has transcended the social; it has become biological:

> This phobia is to be found on an instinctual biological level. At the extreme . . . the Negro, because of his body, impedes the closing of the postural schema of the white man—at the point, naturally, at which the Black man makes his entry into the phenomenal world of the white man.

If we extend Fanon's position, Black men then are phenomenologically "outside" the white man's world until the point of his *physical* entry. It can be seen then that relations with *his* white women become instinctually as well as culturally contradictory. If one understands the universality of this contradiction, the present-day reaction against Black men and white women becomes an unconscious and quasi-biological reaction. The white male (society) cannot deal with the very sexual Frankenstein (Black man) whom he created himself! Such mythology results from a complementary aspect of Euro-America's world view, i.e., the physical versus the intellectual.

The white man is perceived as the intellectual development, the Black man (because of his history) is perceived as the physical development. In spite of the accomplishments and intellectual development (enfranchisement) of Black men, the world outlook relating to them remains biological. That is, Black men do not become more intellectually developed, they become "less" physical. Moreover, America's view of the Black man's change holds that such a change does not result from "things" inside the Black man; rather it holds that Black men have changed only as they are propelled by "things" external to them—the white world (white men). Such absoluteness has decreed in America between Blacks and whites a dichotomy on physical and intellectual attributes. Cleaver has aptly called this matter as it relates to Black and white men the Supermasculine Menial and the Omnipotent Administrator (Cleaver, 1968).

The considerations offered above touch upon many aspects of a situation. Other contributors to this manuscript have dealt with specific parameters of this question. The major question here has been the political ramifications of Black male–white female relationships. In an effort to raise the political consciousness of ALL Black people, every act becomes political. Then too, in a situation where the revolutionary lines are not clear-cut, nothing is counter-revolutionary. That is, unless we can presume that Black men's consciousness (as Black people) is restructured by virtue of this sexual engagement, then the action is meaningless in a political sense. Society will continue then to assume that Black men interact with white women as though it were a conscious decision, i.e., at the expense of Black mates. Secondly, those assumptions will not change appreciably. The polarization between Black and white people will widen causing the reaction to such relationships to become more biologically entrenched; and lastly, the political liberation of Black people will rule out Black men who choose to remain "individuals" in a situation that calls for "we-ness."

References

Clark, Kenneth. *Dark Ghetto*. New York: Harper & Row, 1965.

Cleaver, Eldridge. *Soul on Ice*. New York: Random House, 1968.

Dixon, V., and B. Foster. *Beyond Black or White*. Boston: Little, Brown & Co., 1970.

Fanon, Frantz. *Black Skins, White Masks*. New York: Grove Press, 1967.

Frazier, E. Franklin. *The Negro Family in the United States*. Chicago: University of Chicago Press, 1939.

Hernton, Calvin C. *Sex and Racism in America*. New York: Grove Press, 1966.

Lee, Don L. *Think Black*. Detroit: Broadside Press, 1967.

Myrdal, Gunnar. *An American Dilemma*. New York: Harper, 1944.
Staples, Robert. "The Myth of the Impotent Black Male." *The Black Scholar* 2 (June 1971).
Staples, Robert. *The Black Family*. Belmont, Calif.: Wadsworth, 1971.
Tse Tung, Mao. *On Contradictions*. Peking: Foreign Languages Press, 1966.

Reflecting the Changing Face of America: Multiracials, Racial Classification, and American Intermarriage*

JOEL PERLMANN

If a child has a white mother and a black father, the child is racially . . . what? Presently, on the census form individuals are allowed to declare origins in one race only, and so multiracials must choose one race from the available list or classify themselves as "other." Deciding how the next census should handle the multiracial child is a hot topic now; the directions on how to count are being reconsidered. At issue is more than how just the Census Bureau counts racial origin; every government agency that counts races does so in roughly the same way. The current directions for counting races are found in Office of Management and Budget (OMB) Directive 15; decisions on if and how to change the directive can't be put off for long because the census forms for the year 2000 are needed in the spring of 1998.

Over the past several years the OMB coordinated an interagency task force to study Directive 15, and a good deal of relevant research has emerged, especially from the Census Bureau, on the implications of alternative procedures. In early July of this year the task force issued its recommendations, and the OMB will rule on the issues after considering responses to the report. Congress could intervene in the process; hearings were held in 1993 and this past May, more are scheduled, and there is a bill in committee. Finally, the president has declared a year of discussion on race, stressing the changing racial composition of the country. How to classify the mixed-race child is only one of several issues in the review of OMB Directive 15. In many ways, however, it is the most important; all the others look different after one thinks through the multiracial issue.

Interest groups have lined up on two sides to debate the classification of the mixed-race person.[1] On one side are organizations claiming to represent the American multiracial population; among them are parents in mixed marriages who are

---

* From Joel Perlmann, *Reflecting the Changing Face of America: Multiracials, Racial Classification, and American Intermarriage* (Publications of the Jerome Levy Institute, #35, 1997).
1. For a large sampling of views on this issue, see U.S. House of Representatives 1994. For the range of issues that the OMB has raised for review, see U.S. Office of Management and Budget 1995, 44,673–44,693.

concerned about the way they are asked to identify their children. These organizations demand equal recognition for multiracials in the government's racial classification system; they ask that the category "multiracial" be added to the specific racial categories—white, black, Native American, and Asian/Pacific Islander—that currently appear on the census form. People who select the multiracial category would then indicate from which two, three, or four of these racial groups they are descended. The demand here appears to be more for recognition of multiraciality than for any specific political or economic advantage for multiracials. The advocates do not want to deny a part of their own or their children's origins. I refer to this interest group as the *multiracial advocates.*[2]

The other side in this debate opposes adding a multiracial category and permitting people to list more than one race. This group includes civil rights organizations and representatives of blacks, Hispanics, Native Americans, and Asians/Pacific Islanders. At the core of their opposition is the concern that if individuals are allowed to indicate origins in more than one racial group, the counting of races that undergirds so much civil rights legislation will be muddled and enforcement of civil rights thereby weakened. If, for example, who is black can be counted in various ways, it will be much harder to enforce laws promoting racial equality—antidiscrimination efforts, affirmative action, and voting rights could all be affected. Moreover, some argue, in a society still plagued by strong racial inequality, the tendency of mixed-race people will be to "head for the door," as one spokesperson put it; they will seek to be counted as something other than a member of the minority group in which they are now counted because they think it is to their advantage to do so. I refer to this interest group as the *civil rights advocates.*

Tens of thousands of public agencies, private business enterprises, and non-business institutions (such as colleges) fill out reports on the racial composition of their employees and clients. Consequently, those with the slightest concern for orderly—and equitable—record keeping are also watching the debates carefully.

The key recommendation in the interagency task force's July [1997] report was that individuals henceforth be allowed to declare origins in more than one racial group, but that a new category called multiracial should not be established.[3] The task force did much more than urge a compromise between the two contending positions; this is a case in which the most important demands of both sides can be accepted and, more important, it is in the public interest that they should be accepted. This brief supports the key task force recommendation, although it argues for it from a somewhat different perspective, stressing the need to understand racial intermarriage in the context of ethnic intermarriage generally.

Individuals should be allowed to report origins in more than one racial group, with mixed-race individuals counted in a way as consistent as possible with pres-

2. While the demand may be for recognition, it is worth noting that should the multiracial population be defined as a distinct racial group, it might then become eligible for various benefits.
3. The task force also rejected the need to combine race and Hispanic origin into one question (U.S. Office of Management and Budget 1997, 36,873–36,946).

ent counting procedures and probably with some guarantees that the changes in counting procedures will be pretty much "race-count neutral" in the immediate future. The task force did not resolve the best way to count multiracials in connection with civil rights enforcement, although some of the possible ways were elaborated in an earlier report by Census Bureau staff (Bennett et al. 1997). I add some variations on these suggestions in this brief.

The procedures arrived at may well satisfy both interest groups, but the issue has significance that extends well beyond the concerns of the advocates most directly involved. The way the multiracial issue is being treated, both at the Census Bureau and in the media, tells much about the state of American thinking about race. In the public discussion there is virtually no recognition that racial intermarriage is a form of ethnic intermarriage, despite the fact that most people are familiar with ethnic intermarriage and the Census Bureau has been counting the offspring of such marriages for over a century.

The method used to count ethnic intermarriages cannot be mindlessly adopted as a model for counting racial intermarriages because racial categories, unlike other ethnic categories, are the basis of civil rights legislation. This is the key point to appreciate: Counting the offspring of racial intermarriage would not be harder than counting the offspring of ethnic intermarriage were it not for the legal (civil rights) implications of the racial count. Nevertheless, the ethnic model can suggest guiding principles and the kind of modifications necessary in order to handle racial intermarriage sensibly in counts and in law.

Section 1 of this brief reviews the realities of ethnic blending in the United States, focusing on white immigrants and their descendants, and examines how the Census Bureau has dealt with this blending. Section 2 contrasts the bureau's treatment of ethnicity with its treatment of race. Section 3 provides information on rates of racial intermarriage today. These first three sections, then, explain the issues, setting multiraciality in the context of ethnic blending in general. Sections 4 and 5 are the practical core of the brief, presenting arguments for and against certain policies. Section 4 argues that the context established in the preceding sections provides a rationale for adopting the interagency task force's key recommendation: Allow people to declare more than one racial origin, but do not list a multiracial category on government questionnaires. The remainder of the section considers proposals for counting the responses that the revised race question will elicit on the basis of how the new counts will impinge on civil rights law. Section 5 calls attention to a matter rarely discussed in connection with OMB Directive 15, namely, Census Bureau forecasts of the future racial composition of the United States. This topic regularly makes its way to the front page, but in misleading and confused ways. What links Sections 4 and 5 is the argument that evading discussion of racial intermarriage distorts our understanding of race data, whether we are discussing 1997 or 2050.

Finally, the brief contains two addenda that form extensions of the main argument. The first reviews the experience of racial blending in American history and its implications for the race data covered in present and proposed OMB directives. The second considers briefly another change that has been mentioned in connection with OMB Directive 15, namely, making "Hispanic" one of the race categories.

Ethnic Intermarriage

American as Apple Pie

American history would be unrecognizable without ethnic intermarriage. From colonial times to the present, immigrants typically married their own, the second generation did so much less consistently, and the third generation did so still less consistently, with probably a majority marrying members of other ethnic groups. By the fourth and fifth generations, who even kept track? The evidence for ethnic intermarriage is as overwhelming and unambiguous as for any generalization about the American population: from de Crèvecoeur's observations in the eighteenth century on "this new man, the American" arising out of various European immigrant stocks to the data from census after census in the twentieth century (Heer 1980; Lieberson and Waters 1988).

Intermarriage occurred most often among the descendants of European groups; it was crucial to the making of "Americans" out of the descendants of "hyphenated Americans." It was decidedly less prevalent between these "whites" and other groups, a piece of the story to which I return later. For now, however, notice that among the Europeans the immigrant generation often drew firm lines of division between groups. Moreover, at the turn of the century many influential American thinkers discussed European immigrant groups in terms of different races, such as "Nordic," "Alpine," and "Mediterranean." Arguments for immigration restriction—in congressional debate and across the land—turned in part on the notion that the "racial composition" of the immigrant pool was changing. As late as 1920, telling many Americans that members of all these "races" were "white" would have elicited amused or heated rejoinders that the statement was untrue and that it missed crucial "inherent" divisions among the whites (Higham 1955).

Counting "Multiethnics"

How has the Census Bureau handled the offspring of ethnic intermarriages? It asks respondents to give their country of birth and, often, their parents' countries of birth.[4] When a native-born respondent says that his or her parents were born

---

4. The respondent's birthplace question has been asked in every decennial census since 1850 and the parental birthplace questions in every decennial census between 1880 and 1970. In 1980 and 1990 the parental birthplace questions were dropped. It is to be hoped (probably vainly) that the 2000 census will include the parental birthplace questions, without which we cannot know, for example, whether a 25-year-old native-born individual of Chinese descent is the child of immigrants or the child of descendants who have been in this country since 1870 or before. In any event, the parental birthplace questions continue to be asked regularly on other census enumerations, such as monthly

in two different countries, the bureau records two countries of origin. Both parents born in Italy? Fine. One born in Italy, one in Poland? One in Italy, one in the United States? All fine.

In 1980 and 1990 the Census Bureau also used the ancestry question. Each individual was asked to state with which ancestry he or she identified in order to allow Americans to state an ethnic affiliation even if they were descended from immigrants who had come to the United States many generations back. Three features of the ancestry question are crucially relevant to racial classification. First, the ancestry question asks people to declare the ancestry or ancestries *with which they most closely identify*. Thus a strong subjective element is built into the question. Unlike questions such as "Where were you born?" or "How many years of schooling have you had?" it does not ask for what might be called an objective answer; rather, it explicitly encourages a statement of preferences. The rationale, developed in the late 1970s, for this question leads us back to intermarriage again. Many people are able to trace their origins to numerous ancestries (too many to list) or may not even know about all of them. So they are asked to list the ancestries they consider meaningful.[5]

The second relevant feature of the ancestry question is that it states explicitly that Americans can identify themselves as having *more than one* ethnic ancestry. Many millions of Americans list two ethnic ancestries; millions more list three. The bureau has taken the trouble to code first and second ancestry responses and (in 1980) even to detail the most prevalent combinations of three responses.

The third relevant feature is *how much the ancestry responses have varied* among the same people over time. The question calls for a subjective response about loyalties that for many might be very weak. In 1980 English was listed before German in the bureau's examples of ancestry; in 1990 the ordering was reversed. As a result of this seemingly trivial change, the percentage listing English ancestry declined by a large fraction, and the percentage claiming identity with German ancestry rose by a comparable amount; the percentage claiming Italian ancestry also fluctuated greatly for similar reasons. These examples of confusion in the responses tells us something important about the long-term results of population mixing and the attenuation of connections with the origins of ancestors. Keeping track of American ancestries at the bureau eventually gets messy because of intermarriage patterns—and that is as it should be. A simple answer to the question on ancestry would be a false answer. It would imply that people did not intermarry in American history or that Americans keep careful track of the ethnic origin of distant ancestors whom they never knew (Alba 1995).

Current Population Surveys. For a convenient compendium of the census questions prior to 1990, see Bureau of the Census 1979; for a discussion of the ancestry question, discussed below, see Lieberson and Waters 1988.

5. Another rationale was thought to be that it would tap into putative ethnic loyalties related to the "white ethnic revival" of the late 1970s.

The Hispanic Origin Question

For the past two decades the census form has included a question asking respondents if they are "of Hispanic origin" and, if so, of which specific Hispanic group. Since the answer to this question can be cross-classified with the race question, we often see the categories "non-Hispanic whites," "non-Hispanic blacks," and "Hispanics" (the last with the footnote that "Hispanics may be of any race"). One of the issues in the current review of OMB Directive 15 is whether the Hispanic origin question and the race question should be combined into one question, or, put more crudely, whether Hispanic should be called a race (as discussed in Addendum 2). The point for us here, however, concerns the Hispanic question and intermarriage. Respondents are not told they have to be "entirely of Hispanic origin"; on the contrary, the question clearly permits them to indicate themselves as Hispanic if they are the product of mixed Hispanic and non-Hispanic origin. Indeed, like the ancestry question, the Hispanic origin question leaves it up to the mixed-origin individual to decide whether the "Hispanic" component in his or her background is large enough to answer the question in the affirmative. However, unlike the ancestry question, the Hispanic origin question calls for a direct response on one and only one specific ancestry, thus increasing the likelihood of a positive response.[6]

The Race Question and Racial Intermarriage

The Race Question

On all the questions that deal with ethnic origin—parental birthplace, ancestry, and Hispanic origin—the Census Bureau allows for the possibility that the respondent is of multiple ethnic origins and often tabulates the results of these ethnic intermarriages. On the race question, in contrast, there is an explicit instruction to mark only one category. What if a person demurs and marks two or more? Using certain rules (such as which race is listed first), the bureau recodes the response so that only one race is counted.[7]

For our purposes, this instruction to mark only one race is the most striking peculiarity of the census race question. However, there are others. A second is

---

6. Critics have argued that the information produced by the Hispanic question is already embedded in the ancestry question and that the Hispanic origin question is a useless redundancy propelled by Hispanic interest groups. Defenders of the question note that the question explicitly asks the respondent for a yes or no answer on this *specific* ancestry, which is the only ancestry not covered by the race question that is relevant to legislation. See for example, Lieberson and Waters 1988, 16–18.

7. Similarly, in direct interviews (as opposed to mail-in forms, which most people fill out) "If a person could not provide a single race response, the race of the mother was used. If a single race response could not be provided for the person's mother, the first race reported by the person was used" (Bureau of the Census 1992, Appendix B).

that the question is not labeled on the census form as a question about race; rather, the respondent is simply asked to complete the sentence "This person is . . ." and is given a choice of four specific racial designations—white, black, Native American, Asian/Pacific Islander—and the designation "other." Later, the bureau tabulates the answers under a heading of races. As the bureau's documentation explains, these categories derive from the guidelines in OMB Directive 15. A third peculiarity is that under some of the four specific race designations are listed heterogeneous subgroupings of peoples, for example, the countries of birth or origin in Asia and specific Native American tribes.

The bureau's description of the race question reveals the subjective nature of the racial data it collects and its discomfort about the social scientific standing of what it is collecting. As described by the Census Bureau,

> The concept of race as used by the Census Bureau reflects self-identification; it does not denote any clear-cut scientific definition of biological stock. The data for race represent self-classification by people according to the race with which they most closely identify. Furthermore, it is recognized that the categories of the race item include both racial and national origin or sociocultural groups. (Bureau of the Census 1992, Appendix B)

This statement unequivocally rules out any need for government officials to believe that racial classification has a meaningful basis in biology or to define any objective meaning for a racial category at all: Race is a term in popular usage and whatever it may mean, a person belongs to whatever category of race that person believes he or she belongs to.

An interesting commentary on this process of self-identification appears in a recent joint study by the Census Bureau and the Bureau of Labor Statistics. The authors report on their attempts to learn how respondents distinguished between

> such terms as race, ethnicity/ethnic origin, and ancestry. Despite several attempts to make these questions less abstract and easier to answer, the overwhelming majority of respondents found the questions too difficult. For all but a few, highly educated respondents, it appeared that the terms represented overlapping concepts which draw on a single semantic domain. (Tucker et al. 1996)

Thus the bureau warns us that the term race is not used in a precise "biological" way, but rather subjectively (for self-identification), and that its users do not distinguish it from related terms. Recall also that the term race itself is not mentioned in the question. However, if the answer is based on subjective identification, as in the ancestry question, why can't respondents choose two or more races with which to identify, as they can with ancestry? The answer is clear when one appreciates the current use and origin of the race categories. They emerge from the OMB directive, and they are used in the counts that lie at the heart of a great deal of civil rights legislation.

The great irony here is that data on race are gathered through a more or less slippery and subjective procedure of self-identification and then used as the basis of legal status in an important domain of law and administrative regulation, namely, civil rights. That domain requires legal statuses that are, in the words of the original mandate to the OMB, "complete and nonoverlapping." As a result, the Census Bureau not only uses a subjective definition of race, but also places an unrealistic restriction on that subjectivity—only one race can be chosen (even though it routinely accepts multiple parental birthplaces and ethnic ancestries). In a sense, the race question could just as well be referred to as the "legally protected minority groups question" (although then the Census Bureau would have to add the responses to the Hispanic origin question, a possibility under consideration by the OMB).

The problem with this state of affairs is not just that it may offend the sensibilities of the multiracial advocates; there is something much deeper at stake. In order to have clear-cut racial categories for legal purposes, a system of counting has been created that ignores a widespread reality. Denying that members of different races marry is like treating them as members of different biological species. All the while, the Census Bureau is acknowledging the stunningly high rates of intermarriage among those ethnic groups not designated as racial groups. If racial barriers are to be broken down, racial intermarriage should be treated in the same matter-of-fact way that any other form of ethnic intermarriage is treated, while ensuring that civil rights legislation, which rests on clear counts of racial membership, is not hobbled by ambiguities.

A Kind of Ethnic Intermarriage

Whatever small residue of meaning "race" may still have for anthropologists or biologists today, for our purposes it does have an important meaning, as a subset of ethnicity. Ethnic groupings refer to the different countries or local areas of the world from which people or their ancestors came here during the five centuries since Columbus or to the fact that their ancestors were here prior to that time. Races as a subset of ethnicity are those ethnic groups that were treated in especially distinct ways in the American past (and to some extent are still so treated). This way of defining ethnicity and race may be crude and imprecise, but it drives home two crucial points relevant to this discussion. First, races form a special subset of ethnic groups and therefore racial intermarriage forms a special subset of ethnic intermarriage. Second, a concern with racial classification is legitimate as it arises from such legacies as slavery, the near-extermination of Native American groups, and state laws forbidding interracial marriage—laws that survived in various states until 1967 when the U.S. Supreme Court finally ruled them unconstitutional. If we want to understand problems such as American economic inequality, we cannot ignore people's racial origins; to throw out race classifications in our present censuses would not be smart or fair.[8]

---

8. A variant of the ancestry question could eventually do away with the race question, but that does not seem to be in the works any time soon.

Patterns of Mixed-Race Marriage

How to deal with the mixed-race person depends in part on how common mixed-race marriages are in the United States. To understand these rates we need to appreciate that immigration is rapidly increasing the number of nonwhites who are Asian or Hispanic. Immigrants have always tended to marry their own (many, indeed, arrived as married couples), but their children have been more likely to intermarry. Asians and Hispanics often marry members of other groups. These intermarried couples and their children have not yet had their full impact on social patterns and social statistics because the second generation of the post-1965 immigration is only now reaching marriageable age. A high rate of intermarriage also occurs among Native Americans (although the absolute level is relatively small compared to Asians, Hispanics, and blacks).[9] By contrast, the black intermarriage rate is very low.

Consider, for example, native-born, young (25 to 34 years of age), married people in 1990. Some two-fifths of the Hispanics in this group and over half of the Asians and the Native Americans married members of other groups.[10] Yet more than nine-tenths of the blacks in the group married other blacks. (Nevertheless, even blacks have been out-marrying more than before; the rate for better-educated young black men rose from about 6 percent in 1980 to over 9 percent in 1990.[11]) So there are really two patterns of interracial marriage today: it is uncommon among blacks and common among other nonwhites.

Both of these patterns involve huge numbers of nonwhite Americans. Race has always meant first and foremost the black-white divide—hardly a surprise in a country in which that divide once distinguished slave from master and in which by far the greatest numbers of nonwhites have in the past been blacks. And so, until recently, racial intermarriage meant first and foremost black-white intermarriage. However, that way of thinking about interracial marriage has been made obsolete by the rising number of Asians and Hispanics.

The shifting proportion of blacks and other nonwhites in the United States is crucial to the issues discussed in this brief. It has become common to speak of the increasing share of nonwhites in the American population generally (as the president did in announcing the year of discussion on race). Nonwhites amounted to 16.5 percent of all Americans in 1970 and 24.2 percent in 1990. By 2020, the Census Bureau tells us, that proportion should exceed one-third and by 2050 it should reach one-half. Whatever the value of these specific forecasts (a theme

---

9. The reference is to those who consider themselves Native American by race, not to the much larger group, nearly all of whom consider themselves white, but indicate that they have some Native American ancestry. On the 1990 intermarriage rates for individuals 25 to 34 years old, see Farley 1996, 264–265.

10. Of course, even a Hispanic or an Asian marrying within his or her own "racial" group might well be marrying someone with origins in a different country (a descendant of Chinese immigrants might marry a descendant of Asian Indians, for example).

11. The reference here is to native-born black males, 20 to 29 years of age (Qian 1998; see also Besharov and Sullivan 1996, 19–21).

taken up later), any forecast will show that the proportion of Americans with nonwhite ancestors will be much higher in the next century than it is today.

But also notice that the trend that is transforming the composition of the total American population (rising Asian and Hispanic immigration) is at the same time transforming the composition of *nonwhite* America. The proportion of blacks in this nonwhite population is dropping sharply. Before 1970 meeting a nonwhite American would likely have meant meeting a black person; today the chances are better than even that the nonwhite American will not be black. The percentage of blacks among all nonwhites stood at 66 percent in 1970 and 48 percent in 1990; it is expected to decline to 36 percent in 2020 and to 30 percent in 2050 (Harrison and Bennett 1995; Farley 1996).[12] The high intermarriage rates among the other nonwhites (those who are not blacks) is therefore crucial.

Legislation meant to protect minority races must be viewed from the perspective of these shifting proportions. That legislation was originally designed for blacks and was then extended to other nonwhites. The multiracial challenge to the clarity of civil rights law may still be relatively minor insofar as that legislation applies where it was originally intended to apply. However, the multiracial challenge to the clarity of civil rights law is considerable and rapidly expanding insofar as that legislation also covers other nonwhites.

What will the future pattern of black intermarriage be? Will it accelerate appreciably? That, of course, is impossible to judge with any certainty today. One source of change is the children of today's black-white marriages; these children may intermarry more often than those blacks whose parents and grandparents were all blacks. Even a modest increase in the number of these mixed-race children is likely to increase considerably the number of people who had a black grandparent or parent and are married to a white person. If it seems hard to believe that large-scale intermarriage will ever occur between American blacks and white (or other nonwhite) Americans, consider the situation of blacks in states in which they are a tiny fraction (less than 5 percent of the population). In 12 of these states for which records were available, black intermarriage rates in the 1980s were well above the national norm; indeed, in 10 of these states the rate of black-white intermarriage exceeded 30 percent. These rates, of course, might be dismissed as irrelevant to most American blacks today, who live as part of a large and concentrated minority and consequently meet and marry other blacks. Nevertheless, even in the United States today, black-white marriage is not so strange that it cannot become commonplace when the usual demographic constraint on within-group marriage, namely, the absence of large numbers of potential mates from one's own group nearby, operates strongly (Kalmijn 1993).

12. In 1960 the Census Bureau did not take account of "Hispanics" in discussing race at all; among those it did count as nonwhite, some nine-tenths were blacks. The "chances of meeting" a black or other nonwhite obviously vary dramatically across the country; the example in the paragraph should be thought of as referring to randomly chosen nonwhites selected from the American population.

Whatever the future of black out-marriage, interracial marriage among the native born in the other legally designated nonwhite groups is common. This is the context in which we must assess whether we can oblige people to claim origins in only one racial group.

Counting the Multiracials

People must be allowed to declare themselves as having origins in more than one race. To do otherwise is to deny that interracial marriages exist. Such denial would by implication encourage the dishonest and destructive message that members of different races do not "normally" intermarry. The manner in which mixed marriages are acknowledged, however, also will require careful thinking about how to count for civil rights purposes the individuals who declare more than one racial origin. I return to the civil rights issue later in this section; first we should consider how to handle the individual who lists more than one racial origin.

Arguments against a Multiracial Race Category

Recall that the race question is worded "This person is . . ." and provides five choices with the instruction "Mark one only." One way to change this arrangement is simply to change the instruction—either to "Mark one or more" or to the somewhat stronger "Mark all that apply." Another way is to add a sixth racial category, "multiracial," and then ask individuals to indicate to which of the four specific races they trace their origins.

Should we care about whether we list multiracial as a distinct category? We should care and we should not list it. Learning that someone has black and white origins has meaning; learning *in addition* that the person is multiracial conveys no additional information. The added racial category should be opposed not only because it is redundant, but because it sends the message that somehow something more *is* being communicated, that multiraciality is equivalent to a new racial status. Such categorization tends to solidify the significance of race, instead of simply allowing the statistics on racial intermarriage to reflect how high or low the racial divide is. It suggests that to describe a person as multiracial is to say something important about that person. For some multiracials that status may be important, whether in a positive or negative sense, but for others it may be inconsequential; it may mean only that they have origins in two or more racial groups.

Here the comparison to the way we treat other ethnic origins is helpful. Americans may declare themselves to be, for example, Italian or both Italian and Irish in origin; nobody insists that people of mixed origin place themselves in a special multiethnic category. Children of immigrants can answer questions about their parents' birthplaces without first identifying themselves as "native born of mixed-foreign parentage." For those who want to know how many people list themselves as belonging to more than one race, such information could be obtained from a questionnaire that does not have multiracial listed as a race category.

The ancestry analogy is relevant in another way. It is not unrealistic to think that in the course of one or two generations the descendants of several races may be as uninterested in their racial roots as many whites are in their ancestral roots today. Although people may know that they are descendants of several races, choosing which to list may become as arbitrary to them as listing English or German is to tens of millions today. That time may seem far off for many minority races, especially Americans of black origin; however, the difference between blacks and other nonwhites is important here.

What wording should replace the current instruction on the race question? The analogy to ancestry suggests "Mark one or more," that is, giving respondents the option of indicating multiple origins and allowing them to list as many or as few origins as they identify with. They would not be required to try to list all the ancestries that a tireless genealogist would discover. The many agencies involved also prefer the "one or more" formulation as a less radical departure from the past. In addition, the "Mark all that apply" instruction might encourage people to list distant roots in any number of groups even if they do not feel any kinship with those groups (see Addendum 1, on racial blending). The crucial goals are to eliminate the instruction to mark one only and not to have a multiracial race category.

Implications for Civil Rights Legislation

If we allow individuals to be tabulated in more than one race, how will the resulting counts affect civil rights legislation? The changes in the reporting system should not be undertaken for the purpose of lowering (or raising) the numbers in any racial category, and the changes instituted should leave those numbers close to present counts.

We need to distinguish among the several issues being raised by the civil rights advocates in connection with counting multiracials. One argument sometimes heard attributes motives to the multiracial advocates, namely, that they seek to free multiracials from the burden and responsibility of minority racial status, thereby leaving their full-blooded minority brethren to cope with a still-larger burden. This argument can be dismissed; quite apart from the fact that it misstates the motives of the multiracial advocates, motivations are not at issue; the effect of the proposed changes is what matters. Yet, something more needs to be said on this matter. Once again, the analogy to ethnicity is helpful. Loyal members of ethnic groups—Jews, Italians, Poles, Irish, Japanese—have often seen the person who intermarries as a traitor to their way of life. And when membership in a particular ethnic group carried a potential of discrimination (as was often the case), loyal group members saw the intermarrying or assimilating person as both traitorous and cowardly in the face of ethnic battle, denying his or her own identity to get ahead. The individual for whom ethnic origins were less meaningful than they were for the accusing group members saw the choices very differently. These intraethnic arguments are typically American. Nevertheless, each ethnic (and racial) group and each individual must work them out; government policy cannot be enlisted to firm up the battlements against the erosions of intermarriage. And it is not a valid criticism of government policy to point out that those who propose it are judged less loyal to their group than are others (Spencer 1997).

True civil rights concerns lie elsewhere. The main concern with regard to the reporting system is whether permitting multiple responses to the race question will reduce the total number of people counted as members of minority groups and thereby weaken the range of situations in which violations of civil rights can be tried. Several sorts of legislation are involved.

On the whole, legislation involving the status of a single individual, such as eligibility for affirmative action, should not be much affected (if at all). Past judicial decisions confirming the eligibility of multiracial individuals f' - admission to educational institutions, job-training programs, employment, and set-aside contracts should continue to have standing (Ballentine 1983).

Situations in which people are counted for determining employer discrimination within a firm may be more affected than situations involving the status of a single individual. However, before concluding that this difference is a strong argument against allowing people to list themselves as members of more than one race, two points should be appreciated. First, precedent may again be relevant, and this issue may well have come up before in connection with specific legislation. Even if it has not been discussed in the past, it is likely to come up in the near future, whether or not Directive 15 is changed, given the prevalence of intermarriage and heightened public awareness of it. Second, it is not so clear that the requirement to list only one race favors civil rights in these situations. As multiracial advocates have correctly noted, a worker can be hired as a black and fired as a white. Similarly, the most promising multiracial hires can be classified in the minority column and the least promising in the white column—all to help an employer's civil rights record.

The most obvious area in which a change in the classification system could operate adversely upon civil rights interests is in connection with voting rights legislation and in other legislation that is directly dependent on the census count of the racial mix in local areas (for example, knowing the local racial mix as a context for discussions of possible hires by local firms). The issue, by the way, is *not* that the new legislation will permit (for example) those with some white and some black ancestry to claim *only* white origins for themselves (that option, after all, is no less available with the present race question), but that such multiracial persons might now claim, for example, only black origins and in the future claim white and black origins. How then will they be counted?[13]

13. Relevant but apparently not a subject of discussion, are individuals who think that there are advantages to claiming partial minority status, such as to obtain civil rights protections intended for racial minorities. Presumably, at the level of individual job or school applications, such issues have already arisen or shortly will regardless of the changes to the directive. In the census, this individual has no personal stake in claiming multiple racial origins; however, a person may now choose to do so as a statement about his or her identity.

So How to Count?

The critical point to notice is that the count—the aggregation of answers—is distinct from the race question on the form. The responses to the form will show that some people list themselves in more than one race category. How those responses are aggregated to derive the total number of people in a racial group for purposes of civil rights law is a separate matter.

A recent Census Bureau report points the way (Bennett et al. 1997, 1–15). Most of that report is devoted to determining how people would respond to various formulations of the race question, but the authors also considered how these responses might be aggregated. The authors give three "illustrative approaches to racial classification," which vary from the least to the most inclusive ways of treating people in more than one racial category.

- The least inclusive strategy, the *single race approach,* derives the total number in a racial group by counting only the people who list themselves in that category alone. For example, a person declaring origins in the white and Asian races would not be counted toward the number of Asians or the number of whites, but only toward the number in a "multiple" category, rather like the present "other" category.
- A more inclusive strategy, the *historical series approach*, counts some of those who declare themselves of mixed racial background with minority groups. Specifically, those respondents who list only two races and only one of those two is black, Native American, or Asian/Pacific Islander would be counted with that minority group. Put differently, if the second race listed by an individual is white (or other), the individual's membership in this second race would not be counted.[14] If three or more racial categories are specified or if two minority races are specified, the individual would be counted under multiple race.
- The *all-inclusive approach* counts people as members of all the groups they check. This approach thus permits overlapping category counts that would result in aggregate counts totaling more than 100 percent. A person who checks white, black, and Native American, for example, would be counted three times.

The single race approach has the potential to be punitive to civil rights counts, because people of mixed racial descent who currently list themselves as members of a minority group would not be counted as members of that group if they added their other racial origin in the future. It is likely that the effect would be small, at present, but it would exist.

The historical series and all-inclusive approaches do not have that limitation and are thus much more likely to be taken seriously. Indeed, the authors of the bureau report comment that the historical series approach "might be useful to . . . federal agencies that use data on race and ethnicity to monitor civil rights legislation because it emphasizes classification into the race categories that have

---

14. If white and other were the two listed races, the individual would be counted as white.

been used to monitor changes under extant legislation" (Bennett et al. 1997, 1–12). This approach also seems attractive because it preserves the concept of non-overlapping races whose total number equals 100 percent of the population.[15]

Whether the preservation of nonoverlap is really so valuable is debatable, because it reinforces the myth that people of mixed descent can in fact be neatly placed in one racial category. It does so by ignoring their white (or other) descent. That simplification may not matter for civil rights law at the moment, but it may have long-term consequences.

Moreover, the historical series approach does appear to exclude one type of person who would be counted today as a member of a minority group, namely, a person descended from more than one minority group. For example, a person who today lists himself as black but who, given the chance, would list himself as black and Native American would not be counted as black or as Native American.

The all-inclusive approach may seem bizarre at first glance, and it may be problematic in the legal arena, but we should appreciate that it is in fact a sensible way to think about group origins in the context of intermarriage; that is why ethnic ancestries are treated in this manner. When many people trace their descent to more than one origin, the total of proportions descended from all origins will of necessity add up to more than 100 percent and origins will of necessity overlap. That mixed-race people are counted as white and as minority group members or as members of more than one minority group is an advantage as well. If ethnic ancestries are treated this way, why not racial origins? The answer, of course, is that legal status is not determined by answers to the ancestry question, but it is determined by answers to the race question. Can the demand for clear definition of legal status permit overlap and totals of over 100 percent?[16] I suspect it can. In any case, this is the question that needs to be confronted in aggregating responses for civil rights law.[17] Either the historical series or the all-inclusive approach should quite fully protect civil rights interests in the short run.

15. The authors stress that the specific individual might not end up being classified in the same category as under current enumerations, since given the choice of one race only, an individual might mark white rather than Asian, but under the historical series someone who marked white and Asian would be classified Asian. However, the resulting aggregate numbers are similar. Note also that my discussion is based on the premise that the instruction to respondents on the race question should be "Mark one or more" or "Mark all that apply." The authors also consider the possibility that a multiracial race category be added. They suggest that a person who marked only one of the indicated minority groups and multiracial would be classified with the marked minority group.

16. At the individual level, in fact, this strategy is probably the one in effect now: the triracial person in our example might be able to claim federal benefits as a member of a Native American tribe and file suit against an employer suspected of discrimination against blacks. However, presumably in a suit against an employer accused of discriminating against blacks and Native Americans, our triracial example would not be counted as two people.

17. In addition to the problems already raised, the treatment of such situations as Hispanics suing over voting domination by blacks should be considered.

Effect of Changes on the Counts of Nonwhites

In order to find out how changes in the race question and aggregation approaches would affect racial counts, the Census Bureau carried out detailed surveys over the past year. In the most important of these surveys, areas with high concentrations of racial minorities were targeted. In the target areas, samples of people responded to one or another variant of the race question. These variants of the race question included (1) listing a multiracial category; (2a) not listing a multiracial category but giving instructions to mark one or more categories of race or (2b) not listing a multiracial category but giving instructions to mark all that apply. Also included were different ways of listing Hispanics (discussed in Addendum 2). The bureau tabulated these results in accord with the three illustrative approaches described (single race, historical series, and all-inclusive).

The results of these extensive tests showed relatively little change in the counts of racial minority groups. Even the single race approach had no statistically significant impact on the number of individuals who said they were white, black, or Native American. There was a statistically significant, although modest, difference in the count of Asians/Pacific Islanders (as well as among Native Alaskans) when counts were derived using the single race approach (the least inclusive of the three approaches (Bennett et al. 1997, 1–31).[18] These results from target areas confirm results of earlier, less detailed queries in a national sample of the population in which minimal changes to the racial minority counts were found when multiraciality was provided as a race option.[19]

A Ceiling for Short-Term Changes?

Thus we have some evidence that we can expect minimal immediate changes if we do change the instructions on the race question from "Mark one only" to "Mark one or more." Nevertheless, predicting policy outcomes is not exactly a

18. In the target areas for Asian/Pacific Islander, 58.3 percent of respondents declared that they were Asian/Pacific Islander when given the instruction "Mark all that apply"; 65.0 percent did so when instructed to mark one only. The fraction was virtually identical (64.8 percent) when they were instructed to mark one or more (Bennett 1997, Panels A, C, and H, 1–31).

19. As a supplement to the Current Population Survey (CPS) for May 1995, the bureau asked the race question with and without a multiracial category as well as with and without listing Hispanic as a racial category. When the race question included a multiracial category, the instruction was changed from "Mark one only" to "Mark one or more." However, the option I am urging (changing the instruction without including a multiracial category) was not administered in this national sample. Nor were illustrative approaches to counting provided in reporting the results of this CPS supplement (Tucker et al. 1996). In this survey the major difference in racial counts (presumably using the single race approach) was that the proportion of Native Americans dropped from 0.97 to 0.73 of 1.0 percent when the multiracial category was included in the race question. The difference may seem trivial, but in relative terms, it is large for that small population. Nevertheless, it is not reflected in detailed, targeted counts of the second survey (Bennett et al. 1997, 1–29), and it would presumably not have emerged given less exclusive approaches to the count in the CPS supplement.

procedure we've perfected, nor are those concerned with the policy likely to feel fully reassured by any test of its expected effects. Therefore a mechanism for restricting the impact of whatever change the numbers produce should be considered in connection with any approach to counting for legislative purposes. For example, any change resulting from new counting procedures could be introduced in steps over three years or that change could be limited to 10 percent until 2005. Even though changes will probably not be large, the provision for a ceiling might be reassuring.

A ceiling on changes due to changes in the race question implies comparisons between current and revised methods of classification and such a comparison in turn implies that the Census Bureau continue to use the current form of the race and Hispanic origin question for several more years in canvassing subsamples of the population. The Census Bureau has a long history of formulating question variants on the Current Population Survey (CPS), which is administered to some 50,000 households monthly. There is also a solid precedent for giving different questions to subsamples of households who receive the bureau's long form (detailed questionnaire) in the decennial census: in 1970 the bureau used two different long forms.

A Dilemma for the Long Term

In the long term (a generation or two) the effects of the Census Bureau's illustrative approaches might change dramatically from their apparently minimal effect today. Racial intermarriage may well become much more prevalent than it is today, and then the number of people whose classification depends on these rules (the children of racial intermarriage) would be much larger than today. It is also possible that individuals' responses to the race question will be more mutable than they are today (just as the responses to the ancestry question are today, reflecting weak affiliations among many of mixed origin).

In such a situation, how will the race count serve as the basis for civil rights law? It is not only that the numbers may be much less stable than today. It is also that the relevance of membership in a group will become harder to judge. Will it then be meaningful, for example, to treat a person who had one black grandparent as black for purposes of civil rights enforcement? The answer to that question surely turns on how we think people with one black grandparent will then be treated in American society. If they will suffer discrimination, they should probably be treated as members of the relevant minority race in the count. If they will not suffer discrimination as members of the group, should they still be counted as group members for civil rights purposes?

This is the long-term time bomb we leave in place with any of the bureau's illustrative approaches, and probably with any other approach. The single race approach excludes these mixed-race people from minority counts altogether, the historical series approach includes most, and the all-inclusive approach includes all of them in the count. We must hope that the civil rights of those with origins in racial minorities will have evolved a great deal in a generation or two and that civil rights law will have worked out better solutions for treating those of mixed descent by then. Nevertheless, it is well to remember that at least in our time changing the arrangements for civil rights–related counts has not been easy.

The authors of the bureau's report did not discuss, even for illustrative purposes, a variant of the all-inclusive approach in which a person would be allocated to each racial category that he or she listed, but would be counted in each category as a fraction of a person. Someone who listed white and black, for example, would be counted as one-half of a person in each racial category; someone who listed white, black, and Native American would be counted as one-third of a person in each of the three categories.

The fractional strategy has many disadvantages. It runs the risk of being too gimmicky to command legitimacy in civil rights law; it recalls the distasteful antebellum congressional apportionment counting, in which each slave was tallied as three-fifths of a person; it may remind people of past racial laws in which a person was considered a member of a minority race by virtue of the fraction of "blood" he or she had inherited from that race; and, like the single race approach (but to a smaller extent), it might slightly reduce the number of people counted today as members of a minority group. For example, under current instructions someone who lists herself as black is counted as one person in the black category. With the fractional strategy, if she listed herself as having black and white origins, she would be counted as one-half in the black category and one-half in the white category. While the effect would be small at present, it would be hard to dispel the mistrust that the potential for a decline would engender.

On the other hand, fractional counting does have the advantages of the all-inclusive approach, while preserving the 100 percent total of nonoverlapping categories (without ignoring the impact of intermarriage). And, fractional counting does deal, however imperfectly, with the long-term danger of counting huge numbers of mixed-origin people as though they were only members of a minority group. Consequently, fractional counting should at least be discussed for heuristic reasons. Of the three approaches illustrated by the Census Bureau staff, the all-inclusive strategy may be preferable to the historical series in dealing with this long-term time bomb. While it will inflate the number of people counted as minority group members even more than the historical series approach does, the all-inclusive approach will also count the mixed-race people in all relevant groups, whether or not the groups are racial minorities. As the number of mixed-race responses increases, the amount by which the total number of responses exceeds 100 percent of the population will also increase. These counts should draw increasing attention then to the need to rethink the counting procedures.

Recognizing Racial Intermarriage:
Long-Term Gains for Racial Minorities

Civil rights advocates are right to scrutinize the short-term implications of the proposed changes to OMB Directive 15. However, it would be a mistake to ignore the long-term potential advantage of these changes. Our present system of classifying races has been constructed on the principle that racial categories are immutable; continued use of such a principle is no way to end a racist legacy and no way to think realistically about our present and future society. Racial inter-marriage inevitably confuses and distorts the racial divisions in the country, and in the present context it is natural to see that confusion simply as a threat to civil rights' gains. However, if racial intermarriage comes to be treated as analogous to ethnic intermarriage generally, the country should profit from the confusion of racial identity. If mixed-race people come to be numerous and are treated like other people of mixed ethnic ancestry, it will be harder for racial divisions to remain strong. Surely we already find some of that happening in the *faux pas* over Tiger Woods's racial origins.[20] The present debate over the race question and the resolution of those debates also have the potential to contribute to the erosion of the racial divides.[21]

Forecasting "the Browning of America"

Public discussion about listing the multiracials goes on separately from discussions about the future racial composition of the American people. Yet both issues turn on the same inadequate treatment of intermarriage by the Census Bureau and other government agencies. The projections of race drew the attention of the American people seven years ago as a result of a *Time* magazine article in which the phrase "the browning of America" was coined.[22] *Time* followed the Census Bureau in telling Americans that their country will be more than half nonwhite by the middle of the next century. This message invokes different reactions from different people. To some it says that the United States had better wake up to the needs of its "minorities"; they are soon to be its majority. To others it says the United States had better restrict immigration to avoid reaching the nonwhite majority. But any message drawn from that text will be misguided, because the projections are misguided. They ignore intermarriage.

The branch of the Census Bureau that undertakes several important projections (for example, of age, sex, and total population) somehow got saddled with making racial projections. Dedicated and discerning demographers became linked to a sadly misguided effort. The racial projections are based on the bizarre assumption that there will be no further intermixing of peoples across racial lines. Specifically, they assume that a child born to an interracial couple today will take the race of the mother and that, starting tomorrow, neither that child nor any other American

---

20. *Time*, May 5, 1997, 32.
21. Some observers of racial patterns worldwide fear the flip side of the scenario I've just outlined. In a society of strong racial divisions, they argue, multiracials may come to be defined (as they were in apartheid South Africa and in some other societies) as the "new colored people," with a distinct legal status. Instead of preserving the firm race line by the "one drop rule," we will, these people argue, do as South Africa did, by creating, instead of two sharply delineated races, one or two more, all with a standing in law (Spencer 1997). This scenario seems to me unrealistic because it ignores the difference between our moment in the evolution of race relations and the situation in South Africa in 1900 or 1950. It is true, however, that the legal recognition of a multiracial race category is subject to criticism from this perspective more than the alternative of allowing people to indicate more than one racial origin.
22. *Time*, April 9, 1990.

will marry across race lines. If an Asian-American woman and a non-Hispanic white man marry today, the bureau projects that *all* of their descendants in the year 2050 will be Asian-American and will *only* be Asian-American. If two immigrants arrive from Guatemala today, the bureau projects that *all* of their descendants will marry *only* Hispanics through 2050 and beyond. Such assumptions are wonderfully simplifying and have some short-term political use to a few interest groups, but they are ludicrous—or would be if they were not taken seriously and did not contort our view of where we are.

Realistic assumptions about future intermarriage levels imply both more and less ethnic transformation in the United States than the projections suggest. If the descendants of Guatemalans marry non-Hispanics, it means that many more people will have some "Hispanic origin" by 2050 than would be the case if the descendants of Guatemalans married only other Hispanics. And yet, at the same time, many of these descendants will be only one-quarter or one-eighth Hispanic, with the other three-quarters or seven-eighths some other ethnic origin; very likely they will be part non-Hispanic white.

A recently completed study of immigration by a panel of the National Research Council takes a great step forward in confronting these limitations. The council's panel went on to make its own projections by building in assumptions about the extent of future intermarriage and its impact on future racial identification (Smith and Edmonston 1997). However, by laying bare the assumptions behind the panel's procedures, we come to the central problem inherent in their efforts. The panel assumes that the "Mark one only" instruction will remain in effect for the next six decades and that whatever the level of intermarriage, the children of the racially intermarried would remain members of one race only. The question that the panel therefore sets out to address in its projection is "What will our mixed-race descendants of 2050 mark when instructed to 'Mark one only'?" The answer to that question, to put it gently, is a long way from an adequate statement about how our descendants will relate to their racial origins.

Consider a fairly extreme, but not unreasonable case. In 1990 the 10-year-old child of an Asian-white marriage is listed under one race; in 2000 this person marries the offspring of a Hispanic-white marriage (who also chooses one race). Their own child, born in 2005, is listed under one race, and in 2030 marries the offspring of a black-white marriage. The child of this marriage marries the offspring of a white–Native American marriage, and this couple has a child just as the long form of the 2050 census arrives in the mail; the form instructs them to mark the newborn under one race only. Just how meaningful can their response be? Notice that this example is only "fairly" extreme. On one side of the family there has been racial intermarriage in every generation since 1990, but I have not even specified the racial background of the other side of the family, except for the newborn's parent.[23] The point is not whether the panel correctly projects

---

23. Notice, too, that the panel is obliged to assume that the racial choice for mixed-origin people will be made in the same way as it is today, although the number of races from which parents, grandparents, and great-grandparents descend may be larger on average than today.

which race these parents of 2050 will mark for their newborn; rather the point is that the result of a "Mark one only" instruction on the race question cannot have a recognizable meaning in the society of 2050, any more than that instruction could produce meaningful results if used on the ethnic ancestry question today.

There is another kind of difficulty with such projections, one that would not go away even if the instruction were changed to "Mark one or more." Will Americans in 2050 perceive the major ethnic and racial groupings as they do today? Suppose the Census Bureau in 1900 or even in 1930 had projected the racial composition of 1997, while ignoring the subjective element in racial identity, the reality of intermarriage, and the coming shift in countries sending emigrants. It would not have fared too well. The bureau might have classified most of us as Nordic, Alpine, and Mediterranean, for example. Suppose that during the coming decades many new Slavic immigrants arrive from the countries of eastern Europe: would we be content to simply subsume these recent Slavic arrivals under the category white, along with those whose ancestors came from many lands eight or ten generations back? More likely we would create a subdivision "non–Slavic white" (or would it be "non-recent-Slavic-white"?). Or suppose that as a result of political and economic developments in Asia, immigrants from India and Pakistan increase sharply and arrivals from China, Taiwan, Korea, and the Philippines decline sharply. Will we still speak of Asians or will we make some distinction between the Indian subcontinent and the countries to its east? Admittedly, the difficulty of predicting the big "racial" divides might be seen as analogous to other difficulties that arise with any projections. The objection to predicting identity with just one race is the fundamental objection because it highlights the internal contradiction arising when we define race as "one only" and stresses the need for realistic assumptions about racial intermarriage.

I do not mean to suggest that the National Research Council's panel was unaware of such issues; it mentions caveats directly relevant to most of them; but caveats do not go into the model, and the public hears the count the model produces, not the caveats. Moreover, while the panel is indeed aware of most of these issues, it gives only the weakest of hints that the whole notion of estimating membership in one race only is not productive for a population that will include so many with multiple racial origins. The panel makes a great contribution in drawing public attention to the fact that the current bureau projections ignore intermarriage; but intermarriage cannot be meaningfully incorporated into the projections unless mixed racial membership is also incorporated. Intermarriage changes the salience, the meaning, of race.

Desideratum: The Genealogist's Projection

There is another kind of projection that could be undertaken and it would serve a truly educational purpose. We could estimate the true racial origins of Americans in 2050—the origins a genealogist would discover. This exercise would turn away from the subjective responses people must make when instructed to mark one only or even to mark one or more. The ancestry data show that even the latter instruction will be a simplification. The genealogist's forecast would underscore for the public just how much intermarriage is expected. It would also bring to center stage the uncertainties about the future prevalence of black-white intermarriage. The National Research Council, for example, projected it to remain at 1970 to 1990 levels through 2050.[24] Moreover, this sort of genealogist's exercise is much closer to what the public thinks it is getting in projections about the future racial composition of the country, namely, actual origins rather than subjective simplifications of misguided instructions. If media discussion of Tiger Woods is any measure, awareness of multiraciality is rising; however, the public may still be surprised to learn the extent to which actual origins will be blended. Whatever the precise numbers, our genealogist will surely find that by 2050 many more Americans than today will have nonwhite parents, grandparents, or great-grandparents and that Americans with such nonwhite ancestors will also be more likely than today to have white parents, grandparents, or great-grandparents.

However, why should the Census Bureau be in the business of making long-term racial projections at all, beyond the next decade or so? Nongovernmental researchers can run these simulations. The bureau's other population projections, notably of age, sex, and population, are used in a variety of endeavors. But racial composition? Is the racial projection an atavism from a more racist era, or is it a misguided effort to forecast how many Americans in 2050 will be covered by the legal statuses inherent in the civil rights legislation of today?

The low quality of racial projection data is not the most serious outcome we can expect if we deny that races mingle and treat them differently than other ethnic groups in this regard. The greater danger is the perpetuation and strengthening of a barely articulated idea underlying the present way of counting races: that racial groups live in isolation from one another, that their members must be counted as members of different species might be counted. The Census Bureau does not just count; in choosing what to count and how to count, it is in danger of propping up barriers that would otherwise not be so high or so foolishly placed.

Addendum 1. Race Mixing in the American Past: Legacies and Implications for Today's Counts

In some sense, everyone has mixed origins. In terms of one or another of the differing definitions of race that have operated in this country since 1900, most Americans are of mixed "racial" origin; recall that at the turn of the century Nordic, Alpine, and Mediterranean were often classified as races. Even if we restrict ourselves to the current OMB definitions of race (black, white, Native

24. In each racial group the panel distinguishes immigrants from the native born and distinguishes the native born in terms of how many generations back (one, two, three, four, or more) ancestors immigrated. The panel then applied rates of intermarriage (based on data from our own time) to these subcategories of the population. What, then, does the panel assume about the descendants of blacks brought here in the seventeenth and eighteenth centuries, that is, most American blacks? It assumes that since these blacks have been in this country for four or more generations, they will intermarry in the future no more often than they intermarry today (Smith and Edmonston 1997, chap. 3, section on "Exogamy Assumptions" and Table 3.B.3, "Exogamy Estimates").

American, and Asian/Pacific Islander), there is a good deal of mixed-race descent if one takes the long view. Will this long history of racial mixing distort responses to the race question when people are told they can fill in more than one race, as they can fill in more than one ancestry? The answer in a word is no. First, people do not list every possible response to the ancestry question; rather, they list only those ancestries with which they identify. Second, the Census Bureau tests of the relevant variants of the race question give us empirical evidence that the long history of racial mixing does not much influence responses.

The long view of racial mixing is especially important in considering the historical experience of blacks, Native Americans, and Hispanics (Williamson 1995; Davis 1991; Snipp 1989; Nash 1995). The importance of a clear-cut difference between free and slave and later between subjugated blacks and subordinating whites meant that the black-white color line was sharply and unambiguously drawn. From early colonial times, for example, black-white marriages were illegal. However, notwithstanding the law and the ideology of race, black-white sexual unions occurred in a wide variety of social circumstances, including the sexual exploitation of the enslaved. An extensive mulatto population was documented when the census of 1850 first explored their prevalence nationally. Over the long course of slavery, these mixed-race people came to be defined as black in law and custom, according to the "one drop of blood" rule, by which membership in the white race was limited to those without any black ancestors. Not all societies built around a racial divide have been organized in this way; South Africa, for example, recognized the population of mixed-race descent as a separate legal status labeled "colored." In the United States those in the middle were moved over the line to the black category.

Because a substantial mulatto population intermarried into the rest of the black population, demographers estimate that extraordinarily high proportions of "black Americans" in the United States in fact have some white ancestry (quite apart from any recent trends in interracial marriage). Moreover, some fraction of mulattoes fair-skinned enough to "pass for white" did so; and since they typically married into white America, a nontrivial proportion of "white Americans"— amounting to tens of millions of "white" people—have some black ancestry. Thus the black-white line was preserved, until recently, in law, in race theory, and in much of popular culture, but not in the true genealogical legacies of the population.[25]

Among Native Americans, a somewhat different pattern emerged; there are many reasons for the difference, but certainly a crucial one is the absence of institutionalized slavery for the Native American. By the early twentieth century many people who said they were Native American by race also noted that they were of mixed descent, with some white or black ancestors as well. When government dealt with tribal communities in the twentieth century for various purposes, tribal membership was defined in terms of the proportion of an individual's

25. Until very recently indeed! Laws against intermarriage were not ruled unconstitutional by the Supreme Court until 1967, and such laws were on the books in many states in the 1950s.

ancestors who had been tribal members. The required proportion differed from tribe to tribe: a quarter, an eighth, or less. In addition, the individual had to be recognized by the tribe as a part of the community. Thus, the definition was much more complex than the "one-drop rule"; it included both a "blood quantum" (a specific fraction of Native American ancestry) and a subjective element of communal recognition.

There is also another noteworthy difference between the black–white and red–white situations. Native American is a category on the census race question and on the census ancestry question. When the Census Bureau began using the ancestry question in 1980, it found that millions of people who declared they had some Native American ancestry listed themselves as white on the race question. By 1990 the number of such people had risen to nearly 9 million, while those who declared themselves as Native American on the race question numbered only about 2 million (Harrison and Bennett 1995, 209). In contrast, very few who identified themselves as black on the race question mentioned any European ancestry, and very few who identified themselves as white on the race question mentioned any African ancestry. If people knew and reported their family origins fully, presumably tens of millions would be reporting both black and white ancestry, just as millions report red and white ancestry.

Hispanic Americans present a third variant. The intermingling of Africans, Europeans, and native peoples in the societies of Latin America occurred under a variety of circumstances, but the upshot was that many Hispanic immigrants arrive in this country knowing that they have origins in two or more of these different peoples. At the same time, they learn that in the United States black and white are sharply divided. Which category of the race question, then, should the Hispanics mark? It is hardly surprising that many Hispanics mark other for their race.

It is one thing to appreciate that a great number of Americans have remote genealogical origins in more than one of the categories we label as racial today. It is quite another thing to believe that people today will in fact change the way they answer the race question in order to capture that long ago racial mixing. In fact, the evidence suggests that the reverse is the case. The ancestry data from the censuses of 1980 and 1990 show us that whites rarely identify with an African ancestry and blacks rarely identify with a European ancestry (Farley 1990, 41–46).[26] In addition, the surveys conducted by the Census Bureau in connection with the current OMB review show that the results tabulated using different approaches generally did not yield statistically significant differences from the current method of tabulation. In sum, responses to the race question do not elicit an awareness of the high levels of multiraciality created over the long sweep of

26. The picture is more mixed with regard to Native Americans. In 1980, for example, in addition to the large number of whites claiming some Native American ancestry, about 22 percent of those claiming Native American racial status also claimed some European Ancestry (Snipp 1989, 51). However, the crucial point is that the counts of Native Americans do not change in statistically significant ways when the instructions to the race question change.

American history. To put it differently, the subjective element in the way we determine racial membership allows us to bypass the complexity that is inherent in the genealogical record; what we get for the most part is responses based on an awareness of recent family history.[27]

Addendum 2. Are Hispanics a Race?

Race is subjectively defined by the Census Bureau, with the available categories from which to choose determined administratively by the OMB directive. This arrangement is important for civil rights laws, which cover Hispanics. Hispanics have a hard time knowing what to call themselves in those administratively determined categories. For one thing the awareness of and feelings about a multiracial legacy vary from one society to another, and multiracial immigrants do not necessarily relate to their origins in the same way as the native born. It may well be harder for these immigrants, then, to choose one category. But more important, because of the way Americans talk about race, neither the black or white category seems to include Hispanics easily (thus, "non-Hispanic white"). With what race, then, is the Hispanic supposed to "subjectively identify"?

In the 1990 census, 57 percent of those who identified themselves as Hispanic (on the Hispanic origin question) selected one of the four specific racial categories listed on the census form. Of the 43 percent who did not do so, many placed themselves in the "other" race category, and they constitute the vast majority of the people who chose this category. When a major population group cannot meaningfully identify with an important question, it is natural to wonder whether the question is misstated. Would it help to add "Hispanic" as a new racial category (Farley 1996, 211; Smith and Edmonston 1997, chap. 3, n. 17)? The government's interagency task force recommended against this change, and their recommendation should be supported. The task force suggested instead that listing the Hispanic question before the race question would help reduce the confusion of Hispanics when they confront the race question, and that is the only change that should be made.

On the one hand, it seems strange to treat Hispanic as a race, given the history of that term and the obvious connection of the term "Hispanic" to ethnicity; is "Slavic-American" then a race? Also, the racial count of "others" does not much

---

27. In another test the Census Bureau asked people who said that they were multiracial whether they said so because their parents were of different races, because more distant ancestors were of different races, or because the nature of their group was multiracial. Some three-quarters chose the first reason (Tucker et al. 1996). But with regard to the second response, which concerns us here, the real point is that only a tiny fraction of those who could conceivably have declared a multiracial legacy did so. For example, in the black population alone a substantial majority would have had some rational basis for marking more than one category, if they were inclined to do so; had they done so, the number of multiracials would have been many times greater than it was. Similarly, Hispanics may be confused about whether to mark black, white, or other, but the confusion is not based on a desire to resolve their problem by marking two or three of the available race choices instead of one; rather, they are uncomfortable being labeled in any of the available race groups.

complicate legal issues, since Hispanics are separated from whites and blacks by virtue of the Hispanic origin question. On the other hand, one can argue that the race question is no longer meant to elicit what used to be called race, so that it makes little difference if it is extended to cover Hispanics. Indeed, the race question nowhere mentions the word race, and the tabulation headings could easily be made to refer (as they already often do) to "race and Hispanic origin."

There is, however, another consideration. People tend to ignore subtleties, and listing Hispanic as a category in the race question may contribute to a more widespread willingness to refer to Hispanic as a race. Consider the following examples, taken from the two important technical reports recently produced on the race question changes by the Census Bureau and the Bureau of Labor Statistics.

> ". . . when Hispanic was included as a racial category . . ."
> ". . . where Hispanic was a racial category . . ."
> "Preference for Including Hispanic as a Racial Category" [section title] (Tucker et al. 1996, 5, 41)
> "Hispanic origin is included in the list as though it is a race group" (Bennett et al. 1997, 1–13)

It is easy to understand why the terms are used in this way by responsible analysts; but the eliding of "Hispanic" and "race" is well underway in such usage. The rest of us are likely to be less, not more, careful than Census Bureau officials in eliding "Hispanic" and "race."

Finally, there is the matter of precedent. Because the OMB is going to tell us which groups will be listed as races, it is understandable that ethnic groups other than those already discussed might request consideration for race status (U.S. Office of Management and Budget 1995, 44,681). If an ethnic group, such as one representing Arab-Americans, believes it is in its interest to have its progress scrutinized by government, then being listed as one of the racial groups is a big step in that direction. The subjective nature of the list, the fact that the list is determined by administrators, and the fact that the list is used to define legal status all make it hard to tell groups that they *cannot* be listed as a category in the race question. Including Hispanics will make it harder still to do so.

References

Alba, Richard D. 1995. "Assimilation's Quiet Tide." *The Public Interest* 119 (Spring): 5.

Ballentine, Chris. 1983. " 'Who Is a Negro?' Revisited: Determining Individual Racial Status for Purposes of Affirmative Action." *University of Florida Law Review* 35 (Fall).

Bennett, Claudette E., Bureau of the Census Population Division, and Bureau of the Census Decennial Statistical Studies Division. 1997. *Results of the 1996 Race and Ethnic Targeted Test.* Population Division Working Paper No. 18. Washington, D.C.: U.S. Department of Commerce, Economics and Statistics Division, Bureau of the Census.

Besharov, Douglas J., and Timothy S. Sullivan. 1996. "One Flesh: America Is Experiencing an Unprecedented Increase in Black-White Intermarriage." *The New Democrat*, July/August: 19–21.

Bureau of the Census. 1979. *Twenty Censuses: Population and Housing Questions, 1790–1980*. Ortina, Wash.: Heritage Quest.

———. 1992. Census of Population and Housing, 1990: Public Use Microdata Samples U.S. [machine readable data files]. Washington, D.C.: Bureau of the Census. Appendix B, "Definition of Subject Characteristics," B-30: 'Race.'

Davis, F. James. 1991. *Who Is Black? One Nation's Definition*. University Park: Pennsylvania State University Press.

Farley, Reynolds. 1990. *Race and Ethnicity in the U.S. Census: An Evaluation of the 1980 Ancestry Question*. Ann Arbor, Mich.: Population Studies Center.

———. 1996. *The New American Reality: Who We Are, How We Got There, Where We Are Going*. New York: Russell Sage.

Harrison, Roderick J., and Claudette Bennett. 1995. "Racial and Ethnic Diversity." In Reynolds Farley, ed., *State of the Union: America in the 1990s*. Vol. 2: *Social Trends*. New York: Russell Sage.

Heer, David M. 1980. "Intermarriage." In Stephan Thernstrom, ed., *Harvard Encyclopedia of American Ethnic Groups*. Cambridge, Mass.: Belknap Press of Harvard University.

Henry, William A. 1990. "Beyond the Melting Pot: 21st Century U.S. Population." *Time* 135 (April 9): 28–31.

Higham, John. 1955. *Strangers in the Land: Patterns of American Nativism, 1860–1925*. New Brunswick, N.J.: Rutgers University Press.

Kalmijn, Matthijs. 1993. "Trends in Black/White Intermarriage." *Social Forces* 72, no. 1 (September): 127–129.

Lieberson, Stanley, and Mary Waters. 1988. *From Many Strands: Ethnic and Racial Groups in Contemporary America*. New York: Russell Sage.

Nash, Gary B. 1995. "The Hidden History of Mestizo America." *Journal of American History* 82, no. 3 (December): 941–964.

Perlmann, Joel. 1997. " 'Multiracials,' Racial Classification, and American Intermarriage—The Public's Interest." Working Paper No. 195, The Jerome Levy Economics Institute of Bard College.

Qian, Zhenchao. 1997. "Breaking the Racial Barriers: Variations in Interracial Marriage Between 1980 and 1990." *Demography* 34: 263–276.

Smith, James P., and Barry Edmonston, eds. 1997. *The New Americans: Economic, Demographic and Fiscal Effects of Immigration*. Washington, D.C.: National Academy Press.

Snipp, C. Matthew. 1989. *American Indians: The First of This Land*. New York: Russell Sage.

Spencer, Jon Michael. 1997. *The New Colored People: The Mixed-Race Movement in America*. New York: New York University Press.

Tucker, Clyde, et al. 1996. *Testing Methods of Collecting Racial and Ethnic Information: Results of the Current Population Survey Supplement on Race and Ethnicity*. Bureau of Labor Statistics, Statistical Note No. 40. Washington, D.C.: Bureau of Labor Statistics.

U.S. House of Representatives. 1994. *Review of Federal Measurements of Race and Ethnicity Hearings before the Subcommittee on Census, Statistics, and Postal Personnel of the Committee on Post Office and Civil Service, House of Representatives, 103d Cong., 1st sess., April 14, June 30, July 29, November 3, 1993.* Washington, D.C.: Government Printing Office.

U.S. Office of Management and Budget. 1995. "Standards for the Classification of Federal Data on Race and Ethnicity; Notice." *Federal Register* 60, no. 166 (August 28): 44,673–44,693.

————. 1997. "Recommendations from the Interagency Committee for the Review of the Racial and Ethnic Standards to the Office of Management and Budget Concerning Changes to the Standards for the Classification of Federal Data on Race and Ethnicity; Notice." *Federal Register* (July 9): 36,873–36,946.

White, Jack E. 1997. "I'm Just Who I Am." *Time*, May 5, 33–36.

Williamson, Joel. 1995. *New People: Miscegenation and Mulattoes in the United States.* Baton Rouge: Louisiana State University Press (New York: Free Press, 1980).

For Further Reading

Judith R. Berzon. *Neither White Nor Black: The Mulatto Character in American Fiction.* New York: New York University Press, 1978.

Helen Tunicliff Catterall, ed. *Judicial Cases Concerning American Slavery and the Negro.* 1926; repr. New York, 1968.

William Bedford Clark. "The Serpent of Lust in the Southern Garden: The Theme of Miscegenation in Cable, Twain, Faulkner and Warren." Ph.D. Diss., Louisiana State University, 1974.

Virginia R. Domínguez. *White by Definition: Social Classification in Creole Louisiana.* New Brunswick, N.J.: Rutgers University Press, 1986.

Doreen Fowler and Ann J. Abadie, eds. *Faulkner and Race.* Jackson and London: University of Mississippi Press, 1987.

Susan Gillman. *Dark Twins: Imposture and Identity in Mark Twain's America.* Chicago and London: University of Chicago Press, 1989.

Susan Gillman and Forest G. Robinson, eds. *Mark Twain's Pudd'nhead Wilson: Race, Conflict, and Culture.* Durham, N.C., and London: Duke University Press, 1990.

Elaine K. Ginsberg, ed. *Passing and the Fictions of Identity.* Durham, N.C.: Duke University Press, 1996.

Susan Gubar. *Racechanges: White Skin, Black Face in American Culture.* New York: Oxford University Press, 1997.

Wen-Ching Ho. "Miscegenation in William Faulkner: A Synecdoche for Slavery/Caste System." Ph.D. Diss., University of Michigan, 1989.

Martha Elizabeth Hodes. *White Women, Black Men: Illicit Sex in the Nineteenth-Century South.* New Haven, Conn.: Yale University Press, 1997.

Martha Elizabeth Hodes, ed. *Sex, Love, Race: Crossing Boundaries in North American History.* New York: New York University Press, 1999.

James Hugo Johnston. *Race Relations in Virginia and Miscegenation in the South, 1776–1860.* Amherst: University of Massachusetts Press, 1970.

James Kinney. *Amalgamation! Race, Sex, and Rhetoric in the Nineteenth-Century American Novel.* Westport, Conn.: Greenwood Press, 1985.

Charles S. Mangum, Jr. *The Legal Status of the Negro.* Chapel Hill: University of North Carolina Press, 1940.

Byron Curti Martyn. "Racism in the United States: A History of Anti-Miscegenation Legislation and Litigation." Ph.D. Diss., 3 vols., University of Southern California, 1979.

John G. Mencke. *Mulattoes and Race Mixture: American Attitudes and Images.* Studies in American History and Culture no. 4. Ann Arbor: University of Michigan Research Press, 1979.

Pauli Murray. *States' Laws on Race and Color: And Appendices Containing International Documents, Federal Laws and Regulations, Local Ordinances and Charts.* Cincinnati, Ohio: Women's Division of Christian Service, 1950, © 1951 Rogers.

Werner Sollors. *Neither Black Nor White Yet Both: Thematic Explorations of Interracial Literature.* New York: Oxford University Press, 1997; pbk., Cambridge, Mass.: Harvard University Press, 1999.

Eric J. Sundquist. *Faulkner: The House Divided.* Baltimore, Md., and London: Johns Hopkins University Press, 1983.

Joseph R. Washington, Jr. *Marriage in Black and White.* Boston: Beacon Press, 1970.

Doris Y. Wilkinson. *Black Male/White Female: Perspectives on Interracial Marriage and Courtship.* Cambridge, Mass.: Schenkman, 1975.

Joel Williamson. *New People: Miscegenation and Mulattoes in the United States.* New York and London: Free Press/Collier Macmillan, 1980.

Index

Page numbers in **boldface** refer to indexed contributions to this volume. Page numbers in *italics* indicate extensive or important discussions of a topic.